Costa Rica

timeout.com/costarica

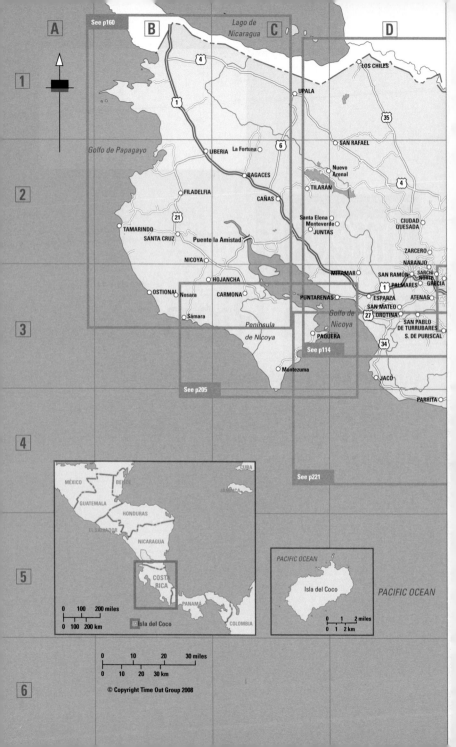

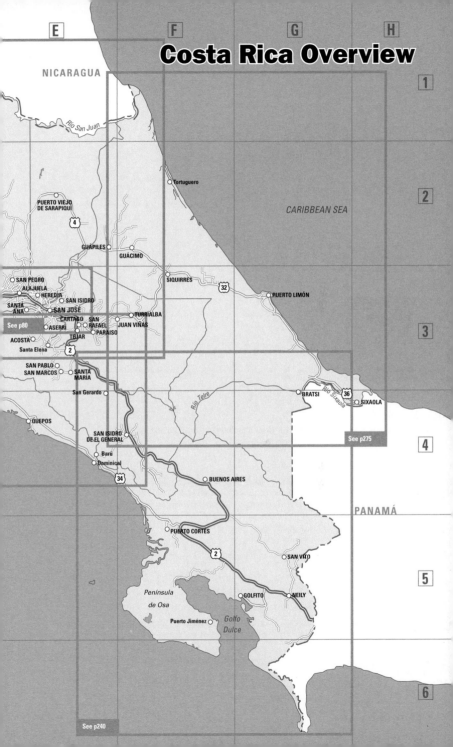

Costa Rica Overview

NICARAGUA

CARIBBEAN SEA

Río San Juan

○ Tortuguero

PUERTO VIEJO
DE SARAPIQUÍ

4

GUÁPILES ○
GUÁCIMO

SIQUIRRES ○
32

○ PUERTO LIMÓN

SAN PEDRO ○
ALAJUELA ○
HEREDIA ○
SANTA ○ SAN ISIDRO
ANA ○ SAN JOSÉ
CARTAGO ○ SAN
ASERRÍ ○ RAFAEL ○ TURRIALBA
ACOSTA ○ TEJAR PARAÍSO
Santa Elena
2

See p80

Río Teire

BRATSI ○
Río Sixaola
36
○ SIXAOLA

See p275

SAN PABLO ○
SAN MARCOS ○ SANTA
MARÍA
San Gerardo ○

○ QUEPOS

SAN ISIDRO ○
DE EL GENERAL
○ Barú
Dominical ○
34

○ BUENOS AIRES

PANAMÁ

○ PUERTO CORTÉS
2

○ SAN VITO

Península
de Osa

○ GOLFITO ○ NEILY

Puerto Jiménez ○

Golfo
Dulce

See p240

Published by Time Out Guides Ltd, a wholly owned subsidiary of Time Out Group Ltd.
Time Out and the Time Out logo are trademarks of Time Out Group Ltd.

© **Time Out Group Ltd 2008**

10 9 8 7 6 5 4 3 2 1

This edition first published in Great Britain in 2008 by Ebury Publishing
A Random House Group Company
20 Vauxhall Bridge Road, London SW1V 2SA

Random House UK Limited Reg. No. 954009

Random House Australia Pty Limited 20 Alfred Street, Milsons Point, Sydney, New South Wales 2061, Australia
Random House New Zealand Limited 18 Poland Road, Glenfield, Auckland 10, New Zealand
Random House South Africa (Pty) Limited Isle of Houghton, Corner Boundary Road & Carse O'Gowrie,
Houghton 2198, South Africa

Distributed in the US by Publishers Group West
Distributed in Canada by Publishers Group Canada

For further distribution details, see www.timeout.com

ISBN: 978-1-84670-091-0

A CIP catalogue record for this book is available from the British Library.

Printed and bound by Firmengruppe APPL, aprinta druck, Wemding, Germany.

The Random House Group Limited supports The Forest Stewardship Council (FSC), the leading international forest
certification organisation. All our titles that are printed on Greenpeace approved FSC certified paper carry the FSC
logo. Our paper procurement policy can be found at www.rbooks.co.uk/environment.

Time Out carbon-offsets all its flights with Trees for Cities (www.treesforcities.org).

Edited and designed by
Time Out Guides Limited
Universal House
251 Tottenham Court Road
London W1T 7AB
Tel + 44 (0)20 7813 3000
Fax + 44 (0)20 7813 6001
Email guides@timeout.com
www.timeout.com

Editorial
Editor Daniel Neilson
Managing Editor Mark Rebindaine
Consultant Editor Ana Wajsczuk
Copy Editors Patrick Welch, Matt Chesterton
Editorial Assistant Celeste Bustelo
Listings Checker Lilita Kloster
Proofreader Emma Clifton
Indexer Anna Norman

Managing Director Peter Fiennes
Financial Director Gareth Garner
Editorial Director Ruth Jarvis
Deputy Series Editor Dominic Earle
Editorial Manager Holly Pick
Assistant Management Accountant Ija Krasnikova

Design
Art Director (Buenos Aires office) Gonzalo Gil
Designer (Buenos Aires office) Javier Beresiarte
Art Director Scott Moore
Art Editor Pinelope Kourmouzoglou
Senior Designer Henry Elphick
Graphic Designers Gemma Doyle, Kei Ishimaru
Advertising Designer Jodi Sher

Picture Desk
Picture Editor Jael Marschner
Deputy Picture Editor Katie Morris
Picture Researcher Gemma Walters
Picture Desk Assistant Marzena Zoladz

Advertising
Commercial Director Mark Phillips
International Advertising Manager Kasimir Berger
International Sales Executive Charlie Sokol
Advertising Sales (Costa Rica) Franklin Cortés,
Maximo Palma
Advertising Assistant Kate Staddon

Marketing
Marketing Manager Yvonne Poon
Sales & Marketing Director, North America Lisa Levinson
Senior Publishing Brand Manager Luthfa Begum
Marketing Designers Anthony Huggins, Nicola Wilson

Production
Group Production Director Mark Lamond
Production Manager Brendan McKeown
Production Controller Damian Bennett
Production Coordinator Julie Pallot

Time Out Group
Chairman Tony Elliott
Group General Manager/Director Nichola Coulthard
Time Out Communications Ltd MD David Pepper
Time Out International Ltd MD Cathy Runciman
Group IT Director Simon Chappell
Head of Marketing Catherine Demajo

Contributors
Introduction Daniel Neilson. **History** Luis Chaves (*Bitter fruit*; *The real pirates of the Caribbean*; *Key events* Emmet Boland).
Costa Rica Today John McPhaul (*The beautiful game* Daniel Neilson). **Wild Costa Rica** Gregory Basco. **Arts & Culture** Henry
Bastos (*A whole lot of bull* Ben Lerwill; *Musical differences* Ruth-Ellen Davis). **Eating & Drinking** Andy Hume (*Spice up your rice*
Caroline Bennett). **Festivals & Events** Ben Lerwill. **National Parks & Trekking** Andy Hume. **Adventure Sports** Caroline Bennett.
Birdwatching Gianfranco Gomez, Tracie Stice (*Birdwatching guide* Gregory Basco). **Diving & Snorkelling** Caroline Bennett.
Fishing Todd Staley. **Surfing** Ellen Zoe Golden. **Rafting & Kayaking** Caroline Bennett. **Getting Started (San José)** Daniel
Neilson. **Downtown** Claire Saylor. **East San José** Erin Raub. **West San José** Claire Saylor (*Sounds of the city* Erin Raub). **Central
Valley (Getting Started)** Ruth-Ellen Davis **Alajuela & Around** Ruth-Ellen Davis. **Heredia & Around** Daniel Neilson. **Cartago &
Around** Ruth-Ellen Davis. **Central Valley North** Ruth-Ellen Davis (*The quest for the quetzal* Gregory Basco). **Getting Started
(Pacific North)** Cat Scully. **North Guanacaste** Dave Casey. **South Guanacaste** Georgina Gil, Andrés Castro, Ruth-Ellen Davis,
Cat Scully. **Península de Nicoya** Ana Wajsczuk, Cat Scully. **Central Pacific Mainland** Andy Hume (*Endless summer of love* Ellen
Zoe Golden). **Southern Pacific** Cat Scully (*A bug's life* Daniel Neilson). **Getting Started (Caribbean)** Cat Scully. **Caribbean**
Caroline Bennett. **Panama** Cat Scully. **Bocas del Toro** Mark Rebindaine. **Nicaragua** Ana Wajsczuk. **Directory** Daniel Neilson,
Ruth-Ellen Davis, Ana Wajsczuk.

The Editor would like to thank: Emma Clifton, Matt Chesterton, Jack and Ena Neilson, Lilita Kloster, Instituto Costarricense
de Turismo, Claire Rigby, James Holland, Jack Ewing, Franklin Cortés, Maximo Palma, David L. Gann, Bob and Helena Myers,
Todd Staley and everyone at Tribalwerks.

Maps by Nexo Servicios Gráficos, Luis Sáenz Peña 20, 7ͬ B, Buenos Aires (www.nexolaser.com.ar).

Photography: Pages 7, 8, 30, 32, 33, 34, 35, 36, 37, 38, 62, 64, 65, 119, 138, 142, 149, 156, 256 Gregory Basco; pages 5,
26, 39, 46, 51, 54, 58, 74, 79, 81, 82, 86, 87, 90, 124, 127, 129, 130, 239, 243, 244, 246, 247, 248, 249, 251, 257,
259, 261, 262, 264, 266, 268, 271, 309 Daniel Neilson; pages 9, 159, 153, 154, 158, 162, 163, 165, 166, 168, 171, 175,
176, 178, 179, 181, 187, 188, 191, 200 Gonzalo Gil; pages 13, 19, 113, 115, 117, 132, 136, 137, 145, 150, 151, 155,
162, 163, 166, 168, 175, 176, 178, 179, 181, 185, 187, 188, 191, 192, 193, 196, 197, 198, 200 Ruth-Ellen Davis; pages
201, 202, 210, 214 Belen Garcia; pages 16, 23, 48, 60, 73, 273, 274, 278, 280, 283, 286, 289, 290, 293, 296, 298, 301,
303 Caroline Bennett; pages 252, 253, 254, 256, 307 Mark Rebindaine; page 20 Ronald Perez; pages 14, 15, 18 private
archive of Andrés Fernández; pages 41, 71, 134, 172, 194, 260 Instituto Costarricencse de Turismo; pages 42, 43, 171
Papaya Music; pages 44, 230, 231, 233, 235, 236 Andy Hume; page 66 Martin van Gestel Rich Coast Diving; pages 68, 69,
70 Rio Parismina Lodge and Crocodile Bay Resort; pages 76, 140 Pacuare River Tours; pages 89, 101, 104, 111, 112 Claire
Saylor; pages 95, 97 Fabián Cordero González; page 152 Charles H Smith; page 120 Café Britt; pages 206, 207, 209 Hotel
Punta Islita; page 213 Javier Fernandez de Leon; pages 216, 220, 222, 224 Georgina Gil; page 226 Ellen Zoe Golden; pages
David L Gann 305, 306, 308. The following images were supplied by the featured establishments 164, 185, 227, 269.

Contents

Introduction

'*Pura vida!*' It's a phrase that is heard endlessly throughout Costa Rica. 'Fancy a beer?' '*Pura vida!*', 'How are you?' '*Pura vida!*' 'Can I buy two tickets to Monteverde?' 'That will be 700 colones. *Pura vida!*' Roughly translated as 'pure living', it is a refrain that defines the people of this amazing country: always welcoming, relaxed and open. Ticos, as they are fondly known, will offer you a beer on the beach as they watch the sunset; invite you for dinner; heck, sneeze on a bus and chances are most people sat around you will say '*salud*'. These are friendly people.

Costa Rica may be one of the most stable countries in Latin America, but it is still far from being as wealthy as North America or Europe. Life can often be very difficult for Ticos, and their catchphrase is a response to this. Living, that's what life is all about, right? Visitors to Costa Rica certainly think so. Beach bums rhapsodise about the perfect Pacific and Caribbean *playas*. Any surfer knows that two of the longest left hand breaks in the world crash on Costa Rica's shores. And then there is the wildlife. A much-quoted statistic is that the country contains six per cent of the world's biodiversity in a landmass that occupies only 0.03 per cent of the globe. You might imagine

that Costa Rica teems with all manner of unavoidable bugs, birds and mammals. Well it does. With the obvious exception of downtown San José, the chances of seeing some exotic looking creature, or at least a worryingly large insect, are almost guaranteed. This, though, is part of Costa Rica's problem. Tourism has become one of the biggest industries in the country, with an influx of more than one million visitors a year. This is a huge footprint, and one that has led critics to complain that Costa Rica is becoming overdeveloped, quashing its 'green' credentials. Occasionally it does seem as though every hotel or tour comes with the almost obligatory 'eco' prefix. They may not all be bonafide, but what is certain is that for the most part Costa Rica is leading the way in sustainable tourism.

In this first edition of *Time Out Costa Rica*, our experts have endeavoured to investigate the claims of each place we recommend. This is undoubtedly one of the most beautiful countries on the planet, and we want to keep it that way. And well-managed and carefully-planned tourism can pay for some of the nation's shortcomings, such as poor infrastructure, and also benefit its lovable population. Costa Rica is paradise. Welcome.

Search out Costa Rica's wealth of fauna, such as this Spider monkey.

The best Costa Rican attractions

Parque Nacional Tortuguero. *See p279.*

Boarding time

The Pacific waves of **Tamarindo** (*see p186*) are perfect for the apprentice surfer and there are plenty of schools eager to introduce beginners to the world of wave catching. At high tide, **Witch's Rock** (*see p173*) off Playa Naranjo offers some of the most famous breaks in the country. Held in equally high kudos among the surfing community are **Dominical** (*see p247*), the Southern Pacific destination **Pavones** (*see p272*) and the Caribbean **Playa Cocles** (*see p294*). Puerto Viejo's **Salsa Brava** (*see p293*) is only to be tackled by the most advanced surfer.

Shore thing

While busy busy busy, the rainforest-lined **Playa Manuel Antonio** (*see p233*) still stands out from the miles of Caribbean and Pacific coastline as a hotspot, and a gay-friendly one too. For seclusion try **Mal País** (*see p210*) on the Península de Nicoya, or laze on white sands at **Punta Uva** (*see p294*) on the Caribbean coast – which is also great for swimming. Guanacaste's clean **Playa Sámara** (*see p196*) is another spot for beach bums.

Heroes in a half shell

Parque Nacional Tortuguero (*see p279*) is a prime location for the endangered green sea turtle, which nests in the Caribbean reserve from July to October. Loggerheads, leatherbacks and hawksbills also frequent this strip of coastline. On the other side of

the isthmus, the leatherback regularly visits Guanacaste's Playa Grande at **PN Marino Las Baulas** (*see p190*). The olive ridley turtle favours Playa Nancite in **PN Santa Rosa** (*see p170*), and when sailing the wetlands of **Caño Negro** (*see p157*) look for the yellow turtle.

Summit special

The bumpy mountain ascent is worth every jolt to experience the cool surrounds of the lush, misty **Bosque Nuboso de Monteverde** (*see p144*). Find gruelling hikes in **PN Chirripó** (*see p243*) which is Costa Rica's highest peak. Sparks fly north of the Central Valley as **Volcán Arenal** (*see p151*) continues to hold its place as one of the ten most active volcanoes on the planet. And in the heart of the Central Valley, **Volcán Poás** (*see p118*) offers visitors closer views at an active crater.

Feathered focus

PN Palo Verde (*see p184*) and the northern wetlands of **Caño Negro** (*see p157*) are renowned for their wealth of avian life. For a glimpse of the declining scarlet macaw try the Central Pacifc's **PN Carara** (*see p222*) and **PN Corcovado** (*see p258*) on the Península de Osa. Good destinations for catching a flitter of the shy but famous resplendent quetzal include **PN Braulio Carrillo** (*see p128*), **PN Volcán Poás** (*see p118*), **PN Chirripó** (*see p243*), the entrance to the **Bosque Nuboso de Monteverde** (*see p144*) and parts of the dense **PN Tapantí** (*see p135*).

ABOUT TIME OUT GUIDES

This is the first edition of *Time Out Costa Rica*, one of an expanding series of Time Out guides produced by the people behind the successful listings magazines in London, New York and Chicago. Our guides are all written by resident experts, who have striven to provide you with all the most up-to-date information you'll need to explore the country or read up on its background, whether you're a local or a first-time visitor.

THE LIE OF THE LAND

We have divided this guide into seven geographical zones: San José & Around, Central Valley, Pacific North, Central Pacific, Southern Pacific, the Caribbean Coast and Further Afield which includes Nicaragua and Panama, and the much visited Bocas del Toro. Each section begins with a map of the region; more detailed maps of major towns and some national parks are included within each chapter.

THE LOWDOWN ON THE LISTINGS

Above all, we've tried to make this book as useful as possible. Addresses, telephone numbers, websites, transport information, opening times, admission prices and credit card details are included in our listings where possible and relevant.

And, as far as possible, we've given details of facilities, services and events, all checked and correct as we went to press. However, this is Costa Rica and venues can change their arrangements, and during holiday periods some businesses and attractions have very variable hours. And in foreign owned places it is not rare to close for a month or two. Where closure has been stated we have included it in the listings.

While every effort has been made to ensure the accuracy of information contained in this guide, the publishers cannot accept responsibility for any errors it may contain.

ADDRESSES

There is a joke in Costa Rica when someone is asking for directions. A typical reply goes something like this: 'walk 100m north of the soccer field and turn left at the sitting dog'. Ticos, you see, don't really use addresses. In larger cities such as San José and Liberia street names tend to be imaginatively titled by number, with *Avenidas* (avenues) running one way while *Calles* (streets) cross them. The *Avenida* and *Calle* numbers usually spread outwards from *Calle* Central (sometimes also called *Calle* 0), and *Avenida* Central (again also known as *Avenida* 0). Odd numbers will go in one direction and even numbers in the other. Confused? Well, few Ticos actually use this

Maps

Area name.. **LIBERIA**	
National park/Protected area	
Place of interest and/or entertainment	
International boundary	
Regional/provincial boundary	
Highway	
Main road	
Important other road	
Unpaved road	
Very rough road	
Footpath	
Railway	
Town or village	○
Mountain/volcano	▲
Bridge	⤳
Hospital	➕
Church/cathedral	➕
Tourist information...	ⓘ

system, and rely heavily on landmarks to give directions. These can be banks (for example the towering Scotiabank in San José), parks, restaurants or bars. Outside major towns there are few signposts and most roads are not named. Again, landmarks are relied upon, most commonly the football field. Occasionally kilometre markers on the side of highways will be given. Where possible we have given accurate directions, in Spanish (*entre* means 'between' and *y* means 'and'), that the locals and taxi drivers will most likely recognise. In small towns, or in areas that stretch along a road we list the restaurants, hotels and sights in a logical order, and give detailed directions in English, using the most common landmark.

PRICES AND PAYMENT

The prices we have supplied should be treated as guidelines; volatile economic conditions can cause prices to change. For most services we have published prices as they were quoted to us – in US dollars (US$) or occasionally in Costa Rican Colones (CRC). Nearly everywhere listed in this book accepts dollars, with the exception of local buses. At the time of going to press, a US dollar was worth just over CRC500.

We have noted whether venues such as shops, hotels and restaurants accept the following credit cards: American Express (**AmEx**), Diners Club (**DC**), MasterCard (**MC**) and Visa (**V**). A few businesses take travellers' cheques.

TELEPHONE NUMBERS

To phone Costa Rica from abroad, dial your country's international code, then 506 (for all areas) and finally the local eight-digit number, which we have given in all listings. Warning: in April 2008 an eigth digit was added to all numbers. The number 2 was added before all fixed lines and 8 before all mobile telephone numbers, however, most cards, leaflets or posters in the country not yet reflect the change.

ESSENTIAL INFORMATION

For all the practical information you might need for visiting the country – including visa and customs information, emergency phone numbers, health, medical and police contacts, details of local transport, language tips, important books and a selection of useful websites – turn to the **Directory** chapter at the back of the guide. It starts on page 311.

LET US KNOW WHAT YOU THINK

We hope you enjoy the *Time Out Costa Rica Guide*, and we'd like to know what you think of it. We welcome tips for places that you consider we should include in future editions and take note of your criticism of our choices. You can email us at guides@timeout.com.

Hotels & restaurants

HOTELS

Throughout this guide we have generally listed the price range for a double room in US dollars as the best indication of the hotel's price bracket. These are the high season rates because they are applicable for the majority of the year. Occasionally we have given prices per person, this is particularly useful for all inclusive resorts. Sometimes establishments charge for villas, cabins and bungalows which have multi occupancy, and the total price is given. Beds in dorm rooms in hostels are also individually priced. There will always be some price variations: for holiday weekends, and especially over Easter, prices can double.

All prices for hotels have been quoted to us directly by the hotel and are accurate at time of going to press. If prices vary wildly from those we've quoted, ask whether there's a good reason.

RESTAURANTS

For restaurants we have quoted the average cost for a main course in US dollars to indicate the general price bracket of the restaurant. We have given amounts for the evening menu, lunch menus will often be cheaper than the price listed. While most restaurants will accept US dollars, some of the smaller eateries, such as *sodas* and market stands, may only take Colones. Drinks and service are additional. See *pp44-47* **Food & Drink** for more on service charges, tipping and tax.

Advertisers

We would like to stress that no establishment has been included in this guide because it has advertised in any of our publications and no payment of any kind has influenced any review. The opinions given in this book are those of *Time Out* writers and entirely independent.

There is an online version of this guide, along with guides to more than 50 international cities, at **www.timeout.com**.

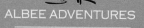

In Context

Features

Victory parade in Sabana, San
José, after the 1948 civil war.

History

Not your average banana republic.

'Nothing has happened in Costa Rica since the Big Bang,' deadpans Carlos Cortés, one of the country's most respected writers, in the opening line of his 1999 novel *Cruz de Olvido*. Like most ironists, Cortés has a deadly serious point to make: when Costa Rica looks in the mirror it sees a small, modest and quiet country, the Switzerland of Latin America. While the work of recent generations of Costa Rican historians has weakened this tongue in cheek classification, many Ticos have learned to live with it – and looking around at some of the history-rich but hopelessly underachieving states with which they share a continent, who can blame them?

BEFORE COLUMBUS

The first inhabitants of what is now Costa Rica can be traced back to between 12,000 BC and 8000 BC. They shared and disputed the dense tropical land with prehistoric (and now largely extinct) animals such as giant sloths and mastodons. They hunted them too, as is suggested by the stone, bone and wooden

spearheads found in the Turrialba region, 55 kilometres (34 miles) east of downtown San José. Tired of chasing dinner, the domestication of food plants began to develop around 4000 BC. Being located in the fertile waist of the American continent, pre-Columbian Costa Ricans had, without realising it, lucked out and could farm root tubers (sweet potato, yam, cassava) typical of South American tropical regions, as well as grains (corn, beans) native to the semi-arid zones of the north. It was a highly fibrous and healthy diet.

This era of consolidation of agriculture, and the changes it implies – sedentism, crafts-manship, social and political organisation – took place between 1000 BC and AD 800 and established a more permanent basis of trade between the north and south and Mesoamerican and Andean peoples. However, it was not the foundation of what are sometimes known as 'high civilisations'. In this epoch, Costa Rica was, in fact, sparsely populated, a backwater land of swamp, jungle and forest. There is scant evidence to suggest that large communities were the norm for pre-Columbian Ticos, and archaeologists have unearthed little of the imposing stone architecture that characterised the developed civilisations of Mesoamerica to the north and the Andes to the south.

The most telling relics that do remain are located at Guayabo on the hills of Turrialba (*see p139*). Scholars believe the ruins were once home to as many as 10,000 inhabitants who lived here from c1000 BC to AD c1400. The most important of Costa Rica's archaeological finds are ceramic and jade objects. Evidence of metalworking has also been uncovered, such as the goldsmithing that was common practice across the Costa Rican territory for possibly 1000 years before the Spanish conquest. Furthermore, sites in the central highlands and Peninsula de Nicoya suggest the influence of the Mexican Olmec and Nahuatl civilisations. Other intriguing archaeological discoveries are stone spheres still scattered across burial sites in Isla del Caño, across the Southern Pacific (*see p260* **Circling the square**) and the valley of Río Terraba. These spheres, some as small as a golf ball, others the size of a small family saloon, are a mystery and historians are puzzling over them in much the same way as future archaeologists will no doubt puzzle over skateboards and electric toasters.

In the early 16th century, the Costa Rican territory was inhabited by approximately 400,000 natives, most of them living in the Central Valley and North Pacific regions. The four major indigenous tribes at the time were the Caribs on the east coast and the Borucas, the Chibchas and the Diquis in the south and north-west areas. They could have had no idea of what was about to hit them.

RICH COAST, POOR COAST

The Spanish conquest of Costa Rica was partly accomplished by the sword but mostly by the microbe. The *Conquistadores* carried diseases for which native Latin Americans had no natural immunity, and it was this, rather than the burning and looting of the popular imagination, that ultimately decimated the indigenous population. Of the 400,000 inhabitants occupying the territory in the early 16th century, by 1569 only 120,000 remained. By 1611, there were just 10,000 native Costa Ricans left. Although warfare and exploitation took their toll, the demographic catastrophe was mainly the work of tuberculosis, measles, typhus, influenza and, above all, smallpox.

On his fourth and last voyage to the New World, Christopher Columbus arrived in the Bay of Cariari, near what is now Puerto Limón on the Caribbean coast, on 18 September 1502. The admiral anchored his caravel in front of an island known as Quiribrí (present-day Isla Uvita) and renamed it La Huerta (the Orchard). The official version states that a crowd of local Carib indigenous inhabitants paddled out in canoes and greeted the crew warmly. Probably not too moved by this gesture but secretly impressed with the gold the natives sported in their noses and ears, it didn't take long for

Drawing depicting victorious troops in San José after defeating William Walker in 1856.

Bitter fruit

The United Fruit Company (UFC), it has been alleged, bribed government officials, got itself involved in invasions and coups, played a role in Kennedy's Bay of Pigs fiasco, and was even involved in the making of a propaganda film called *Why the Kremlin Hates Bananas*. Roll up, Roll up, and Welcome folks, to the United Fruit Company show.

The company was born out of the merger of Andrew W Preston's Boston Fruit Company with Minor C Keith's railway venture. Keith, having found that passenger numbers between San José and Puerto Limón were low, began to grow bananas beside railway concessions. The bananas flourished, and by shipping them to the US he finally found a way to pay off his railway debt. In 1899, the UFC was founded, bolstered after the Costa Rican government defaulted on payments for the railway project, and agreed to hand over 3,200 square kilometres (1,300 square miles) of its land to the UFC, throwing in a 99-year lease on train line concession.

The company prospered (by 1930 it was the biggest employer in Central America) and started to make serious political as well as economic waves in the region. Its future president, the imaginatively monikered Sam 'the Banana Man' Zemurray, had helped to plan the 1911 US invasion of Honduras, and the sheer size of the company and its government concessions allowed it to muscle those same governments into curbing policies deemed to be of harm to its interests. And if that didn't work, there was always plan B.

In 1954, the company participated in the coup which toppled the democratically elected Guatemalan government of Colonel Jacobo Arbenz Guzmán. Led by the CIA (no, not a conspiracy theory: the UFC had bolstered its credentials as a corporate 'Cold warrior' after the company's top public relations officer made a film called *Why the Kremlin Hates Bananas*), the wheels of the operation were oiled by one of the fathers of public relations, Sigmund Freud's nephew Edward Bernays, who was hired by the company to help persuade journalists, and consequently most of the US population, that Guatemala was – horror of horrors – a hotbed of communist subversion.

Not content with that foray, the UFC then lent boats to its pals over at the CIA for 1961's Bay of Pigs snafu. The company was angry at Castro, who had the cheek to redistribute some of the UFC's land to Cuban farmers, much to the glee of the populace.

Mismanagement from the 1950s led to the company's decline and the death knell was sounded on the uncovering of a plan by the UFC's successor, United Brands, to bribe Honduran President Oswaldo López Arellano with a total of US$2.5 million upon the reduction of certain export taxes. In 1971, the head of United Brands, Eli M Black, took the nearest exit: the window of his 44th floor office in the Pan Am Building, New York.

The legacy of the company is extensive and controversial. In the credit column: free schooling, health care programmes and decent pay levels for many workers. On the debit side: severe restrictions on workers' rights, interference in the political affairs of its host countries and brutal suppression of strikes. No wonder the UFC was referred to just as the 'the Octopus' – its tentacles reached about every part of Costa Rican life.

Columbus to spread rumour of the vast riches this land contained (and which would later inspire the Spaniard conqueror Gil González Dávila to name the country Costa Rica, the 'rich coast'). The promise of loot, triggered by this erroneous perception, resulted in large numbers of fortune-hunters – not necessarily known for their cultural sensitivities – descending on Costa Rica. However, to these adventurers the name Costa Rica must have seemed a cruel joke. They were prey to swamp lands, floods, adverse weather and tropical diseases. Fierce and elusive indigenous groups constantly harassed them and, but for a few exceptions, there was no gold at all to be found in this green and humid territory.

CONQUEST

The inevitable conquest of Costa Rica took place between 1519 and 1523. The first intrusive wave started on the Pacific coast with the haughty Hernán Ponce de León, but he was fended off trying to disembark in the Gulf of Nicoya. In 1522, Gil González Dávila followed suit but with much more success. He managed to explore the land, and even got as far as trading with the locals. In 1524, Francisco Fernández de Córdoba founded Villa Bruselas (near current-day Puntarenas), the first successful foreign settlement in Costa Rican territory. This development was the beginning of a violent process of dismantling native societies – what would now be termed 'ethnic cleansing' – in the North Pacific region. Tribal villages were burned, women and children stolen or killed and the men used as slaves. On the other side of the country, the Caribbean coast presented an even bloodier and more difficult conquest, as the people of the region were more accomplished warriors and used the untamable geography to their advantage. They were, however, eventually destroyed. In the Central Valley, Juan de Cavallón is remembered for leading the first expedition in 1561, but the real conqueror was Juan Vázquez de Coronado who in 1563 founded the first colonial capital of the country, Cartago. It was an area known as Nuevo Cartago y Costa Rica, and a designated province of the Kingdom of Guatemala, under the reign of King Charles I of Spain. Yet the Spanish were not fully in control of the territory until the end of the 16th century, when the combined power of horse, steel weaponry and gunpowder made the conquerors unbeatable.

THE FORGOTTEN COLONY

During the 17th and 18th centuries, the colonisation of Costa Rica increased at a very slow pace. The social and economic development of the Spanish provinces was primarily the work of the military personnel, who were granted *encomiendas* – land holdings that included rights for a feudal ownership of serfs. Even with all this 'help', colonists still struggled to grow their own crops. Trade with other colonies was rare and at one point money became so scarce that the settlers had to revert to the traditional indigenous method of using cacao beans as currency. These impoverished colonies grew slowly and were virtually ignored by the Spanish rulers in Guatemala. After the brief flurry of excitement that accompanied its discovery, Costa Rica turned into a forgotten zone of the Spanish Empire.

> **'This was the beginning of a violent process of dismantling native societies – what would now be termed ethnic cleansing.'**

A growing intermixing of the races (*mestizaje*) took place in the 18th century. Descendants of poor *encomenderos* (feudal landlords) and *mestizo* (mixed race) farmers started to inhabit the Central Valley, specifically the fertile lands of Villanueva de la Boca del Monte (present-day San José, founded in 1736), Cubujuqui (present-day Heredia, founded in 1706) and Villa Hermosa (current-day Alajuela, founded in 1782). They farmed tobacco and wheat. This, combined with the ecclesiastical edict that ordered the populace to resettle near churches, resulted in towns taking shape, starting the inexorable (though slow) process of urbanisation. Soon afterwards, the income from crop exports made economic conditions somewhat better, but it was the arrival of the coffee bean and its financial impact that would forever change life in Costa Rica.

BIRTH OF A NATION

The independence of the Central American colonies from Spain on 15 September 1821 came after Mexico's rebellion against the Spanish Crown. For most Costa Ricans, however, life went on as usual; in fact, news of independence didn't reach Costa Rica until a month after it had happened. The country soon found itself in a dilemma: should Costa Rica join the newly independent Mexico or join a new confederation of Central American states? A bitter quarrel took place between the liberal leaders of San José and Alajuela and their conservative pro-Mexican counterparts in Cartago and Heredia. This led to a brief civil war in 1823. The liberals swiftly won the battle and Costa Rica joined the confederation with full autonomy over its own

A coffee plantation in the early 1900s.

affairs. Guanacaste, which had previously remained independent, voted to secede from Nicaragua and join Costa Rica the following year, but even today some Guanacaste residents still harbour secessionist ambitions. From this moment on, liberalism was pushing at an opening in Costa Rica.

Elsewhere in Central America, conservative groups tied to the Church and the previous colonial bureaucracy would go to war against anticlerical and laissez-faire liberals, and a cycle of civil wars came to dominate the region. In Costa Rica, however, colonial institutions had been relatively feeble and early modernisation of the economy thrust the nation out of poverty, laying the foundations of democracy far earlier than was the case elsewhere in the region.

While other countries turned to repression to deal with social tensions, enlightened Costa Rica moved towards reform. And though military plots and coups weren't unknown, generals were usually no more than the cat's-paws of individuals (often progressive civilians) representing the interests of particular groups.

COFFEE TIME

By 1848, Costa Rica had left the Confederation of Central American States and was an established coffee-producing and agro-exporting independent country. This new society was also part of the world trade market. In the same year – one with revolutions across Europe – the República de Costa Rica was proclaimed by President José María Castro Madriz. One of the first countries to recognise the baby republic was Great Britain, whose caffeine addicted empire was buying most of Costa Rica's coffee. Success in the bean trade improved the nation's economic relations with the rest of the world (*see p120* **Coffee fables**). Castro Madriz, an active Freemason and critic of the Catholic Church, was a liberal reformer who believed in a free press at a time when, in Costa Rica at least, censorship was the norm. Madriz was succeeded, however, by a very different kind of leader: coffee oligarch Juan Rafael Mora. Mora presided over a period of remarkable economic growth and directed the force of Costa Rican volunteers who defeated US filibuster William Walker in 1856 (*see p168* **Making of a hero**), dealing the death blow to Walker's ambition to turn Central America into a slave state and annex it to the United States.

After more than a decade of political confusion, General Tomás Guardia Gutiérrez led a group of officers that seized power in 1870, overthrowing the elected government; Guardia Gutiérrez ruled until his death in 1882. Paradoxically, the liberal state was consolidated during his office: though Guardia Gutiérrez ruled as a dictator, his 12 years in power were marked by progressive policies like free and obligatory primary school education, abolition of the death penalty, progressive taxation on coffee profits to finance public works and a reining-in of the power of the army. He also contracted US magnate Minor

Keith to build the Atlantic railroad from San José to the Caribbean ports, opening up the possibility of the cheap exportation of bananas. Keith, with his flourishing banana business, was soon to merge with Andrew W Preston's Boston Fruit Company to become the United Fruit Company; *see p16* **Bitter fruit.**

The shift to democracy was first witnessed in the election called by President Bernardo Soto in 1889, viewed by most as the first 'honest' election in Costa Rica's history, with popular participation (if not anything close to universal suffrage: women and black people were still excluded from voting). To Soto's surprise, his opponent José Joaquín Rodríguez Zeledón won. The Soto government decided not to recognise the new president, but the masses rose to support their chosen leader, forcing Soto to step down.

SOCIAL REFORM AND CIVIL WAR

The beginning of the 20th century saw liberal policies fail, largely due to the effects of the Great Depression. It drove the country to the threshold of social and economic crisis. The 1940s, and particularly the civil war of 1948, were a watershed in the history of Costa Rica, marking the country's shift from a 'caffeinocracy' ruled by a paternalistic rural oligarchy to a more urban-based, centralised state, with a fully fledged bureaucracy and greater industrial and agricultural diversity.

> **'Success in the bean trade improved economic relations with the rest of the world.'**

One individual stands out as the personality of the new era: Rafael Ángel Calderón Guardia, a practising physician who was president from 1940 to 1944. While neighbouring Central American nations struggled under the yolk of tyrannical dictators, Calderón Guardia enacted a series of visionary reforms. His ambitious programme included a reasonable stab at land reform (the landless could gain title to unused land by cultivating it), establishment of a guaranteed minimum wage, paid holidays, unemployment compensation, progressive taxation, plus a series of constitutional amendments codifying workers' rights. He also founded the University of Costa Rica (1940); state-administered social security known as Caja Costarricense de Seguro Social (1941); the social contract known as Garantias Sociales (1942); and the Code of Employment (1943).

Opposed by the conservative coffee barons who had elected him in the first place and by their political pawns, Calderón Guardia and his Social Christian Party entered into a bizarre but useful political ménage à trois with Costa Rica's communist party and the Catholic Church. On the other side, intellectuals, distrustful of this 'unholy' alliance, joined with businessmen, *campesinos* (farmers) and labour activists to form the Social Democratic Party. It was a party dominated by the emergent professional middle classes vying for economic diversification and modernisation. In its own odd coupling, the Social Democratic Party formed an alliance with the traditional oligarchic groups. In 1944, Calderón Guardia, constitutionally ineligible, supported Teodoro Picado Michalski to succeed him. Calderón was accused of electoral fraud, but Picado Michalski won twice as many votes as his opponent anyway. Calderón Guardia stepped up to run again in 1948, but was defeated by Otilio Ulate Blanco. Calderón and his party decreed the result void and promptly seized power. Civil war erupted. The anti-Calderón Guardia forces, led by José Figueres Ferrer (whom Costa Ricans called Don Pepe and who had been exiled to Mexico in 1942), were supported by the governments of Guatemala and Cuba. The war lasted five days and cost 2,000 lives, mostly civilian, but was won comprehensively by Figueres Ferrer's forces. And although the 42-year-old coffee farmer, engineer, economist and philosopher claimed he had raised a 'ragtag army of university students and intellectuals' to topple the government, Don Pepe had been in reality planning his revolution for several years: the 1948 election controversy was merely the spark that lit the powder keg.

Monument to Battle of Rivas.

In Context

President Óscar Arias Sánchez.

THE MODERN STATE

After becoming president, Figueres Ferrer established a military junta that administered the transition to democracy for a year and a half from 8 May 1948 to 8 November 1949. During this period, the Junta abolished the armed forces (one of the rare examples in world history of an army abolishing itself and something Costa Ricans today are very proud of), established a term limit for presidents, nationalised the banks and insurance companies and founded the state-owned Institute of Electricity (ICE).

Later that year, the Constituent Assembly of 1949 approved the right for women to vote, granted full citizenship to blacks, founded the modern civil service, and created the Supreme Tribunal of Elections (to impede future election frauds) and the National Comptroller's Office.

Then, honouring the pledge he had made 18 months previously when establishing the interim military junta, Don Pepe returned the reins of power to Otilio Ulate, the genuine winner of the 1948 election and a man not even of Figueres Ferrer's own party. Costa Ricans later rewarded Figueres Ferrer with two terms as president, in 1953-57 and 1970-74. He dominated politics for the next two decades, founding (in 1951) and then leading the Partido de Liberación Nacional (Party of National Liberation). It became the primary promoter

of state-sponsored development, and a popular force for reform.

Calderón Guardia and Figueres Ferrer are considered the two fathers of the modern Costa Rican state, who laid the groundwork for the social and economic progress that would earn the country a reputation as a peaceful and stable island of democracy in one of the world's most politically unstable and war-torn regions.

A STRONG MIDDLE CLASS

Broadly speaking, Costa Rican voters have ritualistically alternated between presidents belonging to the Party of National Liberation (PNL) and the Social Christian Party (SCP). Successive PNL governments have built on the reforms of the Calderonista era, and the 1950s and 1960s saw a substantial expansion of the welfare state and public school system, funded by economic growth. The conservative SCP governments, however, have encouraged private enterprise and economic self-reliance through tax breaks, protectionism, subsidised credits and other macroeconomic policies. Regardless of the ideological hue of the government in power, economic growth has generally been accompanied by an expanding welfare state, which had grown by 1981 to serve 90 per cent of the population, absorbing 40 per cent of the national budget in the process and granting the government the dubious distinction of being the nation's biggest employer.

By 1978, Costa Rica's social and economic metrics were way above third world averages – 70 years life expectancy; two per cent child mortality; 90 per cent literacy; five per cent unemployment; and 75 per cent of the labour force covered by state-owned social security – all this despite a population explosion that saw the number of Costa Ricans climbing from 800,000 in 1953 to two million in 1973.

PEACE BUT NO PROSPERITY

By 1980, the good times were over. Costa Rica was mired in an economic crisis. Inflation was oscillating between 80 and 100 per cent. The currency was dropping in value, along with coffee, banana and sugar prices. Worst of all, perhaps, were the disruptions to trade caused by the neighbouring Nicaraguan war. When large international loans became due, Costa Rica found itself weighed down overnight with one of the world's greatest per-capita national debts. Both wages and unemployment went in the wrong direction, the former dropping 40 per cent, the latter rising by ten per cent.

In February 1986, Costa Ricans elected as their president a relatively young sociologist and economist-lawyer called Óscar Arias

The *real* pirates of the Caribbean

From the late 16th century to the early 18th century, the Caribbean was a rum place where buccaneers, freebooters, privateers, filibusters and pirates, mainly English and French, sailed around, twiddled their moustaches, downed moonshine, struck matches on their stubble and generally looked menacing. The era was born of the opening up of the trade routes and thrived as the European powers kicked each other around on the old continent, until pirating was eventually made to walk the plank as these same powers enforced their will.

The game plan was simple: boat around in search of either booty (goods and treasure) to steal, or booty (people) to ransom later with whoever would cough up the cash. Strict codes of discipline (lights off after eight while drinking on the deck) were often kept and one such pirate, Bartholemew Roberts, and his crew proclaimed themselves ever ready with an article that read: 'Each man shall keep his piece, cutlass and pistols at all times clean and ready for action'.

And Costa Rica – somewhat ironically named, the pirates might have thought – was very much on the corsair circuit. Although not the magnet for pirates that other gold- and silver-producing regions were, the country had its fair share of timber-shivering types such as Captain Edward Davis and the dreaded Henry, or Hari, Morgan.

Davis was an English buccaneer who is said to be one of the first to stash treasure on Isla del Cocos, sailing in his aptly named flagship, the *Bachelor's Delight*, and alighting at Chatham Bay, on the island, in 1684. Further deposits were apparently made by William Davies (again 1684) and the prettily named Benito Bonito, also known as 'Espada Sangrienta' (Bloody Sword), in 1869. Numerous – some say as many as 350 – expeditions have been made to the island to hunt for the treasure, but none, as yet, has found the loot. *See p59* **Treasure Island**.

Henry Morgan, for his part, was a bit of a lad. Born in Wales, he spent many years in the Caribbean sacking and swearing, eventually to retire from piracy and die, possibly of dropsy, in 1688. And the punishment for all this rape and pillage? A knighthood in 1674.

In 1670, Morgan (later to be the inspiration for the 1935 film *Captain Blood* starring Errol Flynn) sacked Portobello in Panama and boldly told survivors he would return in a year to loot Panama town itself. True to his word, he returned in 1671, defeated the Spanish and looted the city, but missed 700 tons or so of treasure that the wily Church had shipped out. (According to one legend, the clerics heaved it up to the hills of Manuel Antonio.) The treasure is yet to be found, and many locals believe that a mass of precious metal is to blame for poor television and radio reception in the area.

The residents of Esparza, near Puntarenas, also have reason to recall Morgan. Having been tipped off about his impending arrival, they stayed guard for seven days and nights to protect the jewels of the town: two large golden bells hanging in the main church. However, the Welsh wizard outwitted them and made off with the treasure. Local lore has it that the fortunes of the country will only pick up when the bells, wherever they are, are returned to their rightful position.

Sánchez. Arias Sánchez's electoral pledge had been to work for peace. Immediately, he put his energies into resolving Central America's regional conflicts. He attempted to expel the Contras from Costa Rica and, much to the chagrin of the Reagan administration, enforce the nation's official proclamation of neutrality made in 1983 during Luis Alberto Monge's presidency. Arias Sánchez's vigorous efforts were rewarded in 1987, when his Central American peace plan was signed by the five Central American presidents in Guatemala City; an achievement that earned the Costa Rican president the 1987 Nobel Peace Prize, something the whole nation takes pride in.

The 1990s, with Rafael Ángel Calderón Fournier (son of Calderón Guardia) in office, was a decade in which Costa Rica's huge trade deficit reached unsustainable levels, leading to unpopular austerity measures. Memorable countrywide celebrations after the glorious debut of Costa Rica's national football team in the 1990 World Cup were rapidly forgotten as the middle and lower classes began to experience a weakened model of development.

The income from traditional commodity exports like coffee proved to be insufficient to finance the country's welfare state. Agricultural diversification was stepped up. At the same

Key events

12,000 BC – 8000 BC First inhabitants.
1000 BC – AD 1400 Guayabo settlement home to up to 10,000 inhabitants; mysteriously abandoned.
1500 Population of territory: 400,000.
1500 – 1569 Indigenous population decimated by Spanish conquest and its attendant bacteria, plunging from 400,000 to 120,000 (with only 10,000 left in 1611).
1502 Columbus moors in the Bay of Cariari.
1519 Hernán Ponce de Léon unsuccessfully tries to invade from the Gulf of Nicoya; Gil González Dávila makes a more successful effort in 1522.
1524 Francisco Fernández de Córdoba sets up Villa Bruselas (near current-day Puntarenas) – first successful settlement.
1563 Juan Vázquez de Coronado founds the first colonial capital of the country, Cartago.
1600 The Spanish seize control of the entire territory – without asking if anyone minds.
1600 – 1800 Costa Rica remains a backwater of the Spanish Empire, ignoring, and being ignored by, the governors in Guatemala.
1719 Described as 'the poorest and most miserable Spanish colony in all the Americas' by a Spanish viceroy.
1736 San José – then called Villanueva de la Boca del Monte – founded.
1821 With other Central American provinces, Costa Rica declares its independence from the Spanish crown.
1823 – 1839 Costa Rica becomes part of the Federal Republic of Central America.
1848 President José María Castro Madriz formally declares Costa Rica a republic.
1856 Costa Rican volunteers defeat William Walker in his attempt to annex Central America for the United States and create a slave state.
1870 General Tomás Guardia Gutiérrez seizes power in a military coup. A dictator, he nonetheless initiates progressive social and economic policies including the building of the 'banana line': the railroad from San José to the Caribbean.
1889 A tentative step towards democracy as the first 'honest' election is called by President Bernardo Soto; he is defeated, refuses to accept the result, but is then forced to acquiesce in the teeth of popular protest. José Joaquín Rodríguez Zeledón takes over the reins.
1917 – 1919 Dictatorship of Federico Tonoco Granados wins backing of the upper classes. US president Woodrow Wilson is less of a fan. Costa Rica then moves back to democracy.
1948 Civil war. Social reformer Rafael Ángel Calderón Guardia, president from 1940 to 1944, runs for the main prize again and refuses to accept defeat. He seizes power but is forced out by José Figueres Ferrer. some 2,000 people die in the violence.
1949 True to his word, Figueres cedes power after dismantling the armed forces, among other key reforms.
1953 Figueres elected as president for the first time, holding office from 1953 to 1958 and 1970 to 1974.
1986 Óscar Arias Sánchez starts first of two terms as president. Wins Nobel Peace Prize in 1987 for his part in the Central American peace plan.
2004 Former Presidents Rafael Ángel Calderón Fournier and Miguel Ángel Rodríguez Echeverría arrested on corruption charges.
2006 Óscar Arias Sánchez re-elected.

time, tourism began to grow and became one of Costa Rica's primary sources of revenue.

The last 15 years of the 20th century were tough ones for Costa Rica. The failure to maintain previously high standards of healthcare and education, the increasing gap between rich and poor, and the first cases of narcopolitics have changed the way Ticos think of themselves. Tales of an island governed by peace and integrity began to read less like the history books and more like a fairytale.

The new millennium began with the indictment of two former presidents, Calderón Fournier and Miguel Ángel Rodríguez Echeverría, for corruption. Both spent time in jail and are now awaiting trial. Figueres Olsen (son of Figueres Ferrer and a former president) was also accused, but the case was dismissed.

Ticos today are tired of old-school politicians, an attitude reflected by high turnouts in the elections of 2000 and 2006. Yet the flip-flopping stalemate of the two parties remains, and the further polarisation of society seems inevitable even though Costa Rica continues to be peaceful and relatively progressive. It is facing an urgent, unavoidable challenge: how to contend with the changes brought by globalisation without losing the benefits of its unique brand of social democracy.

Teatro Nacional

Costa Rica Today

Conservation or expansion? Traditional customs or globalised trends? Costa Rica is a country on the edge of change.

Costa Rica is a country no longer content to just ship coffee. A nation once dependent on its famous beans and other agricultural exports is now pushing more diverse products and a successful tourism industry. While this shift is making it a busier and more vibrant place, some locals are worried that these changes are threatening traditional ways of life. This kind of cultural uncertainty is epitomised by the *carreta* (ox cart), traditionally a method for hauling coffee but now more likely to be dolled up in bright colours and stationed outside a hotel. The pastoral has become the picturesque. In the end, it is a question of balance. How can a country so lavishly gifted with tropical beaches, spellbinding volcanoes and primeval forests

eschew a short-term cash bonanza and turn such natural riches into material wealth in a sustainable way?

IT AIN'T EASY BEING GREEN

It is a question that is on the minds of the country's people and their politicians, and one that is being openly addressed. In 2007, Costa Rican president and Nobel Peace Prize laureate Óscar Arias Sánchez declared the 'Peace with Nature' initiative, a sign, if nothing else, that the country aims to preserve its natural beauty even while it sets its sights on becoming a member of the 'developed' world.

Costa Rica currently safeguards more than 25 per cent of its national territory in some form of protected land. Green measures, however, do get squeezed to the sidelines with the onslaught of development, largely built to meet the needs of the high-end tourist industry.

Nowhere is this more apparent than along the Pacific coastline. When the Daniel Oduber International Airport, in the northern town of Liberia, tarmacked its runways in the 1990s, the province of Guanacaste changed forever. Once-pristine beaches are now inundated with beach hotels, condominium complexes and marinas. Arias's 'crusade to protect the environment' raises environmentalists' eyebrows when condo development along the Pacific coast proceeds at breakneck speed. There is no denying that this enhanced infrastructure has injected money into the economy, but the advent of hotels, highways and second homes does not *ipso facto* improve the lives of small-town Costa Ricans.

Local residents complain about being priced out of their homes as booming beach towns like Tamarindo and Jacó become enclaves for foreigners more attracted to the fun-and-sun side of Costa Rican life than to the low-impact natural heritage tourism favoured by environmentalists and conservationists. Take a look around the corner from that stylish hotel complex, and instead of polished wood and granite you'll often find ramshackle huts that serve as housing for the hotel's staff. Are tour companies and hotel owners the only ones benefitting from this cash infusion?

'Costa Rica's beauty is found in its traditional lifestyles as much as in its unblemished scenery.'

These issues, however, are nothing new; foreign cash does not put food on everyone's table, but what it can drive is improvement. Growth in tourism challenges local authorities

Children in the Uatsi indigenous community.

By numbers

Geography
Area 51,100sq km (19,729sq miles)
Coastline 1,290km (802 miles)

Population
Costa Rica 4,195,914 (July 2008 est.)
Age structure 0-14 years 27.2%; 15-64
years 66.8%; 65 years and over 6%.
Ethnic groups White (including mestizo)
94%; black 3%; Amerindian 1%; Chinese
1%; other 1%.
Religion Roman Catholic 76.3%;
Evangelical 13.7%; Jehovah's Witness
1.3%; Protestant 0.7%; other 4.8%;
none 3.2%.
Health Life expectancy male 75 (76 in UK);
female 80 (81 in UK). Infant mortality 9
deaths/1,000 live births (4.93
deaths/1,000 live births in UK).

Economy & finance
Currency Colón (CRC)
Exchange rates (as of 30 May 2008)
One pound = CRC1,021.20. One euro
= CRC798.86. One dollar = CRC517.93.
Real GDP growth 6.1% (2007)
Inflation 12% (2007)
Unemployment 5.5% (2007)

to provide adequate water, electricity and
sewage systems, in towns where building
cranes compete with high-rise condos. And with
two million visitors a year, tourism is Costa
Rica's biggest source of foreign exchange,
meaning that, for many living in poverty,
development equals better living standards.

LIFE IN PARADISE
Hard-working Ticos have a right to be ticked off
by the torrent of tourism projects and the
government's modernisation agenda. The truth
is that this country is a paradise, and tucked
away among its forests are molasses-paced
towns where customs and traditions have not
been swept away by condos or software plants.
Costa Rica's beauty is enshrined in the
traditional, unhurried lifestyle of its people as
much as in the unblemished scenery, and
visitors to the country tend to be as charmed by
the population as they are dazzled by the
natural landscape.

When it comes to natural beauty, tourists are
not the only ones who head to Costa Rica's
sandy beaches. Ticos care equally as much
about bikinis and beach volleyball, and less
devout Catholics spend every holiday they can

scrape heading to the coast. Semana Santa
(Easter week) is a particularly heady few days
of beach, booze and boogying. Families pile into
cars laden with coolers, tents, towels and beer
and head to normally isolated beaches where
they set up their stereos and barbecues.
Christmas is another time to enjoy the beach,
it being part of the dry season, which begins in
December and typically lasts until early March.
It's a time of year when Costa Rican joie de
vivre – known as *pura vida* – is on full display
as beach and music festivals flourish.

'Poised between a bucolic past and a dynamic future, Costa Rica's road to modernity is a bumpy one.'

Other entertainment includes parades,
festivals, horse shows and bullfighting (*see p41*
A whole lot of bull), the latter commonly
held in Palmares, Limón and Zapote. Unlike
in traditional Spanish bullfights, the bulls in
Costa Rica do not get hurt. Instead it is the
bullfighters who jump into the ring to challenge
the beast who come off worse. It's not unusual
for a bull to run down a poor amateur *torero*
(bullfighter), launching him into the air in a
scene that manages to be simultaneously
farcical and horrifying. Those who are chased
down rarely suffer more than minor injuries,
though fatalities have been known to occur.
It's a popular family outing.

OPEN DOORS
With an army-less nation, a stable economy
and fertile land, it's no wonder that in recent
years Costa Rica has become a magnet for
immigrants. An estimated 500,000 Nicaraguans
live in the country holding down domestic and
agricultural jobs. Like most immigrant groups,
Nicaraguans are often victims of xenophobia
(unlike the term Tico, Nico – referring to
Nicaraguans – is derogatory) at the same time
as being accepted as important contributors to
the national economy. But it's not just workers
who are crossing the border. More and more
North Americans are moving to Costa Rica,
either on a permanent basis or to spend part of
the year in their second homes. It is estimated
that between 30,000 and 40,000 US citizens live
in the country, and a smaller number of, mainly,
Europeans and Israelis are also moving in.
With property prices rising, local grumbling
can be forgiven, but forward-thinking President
Arias has drafted legislation that recognises the
economic importance of all those that come to
Costa Rica, and seeks to normalise the status
of illegal immigrants.

THE POLITICS OF DEVELOPMENT

Poised between a bucolic past and a dynamic future, Costa Rica's road to modernity is sometimes a bumpy one. A hotly contested debate over whether to join the Central American Free Trade Agreement (CAFTA) might have concluded with a narrow approval in an October 2007 referendum, but the story didn't end there. The opposition party in Congress has blocked the laws that were needed to implement the agreement. The government was forced to seek an extension of the 29 February 2008 deadline to pass the accord. In the meantime, delay in its implementation has forced some businesses, particularly those that export textiles, to close as foreign customers travel elsewhere.

> **'The government has taken steps to open up Costa Rica to the new era of globalisation.'**

Opponents of the agreement insist that increased competition through CAFTA will wreak havoc on the tiny businesses that have traditionally been such an important part of the country's economy. This is especially true in the countryside, where sweet-natured neighbourliness blended with a hard-scrabbled self-reliance is the norm. Those opposing CAFTA also say that the agreement threatens the country's welfare state, a bulwark of the stability Costa Rica has enjoyed for more than 50 years. Supporters of the accord (including President Arias) are equally insistent that Costa Rica, with its high standards of education and hard won democratic institutions, is ready to compete in the globalised economy and poised to join the ranks of the developed world – *if* it takes advantage of CAFTA's trade opportunities.

Costa Rican foreign policy is not restricted to North American issues. In 2007, it broke ties with Taiwan, changing allegiance to the People's Republic of China and thus adding a potential market of three billion people to Costa Rica's portfolio. Furthermore, a free trade agreement with the European Union (EU) is being negotiated in concert with the rest of Central America. This, in theory, would see a joint Central American parliament making political decisions that would directly affect relations between the region and the EU. The EU's desire for Costa Rica to join the Central American Parliament and Central American Court of Justice has not been unequivocally reciprocated, and demonstrates its character as a country that traditionally holds itself at arm's length from its neighbours when it comes to political union. For Costa Ricans concerned about foreign competition and the diminishing power of local communities, there is much to fret about.

Against some concerted opposition, Arias has made several efforts to extend Costa Rica's international ambit. He reached out to the Arabic world, moving Costa Rica's Israeli Embassy from hardline Jerusalem to the moderate Tel Aviv, and renewing relations with the Muslim population that were severed when Jerusalem was chosen as its location in the early 1980s. At the same time Arias recognised Palestine as a state and opened diplomatic relations with the territory, in the hope it will be brought closer to the international community and in some measure contribute to a peaceful resolution of the Arab-Israeli conflict.

Overall, the government has taken steps to push Costa Rica into the new era of globalisation, with the ultimate aim of attracting enough investment to provide young university graduates with high-paying jobs and integrate the country for good into world markets. The pace of life in cities such as San José has already quickened as the country shifts into a higher gear, readying itself for competition. Along the west side of the capital a glimpse of the future is emerging with new industrial parks, glittering malls, upscale bistros and five-star hotels. Those university graduate jobs are already out there in cities like San Antonio de Belén, where microchip giant Intel set up shop in the late 1990s and whose presence has encouraged other software companies to move in. The city of Heredia is another example of software success.

THE TRUE COST OF GROWTH

Change, however, does take some getting used to. Not everything is a rosy picture of paradise and progress. In days gone by Costa Rican police carried screwdrivers in their holsters to remove the licence plates of illegally parked cars. But in recent years, the streets have got meaner. Small town homeyness is rapidly disappearing from the environs of San José, the bustling capital city where, regrettably, the growing pains of an expanding megalopolis, such as theft, robbery and vandalism, is becoming more and more felt. Driving around the city, first-time visitors often wonder what they've signed up for when they see row after row of houses barricaded with razor wire, broken glass-topped walls and iron gates.

The rise in crime in urban areas is a trend dominating the media. Although never ones to shirk at exaggerating the perceived threat, newspapers of all political leanings are placing this at the top of their editorial agenda. It doesn't help, of course, that Costa Rica lies

The beautiful game

Most Central American countries' favourite ball game is baseball. In Costa Rica, however, it is soccer that obsesses the nation.

Taking their inspiration from Brazil, Argentina and Italy, Ticos' level of fanaticism for football is well above the neighbouring countries' obsession with baseball, and Costa Rica's national team has correspondingly done well. Any conversation about football will result in fond reminiscing of reaching the last 16 in the 1990 World Cup (OK it's not Brazil, but it's only a small country). A good position in more recent World Cups has proved frustratingly elusive, and as a result, much of the Costa Rican international footballing pride was focused through the success of Paolo Wanchope, whose memorable tenure at West Ham, Derby County and Manchester City will have fixed him in British football fans' minds.

The Tico fans, while lamenting their international success, turn to the domestic league for necessary boasting. The purple and orange of Deportivo Saprissa is the colour painted on most Ticos' chests. (Their rare purple shirts were said to have appeared when their previous kit, red shirts and blue shorts, were washed together.) Today there are more devotees of El Monstruo Morado (the Purple Monsters) than any other team. Not that you should ever say that to a Liga Deportiva Alajuelense fan. Arch rivals of Saprissa, Alajuelense are also their poorer cousins in terms of titles (24 as opposed to 26), if not the financial well-being of their fans who are traditionally middle class. But when these teams meet in the league, it all but stops the nation. The intense competition between the two sides began in 1949, when Alajuelense beat Saprissa 6-5 in El Estadio Nacional. The friendly banter between Costa Rica's two most supported teams turned violent during the late 1990s, when, copying the trouble of South America and Europe, the fans formed hooligan groups, known as *barra bravas*.

Saprissa's *barra brava*, La Ultra Morada or the Purple Ultra, was formed in 1995. They quickly developed a reputation for violence, particularly against Alajuelense's die-hard fans, know as La Doce, or the Twelfth Player, for their perceived status of being like an extra man.

Both clubs appear to have controlled the issue and the 'Costa Rican classic' makes for an exciting evening, with firework displays and a party atmosphere thrown in for free. While the Purple Monster bounces at one end of the stadium, the red and black mass at the other end counters every insult and noise-making, doubling their effort.

It is a truly Latin-style sporting event. Even if the derby game isn't scheduled while you are in Costa Rica, a trip to a football match is an undeniably important part of Tico culture. And at least this way, you can hold a conversation with any Costa Rican. Just have a look which shirt they are wearing first.

squarely on the drug trafficking route between South America and the US. Consequently, the country has become a trans-shipment point for drug barons, which has led to an upsurge in drug related violence. Substance abuse has also increased, resulting in more robberies and car jackings – daily crimes that contribute to a general mood of insecurity. But now, gone are the dumpy Keystone Kops with holstered screwdrivers, supplanted by a more professional, better equipped force that routinely stages raids on drug havens.

Of more concern is the growth in sex tourism, particularly with under-age boys and girls. Human rights groups continue to work in the country to combat the problem, but with prostitution completely legal, wiping out the problem of under-age sex tourism is proving a major challenge. San José is the main centre for child sex tourism, but some coastal towns, in particular Jacó, are also blighted. The government is, to some extent, beginning to crack down on the problem and educate people often involved in the trade such as hotel staff and taxi drivers. Tourists, usually, don't witness this side of life and go straight from the airport to descend upon the country's most stunning regions. To many living in the country, it seems the tourist desire for untouched beauty stretches to every corner. There is worry that with such a large draw, Costa Rica's unique natural destinations will be overwhelmed by the 'Machu Picchu' effect. But if Costa Rica wants to play with the big boys of the developed world, change is going to continue. Let's hope the government's 'crusade to protect the environment' is taken seriously.

Red-eyed tree frog.

Wild Costa Rica

All creatures great, small, prolific – and endangered.

Eyesight and fog permitting, the entire southern half of Costa Rica can be seen from the country's highest peak, Cerro Chirripó. At only 51,300 square kilometres (19,807 square miles) in area, the country makes up only 0.03 per cent of the planet's land mass. In its environs, however, are found six per cent of the planet's animal and plant species. It is an oft-repeated phrase but Costa Rica is probably the most biodiverse country on Earth. There are 870 species of bird, more than in all of the continental US and Canada combined, 1,500 species of orchid, 280 types of mammal, 380 species of reptile and amphibian and tens of thousands of insects (and counting).

This incredible diversity is due to a number of factors. The most important are the country's geographical position as a land bridge between North and South America and the varied topography that provides for a multitude of different tropical life zones and microclimates.

NATURE'S BEAKS AND TWEAKS

While topography and microclimate are important, there are a number of other factors common to many tropical ecosystems that contribute to Costa Rica's off-the-chart biodiversity. Firstly, the lack of a winter season means that plants and animals can grow and reproduce all year long. Secondly, the physical structure of the tropical forests means wildlife that thrives at different altitudes can come together in small areas. Thirdly, with so many different organisms inhabiting the same space, those at the upper end of the food chain have a feast day. This has led to the development of some impressive predator-avoidance strategies such as walking stick insects and bright warning colours in poisonous frogs. Finally, evolutionary developments and natural selection have led to a wide variation in species. The long, curved beaks of hummingbirds have developed to reach the nectar inside heliconias.

PROTECTING BIODIVERSITY

Costa Rica was originally 99 per cent forested. In 1950, only half of the country was covered by trees, and by 1984 only 19 per cent of the original forest cover remained. At this time, the country had one of the highest deforestation rates in the world. It was also during the 1980s that environmentalists urged political leaders to respond. The government forged one of the most extensive protected area systems in the tropics. Today an estimated 25 per cent of the country's land is protected by law as national parks, reserves and refuges. These protected areas contain an excellent cross-section of the country's ecosystems. Nevertheless, like all developing countries, Costa Rica is saddled with high foreign and internal debt and is subject to the process of globalisation, which often places macroeconomic goals above those of a social or environmental nature. These circumstances – together with socio-economic inequality, the lingering effects of high population growth, inefficient planning and failure to enforce environmental laws – conspire to put pressure on natural resources.

Thus, Costa Rica's protected areas face a number of challenges. The parks are increasingly fragmented, as agricultural and timber interests continue to encroach. Of Costa Rica's total land area today, nearly 60 per cent is dedicated to agricultural production. Of this agricultural land, 1,200 square kilometres (463 square miles) are dedicated to production for domestic consumption while 2,200 square kilometres (850 square miles) are dedicated to export crops, making it the only Central American country in which more agricultural land is dedicated to production for foreign markets as opposed to national ones.

And while it has brought many benefits, tourism itself can have negative environmental consequences as the increasing numbers of visitors adversely affect wildlife, not least because government policy tends to favour larger-scale tourism development. Finally, urban ecological problems such as water and air pollution are reaching critical proportions.

SEEING BIODIVERSITY

Despite the environmental and conservation issues described above, wildlife is indeed abundant in Costa Rica, and wildlife-lovers, birdwatchers and photographers visiting the country will be in nature nirvana. There are five main areas that stand out in terms of habitat for wildlife viewing.

The dry forests of the northern Pacific coast are a great place to view magpie jays, howler monkeys, acacia ants, and turquoise-browed motmots. And the coastal areas and river deltas offer fantastic habitat for birds such as black-necked stilts, roseate spoonbills and frigatebirds. Marine fauna such as golden rays and whale sharks also can be spotted off the coast, and olive ridley turtles come to lay their eggs on the beaches.

The Caribbean plains offer fantastic wildlife viewing opportunities both in the forest and along the various rivers and black water canals that meander through the area. Poison frogs, tree frogs, spider monkeys, sloths and toucans inhabit the forests. Spectacled caiman, anhingas, kingfishers and agami herons live near the water. Endangered green sea turtles lay eggs on the beaches along the northern Caribbean coast.

'Plants have evolved in concert with a staggering number of shimmering hummingbird species.'

Another lowland rainforest area, found on the Península de Osa in the Southern Pacific part of the country, was considered by the late botanist Al Gentry to be one of the best rainforests in the world in terms of structure and botanical diversity. The hot, steamy rainforests of the Península de Osa also constitute the most important refuge for large but highly endangered species such as jaguars, Baird's tapir and the huge harpy eagle. For a full-on jungle experience, the Península de Osa is the place to go.

Cloud forests are a birdwatcher's paradise, an enchanted habitat that is home to emerald toucanets, resplendent quetzals, and golden-browed chlorophonias. Because these forests are enshrouded with cloud cover much of the year, epiphytic plants such as orchids, bromeliads, tropical violets and tropical blueberries reach their peak of abundance and diversity. These plants have evolved in concert with a staggering number of shimmering hummingbird species, ranging from the tiny green scintillant hummingbird to the large purple violet sabrewing.

The sub-alpine habitat, or *paramó*, that occurs on the highest peaks of Costa Rica is a different world altogether. Stunted trees and native chusquea bamboo harbour intriguing and rarely seen species such as fiery-throated hummingbird and volcano junco sparrow. The *paramó* is also home to dozens of endemic species of flower.

BEYOND THE PARKS

While famous, Costa Rica's national park system may not be the best option for viewing

The **boa constrictor**, Costa Rica's largest snake.

or photographing wildlife. The visiting hours are the first problem; the parks are often closed during early morning and late afternoon, precisely the times when the wildlife is most active. In addition, it can be exceedingly difficult to spot wildlife in deep forest. Good lodges often have their own private reserves, which are likely to be accessible at the best times for wildlife viewing. And because these lodges are often at the forest edges, wildlife can be easier to see. A good itinerary might balance visits to national parks with eco-lodges handpicked for their wildlife viewing opportunities and facilities.

Wherever you go, you will need to give careful consideration to the lodges that you visit and the companies that you contract for your travel arrangements. Good guides, travel companies and the staff at quality eco-lodges know where you need to be, and when, in order to see wildlife. These lodges are highlighted in the various sections throughout the guide.

There are also many travel companies that offer general travel, and others that offer specialised travel for birdwatchers and wildlife enthusiasts. The most recommended are:

Caravan Tours *(www.caravan.com, 312 321 9800 from US).*
Established for more than 50 years, it has organised eco-tours at a good price. It covers both coasts and the Central Valley.

Costa Rica Expeditions
(www.costaricaexpeditions.com, 2257 0766).

There are numerous options from rafting expeditions to remote national park exploration.

Foto Verde Tours *(www.fotoverdetours.com, 2253 1611).*
This highly recommended operator specialises in photographic tours of Costa Rican wildlife and scenery. It offers full trips, tailored tours and one- or two-day workshops in the Central Valley town of Zarcero.

GeoPassage *(www.geopassage.com, 2244 9885).*
An online tour agency, based in Austin, Texas, with several Costa Rican packages specialising in wilderness guided tours.

Reef and Rainforest *(www.reefand rainforest.co.uk, 01803 866965 from UK).*
Arranges tailor-made nature tours. Trips include rainforests, national parks and beaches around Costa Rica. 'Romantic' and 'deluxe' nature trips are also offered.

Sunbird Tours *(www.sunbirdtours.co.uk, 01767 262522 from UK).*
Two-week nature tours focusing on birdwatching. Expert guides will take small groups to prime birdwatching sites such as those within the Talamaca region, Monteverde cloud forests and PN Baurillo.

Tropical Nature Travel *(www.tropical naturetravel.com, 1-877 888 1770 from US).*
This company offers three Costa Rican tours but its 'tree top' tour is the best for wildlife watching and includes visits to PN Arenal.

Wildlife guide

MAMMALS

Agouti

Common name Agouti
Scientific name *Dasyprocta punctata*
Habitat Dry forests, rainforests and cloud forests throughout Costa Rica.
The agouti is a very large and strangely handsome rodent that plays an important role dispersing seeds in the tropical rainforests of Costa Rica. A solitary ground-dweller, this cinnamon-coloured rodent hoards seeds in random places, like a squirrel, throughout the forest to make them harder for peccaries to find and dig up. The agouti never finds all of its food, so many of the seeds sprout in places far from the parent tree.

Humpback whale

Common name Humpback whale
Scientific name *Megaptera novaeangliae*
Habitat South Central Pacific coast, especially PN Marino Ballena and Bahía Drake.
Humpback whales grow to 16 metres (53 feet) in length and can weigh over 36,000 kilograms (79,000 pounds). Despite their size, humpbacks are agile travellers; indeed, recent studies show that they make the longest migration of any mammal on the planet. After travelling over 8,000 kilometres (4,970 miles) from the west coast of Antarctica, humpback whales arrive at Costa Rica's Pacific coast to breed from July to September. Humpback whales from the North Pacific arrive from December to February.

Three-toed sloth

Common name Three-toed sloth
Scientific name *Bradypus variegatus*
Habitat Dry forests, rainforests and cloud forests throughout Costa Rica.
With a top speed of 0.25kph, the three-toed sloth lives up to its name, sometimes remaining in the same tree for days. Part of the sloth's lethargy is due to the leaves it consumes, which are low on energy. Sloths are the most abundant mammals in intact rainforests, and in Costa Rica they are one of the few forest mammals whose survival may have been enhanced by forest fragmentation and habitat degradation. This is because sloths' traditional predators are the jaguar and the harpy eagle, large animals that require extensive areas of undisturbed forest.

▶

Mantled howler monkey

Common name Mantled howler monkey
Scientific name *Alouatta palliata*
Habitat Dry forests, rainforests, and cloud forests throughout Costa Rica.

Male howlers begin their calling before dawn, and their roar carries two kilometres through dense jungle to let nearby troops know the extent of the other troop's territory. Howlers are vegetarians; about two thirds of their diet consists of leaves and the other third of fruits and flowers. Howlers are intelligent and have been observed eating the leaves of the ron-ron tree (*astronium graveolens*), after feeding on fruit. Fruits contain sugars, and studies show that ron-ron leaves help to prevent cavities and gum disease as they have anti-bacterial properties.

White-faced capuchin monkey

Common name White-faced capuchin monkey
Scientific name *Cebus capucinus*
Habitat Dry forests, rainforests and cloud forests throughout Costa Rica.

White-faced monkeys are really the goats of the New World rainforest. Climbing from the forest floor to the top of the canopy, these agile monkeys eat everything – plant leaves and branches, ripe fruits, flowers, caterpillars, ants, grasshoppers, small lizards, bird chicks and eggs, even coconuts growing in the rubbish dump outside PN Manuel Antonio. Yet they are important seed dispersers and also help to reduce insect infestation on certain tree species by eating large quantities of larvae. They live in groups, sometimes of up to 30 individuals.

White-nosed coatimundi

Common names White-nosed coatimundi, coati
Scientific name *Nasua narica*
Habitat Dry forests, rainforests and cloud forests throughout Costa Rica.

Coatis are perhaps the most commonly seen mammal in Costa Rica. A relative of the raccoon, coatis are active during the daytime when they roam the forest from floor to canopy using their acute sense of smell to locate their invertebrate prey. At certain times of year, they will supplement their diet with wild fig, mountain almond and hog plum fruits. Adult coati males are generally solitary, but youngsters and females can be seen in groups of ten or more. Their predators include boa constrictors, large raptors and jungle cats. Coatis have double-jointed ankles and are able to descend trees head first.

AMPHIBIANS AND REPTILES

Boa constrictor

Common name Boa constrictor
Scientific name *Boa constrictor*
Habitat Dry forests and rainforests
throughout Costa Rica.

The boa is Costa Rica's largest snake, with
specimens occasionally growing to over 3.5
metres (12 feet) in length. The boa kills its
animal prey – iguanas, coatis, monkeys, and
even deer – via constriction rather than
venom. After seizing an animal with its sharp,
decurved teeth, boas squeeze until the prey
is suffocated and then swallow their meal
head first. Boas are hard to spot in the forest
but can be quite common near human
dwellings in rural areas as they are attracted
to the abundant supply of rodents and small
agricultural animals.

Emerald basilisk lizard

Common names Emerald basilisk lizard,
Jesus Christ lizard
Scientific name *Basiliscus plumifrons*
Habitat Rainforests of Caribbean plains.

Basilisk lizards, of which there are three
species in Costa Rica, can run on water in
order to flee from predators. This fantastic
escape behaviour is made possible by a
moveable flap of skin on the basilisk's feet.
This flap increases the surface area and
forms air pockets under the feet while the
basilisk runs through the water on its hind
legs. Due to this ability, they are also called
Jesus Christ lizards. It has been calculated
that for a man to sprint like a basilisk lizard
does on water, he'd have to dash at 100kph
(62mph). The emerald basilisk is an
opportunistic feeder and dines regularly on
insects, frogs and even smaller lizards.

Eyelash viper

Common name Eyelash viper
Scientific name *Bothriechis schlegelii*
Habitat Rainforests throughout Costa Rica.

Eyelash vipers are fascinatingly beautiful, yet
potentially lethal, arboreal snakes with
triangular-shaped heads and scales over their
eyes that look like eyelashes. Sit-and-wait
predators, they usually strike mice and frogs
but a handful of people die every year in
Costa Rica from their bites. The species
comes in a variety of colours, each of which
has adapted to camouflage itself within its
surroundings. Perhaps the most attractive is
the yellow eyelash viper, which can be seen
frequently near Tortuguero and Carara
national parks.

▶ Fleischmann's glass frog

Common name Fleischmann's glass frog
Scientific name
Hyalinobatrachium fleischmanni
Habitat Rainforests and cloud forests
throughout Costa Rica.

Glass frogs receive their name from the
translucency of their skin, particularly on their
undersides, where the heart and other vital
organs are sometimes visible. Fleischmann's
glass frogs are found most often near fast-
flowing streams. Males call from leaves
overhanging the water on rainy nights. After
mating, the eggs hatch, and the tadpoles fall
directly into the water. Hatching is triggered
by rain, which disturbs the water surface
below and decreases the probability of fish
detecting and eating the tadpoles as soon as
they hit the water.

Green iguana

Common name Green iguana
Scientific name *Iguana iguana*
Habitat Dry forests and rainforests
throughout Costa Rica.

The trade in their meat (yes, reputed to taste
like chicken) and their sale as pets have
reduced their numbers in decades past,
but now green iguanas are quite commonly
observed in many parts of Costa Rica.
Despite its name, only juvenile green iguanas
are green. Older iguanas turn brownish grey,
with males sporting a golden orange colour
during the breeding season (September to
November). Juveniles eat all manner of
invertebrates but switch to a vegetarian diet
as they mature. A common behavioural trait is
the iguana's 'head bob', which they will do as
an act of aggression or in mating ritual.

Olive ridley sea turtle

Common name Olive ridley sea turtle
Scientific name *Lepidochelys olivacea*
Habitat North Pacific beaches in
Guanacaste province.

The smallest of the sea turtles that nest on
Costa Rican beaches, the olive ridley arrives
en masse to lay eggs from June to December.
During these brief but furious *arribadas*
(arrivals), pregnant females emerge on rainy
nights from the ocean to dig pits on the sandy
beaches at Playa Ostional and Playa Nancite.
After depositing their eggs, they return to the
ocean, leaving the eggs and the future
hatchlings at the mercy of human predators
and animals such as vultures and raccoons.
Like all sea turtles they are threatened by
fishing nets and coastal development.

Red-eyed tree frog

Common names Red-eyed tree frog or gaudy
leaf frog
Scientific name *Agalychnis callidryas*
Habitat Lowland rainforest of Caribbean and
Península de Osa, mid-elevation cloud forests.
During the day, this nocturnal frog often
appears as a smallish green bump on the
underside of a heliconia or banana leaf. The
frog's garish colouring is a predator-avoidance
strategy called 'flash and dazzle' or 'startle
colouration', which is thought to cause a vital
second or two of confusion that helps it to
leap away. Birds, bats and snakes are all
predators, apparently undeterred by the weak
toxins found in the frog's skin. In the evening,
the male's call can be heard, a 'chack chack'
that acts as a way of scaring other males off
their territory.

Short-nosed vine snake

Common name Short-nosed vine snake
Scientific name *Oxybelis brevisrostrus*
Habitat Rainforests and cloud forests of
Caribbean plains and slopes, scattered
populations in Pacific slope cloud forests
of Tilaran mountain range.
The Short-nosed Vine Snake camouflages
itself by looking like the green stems of
vines. On windy days, the snakes even add
a swaying effect to their typical slithering
motion in order to enhance this camouflage,
increasing their chances of catching small
lizards and tree frogs. Although fangless and
not classified as venomous, vine snakes
actually do produce a mild venom that
consists primarily of anticoagulants and
digestive enzymes, which help to immobilise
their prey. The snakes are long and thin and
grow up to 1.5 metres (five feet) in length.

Specatacled caiman

Common name Spectacled caiman
Scientific name *Caiman crocodilus*
Habitat Lowland rivers and wetlands
throughout Costa Rica.
Caimans are alligator relatives commonly
observed near slow-moving rivers and
wetlands, particularly at the end of the dry
season when low water levels produce greater
concentrations of caimans. Though they can
grow to be 2.5 metres (eight feet) caimans
are not considered to be dangerous to
humans, and instead spend their days in
search of fish and waterbirds. Until the
1980s, caiman populations were on the
decline in Costa Rica due to the pet and
animal skin trade, but increased protection
measures have led to a population rebound.
When they reach full size caimans have
almost no predators to worry about, though
their hatchlings are often eaten by hawks.

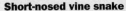

Strawberry poison frog

Common names Strawberry or blue jeans
poison frog
Scientific name *Oophaga pumilio*
Habitat Lowland rainforest of Caribbean
slope and plains.

Strong toxins in the strawberry poison frog's
skin glands are derived from its diet of ants
and the frog's bright red colour warns its
potential predators to find another snack.
Post-natal care in this frog is unusual. After
the eggs hatch, usually between three and
ten days the mother takes the tadpoles, one
at a time, for a piggyback ride up into the
trees where water collects in bromeliads. She
returns periodically to feed her babies with
her own unfertilised eggs, which provide the
tadpoles with extra protein. Metamorphosis
takes about six to eight weeks. Males are
territorial and will wrestle a rival mate until he
is defeated.

Yellow-eyed leaf frog

Common name Yellow-eyed leaf frog or
blue-sided tree frog
Scientific name *Agalychnis annae*
Habitat Coffee plantations and gardens in
the Central Valley.

The Yellow-eyed leaf frog is highly endangered.
Formerly common in cloud forests throughout
the Central Valley and the north-central
mountains, the yellow-eyed leaf frog now
survives only in coffee plantations and gardens
near San José. The frog breeds in the polluted
streams in San José, a behaviour that some
ecologists speculate may provide it with
protection against the deadly chytrid fungus
that is decimating amphibian populations
worldwide. Although an adaptable species,
the frog is in decline due to a loss of habitat.

INSECTS

Morpho butterfly

Common name Blue morpho
Scientific name *Morpho peleides*
Habitat Dry forests, rainforests and cloud
forests throughout Costa Rica.

Morpho butterflies dazzle visitors to rainforest
and cloud forest areas throughout Costa Rica
with their electric blue wings. Their shimmering
colours and erratic flight patterns help them to
avoid predators, such as jacamar birds, which
find it difficult to visually track these flying
jewels of the forest. Morpho butterflies feed
mostly on fallen fruit including wild figs and
cocoa pods. They have a large wing span for
a butterfly and indigenous peoples sometimes
use their wings as decorative accessories,
such as on ceremonial masks.

Arts & Culture

The cultural revolution has just begun.

Mexico has its mariachi bands and moustaches, Cuba has its salsa and cigars and Colombia has cumbia and Shakira. Costa Rica, on the other hand, is defined by many foreigners by its wildlife and its beaches, and not any great cultural contribution on an international level. Until now. The country is undergoing a cultural revolution. Modern art, intelligently updated traditional music, a significant classical music and opera scene and hundreds of festivals are all becoming well supported. The country's nuggets of cultural heritage have, over time, evolved into a special brand of what it means to be Costa Rican, and have defined this nation beyond its natural beauty.

Located on the Central American isthmus, the north of the country is influenced by currents from Mexico and Guatemala. Remnants of these prominent Mesoamerican cultures can be seen today in Costa Rican folk music and dance (*see p171* **A folk tale**). During celebrations, instruments like the *quijongo* (a single stringed bow and gourd) accompany women in colourful long skirts dancing the *Danza del Sol* and *Danza de la Luna* that exhibit elements of a pre-Colombian past. To the south, the provinces of Puntarenas and Limón have a Caribbean tone. The music of choice is reggae, language has inflections of patois (*see p285* **Patois patter**) and cooking ingredients include curry and coconut (*see p45* **Spice up your rice**).

Although there are noticeable differences in the cultures of its people, Costa Rica is not a divided nation and any distinctions fade completely during the country's many festivals (*see pp48-50* **Festivals & Events**), when Tico traditions and customs are celebrated and strengthened with each passing year.

AY, MARIMBA!

During festival time, towns transform from dusty backwater stops to colourful gathering points where traditional costumes, foods, parades, and most enjoyable of all, folk music are displayed. Traditional music in Costa Rica is inextricably linked to the marimba, a musical instrument popular across Latin America during the colonial era. Franciscan missionaries introduced the marimba to Costa Rica from Guatemala and its use spread throughout the region of Guanacaste and the Central Valley. Such is the importance of the percussion instrument, it was declared a national symbol in 1996. The high and velvety tones of the marimba form the basis of the compositions for traditional dances such as the *Caballito Nicoyano* (Little Nicoya Horse). In the dance, the men dress in white and carry red handkerchiefs (representing *campesinos* – peasant farmers) and they court the women while symbolically trying to lasso them. *El Punto Guanacasteco* (The Guanacaste Point) is another popular dance. It is accompanied by double-entendre filled verses that the couples sing to each other.

> **'Since 2000, there has been a boom in contemporary art attracting international attention, and money.'**

A love of dance is in Tico blood and when the sounds of strumming guitar, resonating marimba and woops and hollers ripple through the air, it makes an ordinary bank holiday back home look like a damp squib.

RURAL KITSCH

A centrepiece for many festivals is the ubiquitous Costa Rican *carreta* (ox cart). It is a national symbol (and popular tourist souvenir in miniature) and in 2005 UNESCO declared the *carreta* a 'Masterpiece of the Oral and Intangible Heritage of Humanity' (we're not sure what that means, either). The construction of *carretas* is a specialised Costa Rican craft, but they were originally used to transport coffee beans (*see p124* **Cart wheeling**). The tradition of the ox cart has also been turned into a festival of its own – *Día de los Boyeros* (Day of

the Ox Cart Driver) celebrated during March. The biggest celebration is held in Escazú.

An equally fragile souvenir is a piece of Chorotega-style pottery. The Chorotega were an indigenous group from the Guanacaste province, who lived around the town of Guatil (*see p184*). Their process of making the pottery is thought to date back 4,000 years. While the group were largely decimated after the *Conquistadores* walked down the gangplank, this Mesoamerican aesthetic has thankfully survived. Unfortunately, their language hasn't.

LIFTING LITERARY STANDARDS

Unlike many Latin American countries, Costa Rica has never been at the forefront of the literary scene. It has not produced radical writers or new schools of literature at the level of the Colombian Gabriel García Márquez and magical realism, for example. Carlos 'nothing has happened in Costa Rica since the big bang' Cortés is among those who have criticised writers for being too pedestrian. They theorise that Costa Rica's artistic conformity is because the country has not been as hit with the major struggles of dictatorships or civil war.

> **'There is a confident new generation of creative minds. Writers, performers and artists.'**

In the last 20 years, however, the literary bar has been raised and the government has been promoting the arts through prizes, scholarships, international book conferences and youth writing programmes. Contemporary authors who have attracted a lot of attention include the poet Alfonso Chase and Fernando Contreras Castro whose 1994 book *Única Mirando al Mar* looked at the sense of community found among the poor of San José. Tatiana Lobo is one of the very few Costa Rican writers whose work has been translated into English. Her historical novel *Assault on Paradise* (1998) takes an entertaining look at the 'gossipmongers and backbiters' of 18th-century Costa Rica, while taking a hefty swipe at the Catholic Church.

Anacristina Rossi's *The Madwoman of Gandoca* (1992) is set in the Gandoca-Manzanilla protected area of the Caribbean. It tells the story of a woman trying to cling on to her home when threatened by encroaching development. The most recent Tico author to have a book translated is Óscar Núñez Olivas. His journalistic storytelling craft is evident in his 2007 true crime novel *Cadence of the Moon*. One of the most famous novels is *The Island of Lonely Men* by José León Sánchez, which

A whole lot of bull

Internationally, bullfighting doesn't get a whole lotta love. What its proponents would define as a vital cultural legacy translates in the eyes of others as plain old cruelty. And for many visitors to Costa Rica going to check out the local bullfight is a step too far when it comes to immersing oneself in local culture. Rice and beans every day for breakfast, yes please; wheezing, bleeding bulls, no gracias.

While bulls here aren't killed or intentionally injured, there are not many animal-lovers who would consider the industry a fine service to human-taurine relations. Likewise, the risks for those going head-to-head with 700 kilos of meat and horn are real ones, and fatal gorings are far from unheard of. It's possible to see why some find it thrilling, just as it's possible to see why some find it appalling. Put simply, it's up to you. The fact is this: like them or loathe them, bull sports form an integral part of a large number of annual fiestas.

The tradition of bullfighting in Costa Rica is long-founded. Guanacaste's grassy ranches are their spiritual home – it was here that *sabanero* (cowboy) culture first took hold, with 18th- and 19th-century cowboys banding together seasonally to herd up their cattle at round-up time. Job done, they would then cut loose with hard-drinking parties and balls-out contests of masculinity. In *sabanero* terms, pitching their wits against the thunderous hulk of an infuriated bull – whether straddling it or outsmarting it – was pretty much the dictionary definition of 'macho', and the sport's popularity swelled.

These pastimes evolved over the years to the point where bull-running, rodeo-riding and Tico bullfighting began to occupy central roles as spectator events at northern festivals. The trend spread southwards as bullfighting heritage status hardened, and today few corners of the country are strangers to bucking hooves, quick-stepping *matadors* or iron-cheeked rodeo riders.

The local *redondel* (bullring) can constitute anything from a thatched wooden clearing to a smart new building, and at larger festivals you'll encounter a suitably red-blooded attitude to drinking and dancing after the event. It's said that recent legislation was introduced to ensure participants abstained from alcohol prior to stepping into the ring – although quite why anyone with a brain would choose to do so sober is anyone's guess.

recounts his life in a Guanacaste island prison; *see p218* **Isle of fright**.

A BRUSH WITH MODERNITY

Like the literary arts, the story of Costa Rican painting has not been a globally influential one, until very recent times. Most of the country's art history can be traced back to the school of one man, Tomás Povedano de Arcos (1847-1943), a Spanish painter who was invited to Costa Rica by the then president Rafael Iglesias Castro, to promote the arts. Povedano de Arcos founded the Escuela de Bellas Artes (School of Fine Arts) in 1897 and was its director for 40 years. The most significant artists from the first half of the 20th century to pass through the school's classrooms include Francisco Amighetti, Ezequiel Jiménez and Teodorico Quirósi whose work *El Portón Rojo* – The Red Gate – can be seen in the **Museo de arte Costarricense** *(see p101)*. During this time landscape painting was the most popular genre, and picturesque mountain towns were depicted in watercolour and muted oils. Key landscape artists include Margarita Bertheau, Juan Luis Rodriguez and Francisco Zúñiga.

Musical differences

With a bank of artists as equally home-grown and vibrant as the orange fruit from which it takes its name, Costa Rica's leading world music label, Papaya Music, provides a deserved platform for Central America's talented and largely underexposed musicians. Since the label's 2003 inception, the region's finest – including popular group Malpaís, the late Ray Tico and the Caribbean sounds of Walter Ferguson – have been receiving the full treatment from Papaya's team of top graphic designers, sound technicians, photographers and researchers. And the result? A collection of beautifully crafted albums fusing traditional Mesoamerican influences with contemporary sounds.

Lending their wealth of experience to the cause are art curator Virginia Pérez-Ratton,

MALPAÍS Uno

MANUEL OBREGÓN Y
LA ORQUESTA DE LA ___

filmmaker and producer Luciano Capelli and producer Yazmín Ross. 'Every Papaya Music album is a celebration,' says Ross. 'Each is a piece of Central America's musical identity that brings together traditional and contemporary performers, well-known artists and writers to blend music, images and lyrics, making each CD a small, unique work of art.'

The Papaya label was the idea of pianist, composer and all-round music maestro Manuel Obregón. The San José-born musician began tinkling the ivories aged seven, and his interest in jazz has taken him to Barcelona and Switzerland. He has a veritable catalogue of music to his name, both solo musician and composer, and his awards' cabinet is bursting courtesy of the Costa Rican Music Composers and Authors

During the 1960s, artists reacted against the subjects and techniques of their forefathers as magical realism cast its wand across Latin America. Abstract expressionism and the use of bright colours were explored in order to express new themes. Manuel de la Cruz González played a fundamental role in the introduction of modernist art to the country.

In 1961, together with Luis Daell Avila and Felo García, he founded *Grupo Ocho*, which searched for a way out of figurative art; *see p112* **Local colours**. In 1964, Cruz González formed *Grupo Taller* with Carlos Moya, Rafa Fernández and Claudio Carazo. Their aim was to share artistic experiences while respecting the individual style of each group member. A good example of modern Costa Rican artistic style is in the work of Puntarenas-born Isidro Con Wong. He says his art is influenced by the Costa Rican's natural surroundings and is best represented through magical realism, which renders the natural world in a swirl of bright colours and bizarrely rendered animals.

HOLDING UP THE EASEL

Institutional and state support for new artistic trends began with the foundation of San José's **Museo de Arte y Diseño Contemporáneo** (MADC) (*see p86*) in 1994. It quickly became the

spearhead for the local avant-garde in the 1990s with its goal to disseminate and promote the most recent and dynamic in contemporary art and design. MADC's permanent collection brings together the most important Central American contemporary art, with works by recognised Costa Rican, Central American and international artists.

The private gallery **Jacob Karpio Galería** (Cuesta de Núñez, San José, www.jacobkarpio-galeria.com, 2257 7963) has been instrumental in promoting Costa Rican art at an international level. It was the first gallery to represent Costa Rican artist Federico Herrero (born in 1978), who won the Golden Lion prize for a young artist at the 49th Venice Biennale in 2001, and is currently the Central American artist most widely promoted by galleries and museums in Germany, Spain, England and Japan. Jacob Karpio Galería also represents Priscila Monge (photography), Lucía Madriz (installations), Guillermo Tovar (drawing) and Alejandro Ramírez (performance), all of whom are known at an international level. Next door to this space is **TEOR/ética** (www.teoretica.org), an NGO that promotes new artistic ideas from a non-commercial point of view.

Since 2000, there has been a boom in contemporary art. There are several art fairs

Association. Trophies include best composer and best album. He is also a member of the much-loved band Malpaís.

Obregón's Papaya label celebrates the relationship between Central American music and the natural world, and continues the work of his Orchestre de la Papaya in publicising the region's music. Formed in 2002, the orchestra saw the coming together of 14 musicians from seven Central American countries, in a melting pot of indigenous, European, African and world urban sounds. Their tracks include samples of the Panamanian violin, Nicaraguan marimbas alongside *tinajas* from Guatemala and drums from Honduras. February 2006 saw the orchestra lead the first ever Papaya Music Festival and draw crowds across the isthmus to San José. Although not yet an annual event, there are plans for more sporadic festivals of its type. Papaya Music may currently be based in the Costa Rican capital San José, but future ambitions involve expanding throughout Central America, continuing the search for unreleased and under-publicised Central American music.
www.papayamusic.com

throughout the year. **Valoarte** is an annual art auction that has acted as a weather vane for artistic trends in Costa Rica. MADC's **Bienal de Artes Visuales (Bienarte)**, which takes place every other year, is a commercial exhibition responsible for selecting Costa Rican representatives to attend the Central American Biennale. Other important festivals include the **Festival Internacional de las Artes** (www.festivaldelasartescostarica.com) held in April, **Festival de Musica Credomatic** (www.credomatic.com) in August, the film festival at the Café Britt theatre **Festival de Cine y Video Documental Terruño Espressivo** (www.terrunoespressivo.com) and the **Fiesta de la Musica** (www.msj.co.cr), a street music festival held in San José in the third week of June.

THE FAT LADY SINGS

The government of Costa Rica is a keen supporter of the arts, funding Orquesta Sinfónica Nacional, its choir Coro Sinfónico Nacional and the **Teatro Nacional** (*see p86*), various performing arts groups, youth programmes and village art projects. Sponsorship falls under the Ministry of Culture and Youth (MCJ). The head office is located in the Centro Nacional de la Cultura (Antigua Fábrica Nacional de Licores, Avenida 3, entre Calles 11 y 15, www.mcjdcr.go.cr, 2255 3376).

Costa Rica also rolls out the red carpet for acclaimed touring companies, a recent example of which was the Julliard String Quartet. Universities are active in promoting the arts. The **Universidad de Costa Rica** (*see p95*) even has its own arts channel on AmNet that broadcasts recitals and other performances. There are also many cultural and artistic surprises tucked away unlikely places: San José's underground theatre scene, Heredia's amateur opera company, Caribbean cooking lessons in Tortuguero and an open-air art museum in Punta Islita, Guanacaste (*see p206* **Frescoes al fresco**).

During the past 50 years, Costa Rican writers, performers and artists have woken up and smelled the scent of their native coffee, so to speak, leading to the emergence of a confident new generation of artistic minds. The bizarre Tico saying 'Costa Rica does not have an army but does have violins' may well become a bumper sticker yet as the arts continue to grow. And while its biodiversity and its beaches are still the major attractions for most tourists, it is the nation's artistic endeavours that are beginning to redefine how the country is seen from abroad.

Fish supper at **Iguana Verde**.
See p270.

Eating & Drinking

Prime local ingredients, simply prepared, Caribbean-style.

Depending on which area of the country you visit, you'll find a variety of dining choices in Costa Rica. Along the coasts, needless to say, seafood dominates. In the north the menu is more typically indigenous and very (and we mean *very*) corn-based. On the Caribbean you'll taste more African influences: spicier dishes cooked in coconut oil or milk with tubers, such as yams.

As in most countries, the food is generally better in the more densely populated areas, like San José, Guanacaste, Limón and the Central Pacific coast. However – and partly thanks to the tourism boom – you can find good eateries throughout the country, even in very remote towns. There are many Chinese restaurants, ranging from excellent to atrocious, and also a surprising number of Italian restaurants, usually offering home-made pastas and recipes passed down from *nonna*.

RICE AND BEANS

The Costa Rican national restaurant would have to be the ubiquitous *soda*, a Central American version of the café or diner. The food is usually cheap, and *sodas* offer bargain daily specials. Often they don't even have menus and simply offer what happens to be in stock that day. A good choice will generally be one of the many varieties of *casado* (literally, 'married') – usually chicken, beef or fish fried or cooked in sauce and served with rice, stewed black beans, a small oil-and-vinegar dressed salad and fried plantains. Sodas can vary enormously in price and quality, but the most popular one in each town is by and large a good choice. Just be aware that almost everything is fried in a tanker disaster's worth of vegetable oil.

Costa Rica's most famous native dish is *gallo pinto* (literally, 'spotted rooster'). It's eaten for breakfast and consists of diced and sautéed onion and bell pepper mixed with seasoned white rice and black beans. (Vegetarians: beware of any Tico bean dishes, as the beans are sometimes stewed in lard or bacon grease.) Costa Ricans are so proud of this popular national dish that many towns have annual *gallo pinto* festivals, and an oft-spoken saying in the country is '¡*El/ella es mas tico que gallo pinto!*' (He/she is more Costa Rican than *gallo pinto*!) It's a good, hearty breakfast, full of energy for the day, but many foreigners will find the dish's weight difficult to stomach at this hour and may quickly tire of rice and beans, as they are served with every meal.

Other popular soda dishes are the various fried rices: *arroz con pollo* (chicken fried rice), *arroz con camarones* (prawn fried rice) and *arroz cantonese* or *arroz mixto* (usually rice fried with vegetables, chicken, ham, and fish or prawn). A good, standard choice for vegetarians and vegans may be *arroz con vegetales* because, unless it is sautéed in butter or chicken stock, it usually doesn't contain animal products (but never assume anything). Also common in the sodas are *patacones* (smashed and fried green plantain chips) and ceviche – chopped raw fish or lightly cooked prawn 'cooked' in lime juice with diced vegetables and chillies.

FRUITS OF THE SEA

Costa Rica is a seafood-lover's paradise. For fish, the coastal menus usually include *dorado* (mahi-mahi or dolphin fish), various other species of *atún* (tuna), *corvina* (sea bass), *róbalo* (snook) and *pargo rojo* (red snapper), served in fillets, steaks or whole. There is also a large variety of shellfish available ranging from the delicious *piangua* (black clam) ceviche to the enormous *camarón jumbo* (king prawn). Depending on your tastes, seafood cooked soda-style can sometimes be a little bland and you may want to try some of the more interesting 'Costa Rican fusion' restaurants popping up.

Although hardly a gourmet's paradise, Costa Rican cuisine can be tasty and diverse, particularly along the Caribbean coast, and many people return home looking for a recipe for *gallo pinto*.

FRUITS OF THE FOREST

Delicious tropical fruits, like mango, banana, *guayaba* (guava), papaya and various melons, are readily available throughout the country. They are often mixed with sugar and water to make *naturales* (natural fruit drinks), or blended *con agua* (with water) or *con leche* (with milk) and ice to make *batidos* (smoothies).

Spice up your rice

Think you can't get enough rice and beans? You'd be surprised. Endlessly chowing down on this combo can dull the palate, not to mention put a strain on intimacy. Most visitors to Costa Rica will therefore delight in the spicier offerings of the African-influenced Caribbean coastal region. Zesty Creole-inspired dishes are prepared with an imaginative use of African spices, exuding hints of coriander, cumin, black pepper, chillies and ginger. Coconut milk is used in many dishes to transform the most basic of ingredients into exotic culinary masterpieces. Fish, chicken and pork concoctions are simmered for hours until the meat is tender and saturated in a seductively sweet and spicy coconut cream.

Caribbean cooking incorporates vegetables and starchy tubers common in Africa and Jamaica such as yucca, potatoes and *fruta de pan* (breadfruit) – a native African crop with a whitish flesh that is usually boiled or baked. Ackee – a spongy yam-like fruit that is poisonous when unripe – tastes a bit like scrambled eggs and is often served with salted fish for breakfast. Though cast to

the pigs in other parts of the world, *pejibaye* – a bitter green or orange fruit the size of a small lime – is sold at roadside stands and eaten with salt. Patties are another grab-and-go food. They are spicy meat pies sold on the street with *pipas* – green coconuts with the top whacked off so you can drink the sweet liquid with a straw – to wash them down.

The most common regional plate is rice and beans – red or black beans and rice stewed in coconut milk. Rich enough to call a meal but often served as a side dish with other plates, it's a tasty twist on the common highland fare. Equally authentic is *rondon* ('run down' or in to cook down), a spicy coconut milk-based stew made with tropical roots such as yucca, potato and plantains, plus veggies, fish, seafood or meat, and just about anything else the cook has lying around.

Coconut, erm, nuts can end their meal with *bolitas de coco*, an alarmingly sweet dessert of balls of dried grated coconut pasted together with condensed milk and fried in butter. Other sweet delights are johnnycakes (fried sweet dumplings), *budín* (a moist fruitcake) and *pan bon* (glazed sweet bread).

Or try a drink from the passing *copero*, who will offer you *pipas* – cold peeled coconuts with a hole in the top for a straw – or one of his many other flavoured *copos* (shaved ice drinks). There are also some rather strange-looking exotic fruit treats to sample, like the *mamón* (rambutan) and *manzana de agua* (water apple). When eating fresh fruits be conscious that they may often contain pesticides or other chemicals and should be washed accordingly.

There has been a movement in recent years to promote organic farming, and many organic fruits and vegetables are readily available. However, as government regulation is lax, you should not assume that produce advertised as *organico* is truly chemical free.

TAX INSPECTOR

Costa Rican restaurants are required to add ten per cent sales tax, three per cent tourism tax and ten per cent service tax to their bills. If you find 'IVI' (*impuestos vienen incluidos* or taxes included) printed on your menu it means that the first 13 per cent is already included in the printed price. If it says *servicio incluido* (service included) it means the ten per cent service tax (which goes directly to the waiting staff) is also included. If neither of these is listed you may have to pay 23 per cent more than the printed price. Ask if you're unsure. Tipping is certainly not the norm among Ticos, but it's definitely always appreciated; most foreigners go with the ten per cent rule. All taxes should already be included for alcoholic drinks in bars.

BLACK MAGIC

Long one of the country's most important cash crops, Costa Rican coffee beans are regarded among the world's best varieties. The beverage itself is usually served black with sugar and is strong. Recently, there has been an upsurge of speciality cafés serving espresso drinks or iced coffees. If you're in a small town, the local Italian restaurant is generally a good bet for plain or mixed espressos. Coffee is grown in the highland areas throughout the country, and Ticos often have a brand preference – most often what's produced in their region. In the north they like what's grown around Poás or Heredia, while the southerners prefer beans from San Vito.

BOOZE CRUISE

Costa Rica has two main beer brands: Imperial and Pilsen. Imperial, the most popular with Ticos, is also by far the most drunk among tourists. However, if you want to try to blend in more easily with the local fishermen, cowboys and toughies, we'd recommend a Pilsen. (And remember, it's 'Pil-*sen*' not 'Pils-*ner*'). The other leading national beers are Bavaria and Rock Ice (regular or with lime). Both Imperial and Bavaria also offer a variety light in alcohol. Beers in bars range in price throughout the

A traditional soda breakfast of *gallo pinto*, tortillas, spicy sauce and, of course, coffee.

country from about US$1 a bottle in less populated areas to more or less the national standard of about US$1.60, but can be as much as US$4 in popular tourist areas. North Americans, especially, are warned to be careful, as the average alcohol content is five per cent, higher than many US beers. Carbonated, alcohol-infused drinks are also available in cans, the two most popular being Cuba Libre and Bamboo. Both are rum and cola mixes and contain about nine per cent alcohol.

Most bars have a good variety of Central American and international spirits – vodka, gin, rum, tequila and various brands of whisky are available almost everywhere, though certain mixers may be difficult to come by. Coca-Cola is pretty much the standard mixer for any of the above, but other non-alcoholic drinks – *frescos* (soft drinks) and *jugos* (juices) – are also widely available from sodas and *pulperías* (stores).

Costa Rica's national spirit is generally recognised to be *guaro*, a distilled, un-matured sugarcane liquor. However, *guaro* in common conversation could mean any liquor (think 'booze'). Real sugarcane *guaro* is sometimes labelled as vodka or rum, and while by no means tasty, is usually gluggable. The most popular brand is Cacique, but other well-known labels are Apaché and Cañita. Bottles can be as cheap as US$2 a litre and many tourist-oriented bars offer speciality drinks made with Cacique, though you'd probably be better off substituting it for vodka.

One of the favourite good-tasting Costa Rican liquors, on the other hand, is Centenario, a (slightly) dark rum, delicious on the rocks or mixed to your liking. A shot usually costs about the same as a beer in most establishments. There are also many locally made liqueurs, such as Café Rica, a coffee infusion similar to Mexico's Kahlua. Costa Rican wine is about as bad as you'd imagine, but cheap imports from Chile and Argentina are great.

In your travels you may also come across *chicha*, an indigenous fermented drink. The main ingredient in *chicha* is usually boiled corn, banana or yucca, which is made into a dough and mixed with water and sugar until it ferments. Costa Rican indigenous communities still frequently drink *chicha* for special occasions. Or you could go the bootlegger's route and search out some Costa Rican moonshine, but this is only for the hardy imbibers. Popularly called *contrabando* or *pedo de chancho* ('pig fart'), this illegal spirit is still quite common and often available from fruit trucks or under the table in your local *pulpería*.

Be warned: pig fart or no pig fart, 32-degree heat, high humidity and glaring sun do not mix well with a hangover.

The menu

Basics

Carta/menú/lista menu; **la cuenta** the bill; **desayuno** breakfast; **almuerzo** lunch; **cena** dinner; **entrada** starter; **plato principal** main course; **postre** dessert; **casero** home-made; **pan** bread; **agua** water; **cerveza** beer; **vino** wine.

Cooking styles & techniques

A la parrilla barbecued; **a la plancha** on griddle; **al horno** baked; **frito** fried.

Carne y aves (Meat & poultry)

Albóndigas meatballs; **bife de lomo** tenderloin; **cerdo** pork; **chivito** kid; **chorizo** sausage; **ciervo** deer; **conejo** rabbit; **cordero** lamb; **jamón** ham (**cocido** boiled, **crudo** Parma-style); **lechón** suckling pig; **pato** duck; **pollo** chicken.

Pescados & mariscos (Fish & seafood)

Anchoa anchovy; **almeja** clam; **atún** tuna; **bacalao** cod; **camarón** prawn; **cangrejo** crab; **ceviche** raw fish 'cooked' in citrus fruits; **choro** mussel; **corvina** sea bass; **dorado** mahi-mahi or dolphin fish; **lenguado** sole; **mejillón** mussel; **ostra** oyster; **pargo rojo** red snapper; **piangua** black clam; **pulpo** octopus; **róbalo** snook.

Verduras, arroz & legumbres (Vegetables, rice & pulses)

Arroz rice; **berenjena** aubergine/eggplant; **calabaza** pumpkin/squash; **cebolla** onion; **vainica** green beans; **elote** sweetcorn; **frijoles** black beans; **palmito** palm heart; **aguacate** avocado; **papa** potato; **puerro** leek; **zanahoria** carrot.

Fruta (Fruit)

Ananá pineapple; **cereza** cherry; **fresa** strawberry; **manzana** apple; **naranja** orange; **toronja** grapefruit.

Local specialities

Casado traditional meal with beans and rice; **chincharrones** pork crackling; **chorreadas** cornmeal cake with sour cream; **gallo pinto** mixed beans, rice, peppers and onion for breakfast; **patacones** smashed and fried plantain crisps; **rondon** seafood soup in coconut milk; **tamales** cornmeal pies with rice, meat and vegetables cooked in banana leaf; **vigoron** tortillas stuffed with cabbage.

Limón Carnival. *See p50.*

Festivals & Events

Parties, dancing, drinking – and that's just the mango festival.

It's no surprise to learn that Ticos like to party – this is Latin America, after all. As with much of the region, Costa Rica's calendar is packed with fairs, fiestas and religious knees-ups and, like many of their neighbouring countries, Catholicism and agriculture tend to provide most of the focal themes. While events aren't generally as frenzied as many of their counterparts in, say, Mexico, they still give an animated insight into the national psyche. If you're after liberal helpings of late nights and Latino zeal, you won't be disappointed. All good things come with a caveat, of course, and the bigger festivals can bring daily life to a grinding halt – no banks, no post offices, and buses that are either not running or sardine-crowded. Hotels, cabins and even vacant spots on derelict ground also fill up quickly. If you're keeping to a tight schedule, do a bit of logistics homework first and try to take in at least one festival.

January-March

Fiestas de Palmares
Palmares, Alajuela. **Location** *p117.* **Date** early Jan.
A fortnight of folk dancing, concerts, carnival rides, *tope* (horse parades) and bullfighting in what at most other times of the year is a sedate village.

Fiestas de Alajuelita
Alajuela. **Location** *p117.* **Date** mid Jan.
The token ox cart parade and pilgrim procession to the iron cross overlooking town is in honour of the Black Christ of Esquipulas. There's no shortage of music, food and drink to accompany this province's godly goings-on.

Fiestas de Santa Cruz
Santa Cruz, Guanacaste. **Location** *p183.*
Date mid Jan.
Lots of marimba music, with bullfighting and dancing. As in Alajuelita, the Black Christ of Esquipulas takes centre stage.

Fiestas de San Isidro de El General
San Isidro. **Location** *p242.* **Date** early Feb.
Agricultural fair with livestock shows, flower exhibitions and bullfighting in this colourful hub in the southern zone.

Carnaval de Puntarenas
Puntarenas. **Location** *p220.* **Date** last wk of Feb.
Music, food and fun in the sun. Repeat vigorously for seven days and you'll know what's hit you. Superb fun in this otherwise sleepy town.

Bonanza Cattle Show
Bonanza Fairgrounds, San José. **Location** *p95.* **Date** 1st wk of Mar.
Lively annual gathering of the nation's cattlemen, featuring bullfights, rodeos and horse races.

Día del Boyero (Day of the Ox Cart Driver)
Escazú, San José. **Location** *p107.* **Date** 2nd Sun in Mar.
Ox carts a-go-go. Hand-painted carts parade the streets while local priests shower blessings on the produce and animals. *See p124* **Cart wheeling**.

Festival Internacional de las Artes
San José and surrounding towns. **Location** *p81.* **Date** Mar in even-numbered years.
Taking place every other year, this arts festival showcases a variety of performance theatre, dance and artwork. Participation can be expected from both national and international artists.

Festival de Frutas
Orotina, Alajuela. **Location** *p117.* **Date** mid Mar.
Bump up your vitamin C levels with a visit to Orotina's annual celebration of the fruitier side of life. Bizarre fruits and soups are available. As well as food stalls there are fairground rides and concerts, while a series of talks are also held.

Día de San José
San José and across Costa Rica. **Location** *p81.* **Date** 19 Mar.
St Joe's big day. Celebrated around the country in all towns and villages that share his name, it's a time for fairs, church masses, bullfights and food.

April-June

Semana Santa (Holy Week)
Across Costa Rica. **Date** Mar or Apr.
If you're here at this time, you'll know about it. Costa Rica closes down pretty much entirely in the run-up to Easter Sunday – prices are often hiked and hotel space can be limited. Large-scale religious processions take place across the country, with Cartago being the major focal point. *Semana Santa* is the nation's most important holiday period.

Día de Juan Santamaría
Alajuela and across Costa Rica. **Location** *p117.* **Date** 11 Apr.

Parades, concerts and dances in commemoration of the country's national hero, drummer boy-turned-war valiant Juan Santamaría. The city of his 1831 birth, Alajuela, is at the hub of the celebrations.

Día del Trabajador (Labour Day)
Puerto Limón and across Costa Rica. **Location** *p284.* **Date** 1 May.
May Day means a state of the nation address by the president, congress elections and more marches than you can shake a stick at. Celebrations in Puerto Limón incorporate picnics and cricket matches.

Feria de Artesanía
San José. **Location** *p82.* **Date** last wk of Apr or 1st wk of May.
Large craft fair in the capital, popular with locals and souvenir-hunters alike.

Día Corpus Christi
Across Costa Rica. **Date** 29 May.
Ticos all over the country get a day off for this religious festival.

July-September

Fiestas de la Virgen del Mar
Puntarenas. **Location** *p220.* **Date** Sat closest to 16 July.
The usual array of parades, music and religious activities, headlined by a regatta of decorated boats in the Gulf of Nicoya. Held in honour of the Virgin of Mount Carmel, Puntarenas's patron saint.

Día de la Anexión de Guanacaste
Guanacaste province. **Location** *p163.* **Date** 25 July.
Focused largely but by no means entirely on Liberia, the Día de la Anexión commemorates Guanacaste's decision in 1824 to join Costa Rica, rather than neighbouring Nicaragua, although independent sentiments still remain. Bullfights, fiestas and parades are held.

Feria de los Mangos
Alajuela. **Location** *p117.* **Date** end of July.
Music, parades and craft fairs in Alajuela with a special focus on, yes, the mighty mango.

Día de la Virgen de los Ángeles
Cartago and across Costa Rica. **Location** *p133.* **Date** 2 Aug.
A nationwide pilgrimage wends its way to the basilica in Cartago, with some of the more devout travelling on their knees. More than a million people make the spiritual journey.

Día de la Independencia
Across Costa Rica. **Date** 15 Sept.
The full works: beating drums, national anthems, lantern parades and suitably raucous festivities. Students carry a 'Torch of Liberty' from Guatemala to Costa Rica, ending their journey at Cartago.

October-December

Aniversario de San Isidro

San Isidro de El General. **Location** *p242.*
Date 9 Oct.

Party held to celebrate the founding of this important southern city, an event enthusiastically seen in by locals every year.

Carnaval de Puerto Limón

Puerto Limón. **Location** *p284.* **Date** early to mid Oct.

The east coast often brings with it a suitably Caribbean ambiance, and never more so than in Puerto Limón in October. The city carnival is a week-long jump-up of costumed dancers, Mardi Gras-style parades and live bands. Columbus Day (12 October), aka Cultures' Day, is a focal point.

Día de la Virgen del Pilar

Tres Ríos, Cartago. **Location** *p133.* **Date** 12 Oct.

Held to honour the patron saint of the Tres Ríos district, chiefly by way of a parade with elaborate costumes and dancing.

Fiesta del Maíz

Upala, Alajuela, nr Costa Rica's northern border. **Location** *p117.* **Date** 12 Oct.

A spirited observance of all things maize. As well as a farmer-centric exhibition of the produce in question, there's also a Corn Queen contest and a procession of costumes fashioned entirely from corn husks and silk.

Día de los Santos Difuntos

Across Costa Rica. **Date** 2 Nov.

All Soul's Day, also known as *El Día de los Muertos* (The Day of the Dead), is when Costa Ricans to pay their respects to the dearly departed with graveyard visits, taking along all manner of offerings.

El Desfile de Carretas

San José. **Location** *p81.* **Date** late Nov.

A major parade of ox carts down the capital's Paseo de Colón, which started in 1997 to honour the cart's long heritage in the country. Participants come to San José from all over Costa Rica.

Fiesta de la Luz

San José. **Location** *p81.* **Date** begins 1st wk of Dec.

Let there be light. The city sees in December by decorating homes and businesses – parts of San José positively groan with lights – as well as with concerts and firework displays.

Fiesta de los Negritos

Boruca. **Location** *p252.* **Date** wk of 8 Dec.

The village comes alive with a mixture of indigenous ritual and Catholic tradition, culminating in one of the country's most absorbing celebrations, in which music is a key element. The fiesta is held to honour the Virgin of the Immaculate Conception.

Fiesta de la Yegüita

Nicoya. **Location** *p181.* **Date** 12 Dec.

The parade itself centres on a statue of the Virgin of Guadalupe, while the wider celebration takes in dancing, local delicacies, fireworks and concerts. Indigenous customs also play a large part.

Carolers' season

Across Costa Rica. **Date** from 15 Dec.

Tuneful *posadas* (carol singers doing the rounds door-to-door) begin in the middle of the month, often with the aim of raising money as they go – charitable causes are usually the beneficiaries.

Festejos Populares (Year-end celebrations)

Zapote Fairgrounds, San José. **Location** *p95.*
Date late Dec.

The Zapote Fairgrounds in the south of San José host a week of high-octane merrymaking, with a cavalcade of music, rides, fireworks and seasonal foods. Notable for its questionable bull-teasing antics, which can see as many as 200 people in the show-ring at any one time.

Christmas celebrations

Across Costa Rica. **Date** from early Dec.

As with elsewhere in the Christian world, Christmas for Ticos centres on spending time with families, and many of the traditions – nativity scenes, present-giving and so on – will be familiar. Festive food and drink, on the other hand, comes in the form of eggnog, *tamales*, corn beer and unfeasible amounts of apples and grapes.

Misa de Gallo

Across Costa Rica. **Date** 24 Dec.

Catholic churches mark Christmas Eve with the *Misa de Gallo* – literally, Mass of the Rooster – at the stroke of midnight.

Tope (Horse Parade)

Downtown San José. **Location** *p82.* **Date** 26 Dec.

Equine entertainment, with a large horse parade through the centre of the capital. The procession marks the end of the year's equestrian events. TV cameras transmit the spectacle to households around the country, with many top riders (and more than 4,000 horses) taking part in the proceedings.

Carnaval San José

San José. **Location** *p81.* **Date** 27 Dec.

This can be quite a sight. San José's huge December carnival combines eye-popping floats and live music with some distinctly Costa Rican flavouring. If your feet aren't moving and you're not wearing a smile, you're at the wrong parade.

Fiesta de los Diablitos

Boruca. **Location** *p252.* **Date** 30 Dec-2 Jan.

Dramatic re-enactment of a battle between Spaniards and indigenous groups, with flutes and drums, and using the Boruca's famous masks. *See p252* **Facing the past.**

Outdoor Pursuits

A | B | C | D

Lago de Nicaragua

1

- R B
  Isla Belaños
- R V S
  Bahia Junquillal
- P N
  Santa Rosa
- P N
  Guanacaste
- Estación
  Horizontes
- UPALA
- P N
  Rincón de la Vieja
- Z P
  Volcán Miravalles
- P N
  Volcán Tenorio
- LOS CHILES
- R V S
  Caño Negro
- Río Frío
- SAN RAFAEL
- R F
- Nuevo
  Arenal
- Z C Volcán Arenal
- La Fortuna
- LIBERIA
- R V S
  Iguanita
- Río Liberia
- BAGACES
- TILARÁN
- CAÑAS
- Z P
  Tenorio

2

- FILADELFIA
- P N
  Palo Verde
- Santa Elena
  Monteverde
- Z P
  Arenal
  Monteverde
- P N Arenal
- Z P
  Arenal Monteverde
- CIUDAD
  QUESADA
- P N
  Castro Blan
- R B
  Alberto Manuel
  Brenes
- ZARCERO
- NARANJO
- P N
  Marino
  Las Baulas
- R V S
  Tamarindo
- TAMARINDO
- SANTA CRUZ
- Puente la Amistad
- P N
  Diriá
- NICOYA
- P N
  Barra Honda
- JUNTAS
- MIRAMAR
- SAN RAMÓN
- SARCHÍ
  NORTE
- PALMARES
- GRE
- ATENAS

3

- OSTIONAL
- Nosara
- R V S
  Ostional
- HOJANCHA
- CARMONA
- R B
  Isla Pájaros
- PUNTARENAS
- R V S
  Isla San Lucas
- ESPARZA
- SAN MATEO
- OROTINA
- SAN PABLO
  DE TURRUBARES
- S. DE PURISC
- Sámara
- PAQUERA
- R B
  Isla Guayabo
- R V S Curú
- R B
  Isla Negritos
- P N
  Carara
- P N
  Cerro d
  La Cangre
- Montezuma
- R N A
  Cabo Blanco
- JACÓ
- PARRITA

PACIFIC OCEAN

4

- MÉXICO
- BELICE
- CUBA
- JAMAICA
- GUATEMALA
- HONDURAS
- EL SALVADOR
- NICARAGUA
- COSTA
  RICA
- PANAMA
- COLOMBIA
- Isla del Coco

PACIFIC OCEAN

Isla del Coco

0 1 2 miles
0 1 2 km

5

0 100 200 miles
0 100 200 km

6

0 10 20 30 miles
0 10 20 30 km

© Copyright Time Out Group 2008

🏄 Surfing 🎣 Fishing 🤿 Diving 🚣 Rafting 🦜 Birdwatching 🥾 Trekking 🪂 Adventure Sports

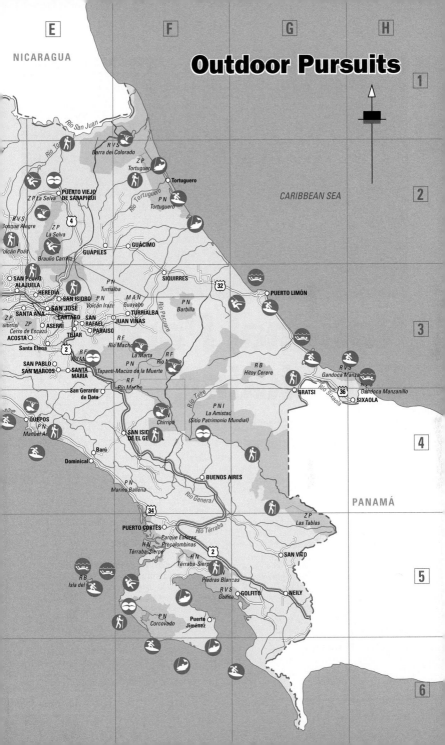

Outdoor Pursuits

NICARAGUA

CARIBBEAN SEA

PANAMÁ

E   F   G   H

1
2
3
4
5
6

Rio San Juan

Rio Tori

R V S
Barra del Colorado

Z P
Tortuguero

Tortuguero

Rio Tortuguero

P N
Tortuguero

Z P La Selva

PUERTO VIEJO
DE SARAPIQUÍ

R V S
Bosque Alegre

Z P
La Selva

Volcán Poás

Braulio Carrillo

GUÁPILES

GUÁCIMO

SIQUIRRES

32

PUERTO LIMÓN

SAN PEDRO
ALAJUELA

HEREDIA

SAN ISIDRO

P N
Turrialba

M A N
Guayabo

P N
Barbilla

SANTA ANA

SAN JOSÉ

CARTAGO

SAN
RAFAEL

SAN
ASERRÍ

P N
Volcán Irazú

TURRIALBA

JUAN VIÑAS

Z P
urbicisí

Z P
Cerro de Escazú

PARAÍSO

ACOSTA

TEJAR

R F
Río Macho

Santa Elena

R F
Río Ma

PABLO

P N
Tapantí-Macizo de la Muerte

La Marta

R F

R F
Río

R B
Hitoy Cerere

Gandoca Manza

R V S

SAN PABLO
SAN MARCOS

SANTA
MARÍA

R F
Río Macho

BRATSI

Rio Sixaola

Gandoca Manzanillo

36

San Gerardo
de Dota

Rio Telire

SIXAOLA

P N I
La Amistad
(Sitio Patrimonio Mundial)

QUEPOS

P N
Manuel A

Chirripó

SAN ISIDRO
DE EL GE

Barú

Dominical

BUENOS AIRES

P N
Marino Ballena

Rio Genera

Z P
Las Tablas

34

PUERTO CORTÉS

Rio Térraba

Parque Esferas
Precolombinas

H N
Térraba-Sierpe

H N
Térraba-Sierpe

2

SAN VITO

R B
Isla del

P N
Piedras Blancas

R V S
Golfito

GOLFITO

NEILY

P N
Corcovado

Puerto
Jiménez

Esquinas Rainforest Lodge.
See p265.

National Parks & Trekking

Enjoy one of the planet's largest national park networks.
Just bring insect repellent.

Costa Rica's main industry has become tourism. As a visitor in a not-quite third world country catering to mostly wealthy foreigners, you can expect anything from a dirt floor canvas hovel with (literally) little more than a pot to pee in to five-star extravagance with friendly and attentive all-inclusive service. This dichotomy is clearly evident in the country's many national parks. Whether you want to trek unhindered and unguided in the rough jungle with just a bivouac for shelter or lounge at the 'wet bar' of your lodge's spring-fed pool with a fruit-tini in each hand, you'll find it all – and everything in between – in Costa Rica's vast parks and forests.

THE PROMISED LAND
The birth of Costa Rica's conservation movement is credited to two people: Swedish-born Nils Olaf Wessberg and Costa Rican national Mario Boza. Wessberg and his wife, Karen Morgensen

Fischer, moved to Costa Rica in 1955 and purchased a farm in Nicoya. The couple became dismayed as they witnessed the devastation of previously untouched, ancient forest. Wessberg began a letter writing campaign and three years later had raised enough funds to purchase 12 square kilometres (4.6 square miles) and create what is now the **Reserva Natural Absoluta Cabo Blanco**. Tragically, the Swedish naturalist was murdered in 1975 by opponents of his plans to create a similar reserve on the Península de Osa.

Mario Boza became interested in conservation as a young student, in particular during a trip to the United States in the 1960s, when he was inspired by a visit to the Great Smoky Mountains. Boza returned to Costa Rica to begin work on his Masters thesis: a management plan for Volcán Poás. His plan would result in the Monumental Nacional Santa Rosa, and when the Servicio de Parques

In Context

Nacionales (SPN) was established in 1969, Boza became the organisation's first director. Yet despite the creation of the SPN, the area continued to be threatened by squatters, cattle ranchers and legislation that proposed the area be turned over to the national tourism institute. With the help of national news organisations and the National Association of Biologists, Boza and the then-president's wife, Karen Olsen Figueres, vigorously lobbied all 57 assembly members. The bill was quashed and Santa Rosa remained under the jurisdiction of the SPN.

THE PROTECTED LAND

Today some 8,240 square kilometres (3,180 square miles), which is 16 per cent of Costa Rica's entire land mass, are officially protected by the **Ministerio del Ambiente y Energía** (MINAE) and other public organisations. However, if you include mangrove forests (all of which are declared national forest reserves) and other semi-protected areas (which allow for restricted land usage), the total protected area jumps to 12,560 square kilometres (4,850 square miles) or about 25 per cent of the country. On top of this are near countless other areas cared for by private and non-profit agencies. In addition, some protected zones are reserved for research or for indigenous communities.

The **Sistema Nacional de Areas de Conservación** (SINAC) works with individual organisations to link the country's nearly three dozen protected areas into 11 conservation areas: Guanacaste, Tempisque, Cordillera Volcánica Central, Llanuras del Tortuguero, Amistad Caribe, Amistad Pacífico, Osa, Pacífico Central, Arenal-Tilarán and Arenal-Huetar Norte.

BIODIVERSITY BOASTING

Costa Rica, often considered to be the birthplace of the term 'eco-tourism', is a magnet for both biological researchers and amateur nature-lovers. Few, if any, countries have so much biodiversity in such a comparatively small area. Costa Rica, for example, is surely a birdwatcher's paradise; the country is home to 850 (and counting) avian species. To put this into perspective, this is more than in any one of the continents of North America, Australia or Europe. It is also home to some 220 mammals, 170 amphibians, 215 reptiles, more than 1,000 fresh and saltwater fish, 35,000 species of insects and 12,000 vascular plants; 1,600 of the latter are orchids (about four per cent of the world's species).

The land rises from sea level to just over 3,800 metres (12,460 feet) in the high mountain areas and contains almost all of the world's vegetation macro types: deciduous woodland,

forest savannah, evergreen forest, flooded forest, cloud forest, *páramos* (moorland) and herbaceous swamps. In addition, the country includes ecosystems like coral reefs, sandy beaches, marshes, rivers and streams. In little more than a day, in certain areas, you could conceivably do an 'ecosystem crawl' – from coastline to mangrove swamp and low rainforest, into higher cloud forests, and finally up on to the drier vegetation of the *páramos*.

Contact SINAC (2256 0917) for up-to-date information on park hours and pricing, or you may find a more specific phone directory on its website (currently in Spanish only) at www.sinaccr.net.

LOSING PARADISE

Although Costa Rica has made advances to conserve its natural environment and is now perhaps the most forward thinking of Latin American countries in this respect, many problems remain. In the 1940s, nearly 90 per cent of the country's land was forested; today the proportion is 25 per cent. Unfortunately, the government has little funding for enforcing forestry protection, and unknown amounts of land are still illegally forested.

> **'The country is home to 850 (and counting) avian species... this is more than in North America, Australia or Europe'**

One of the largest problems facing Costa Rica is pollution. Livestock rearing, farming and under-regulated factory production send toxins into rivers and watersheds where they contaminate fragile ecosystems. Litter is also a major problem. People often think nothing of throwing wrappers and plastic bottles on the ground, which then often find their way into rivers and on to beaches.

Another issue is illegal fishing, be it large (sometimes international) boats pulling in hundreds of kilograms of fish, or individual fishermen, just offshore, using nets from their small launches. Overfishing (possibly coupled with global warming) is beginning to have an impact on Costa Rican fish populations. And despite the efforts of ecologists and national and international volunteers working to maintain the sea turtle population, it's still a common occurrence in much of Costa Rica to find sea turtle eggs for sale at the local bar or *pulpería* (general store). It is believed the eggs increase sexual stamina, and they are often eaten as a direct act of rebellion against the

The best Treks

Cerro Chirripó

Scale Costa Rica's highest peak. Leave from the charming mountain village of San Gerardo de Rivas (see p245) and take two days to explore the peak and the surrounding national park. If your luck's in, you might spot quetzals and coyotes.

Parque Nacional Corcovado

Experienced trekkers adore this superlative national park. A minimum of two days is required to hike between the three ranger stations through the dense jungle, with one of the highest rates of biodiversity on the planet. See p258.

Cloud forests of Monteverde

Numerous day hikes and a few longer treks along the misty trails of Monteverde are a great way to see the vast array of wildlife in the area. See p142.

powers wishing to keep the practice illegal; see p196 **Turtle power**. Other problems include pumas being killed to protect livestock, birds trapped by poachers and sold illegally and dogs and cats killing defenceless prey like sloths.

Even so-called 'eco-tourism' can cause environmental problems, as more and more people are tramping through previously virgin wilderness, sailing in previously unexplored waters, and staying in 'environmentally friendly' eco-lodges that, however nicely designed, can never be as beautiful as the landscapes they inevitably displace. Not to mention the increased amount of development and infrastructure needed to cope with Costa Rica's millions of visitors every year.

Given all these problems, Costa Rica is still making a fine job of it. Thanks to education, public sentiment is rising in favour of environmentalism. Bear in mind that this is still a developing country; many of the problems of pollution and land destruction result directly from the sudden influx of crowds. The infrastructure to deal with them is simply not present. Still, Costa Rica's environmental record puts that of most first world countries to shame. With the help of national visionaries and foreign biologists, parks volunteers and educated tourists, Costa Rica looks likely to continue to be a haven for naturalists, trekkers, surfers, wildlife watchers, and, of course, unrepentant boozehounds, for generations to come.

WHEN, WHERE AND HOW

Although Costa Rica is one of the more popular tourist destinations in the world, there is no need to be overly concerned about crowded parks; there is still a lot of land to absorb the number of visitors. Park entrance fees vary from zero to around US$15. Each park zone has its own guides and tours associated with it, and there are good companies working in almost all of the key areas.

Many park authorities allow guests to trek and camp, unguided, within the park's boundaries. However, it is often advisable to go with a guide. Not only will this put funds into the park's coffers and that of the local community, but also your guide will be able to identify subtly camouflaged fauna and flora that the average tourist would miss.

If you plan to go it alone be sure to research the flora and fauna of the area for easier identification. Furthermore, it is wise to be aware of any dangers, such as flash floods, unmarked trails or venomous plants and animals that you may come across. Costa Rican mountains and swamps are home to, among other beasties, the feared fer-de-lance snake, the most poisonous snake in the Americas. It won't be long before you hear long tales of sights and bites. Most parks and reserves can be entered without a permit; for the exceptions, get a permit from a public information office.

While it may vary slightly between different zones, Costa Rica essentially has two seasons: dry (December to mid April) and green (read 'wet' – mid April to December). However, any given day in the 'wet' season may be quite clear and sunny, and vice versa.

Most parks and reserves offer day treks, and tourists can opt to stay a night or two in any given area before moving, by bus or car, on to the next. There are also many options for longer camping trips.

Good topographical maps of Costa Rica are available to buy online at www.omnimap.com or in San José from the **Instituto Geográfico Nacional** (Avenida 20, entre Calles 9 y 11, 2257 7798), inside the gates of the Ministerio de Obras Públicas. The office is open from 8.30am to 11.30pm Monday to Friday.

WHAT TO TAKE AND OTHER TIPS

Costa Rica's terrain and climate vary tremendously, from mountains, to ocean and wet rainforest, to dry plains – so it is difficult to give a definitive list of necessary gear to take. Be certain to research your particular destination(s), as phrases like 'dry season', 'marked trails' and 'easily accessible' are essentially subjective statements.

National parks at a glance

Costa Rica has 25 national parks. Along with the 136 biological reserves and hundreds of privately owned parks, the list is extensive. Here are some highlights.

Central Valley
Reserva Biológica Bosque Nuboso de Monteverde Excellent trails through the cloud forest; see quetzals, 30 species of hummingbird and many orchids. *See p144.*
PN Braulio Carrillo Rugged trekking along Los Niños Circular and Los Guarumos trails. The most accessible point is to the Volcán Barva, with its misty lakes and paths around the peak. There are jaguars, pumas and monkeys. *See p128.*
Monumento Nacional Guayabo On the southern slope of the Turrialba volcano. This is probably the most important archaeological site in Costa Rica with aqueducts and tombs dating as far back as 1000 BC. *See p139.*
PN Volcán Irazú The largest and tallest volcano in the country, with five craters on top. Beautiful views into the main crater, which has a diameter of 1,050 metres (3,445 feet), and is 300 metres (984 feet) deep. *See p133.*
PN Volcán Arenal Walk through the greenery around the base of the volcano and then step back and watch its incredible night-time eruptions from a distance. *See p152.*

Pacific north
PN Marino las Baulas One of the world's most important nesting grounds for Atlantic leatherback turtles. *See p190.*
PN Palo Verde More than 12 different habitats and great birdwatching wetlands to boot. *See p184.*
PN Rincón de La Vieja Check out Cataratas Escondidas (Hidden Falls), an amazing chain of 60- to 70-metre-high (200- to 230-foot)

waterfalls, and the thermal springs and solfataric lagoons in Las Pailas. *See p169.*
PN Santa Rosa and PN Guanacaste Two neighbouring parks with a shared administration in the area known as Dry Pacific. Parks cover land from sea level to almost 1,700 metres (5,600 feet) – some of the most diverse habitat in the country. Trek through Orosí and Cacao volcanoes to see ancient petroglyphs. *See p170.*

Central Pacific
PN Carara Contains Costa Rica's major evergreen forests; great trekking through the trees and wetlands. *See p222.*
PN Manuel Antonio Perhaps the most popular single site in Costa Rica, due to its incredible views and beaches – lots of monkeys, coatis and kinkajous. *See p233.*

Southern Pacific
PN Corcovado One of the most impressive parks in Costa Rica; there is a huge amount of trekking territory and a wide variety of wildlife. It was once described by *National Geographic* as the most biologically diverse place on the planet. *See p258.*

Caribbean
PN Cahuita Beautiful white-sand beaches, and the best coral reef on the Caribbean coast. *See p290.*
PN Tortuguero and Refugio de Vida Silvestre Barra del Colorado Together they protect 1,120 square kilometres (430 square miles) of land and 520 square kilometres (200 square miles) of marine habitat. Important nesting site for Caribbean green turtles, Atlantic leatherback, hawksbill and loggerhead turtles also lay their eggs here. Ocelots and otters can also be found, as well as more than 60 species of frog. *See p279.*

Wherever you may go (apart from high altitudes), it is likely there will be bugs – so take some repellent. It's also usually very hot; you'll need to carry plenty of water. As a general rule, you'll want to take light trousers, a waterproof, some long-sleeved shirts and waterproof boots (if you plan to go trekking), a hat, sunglasses and sunscreen.

If you are an inexperienced hiker on unmarked trails it's not prudent to go without a guide, especially in largely uninhabited areas where there may not be a soul within miles and rescue teams are virtually non-existent. If you

are knowledgeable, however, there is a huge amount of wilderness to explore, much of it on private land. The majority of private landowners allow trekkers in. If you request permission and offer to pay (you probably won't have to) you will likely be welcome. The same goes with hitchhiking; just be a little wary of whom you are thumbing a lift from. *See p312* **Hitchhiking**.

PICK OF THE PARKS
With such a great variety of parks and trails, it is nigh on impossible to give a full description

Deserted beaches in **PN Marina Ballena**, for the Robinson Crusoe experience. *See p250*.

of each one, but the following are some of the best in the country.

One of the most popular parks in Costa Rica is **PN Volcán Arenal** (*see p152*), home to the eponymous, still active volcano, which can often be seen spewing lava high into the night sky. The park is rich in biodiversity, containing half of Costa Rica's land-dwelling vertebrates (mammals, birds, reptiles and amphibians). The land is rough, but trails abound in the area directly below and surrounding the volcano. There are also many spots to enjoy volcanic hot springs. Some of the best views, especially at night, can be found to the west and north of the volcano. Access to PN Volcán Arenal is via a sealed road from San José, through Ciudad Quesada and towards La Fortuna. There are also direct bus services to La Fortuna from San José. The administration office has a car park, toilets and visitor centre; many trails begin from there. There are also a variety of hotels and camping areas within the park (call PN Volcán Arenal, 2466 8610).

In the far south of Costa Rica, near the Panama border, sits the Península de Osa, home to **PN Corcovado** (*see p258*). One of the wettest areas in Costa Rica, PN Corcovado is a trekker's and wildlife watcher's nirvana. The park is home to 140 species of mammals, including protected animals such as baird's tapir, giant anteaters, jaguars, ocelots, puma-like jaguarundis and margays, as well as the country's largest population of scarlet macaws and all four species of native monkey. The park has some of the most untamed wilderness in the entire country and hundreds of kilometres of trails (beginner trekkers be warned: many are

unmarked and difficult to follow). Arrival in Corcovado is easiest by small aeroplane or boat to **Puerto Jiménez** (*see p260*) or **Bahía Drake** (*see p255*), then continue into the park via taxi (some bus services are available) or along a rocky road to Carate. There are many hotels, restaurants and markets in Puerto Jiménez as well as some nice lodging. The area directly surrounding the park has campsites and privately owned nature reserves with cabins. There are several ranger stations that offer basic lodging. Contact PN Corcovado park office on 2735 5382.

PN Santa Rosa and **PN Guanacaste** are adjoining parks in a region known as Dry Pacific. They work under shared management and are divided into nine sectors. The land within the two parks goes from sea level to almost 1,700 metres (5,600 feet) and has some of the country's most diverse range of species.

PN Santa Rosa contains perhaps the most important example of dry tropical forest in all of Central America and has become one of the foremost research centres for this type of ecosystem. It is also a location of great historic importance to Costa Rica, as the site of the country's victorious battle against American filibusters on 20 March 1856. Parque Nacional Santa Rosa (includes extensions for PN Guanacaste) 2666 5051.

PN Guanacaste's most emblematic features are the Cacao and Orosi volcanoes, neither of which have been active during the last few thousand years and are now covered with thick evergreen and cloud forest. The Río Tempisque, one of the longest rivers in the country, runs through the mountains and hills here. Also in the

Treasure Island

'Bloody Sword' is a great nickname for a pirate. This early 19th-century swashbuckler – whose 'real' name was Benito Bonito – was reported to actually be a British naval officer-turned-pirate. Old Bloody Sword may have had a fierce temper, a scarred face and, well, a bloody sword, but he also had great taste in tropical islands. How else to explain his choice of such a divine location as Isla del Coco in which to stash his precious booty?

The 'Loot of Lima' is the Holy Grail for treasure-seekers. Legend has it (as legend always does) that a hoard of gold and silver bars, gold laminas from church domes and two life-size gold statues of the Virgin Mary, all worth US$300 million today, was entrusted to William Thompson, a British brig captain, by the clergy of Lima. Thompson's assignment was to hide the stash in Mexico.

Instead Thompson did what any sensible man would: a runner. He had every person on the ship murdered, hooked up with (fellow British naval officer?) the one and only Benito 'Bloody Sword' Bonito, and sailed to the Isla del Coco to bury their prize. A British crew eventually captured Thompson, while Benito Bonito supposedly fared better and managed to escape to either Canada or Australia (good luck finding that treasure).

Today the jewel of the Parque Nacional Isla del Coco is its wildlife and scenery, deemed stunning enough to be used for the opening scene of the film *Jurassic Park*. Known as the 'Costa Rican Galapagos', it sits just over 500 kilometres (310 miles) south-west of Costa Rica (750 kilometres – 466 miles – north-east of the Galapagos Islands) and was declared a national park in 1978. With 20 square kilometres (eight square miles) of land and 972 square kilometres (375 square miles) of marine habitat, it is the world's largest uninhabited island. It became a UNESCO World Heritage Site in 1997.

The island is a craggy piece of volcanic formation, part of the underwater column known as the Coco Seismic Ridge, with an annual 7,000mm (275 inches) of rainfall, providing water for its many beautiful waterfalls. There are three endemic bird species: Isla del Coco cuckoo, Isla del Coco flycatcher and Isla del Coco finch.

The island is perhaps best known for diving. Famous diver and researcher Jacques Cousteau once called Isla del Coco 'the most beautiful island in the world'. The waters and reefs surrounding the island boast some 18 species of coral, at least four species of dolphin and huge shoals of sharks. It is also home to many sea turtles, California sea lions and whale sharks – the biggest fish in the world. The diving visibility is extraordinary.

Although no humans currently inhabit the island, many have tried. It was a frequent stop off in the 1700s for whalers in search of fresh water. And, as mentioned, it is purported to have been the hiding place for many famous pirates' booty too. In September 1869, the Costa Rican government organised an official expedition to find treasure, but to no avail. However, it did officially claim the island for its flag on 15 September of the same year.

From 1864 to 1872, Coco was an island prison. Subsequently, two attempted settlements failed, but the colonisers' animals remained, and the island is now home to some slightly less than domesticated goats, pigs and cats.

Only about 1,000 tourists visit the island each year. There are some trails, but camping is prohibited and permission from the parks service is required for a visit. Most travellers to the island stay overnight on their boats; it takes over 36 hours to reach the island from Puntarenas, where specialist boat tours are offered; but be warned, they can be pricey. To apply for visitor permission and to enquire about travel to the island, contact Área de Conservación de la Isla del Coco (2258 7350) in San José.

park is the Maritza Biological Station, home to *los petroglifos* – an area famous for its (yup) pre-Columbian petroglyphs. The parks are accessible from the Interamericana highway north of Liberia (bus service available from Liberia). PN Santa Rosa has two campsites with facilities and drinking water. On Playa Naranjo, Estero Real and Murciélago camping is permitted but there are no facilities or drinking water. From the administration office and Cacao and Pitilla Biological Stations there are trails throughout the parks and to the tops of the volcanoes.

Costa Rica is a country where fabulous wildlife and scenery are practically unavoidable. Costa Rica's national parks might not be rolling in cash but when it comes to nature they're one of the richest places on earth.

Puerto Viejo. See p193.

In Context

Adventure Sports

Imagine what Tarzan could have done with a zip-line...

Whether you choose to zip, flipper, paddle or pedal your way around, Costa Rica has become a fantasyland for the adrenaline fiend. Wildly diverse geography concentrated in a relatively small land mass, accessible terrain, a variety of water courses and solid tour operators make it an ideal destination to practise edgy endeavours or try something entirely new.

You can whitewater raft down Class IV rapids, zip-line through the treetops for a bird's eye view of the rainforest canopy, view the Central Valley from a hot-air balloon, mountain bike through coffee plantations, surf head-high breakers in the tropical waters of the Pacific, abseil down waterfalls in the Caribbean lowlands or jump off a bridge into the gorge of the Rio Colorado. Blood still not pumping hard enough? Plunge deep into crystalline seas to explore life-rich underwater worlds, hike into the caldera of an active volcano, scale ancient 20-metre-high trees, catch the big one on a deep-sea fishing adventure, windsurf one of the world's best freshwater spots, hang-glide over the Pacific, horseride, kayak…then crash and rejuvenate on a pristine beach. It might be a

marvellous place to relax too, but most people don't come to Costa Rica to do nothing – with such an impressive list of activities, adventure junkies can really live it up.

OUTFITTERS

Costa Rica's small size and reasonable tourism infrastructure make doing it all, well, doable. There aren't many places on the planet where you can experience such a variety of spectacular landscapes and activities in one trip, and the tourism industry has cashed in on this, offering scores of multi-adventure excursions. Book the full expedition in advance, or piece together a few tours once in country. Reputable outfitters include **Costa Rica Expeditions** (2257 0766, www.costarica expeditions.com), one of the longest standing operators specialising in natural history and adventure travel. **Horizontes** (2222 2022, www.horizontes.com) has been offering multi-sport trips since 1984, and **Coast to Coast Adventures** (2280 8054, www.ctocadventures. com) will have you hiking, biking and rafting in some unique remote locations. **Serendipity**

Adventures (2226 5050, www.serendipity adventures.com) is a US-based company that operates all its own tours with its own equipment. If you have more time, the **Costa Rica Rainforest Outward Bound School** (2278 6062, www.crrobs.org) offers multi-sport, kayaking, hiking and surfing excursions for university credits or just for fun.

ZIPPING, GLIDING AND FLYING

Parasail or paraglide over the golden beaches of the Pacific, watch the changing scenery from a helicopter or hot-air balloon, or spread your own wings as you take the bungee plunge. A range of exhilarating aerial adventures means you could easily spend much of your holiday airborne. Canopy tours have become practically synonymous with adventure tourism in Costa Rica. Zip-lines are scattered about the nation's many forests and new tour operators pop up constantly, and for good reason: it's incredibly good fun. Nothing will prepare you for the thrill of zooming through the trees some 20 metres (60 feet) above the ground, or spotting plants and wildlife from the swaying canopy roof as you sit in your harness awaiting the ride to the next treetop platform. While much of the rainforest's life hangs out high in the canopy, note that many tours are geared towards giving a wild ride rather than appreciating wildlife.

For a slower, more cerebral experience and more chances to spot monkeys and birds, head to an aerial tram. Gondolas lift passengers high over the trees at cruising speed via a system of cables of varying heights, leading you through the different layers of rainforest life. See regional chapters for local operators, but worth recommending here are: **Original Canopy Tour** (2291 4465, www.canopytour.com) in Monteverde, with additional locations in Liverpool, Bahia Drake and Mahogany Park. **Turu Ba Ri Tropical Park** (2250 0705, www.turubari.com) comprises a large tropical park near Jacó on the Pacific coast with an aerial tram, zip-line, 'Sensational Cable' (50 seconds of flying across a 1,000-metre (3,280-foot) cable at 80 kph/50mph), rappelling and climbing wall, and Tarzan swing. **Rain Forest Aerial Trams** (2257 5961, www.rfat.com) is a well-established affair with locations on both the Atlantic and Pacific coasts. It is a much more gentle excursion.

Hot-air balloon flights can be arranged in San José, and **Helitours by Aerodiva** (2296 7241, www.aerodiva.com) offers helicopter tours for the thick walleted. **Tropical Bungee** (2248 2212, www.bungee.co.cr) organises jumps off the Old Colorado River Bridge into the 80-metre-deep (265-foot) river gorge below, while the newer **Arenal Bungee** (2479 7440,

www.arenalbungee.com) in La Fortuna is home to the unique 'Extreme Machine' bungee construction, along with a 'Rocket Launcher' and 'Big Swing' airborne adventures.

TWO WHEELS BETTER THAN FOUR

Landlubbers will find plenty to do close to the earth with a myriad of mountain biking, motorcycling, horse riding, caving and canyoning opportunities. Some of the best cycling can be found around the flanks of Volcán Arenal in the La Fortuna (*see p151*) area and across the Central Valley, where countless kilometres of dirt roads traversing a variety of terrain could keep novice and serious bikers rolling for weeks. Quality bikes can be rented in most tourist towns and several outfitters offer day-to-multi-day excursions. Be wary of potholes and careless drivers; the main highways are heavy with traffic and some of the nation's back roads make Swiss cheese look solid. **Costa Rica Biking Adventures** (2225 6591, www.bikingcostarica.com), **Adventuras Naturales** (2225 3939, www.adventure costarica.com) and **Bike Arenal** (479 9454, www.bikearenal.com) have been doing good business for years.

Looking for power behind your pedal? **Wild Rider** (2258 4604, www.wild-rider.com), **Costa Rica Motorcycle Tours** (2225 6000, www.costaricamotorcycletours.com) and **Harley Rentals** (2288 6362, www.harleytours costarica.com) offer motorcycle and four-wheel-drive tours, or you can rent and go at your own pace. **MotoDiscovery** (from US 800 233 0564, 830 438 7744, www.motodiscovery.com) features motorcycle tours though Central America, including a trip from Rio Grande to the Panama Canal (riders then fly back home).

WARNING

Many of these adventures contain an element of danger, so be selective when choosing a company. After a spate of deaths among tourists, in 2003 the Costa Rican government passed a set of safety standards that all adventure tour companies had to adhere to. But rules are only as good as their enforcement.

Each tour should have a certificate from the **Instituto Costarricense de Turismo,** which, after an inspection of safety measures, binds them to adhere to the '*Reglamento para la Operación de las Actividades de Turismo Aventura*' (Rules for the Operation of Adventure Tourism Activities) after an inspection of safety measures. Ask to see it. The outfitters we have recommended have been operating in Costa Rica for years and have good safety records. Seek out a tour that will not only be thrilling, but also safe.

The resplendent quetzal.

Birdwatching

Twitchers are flocking to catch a glimpse of Costa Rica's abundant bird life.

With more than 850 recorded bird species, Costa Rican forests are alive with colour and song. Both the novice and professional will find it a fine stage for observing prized species such as the resplendent quetzal (*see p156* **The quest for the quetzal**), the scarlet macaw or the keel-billed toucan. Some of the rainforest's greatest spectacles involve birds and will fascinate even the most casual observer. A day's hike might be enlivened by a group of male hummingbirds striking their best notes, male manakins dancing and singing, as they vie for a female's attention, a frenzy of birds cashing in on fleeing insects or the sudden arrival of a mixed flock – a true birding bonanza. A good day's twitching in Costa Rica can yield between 85 and 150 species sightings.

FEATHERED FRIENDS

With lowland tropical rainforests on the Caribbean and Pacific coasts climbing to lush volcanoes draped in cloud forest and *páramo* (moorland) peaks reminiscent of the Andes, Costa Rica encompasses 12 of the planet's 18 different life zones. These micro-habitats, isolated by the mountain ranges that bisect

the country, have protected the great variety of species that breed throughout Costa Rica, including three endemic species: the mangrove hummingbird, the coppery-headed emerald and the black-cheeked ant-tanager.

Many other birds are only found in Costa Rica and western Panama including: beryl-crowned hummingbirds, fiery-billed aracaris, fiery-throated hummingbirds and baird's trogons, to name but a few. Costa Rica represents 0.03 per cent of the world's land surface, and is about the size of West Virginia or Switzerland, yet it is home to eight per cent of the world's bird species. More have been identified in this tiny country than in all of the United States and Canada combined.

The country's abundance of birdlife means that it is possible to birdwatch in the morning at any given location, drive for a few hours, and enjoy an afternoon birding session featuring many different species. And the well-established national park system, with accommodation for every budget, make it easy, as well as comfortable, for visitors to enjoy their avian encounters.

In Context

WATCH THE BIRDIE

One of the best destinations for birders is **La Selva Biological Station** (*see p131*), where more than half of the country's bird species have been registered. Located on the Caribbean foothills, near the town of **Puerto Viejo de Sarapiquí** in Heredia province, La Selva is a world famous tropical research station operated by the Organisation for Tropical Studies. It is considered among the top five most biologically diverse lowland forests on the planet, attracting more than 350 researchers from more than 25 countries every year. La Selva consists of more than 160 square kilometres (60 square miles) of protected primary and secondary forest and reaches its southern limit at **PN Braulio Carrillo**, making it a vital wildlife corridor connecting the Caribbean lowlands to the cloud forests of the Barva, Cacho Negro and Zurqui volcanoes. Most of the trails around the station are paved and the terrain is flat, making birdwatching easy and enjoyable. Also available is a 'Bird Watching 101' course. This full-day activity is a good introduction to birdwatching for all ages.

Also run by the Organisation for Tropical Studies is the **Wilson Botanical Garden** (*see p268*), located near the town of San Vito. **PN La Amistad** (*see p268*), on the Panamanian border, is Costa Rica's largest park and a UNESCO World Heritage Site, where more than 330 species have been sighted. The reserve also runs **PN Palo Verde** (*see p184*). Located on the Tempisque river basin in Guanacaste province, this is a 200-square-kilometre (77-square-mile) national park made up of seasonal wetlands and tropical dry forest. About 300 bird species have been reported here, including 60 species of wading and aquatic birds, which live here from September to March.

Birdwatchers interested in tropical dry forest species will find a visit to **PN Santa Rosa** (*see p170*) in the north-west of the country deeply rewarding. Over 250 species of bird have been recorded here including white-throated magpie jays, long-billed gnatwrens, barred antshrikes, rufous-naped wrens, turquoise-browed motmots, long-tailed manakins, scrub euphonias, elegant trogons and Pacific screech-owls.

Linking the dry northern Pacific lowlands to the wet southern Pacific lowlands, **PN Carara** (*see p222*) emerges as a crossroads for Pacific dry forest species and Pacific rainforest species, and is therefore a comprehensive birding site.

Further south, **PN Corcovado** (*see p258*), on the Península de Osa, offers Costa Rica's best representation of Pacific lowland rainforest species. Located in the South-west of the country, this 425-square- kilometres (164-square-miles) national park is one of the sparkling jewels of Costa Rica's national park system and protects one of the finest stretches of Pacific rainforest in Central America. Over 500 species of tree have been identified, some growing to dizzying heights. Endangered harpy eagles and other large and rarely viewed raptors survive here.

> **'Costa Rica represents 0.03 per cent of the world's land surface, yet is home to eight per cent of its bird species'**

The cloud forests around **Monteverde** (*see p142*), home to some of Costa Rica's most spectacular species, are an essential stop on a birdwatcher's tour. Three-wattled bellbirds, bare-necked umbrellabird, resplendent quetzals, red-headed barbets, and over half of the country's 45 resident hummingbird species make their home in forests on these Caribbean and Pacific slopes.

Another recommended cloud forest destination is **Cerro de la Muerte** (*see p242*). Here cloud forest gives way to *páramo* as Cerro de la Muerte, one of Costa Rica's highest peaks, climbs above the timberline. San Gerardo de Dota, on the peak, is considered to be one of the most reliable places to see the resplendent quetzal. On this massif you may encounter cloud forest species such as emerald toucanets, black guans and golden-browed chlorophonias as well as birds that dwell at higher elevations such as volcano Hummingbirds, sulphur-winged parakeets and dusky nightjars.

RESOURCES

Essential to a successful twitching trip is a pair of binoculars. High-end brands such as Swarovski and Carl Zeiss are expensive but well worth the investment. A good guidebook is F Gary Stiles and Alexander F Skutch's *A Guide to the Birds of Costa Rica*.

An experienced guide can make a huge difference to your birdwatching experience. In general, hotels and reserves have guides that they recommend; just make sure that birds are their speciality and ask about their experience. On average an expert guide costs US$60 per day, or around US$20 for a two- to three- hour hike. A good place to start for resources and contacts is the Costa Rican Birding Club (www.camac donald.com/birding/cencostaarica.htm). Its website lists tour operators, events and longer courses available in the country. Birding Pal (www.birdingpal.org/Costarica.htm) also can put fellow twitchers in contact with one another, but they are not paid guides.

Six not to miss

Golden-browed chlorophonia

Common name Golden-browed chlorophonia
Scientific name *Chlorophonia callophrys*
Habitat Cloud forests on both Pacific and
Caribbean slopes.

The Golden-browed chlorophonia is one of
the most striking birds inhabiting the misty,
moss-laden cloud forests of Costa Rica.
These attractive green, yellow and blue
birds eat insects, the small fruits of tropical
mistletoes, tropical blueberries and wild
figs. Chlorophonias are some of the most
important seed dispersers in tropical forests
throughout the country. The female is a little
duller in colour, can have spotmarkings and
doesn't have a yellow patch over its eye.

Green honeycreeper

Common name Green honeycreeper
Scientific name *Chlorophanes spiza*
Habitat Forests and forest edges of
lowlands and foothills throughout the country.
Green honeycreepers have long, curved
beaks that are perfect for dipping into the
centre of a flower for a sweet snack, in the
process transferring pollen from one flower
to another. Thus the green honeycreeper is
important ecologically in helping to pollinate
many species of shrub and tree, including the
Ice-cream bean (*Inga sp.*) and coral bean
trees (*Erythrina sp.*). One of the best places
to see green honeycreepers and their other
honeycreeper and dacnis relatives is at the
birdfeeders of many eco-lodges. Fruit is their
main diet but they also feed on nectar and
insects. Their call is a sharp cheep.

Keel-billed toucan

Common names Keel-billed toucan, the bill
bird (any toucan)
Scientific name *Ramphastos sulfuratus*
Habitat Lowland rainforests and mid-elevation
cloud forests of northern plains and
Caribbean foothills.

The keel-billed toucan – the best-known
of Costa Rica's seven toucan species –
inhabits rainforests and cloud forests, where
it disperses the seeds of trees such as the
wild nutmeg. In addition to the fruit that
constitutes most of its diet, the keel-billed
toucan feeds on insects, small lizards and
frogs, and even the eggs and baby chicks of
other birds. Its call sounds exactly like the
croak of a tree frog and its bill can be up to
12cm (6in) long.

Macaws

Common names Scarlet macaw, great
Green Macaw
Scientific names *Ara macao, ara ambigua*
Habitat Lowland rainforest of northern plains
and southern Pacific coast for scarlet macaw
and lowland rainforest of northern plains for
great green macaw.

Costa Rica's two macaw species are large,
loud and colourful, and they can grow up to
96cm (36 in) long, most of which is their tail.
Their gregarious nature and multi-hued
plumage make them desirable as cage birds:
poachers steal young chicks from nests in the
rainforest canopy to sell as pets on the black
market in Costa Rica and abroad, decimating
local macaw populations, almost to the point
of extinction. Nevertheless, conservation
measures targeting these charismatic
animals have led to a comeback of sorts,
and today there are more than 1,600 scarlet
and 200 green macaws in the wild.

Summer tanager

Common name Summer tanager
Scientific name *Piranga rubra*
Habitat Lowland and cloud forests,
farms and gardens throughout Costa Rica.

The summer tanager breeds in the southern
United States but lives in Costa Rica from
September to April taking advantage of the
abundant food sources found in the tropical
forests year-round. A beautiful bird, the
summer tanager joins mixed flocks of
resident tanagers and warblers to forage for
insects and fruit. Though shy, this brilliant red
bird can be observed easily at birdfeeders
that offer bananas, plantains, papaya or
watermelon to feed on. Their song consists
of melodic units, usually in a constant flow.

Violet sabrewing

Common name Violet sabrewing
Scientific name
Campylopterus hemileucurus
Habitat Cloud forests on both Pacific
and Caribbean slopes.

Of Costa Rica's nearly 60 hummingbird
species, the violet sabrewing is one of the
largest and most attractive. Often seen as
nothing more than a rich purple iridescent
flash in the cloud forest, the violet sabrewing
pollinates many flowers, including those of
heliconias, columneas (an African violet
relative) and bromeliads. Violet sabrewings
are eager visitors to garden hummingbird
feeders in cloud forest areas. A sharp
twitter defines their song.

Up close and personal with the turtles of the Pacific.

Diving & Snorkelling

Costa Rica's great Poseidon adventure.

Although Costa Rica doesn't have the crystalline waters and coral life of its neighbours Belize and Honduras, there is good diving and snorkelling to be had beneath its pleasantly temperate waters, rich with tropical fish and large marine life. Sites off both the Pacific and Caribbean coasts are home to numerous species of small fish and crustacean, but sightings of larger sea creatures such as mantas, morays, jewfish, turtles, eagle rays, giant jellyfish and sharks are the real draw for divers.

Visibility varies with the season and location and is generally pretty poor (6-24 metres/20-79 feet) during the rainy season, when rivers swell and pour out into the ocean, making it murky. Banana plantation runoff is also a major problem and has destroyed much of the Caribbean reef, although there is still worthwhile diving around Isla Uvita off the coast of Puerto Limón and further south at Cahuita and Manzanillo. Most dive-site development and dive outfitters can be found along the Pacific coast, but there's not much coral life here. Body-temperature waters and

an astounding array of marine life make up for it. With waters a consistent 24°C to 29°C or higher (and a mild 23°C at the thermocline some 20 metres – 65 feet – below the surface), shallow divers and snorkellers may not need a wetsuit.

TAKE THE PLUNGE
Isla del Coco (*see p59*), some 500 kilometres (310 miles) south-west off the shore of Costa Rica, is hands down the best diving spot in the country, though getting there requires 36 hours by live-aboard boat, and there is no accommodation on the island. For hardcore divers it's worth it – 18 species of coral reef, 156 species of fish, more than 55 types of crustacean and a myriad other marine mammals inhabit the waters surrounding the island. Mantas, whale sharks, hammerheads and other big creatures are often spotted in impressively large shoals. Diving here requires experience and is for intermediate to advanced levels.

A SHORE THING
The best shore-based dive spots on the Pacific coast are at **Bahía Drake** and **Isla de Caño**

In Context

(*see p254*) and **Playa Ocotal** (*see p174*). Diving is mostly around underwater rock formations, and you're likely to encounter grouper, rays, parrotfish, eagle rays, morays, giant jellyfish and a host of other fish, invertebrates and larger marine life.

By Isla de Caño, **El Bajo del Diablo** (the Devil's Pinnacle) is one of the most interesting sites in the country, with towering rock pinnacles rising up more than 46 metres (150 feet) from the sea bed, creating a fascinating maze of peaks and valleys rich with barracuda, eels, reef sharks, giant mantas and tropical fish. Waters around the islands can be challenging because of strong currents and surges; less experienced divers should take special care. Punta Gorda, about six kilometres (3.5 miles) west of **Playa Ocotal** (*see p174*), is famed for whale shark and black marlin sightings. To the south, the reef of Isla de Caño off the Osa Peninsula is home to a vertical wall where an astounding array of pelagic fish and rays hang out. The island is reached via dive boats departing from **Bahía Drake**, **Golfito** (*see p254*) and **Quepos** (*see p230*).

To the east, on the Caribbean coast, **Isla Uvita** (*see p284*), **Cahuita** (*see p288*) and **Manzanillo** (*see p299*) all have decent diving and snorkelling opportunities, though infrastructure for the sport is less established than on the Pacific coast. Isla Uvita is easily accessible from Puerto Limón and there's a wreck, the *Fenix*, to explore.

There is a fan-shaped reef covering six square kilometres (2.3 square miles) and incorporating 35 species of coral that wraps around Cahuita point, although much of the coral has been severely damaged. Still, a variety of fish life and two shipwrecks make for decent dives, and even better snorkelling since most of the interesting life here lives close to the surface. Further south, the **Refugio Gandoca-Manzanillo** (*see p300*) protects a southern extension of the reef and is less visited and in better shape. Check with park rangers and outfitters about conditions, as the area is notorious for quickly changing tides.

Rain runoff and wave conditions make shallow waters rough, murky and bad for snorkelling. The best snorkelling is off the southern Caribbean coast in Manzanillo where the reef is less damaged, especially during the months of September and October. The Pacific coast isn't so good. Even though there are many safe bays, you aren't likely to see much of interest through the silt-obscured waters.

PRACTICALITIES AND PRECAUTIONS

Underwater explorers should remember that coral is very delicate and should not be touched: doing so destroys the mucus membrane that protects it from deadly bacteria. Sunscreen is also toxic to coral; wear a white shirt for protection when snorkelling instead. Divers who are bringing their own equipment should wash it well before using it in Costa Rican waters, as items used in other locations can introduce foreign bacteria and algae that damage the delicate ecosystem.

The **Professional Association of Diving Instructors** (PADI, US office + 1 949 858 7234, www.padi.com) and **National Association of Underwater Instructors** (NAUI, US office + 1 800 553 6284, www.naui.org) are good resources for diving information in Costa Rica and worldwide. **Divers Alert Network** (US office + 1 800 446 2671, 919 684 2948, www.diversalertnetwork.org) provides diving insurance and support. There's a hyperbaric chamber at Cuajiniquil in Guanacaste.

Here are a few recommended outfitters around the country (also check listings in regional chapters). **Costa Rica Adventure Divers** (2385 9541, www.costaricadiving.com) offers diving and snorkelling around Bahia Drake and Isla de Caño. **Diving Safaris de Costa Rica** (2672 0012, www.costaricadiving.net) is one of the larger operations based in Playa Hermosa. As is **Rich Coast Diving** (2670 0176, www.richcoastdiving.com), Playas del Coco. On the Caribbean coast, **Aquamor** (2759 9012, www.greencoast.com/aquamor), within the PN Gandoca-Manzanillo, offers tours, certification courses, night and nature dives. **Diving Mania** (2291 2936, www.divingmania.net) in San José rents equipment and gives classes and tours.

The best Diving sites

Isla del Coco

500 kilometres (310 miles) off the Pacific coast is the 'Costa Rican Galapagos' and the country's best and most untouched diving site. An added incentive for divers is the rumour of hidden treasure. See p59.

Isla Uvita

Clear waters, abundant marine life and wrecks are just part of the attractions on this historic Caribbean island where Christopher Columbus landed. See p284.

Isla de Caño

The underwater rock formations around this island near Bahía Drake make it a great place to see rays and parrotfish. Most lodges in the area can organise excursions to the island. See p254.

Fishing

Battling the beasts of the ocean.

A million or so years ago volcanoes erupted on the ocean floor, and the constant spurting of lava created the beautiful mountain ranges in the isthmus of Central America. In Costa Rica some of these mountain ranges never reached the surface. Whatever power orchestrated this underwater mosaic must have been fond of fishermen. The volcanic shoreline and undersea ranges are great refuges for sea life.

CARIBBEAN CATCHES

Many rivers flow into the Caribbean. They carry tons of silt washed down from the mountains during heavy rains. As a result most of the near shore reefs have been covered up over the years, but it makes for perfect conditions for species that thrive on a mix of salt and fresh water, like tarpon and snook.

Many of the lodges that specialise in these species are in isolated areas and are only accessible by plane or by boat. **Barra del Colorado** (*see p278*), **Parismina** (*see p281*) and **Tortuguero** (*see p281*) are the most popular destinations. The heritage of the eastern seaboard is Jamaican and they settled here after completing the railroad between Puerto Limón and San José; consequently, almost all guides speak a Caribbean English. December starts the run of *calba* (fat snook) and catches of over 50 a

day are common, though the fish average only one to three kilograms (2.2 - 6.6 pounds). From August to October is when most of the monster snook are taken, including the all-tackle record of a 24-kilogram (53-pound) fish.

Tarpon are available year-round and swim in small pods in the rivers and in giant shoals in the ocean. They average around 35 kilograms (80 pounds) but have been weighed in at more than 90 kilograms (200 pounds) on occasion. Crossing the sandbar at the river mouth to get to the ocean can be an exciting ride and at times the breaking waves prohibit the voyage. When this happens, boats are restricted to fishing the rivers. Anglers then have a choice to fish tarpon in the river or venture back into the creeks and lagoons and search for freshwater species like rainbow bass, guapote (mojarra) or machaca. All are a test of angling skill on light tackle or fly equipment. Prices start at around US$1,800 for a five-day package with three fishing days. Accommodation is usually included.

PACIFIC PULLS

Some 20 years ago there were only a handful of boats that took tourists out into the Pacific in search of game fish. Marlin, sailfish, yellowfin tuna, dorado (dolphin fish) and wahoo are the target species in these waters. Today there are hundreds of operators and local fishermen running trips, plus marinas in Flamingo, Los Suenos, and two under construction in Quepos and Golfito. Or you could stay in all-inclusive hotels like **Crocodile Bay Resort** (*see p260*), **Golfito Sailfish Ranch** (www.golfitosailfish rancho.com) and **Zancudo Lodge** (Zancudo, 2772 0008, www.thezancudolodge.com) in the southern zone.

> ### 'Set at the base of one of the most active volcanoes, you can often witness an eruption as you fish.'

Costa Rica has become famous for its sailfish and small size marlin that can be taken with a fly-fishing rod. Most marlin average from 65 kilograms (150 pounds) to 130 kilograms (300 pounds), although fish of 450 kilograms (1,000 pounds) have been caught. Peak periods for different species vary depending on the region so it is always best to ask when booking a trip.

The inshore action is consistent year-round. Roosterfish are the most prized of inshore species. They live only in the waters between southern Mexico and Ecuador, so Costa Rica's position is ideal. The big tides on the Pacific side keep the inshore reefs swept clean of river silt and, although the reefs are volcanic and not coral, they are teeming with life. Cubera snapper, African pompano, bluefin trevally, jacks and grouper are on constant patrol.

FRESHWATER FINDS

The source of most of Costa Rica's electricity, Lake Arenal, is also a popular fishing spot. Set at the base of one of the country's most active volcanoes, you can often witness an eruption as you fish. Some of the largest guapote come from this lake, as do tilapia and machaca. The **Rain Goddess** (www.bluwing.com) is a six-room houseboat that offers fishing tours and luxury dining in front of the volcano. Some of the best lava shows can be seen at night from the roof-top deck. There are several operators that do tours in the Caño Negro area, where tarpon have ventured from the sea as far up as Lake Nicaragua and as far down as Rio Frío.

FACTS & FIGURES

A fishing trip in Costa Rica can cost as little as US$100 with a local fisherman in a small boat (check to see if it at least has a life jacket) to US$3,000 a day on a multi-million-dollar sport fishing vessel. The average is US$700 to US$1,200 for an offshore trip, perhaps a little less for smaller boats specialising only in inshore fishing. The best results come with research. Ask lots of questions and don't assume anything. Many operations can handle special requests such as for fly fishing or light tackle, but ask what is supplied and what you are expected to take.

Two fishing travel specialists that have offices in Costa Rica and over 15 years' experience apiece are: Rob and Steve Hodel (www.ticotavel.net) and Richard Krug (www.americanasportfishing.com).

The one that didn't get away…Bringing in a Roosterfish.

Fishing guide

Billfish

Common names Marlin, sailfish, spearfish
Scientific names *Istiophoridae, Istiophorus*
The Pacific coast is world renowned for billfish and they can be caught any day of the year. They are a sought-after and fairly common game fish in these waters. Blue marlin, black marlin, striped marlin and sailfish are taken within the sight of land. All fishing is catch and release. The action peaks in different areas at different times of the year, so check ahead when booking a trip. These fish can swim up to 80kph (50mph).

Roosterfish

Common name Roosterfish
Scientific name *Nematistius pectoralis*
Roosterfish prowl the Pacific coastline and inshore reefs as loners or in packs. They are the wolves of inshore waters and most other fish move out of their way. They are exotic-looking fish, whose combed dorsal fin and sheer power make them the most popular of inshore targets. They usually weigh a hefty nine kilograms (20 pounds) but can get up to as much as 45 kilograms (100 pounds).They are available in good numbers year-round, a pretty reliable catch, best with live bait.

Snook

Common names Snook, snoek
Scientific names *Sphyraena, gempylidae*
There are eight different species of snook in Costa Rica: four are found on the Caribbean coast and four found on the Pacific coast. The Atlantic common snook and the Pacific black snook can reach 23 kilograms (50 pounds) and the world record for each came from Costa Rican waters. Don't expect to catch large numbers of these tasty game fish; what you do have, though, is a chance to catch a trophy. They occur singly or in shoals.

Tarpon

Common names Tarpon, sábalos
Scientific name *Megalops*
Tarpon are found along the entire Caribbean seaboard. They also enter coastal rivers and venture as far up as water depth allows. Known as 'silver rockets', because they are airborne within seconds of being hooked, these prehistoric survivors are a true test of an angler's stamina and therefore one of the most sought-after and enjoyable catches along the coasts of Costa Rica.

Punta Cocles, South Caribbean. *See p294.*

Surfing

Fifty breaks, two coasts and a lot of chilled locals. This is surfing Tico style.

'We are mellow, we are *pura vida*, and that comes out when we are surfing,' says Diego Naranjo, Costa Rican surf champion. 'We say "hi" to everyone and just have fun.'

'There's not much localism like in Hawaii where you might get your ass kicked,' he continues. 'You might find some crazy guys in some spots, but you can pretty much surf anywhere peacefully unless you do something really wrong.'

This is one of the reasons Costa Rica has become one of the world's top surfing destinations. But as Naranjo admits, while friendly locals help, the real reason surfing is flourishing is that there is just so much of it.

Along Costa Rica's two coasts, crashed and crunched by the Pacific Ocean and the Caribbean Sea, are at least 50 breaks, including what is reportedly the second longest left-hand break in the world. There are extreme tube spots for experts; soft, inviting beginners' bays; and everything else in between you can imagine. And surfer lore has it that there are many more breaks to be found. Using sophisticated tools such as Google Earth,

new breaks, many almost impossible to get to, are being discovered. And just as every break is unique, so is every location. Whether you're a surfing family or a student looking for your first wave, you'll find a variety of surfer-friendly lodging, restaurants, schools and services along the Pacific and Caribbean coasts.

Costa Rica is without doubt a surfing centre. But it isn't quite what you would expect. Sure, the country still welcomes its fair share of backpacking dudes, out for the freewheeling, carefree, 'let's see where the wind and the waves take us' holidays, the kind of trips made famous by surfers in flicks such as *Bikini Beach* and *Fast Times*. But this kind of surfer is increasingly in the minority. Surf tourism is beginning to attract big bucks from the pockets of those willing to shell out for the goods and services that come with a top-notch surf trip.

A survey by the Institute of Costa Rican Tourism (ICT), carried out in airports (it's not difficult to spot a surfer), found that 100,278 surfers visited Costa Rica during the first half of 2006, remaining in the country for an average of 17 nights and spending US$122 every 24

Making waves

Legend, hearsay and broken pacts are the stuff most surfing anecdotes are made of. The discovery of a new break, for example, such as the one that emerged after a recent earthquake at the Caribbean coast's peeling reef Salsa Brava, is the kind of semi-apocryphal nugget surfers love to trade in. Tico surfers are no exception; they all have a tale to tell. A typical episode of discovery goes something like this:

Down in Guanacaste sits an odd geological formation known as Witch's Rock. Today it swells up a world-renowned surf break, but a mere 40 years ago, only two brothers knew it existed.

The brothers, Randy and Louis Wilson, the former now owner of Tamarindo Sportfishing, the latter the proprietor of Playa Grande's Las Tortugas Hotel, arrived from Florida in the early 1970s. Back then Tamarindo was a town of three Tico families, none of whom were surfers. According to Randy, in those days the estuary was in a different place, with a longer and more consistent break. Then came 'Puca Madness', when folks flooded the village to gather a hot new commodity: the beautiful and profitable Puca shells that lay on the beach. 'From then on,

the entire economic structure of the area changed,' Randy recalls. The first group of developers followed, taking sand directly off the beach for landfill to build homes between Tamarindo and Langosta. As a result, the surf break moved to the mouth of the Tamarindo river.

The Wilsons continued the search for the area's best waves. 'We knew about an undiscovered area from looking at maps of the northern shore. So we dug our car through the bush to what is now known as Witch's Rock. When we got there, we saw these Californian guys surfing. Around the fire that night, we made a pact that no one would say a word.' It didn't last long. The beans were spilled by some Californian friends of the Wilsons to whom the brothers had shown the beach – and presumably (and pointlessly) sworn to secrecy.

Witch's Rock gospel spread as fast as the waves that hit its shore; and as soon as the locals realised they could make money from visitors, the beach was actively promoted. Many years passed and the information travelled. In 1991, however, Costa Rica's place in surfing folklore was cemented with the arrival of Robert August, the star of the

quintessential surf film *Endless Summer*. And his first trip to Jacó changed his life forever.

'I had already travelled a lot,' says August. 'But there was something about Costa Rica that felt really good. There was nothing in Tamarindo; we ate fish, went to fiestas and surfed like crazy.

After this trip, August decided to make his second home in Tamarindo and when Bruce Brown finally decided to film the sequel to *Endless Summer*, starring Robert 'Wingnut' Weaver and Patrick O'Connell, the movie began with August taking them to Tamarindo.

'The Costa Rican thing up to then was brand new, and it showed that the surfing and the country was manageable. People thought "Wow, I can do that".'

Of course, after *Endless Summer II* was released in cinemas in 1994, Costa Rica as a surf destination exploded, and the sport would never be the same again. August noticed the difference immediately but was quick to point out that it was, and still is, the locals who impress him the most.

In 2008, one of the best surfers in the water at the professional level is Gilbert Brown from Puerto Viejo. The 25-year-old Caribbean-coast surfer already has the 2001-02 Circuito Nacional de Surf championship under his belt and at the time of writing is ranked first in Costa Rica.

Born in Puerto Viejo, he spent eight years as a 'fisherkid', but at the same time was hanging out in the parks climbing trees to watch the older Salsa Brava surfers in action. The Salsa Brava wave is considered the most challenging in all the country.

But, along with Costa Rican surf champion Diego Naranjo, Brown is part of a new wave of surfers. 'Now, the professional surfers are all responsible people working in the sport,' asserts Naranjo. 'We now have more support in Costa Rica than from the international companies. And the kids are looking up to us, seeing that we can make a living from surfing, and they can do it too. It does not just have to be a sport for hippies.'

The history of Costa Rica's surf culture seems far from finished. Not only are there more breaks to be found, but a new generation of Ticos and visitors will be there to surf them.

Surfers start early on the **Península de Osa**.

hours. The vast majority come from the US, but an increasing number are arriving from the chillier waters around Europe, particularly during the winter months.

José Ureña, president of the Costa Rican Surf Federation, welcomes the influx. 'The great amount of money these people leave here forms a vital part of the economy in places like Tamarindo, Jacó (on the central Pacific coast) and Puerto Viejo (on the southern Caribbean coast), but there are many more.

'All of this data indicates clearly that we are in the forefront of great economic strength for the country because, in addition to these high tourist numbers, the type of surfer who comes here has changed,' Ureña continues. 'No longer are they visitors with just a little money, but young professionals, managers of companies, real estate developers. In short, the country is being positioned in the surf world as an attractive destination for clients of high purchasing power.'

Why is it that all these people are picking Costa Rica as the place to come on a surf trip? 'The two best reasons that Costa Rica is a mecca for surfing are that we have warm water all year round and our waves are consistent,' answers Ureña. 'I mean, we have waves 365 days a year somewhere along the Pacific. Another advantage is that there is a variety of our breaks – beach breaks, reef breaks, point breaks – we can cover every level of surfer.'

And it's these same waves that have spawned a national surf team that was ranked number eight in the world at the International Surfing Association's World Surfing Games in Huntington Beach, California. At the Pan American Surf Games – second only to the Olympics in stature – surfers from Costa Rica won an historic gold medal for juniors in 2005 (Jason Torres from Jacó) and a bronze medal in the open in 2007 (Gilbert Brown from Puerto Viejo). But the most recognisable Tico to surf on the world stage is Tamarindo's Federico Pilurzu, a two-time Central American Surf Champion, now ranked among the top 50 in the world. It's a golden time for surfing in Costa Rica, but with these resources, how could it fail?

Landscaped with gardens, jungles, mountains and beaches, with sand ranging from black to white, fanned by a spectrum of warm water waves, the Costa Rican surfing experience is decidedly of that same *pura vida* experience that Naranjo is talking about. As with all surfing adventures around the globe, the discovery of Costa Rica's waves is an opportunity to immerse yourself not only in exceptional waters but also the friendly Tico culture, and to revel in one of the most beautiful natural environments on the planet.

TAKE ME TO THE BEACH
Getting to Costa Rican beaches quickly can be simple if you prepare yourself in advance. It is best to fly into San José's Juan Santamaría International Airport, or Liberia's Daniel Oduber International Airport, and arrange a van or taxi transfer directly to your surf break. It is also easy to rent a car (a four-wheel drive is absolutely necessary for the bad roads) or hop on a bus (see **Getting there** section in each area). Most are happy to take boards, but they may not be treated quite as carefully as they should and you will need to keep an eye on them. There are two national airlines, **Sansa** (www.flysansa.com) and **Nature Air** (www.natureair.com), that offer multiple flights each day to various beach towns around the country, but ask in advance if they will take your surfboards – longboards are very difficult to transport. Nature Air will accept boards only if there is space and will charge US$40 for each one. Sansa will only take two surfboards on each flight for US$10. Boards exceeding 2.1 metres (6.9 feet), windsurfing boards and kayaks are not accepted. In each town, even those with just a bit of surf, there will be private tour services offering surf lessons, surfboard rentals and surf trips. In addition, you will find comfortable lodging, restaurants, stores, and a vibrant nightlife to supplement your inevitably thrilling water life.

The best Surfing destinations

Guanacaste

A strong northerly offshore wind blows consistently during the dry season months from December to March and big storms in the rainy season create regular swells, making breaks along this coast ideal, particularly from April to November.

Potrero Grande (Ollie's Point) A long right point break accessible by rented boat from Playas del Coco. *See p173.*

Playa Naranjo (Witch's Rock) This world-famous geological formation acts as a point for strong offshore winds, particularly from December to March, and creates beach breaks in all directions, which work best with the incoming high tide. *See p173.*

Playa Grande Offers a long, pristine beach break, with lefts and rights, featuring consistent offshore winds. *See p190.*

Tamarindo The best place to learn to surf. With the bay enclosed on all sides, there is a slow beach break out front. *See p186.*

Langosta The largest and strongest wave of Tamarindo, a right and left point break that curls off a rivermouth. *See p186.*

Nosara This beach break produces rights and lefts with some shallow-rock reef lefts that get barrelling with swell. *See p193.*

Playa Guiones A left point beach break. Consistent year-round. *See p193.*

Mal País A specific beach break as well as a catch-all name for spots including El Carmen, Los Suecos, Punta Barrigona, Santa Teresa, Playa Hermosa and Manzanillo. *See p210.*

Central Pacific

Only two hours away from San José, these beaches are best during the rainy season from April to November.

Boca Barranca The dark water is only rainwater runoff, and that's great because this rivermouth break is a high-regarded very long left. *See p225.*

Puerto Caldera A very good left. Three kilometres (two miles) south of Boca Barranca. *See p225.*

Playa Escondida Accessible only by boat from Playa Herradura, but on a good swell, this excellent point break peaks up forming a very good left and a nice right. *See p225.*

Playa Jacó Another excellent learners' spot that is a fun beach break. *See p225.*

Playa Hermosa The crown jewel of the area. A very strong and long stretch of beach break

best when the tide is rising. The pros love this spot because it's the most consistent beach break on the Pacific coast. *See p210.*

Playas Esterillos Este/Oeste, Bejuco, Boca Damas All of these beach breaks provide good waves, and are located very close to Playa Hermosa. *See p230.*

Southern Pacific

The Southern Pacific is for the adventurous but the prize might be worth it; it includes the world-renowed Pavones left break.

Playa Dominical Surf this powerful beach break, with lefts and rights. *See p247.*

Bahía Drake With access only by boat, this wild region of Costa Rica offers long, powerful waves when there's a big swell. *See p254.*

Pavones If the swell is going, the left can be as long as 800 metres (2,624 feet). Excellent ride, considered world-class, with good shape, and fast. A must-visit wave. *See p272.*

Punta Burrica These are very remote reef breaks accessible only by boat. This is the last beach in the south.

Caribbean coast

Flavoured by exotic culture that is distinctly Caribbean, the surf experience on the east coast is special. The waves along the coast are for expert surfers. They are treacherous, breaking above coral reefs, and forming into the biggest surf in the country. The prime months are from January to April. In the summer, tropical storms move throughout the Caribbean seas creating huge surf. It is best to surf with the locals.

Manzanillo Secluded, exotic, consistent and fast beach break with right and left point breaks, both with tubular sections. *See p299.*

Salsa Brava The King of Costa Rican waves, so be careful and only paddle out if you are an experienced surfer. This is a thick, voluminous, Hawaiian-style wave that comes from deep water on to a shallow reef. Salsa Brava gets very big, steep and tubular. Bring more than one board. *See p299.*

Black Beach, Cahuita A good private spot, and an excellent beach break that seems to get waves year-round. *See p288.*

Playa Bonita Another thick, powerful and dangerous left, point and reef break north of the town of Puerto Limón. *See p284.*

Isla Uvita A 20-minute boat ride from Puerto Limón only at certain times of the year. The wave is a powerful left. *See p284.*

The **Río Pacuare**. *See p141*.

Rafting & Kayaking

Up the creek with a paddle and some very soggy clothes.

Home to some of the best white water in Central America and with a few runs that could take world-ranked rivers for a ride, Costa Rica is an aquatic playground for paddlers. Renowned rivers featuring Class I to V rapids, calm ocean bays and wilder surf on both coasts offer first-timers, families and seasoned rafters exhilarating opportunities through a variety of quickly changing landscapes. Well-established professional tour operators offer half-day to multi-day adventures, generally providing transportation and accommodation, bilingual English-speaking guides and modern equipment at reasonable rates. Rapids are generally wildest during the wet season from June to October, although the drier months from November to April provide the best runs for river runners of all levels, and decent waters can be found around the country year-round.

FLOAT ON

The most popular trips are along the **Río Pacuaré** (*see p139*), one of the world's top white water runs originating deep in the Cordillera de Talamanca in Cartago province, and flowing some 100 kilometres (62 miles) to the Caribbean. Rafters enjoy Class III to IV

rapids while tumbling down through some of the most varied scenery the region has to offer, as the mighty river snakes through wildlife-rich virgin rainforest, wraps around waterfalls draped over rocky cliff walls, and rushes out to the Caribbean plains where villages and pasturelands dot the upper banks. There are several stretches of technically demanding rapids, including a 250-metre (800-foot) vertical drop through Class II to IV rapids over the 25-kilometre (16-mile) stretch downriver from the popular Tres Equis launching point.

Another favourite, the Río Reventazón in the Caribbean lowlands, dishes out Class II to V waters and is good for both beginners on day trips and seasoned adventurers. This river is home to the renowned Class V runs in the Guayabo section, although the building of a hydroelectric dam has destroyed some of the higher-class stretch. The river is full year-round but June and July are the best rafting months.

Several tour operators feature 'Rafting Safaris', multi-day camping excursions along longer rivers of varying difficulty. The lengthy Río General is among the more famous world-class rivers in Costa Rica thanks to its complex network of choppy rapids, big waves and sheer volume of water. The river runs along **San Isidro de El General** on the slopes of the Talamanca Mountains south-east of Manuel Antonio, winding its way through narrow gorges and green forest for kilometres, full of birds and wildlife. The river boasts stretches of Class III and IV rapids and is long enough for multi-day adventures.

PACIFIC RUNS

On the Pacific side of the country, the mostly Class III to IV waters of the **Río Naranjo** step it up a notch in a section dubbed 'the Labyrinth', an exciting Class V expert-only segment generally untamed from December to March, although notoriously inconsistent. Less experienced rafters enjoy calmer waters and a change of scenery downstream where the river leaves the rainforest and climbs out through farmland and **Parque Nacional Manuel Antonio** (see p233) before making its way to the Pacific. The nearby Río Savegre is one of the nation's cleanest and offers Class III to IV expeditions. Its quieter neighbour, the Class II Río Parita, is lined by lush tropical forest home to a diversity of wildlife, a popular route for first-timers and families looking more to float and birdwatch.

> **'Sea kayaks are an excellent means to explore more remote nooks not easily accessible by land.'**

Also worth a run, the crystal-clear Class III **Río Sarapiquí** (see p131) runs along the Cordillera Central before spilling out into the Caribbean lowlands to the east, with trips from May to December. Rio Chirripó (Class III to IV) runs down from **Chirripó** (see p242) and along the south-west Pacific slope, and won't disappoint seasoned paddlers searching for volumes of fast moving water.

Costa Rica regulates rafting companies. Participants must wear life jackets and helmets (provided). You should take a swimsuit, T-shirt, sports sandals or tennis shoes, sunscreen, and an extra set of clothes for the return. Most places carry a dry bag for cameras and other things that shouldn't get wet.

KAYAKING

Over 1,200 kilometres (745 miles) of varied coastline, numerous estuaries teeming with life and the exciting rapids of the aforementioned rivers make Costa Rica a superb location for kayakers. Varied conditions and watercourses

make for great river kayaking, particularly on the Pacuaré, General, Sarapiquí and Reventazón rivers. Specialised tour agencies operate out of **Turrialba** (see p139) and **Puerto Viejo de Sarapiquí** (see p131), and the small towns make good bases for exploring the rivers and meeting other shoulder-sore paddlers.

While white water kayakers enjoy much of the same river terrain frequented by rafters, sea kayakers are an excellent means to explore more remote nooks not accessible by land, and to to sneak up quietly on wildlife.

On the Pacific coast, **Parque Nacional Manuel Antonio** (see p233) offers spectacular paddling along sandy coves and there are several interesting islands to explore just offshore. The **Refugio Nacional de Vida Silvestre Curú** (see p219), located on the Peninsula de Nicoya, is another ideal spot to set to sea, with long stretches of pristine beaches, rocky walls and quiet estuaries. The mazy waterways and lush mangroves of **Parque Nacional Tortuguero** (see p279) are also great for paddling and wildlife spotting.

OPERATOR PLEASE

Many outfitters on both coasts rent equipment allowing you to explore at leisure, or take a tour with a naturalist guide who will point out wildlife you may miss on your own. Be careful when kayaking in the ocean, as heavy currents can make for dangerous conditions. If you aren't sure, hire a guide.

A few worthy tour operators are **Costa Rica White Water**, part of Costa Rica Expeditions (2257 0766, www.costaricaexpeditions.com), one of the first and still one of the best for day and multi-day trips on a host of rivers. **Pacuaré River Tours** (2291 6844, www.pacuareriver tours.com) has a day trip deal for US$75 per rafter for groups of four or more. **Costa Sol Rafting** (2293 2150, www.costasolrafting.com) offers more challenging excursions and special trips for kayakers. **Aguas Bravas** (2292 2072, www.aguas-bravas.co.cr) is a smaller company specialising in family adventures on the Saraquipi and more challenging trips into the Class IV-V section for advanced paddlers. **Ríos Tropicales** (2233 6455, www.riostropicales. com) has been in business since 1985 and runs a number of trips for all levels on most raftable rivers. Overnight stays on the Rio Pacuaré are in a nice riverbank lodge. **Exploradores Outdoors** (2222 6262, www.exploradores outdoors.com) operates from several major tourist hubs around the country and integrates activities like canopy tours and snorkelling with rafting trips. Other local companies can be found throughout the country; for more information see regional sections.

San José
& Around

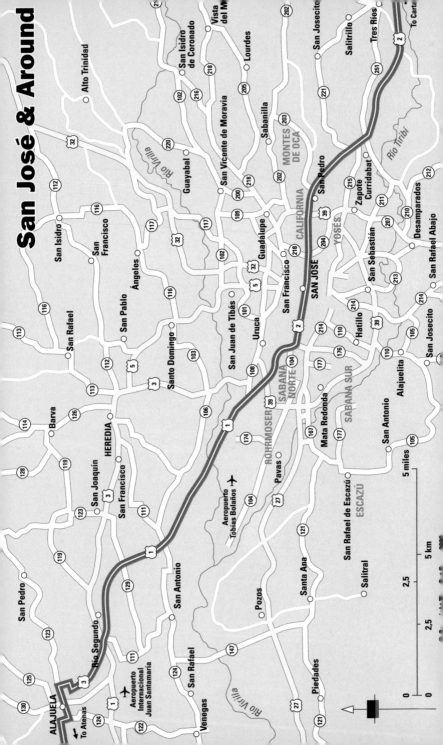

Getting Started

San José gets a bad rap, but it remains Costa Rica's cultural capital.

San José is often derided by visitors. True, it isn't the prettiest of cities. Its downtown area is a metropolitan mash-up of busy people, careless bus drivers and angry taxi drivers. Of the attractions that draw most tourists to Costa Rica – beaches, volcanoes, wildlife and surf breaks – there are none. San José, on first sight, often scares people.

So why stay here? Because, despite all of its shortcomings, San José is still a vibrant cultural centre and the country's capital. Within the city's boundaries are Costa Rica's finest restaurants, its best museums, its most exciting nightlife and most of its extant colonial architecture. It is also decisively Latin – something that cannot be said of most of the foreign-owned resorts. For anyone who wants to see the 'real' Latin America, warts and all, San José is where to go, even if only en route to somewhere more attractive.

We've divided this chapter into three sections: **Downtown**, **East San José** and **West San José**. Each of these districts has its own distinct character and visitor attractions. Most expats live in the wealthy west in the neighbourhoods of **Escazú** and **Santa Ana**. Art buffs and foodies should head directly to this area, in which private galleries and design studios showcase the best of contemporary Costa Rican creativity and restaurants such as **Chateau 1525** (*see p87*) and **La Luz** (*see p107*) serve up inventive cuisine inspired both by traditional Tico food and international classics. The west of the city has some of the best luxury accommodation such as the **Marriott Courtyard** (*see p111*) and the **Real Intercontinental** (*see p111*). But there are many more quality hotels in this affluent area that is very close to the airport.

The east of the city is where you'll find most of the best nightlife. The high student population gives the **Los Yoses** and **San Pedro** neighbourhoods their lively atmospheres. San José's best bars are in these *barrios*, which are quickly gaining a reputation among backpackers as the places to party before hitting the surf. There are also several decent hotels and B&Bs in the area.

Street vendors and lottery ticket sellers pack the centre of San José. Reggaeton blasts from shop doors and fervent salespeople try to sell you sportswear. The epicentre of downtown is the **Mercado Central** (*see p83*), which should

Teatro National.

be on everyone's list of places to see in San José. Here, cheap *sodas* serve up huge *casados* and big bowls of ceviche. A little further away is the opulent, neo-classical **Teatro Nacional** (*see p86*). Next door to the Teatro Nacional is the fascinating **Museo de Oro Precolombino** (*see p86*), which offers visitors an insight into Costa Rica's often forgotten indigenous heritage. The **Museo de Jade** (*see p86*), with its beautifully smooth crafted pieces, serves a similar purpose. And the nearby area of **Amón** is made up of tidy houses, some lovely cafés, and restaurants in converted colonial buildings.

San José & Around

Downtown

It may be chaotic and dirty but the city centre is exciting and unfailingly Latin.

Teatro Nacional. See p86.

San José is a blue-collar city without frills or airs. The buildings are square and predictable and the people strong and hard-working. A handful of Victorian and neo-classical mansions left over from the days when coffee barons ruled the town have been converted into boutique hotels and restaurants targeting international businessmen and tourists, and are adding flair to the grey city.

A population boom after World War II gave way to rapid, unplanned growth that all but wiped out the remaining colonial architecture. Historic buildings were replaced by no-nonsense office blocks, and residential areas sprang up to meet the sudden demand, consisting of rows of small homes made from corrugated iron and concrete. Owing to rising crime, the upper classes migrated from the centre to neighbourhoods like Escazú and Santa Ana, leaving the city economically neglected until recent years.

Metal bars and barbed wire encase windows and doors, offering visible evidence of the lack of security felt by the population. Indeed, if you turn the wrong corner and wander into Barrio México, near the Coca-Cola bus station, you will find painful reminders that even the most forward-thinking government in Central America cannot reach all of its citizens.

Still, the city has inevitably grown as a centre of commerce and government. The buzzing crowds around the Mercado Central prove that the economy is alive and well. Just about any product you can imagine is available within the century-old structure and along adjacent side streets, from fresh fish to tacky trinkets and colourful exotic fruit.

Further east, in the Parque Nacional, you will find politicians, street vendors and university students hanging around remnants of the country's strong democratic past. Here, the large, distinguished civic buildings dating back to the 19th century will make you forget that you are in a third world country.

New social programmes, stricter treatment of criminals and a municipal beautification and re-urbanisation plan called 'San José Posible' promise to bring light back into the city that was the third in the world to install electric lighting in public areas. The pedestrian walkway along Avenida Central is being enlarged, pavements widened and businesses opened up to include outdoor seating at restaurants and large open storefronts. With such a pro-tourism administration, San José's beauty is likely to be brought into the foreground in the coming years.

With a cool temperate climate, San José is a great place to spend a day outdoors wandering from plaza to side street, getting a sense of the daily lives of its residents.

THE BIRTH OF A CITY

San José was first established in 1737, long after the foundation of the country's first provincial capital, Cartago, in 1564. In the beginning, San José held little importance except as a stop on the tobacco trading route. Its original inhabitants were nationalist merchants, many of whom had been exiled from Cartago. Their business savvy helped create a thriving economy, in large part due to the country's near monopoly on the region's tobacco trade. When Costa Rica's independence from colonial rule was declared in 1821, the citizens of San José took up arms against their less liberal-minded compatriots in Cartago, who wanted to become part of a Central American federation. San José won, and claimed as the capital in 1823.

Public education and the profitable coffee industry became priorities in the new city. The members of the new elite, mostly wealthy coffee barons, were, generally speaking, a force for good in the country. They even taxed their own exports to raise money for projects such as a university, the Teatro Nacional (*see p86*), cobbled roads, a tramway and outdoor lighting.

A series of progressive presidents and a well-educated upper class laid the groundwork for the relative prosperity that the country enjoys today, in a region often plagued by war and poverty. The only large uprising in the country occurred in 1948 after President Rafael Ángel Calderón Guardia refused to step down after losing his re-election. José Maria Figueres Ferrer defeated him in a one-month battle and began his mission to modernise the country's social, economic and political institutions.

Today San José is one of the largest and most cosmopolitan cities in Central America. Since the army was abolished in 1949, 12 peaceful, democratic and relatively corruption-free elections have been held. The latest re-election of Nobel Peace Prize winner Óscar Arias Sánchez has helped attract foreign investment, and the tourism industry is flourishing. Though crystal-ball gazing is generally unwise in Latin America, Costa Rica's future looks bright.

Sightseeing

Heirs to proud and accomplished civilisations – indigenous, colonial or both – many Latin American cities exude self-confidence and dazzle visitors with their grand civic piles, broad thoroughfares and lush parks. San José is not like this. Most of the city's architecture, fashion and pop culture is a hybrid of foreign paradigms. Just below the surface, however, there is a distinct cultural pride that comes out in full colour during national holidays and local festivals. Outside of the fiestas season the following sights are some of the best places to visit if you want to learn more about the Tico mentality and national identity. The excellent museums offer fine examples of pre-Columbian artefacts.

Mercado Central

Avenida Central, entre Calles 6 y 8. **Open** 6.30am-6pm Mon-Sat. **Credit** varies.

As the giant numbers over the main entrance tell you, the central market was first opened in 1880 and has served as a commercial hub since. Stalls line the building, turning a high airy space into a claustrophobic maze of people and random goods from top hats to guitars to fresh seasonings and restaurants. Follow the aroma to the food stands and you will find small stalls filled with hanging vegetables and

 The best **San José**

Things to do

Gawp at the incredible jewellery on display at the superlative **Museo de Jade** (*see p86*). Continue your studies of Costa Rican indigenous life with further opulence and glittering gold artefacts at the **Museo de Oro Precolombino y Numismática** (*see p86*). For later Costa Ricans it was coffee that was the true bounty, money from which helped build San José's loveliest building, the **Teatro Nacional** (*see p86*).

Places to stay

Escape the fug and fumes at **La Paseo del Rosa** (*see p94*), a building dating back to 1897. Centred around a verdant courtyard that attracts exotic birds, this reasonably priced boutique hotel will either provide a taste of your trip to come or preserve the relaxed pace of life as your holiday comes to an end. If it's Western-style modernity you're craving, consider the modern **Hotel Parque del Lago** (*see p93*), which offers stylish and clean surroundings and all modcons; it's great for business travellers. However, the pick of the bunch is **Hotel Grano de Oro** (*see p93*).

Places to eat

The **Hotel Grano de Oro** (*see p89* **Golden delicious**), set in a three-storey mansion, wins the food accolades too. Its French chef adds a Gallic touch to international fare. Follow your nose directly to the **Mercado Central** (*see left*). A bustling and random mix of market stalls compete with a wealth of sodas offering a hearty traditional mix of anything as long as it comes with beans and rice. The ceviche is excellent at almost every venue. **Tin Jo** (*see p89*) offers quality South-east Asian food.

Nightlife

San José has an energetic nightlife scene. If you have a date on your arm, grab a table at **Rapsodia** (*see p90*), a cool and modern bar. Drinking tasty cocktails out on its stylish terrace is a surefire way to impress your companion. But if it's dancing and drinking you're after then **Vertigo** (*see p90*) will get the pulse racing. For frothy beers and a good-time vibe, the bars in the studenty east of the city make for a fun pub crawl, especially along the **Calle de la Amargura** (*see p99*).

San José & Around

Downtown

Parque
La Sabana

PASEO COLÓN

Parque

AVENIDA 17

AVENIDA 15

AVENIDA 13

Plaza

AVENIDA 13

AVENIDA 11

AVENIDA 7

AVENIDA 7

AVENIDA 5

AVENIDA 5

AVENIDA 3

AVENIDA 5

AVENIDA 3

AVENIDA 3

AVENIDA 1

PASEO COLÓN

AVENIDA 1

AVENIDA CENTRA

PASEO COLÓN

AVENIDA 2 CENTENARIO

Hospital
Nacional
de Niños

Hospital
San Juan
de Dios

Parque
La Merced

AVENIDA 4

AVENIDA 6 CASTRO MADRIZ

AVENIDA 6

AVENIDA 6

Parque

AVENIDA 8

AVENIDA 8 SIMÓN BOLÍVAR

MERCED

AVENIDA 10

AVENIDA 10

AVENIDA 12

AV. CAMPOS

AVENIDA 24

AVENIDA POCHET

AVENIDA 14

AVENIDA 26

AVENIDA 18

AVENIDA 20

AVENIDA 20

Parque

AVENIDA 20 BIS

AVENIDA 22

AVENIDA 24

AVENIDA 28

AVENIDA 28

AVENIDA 26

AVENIDA 26

AV. 26

AVENIDA 28

AVENIDA 30

AVENIDA 32

AVENIDA 34

Río María Aguilar

0   500 m
0   500 yds

© Copyright Time Out Group 2008

herbal cures for all your ailments. Market food stands serve up the freshest and tastiest typical Costa Rican dishes. The area around can be dangerous, especially after 6pm.

Museo de Arte y Diseño Contemporáneo (MADC)

Calle 15, y Avenida 3 (2257 7202/www.madc.ac.cr). **Open** 10.30am-5.30pm Tue-Sat. **Admission** free.
This museum is set in the former National Liquor Factory that was built in the mid 19th century. It plays host to an international sampling of modern artists, the majority from Costa Rica and Latin America. Ponder the wide variety of media as you learn more about the artists' lives and inspirations. The usually excellent temporary exhibits demonstrate a new appreciation of modern Costa Rican artists, sculptors and photographers.

Museo de Jade

Avenida 7, entre Calles 9 y 11 (2287 6034). **Open** 8am-3.30pm Mon-Fri; 9am-1pm Sat. **Admission** US$2; free under-12s.
Recently reopened on the ground floor of the Instituto Nacional de Seguros (INS) building, this is one of Costa Rica's most famous museums displaying a jaw-droppingly large collection of jade artefacts dating from between 500 BC and AD 800. It offers a unique insight into the lives of Costa Rica's indigenous population, and especially into the trade routes they developed (jade is rarely found in Costa Rica itself, but was considered the most precious of stones). Alongside the lovingly displayed pieces are fine examples of pottery, bowls and figures, some of which use human teeth for decorations.

Museo de Oro Precolombino y Numismática.

Museo Nacional

Calle 17, entre Avenidas Central y 2 (2257 1433/www.museosdecostarica.com). **Open** 8.30am-4.30pm Tue-Fri; 9am-4.30pm Sat, Sun. **Admission** US$4.
Set in an ex-military fortress on a hill, this national museum offers one of the best views from within the city. From the outside, you cannot miss its battered wall, reminders of the revolution of 1948. Inside, the museum takes a look at Costa Rican identity from its pre-Columbian inhabitants starting in 12,000 BC to its modern day government, religion and natural wonders. Don't miss the gold display, or the downstairs secret garden that houses a number of native butterfly species including the elusive Blue Morpho among many others.

Museo de Oro Precolombino y Numismática

Calle 5, y Avenida Central (2233 4233). **Open** 9am-4.30pm Tue-Sat. **Admission** US$6.
If the Museo Nacional is at the top of the city, the Museo de Oro Precolombino is at the bottom: underground to be exact. Located beneath the Plaza de la Cultura, the museum's three subterranean floors display more than 2,000 glittering pieces of pre-Columbian gold, often representing animals or anthropomorphic designs. It is one of the largest collections of its kind in the Western hemisphere, and a highlight of San José. The pieces range from intricate jewellery to headpieces; from weapons to fertility symbols. There is also an interesting display about the history of Costa Rican money.

Teatro Nacional

Calle 5, y Avenida Central (2221 1329/www.teatro nacional.go.cr). **Open** 9am-5pm Mon-Sat. **Admission** US$3. **Credit** MC, V (online only).
The national theatre is a diamond in the rough in downtown San José's Central Plaza. The building sits in front of the Gran Hotel Costa Rica as a testament to the days when coffee barons ran the town and decided to tax their own coffee exports to bring a little culture to the city. The theatre was constructed throughout Europe in parts and shipped to Costa Rica for reassembly in the 1890s. Its interior includes murals and paintings by Italian artists, while the structure was built from Belgian metal. Today you can wander about its halls or visit the coffee shop to explore the walls of local and European art, or catch a play or concert.

Where to eat

Like the architecture, the food options in San José are mainly conventional. Most *sodas* will serve a bountiful plate of the day for as little as US$3 or US$4. Expect the bounty to consist mostly of rice and beans. There is little rhyme or reason to how restaurants are dispersed throughout the centre. The business centre along Paseo Colón has a variety of ethnic restaurants,

Tacky souvenirs and excellent food at the **Mercado Central**. *See p83.*

North American fast food chains and a few high-end establishments, while in the East restaurants vary between catering to tourists, government officials and the student crowd. For a truly Tico experience, eat at a stand in the **Mercado Central** (*see p83*), where national dishes are pieced together from the same fresh ingredients on sale all around you. What you see is not always what you get in San José, so don't be scared to poke your head in and ask to see a menu before you pass up treats like **Machu Picchu** (*see p89*), **Lubnan** and **Chateau 1525**.

Café Mundo

Calle 15, y Avenida 9 (2222 6190). **Open** 11am-11pm Mon-Thur; 11am-midnight Fri; 5pm-midnight Sat. **Main courses** US$10. **Credit** AmEx, MC, V.

Café Mundo is a classy bar-restaurant in Barrio Amón that is housed in a restored mansion and attracts an international crowd. There are multiple seating areas from the outside terrace to the back patio, and all enjoy views of bright, stylish art and the lovely house itself. Service is a bit slow, but the international menu is vast and delicious. *Photo p90.*

Chateau 1525

Behind Biblioteca Nacional, 125m east of yellow house (2248 9337/www.chateau1525.com). **Open** 11.30am-3pm, 6-10pm daily. **Main courses** US$30. **Credit** AmEx, MC, V.

This modernly elegant edifice faces a side street behind the Biblioteca Nacional and offers patio and indoor seating. Chateau 1525 is one of three dining options in the building, which also includes the more casual Rogue Kitchen and Bar, a private conference room and an art gallery. Specialities include duck with polenta, beef tenderloin in an espresso sauce, salmon with papaya and mint sauce and sweet chillies, and rabbit stuffed with apples and cinnamon and wrapped in cheese and bacon. There is Wi-Fi available.

La Esquina de Buenos Aires

Calle 11, y Avenida 4 (2223 1909). **Main courses** US$22. **Open** noon-midnight daily. **Credit** AmEx, DC, MC, V.

This renowned Argentinian restaurant could only be more authentic if your steak was brought to you by a tangoing *gaucho* with a Boca Juniors scarf round his neck. Fortunately, there are no such gimmicks; this place does what restaurants on the River Plate do best: sublime steaks perfectly grilled thanks to Argentinian chef Mauricio Cabado. To accompany the meat you can choose from 80 varieties of wine from the motherland. For those not so carnivorously inclined, pastas, empanadas, seafood and fish dishes are also available. Highly recommended are the artichoke-stuffed sorrentinos.

Hotel Grano del Oro

Calle 30, entre Avenidas 2 y 4 (2255 3322/www.hotel granodeoro.com). **Open** 6-10am, 11.30am-3pm, 5.30-10pm daily. **Main courses** US$15. **Credit** AmEx, DC, MC, V.

This is one of the most highly acclaimed restaurants in Costa Rica. This hotel restaurant is set in an artistically refurbished colonial house and serves fine Gallic dishes. *See p89* **Golden delicious.**

Lubnan

Paseo Colón, entre Calle 22 y 24 (2257 6071). **Main courses** US$8. **Open** 11am-3pm, 6pm-1am Tue-Sat. **Credit** AmEx, DC, MC, V.

Golden delicious

The **Hotel Grano de Oro** (*see p87*), with its sophisticated blend of the antique and the contemporary, is a welcome relief from the eyesore that is much of San José. The three-storey mansion towers over the street with a wide staircase flanked by parallel-tiered fountains flowing down from the entrance. A tinted glass door slides out of the way to make room for the guests, who exude an air – and who can blame them? – of being omnipotent. No need to envy them: you'll feel the same after only an evening here.

The restaurant sits just beyond the lobby, and includes a sunken, open-air patio with a large white fountain in the centre that gazes up to the second-storey windows above. The patio is decorated with ivy and potted shrubs and lit by a mixture of white lights, candles and sconces. Large yellow stained-glass windows face the well-stocked bar on the other side of the patio, which is framed by a slightly more formal area with hard wood floors littered with oriental rugs that whisper opulence when coupled with heavy maroon floor to ceiling drapes. Comfortable velvet U-shaped booths or antique table and chairs welcome travel-weary guests. As a welcome gesture, diners receive a *regalo de la casa* or house gift – a small amuse-bouche such as whipped asparagus mousse with fresh bread and herb butter. Next, choose from a menu featuring everything from chicken vol-au-vent to dishes like rabbit wrapped in bacon, and duck liver pâté, a speciality of French chef Francis. The drinks are equally as good, ranging from caiparhinas to Irish coffee to national beers. Finish with a beautifully presented chocolate cake and ice cream, or enjoy a cool San José evening and a nightcap by the bar.

Lubnan is a Lebanese restaurant that has stood alone opposite the Scotia Bank on Paseo Colón for 13 years. Half-hearted Middle Eastern decorations do a disservice to the high quality food. The adjacent bar has quaint cave-like decor and is a local favourite on Wednesday nights with occasional music performances. Hookahs and drinks are available in either setting, while the food is limited to the front room. Try the meze plate for two (US$25).

Machu Picchu

Calle 31, entre Avenidas 1 y 3 (2222 7384). **Open** 11am-3pm, 6-10pm Mon-Sat. **Main courses** US$12. **Credit** AmEx, DC, MC, V.
Machu Picchu is an excellent Peruvian restaurant situated on a nondescript street north off Paseo Colón. The service is excellent from the moment the door opens to when the bill arrives. House specials include *aji a la gallina* (chilli chicken), ceviche and, of course, the pisco sour, made from Peru's strong grape-based spirit with sour mix and egg white.

Manolo's

Calle 2, y Avenida Central (2221 2041). **Open** 24hrs daily. **Main courses** US$8. **Credit** AmEx, MC, V.

This Avenida Central stalwart has been open for over half a century and serves dinner specials round the clock. Try the Tico breakfast of *gallo pinto* for dinner, or a steak sandwich for breakfast as you watch the crowds passing by from the outdoor patio.

Nuestra Tierra

Calle 15, y Avenida 2 (2258 6500). **Open** 24hrs daily. **Main courses** US$12. **No credit cards.**
The restaurant's decor will take you back to the early 20th-century Costa Rican countryside, when cowboys and cattle roamed the lands. Brush up on your history as you review the old photos of downtown San José that are encased in each table while you wait for typical Costa Rican fare. Be sure to order a regular coffee, which is filtered in front of you using the traditional Tico-style with a cloth pouch suspended over a beat-up tin coffee pot.

Tin Jo

Calle 11, entre Avenidas 6 y 8 (2221 7605/www. tinjo.com). **Open** 11.30am-3pm, 5.30-10pm Mon-Sat; 11.30am-10pm Sun. **Main courses** US$10. **Credit** AmEx, MC, V.
Tin Jo is often declared one of the top dining options in San José. It offers a unique combination of cuisine

Let them eat cake at **Café Mundo**. *See p87.*

from all over South-east Asia, and it also has decorations to match. The decor is as authentic and elegant as the food and the service is prompt and polite. A range of curries include both Thai specialities such as fish curry in coconut milk and a spicy green curry, while from the other side of the Bay of Bengal comes masala chicken, made using authentic spices and cooking methods.

Where to drink

Castro's

Avenida 13, y Calle 12 (2256 8789). **Open** 11am-3am daily. **Credit** AmEx, MC, V.
Castro's is a giant three-storey club featuring Latin and tropical beats, and is very popular among the locals. Tables and chairs are pushed to the side by evening as people come here to get a serious groove on, despite being packed into the dancefloor like sardines. Tables are still accessible for those who would rather watch than take part in the action, and food is served all night. The inviting entrance sits in a dodgy neighbourhood, so best to take a taxi and leave your valuables behind.

Rapsodia

Paseo Colón, y Avenida Central (2248 1720). **Open** 5.30pm-1am Tue-Thur; 5.30pm-3am Sat, Sun. **Main courses** US$12. **Credit** AmEx, DC, MC, V.
Rapsodia is a new, stylish addition to San José's centre. It was recently opened in a renovated house; the dark grey modern façade is easy to overlook next to the Centro Colón building. The blue lights, white and black leather sofas and outside patio seating are unique in the city. Despite a decent dinner menu, with options ranging from pizza to steak, the place is usually empty until around 11pm. The loud

electronic music gets the young, trendy crowd on their feet until the early morning.

Shakespeare Bar

Calle 28, y Avenida 2 (2258 6787). **Open** 5-11.30pm daily. **Credit** AmEx, MC, V.
Shakespeare Bar is one of the few popular night destinations that doesn't blast loud music into the early hours. The sophisticated set-up is reflected by the clientele, who are often on their way to or from a show at the adjoining Sala Garbo cinema or next door's Laurence Olivier Theatre.

Vertigo

Centro Colón Building, Paseo Colón (2257 8424/www.vertigocr.com). **Open** 10pm-6am Thur-Sat. **Credit** AmEx, MC, V.
Vertigo is a modern electronic dance club that is a favourite among students and anyone who enjoys disco balls, flashing lights and watching professional dancers on stage work it out to the sounds of popular local DJs. This is a place to be seen and to dance, although upstairs has a slightly calmer atmosphere with cushioned seating. By midnight, however, everyone here will also be on their feet. ID is required upon entering, no matter your age.

Where to stay

With little international appeal, San José is lagging a bit behind other Costa Rican destinations when it comes to sophisticated lodging. With a few exceptions, hotels here have average prices, and facilities to match. However, with a growing demand for rooms – since most tourists must spend a night or two in the city whether they like it or not – comes the need for

Democratic movements

Start: Plaza de la Democracia
Finish: Plaza de la Cultura
Length: 2 kilometres (1.2 miles)

Despite being the youngest capital in Central America, San José has a strong democratic history and a new artistic revival can be felt pushing up through the dust and debris left by years of cultural identity. This walk will help you to get a feel for the current national character and how it developed.

Start your morning by pulling up a bench at **Nuestra Tierra** (*see p89*), a two-storey traditional restaurant on the corner of Avenida 2 and Calle 15. Read about historic landmarks in the photos lining your table while your coffee seeps through an old-fashioned cloth sieve called a *chorreador*.

Walk off your *gallo pinto* breakfast while you explore the artisan market in the **Plaza de la Democracia**. Explore the tunnel of stands displaying hammocks, wooden trays, jewellery and masks. Once you've bartered your way to souvenir ownership, make the short ascent to the entrance of the ex-military fortress at the east end of the plaza, now the **Museo Nacional** (*see p86*). Spend an hour exploring the exhibits that take you from 12,000 BC to present day Costa Rica, before enjoying the best view of San José from within the city.

Next, head north along the palm tree-lined pedestrian walkway to the **Parque Nacional**. This is the most prominent green space in the city, with the **Legislative Assembly**, **National Library**, **National Cultural Centre** (Cenac) and the **Electoral Assembly** all ranged around it. Pass the giant statue depicting the Battle of Rivas, where Costa Rica defeated the US

filibuster William Walker and his troops, and head to the north-west corner of the park to explore the **Museo de Arte y Diseño Contemporáneo** (*see p86*).

From fine art to gastronomy: your next stop is lunch. Upon exiting the museum, head north for two blocks into the quaint historic district of Barrio Amón. After the road bears left, make a sharp right up to **Café Mundo** (*see p87*) in a restored mansion.

Next, head back to Avenida 7 and turn right, going west. On the first corner, check out **Ñ**, a commercial art gallery that sells work by young artists and hosts music and poetry readings. The heavy black door around the corner leads to an underground showroom called **Dar(t)do**. Owned by an amiable old Tico, the room is open by appointment only. The dartboard in the window isn't just symbolic of the name; it signals to the art community when a show is in progress. If the dart in the centre is green, there's an exhibition on; if red, the showroom is closed.

On your way out, pass by the **Casa Amarilla**, a historic landmark that houses the Ministry of Foreign Affairs, and enjoy the shade of tropical trees in **Parque España**. The adjoining **Parque Morazán** is anchored by the **Templo de Musica**, which was constructed in 1920 as a replica of the Temple of Love and Music in Versailles and has played host to orchestras and important political speeches. If you're lucky, you might catch a music or art festival put on by the municipality in the area.

Turn left (south) at the far end of Parque Morazán and venture several blocks to the wide-open **Plaza de la Cultura**. Enjoy the sunset while watching pigeons flutter about in the pink sky. Make your way over to the crowning point of the plaza, the green-domed **Teatro Nacional** (*see p86*). Enter to see San José's most impressive structural design, or grab a table at Gran Hotel Costa Rica's open-air café, **Café 1830**, for a cappuccino break.

Next, head west down the pedestrianised street, window shopping until you reach **Manolo's** (*see p89*) for a diner-style dinner. This local favourite opened in 1958 and has been serving typical cuisine 24 hours a day ever since. It has two floors of prime people-watching patios where you can see today's San José pass by.

higher international standards and service. Spotting this gap in the market, chains like Sleep Inn, Radisson and Holiday Inn have all positioned themselves close to important cultural landmarks, while retaining their North American characteristics. Other hotels have hopped on board with renovations, enlargements and the hiring of English-speaking staff.

Aurola Holiday Inn

Avenida 5, entre Calles 5 y 7 (2523 1000/ www.aurolahotels.com). **Rates** US$160-$800 double. **Rooms** 200. **Credit** AmEx, DC, MC, V.
This modern lodging option towers over the city with its 200 rooms spread over 17 floors, topped with the gourmet Mirador restaurant. It is located in front of the Parque Morazán, a great spot for jetting off to the many nearby cultural sights. Expect generic yet reliable chain hotel style and comfort.
Bar. Business centre. Gym. Internet. Pool (indoor). Restaurants (2). Room service. Spa. TV.

Clarion Amón Plaza

Avenida 11, y Calle 3 (2523 4600/www.hotel amonplaza.com). **Rates** US$80-$100 double. **Rooms** 87. **Credit** AmEx, MC, V.
Aiming to position itself as one of the leading downtown hotels, the Amón Plaza – with its modern colonial style and reasonable prices – is as good as you can find in the area. Among its extras, it has a large casino, an open-air restaurant and, best of all, large, modern bedrooms. Guests vary from visiting corporate executives to families looking for comfort and security in an area that can be dodgy after 6pm.
Bar. Internet. Parking. Restaurant. Room service. TV.

De Luxe Backpackers

Calle 7, y Avenida 9 (2223 9414/www.gruporeal internacional.com). **Rates** US$10 dorm bed. **Rooms** 10. **No credit cards**.
Located near to Tranquilo Backpackers, this hostel has a calmer, more relaxing atmosphere. The old mansion has high arched windows inside between the common areas that include cable TV and tables topped with stylish chess and checker sets. The ten bedrooms have two or three bunk beds apiece. Three private rooms also have space for four people at the same price.
Parking. TV.

Gran Hotel Costa Rica

Calle Central, y Avenida 2 (2221 4000/www. granhotelcr.com). **Rates** US$94-$112 double. **Rooms** 104. **Credit** AmEx, DC, MC, V.
In one of the best locations in the city, the hotel anchors the busy Plaza de la Cultura directly in front of the Teatro Nacional. The downstairs café and restaurant maintain a formal, old-school ambience in a beautiful setting. The grandeur, unfortunately, has since faded from the hotel rooms, which are noticeably ageing, but still adequate.
Bar. Business centre. Concierge. Gym. Internet. Parking. Restaurants (3). Room service.

Hotel Balmoral

Avenida Central, entre Calles 5 y 7 (2222 5022/ www.hotelbalmoral.travel). **Rates** US$80-$144 double. **Rooms** 112. **Credit** AmEx, DC, MC, V.
Hotel Balmoral's central location should be the highlight, but this is a well-equipped four-star hotel, and, at these prices, a bargain. Restaurants, meeting rooms and a gym make it popular with passing business travellers, but tourists are far from forgotten about and staff can help with all manner of queries. The clean rooms are basic but of ample size.
Bar. Business centre. Concierge. Gym. Internet (shared terminals, wireless, free). Parking (free). Restaurant. Room service. Spa. TV.

Hotel Britannia

Avenida 11, y Calle 3 (2223 6667/www.hotelbritannia costarica.com). **Rates** US$77-$147 double. **Rooms** 24. **Credit** AmEx, DC, MC, V.
The Hotel Britannia is housed in an early 1900s mansion and includes a modern extension with 14 additional rooms. The decor includes combinations of high ceilings, thick brick walls, oriental rugs and mosaic tiles. A restaurant serving international cuisine can be found in the original cellar.
Internet (shared terminals, wireless, free). Restaurant. Room service. TV.

Hotel Dunn Inn

Calle 4, y Avenida 11 (2256 1134/www.hoteldunninn. com). **Rates** US$49-$99 double. **Rooms** 26. **Credit** AmEx, MC, V.
A bright yellow Victorian-style building is actually two houses converted into one hotel. There is a bar and open-air restaurant with international food options. In front of the Lucky Horseshoe Casino, and near the Parque Morazán, the location is convenient during the day but can become a bit rough at night.
Bar. Gym. Internet. Parking. Restaurant. Room service. TV.

Hotel Grano de Oro

Calle 30, entre Avenidas 2 y 4 (2255 3322/www. hotelgranodeoro.com). **Rates** US$88-$105 double. **Rooms** 35. **Credit** AmEx, DC, MC, V.
A resounding favourite, the Hotel Grano de Oro is nearly flawless in its delivery. The hotel restaurant is one of the best in the country (*see p89* **Golden delicious**), with excellent service that filters over into the room service and hotel staff. The converted mansion maintains its distinguished character of years past with its antique furnishings, freshly painted walls and colonial charm. An upstairs balcony includes a jacuzzi and offers sweeping views of the city and surrounding mountains. Standard rooms are elegant and simple, while the suites are spacious and luxurious with hand-painted tiles, seating areas and garden or city views.
Bar. Parking. Restaurant. Room service. TV.

Hotel Parque del Lago

Paseo Colón, y Calle 42 (2257 8787/www. parquedellago.com). **Rates** US$114-$194 double. **Rooms** 40. **Credit** AmEx, DC, MC, V.

San José & Around

With modern conference halls, free Wi-Fi and a crisp, professional atmosphere, this hotel is popular with business travellers. The rooms are new, stylish and pristine, and its location next to the Sabana Park and a multitude of chain restaurants offers opportunities for relaxation and convenience.
Bar. Business centre. Concierge. Internet (wireless, free). Parking. Restaurant. Room service. TV.

Hotel Rincon de San José
Calle 15, y Avenida 9 (2221 9702/www.hotelrinconde sanjose.com). **Rates** US$48-$74 double. **Rooms** 27. **Credit** AmEx, DC, MC, V.
This comfortable hotel is located in an interesting little corner of San José, just north of Parque España in the historic district of Barrio Amón. Stained-glass windows adorn the bright, casual dining area, while the 27 rooms are a bit darker, with worn bedding.
Internet. TV.

Pangea
Calle 3, y Avenida 11 (2221 1992/www.pangea. hostel.com). **Rates** US$12 per person dorm; US$24 double. **No credit cards.**
Pangea is a party hostel with a unique, modern design and fun atmosphere. While thin walls and mattresses come with the hostel scene, Pangea makes up for these minor details with a pool table, free internet, a patio and a swimming pool. The open-air rooftop restaurant and bar serves surprisingly delicious food and unsurprisingly strong drinks.
Bar. Internet (shared terminals, free). Parking. Pool. Restaurant. TV.

La Paseo del Rosa
Paseo Colón, entre Calles 28 y 30 (2257 3258/ www.rosadelpaseo.com). **Rates** US$75-$90 double. **Rooms** 18. **Credit** AmEx, MC, V.
Once the residence of the Montealegre coffee baron family, this delightful 1897 mansion has been converted into a boutique hotel offering a relaxing escape from the bustle of San José. Based around a flower-filled courtyard, it is impossible to know you are right in the centre of town on the principal Paseo Colón. The basic but well-appointed rooms integrate modern amenities (cable TV, orthopaedic mattresses) while reflecting the hotel's heritage. And taking breakfast on the patio, with excellent coffee, while hummingbirds flitter around you, is a delight. It was also the first small hotel to be awarded accolades for its environmentally sustainable management.
Bar. Internet (shared terminal, US$1.50/hr). Room service. TV.

Resources

Hospital
Hospital San Juan de Dios *Paseo Colón, y Calle 14 (2257 6282).* Free public hospital.

Internet
CyberCafé Las Arcadas *Round the corner from Gran Hotel Costa Rica on Avenida 2 (2233 3310).* US$1/hr. **Open** 7am-11pm daily.

Police
OIJ (Judicial Investigation Organisation)
Calle 15, entre Avenidas 4 y 6 (2295 3643).

Post office
Calle 2, entre Avenida 1 y 3 (2258 8762). **Open** 8am-5pm Mon-Fri.

Tourist information
Costa Rican Tourism Institute (ICT) *Under the Plaza de la Cultura (2222 8251).* **Open** 9am-5pm Mon-Fri.

Getting there & around

By air
From the centre you have access to San José's Juan Santamaria International Airport (20mins west of the centre), and the domestic Tobias Bolaños Airport in Rohrmoser. **Nature Air** (www.natureair.com) and **Sansa** (a domestic branch of TACA, www.flysansa. com) have domestic flights departing daily to most parts of the country, with prices starting at US$42.

By bus
Bus routes in Costa Rica are owned by dozens of private companies, which can be hard to figure out. Route start and end points are marked on the front of the bus, and each has a designated departure point in the centre of the city. Intercity buses cost around CRC250-350 (US$0.50-$0.75), whereas a 3-4hr trip to the beach could cost US$5 (see relevant destinations for prices and more details). Most national buses leave from the Coca-Cola bus station or the streets perpendicular to Avenida Central around Calle 12. Ask around, and be sure to verify the departure time the day before any trips outside of San José, as some buses only leave twice a day. Semi-private shuttles can be reserved through www.interbusonline.com. International bus companies, such as **Tica Bus** (www.ticabus.com) and **Transnica** (www.transnica. com), can take you as far as Mexico with several overnight stops.

By car
There are numerous car hire agencies along Paseo Colón, where you can either return your car, or pick one up on your way out of the city. Driving in the city is not desirable as one-way roads are poorly marked and street signs are as non-existent as car parks.

By taxi
City taxis are red with yellow triangles painted on the side, while airport taxis are orange and more expensive. The current price for the first kilometre is CRC405 (almost US$1), as marked on the *maria* or taxi meter. Taxi drivers often take advantage of tourists' unfamiliarity by charging random exorbitant fees for short trips. If the meter is not on, ask the driver: '¿puede poner la maria, por favor?' (can you please put the meter on?). It is best to get your hotel to call a known taxi service, which isn't going to rip anyone off. Reliable taxi services include: Alfaro (2221 9300) and CoopeTico (2224 7979). Expect to wait a while at peak traffic hours. For more on safety *see p315* **Taxis.**

East San José

Students of good nightlife will enjoy San José's university neighbourhoods.

Former president Daniel Oduber Quirós (1974-78) salutes the flag.

Although just a few miles east of downtown San José, San Pedro and its surrounding area is a world of its own. It is characterised by its prestigious **Universidad de Costa Rica**, its small-town atmosphere, its Western-style malls and its party atmosphere, especially the bar-filled **Calle de la Amargura** (*see p99*). Its unique personality and the welcoming smiles of its inhabitants are a winning combination, and its cosy size allows for easy exploration without getting lost in a maze of one-way streets and dead-end roads.

The road from Los Yoses to Curridabat measures no more than six kilometres (3.5 miles), but East San José manages to pack a lot of activity into a small area. Eclectic and quality restaurants are quietly tucked into residential neighbourhoods and the **Zapote Farmers' Market** (*see p96*) has a delicious selection of fruit. Kilometres of walking trails wind through the tranquil **Parque del Este** (*see p96*), which also offers the exhilaration of an urban canopy tour and beach football – albeit without a real beach.

All the points of interest are centred around two popular neighbourhoods: **San Pedro** and **Los Yoses**. Los Yoses is defined by upscale living, home to university professors and city professionals, while San Pedro is the country's only true university town, known for a hardy nightlife, inexpensive sodas and a musical preference more slanted towards reggaeton than cumbia.

The beat of reggaeton can be heard louder in this area than perhaps anywhere else in Costa Rica. University bars, complete with boisterous drinking games and all-night dancing can be found along the aforementioned **Calle de la Amargura**. But a more sophisticated evening can be had at one of San José's best venues, the **San Pedro Jazz Café** (*see p99*), where you will regularly find some of the country's best bands including the Grammy Award-winning Editus.

There is always the temptation to breeze through San José without a second thought, but East San José's slice of Costa Rican nightlife deserves at least an evening. There are no rainforests or smoking volcanoes here, but the area's perfect mountain temperatures, lively public football fields and chiming church bells within the country's largest university town will grant a greater understanding of Latin American life, love and culture.

Sightseeing

Los Yoses and Curridabat may lack the exotic attraction of Monteverde's ethereal cloud forest or the tropical beaches of the Pacific coast, but as a residential area, greater San Pedro is home to many annual festivals, typical Costa Rican living, and a lively atmosphere only found in a town that many call home. The following recommendations will allow you to experience the 'real' San José for a day or two. It's easy to overlook, but eating, partying and playing like a Tico should be an integral part of a holiday in Costa Rica.

Feria de Zapote
Campo Ferial de Zapote, Zapote Fair Grounds.
Open 6am-noon Sun. **Admission** free.
The Zapote Farmers' Market is one of the city's finest, with more than 100 stalls loaded with familiar favourites such as mango and cucumber, and more exotic offerings like juicy *guanabana* (soursop) and *granadilla* (passion fruit). This is one of the best places to test your bargaining skills, and the deals get better as the hours pass. Bear in mind, however, that as time goes by, the goods get picked over, so if you want the best of the best, arrive early and compare prices. If you are going to be in the area for several days, the Feria can be your best friend – a week's worth of fresh and colourful fruit and vegetable booty can easily cost less than US$10.

At the end of every year, the **Fiestas de Zapote** take place in the same location as the weekly Farmers' Market. They are among the area's best-loved annual festivals, offering about a week and a half of good Costa Rican fun. *Chinamos* – small stands offering typical fare from all over Central America – line the festival's streets. Rides fly through the air, and the *megabares* – huge, portable dance clubs sponsored by Costa Rican companies – keep the partygoers lubricated. And, as in many other major Costa Rican festivals, a giant bullring is built, where Ticos test their agility by taunting, but never killing, a raging bull.

Museo de Insectos
In the basement of the Universidad de Costa Rica Music School building (www.miucr.ucr.ac.cr).
Open 1-4.45pm Mon-Fri. **Admission** US$2.
Housing one of Central America's largest insect collections, this museum in the Universidad de Costa Rica is an insight into the bizarre world of six-legged creatures, impressive arachnids and flying insects. A great change of pace from the country's typical beauty, and the size of some specimens is shocking.

Parque del Este
300m west of the Christ statue in Sabanilla. **Open** 8am-4pm Tue-Sun. **Admission** US$1.50.
This is a green oasis tucked into a residential area near San Pedro. A short ride on any bus marked 'San Ramón' will take you to kilometres of well-groomed walking and biking trails that wind through the park's land where, even on a weekend, you're unlikely to encounter more than a few fellow hikers. For the sports enthusiast, the park offers beach football, basketball courts, outdoor swimming pools and football pitches. Take a break at one of the park's many picnic tables and barbecue pits, and when you get up the courage, fly through the air on an urban canopy (2215 2544/8842 8752) for US$20.

Planetario de San José
400m north of Muñoz y Nanne (2202 6403/www. planetario.ucr.ac.cr). **Open** presentations at 8.30am, 9.30am, 10.30am Mon-Sat. **Admission** US$3.
Not all Costa Rican adventures begin outside, and the Universidad de Costa Rica's Planetarium proves this point. There are five main shows on the Planetarium's roster – the Travelling Astronomer, the Celestial Zoo, the Sun and the Planets, the Solar System's Ghosts and the Firmament's Jewels – and all are available at regular intervals from Monday to Saturday. For the serious stargazer, the Planetarium organises urban telescoping meetings on the first Tuesday of each month between December and May. If you have even a passing interest in the sky above, plan a stop here and learn a bit about the stars above, and the night sky view from, Costa Rica.

Where to eat

East San José is heavily sprinkled with familiar fast-food chains, so if you get a craving for a cheeseburger in the land of rice-and-beans, your desires will not go unfulfilled for long. Not that the area is shy of local flavour: there are plenty of sodas where typical *casados* are served for about US$3 and a snack-worthy meat or cheese-filled empanada for US$1. However, there are also some recommended restaurants for when you want to dig a little deeper, and try other Latin American cuisine.

A La Leña
Next to San Pedro Más X Menos (2225 5583).
Open 11am-11pm Mon-Sat; 11am-10pm Sun.
Main courses US$8. **Credit** AmEx, DC, MC, V.
Tucked back into an unassuming storefront, it would be easy to miss this lovely little Italian restaurant if you didn't know what to look for. A La Leña's service is friendly, if not entirely quick, but the restaurant's natural drinks are good. Large portions of pasta, oven-fired pizzas dripping with fresh cheese and complimentary sauces are just some of the highlights. For the hungry, start with a caprese salad and ask for the delicious chef's pizza.

La Casita Azul

800m south of San Pedro's Banco Nacional (2283 2740). **Open** noon-10pm Mon-Fri; 6-10pm Sat. **Main courses** US$13. **Credit** AmEx, DC, MC, V.
La Casita Azul is one of the region's better *comida típica* restaurants, offering excellent Central American favourites and Costa Rican specialities. The best dishes include economical *casados* and *corvina a la Caribeña* (Caribbean sea bass), the latter a mildly spicy, coconut-milk covered creation straight from the Caribbean coast.

Chancay

200m south of Pops ice-cream parlour, Curridabat (2234 3257). **Open** noon-3.30pm, 6.30-10pm Mon-Thur; noon-10pm Fri-Sun. **Main courses** US$14. **Credit** AmEx, DC, MC, V.
Riding on the unstoppable rise in popularity of ceviche, Chancay offers a high-end option. The restaurant's small interior is quietly decorated with Peruvian masks and artefacts, and the staff are mainly native Peruvians with in-depth knowledge of their country's national cuisine. Specialising in seafood and fish, Chancay's most famous dish is the *trilogia de causas*, a mixture of octopus, prawn and tuna with traditional potatoes.

Comida Para Sentir

150m north of San Pedro Church (2224 1163). **Open** 10am-6pm Mon-Fri. **Main courses** US$5. **Credit** DC, MC, V.
This small vegetarian restaurant is an area favourite, choosing to centre on a small number of daily specials. Walking through the unassuming front gate feels like entering a normal Costa Rican home, complete with an adoptive mother ready to feed you this week's farmers' market specialities.

Jurgens

250m north of Los Yoses Subaru dealership (2280 9148). **Open** noon-2.30pm, 6-10pm Mon-Fri; 6-11pm Sat. **Main courses** US$18. **Credit** AmEx, DC, MC, V.
Specialising in French continental cuisine, Jurgens is one of East San José's best-loved fine dining restaurants. Recommended chef specialities are the *lomito berner* (tenderloin), *pato a la naranja* (duck à l'orange), and the restaurant's unique take on sea bass, which comes prepared in a variety of ways.

Malaysa Grill & Lounge

On the road to Sabanilla, 50m west of the University of Costa Rica's sports facilities (2253 9082). **Open** 11am-3pm, 6-11pm Mon-Sat. **Main courses** US$8. **Credit** AmEx, DC, MC, V.
Specialising in grilled meats, Malaysa Grill & Lounge also extends its offerings into pastas and seafood dishes. For the hardy omnivore, this restaurant offers more than five cuts of red meat, a lobster and fish grill, plus green salads and soups.

El Novillo Alegre

Plaza Freses Commercial Center, opposite Pops, Curridabat (2524 0353). **Open** noon-2.30pm, 6.30-10.30pm Mon-Thur; noon-3pm, 6.30-11pm Fri; noon-11pm Sat; noon-9pm Sun. **Main courses** US$27. **Credit** AmEx, DC, MC, V.
A good choice for upscale dining in East San José, El Novillo Alegre offers international cuisine with an emphasis on native Argentinian dishes. A patron favourite is the excellent *parrillada argentina*, or

It may not look exotic but the fruit certainly is at the **Feria de Zapote**.

San José & Around

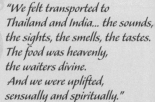
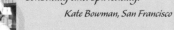

Argentinian grill. Take your choice from succulent beef tenderloin, tender rump roast, and many other beef, chicken and offal specialities.

Olio
200m north of the Barrio Escalante Bagelmens (2281 0541). **Open** 11.30am-12.30am daily. **Main courses** US$8. **Credit** AmEx, DC, MC, V.
This upscale Mediterranean restaurant offers some of the area's best tapas, as well as a varied menu that includes Greek treats such as hommous and fresh pita bread, Italian delicacies like fresh pasta marinara, and the recommended *hongos Madrileños*.

Ozaki
25m south of San Pedro Mas X Menos (2224 7985). **Open** noon-10pm Mon-Wed; noon-11pm Thur-Sat; noon-8pm Sun. **Main courses** US$16. **Credit** AmEx, DC, MC, V.
Ozaki offers a fusion of Peruvian and Japanese flavours. The chef understandably recommends his *ceviche tres banderas* (three flags ceviche), a trio of Costa Rican, Peruvian and Japanese ceviches. The combination sushi platters are also good.

Where to drink

As the only true university town in the country, San Pedro and its environs are full of bars and small discos. Synonymous with student party life, the **Calle de la Amargura** (www.calleamargura.com) can either mean 'Street of Bitterness' or more often 'Street of Extreme Drunkenness'. Just south of the University of Costa Rica's main entrance, it is one of the best places to party. The most popular places for drinking and dancing are the well-known bars **Terra U** and **Tavarua**. **Caccio's** and **Congos** are two of the favourite spots for putting away pitchers of beer. These venues are usually safe, but remember to keep an eye on your belongings in the bars and in the surrounding areas. Also, regardless of where you're headed, ID is frequently requested, so bring a photocopy of your passport. If you can't prove you're over 18 you won't get past the bouncers, no matter how old you look.

El Cuartel de la Boca del Monte
Diagonally opposite Barrio La California's Cine Magaly (2221 0327). **Open** 11.30am-2.30pm, 6pm-1am daily. **Credit** AmEx, DC, MC, V.
With a huge menu of 150-plus cocktails, live music on Mondays, and a central location in Barrio La California, it's no wonder El Cuartel is popular among both locals and tourists. The bar is one of the most diverse and renowned in the country.

Latino Rock Café
On the southern corner of Barrio La California's La Primavera petrol station (2222 4719/www.latinorock cafe.com). **Open** noon-3pm, 7pm-2.30am Mon-Sun. **Credit** AmEx, DC, MC, V.

Another beloved live music location, the Latino Rock Café is a full-service stop, promising a good menu, strong drinks and some of the area's best live rock music. Like the Jazz Café, if popular bands are playing, book in advance.

San Pedro Jazz Café
On the San Pedro main road, next to Banco Popular (2253 8933/www.jazzcafecostarica.com). **Open** 6pm-2am daily. **Credit** AmEx, DC, MC, V.
Offering live music every day, strong spirits and chef specialities like the shrimp-stuffed sea bass and cheese fondue, it's not hard to see why San Pedro's Jazz Café is one of the area's most frequented after-hours hotspots. Check its website for a schedule of upcoming events and if Costa Rica's well-known Malpaís or Editus are on the bill, reserve several weeks in advance. Food is a bit expensive, so stop at one of our recommended restaurants before heading to Jazz Café. *See p108* **Sounds of the city**.

Where to stay

East San José is home to hotels ranging from dorm-style hostels to upscale boutique establishments. Don't expect five-star luxury, but the amenities on offer are good enough for all but the fussiest of travellers.

Casa Cambranes
150m south of Los Yoses Spoon Coffee Shop (2253 8858/www.casacambranes.com). **Rates** US$70-$80 double. **Rooms** 12. **Credit** AmEx, DC, MC, V.
This four-star hotel is popular among business travellers. Each of its comfortable 12 rooms sports a different colour scheme, and five have a jacuzzi. Danish design touches give the place a light and minimal feel, but it's also warm and cosy.
Business centre. Internet (wireless, shared terminal, free). Spa. TV.

Hostel Bekuo
100m south and 25m east of Los Yoses Subaru dealership (2234 1091/www.hostelbekuo.com). **Rates** US$12 dorm; US$30 double. **Rooms** 5 double; 1 female, 1 male, 2 mixed dorms. **Credit** AmEx, DC, MC, V.
Widely considered to be one of the best and most attractive hostels in Costa Rica, Hostel Bekuo is owned by two Costa Ricans, one of whom studied interior design. The hostel's name comes from the indigenous Bribri word for 'constellation' and the lodgings, with paper lanterns hanging from ceilings, are as bright as the night's starry sky. The hostel's walls are lined with photographs of the country's flora and fauna, and cosy seating areas add to the communal feeling.
Internet (shared terminal, wireless, free).

Hotel 1492
300m east of Cine Magalys (2225 3752/www. hotel1492.com). **Rates** US$42-$90 double. **Rooms** 10. **Credit** AmEx, DC, MC, V.

Snuggled into the upscale Barrio Escalante, this cosy hotel is small enough to offer a tranquil ambience, but is big on hospitality and convenience. The hotel has quaint interior arches, high ceilings, original Portuguese-tile floors and colonial-style architecture. The original owner of Hotel 1492 – then called Hotel Jade y Oro – was an artist who had grown up in the house; her legacy endures in the form of art and bright decoration.

Hotel Boutique Jade

250m north of Los Yoses Subaru dealership (2224 2455/www.hotelboutiquejade.com). **Rates** US$117-$152. **Rooms** 30. **Credit** AmEx, DC, MC, V.
Offering newly remodelled rooms with all the bells and whistles, Hotel Boutique Jade is in an ideal location in the upscale Los Yoses. In addition to the hotel's amenities, it shares real estate and an owner with Jurgens (*see p98*), one of the area's most prestigious restaurants. If you feel like treating yourself to a bit of luxury and sensory satisfaction, this is the place to do it.
Internet (wireless, free). Pool (outdoor). Restaurant. Room service.

Hotel Don Fadrique

700m west of San Pedro Burger King (2225 8186/ www.hoteldonfadrique.com). **Rates** US$60-$80 double. **Rooms** 16. **Credit** AmEx, DC, MC, V.
If you're aiming for style and class on a budget, the Hotel Don Fadrique is the place to be. Surrounded by tropical gardens, and known for one of the best art galleries in San José, the hotel is ideally located and flawlessly appointed, offering a quiet atmosphere and familial ambience. A relaxed colour palette complements the understated rooms, and the friendly staff only serves to improve your impressions of this small hotel.
Internet (shared terminal, free). Parking (free).

Hotel Le Bergerac

200m east of Barrio La California Kentucky Fried Chicken (2234 7850/www.bergerachotel.com). **Rates** US$83-$157. **Rooms** 26. **Credit** AmEx, DC, MC, V.
One of the area's dwindling number of colonial-style homes, the Hotel Le Bergerac is decorated in a French style, bringing some elegance and good breeding to Barrio Escalante's hotel scene. Though upscale, the hotel prides itself on being a tranquil getaway; you'll find yourself feeling relaxed and comfortable the moment you walk into your room or see the surrounding tropical botanical gardens. The hotel is home to the area's leading French restaurant, L'Ile de France.
Room service. Internet. TV.

Hotel Las Orquídeas

75m east of Los Yoses AutoMercado (2283 0095/www.lasorquideashotel.com). **Rates** US$12 dorm; US$55 double. **Rooms** 18. **Credit** AmEx, DC, MC, V.
The hotel building dates back to the beginning of the 20th century and was home, for 80 years, to one of the region's wealthiest coffee families. Today

serving as a boutique hotel, the rooms are individually decorated, promising the comfortable atmosphere that every home should have. Prices are good, especially considering the hotel's location in the sought-after Los Yoses neighbourhood. The rooms are decorated and decked out in a simple manner but are comfortable enough.
Bar. Internet (shared terminal, free). Parking (free). Restaurant. TV.

Hotel Milvia

100m east of Muñoz y Nanne (2225 4543/www. novanet.co.cr/milvia). **Rates** US$59-$75 double. **Rooms** 9. **Credit** AmEx, DC, MC, V.
Built in 1930, this San Pedro hotel was once one of the area's most prestigious homes. Today, fully restored, its heritage is evident in the exquisite wooden floors, artisan staircase and old-world charm present throughout. Walk out to the balcony for great views of Volcán Irazú, or contemplate life in the hotel's own Zen garden. Although all the rooms are spacious and comfortable, if you want to feel like a celebrity, ask for the room Julia Roberts and Susan Sarandon stayed in (not at the same time, incidentally). Lunch and dinner are also available and drinks are served all day.
Bar. Internet (wireless, free). Restaurant. TV.

Resources

Hospital

Hospital Calderón Guardia *200m north of Parque Nacional (2257 7922).* Free public hospital and clinic.

Internet

San Pedro's Calle de la Amargura (*see p99*) has several small internet cafés.

Post office

First floor of American Outlet Mall. **Open** 9am-4pm Mon-Fri; 9am-12pm Sat.

Getting there

By bus

East San José is very well served by the country's inexpensive and reliable bus system. You can catch the Sabanilla, San Pedro and Curridabat bus lines from the eastern end of Avenida Central's pedestrian area – front windscreens are marked with the most important stops, but if you're ever in doubt, just ask the bus driver and he will nod to tell you whether he's heading to your intended stop.

By taxi

Area taxis are common and relatively cheap, so if you're looking to get from A to B in a hurry, just stick your hand out to hail a taxi. As in the rest of San José, only use official taxis, which are marked with a yellow triangle painted on to the taxi's red exterior. Reliable taxi services include Alfaro (2221 9300) and CoopeTico (2224 7979). For more on safety, *see p311* **Taxis**.

West San José

For quality cuisine, luxury lodgings and green spaces, west is best.

It's hard to believe that **Parque La Sabana** was once the city's airport.

Compared to the urban sprawl of central San José, the neighbourhoods that spill out to the west enjoy much more green space and a residential-focused design, making them a favourite among the country's elite. This area, starting at the recreational centre of **Parque La Sabana** and fanning out into the neighbourhoods of **Rohrmoser**, **Pavas**, **Escazú** and **Santa Ana**, has the country's best mix of trendy accommodation options, diplomatic residential area and a good supply of restaurants, bars and nightlife.

La Sabana, Rohrmoser & Pavas

La Sabana, set just west of the San José city centre, is generally separated into the four cardinal points depending on which side of the large **Parque La Sabana** you are referring to. The park, once the country's major airport, is the largest green space in the city, bringing some fresh air into San José and making real estate prices in the surrounding areas higher than elsewhere. North and south of the park are important office buildings and a residential mix of small homes and apartment complexes dotted with several hotels and restaurants, all with great access to the major motorways.

Further west is the suburban neighbourhood of **Rohrmoser**. Also the home of current president Óscar Arias Sánchez, this area is known for its concentration of old money. Foreign embassies have also helped attract some classy restaurants, excellent grocery and clothing stores, as well as the usual mix of fast-food dining options. The main artery through the region is the tree-lined **Rohrmoser Boulevard**, which shoots downhill with the added charm of a small park every four blocks. With its neighbour to the south, **Pavas**, the prosperity here diminishes the further west you go and gives way to sprawling middle-class neighbourhoods with dodgy reputations. Pavas does, however, have a good mix of ethnic eateries, including a growing Chinatown just west of the US Embassy.

Sightseeing

Museo de arte Costarricense
Parque La Sabana (2222 7155/www.musarco.go.cr).
Open 9am-5pm Tue-Fri; 10am-4pm Sat, Sun.
Admission US$5; students US$3; free Sun.
Set in the terminal of the original San José airport, the Museo de arte Costarricense crowns the Parque La Sabana at the east end, inviting those out for a stroll in the park to learn a little more about Costa Rican art. The building is whitewashed and Spanish

in style with cast iron railings and a handmade tile roof. The museum houses several permanent exhibits including an outdoor sculpture garden and the upstairs Salon Dorado, which is covered in murals depicting the history of Costa Rica created by artist Louis Feron. Displays include photography, paintings and several interactive pieces. Themes covered in the exhibition include interpretations of the Costa Rican countryside and the Tico identity. Alongside is the Museo de la Miniatura, a project in which dozens of Costa Rican artists contributed artworks in mixed media no bigger than 17cm (7 in). *Photo p104.*

Parque La Sabana

Parque La Sabana is the largest park in the city and enjoys a central location on the site of the original international airport. The park is home to a large, man-made lake, the national stadium, the national gymnasium and the Museo de arte Costarricense (*see p101*). Art festivals, parades, football games, concerts and the like have all been held in this lively destination, which, given its importance to the city's residents, could be compared to New York's Central Park. Daily football games are held on the park's plentiful fields; joggers enjoy the maze of paths; and makeshift fishermen can be seen trying their luck in the lake while shooing away the giant ducks that claim it as a seasonal home. The park is currently undergoing a major facelift with the renovation of the stadium (a gift from the Chinese government) and the removal of the park's abundant eucalyptus trees, which will be replaced by native species.

Where to eat & drink

Los Antojitos

Road to Pavas, next to Banco Cuscatlan, Pavas (2231 5564). **Open** 11.30am-10pm daily. **Main courses** US$8. **Credit** AmEx, MC, V.
This corner restaurant has an extensive menu of Mexican food and specialises in barbecued tacos. Not quite authentic with the menu, it still manages to please the average visitor with a good variety that include a nice selection of diet-conscious food.

Benihana

Opposite Parque La Sabana (2296 0041/ www.benihana.com). **Open** noon-3pm, 6-11pm Mon-Fri; 1-5pm, 6-11pm Sat; 2-11pm Sun. **Main courses** US$14. **Credit** AmEx, MC, V.
Since 1964, this sushi restaurant has stood out from the pack thanks to its beautiful and tranquil setting. Its unique three-storey wood building enjoys a great vantage point over Parque La Sabana. The upscale venue comes with classy interior and authentic sushi and Japanese cuisine. The owners pride themselves on a presentation style they call 'eatertainment' based around hibachi grills. Once you've had your fill of teppanyaki go for the full Tokyo experience and hire one of the available karaoke rooms.

Café Mediterraneo

Road to Pavas in front of Banco Banex, Pavas (2290 5850). **Open** noon-10pm Mon-Sat; noon-4pm Sun. **Main courses** US$10. **Credit** AmEx, MC, V.
This classy boutique restaurant offers pastas and thin crust pizzas with rich ingredients, fresh bread and a good wine selection. Recent renovations offer upstairs balcony seating.

El Chicote

Opposite Parque La Sabana (2232 0936/ www.elchicote.com). **Open** 11am-3pm, 6-11pm Mon-Fri; 11am-11pm Sat, Sun. **Main courses** US$16. **Credit** AmEx, MC, V.
This Sabana Norte stalwart faces Parque La Sabana and specialises in ribeye steak and Argentinian *chorizos* (sausages). It's nice on a lazy Sunday afternoon with live piano music from 1pm to 4pm. The atmosphere is formal yet friendly.

Fogoncito

Rohrmoser Boulevard, in front of Plaza Mayor, Rohrmoser (2290 0910/www.elfogoncito.com). **Open** 11am-1pm Tue-Sat; 11am-11pm Mon, Sun. **Main courses** US$8. **Credit** AmEx, MC, V.
This Mexican steakhouse offers a large selection of burritos and meaty dishes, served in portions just big enough to fill you up. Like your favourite Mexican place back home, nachos are served before your meal with three fresh dipping sauces to whet the palate. Wash them down with a margarita.

Kabana Classic

In front of Plaza Rohrmoser, Rohrmoser (2291 6310). **Open** 3pm-2am daily. **Credit** AmEx, MC, V.
This popular after-work destination with big open windows turns it up after hours with popular music videos from the 1980s, 1990s and today playing on numerous large flat-screen TVs. It can get very crowded after 10pm, so try to get there earlier if you want a table. An upstairs VIP area charges a US$25 entrance fee.

Little Seoul

50m north of Plaza Mayor, Rohrmoser (2232 5551). **Open** noon-3pm, 5.30-10pm Tue-Sat; noon-9pm Sun. **Credit** AmEx, MC, V.
A Korean-owned restaurant that stands alone just off the Rohrmoser Boulevard, Little Seoul offers an Asiatic mix of food including teppenyaki, sushi and the Korean classic and customer favourite Bi bim bop, a fresh rice and vegetable dip with a spicy red sauce. All flavours are authentic, and the service is polite and professional from the presentation of the steamed towels to the delivery of the bill.

Mac's American Bar & Rest

Sabana Sur (2231 3145). **Open** 9am-2am daily. **Main courses** US$7. **Credit** AmEx, MC, V.
Mac's is an American-style sports bar with a Tico twist on typical fried bar food like wings, nachos and burgers. When a competition isn't on one of the many television screens, guests can try their hand at table football or pool.

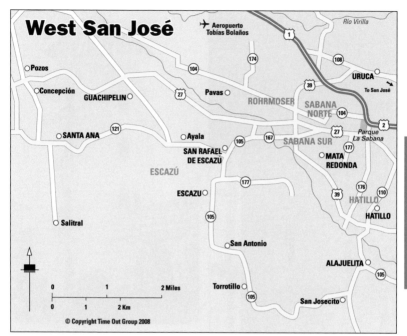

West San José

Pan e Vino

Plaza Rohrmoser, Rohrmoser (2231 3917).
Open noon-midnight Mon-Sat; noon-10pm Sun.
Main courses US$8. **Credit** AmEx, DC, MC, V.
Set next to the food court in Plaza Rohrmoser, Pan e Vino is a quaint Italian restaurant serving pastas and over 40 varieties of thin crust pizza with the freshest of ingredients, best washed down with a glass of the house *vino tinto*.

Pollo Cervecero

Pavas (2232 2727). **Open** 11.30am-2am daily.
Main courses US$7. **No credit cards**.
A truly classic Costa Rican after-work bar, Pollo Cervecero's open-air wooden patio and seating is a hit with locals, who roll in here every day of the week after 5pm. At the weekends the music is turned up a bit, but it still remains a destination for eating and drinking only. Typical fried bar food Tico-style rules the menu, including *patacones* (fried plantains), fried cheese cubes and Mexican meat dishes.

Rincón de mi Tata

100m south, 400m east of Jack (2296 1590).
Open 4pm-2am daily. **Credit** AmEx, MC, V.
This is a semi-open-air bar and dance club with a fun Latin atmosphere. DJs mix up a combination of reggaeton, salsa and merengue, among other Latin sounds, as the clientele and the occasional professional dancers heat up the dancefloor. While the music is loud and sure to get you in the dancing spirit, there is plenty of seating, so you can just sit and watch if you prefer.

El Van Gogh

In front of Plaza Rohrmoser, Rohrmoser (2291 4308). **Open** 4pm-2am daily. **Credit** AmEx, MC, V.
This student-oriented bar gets rowdy at the weekends and on Tuesdays when live music or an open bar are offered. The menu includes an array of tapas and sandwiches, and hookahs are available on request. The staff are young, and the interior design reflects the name with murals of Van Gogh's popular paintings covering the walls and exterior.

Where to stay

Casa Roland

Rohrmoser Boulevard, Rohrmoser (2231 6571/ www.casa-roland.com). **Rates** US$95-$200 double.
Rooms 27. **Credit** AmEx, MC, V.
There is nothing commercial or common about this hotel. Casa Roland is a unique, artistic boutique hotel, between the elite neighbourhood of Rohrmoser and more down to earth *barrios*. The plentiful artwork and colourful design of this 27-room converted townhouse adds a charming and sophisticated touch to the friendly service. Its Paragon 'American Bistro' restaurant is in a modern well-appointed room and serves up good international cuisine.
Bar. Internet (shared terminal, free). TV.

Sculpting the Costa Rican identity at the **Museo de arte Costarricense**. *See p101.*

Colours Oasis Resort

200m from end of main boulevard (2296 1880/ www.colours.net). **Rates** US$59 double; US$169 apartment. **Rooms** 14. **Credit** AmEx, MC,V.

This hotel is not so much colourful as cosy and classy. The restaurant and bar offer poolside seating along with a well-appointed dining area that has a tropical vibe, with paddle fans and wicker chairs. The hotel and bar are predominantly (but not solely) gay-oriented, and rooms offer a comfortable respite from the busy city centre just ten minutes away. Rooms open on to the pool courtyard or tasteful interior gardens.

Bar. Gym. Internet (high-speed, wireless). Restaurant. TV.

Crowne Plaza Hotel Corobici

Sabana Norte, 100m north of Parque La Sabana's north-east corner (2232 8122/www.ichotelsgroup. com). **Rates** US$155-$400 double. **Rooms** 213. **Credit** AmEx, MC, V.

Recently acquired by the Crowne Plaza chain, the interior of this grand 213-room hotel was completely renovated in 2008. Facilities include a casino, conference rooms, Japanese Fuji restaurant and a pool with poolside restaurant. The new owners have brought a fresh new look – from the bedding to the interior decoration – to a great location. The additional extras such as a well-equipped fitness centre, a 24-hour lounge and a sauna make this an excellent option for business visitors and families. The towering exterior, however, still looks like something from out of this world.

Business centre. Concierge. Gym. Internet. Pool (outdoor). Restaurants (2). Room service. Spa. TV.

Hotel Barcelo Palma Real

Sabana Norte, 200m north of ICE building (2290 5060/www.barcelo.com). **Rates** US$125-$171 double. **Rooms** 67. **Credit** AmEx, MC, V.

This business-oriented hotel can be found in a great residential area just north of Parque La Sabana. The 67 rooms include four suites all with either two queen-sized beds or one king-sized bed. The rooms are average in size and motif, and while comfortable, they are beginning to show their age. All amenities that one would expect are available, including conference rooms, a business centre with computers, internet, fax and photocopier. There is a reasonable on-site restaurant called Zabor.

Bar. Business centre. Gym. Internet (shared terminal, wireless). Restaurant. TV.

Isla Verde

Road to Pavas, 200m west of American Embassy (2296 5068/www.hotelislaverde.com). **Rates** US$53 double. **Rooms** 20. **Credit** AmEx, DC, MC, V.

This hotel is better known for the gourmet Chinese restaurant of the same name, specialising in fresh fish with Chinese and Cantonese twists and tastes. Although not in the finest looking buildings, Isla Verde hotel offers good lodging in a commercial area of Pavas that is quickly becoming known as the

city's Chinatown. The 20 rooms are simple, clean and comfortable.

Restaurant. Internet (shared terminal, wireless, free). Parking (free). Room service. TV.

Mi Casa Hostel

100m north and 25m east of the Torre La Sabana (2290 4563/www.micasahostel.com). **Rates** US$12 dorm; US$26 double. **Rooms** 4. **No credit cards.**

This hostel makes you feel right at home in a converted, traditional Costa Rican house set in the safe, residential neighbourhood of Sabana Norte. The friendly owners will give you all the tips you need for a great stay in the city. Choose from one of four private rooms, a mixed dorm or a women-only dorm. Open since 1994, the Tico owners have made the stay as lively as possible with table football and DVDs to rent.

Internet (wireless access). Parking (free).

Tennis Club

Sabana Sur (2232 1266/www.crtennis.com). **Rates** US$45-$85 double. **Rooms** 27. **Credit** AmEx, DC, MC, V.

The strength of the Tennis Club is its facilities. This is a great place to stay if you are athletic and like to compete even when away from home. A stay here includes access to all the club's facilities including three pools, 12 tennis courts, a basketball court, a football field, a sauna, and so on. The 27 rooms are simple, and a bit dated. Suites come with private balcony, allowing you to keep an eye on the training below.

Restaurant. Pools (outdoor, indoor).

Getting there

By air

Pavas is home to the **Tobias Bolanos Airport** (2km west of US Embassy, 2232 2820), the main hub for the domestic airline **Nature Air** (2299 6000, www.natureair.com) and several charter companies. Flight options to remote destinations in the country are plentiful and range from US$40 to US$100.

By bus

The La Sabana area can be reached from downtown San José by the Sabana Cementerio or Sabana-Estadio buses, which depart from the Metropolitan Cathedral and stop along Paseo Colón. For Pavas, take Ruta 2 or Lomas bus from Avenida 1 and Calle 20. For Rohrmoser, take the Boulevard/aeropuerto bus that leaves one block west of the cathedral and makes stops adjacent to Parque La Sabana and along Rohrmoser Boulevard to the Tobias Bolanos Airport. Both Santa Ana buses leave from the Coca-Cola bus station in downtown San José (Avenida Central y Calle 12). Their return route leaves from in front of Centro Colón at the west end of Paseo Colón.

By road

If driving, these neighbourhoods are hard to miss as they are directly west of downtown, but beware of the changing one-way streets. Paseo Colón ends on the east side of Parque La Sabana.

Resources

Hospital

Hospital CIMA *500m west of Prospero Fernández toll booth (2208 1000,www.hospitalsanjose.net).* This world-class hospital has a great reputation among foreign expats and has even become a destination for medical tourism thanks to its reasonable prices.

Internet

Speed Net *150m west of Plaza Mayor on the Rohrmoser Boulevard (2296 1915).* **Open** 9am-9pm daily. A reliable internet café that is always open and charges just over US$1/hr.

Escazú & Santa Ana

The wealth in Rohrmoser and Pavas is understated in comparison to that of the neighbouring *cantóns* of Escazú and Santa Ana, the most affluent districts in Costa Rica. They are the most westernised of the country, housing a large foreign population, US chain restaurants and multinational companies, and home to the expansive **Multiplaza Shopping Centre**, the biggest and most exclusive mall in San José. Despite the strong foreign influence, both these towns still preserve a local ambience, especially near their respective centres. You'll see traditional adobe houses, rustic *sodas* and an occasional cow roaming the small, narrow streets. And despite being home to the some of the country's richest people both Escazú and Santa Ana are in fact an interesting blend of social classes; from the wealthy – both foreign and Costa Rican – to the working class.

Like the traditional Costa Rican town, the centres of Escazú and Santa Ana are defined by a church with an adjacent plaza. In Escazú, the districts of San Rafael and San Antonio harbour luxurious residences and social venues, while in Santa Ana the area of Altos de Lindora exhibits the most cash. Escazú and Santa Ana also have a variety of gated residential communities and private schools, the excellent CIMA hospital, the elitist Costa Rica Country Club and some of San José's finest restaurants.

Sightseeing

Cerámica Las Palomas

Alto las Palomas (2282 7001).
Open 7am-5pm Mon-Sat.
Santa Ana is famous throughout the country for its ceramics. The Cerámica Las Palomas, along with around 30 other independent family workshops in the area, exhibits traditional clay-coloured bowls as well as large greenware bowls, vases, coffee mugs and urns. Visitors also have the chance to watch the craftsmen and women make pots and bowls.

Farmers' markets

Santa Ana, north side of football pitch.
Open 6am-10am Sun.
A closer proximity to some of the most fertile areas of Costa Rica and a comfortable residential setting bring added charm to the farmers' markets in the west of San José. The market in Pavas becomes a five-block-long mosaic of people and colourful tarpaulins covering goods from soy blocks to organic herbs to El Salvadoran *pupusas* (tortillas) and bright tropical flowers. Bring a book bag or some other sturdy hold-all if you are shopping for a few days' supplies – you'll need it.

Where to eat

Café de los Artistas

100m south of Plaza Rolex, San Rafael, Escazú (7288 5082). **Open** 8am-6pm Mon-Sat; 8am-4pm Sun. **Main courses** US$8. **No credit cards**.
This petite venue is where it's at for browsing over local art while cradling a hot mug of coffee. It is a North American-style coffee shop, complete with delectable home-made pastries and excellent weekend brunches. Live jazz is often featured on Sunday mornings and there is a small craft store and workshop that exhibits local artwork.

Cerutti

200m south of El Cruce shopping centre in San Rafael, Escazú (2228 4511). **Open** noon-2.30pm, 6-11pm Wed-Mon. **Main courses** US$25. **Credit** AmEx, MC, V.
Cerutti is probably the most formal of all the Italian restaurants in the metropolitan area, as well as one of the most romantic. One would never guess this, though, from a glance at its simple façade. Cerutti's relatively small size contributes to its intimate and cosy ambience. The service is superb, and the food includes a variety of delectable pastas – the meat and fish dishes are also reliable.

Il Panino

La Paco shopping centre, San Rafael, Escazú (2228 3126). **Open** 8am-midnight Sun-Thur; 8am-2am Fri,Sat. **Main courses** US$15. **Credit** AmEx, MC, V.
Il Panino is a fashionable place to enjoy a cup of coffee in the afternoons, perhaps on the open-air terrace. In the evenings, candlelit tables and lounge-style music create the ambiance for cocktails. Il Panino is basically a posh sandwich shop as well as café, serving European-style snacks, fresh salads, drinks and a variety of desserts.

La Luz

Hotel Alta, Alto las Palomas (2282 4160/www. thealtahotel.com). **Open** 6.30am-3pm, 6-10pm Mon-Sat; 9am-4pm Sun. **Main courses** US$18. **Credit** AmEx, MC, V.
Located in Hotel Alta, the splendid La Luz restaurant has been proclaimed by many to be the best restaurant in the country. The decor is exquisite, and

Sounds of the city

You may have thought San José moved to the rhythm of cumbia beats, but a strong local jazz scene is gathering momentum. Popular with young professionals and students, Costa Rican jazz musicians have quickly made a name for themselves in the sweaty nightclubs and chill-out lounges usually frequented by the late-night crowd.

A couple of jazz clubs have opened up in San José, most notably the two **Jazz Cafés**, one in San Pedro (*see p99*) in the city's eastern suburbs and the recently opened bar in Escazú (*see p109*). These hip hangouts, popular and sophisticated venues for live music in Costa Rica, have attracted big names such as Cuba's legendary duo Chucho Valdez and Irakere, the highly acclaimed jazz-fusion drummer Dave Weckl, Australia's jazz-fusion guitarist Frank Gambale and Ralph Irizarry & Timbalaye, a New York-based Latin Jazz project, and popular in Central America.

Afro-Caribbean beats are also staple sounds, and two of the country's most loved bands, Malpaís and the Grammy-winning Editus, play at one of the above-mentioned venues at least once a month.

Jaime Gamboa, the Malpaís bassist, said, 'The east of San José is the most active zone in relation to national music: there are at least five places where you can find live music every night. Among them is the San Pedro Jazz Café, which has a great musical line-up, a good sound system, and a very unique vibe. But there are also places like El Observatorio and Latino Rock Café, which offer great conditions for playing live music.'

The two Jazz Cafés in particular are constantly aiming to keep things fresh, and host a wide assortment of live acts; shows at the two Jazz Cafés include Tuesday Mundoloco (or Crazyworld), one-off specials with alternative, or often purely ethnic music, flamenco, belly dancing, jazz, rock and reggae plus modern takes on the ever-present cumbia and reggaeton beats.

The club's appeal draws in all types, from businessmen and intellectuals to struggling writers and aspiring musicians. Twenty to thirtysomethings find themselves walking through its doors after a day at the office and don't head home until the wee hours of the morning, entranced by what is on offer. Acts are not booked on their availability but rather purely on their quality, breeding a high standard of music in a city that seems only now to be tapping into its creative potential.

Whichever band you manage to catch, you will have caught them in a moment of almost musical epiphany, for Costa Rican musicians are finally beginning to be recognised internationally, and San José seen as a worthwhile music-lover's destination.

---

the large glass windows frame a spectacular view of the valley below. For starters, hand-formed feta cheese tart is recommended. For mains, favourites include shrimp with orange and champagne, Moroccan chicken and grilled beef tenderloin. A popular dessert is the shortbread stuffed with pineapple and macadamia nuts in blackberry sauce.

Machu Picchu

Plaza Paloma shopping centre, Santa Ana (2282 7917). **Open** 11am-10.30pm Mon-Wed; 11am-11pm Sat; noon-6pm Sun. **Main courses** US$12. **Credit** AmEx, MC, V.

Like its sister restaurant near Paseo Colón downtown (*see p89*), Machu Picchu offers a wonderful array of Peruvian foods. The *chicha morada* drink, made with purple corn and spices, is delicious. What sets this Machu Picchu apart from the other is the splendid view it offers from the restaurant's extended balcony.

Más Tequila

Plaza Itskatzu, in front of Multiplaza, Escazú (2228 1815). **Open** 4.30pm-2am Mon-Thur; noon-2am Fri-Sun. **Main courses** US$6. **Credit** AmEx, MC, V.

Más Tequila is a small but fun venue, and it is partly open-air. The restaurant specialises in Mexican food with reasonably priced snacks and meals. This bar and restaurant appeals to a trendy but slightly older crowd, mostly in their late twenties and above. There is live music at weekends.

Le Monastère

On the Santa Ana road from Escazú, (2289 4404/ www.monastere-restaurant.com). **Open** 6.30-10pm Mon-Sat. **Main courses** US$30. **Credit** AmEx, MC, V.

Le Monastère is a magnificent chapel-turned-restaurant with a twinkling view of the San José metropolitan area. From the marble statues that grace the gardens to the thick walls and exquisite antiques, Le Monastère is steeped in elegance. It comprises three different areas: a romantic bar near the entrance, the restaurant (complete with waiters in 19th-century French monk frocks) and a small cosy cellar with live music from Thursday to Saturday. The French chef prepares exquisite meals such as smoked salmon petals and caviar and homemade duck pâté with cognac.

Taj Mahal

Old road to Santa Ana, 1km west of La Paco shopping centre, Escazú (2228 0980). **Open** noon-3pm, 6-11pm Tue-Sat; noon-8pm Sun. **Main courses** US$20. **Credit** AmEx, MC, V.

The Taj Mahal is the only Indian restaurant in Costa Rica and, fortunately, it's a good one. The colourful and elegant converted house is charming as well as spacious. The gardens at the back are home to a lovely pair of peacocks as well as a tandoori oven.

Tiquicia

Escazú (2289 5839). **Open** 5pm-midnight Tue-Fri; 1pm-midnight Sat; noon-6pm Sun. **Main courses** US$8. **Credit** AmEx, MC, V.

Tiquicia (restaurant, bar and mirador) is situated in the mountains of San Antonio, Escazú, and serves Costa Rican fare. What is most spectacular about Tiquicia, however, is the 360-degree view of the entire Central Valley, which has made this restaurant one of the most renowned in the area.

Nightlife

Escazú Jazz Café

On the Próspero Fernández highway, in front of the CIMA Hospital (2288 4740/www.jazzcafecostarica. com). **Open** 6.30pm-2am daily. **Credit** AmEx, MC,V.

One of two branches of San José's best music venues. Opening in 1999 this was the first location and quickly built its success on carefully chosen acts and quality sound systems. *See left* **Sounds of the city** for more information.

Frankie Go

Trejos Montealegre shopping centre, Escazú (2289 5937). **Open** 5pm-2am Tue-Sun. **Credit** AmEx, MC, V.

The clientele dress to impress at this lounge-style pub. The music is Latin pop, some hip hop, as well as a decent dollop of increasingly popular (and elite-preferred) electronic music. Frankie Go is popular among high school and college students, although people in their late twenties are fans too.

Grappa Live

In front of San José bank, Lindora, Santa Ana (2203 7543/www.grappalive.com). **Open** 5pm-1am Mon-Sat. **Credit** AmEx, MC, V.

Grappa Live is a small but trendy venue, especially popular from Tuesday to Thursday for its live music. There's a stage at the back for the performers, although it is a nice place even without music. It is decked out with small tables and a sofa lounge.

Henry's

Plaza San Rafael shopping centre, Escazú (2289 6250). **Open** 3pm-2am Tue-Sun. **Credit** AmEx, MC, V.

Henry's is a fun and colourful bar that appears to have been transplanted from Jacó right into the city. There are dozens of exciting cocktail options, with prices ranging from US$4 to US$8 for drinks.

Living

Via Lindora shopping centre, Santa Ana (2282 0287). **Open** 9.30pm-3.30am Wed, Fri, Sat. **Credit** AmEx, MC, V.

Living is a pre-Utopia (*see below*) venue, and emits a lounge bar feel in contrast to Utopia's club vibe. It is discreet and sofa-filled, playing more electronic music than Latin party hits. Beer costs around US$2, while the average cocktail will set you back US$5.

Privé

Venue 22, Boulevard shopping centre, 300m south of Multiplaza, Escazú (2201 8520/www.privecr.com). **Open** 9pm-3am Thur-Sat. **No credit cards**.

Privé is one of the trendiest and most exclusive clubs in the area. Latin pop and electronic music top the musical menu, and on weekends the hottest DJs in town are often present. All of the seating area is VIP, so be prepared to stand (or dance) all night if you don't have a reservation. Beer costs about US$3, while shots and cocktails range from US$4 to US$7.

Utopia

Via Lindora shopping centre, Santa Ana (2282 0233). **Open** 9.30pm-3.30am Thur, Sat. **Credit** AmEx, MC, V.

Utopia is more spacious than nearby Living (*see above*). It has two storeys, the upper one being the VIP area. It is the flashier and more sophisticated of the two venues, well, it has a giant chandelier, at least. The music policy is Latin pop.

Where to stay

Canal Grande Hotel

On the main road of Piedades de Santa Ana (2282 4089/www.hotelcanalgrande.com). **Rooms** 12. **Rates** US$170 double. **Credit** AmEx, MC, V.

The quaint Canal Grande Hotel is situated in a rather tranquil part of Santa Ana. It has a bar service, swimming pool, a sauna as well as a car-rental service and tours. The rooms are spacious yet cosy and are set among green scenery. A restaurant serves quality Tico cuisine. The decoration is in great taste and will appeal to art lovers. This is an ideal place to enjoy the evening view (sunset free of charge). *Bar. Parking (free). Pool (outdoor). Restaurant. TV.*

Hotel Alta

Alto de las Palomas, on the old road from Escazú towards Santa Ana (2282 4160/www.thealtahotel. com). **Rates** US$160-$390 double. **Rooms** 23. **Credit** AmEx, MC,V.

The luxurious Hotel Alta, with its Spanish-medieval style, is probably the most lavish of all the non-chain hotels in the area. The elegant but unpretentious five-storey building features large balconies and wide stone stairways, as well as a large swimming pool. Looking past the grand century-old Guanacaste tree you will find a spectacular view of San José. It also hosts one of the top restaurants in the country, La Luz (*see p107*). Photo *p111*.

Go stark bathing mad at **Hotel Alta**. *See p109.*

Bar. Business centre. Concierge. Gym. Internet (high-speed, wireless). Parking (free). Pool (outdoor). Restaurant. Room service. TV.

Hotel Quality

Autopista Próspero Fernández, 5mins from Multiplaza, Santa Ana (22046700/www.realhotels andresorts.com). **Rates** US$120 double. **Rooms** 154. **Credit** AmEx, MC, V.

The Quality Hotel is located in Santa Ana's business and financial centre. The rooms are clean, comfortable and spacious, with a minibar and microwave among other standard amenities. It is typical of chain hotels the world over and is best suited to business travellers or those passing through just for the night. For food, however, it's probably best to have a wander around the neighbourhood options. The hotel is also located near the Valle del Sol golf course.

Bar. Business centre. Disabled-adapted rooms. Gym. Internet (high-speed, shared terminals). Parking (free). Pool (outdoor). Restaurant. Room service. TV.

Marriott Courtyard

Autopista Próspero Fernández, next to Plaza Itskatzu (2208 3000/www.marriott.com). **Rooms** 119. **Rates** US$150 double. **Credit** AmEx, MC, V.

The elegant Marriott Courtyard is located across the street from the CIMA Hospital and near the Multiplaza mall and is about 16 km (10 miles) west of downtown San José. The rooms are large and comfortable, with classic stylings. The Marriott Courtyard is also conveniently located next to Plaza Itskatzu, which offers a wide variety of restaurants and shopping options.

Business centre. Concierge. Disabled-adapted rooms. Gym. Internet (high-speed, wireless). Parking (free). Pool (outdoor). Restaurant. TV.

Real Intercontinental

Guachipelin, on the Próspero Fernández highway next to Multiplaza (2208 2100/www.realhotelsand resorts.com). **Rates** US$240 double. **Rooms** 261. **Credit** AmEx, MC,V.

The colossal Real Intercontinental hotel offers everything you could wish for; every modern luxury is installed. There is a well-equipped and up-to-date gym and a business centre. Its three

restaurants are Azulejos, which has an international menu, Alfredo, specialising in Italian food, and the Factory Steak and Lobster. For drinks, the Nau Bar offers a variety of sake cocktails and sushi snacks while the Zambra Bar has a range of national and imported drinks and occasional live music. The Real Intercontinental is conveniently situated next to Multiplaza, Costa Rica's largest and finest mall. The hotel is particularly popular with business travellers.

Bars (2). Business centre. Concierge. Disabled-adapted rooms. Gym. Internet (high-speed, shared terminals, free). Pool (outdoor). Restaurants (3). Room service. Spa. TV.

Villa Escazú B&B

900m west of Banco Nacional, Central Escazú (2289 7971/vescazu@hotels.co.cr). **Rates** US$52-$65 double. **Rooms** 6. **No credit cards**.

Situated on the hillside of Escazú, and overlooking the Central Valley, Villa Escazú is a rustic Swiss chalet-style house surrounded by lush tropical gardens. To ensure tranquillity and a good night's rest the landlady prefers guests to be back in by 10pm, so it's not best suited to those wanting to check out San José's clubs. A minimum two-night stay is required.

Parking (free). TV.

Getting there

By bus

Buses for Escazú and Santa Ana leave from the Coca-Cola bus station (Avenida Central, y Calle 16).There are several buses to Escazú, all passing through San Rafael de Escazú en route to Multiplaza, Bello Horizante and Guachipelin. Buses to Santa Ana go by way of Escazú or Multiplaza, and are marked Antonio de Escazú.

By car

If going by car, take the Prospero Fernandez Highway going west from the centre. The exits for both Escazú and Santa Ana are labelled as such. Otherwise, to get to Escazú you can take the road from La Sabana that parallels the highway and will take you over the Los Anonos Bridge.

Local colours

Costa Rican art varies from indigenous masks and ceramics to traditional painted ox carts and rural paintings and pictures. Throughout history, the country's abundant natural beauty and materials have inspired all forms of national art. During the late 1920s, the Costa Rican 'Landscape Movement' took place. This movement expressed the characteristics of the foggy mountain towns particular to the Central Valley, replete with adobe houses, cobblestone streets and the omnipresent volcanoes in the background. The artists who belonged to this movement called themselves the 'Group of New Sensibility', and they began to depict Costa Rica in vibrant colours.

While the country's scenic landscapes still inspire many artists today, the growing city centres have also become a source of inspiration for modern artists such as Felo Garcia and Carlos Pardo (pictured). Garcia, who studied architecture in London and was once – and notably – Pardo's professor and mentor, brought together a collective of artists called Grupo Ocho that was dedicated to the idea of 'arte por el arte' (art for art's sake) and breaking Costa Rican artists free from thetraditional institutional bounds. His paintings of earth-toned urban settings, with houses stacked on houses criss-crossed with electrical wires, can be seen at the **Museo de arte Costarricense** (*see p101*) in Parque La Sabana.

Pardo, in contrast, uses bright colours to depict a similar urban sprawl, and shantytowns that could be mistaken for Brazilian *favelas* with clothes lines giving life to the otherwise abandoned yet inviting cityscape. His paintings encompass the concept of magical realism with a playful and deceptive use of fictitious shadows and penetrating light that defy the rules of realism. He exchanges rigid lines for shapes that seem to melt together or lean upon each other, ready to topple over if the delicate balance is disturbed. Although the bright colours never fade, his horizons range from cool blues to fiery reds, depending on his mood. In his own more turbulent past, his work often depicted stormy skies with a mixture of cool and bright shades looming over the cities.

Both Pardo and Garcia also play with human figures in some of their non-urban paintings, using strong sweeps and shadows to emphasise dramatic features and characteristics. Pardo's art, along with that of some of the most important artists in the country, can be found at **Amir Art Gallery** (Avenida 5, y Calle 5, 2256 9445, www.amirart.com), off Parque Morazán. The **Café de los Artistas** (*see p107*) is a popular yet petite venue where art can be appreciated any time. Local artwork can also be bought for as little as US$10-$20 from its crafts store and workshop.

Escazú is a hub for artists and hosts a couple of art fairs each year in the field between Plaza Colonial and the Mas X Menos supermarket. Artists from around the country come to exhibit their work.

Central Valley

Getting Started

The coast is amazing, but wait till you see the interior...

The emerald **Laguna Botos** on Volcán Poás. *See p118.*

Descending through the clouds into the Juan Santamaría International Airport, you will see the towering waves of emerald mountains that mark Costa Rica's strikingly fertile hub. A tapestry of cities, mountain towns, national parks, cloud forests, smouldering peaks, coffee *fincas* and fruit plantations carpet this elevated central landscape. Conveniently for the traveller, everything is in such close proximity that most principal attractions can be reached by car from San José in under two hours.

The region owes its spectacular array of plant life to its temperate climate and volcanic soil. Altitudes of up to 4,000 metres (13,000 feet) experience mild conditions of 15°C to 30°C, and the mineral-dense earth is enriched by the sporadic ashy splutterings from the Central Valley's active volcanoes: Poás, Irazú and Arenal.

A short drive north from the airport, past Alajuela and towards Poás, sugarcanes, papaya trees, mangos, flower nurseries and sloping coffee plantations dominate the landscape. This is the heart of the country's coffee industry, and plantations such as **Doka Coffee Estate** (*see p118*) on the slopes of Poás and Heredia's **Café Britt** (*see p127*) run tours into the world of the bean that transformed Costa Rica's economy.

To get up close and personal with the region's diverse flora and fauna, explore one of the Central Valley's national parks. Each differs dramatically. Draped across the north-east of the region, the impressive 440 square

kilometres (170 square miles) of **Parque Nacional Braulio Carrillo** (*see p128*) consists of cloud forests, primary forests, waterfalls and rivers, as well as the lofty **Volcán Barva**. A sparsely vegetated lunar landscape greets visitors to the higher parts of **PN Volcán Irazú** (*see p133*) in the east of the region, while the south-east's **PN Tapantí** (*see p135*), in the Talamanca range, is known for its dense forest. Also in Cartago province is the less visited **PN Volcán Turrialba** (*see p135*), where visitors can descend into one of the craters. Situated north of Alajuela, **PN Volcán Poás** (*see p118*), with its smouldering crater, is the most visited of Costa Rica's parks.

From the air the Central Valley can appear an untouched prehistoric landscape, and aside from a disappointing lack of dinosaurs, the greenery covering the country's heartland does play host to a number of exotic species of wildlife including jaguars, quetzals, hummingbirds, coyotes, tapir, deer, raccoons and monkeys.

As well as simply venturing out into the parks to see what flutters by, butterfly and bird enthusiasts can visit one of the region's many wildlife centres. Alajuela's **Zoo Ave** (*see p119*), located in La Garita, is home to one of the biggest aviaries in Central America; and at **La Guácima Butterfly Farm** (*see p119*), also in the Alajuela area, a rainbow of hundreds of butterflies fills an enclosed tropical garden. Head north towards Poás for **La Paz Waterfall Gardens** (*see p118*).

Central Valley

Things to do

Hike along a trail in the cloud forest of **Monteverde** or whiz above said trail on a zip-line canopy tour (*see p142*). Then kick the adrenaline up a notch with a white water rafting experience down the tumbling rivers around **Turrialba** (*see p141*). After a hard day's kayaking on Lake Arenal, have an epic soak in **Tabacón Hot Springs** (*see p156*) followed by a trip to the **Arenal Observatory Lodge** to take in the nocturnal fireworks of **Volcán Arenal** (*see p155*). Get the energy for all this activity with much sipping of the Central Valley's finest freshly ground coffee.

Places to stay

Immerse travel weary bodies in Alajuela's flowery haven, **El Silencio** (*see p123*). The garden and luxury rooms are packed with idiosyncratic touches, and the meals are delightful. For tranquillity and views, **El Cafetal Inn** (*see p123*), on the outskirts of Atenas, is the perfect getaway. Stroll through the coffee plantation, slide into the pool or simply sit with a book amid the orange trees.

From the attentive service to the flawlessly manicured grounds, quality resonates throughout Turrialba's **Casa Turire** (*see p139*). The gleaming colonial-style mansion, complete with spacious restaurant, wood-furnished cocktail bar and outdoor jacuzzi, is an idyllic setting that even the most jaded traveller would be hard pressed to find fault with.

Places to eat

For top fish dishes, Alajuela's **Princessa Marina** (*see p121*) has it covered. Its ceviche is outstanding. Take a quick taxi west from downtown for probably the best food in the area.

Sitting high in the mountains of Monteverde, the El Establo Hotel's public restaurant, **Laggus** (*see p148*), is a pricey but exquisite way to treat your taste buds. Another culinary high-flyer is the restaurant at Arenal's **Tabacón Hot Springs** (*see p156*). Guests enjoy an array of fresh Costa Rican and international food served buffet style. Those looking for a decent meal in Turrialba should take the ten-minute taxi ride to **Don Porfi's** (*see p141*) cosy Italian and international restaurant.

In the north of the region, the world-renowned cloud forest of **Monteverde** (*see p142*) is a major attraction for nature-lovers and thrill-seekers. It is known worldwide for its biological reserves and is also where the zip-line canopy tour was born, prompting a variety of similar activities in the Monteverde and Santa Elena forests, not to mention a slew of copycat jungle tours all over the globe. A jeep-boat-jeep ride away across the wide waters of Lake Arenal looms the mighty **Volcán Arenal** (*see p151*), whose nightly explosions are a truly unforgettable sight. (Eager observers are at the mercy of the clouds here, so praying to respective Gods for clear skies is highly recommended.) To take pictures of the volcano in the throes of an eruption, take a tripod.

As well as a host of wildlife, looming volcanoes and thriving agriculture, the Central Valley is also home to over 70 per cent of Costa Rica's population. The cities of San José, Alajuela, Cartago and Heredia, the country's four biggest urban areas, and their namesake provinces can all be found in this region. San José aside, the attraction-hungry visitor will find only a handful of worthy destinations within city limits. However, compared with many of the tourist-focused towns in coastal Costa Rica, the Central Valley offers more authentic examples of Tico city life.

First port of call from the airport is Alajuela, a far more tranquil town than the capital. Positioned at a lower altitude than San José, Alajuela is typically a few degrees warmer, and in the heady sunshine is a comfortable and relaxing location. Ten kilometres (six miles) north of the capital is Heredia, a lively university town. Both towns should be considered as alternative bases to San José. The former capital Cartago, 22 kilometres (14 miles) south-east of San José, is steeped in history, and though its current state is moderately depressing overall, the impressive **Basílica de Nuestra Señora de los Ángeles** (*see p133*) is reason enough for a brief stopover. For accommodation in Cartago province head on to the **Orosí Valley** (*see p135*), which is within easy distance of the early colonial **Ujarrás ruins** (*see p138*). Also in the province, on the slopes of Volcán Turrialba, is the most substantial archaeological site in the country. The **Monumento Nacional Guayabo** (*see p139*) is an example of pre-colonial life in a country where traces of the indigenous population are scarce.

Getting about the Central Valley is relatively painless; buses are frequent and reliable. However, heading up the rocky incline to Monteverde is best tackled in a four-wheel-drive vehicle, either self-drive or in one of the many shuttle buses.

Alajuela & Around

Steaming coffee and smoking volcanoes. Oh, and the world's biggest ox cart.

Catedral de Alajuela dominates the lively town centre.

The pleasant urban neighbourhood of Alajuela lies 18 kilometres (11 miles) north-west of sprawling San José and two kilometres (1.25 miles) from **Juan Santamaría International Airport**. The focal point of the country's second largest city is a small but bustling centre, and the handful of attractions makes for a more accessible and less daunting introduction to Tico city life than the capital. The standard of accommodation in this area is typically high, making it a good base for visitors to reach many of the Central Valley's brightest jewels. Close to the city is Costa Rica's much visited **PN Volcán Poás**, complete with a steaming crater and tropical flora. It is best viewed in the clearer skies of early morning, leaving plenty of time to explore the park and visit attractions such as the unmissable **La Paz Waterfall Gardens** (*see p118*) and the famous **Doka Coffee Estate** (*see p118*). Located in the far north-west of the region is the **Los Ángeles Cloud Forest**, which provides a similar yet smaller scale experience to the

famed Monteverde. A popular trio of small towns can be found west of Alajuela, with tranquil **Atenas**, clean bubbling **Grecia** and the craft hub of **Sarchí** each possessing distinctive charms. The artisan town of Sarchí is the birthplace of the famous Costa Rican ox cart (*see p124* **Cart wheeling**), and a good spot for picking up handmade souvenirs.

Alajuela City

The shade offered by the mango trees in **Parque Central** on Avenida Central is a boon for those making their first acquaintance with the Costa Rican sun. Towering beside the plaza, the gleaming white building, flanked by sun-yellow tabebuia trees, is the **Catedral de Alajuela**. This spacious 19th-century edifice marks the burial place of two Costa Rican presidents, Tomás Guardia Gutiérrez and León Cortés Castro. Head down to the cathedral plaza on Thursday evenings and Sunday mornings to hear the concert band of Alajuela belt out some

Alajuela & Around

Parque Nacional
Castro Blanco
Bajos del
Toro

Cerro
Palmira

Parque
Nacional
Volcán Poás

Volcán Poás

Poasito

Fraijanes

SARCHÍ

GRECIA

SAN PEDRO
DE POÁS

Tacare

ALAJUELA

0   1.5   3 miles

0   1.5   3 km
© Copyright Time Out Group 2008

Aeropuerto
Juan Santamaría

tunes, both popular and classical, while families and amorous teenagers look on.

Two blocks west of Parque Central is the **Mercado Central**, a typically bustling indoor market hawking fruits, vegetables, fish and meats. It's best to get there early because unlike its (mildly) cleaner cousin in San José, this one can develop quite a whiff as the day goes on. For a fascinating introduction into the weird and wonderful world of tropical fruit and vegetables, head to **Plaza Ferias**, 14 blocks west of downtown, on Friday afternoons and Saturday mornings. The land surrounding Alajuela is teeming with agricultural produce and growers from the area gather in Plaza Ferias for the largest farmers' market in the country. This feast of colour is best visited around 2.30pm on Friday when things are in full swing and the produce fresh and plentiful.

Lying two blocks south of Parque Central is **Parque Juan Santamaría**. The term 'park' is somewhat loosely applied to what appears more like a wide stretch of paving than inner city greenery. However, the attraction here is a statue of the teenage Alajuela-born war hero. Juan Santamaría died in the 1856 Battle of Rivas after torching the building of the US coffee baron William Walker (*see p168* **Making of a hero**) who wanted to enslave the Central American peoples. Santamaría successfully set El Mesón de Guerra alight, causing the North American filibuster and his men to flee; but the young drummer boy fell to their gunfire. Further information can be found at the

Museo Juan Santamaría, formerly the town jail (Avenida 3, y Calle 2). The modest museum is open from Tuesday to Sunday, from 10am to 6pm, and admission is free. As if sacrificing his life for the liberty of his people wasn't enough, Juan Santamaría's success has also given his fellow countrymen a day off work. In commemoration of the event, 11 April is Juan Santamaría Day and a national holiday.

Across town, five blocks east of Parque Central, lies the Baroque church of **Iglesia de Santo Cristo de la Agonía** built in 1941. For a caffeine stop and to top up on local information, head 100 metres north and 300 metres west of La Agonía to **Goodlight Books**. As well as a good selection of new and used guidebooks, it serves coffee, pastries and has free Wi-Fi. Open seven days a week.

EXCURSIONS

A 40-minute drive through gleaming green surrounds leads you from Alajuela to **PN Volcán Poás** (ranger station 2482 2424). The visitors' centre is open between 8am and 3.30pm and has a US$10 entry charge. From San José buses leave from Avenida 2, between Calles 12 and 14, at around 8.30am. It's about a two-hour trip and a bus returns at 2pm. By car head north out of Alajuela on Highway 130 until you reach the centre. PN Volcán Poás, Costa Rica's most visited national park, was created in January 1971 and features the largest active volcano crater in the country. The viewpoint is a ten-minute walk from the car park, and here observers stand just feet away from the steaming crater with its steely pool of bubbling sulphur-rich rainwater. Get there early for the best chance of clear skies. A 20-minute trek (they say it takes 45 minutes – it doesn't) up a steep shaded path leads to **Laguna Botos** (*photo p115*), a second crater, filled with turquoise-stained rainwater. Birds are the predominant visible wildlife in this area of Poás. There have been quetzal sightings, though few in recent years. Near the car park is a café, souvenir shop and small gallery.

If you're venturing out to Poás, an absolute must is to swing 15 kilometres (nine miles) east to **La Paz Waterfall Gardens** (Vara Blanca, 2225 0643, www.waterfallgardens.com). The butterfly sanctuary, hummingbird feeding area and serpentarium are enough to satisfy the keenest wildlife enthusiast and the five thundering waterfalls are truly spectacular. The volcanic slopes are also home to the **Ark Herb Farm** (Santa Barbara, 2846 2694, www.arkherb farm.com, US$12), housing more than 300 species of medicinal plant, and the **Doka Coffee Estate** finca (three kilometres/two miles east of Sabanilla de Alajuela, 2449 5152, www.dokaestate.com), famous for its insightful tours into the Costa Rican coffee process. If herbs and caffeine aren't stimulation enough, try the zip-line canopy tour at **Las Colinas del Poás** (one kilometre/0.5 miles north of Jaulares Cencerro, 2482 1313, www.colinasdelpoas.com) for a ride through the canopy.

One of the largest aviaries in Central America is just four kilometres (2.5 miles) west of downtown Alajuela. **Zoo Ave** (La Garita, 2433 8989, www.zooave.org, US$15), in the small town of La Garita, is the largest breeding, release and rehab centre for wildlife in Latin America. At the time of writing there was one remaining quetzal from a pair of males donated in 1994. While tropical birds are the star turns, a small zoo is also home to monkeys, crocodiles and deer.

Another popular wildlife watching attraction is **La Guácima Butterfly Farm** (2438 0400, www.butterflyfarm.co.cr, US$15), 14 kilometres (8.5 miles) south-west of Alajuela. Visitors stroll among a flurry of butterflies in the enclosed tropical garden and early birds to the caterpillar room have a good chance of witnessing the transition from chrysalis to newly emerged butterfly. One of Costa Rica's best golf courses is in **La Guácima** (Los Reyes, 2438 0004).

For those not making the hike up to Monteverde's forests, Alajuela province's **Bosque Nuboso Los Angeles** (2661 1600, US$15) is a smaller eight-square-kilometre (three-square-mile) reserve offering a more accessible cloud forest experience. Trails lead around the area, but it can get muddy. There is also a well-regarded restaurant on the premises serving typical Tico dishes and a range of fresh and interesting fruit.

Where to eat & drink

La Casa del Viñedo

La Garita (2487 6086). **Open** 11am-10pm Tue-Sun. **Main courses** US$9. **Credit** AmEx, DC, MC, V.
This Argentinian-styled steak house (tango crackles away in the background) is highly recommended for its meat cuts and speciality Italian and Argentinian wines. The *parillada* (mixed grill) is big enough for two.

Cugini's

Avenida Central, y Calle 5 (2440 6893). **Open** noon-midnight Mon-Sat. **Main courses** US$9. **No credit cards**.
Though pumping nightlife isn't Alajuela's forte, there are a few good watering holes worthy of an evening's attention – and this is one of them. Popular with students and young tourists, the ground-floor bar of this American/Italian eatery has a lively sports bar atmosphere and an extensive cocktail list. Its massive pizzas also make for a good snack.

Mirador del Valle

La Garita (2441 7318/www.miradordelvalle.info). **Open** noon-11pm Mon-Thur; noon-midnight Sat; 11am-10pm Sun. **Main courses** US$9. **Credit** AmEx, DC, MC, V.
Seven kilometres north of Alajuela, towards Volcán Poás, is the perfect place for a Sunday barbecue; but spectacular views of the Central Valley can be enjoyed any day of the week. Grilled meats are a speciality, but there is also a good range of fish dishes.

Princesa Marina

Barrio San José (2433 7117/www.princesamarina. com). **Open** 11am-10.30pm Mon-Thur; 11am-11pm Fri, Sat; 11am-9pm Sun. **Main courses** US$9. **Credit** AmEx, DC, MC, V.

It's not all hot air in **PN Volcán Poás**, the country's most visited national park.

Central Valley

Coffee fables

Considering Costa Rica's caffeine to person ratio, it's a wonder Tico life continues to be so leisurely paced. The country remains one of the world's primary coffee producers and deliciously smooth, steaming *tazas de café* (cups of coffee) are as ubiquitous as the rodent-sized bugs. The introduction of the Ethiopian-born shrub to Costa Rican soils happened without fanfare, and so the precise date – a bean of contention – is some time between 1790 and 1820. Indisputable, however, is the highly apt stimulating effect the mid 19th-century coffee boom had on the country's flagging economy. Single-handedly, this little bean, 'the berry', transformed a financially inconsequential fragment of Central America into its most affluent region.

For Costa Ricans living then, this sudden injection of wealth was a case of about bloody time too. Columbus's 1502 reports of *la costa rica* (the rich coast), in a nod to the native bling, had excited the first wave of settlers. But after the years spent overcoming the indigenous population, recovering from Volcán Irazú's 1723 devastation of the then capital Cartago and slowly populating the Central Valley, the wheat, maize and spice agriculture of colonial life was not proving financially fruitful. But by 1850, coffee accounted for more than 90 per cent of the country's export revenue, bringing in money from across the globe, notably from Britain. Not only did it thrive in the volcanic soils, mild climates and perfect altitude of the Central Valley, but in the days of slow transport the bean's longevity made it an ideal traveller.

Plantations initially surrounded San José and it was a gruelling 115-kilometre (71-mile) trek from the capital to the Pacific port of Puntarenas from where Costa Rica exported most of its coffee crop. It was not long before much of the land around the populated areas of the Central Valley was carpeted with the shrub. The process was helped by the 1824 election of Juan Mora Fernández as Costa Rica's first head of state, who introduced land grants for coffee growers. Although this sped up production and allowed further riches for the country as a whole, the wealth among those involved in the coffee chain was spread unevenly. Sitting smugly at the top, the *cafetaleros* (coffee barons) increased their wealth by controlling credit, purchase prices and processing facilities, leaving the smaller producers at their mercy. And it was not until the early 20th century that an Asian immigrant, the banana, was to knock the berry off the lucrative top spot.

For the past 20 years agriculture has taken an economic back seat, overtaken by electronic components. However, since the 1980s the tourism industry has swelled into one of the country's most significant money makers. Sadly for those who take pleasure in Costa Rica's sloping coffee fincas, more and more growers are selling up their land for the quicker and bigger buck of real estate. But while urban areas continue to expand further into the countryside, coffee still remains an important part of Costa Rica's global identity and the coffee tours around the Central Valley are an essential trip into the past.

For reliable fish dishes try Princesa Marina in the village of Barrio San José, just a five-minute drive west of the centre. Pasta, meat and chicken dishes are available, but the seafood is the shining glory.

Where to stay

Hotel Mi Tierra
Avenida 2, entre Calles 3 y 5 (2441 1974/www. hotelmitierra.net). **Rates** US$30-$40 double. **Rooms** 11. **Credit** AmEx, MC, V.
A basic but clean bed and breakfast in central Alajuela, three blocks east of Parque Juan Santamaría. The floorboards may be creaky but there is a pool in the garden and wireless internet access in the communal area. Shared and private bathrooms. Adventure tours can also be arranged.
Internet (free wireless). Parking (free). Pool (outdoor).

Jardín Tropical
800m west & 100m south of Zoo Ave, La Garita (2433 5045/www.jardintropicalbandb.com). **Rates** US$40-$50 double. **Rooms** 7. **No credit cards**.
This is another reliable mid-range option. Set in a mini botanical garden by Zoo Ave (*see p119*), this is a tranquil spot, basically a suburban B&B rather than a hotel. It is a family home, but the owners are wise to the fact most people want to be left alone. Friendly and clean.
Parking (free).

La Paz Waterfall Gardens
Vara Blanca (2225 0643/www.waterfallgardens. com). **Rates** US$205-$315 double. **Rooms** 3. **Credit** AmEx, DC, MC, V.
At the upper end of the price scale, the Peace Lodge within the incredible La Paz Waterfall Gardens is featured as one of the branded Small and Distinctive Hotels, and deservedly so. Every spacious room is decorated with the flora of the area and has a jacuzzi (sometimes on the balcony). Some have their own waterfall, a 'garden' shower and fireplace. Guests also have out-of-hours access to the La Paz grounds.
Bar. Internet (shared terminals, free). Parking (free). Restaurants (3). Room service. Spa. TV.

Pura Vida
500m from the Punto Rojo factory, Alajuela, on the left-hand side (2430 2929/www.puravida hotel.com). **Rates** US$85-$130 double. **Rooms** 6. **Credit** AmEx, MC, V.
For your bed and breakfast taken with a pinch of flower-laden luxury, try this former colonial style coffee finca just 4km (2.5 miles) from the airport. Views of Volcán Poás or the Itikis Valley can be enjoyed from the rooms, or from the garden. Why sit inside when there are pineapples, plantains, 20 varieties of hibiscus and 40 varieties of orchid growing just inches away? Platters of fresh fruit, smoothies and pastries are served to guests sipping their early morning coffee among hanging orchids. Three-course candlelit dinners on the garden terrace are also available on request for US$25. Hosts Bernie and Nhi provide a personal touch, fusing the key elements of a high quality establishment with a warm and welcoming bed and breakfast.
Internet (shared terminal). Restaurant.

Vida Tropical
2 blocks north of the Tribunales de Justicia, 10th house on the right (2443 9576/ www.vidatropical.com). **Rates** US$45 double. **Rooms** 6. **Credit** MC, V.
For comfortable mid-range accommodation just five minutes from the airport and walking distance from Alajuela centre, this welcoming family-run bed and breakfast ticks all the boxes. It has wireless internet access, cushioned communal spaces and a wonderfully warm, international vibe. Free local phone calls, secure parking and free laundry are included with stays of three days or longer.
Internet (free wireless, shared terminal). Parking (free).

Xandari Resort
3km north of Alajuela towards Volcán Poás (2443 2020/www.xandari.com). **Rates** US$192-$366 double. **Rooms** 22 (villas). **Credit** AmEx, MC, V.
Xandari is the acme of luxurious holidaying in the Alajuela area. The 16-hectare (40-acre) plantation has 22 villas, most of which have two double beds, a jacuzzi and panoramic views. You can swim in one of the two large gleaming pools; saunter through the greenhouse and orchid house; and stumble across the original artworks to be found throughout the resort. The on-site spa village also offers an indulgent medley of pampering treats. Hot stone massages, body wraps and exotic facials are available. Xandari also has a programme to lessen the environmental impact of the hotel.
Pools (2, outdoor). Restaurant. Spa.

Resources

Banks
Banco Nacional *west of the central park (2212 2000).*

Hospital
Hospital San Rafael *east of Mall International on the way into Alajuela from the airport (2440 1333).*

Internet
The post office on the corner of Calle 1, y Avenida 5 has some terminals (no phone). **Open** 7.30am-5pm Mon-Fri; 7.30am-noon Sat.

Police
4 blocks west of Mercado Central (2440 8889)

Tourist information
Goodlight Books *Avenida 3, entre Calles 1 y 3 (2430 4083/www.goodlightbooks.com).* **Open** 9am-6pm daily.
There is no official tourist information but these guys will help with anything.

Getting there

By bus

From San José buses every 15mins or so from the terminal on Avenida 2, between Calles 12 and 14. From the airport red **Tuasa** buses leave frequently for Alajuela. Both arrive at **Alajuela bus terminal** on Calle 8, between Avenidas Central and 1. Take buses to San José and the airport from here.

By road

Alajuela is only a 10min drive from the airport. Taxis cost around US$3. Alajuela is well signposted; take the Interamericana towards San José and turn off north at the first intersection.

Atenas, Grecia & Sarchí

The small village of **Atenas** lies 25 kilometres (15 miles) west of Alajuela. Aside from breathtaking views there are few tourist attractions – but pick up a *toronja rellena* from a roadside seller. This grapefruit filled with honey and condensed milk is an Atenas speciality.

The compact farming town of **Grecia**, voted the 'cleanest little town in Latin America', is 18 kilometres (11 miles) north-west of Alajuela. The focal point of this collection of shops and cafés is the strangely attractive deep red church, the **Iglesia de la Nuestra Señora de las Mercedes**, made from pounded metal. When the previous church fell victim to fire, the town took the rather bizarre though admittedly logical move to construct its Gothic successor out of metal.

One of the most popular excursions from Grecia is to the artisan hub of **Sarchí**, a short bus ride from Grecia's main bus station 400 metres south of the church. Costa Rica's craft capital provokes mixed responses from visitors, with some thinking it simply a touristy souvenir centre. But many find the famous *fabricas de carretas* (ox cart factories) and *mueblerías* (furniture factories) to be a unique day trip and an interesting insight into Costa Rican culture. *See p124* **Cart wheeling**.

Sarchí is split in two by the Río Trojas. The main craft centres, such as the oldest and most famous ox cart producers **Fábrica de Carretas Joaquín Chaverri** and the mall of souvenir shops that makes up **Plaza de la Artesanía**, are located in Sarchí Sur. A new addition to Sarchí Norte is the **Else Kientzler Botanical Garden** (2454 2070, www.elsegarden.com), containing over 2,000 internationally sourced plants. It is open from 8am to 4pm and costs US$12 to enter. Also in Sarchí Norte see the world's largest ox cart (OK, we're not talking about ticking off major life goals here), built in 2006 for the express intention of getting the town's name into the *Guinness World Records*.

Where to eat & drink

The best bet for good food is traditional cuisine. Generous portions await at Atenas's outdoor **Rancho Típico La Trilla** (2446 5637, main courses US$7) on Highway 3, just before the Coopeatenas gas station on the right-hand side. Grecia's **Rancho Nelsons** (2494 1515, main courses US$5) serves local food at extremely reasonable prices. For a bite to eat in Sarchí, try **Las Carretas** (2454 1636, main courses US$7).

Where to stay

The calming greens of the cloud forest encase the luxury suites of **El Silencio** (2291 3044, www.elsilenciolodge.com, US$240 double). The fusion of natural ingredients – used in room furnishings, organic meals and spa treatments – is this establishment's signature. Each of the 16 luxury suites feature a private deck and whirlpool. The package includes three daily meals, using, where possible, fresh, organic and regional products. For that one step further towards nature-induced nirvana there is a large spa, with beauty and relaxation treatments.

El Cafetal Inn B&B (Santa Eulalia, www.cafetal.com, 2446 5785, US$60 double) is the hotel of choice in Atenas. That the immediate surrounds offer little activity is inconsequential for guests at this peaceful hotel and coffee plantation that looks out across a valley of swaying sugarcane. The two-level hotel building has 14 well-appointed and spacious rooms.

La Terraza (2444 3685, www.laterrazab-b. com, US$90 double) is an intimate, well-kept establishment a short taxi ride from central Grecia. It is a peaceful place in which to relax in rocking chairs and stroll through grounds featuring a stream with a wooden bridge.

If staying in Sarchí, try **Hotel Daniel Zamora** (2454 4596, US$35 double). Located on a side street heading east from the football pitch, it has comfortable accommodation.

Resources

Bank

Banco Nacional *main plaza of Sarchí Norte (2212 2000).*

Hospital

San Francisco de Asis *500m west of church in Grecia (2494 5044).*

Internet

Rick's Internet Café *opposite park in Atenas (2446 0810/www.ricksinternetcafe.com).* **Open** 8am-8pm daily.

Police

Grecia (2494 5379).

Central Valley

Cart wheeling

The tale of the humble Costa Rican ox cart is a true Cinderella story. From its origins as a 19th-century method of trudging sack loads of coffee beans across the mountains, with a lick of paint and the arrival of modern transport, *carretas* (ox carts) were catapulted from being large wooden boxes on wheels plus a big cow into artisan stardom. And for the last 20 years, the elaborately decorated ox cart has reigned as the psychedelically festive, official symbol of the country's vibrant craft industry.

It is no wonder the Costa Rican people hold the creation process of *carretas* in great esteem. In the agriculturally dependent colonial times, reliable transportation of goods was paramount to basic survival and solid craftsmanship was required to ensure valuable produce made the distance. For many their trusty cart was also the only means of

transport and so its upkeep and quality became a status symbol.

The painting of the strong lagarto wood wheels began in the early 20th century and the designs indicated in which region the owner lived. These days every grain of wood is painstakingly decorated with bright geometric patterns.

The largest Sarchí ox cart factory, the Fábrica de Carretas Joaquín Chaverri (*see p123*), has been producing ox carts since 1903 and is frequented by a permanent stream of tourists. As well as the full-scale carts, visitors to Sarchí can see the production of miniature replicas, which make predictably popular souvenirs. While the small Alajuelan town remains ox cart HQ, the carts appear at festivals and events all over the country, the most famous being in the streets of Escazú for the Día Nacional del Boyero (National Day of the Ox Cart Driver) on the second Sunday in March. This colourful occasion sees the streets filled with a host of oxen, intricately decorated carts and participants in traditional dress. The festivities begin at 5am for Alegre Diana when a girl dressed up as the protagonist goes around and wakes up the town's residents. And if that wasn't random enough, clowns and kids in fancy dress join the pilgrimage to the Iglesia de San Antonio. The drivers are blessed and the best oxen and cart owners are awarded prizes.

Central Valley

Heredia & Around

White water rafting and tranquil cloud forests, all within an hour of San José.

Heredia is a pizza slice-shaped province fanning out from its namesake capital, north to the border with Nicaragua. The principal city is a mere 20-minute drive from both downtown San José and the **Jose Santamaría International Airport**. It is a relaxed yet pleasingly vibrant town, with a large student population. Bars and cafés serving coffee from nearby fincas dominate the historical centre of the town, making staying here a pleasing option after arriving or just before bidding farewell to the country.

The highlight of this area is, however, the **PN Braulio Carrillo** (*see p128*). This vast protected land is one of the largest national parks in Costa Rica and made up of mostly untouched virgin rainforest. On its border is the famous **Rainforest Aerial Tram** (*see p130*), a low impact 'skytrain' that carries visitors up into the canopy of the forest.

North of PN Braulio Carrillo are the small towns of **Puerto Viejo de Sarapiquí** (*see p131*) and **La Virgen** (*see p131*). Although they may not be as well known or as developed as settlements in the Monteverde and Santa Elena area, they are beginning to offer the full gamut of tourist attractions, including reptile farms and biological reserves, as well as accommodation from luxury lodges to budget cabins.

Heredia is also coffee country and home to one of the most modern tourist centres in the country: the **Britt Coffee Tour**. Shuttle buses bring in java junkies from hotels in San José, Alajuela and Cartago for the centre's entertaining look into the history of the little bean that changed the country's destiny.

Heredia

Heredia is known as the 'Ciudad de las Flores' (the City of Flowers). But before any budding botanists start packing their quadrangles, they should note that the name is due to the city's associations with the Flores family who dominated cultural life here in the early 19th century. (Understandably, the tourist board doesn't make that clear.) Heredia is, nevertheless, a small jaunty town with a friendly population of around 75,000, and provides a great alternative to the sleeping options around the airport. It is the gateway to the PN Braulio Carrillo.

There is no doubting where the centre is: head to **Parque Central** where Calle Central and,

yes, Avenida Central meet. From this leafy park you can easily take in Heredia's historical legacy. There is evidence that the mountain-dwelling Cubujuqui indigenous people settled in the Heredia area from the early 16th century onwards, but the city itself wasn't founded until 1706. Originally it was named Villavieja, only becoming Heredia in 1763.

The **Parroquia de la Inmaculada Concepción**, on the main square, was opened in 1796. And whether by divine intervention or sturdy design, it has survived some city-razing earthquakes. Most interesting are the **Jardíns de la Immaculada** gardens that grow on its west side. Directly north of the church is **El Fortín**, a well-known symbol of the city. Erected in 1876 by the then governor of the province, Fadrique Gutiérrez, the fort shows the influence of both the governor's military experience and his amateur passion for (often quite sensual) sculpture. This small fortress

The best Birdwatching

With hugely diverse habitats sheltered within its borders, Alajuela province is often named the best place to birdwatch in Costa Rica.

La Selva (*see p131*), in the Caribbean foothills, is undoutedly the most famous place in Costa Rica for birdwatching. Run by the Organisation for Tropical Studies, this study centre has, at last count, recorded more than 448 species of bird. It caters both for expert twitchers wanting in-depth specialist guides and for the complete beginner, many of whom take their unique 'Birdwatching 101' course.

Deeper inside the rainforest is the **Tirimbina Rainforest Center** (*see p131*). It is also a tropical research centre and benefits from all the expertise that comes with that. But familes are welcome, with children – OK, everyone – enjoying its chocolate tour.

In the Sarapiquís Valley is a more luxurious offering from **Centro Neotrópico Sarapiquís** (*see p131*). Its botanical garden attracts hundreds of birds.

Explore Costra Rica's flora in Heredia's **Jardíns de la Immaculada**.

never saw any action. You can wander around the site, but unfortunately you can't enter it.

Other interesting buildings are all within a city block of the Parque Central. The educational facility **Liceo de Heredia** is a large two-storey edifice constructed in 1870, and donated to the province in 1904, by the wonderfully named Anita Roy Lordy Pundy. The **Casa de la Cultura** on the north side of the plaza is the former residence of President Alfredo González Flores, president between 1914 and 1917, and exhibits art and photography but little else.

EXCURSIONS

Most visitors, however, come to Heredia for one reason: the **Britt Coffee Tour** (2277 1600, www.cafebritt.com, US$35-$58). The complex is 500 metres north then 400 metres west of the Automercado in central Heredia (don't worry, it is very well signposted). The award-winning attraction takes international coffee aficionados through a genuinely funny interactive and bilingual tour devised by a local theatre troupe. The tour begins with a walk through their mini plantation, with guides explaining how the beans grow, and how the volcanic earth and altitude are tailor-made for high-quality coffee. Then, after a brief but fascinating wander around the working roasting plant (it smells amazing), they explain how the cash crop rescued Costa Rica's ailing economy (*see p120* **Coffee fables**). After a hearty buffet lunch, real bean geeks can have a private lesson on tasting methods, or instruction on how to make the perfect cappuccino. Café Britt is one of the biggest roasters of coffee in Costa Rica and has a series of social programmes for local communities. Tours start at 11am and 3pm between 15 December and 30 April. Reservations are essential.

Where to eat & drink

All around the centre there are cheap sodas offering the usual Tico fare. The pick of the bunch is **Fresas** (Avenida 1, y Calle 7, 2262 5555, main courses US$5), a popular open window eaterie with good salads and smoothies. If you can't make it over to the Caribbean coast, go to **Cocina de Mami**'s bamboo kitchen (Calle Central, entre Avenidas 1 y 3, 2290 6492, main courses US$6) where chefs rustle up beef and grilled fish in their speciality sauces while dancing to the sound of calypso.

El Cholo (Calle 12, y Avenida Central, 2261 1801, main courses US$4) offers good-value Spanish-style seafood and tapas and is popular with students chatting over a lunchtime beer. A short distance away is **La Parrilla** (Calle 12, entre Avenidas Central y 1, 2261 3707, main courses US$8), a slightly more upmarket Argentinian option with the focus squarely

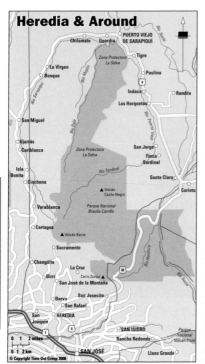

Heredia & Around

PUERTO VIEJO DE SARAPIQUÍ
Chilamate
Guardia
Río Sucio
Zona Protectora La Selva
Tigre
La Virgen
Bosque
Río Macho
Paulina
Río Sarapiquí
Indaco
Rambla
Las Horquetas
San Miguel
Río Puerto Viejo
Ujarrás
Cariblanco
Zona Protectora La Selva
San Jorge
Finca Sardinal
Isla Bonita
Cinchona
Río Sardinal
Santa Clara
Volcán Cacho Negro
Corinto
Varablanca
Parque Nacional Braulio Carrillo
Cartagos
Volcán Barva
Río Hondura
Sacramento
Changüite
La Cruz
Birrí
Cerro Zurquí
San José de la Montaña
San Josecito
Barva
San Rafael
San Joaquín
HEREDIA
SAN ISIDRO
Parque Nacional Volcán Irazú
Rancho Redondo
SAN JOSÉ
Llano Grande

0   1   2 miles
0   1   2 km
© Copyright Time Out Group 2008

on meat, more meat and, for variety, large side portions of offal.

For a quick intake of Costa Rican coffee with some good pastries, **Trigo Miel** (Calle Central, y Avenida 3, 2260 5122) is a clean bakery with a few tables. Another relaxed place is **Café de Flores** (Calle 3, y Avenida 1, 2290 6492).

If something a bit stronger is calling there are several bars along Avenida 1, between Calles 3 and 9. The best is **La Choza**, but the ugly, street-facing **El Bulevar** is usually packed.

Where to stay

Good lodging options in Heredia are slim; fortunately, those that do exist are very good. Nearest to the city is the homely – in the truest sense of the word – **Casa Holanda** (2238 3241, www.casaholanda.com, US$75-$150 double). Run by the New York composer, classical pianist and tenor James Holland, this four-bedroom bed and breakfast is a well-located townhouse in a suburb five minutes from Heredia's centre, and 20 minutes from the airport. The immaculate house, complete with grand piano, offers an intimate haven from the area's bustle. James,

a font of local knowledge, can either tailor your holiday – anything from organising and hosting tours to rustling up a gourmet candlelit dinner – or just leave you to relax. Free Wi-Fi, king-size beds, whopping breakfast and free access to laundry facilities are useful additional extras. And if you are lucky, you'll be there for a classical recital with some of his talented friends.

Further north of Heredia city, beyond the town of **Barva**, is one of Costa Rica's finest hotels. **Finca Rosa Blanca Country Inn and Spa** (Santa Bárbara de Heredia, 2269 9392, www.finca-rblanca.co.cr, US$270-$320 double; *photo p130*). Inspired by Gaudí, this whitewashed luxury hotel and restaurant is high up the Central Valley, with views of coffee plantations and mountain forest that can be admired as you eat in the **Tigre Vestida** restaurant – also one of Costa Rica's best. Each of the 13 rooms, two villas and all common spaces are quirkily decorated by the US proprietors' own art collection. A spa, infinity pool, horse riding and interactive tours of the finca's coffee plantation add to its appeal. It is a lodging that would suit honeymooners rather than families.

Resources

Hospital
Hospital San Vicente de Paul *Avenida 8, entre Calles 14 y 16 (2261 0001).*

Internet
Speedy Internet *Avenida 2, entre Calles 5 y 7 (no phone).* US$1 per hr. **Open** 8am-7.30pm Mon-Sat.

Post office
North side of Parque Central (2443 2653).

Getting there

By bus
Buses leave for Heredia every 10-15mins from Avenida 2, between Calles 12 and 14 in downtown San José. It costs around CRC285 and will leave you by the **Universidad Nacional**, 6 blocks from the Parque Central. As this guide went to print a new central terminal on Avenida 10, between Calles 4 and 8, was being built. Currently, buses leave from the **Mercado Central** at Avenida 6, and Calle 2.

By road
Heredia is on Ruta 3 from San José. Head towards the Parque La Sabana and take the signposted road from there. It is 11km (7 miles) from San José.

PN Braulio Carrillo

This expansive national park extends from the high-altitude primary cloud forest surrounding **Volcán Barva**, near the provincial capital of

Wander lonely as a cloud in **Parque Nacional Braulio Carrillo**.

Artful lodgers adore the **Finca Rosa Blanca Country Inn and Spa**. *See p128.*

Heredia, to the tropical lowland rainforest of the Caribbean. This area is often ignored by visitors to Costa Rica, who tend to be seduced instead by the fiery Volcán Arenal and the surrounding mountain forest. And while 2,906-metre (9,534-foot) Volcán Barva may not be emitting lava, or even a hint of steam (there are two misty lagoons on top), the flora of this cloud forest is unsurpassed. It is also easily accessible from all of the Central Valley's principal cities. The more adventurous can machete further through the park to wonder at hidden waterfalls, enormous plants and swimming holes. Because of its size – 475 square kilometres (183 square miles) – and a variation in altitude of almost 3,000 metres (9,800 feet), there is a remarkable amount of biodiversity. The bare statistics are impressive: 6,000 species of tree and plant (the gunnera leaves are improbably large) provide habitat for more than 500 types of bird including toucans, eagles and the quetzal, and more than 135 species of mammal including jaguars, tapirs and monkeys.

The park was created as a result of an agreement between environmental lobbyists and the government; the latter wanted to create a motorway from the capital to the country's important Caribbean ports. The Guápiles Highway now divides the protected park, but provides access along its routes.

Volcán Barva, which last blew its top in 1772, is the access point closest to Heredia. From the **Barva Sector ranger station** (*see p131*) a 40-minute hike will lead you to Laguna Barva, one of three lakes at the peak of the volcano.

The park is served by two ranger stations that are open to the public (see www.sinaccr.net for details, only in Spanish for now), and are the best access points to trails. They are open daily between 8am and 4pm with an entrance fee of US$8 for foreigners. Each provides toilets and picnic areas. Camping is permitted for US$2 at a site near the peak. Well-maintained paths will take you to two gorgeous lookout points where you can sit and watch the mists roll in and out. Two longer side trails through the forest are highly recommended, and an information booklet and map (in Spanish) is available at the ranger's office. Another muddy two-hour round trip will lead you deep into the clouds and to Laguna Copey, although this is for more experienced hikers. Take good boots.

The **Quebrada González ranger station** is another popular starting point for signed paths through the steamy rainforest. It is also only two kilometres (1.25 miles) from mineral-tinted **Río Sucio** (Dirty River). For further exploration, a guide is strongly recommended.

EXCURSIONS

The **Rainforest Aerial Tram** (Central office, Avenida 7, entre Calles 9 y 7, San José, 2287 8951, www.rfat.com) takes visitors on an 80-minute journey high up through the canopy of the cloud forest bordering PN Braulio Carrillo. Constructed by biologist Don Perry, it offers an opportunity to see wildlife without climbing trees or zip-lining (although it is also available), but rather sitting on a delicate six-person tram hanging from cables. The reserve can also be explored on foot along guided trails. If you miss seeing the wildlife in the wild, a frog and butterfly garden and snake exhibit should sate your appetite. The basic tram trip costs US$55 for adults and US$27.50 for children and students. Other, more expensive, passes are available that include guided tours. To reach the reserve take the Guápiles Highway for 50 minutes from San José, and follow the signs five kilometres (three miles) after crossing Rio Sucio. Buses to Guápiles from San José should be able to drop you off here (ask first) and it is then a two-kilometre (1.25-mile) hike to the centre from the entrance. There are also ten bungalows available for lodging.

Getting there

The **Quebrada González ranger station** is on the Guápiles Highway, two kilometres (1.25 miles) past the Zurquí tunnel. Regular buses between San José and Guápiles will leave you at the entrance. There is also a car park.

The **Barva Sector ranger station** is reached by climbing steeply through the colonial village of Barva and the even smaller San José de la Montaña to Sacramento. The easiest access is by car (four-wheel-drive recommended). Buses from Heredia leave for **Sacramento**, some continuing to the park, from the Mercado Central three times a day: 6.30am, 11am and 4.30pm. Check these times in advance of your trip.

Sarapiquí & around

North of PN Braulio Carrillo are the towns of **Puerto Viejo de Sarapiquí** and **La Virgen**. They are quickly catching up with their better-known neighbours of Monteverde and Santa Elena, and this area is now offering all the tourist infrastructure needed to make this a worthwhile side trip. It is an area best explored by car as most of the attractions are spread out. It is also a very family-friendly zone.

The Sarapiquí river is one of the best places in Costa Rica to go white water rafting. Most lodges in the area will be able to organise a wild and bumpy day trip on the river. **Aguas Bravas** (www.aguas-bravas.co.cr) is one of the most established and professional outfits in the area, taking thrill-seekers down Class II to IV rapids. Prices range from US$50 to $65. Biking, hiking, horse riding and canopy tours can also be organised, as well as guided rainforest walks. Transfers from San José can be arranged.

EXCURSIONS

La Selva (three kilometres/two miles south of Sarapiquí, 2524 0607, www.ots.ac.cr) is a world-famous research centre run by the Organisation for Tropical Studies. Founded in 1953, this centre has since become one of the world's most respected eco-tourism centres. Of course, it is mainly inhabited by students and biologists carrying out research projects, but its facilities for visitors are superb. Half-day and full-day tours are run by leading naturalists, who, as well as pointing out birds, will also give you a glimpse into the research going on in the centre. Tours start at 8.30am and 1.30pm daily. Private night tours and birdwatching tours are also offered, plus a very popular 'Birdwatching 101' introduction to rainforest birds.

Tirimbina Rainforest Center (La Virgen de Sarapiquí, 2761 1579, www.tirimbina.org) is essentially a tropical science centre that has opened up its doors to offer eco-tourism tours to schools, researchers, students and, of course, visitors. A 15-room lodge is also available for longer term visitors at US$64 a room.

Another widely endorsed sustainable eco-tourism centre is the **Centro Neotrópico Sarapiquí** (La Virgen, 2761 1004, www.sarapiquis.org). This comfortable lodge offers visitors an education into rainforest life and the communities that inhabit these areas.

Where to eat & stay

There are plenty of resorts that offer all-inclusive packages or cheaper tent camps and cabins along Route 126 between Puerto Viejo de Sarapiquí and La Virgen. Below are some of the best. Food can be bought at all the resorts.

Going north from La Virgen, the first is the semi-permanent tent camp **Hacienda Pozo Azul**. There are two lodging options on this eight-square-kilometre (three-square-mile) working farm. The **Cuculmeca Tent Camp** has 27 tents, each with four beds, for US$40 a double. The nearby **Magasay Jungle Lodge** has ten comfortable rooms in a hardwood house.

A beautiful lodge is the riverside **La Quinta Sarapiquí Country Inn** (2761 1300, www.laquintasarapiqui.com, US$65-$80 double). A Tico-run family lodge, La Quinta also serves up traditional food from its garden.

Getting there

By bus

Direct buses leave for Puerto Viejo de Sarapiquí 10 times a day from the **Gran Terminal del Caribe** in downtown San José (Calle Central, y Avenida 13).

By car

The easiest way to approach this area is by taking the Guápiles Highway. At the intersection at Rio Frio follow the signs to Puerto Viejo de Sarapiquí (not Puerto Viejo de Limón). This will take you to Puerto Viejo de Sarapiquí. For the La Virgen road turn left at Puerto Viejo de Sarapiquí.

Central Valley

Cartago & Around

Come here for rafting, ruins and religious sites, in a scenic setting.

Play misty for me – **Lago de Cachi** in the Orosí Valley.

While the ambience of the provincial capital is less than seductive, Cartago province features some of the most attractive scenery in the Central Valley. The land here is notably fertile, and it is this, combined with the sturdy figures of **Volcán Irazú** and **Volcán Turrialba** and some of the best white water rafting in the world, that makes it an alluring destination.

The rafting mecca of Turrialba in the east of the region attracts scores of adventure travellers eager to ride **Ríos Pacuare** and **Reventazón** and there are plenty of professional outfitters willing to take visitors along the bumpy waters. The nearby **PN Volcán Turrialba**, with its lush landscape, impressive views and textbook craters, is surprisingly undervisited compared with its

Central Valley counterparts. Irazú is Costa Rica's tallest volcano and the rather arid surrounds near its summit are in striking contrast to the rest of the area.

At the feet of these daunting peaks, amid the bewitching and subtle charms of the **Orosí Valley**, are the relaxed little towns of Cachi and Orosí from where **PN Tapantí** and the **Monte Sky Reserve** are within easy reach. Alongside its natural riches, Cartago province offers a culture-seeker some of the country's most interesting sites: Costa Rica's most sacred church, the **Basílica de Nuestra Señora de los Ángeles**; the colonial **Ujarrás ruins**; and the clearest example of long-gone indigenous life at the **Guayabo excavation site** near Volcán Turrialba.

Cartago City

The history of Cartago (meaning Carthage) is one peppered with misfortune. Costa Rica's capital from 1563 until 1823, the city exhibits fine Spanish colonial architecture but its charm has been systematically destroyed by a series of earthquakes, in particular the 1732 rumblings of nearby Volcán Irazú. It remained the country's capital until 1823 when the honour was transferred to the larger San José.

While Cartago has never regained its former glory, there are, among the rather characterless urban sprawl, some striking historical sites that draw tourists. The architecturally rich Byzantine-styled **Basílica de Nuestra Señora de los Ángeles** is revered as the country's most sacred spot, attracting 1.5 million pilgrims each year. Local legend attests it was built on the site of a miracle by Costa Rica's patron saint, the Virgen de los Ángeles. The dark stone statue of the Virgin, still hidden inside the Basilica, is known affectionately as La Negrita (*see p134* **Myths and miracles**).

Pilgrims trek from across the country, and occasionally further afield, to be touched by the 'black' Virgin's healing powers. Along with the rest of the city, the Basilica has suffered from the forces of nature over the years but has been lovingly restored, most notably in 1926.

A not so fortunate Cartago monument is the **Iglesia del Convento** (Avenida 2, y Calle 2). Built in 1635, this was one of the first churches razed in colonial Costa Rica, and its earthquake-shattered ruins are in the central plaza.

EXCURSIONS

The scenery around Cartago is some of the most striking to be found in the Central Valley. A 19-kilometre (12-mile) drive north-east is the epicentre of the province, **Volcán Irazú** and the national park (2551 9398, US$10) established in 1955 to protect its flora and fauna. The 3,432-metre (11,260-foot) Irazú is the country's highest active volcano, and when you stand amid the sparse lunar landscape found higher up its slopes, the views stretch right to the Caribbean. Although inactive since 1994,

Cartago & Around

Central Valley

Myths and miracles

Key to the history of Cartago's famed **Basílica de Nuestra Señora de los Ángeles** (*see p133*) is a charming piece of local folklore that defies the city's troubled past and keeps it (just about) on the modern-day tourist map. Legend has it that in 1635, a young girl named Juana Pereira stumbled upon a black rock that bore a striking resemblance to the Virgin Mary. Thinking the object was a doll, the girl tried twice to keep it in her bedroom, but each time she stowed it away it disappeared, only to be found later in the exact place in which she first discovered it.

On hearing the tale the priest of Cartago took the tiny statue and locked it away in a vault. When he returned the following day to find an empty basement, and the rock back in its original spot, the priest took the miracle as a sign that this was a sacred place on which a house of worship should be built. And so the soaring Basílica de Nuestra Señora de los Ángeles was built and the 'black' Virgin,

La Negrita, housed with much reverence within its walls. La Negrita, as the statue is affectionately known, was soon made a patron saint of Costa Rica and bestowed with many mystical powers including the ability to protect the country from natural disasters.

With more than a touch of irony, she has since been moved from her original location due to the reconstruction of the Basílica following earthquake damage.

But unlike the land, the belief in the relic's powers has never been shaken. Many Ticos travel to the Basílica to be touched by La Negrita's healing powers and worshippers leave plentiful gifts for their saint.

An annual mass pilgrimage of over a million believers – more than for any other national religious journey – to the Cartago monument takes place on 2 August, marking the Fiesta of the Virgen de los Ángeles, the day on which, nearly 400 years ago, a little girl found a little black rock in Cartago.

Irazú has erupted on several notable occasions, most famously in 1963 when US president John F Kennedy was visiting the country. As a consequence it is often called 'Colossus' in a nod to the destruction it has caused. The volcano features several craters; one is named after a former governor of Costa Rica, Diego de la Haya, and is filled with transfixing green water. A taxi from Cartago to Irazú costs around US$35.

Where to eat

Grabbing a quick *casado* in a soda around town is likely to be the best culinary option. Just out of town, four kilometres (2.5 miles) towards Paraíso, **Casa Vieja** (2591 1165, main courses US$4) serves good international food.

Where to stay

Cartago is best visited on the way to, or as a day trip from, the nearby Orosi Valley. However, if arranging accommodation here is essential, try **San Francisco Lodge** (Calle 3, 25 metres north of the Mercado Central, 2574 2359, US$18-$25 double), which has big rooms and cable TV. Another, slightly pricier option is **Los Angeles Lodge** (Avenida 4, entre Calles 14 y 16, 2551 0957, US$25-$40).

Getting there

By bus
From San José, **SACSA** (2233 5350) buses leave for Cartago every 10 mins or so from Calle 5, between Avenidas 18 and 20. To return from Cartago buses leave from Avenida 4, between Calles 8 and 10.

By road
If driving, Cartago is a 30min drive south on Highway 2. It is very well signposted and the highway practically goes through the centre.

Resources

Bank
Banco Nacional *Avenida 4, y Calle 5 (2212 2000).*

Hospital
Hospital Max Peralta *Avenida 5 (2550 1999).*

Internet
Alta Velocidad *Calle 1, entre Avenidas 1 y 3 (no phone).* **Open** 9am-9pm daily.

Orosí Valley

In the sweeping Orosí Valley is a clutch of small towns amid some of the prettiest greenery the Central Valley has to offer. Considering

The best History sites

Basílica de Nuestra Señora de los Ángeles
This magnificent Byzantine-style structure is without doubt the city of Cartago's shining glory. It is the country's most important pilgrimage destination. *See p133.*

Ujarrás Ruins
Have a picnic in the pleasant park area surrounding the ruins of one of Costa Rica's first colonial churches. *See p136.*

Monumento Nacional Guayabo
See the most comprehensive example of ancient indigenous life at the foot of Volcán Turrialba. *See p139.*

Iglesia de San José Orosi
Find the country's oldest working church in the tranquil village of Orosí. *See p135.*

the area's beauty, it is remarkably unclogged with tourists and offers satisfaction for those harbouring 'getting-away-from-it-all' urges. Explore the coffee-coated surrounds on horseback, mountain bike or, for the more adventurous, quad bike. Unwind in natural hot springs, wander through ancient ruins and marvel at world-class botanical gardens. And head south towards the Talamanca mountain range for the wild **PN Tapantí**.

The village of **Orosí**, a few kilometres south of **Paraíso**, is a quiet collection of dwellings in the heart of the valley. In Costa Rican terms, the weather here can be quite cool and misty, and when clouds are slumped over the surrounding hilltops it could almost be a remote spot in Ireland; that is until you notice the palm tree you're leaning against. This humble village has one main through-road, near the bottom of which sits Costa Rica's oldest functioning church, the **Iglesia de San José Orosí**, built in 1743.

Naturally warmed water has a tendency to pop up a lot around here and several modest hot springs can be enjoyed in and around Orosí village. If heading uphill from the park, take a right at the Hotel Reventazón sign and sample the warm natural pools of **Los Balnearios** (2533 2156, US$2) at the end of the road. In keeping with the area's understated charm, these are a world away from the springs to be found in Arenal (and a lot cheaper).

Generally thought a nicer dip than Los Balnearios, **Los Patios** (2533 3009, US$2) is

Central Valley

Easter parade in the village of **Orosí**.

located a ten-minute walk from the centre of
Orosí along the main road. Pick up details of
the trail to free springs and the nearby 'beach'
(sandy part of the river) on the Río Grande de
Orosí at **Otiac**, a tourist information centre
with postal services, tours and souvenirs. It also
offers some of the best-value Spanish classes in
the country. It is run by the same folk who run
the village's popular **Montaña Linda**
hostel (2533 3640, www.montanalinda.com).

EXCURSIONS

Four kilometres (2.5 miles) from Cartago is
a globally acclaimed botanical garden. The
expansive **Lankester Gardens** (2552 3247,
www.jardinbotanicolankester.org, US$5)
contain a vast collection of plants – mainly
orchids – set up by British naturalist Charles
Lankester in the 1950s, and later donated to
the University of Costa Rica. It is open from
8.30am to 3.30pm.

In easy reach of Paraíso is the working coffee
farm, mill and roastery of **Finca Christina**
(2574 6426, www.cafecristina.com, US$10),
which offers an educational experience (by
reservation only). It can be reached by heading
east from Paraíso to Turrialba. After passing a

white arch on the right, continue 250 metres
and turn right on the next unpaved road; the
entrance is to the left. Continuing on to Orosí,
two kilometres (1.25 miles) from Paraíso, is the
Mirador de Orosí, which has great views.

Once in Orosí village, horse riding (US$10)
and quad tours (US$50) around the valley can
be arranged through Hotel Reventazón (2533
3838, www.costaquadtours.com). A short drive
(or trot) from Orosí leads to Cachi. Take the main
road heading south-east out of the village, away
from Cartago: it curves back up and round,
through Loaiza and on to Cachi. The road
circumnavigating the valley circles the **Laho
Cachi**, created by a dam that provides much of
the Central Valley's electricity. On the way into
the town it is worth stopping off to browse the
mystical coffee-wood carvings at **La Casa del
Soñador** or 'House of the Dreamer' (2577 1186).
Continue around the lake to Ujarrás and the
ruins of the country's first colonial church,
the **Iglesia de la Limpia Concepción de
Nuestra Señora**. Dating back to 1570, the
Ujarrás ruins today are a roofless shell,
hammered by centuries of floods and
earthquakes. It is said that the Virgin had some
hand in helping residents defeat British pirates

Ujarrás church.

in 1666. (Quite how this came to pass is slightly fuzzier). It is a pretty area, teeming with birds, which makes it a nice picnic spot.

Nature-lovers, rejoice! – for the ecological park and waterfalls of **Monte Sky** (2228 0010, www.intnet.co.cr/montesky, US$8, call in advance) and the **PN Tapantí** are just a short journey from Orosi. The thickly forested terrain of PN Tapantí, or PN Orosi as it is sometimes referred to, is located 16 kilometres (ten miles) from Orosi village along the upper part of the **Río Grande de Orosi**. The park, created in 1982, is one of the wettest places in the country with up to 7,000 millimetres (280

inches) of annual rainfall. It is a renowned quetzal nesting area and home to various mammals such as the jaguar. It can be reached easily from Orosi by simply continuing through the town and staying on the road all the way to the park. The park's ranger station is open from 5am to 5pm with information on trails and swimming areas.

Where to stay

For a relaxed and comfortable stay in the heart of Orosi, try **Hotel Reventazón** (2533 3838, www.hotelreventazon.com, US$40 double). All

The impenetrable cloud forests of the **PN Volcán Turrialba**.

seven rooms have TV, refrigerator and free Wi-Fi. The restaurant downstairs serves tasty food at breakfast, lunch and dinner at reasonable prices. Guests from the hotel can also use some private hot springs in the area (US$50 for non-guests, lunch included).

The best backpacker vibe in the area is found at **Montaña Linda** (2533 3640, www.montana linda.com, US$20 double, US$7.50 dorms, US$3 camping), which has a communal kitchen, games and knowledgeable staff.

Where to eat

El Nido (2533 3793, main courses US$5), two blocks north of the football pitch, is good for a quick bite and is a popular spot for a late night drink. On the corner of the field by the main road, **Restaurant Coto** (2533 3032, main courses US$8) is a reliable place to get a decent plate of food. For veggie options head two blocks north of the church to **Tia's Garden** (2533 1454, main courses US$6).

Getting there

By bus

For the Orosí Valley take the bus in Cartago from Calle 6, between Avenidas 1 and 3. The bus leaves every half an hour or so. It takes about 30mins to Orosí and costs around US$0.50.

By car

Head out of Cartago south-east on Highway 10 to Paraíso 8km (5 miles) away. From Paraíso turn south to Orosí, or continue eastwards to Ujarrás and Cachí.

Resources

Internet

PC Orosí *one block north of Otiac (2533 3302).* **Open** 8am-7pm daily.

Police

Corner of the football pitch (2533 3082).

Turrialba

To go to Turrialba and not participate in a splash of white water rafting is like trekking to the North Pole only to snooze through the Aurora Borealis. Well, almost. Flowing from the Cordillera de Talamanca out to the Caribbean, the **Río Pacuare** is a bona fide celebrity of the rafting world, graded from beginners' Class III rapids, up to a jarring Class VI. This storming mass of H_2O offers some of the best white water on the planet, and the surrounding scenery is breathtaking. The country's other acclaimed rafting river, the **Río Reventazón**, also flows Caribbean-wards through the area, and there is

an equally rampant stream of tour companies eager to whet prospective appetites for the sport (*see pp76-77*). Tours here are not just about the water: lining both rivers is a backdrop of tropical greenery hosting an array of super-snappable wildlife.

During the day the town of Turrialba is a good little place in which to sip coffee and decide which of the thundering rafting tours takes your fancy. The main area of town branches off from the **Parque Central** at Calle 1 and Avenida 4. Walking around at night, the vibe can get a little edgy, especially along the strip by the Hotel Interamericana, so if travelling alone it's best to avoid night strolls.

EXCURSIONS

Lying 19 kilometres (12 miles) north of the town is **PN Volcán Turrialba**, which has been in existence since 1955 and, though small, features three craters, cloud forest and rainforest and a good selection of wildlife. The volcano is classified as active, though the last significant eruptions were back in the 1860s. Near the volcano is the **Monumento Nacional Guayabo**, the country's best remaining example of the indigenous lifestyle.

In general, scant evidence remains of Costa Rica's pre-colonial happenings, in part owing to the destructive nature of earthquakes and volcanic explosions and in part because the conquering Spanish were a similarly unhelpful force when it came to preserving the dwellings of their predecessors. Thus the relatively comprehensive indigenous remains found north-east of Turrialba on the southern slopes of its eponymous volcano are rather special.

Nestled in Costa Rica's trademark dense forest, the findings at **Guayabo** (2559 0099, US$10) show a settlement dating back as early as 1000 BC. Thorough excavations began in 1968 (by archaeologist Carlos Aguilar Piedra), and the site was awarded national monument status five years later. Even though excavation of the full area is far from complete, many cobbled paths, an aqueduct system and the remains of conical shaped buildings have been unearthed, along with pieces of pottery and gold artefacts that can be seen at the **Museo Nacional** in San José (*see p86*).

The main points of interest at Guayabo are the detailed petroglyphs (images in rock made by much chipping and scraping). Some are clearly of animals, but the meaning of others remains unknown. Some experts believe that Guayabo was abandoned before the Spanish arrived, but the reason for the population's demise is still unclear. The site, open between 8am and 3.30pm, is maintained by a handful of local residents living near the entrance.

Central Valley

White-knuckle rides with **Pacuare River Tours**.

Information is available at the ranger station and local experts also provide guided tours and ask for a donation at the end of the tour. There is also a picnic area, and camping can be arranged. Some 500 metres south of the site is the **Guayabo Butterfly Garden** (2559 0162, US$2), open between 8am and 4pm.

Loco's Tropical Tours (2556 6035, www.whiteh2o.com) runs rafting tours for US$65 per person if booked through its website. A popular operator is **Costa Rica Nature Adventures** (2225 3939, www.costaricanatureadventures.com), which runs one-, two- and three-day packages, incorporating stays at the lovely **Pacuare Lodge**.

Other recommended companies in the area are **Costa Rica Ríos** (2556 9617, www.costaricarios.com), **Exploradores Outdoors** (2222 6262, www.exploradoresoutdoors.com, US$95) and **Pacuare River Tours** (2291 6844, www.pacuarerivertours.com, US$95), all of which splosh down Pacuare every day.

Just three kilometres (two miles) from Turrialba, along the highway to the Atlantic coast, is **CATIE** (2558 2000, www.catie.ac.cr), one of the world's premier tropical research centres. This Tropical Agricultural Research and Higher Education Centre features a botanical garden with a sumptuous array of tropical fruits. It is open from 7am to 3pm.

For a relaxing coffee tour try the **Golden Bean Coffee Tour** (2531 2008, www.goldenbean.net, US$19) in Atirro, which is located after a turn-off on the route to La Suiza from Turrialba. Coffee aficionados are taken through the centre's own finca to see how the bean is processed. Then they get to try a cup of the finest brew. To experience traditional rural customs, visit **Tayutic Hacienda Experience** (no phone, www.haciendatayutic.com, US$311-$390) in Sitio Mata. This small luxury hotel with well-appointed rooms is designed to harmonise with the surroundings. It also has an open massage room with incredible views across the valley. For US$120 a day, spa treatments including massage, a 'cleansing' lunch and the opportunity to relax in the forest surroundings can be enjoyed. It also offers modern Tico food in its restaurant.

Where to eat & drink

The restaurant at **Turrialtico Lodge** (2538 1111, main courses US$6) is a very popular spot for lunch and dinner and offers an excellent selection of typical food. A ten-minute taxi ride from Turrialba downtown, **Don Porfi's** (2556 9797, main courses US$10) cosy Italian/international restaurant is one of the best in the area and worth the cab fare.

Where to stay

An immaculate palm-lined road leading to pristine grounds backed by the glassy sheen of Lago Angostura is a fittingly idyllic introduction to **Casa Turire** (2531 1111, www.hotelcasaturire.com, US$120-$135 double). Located eight kilometres (five miles) from downtown Turialba this four-star hotel is a sanctuary for those seeking stress-free days.

The colonial-style mansion has 12 rooms and four suites. The hotel's pièce de résistance, however, is the luxurious Master Suite, with two floors, a spacious balcony accommodating up to 15 people and a personal jacuzzi. A first-class restaurant looks over the pool area. During the day, ambient tunes spill out from the restaurant across the sun loungers and shaded seating areas surrounding the pool.

A minute's walk takes guests to the hotel's farm where kids can pet goats, chickens, horses, a rather grumpy goose and a water buffalo (OK, don't pet everything). Fresh produce for the restaurant is grown on a plot just next to the farm as part of the hotel's push towards sustainable tourism. If guests can tear themselves away from their loungers, there are horse rides around the valley and guests can hire mountain bikes, kayaks and canoes.

Turrialtico Lodge (2538 1111, www.turrialtico.com, US$58-$62 double) offers a mountain refuge with stunning views.

Budget-seekers simply after a bed and a hot shower following a hard day's rafting should try **Hotel Interamericana** (2556 0142, US$20 double, shared bathroom; US$35 double, private bathroom). Head to **Volcán Turrialba Lodge** (2273 4335, www.volcanturrialbalodge.com, US$50-$70 double) for easy access to the namesake volcano.

Getting there

By bus

From San José, take the hourly **TRANSTUSA** (222 4464) bus between 8am to 8pm from Calle 13, between Calles 6 and 8. Returning, head to the new terminal on Highway 10 for hourly buses to San José. The journey takes 2hrs.

Resources

Bank

Banco Popular *head right from the park on to Avenida 4 (2556 6098).*

Internet

Dimension Internet *eastern corner of Parque Central (2556 1586).* **Open** 9am-9pm daily.

Central Valley

Central Valley North

The firework display from Volcán Arenal is just one of the region's highlights.

The north of the Central Valley stars some of the Costa Rican tourist industry's biggest players. The conservation efforts and enchanting greenery of Monteverde's cloud forest are renowned worldwide; and braving difficult access, many clamber up the Tilarán mountain range to the Quaker settlements of Monteverde, Santa Elena town and their namesake reserves. This pocket of mountain wilderness was the birthplace of the canopy tour, and today streams of visitors whizz through the treetops, suspended on cables high in the forest canopy among the birds and bugs.

Then there is the vast Lago Arenal. As well as being a key element of a national hydroelectric project, this artificially enlarged expanse of water has great fishing and water sports facilities and enhances an already beautiful landscape. Smoking high above the lake and the nearby town of **La Fortuna** is the mighty **Volcán Arenal**; on a clear night its orange and red lava spurtings are a sight to impress the most jaded observer – unquestionably, one of the best spectacles in a very spectacular country.

Monteverde & around

Just getting to Monteverde and Santa Elena is an experience. The winding and oh-so-undulating 35-kilometre (22-mile) climb resembles baked riverbed more than road, and even in a four-wheel-drive vehicle it's one heck of a bumpy ride. Heading higher and higher the views quickly become commanding, and it's clear you are entering a community quite isolated from the rest of Costa Rica. The area's remoteness was the key attraction for North American Quaker settlers in the 1950s, who came in search of peaceful refuge in response to US involvement in the Korean War. The cool Monteverde climate proved highly conducive to dairy farming, and the Quaker-founded **Monteverde Cheese Factory** still provides much of the country's cheese and ice-cream. The Quakers have played a substantial part in the protection of the area's eponymous slice of cloud forest, having had the foresight to buy up land and donate substantial sums towards its management. Those interested in the Monteverde Quakers are welcome to drop

An eyelash viper crawls through the cloud forest in search of frogs and birds to eat.

Central Valley North

in at the **Friends Meeting House** up near the Reserva Biológica Bosque Nuboso de Monteverde.

One eight-kilometre (five-mile) road, with a good smattering of hotels, restaurants and art galleries along the way, connects the small Monteverde community and the **Reserva Biológica Bosque Nuboso de Monteverde** with Santa Elena. The latter town offers a central triangle of everything required to restock and replenish: internet cafés, a pharmacy, restaurants, a good sized supermarket and a police station. As with much of the country, development is under way, and at the time of going to press several square kilometres of forest are being cleared to make way for a new shopping mall. Yet despite the investment, Santa Elena has managed to maintain the arty, backpacker vibe that made its name, and which has persisted even after the tragedy of March 2005 when a group of armed thieves stormed the Banco Nacional, killing nine people.

EXCURSIONS

The **Reserva Biológica Bosque Nuboso de Monteverde** (2645 5122, www.monteverde info.com, US$15) – 115 square kilometres (44 square miles) of high-altitude greenery, frequently engulfed in hanging clouds – was set up by American biologists in 1972 with the support of the Tropical Science Centre. The perpetual high humidity levels and mild temperatures act as the perfect plant-life incubator, producing layer upon layer of vegetation. With no extreme weather conditions to combat, many plants here have plentiful reserves of energy to produce toxins, protecting themselves against hungry bugs. Roam through the forest and watch insects hopping from plant to plant, nibbling tiny amounts of each one so as not to ingest too much of any one poison.

Three-wattled bellbirds, bare-necked umbrellabirds, resplendent quetzals, red-headed barbets and over half of the country's 45 resident hummingbird species also make their home in the cloud forests of the Caribbean and Pacific slopes. More than 400 bird species have been recorded here. The best time to see the altitudinal migrants such as the resplendent quetzal and the three-wattled bellbird is from March to June when they return to the cloud forest to breed. Other species that may be encountered include: highland tinamous, black guans, emerald toucanets, tiny hawks, spangle-cheeked tanagers, golden-browed chlorophonias and orange-collared trogons. The coppery-headed emerald, another of Costa Rica's endemic species, is also present in Monteverde. Beware: it gets busy.

If you're 'doing' the reserve without a guide, the unchallenging two-kilometre (1.25 mile) Sendero Bosque Nuboso is a pleasant trail. There are other trails cutting across the reserve, such as Sendero Chomogo and Sendero Wilford Guindon, which involve far more legwork.

Cohabiting in the reserve are 400 species of bird, 2,500 forms of plant life and several mammals including five species of cat. But don't expect scenes reminiscent of *The Jungle Book*. The wildlife is generally shy and the foliage thick; typical sightings are of birds fluttering amid the canopies, and small rodents. Taking a guide increases the chances of wildlife spotting and they are also extremely knowledgeable about the diverse plant life. Guided tours are an extra US$15 and reservations need to be made in advance. For those happy to wander alone amid the thick green canopies, with just the mountain breeze and chiming bird calls for company, it can feel like you are the last person on earth.

Monteverde is, however, a good place for spotting the tremendously timid quetzal, and there is normally one flitting about the entrance (being trailed by a swarm of photographers) just before the reserve opens each morning at around 6.30am. The male bird is the more striking of the bright green pair, sporting an impressive trailing tail. A large souvenir shop and adjoining café sit by the entrance.

Located six kilometres (3.5 miles) north-east of downtown Santa Elena, the **Reserva Santa Elena** (2645 5390) may be smaller and less well known than its world-famous contemporary up the road, but many people deem this steeper and higher altitude reserve to be even prettier than Monteverde. It is self-funded and functions with much help from students – both volunteers from abroad, and from the local high school whose boards run the reserve. All proceeds are ploughed back into the forest's conservation programmes. Established in 1992, this attractive chunk of tropical jungle has several trails, and on a clear day Volcán Arenal can be seen from the high observation point. There is a visitor centre (from which waterproof boots can be hired) and a cafeteria open from 7am to 4pm.

A third precious patch of forest is the **Bosque Eterno de Los Niños** or Children's Eternal Rainforest (2645 5003, www.acmcr.org), created through funds raised by schoolchildren around the world. The 220-square-kilometre (85-square-mile) site incorporates primary and secondary zones of evergreen forest, cloud forest and rainforest. The night walk comes highly recommended and is probably the best bet for seeing wildlife. For more information go to the administrative office near the Jardin de Mariposas, or visit the website.

Path to the clouds in the **Reserva Biológica Bosque Nuboso de Monteverde**.

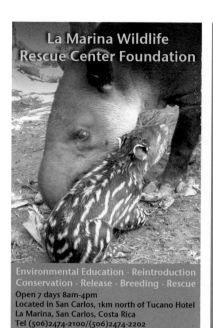

Tours de force

Monteverde tour operators are as plentiful as trees, and while hotel staff are eager to assist in arranging excursions, it's worth remembering that nine times out of ten they will recommend the operator who gives them the best commission. With everything the region has to offer, it's hard to find a truly bad tour in Monteverde, but since you've come this far you might as well employ the services of one of the park's top outfits.

While it's the light of early morning that shows the forest at its most striking, it is as twilight creeps in that you'll have the best chance of seeing many of the forest's inhabitants. Tarantulas, insects, bats, frogs and smaller mammals such as raccoons are regular sightings during night tours – and no, this one probably isn't an enjoyable choice for bug-phobes. There are many night tours to choose from; all of them essentially offer a similar experience. **Bajo del Tigre** (2645 5923, www.acmcr.org, US$20) is part of the Children's Eternal Rainforest, and its night walk comes highly recommended. Bajo del Tigre is a not-for-profit organisation with the money going directly back into preserving the forest.

The ultimate rainforest experiences for those with a penchant for adrenaline are the canopy tours. The Costa Rican-owned **Selvatura Canopy Tour** (2645 5929, www.selvatura.com, US$40) has been running for 15 years. Scream, slide and soar through the treetops on 15 cables, 18 platforms and a Tarzan swing, all in primary forest. **Selvatura's Treetop Walkways** (US$20) are also another way to get right up into the canopies for those wanting a less adrenaline-fuelled experience. The selection of hanging bridges leads visitors through a three-kilometre (two-mile) trail at altitudes ranging from ten metres (36 feet) to 55 metres (180 feet). Another one for the rush seekers is the **Familia Brenestours Canyoning Tour** (2645 5581, www.familia brenestours.com, US$60), which takes folks rappelling down six contrasting waterfalls.

For kids, a great hands-on tour is at **El Trapiche** coffee and sugar finca (2645 5834, www.eltrapichetour.com, US$25, US$10 children). See the coffee and sugar mill processes, take an ox cart ride around the family-run property, and try some freshly made sugary products.

Unless you stay in one of the quite pricey complexes right next to Monteverde, getting to the park requires a steep hike of several kilometres. The easiest and cheapest way to access the reserves is by bus that departs from the centre of Santa Elena at 6.30am, 8.30am, 10.30am, 12.30pm and 3pm. The times for Monteverde are 6.15am, 7.30am, 9.20am, 11.30am, 1.20pm and 3pm. The fare is US$2 for a return trip. Times are posted up in the windows of most tour operators' offices in Santa Elena, so it is worth checking there for any changes. The buses can be waved down on the route, and many drivers will offer walkers a ride. A taxi shouldn't cost more than US$9, but check with the driver before getting in one.

As well as daytime horse rides round the area, **Caballeriza El Rodeo** (2645 5764, US$25-$45) runs beautiful sunset rides from 4pm. The office is located 300 metres south-west of Santa Elena centre and is open from 8.30am to 4.30pm. It's a sturdy and long hike – or a US$10 taxi ride – from Santa Elena to the **Catarata San Luis**; however, once there, the 100-metre-tall (330-foot) waterfall is wonderful, as are the trails that lead up to and around the area. The entrance fee is US$7.

For a close-up look at Costa Rica's amphibious world, check out the **Ranario**, the frog pond of Monteverde (2645 6320, www.ranario.com, US$9), open from 9am to 8.30pm. This indoor exhibition of more than 28 species of frog and toad includes the famous red-eyed tree frog. More cold-blooded life can be seen at the **Serpentario** (2645 5238, US$8), open from 8.30am to 8pm, on the steep slope coming into Santa Elena from the Monteverde road. If you fancy a flutter, check out the **Monteverde Butterfly Garden** (2645 5512, www.monteverdebutterflygarden.com, US$9), open from 9.30am to 4pm. It's a 20-minute walk from Santa Elena, near the Ecological Sanctuary. Head towards Monteverde and take a right at the school and the turn-off for the garden will come up on the left side of this road.

The **Jardín de Orquídeas** (2645 5308, www.monteverdeorchidgarden.com, US$7), just off the Santa Elena triangle, has an impressive collection of more than 425 orchids. Up in Monteverde, the **Paseo de Stella** (2645 6566, http://paseodestella.googlepages.com) is a visitor centre, open from 9.30am to 8.30pm, featuring a 'bat jungle' with a reversed day or night cycle, a museum showing how the

The best Viewpoints

Arenal Observatory Lodge

As the daylight fades, watch the sparkling Arenal lava flow from its peak, from the safety of the hotel's broad viewing platform, drink in hand. A stay in a room offers floor-to-ceiling windows directly overlooking the volcano. *See p155.*

Tabacón Springs

Spend an evening soaking in a tub heated by the volcano's thermal energy, while gazing at the scenery. *See p156.*

Lake Arenal

Take the jeep-boat-jeep ride from Monteverde across Lago Arenal and see Volcán Arenal's mighty form loom over the lake. *See p151.*

Parque Nacional Volcán Arenal

Hike through the lava-strewn fields of the Parque Nacional. Guides will explain words like 'andesitic stratovolcano' – which is exactly what Arenal is, in case you didn't know. *See p153.*

Canopy Tour

See the peak through the treetops with the **Sky Trek Canopy** tour (www.skytrek.com), or speed through the trees on a zip-line.

community has changed over past years, an art gallery and the Caburé Argentine Café, all located in front of the Hotel El Bosque. The nearby **Monteverde Cheese Factory** (cheesefactory@monteverdeinfo.com, US$8) is a significant part of the area's history and has been open since 1953, just two years after the Quakers first settled in the area.

Where to eat

A relatively new addition to the area is the El Establo Hotel (2645 5110, www.elestablo.com, main courses US$20), whose new restaurant, **Laggus**, is open to the public. Though pricey, the food is exquisite, and customers are more than welcome to sit on the terrace and have a cocktail and appetiser while watching the sun sink over the Gulfo de Nicoya. The easiest way to get to the restaurant is from the hotel reception, on the road to Monteverde opposite from Chimera, where a free shuttle bus takes customers up to the restaurant. Taxis can be called ahead to take diners back to their hotel.

Opposite El Establo on the right-hand side of the road towards Monteverde is **Chimera** (2645 6081, main courses US$6), a popular and lively little tapas restaurant. Its fresh selection of dishes is reasonably priced with a couple of interesting concoctions including a dish incorporating chocolate with chicken. (Hmmm.) The menu has some tasty vegetarian options, and for those who like their seafood, the prawn lollipops come highly recommended. A hundred or so metres towards Santa Elena is Mediterranean-influenced **Moon Shiva** (2645 6270), a funky café-restaurant popular with the younger crowd. Situated above a well-stocked bookshop on the way into Santa Elena, **Chunches** (2645 5147) offers a selection of cakes, breakfast dishes and fresh sandwiches. It is a friendly relaxed spot for a reviving coffee, fruit smoothie or snack. Word of advice: try the chocolate brownies. Laptop users can tap into the café's wireless internet free of charge. In the heart of Santa Elena, **Morpho's** (2645 5607) serves pricey yet top of the range local cuisine.

Where to stay

A top backpacker favourite is **Pensión Santa Elena** (2645 5051, www.pensionsantaelena. com, US$6 dorm, US$14 double). It has the bare essentials of hostel living, but the vibe is friendly and welcoming. There's a good sized communal kitchen and a hammock out front for the lazy traveller. On the outskirts of downtown Santa Elena, **Hotel Finca Valverde** (2645 5157, www.monteverde.co.cr, US$65-$70 double) offers basic cabin-style lodging. The on-site restaurant needs to move on from the 1970s but it does have free Wi-Fi and a well-stocked bar.

About ten minutes' walk up (and we mean 'up') the road from Santa Elena to Monteverde is **Manakin Lodge** (2645 5080, www.manakin lodge.com). The rear end of the building is nestled in rainforest and the regular appearance of birds, small animals and the mischievous local monkeys can be seen from the communal living room. A lovely Tico family runs this B&B, and the breakfast spread is somewhat predictably abundant.

Have your wilderness with a good dose of luxury at slick mountainside establishment **El Establo** (2565 1605, www.elestablo.com, US$188 double); *photo p151*. Charmingly furnished rooms, expansive grounds, a spa and well-regarded restaurant await. For those wanting to stay right up near the Monteverde reserve, try the upmarket **Monteverde Lodge** (www.costaricaexpeditions.com, US$128 double), which can also provide guides.

Volcán Arenal's nightly
firework display.

Where there's smoke...

The smooth swirl of smoke rising from the mouth of Volcán Arenal reminds all living in its shadow of its constant activity, with rock and lava making regular sorties down the volcano's steep side. Costa Rica's youngest volcano ranks as one of the most active on the planet, and its explosive nature is the area's main tourist magnet.

To what extent its antics are visible to spectators, however, is dependent on the weather, and clouds can quickly and effortlessly veil the best part of the volcano from view. The only course of action is to embark on much finger crossing and hope for clear skies.

Any attempts to get a closer glimpse from areas other than those points marked on trails and at viewpoints is, almost needless to say, highly, highly dangerous – as made all too tragically clear in 1988 when a reckless young North American male lost his life to Arenal's fiery outbursts while trying to climb the volcano. And this was far from the first life taken by the volcanic giant.

After 400 years of slumber, Arenal woke up in a very bad mood in 1968, killing almost 100 people and flattening the nearby villages of Tabacón, Pueblo Nuevo and San Luis over several turbulent days.

With cruel irony this deadly awakening single-handedly put La Fortuna on the tourist map, drawing flocks of eager spectators from across the globe. While constantly monitored and perfectly safe from a distance, Arenal is a force of nature and is therefore never wholly predictable. But bear in mind that there is, on average, an eruption every five to ten minutes; whether it will be a little spurt or a raging inferno is anyone's guess.

As recently as 2000 an unexpected eruption of gases and ash took the lives of a tour guide and one of his charges. That same month a Sansa Airlines plane crashed into the side of Arenal, killing all ten on board. The plane, it was said, had deviated more than 20 kilometres (12 miles) off its prescribed course, and was thought to have been trying to get a closer view of the erupting volcano. Unbelievably, a second aircraft met a similar fate two months later, seemingly for the exact same reason. So if logic doesn't suffice, history shows that Arenal's magnificence should be appreciated from a safe distance. And as well as the typical volcano hikes there are several places, such as the **Arenal Observatory Lodge** (*see p155*) and **Tabacón Grand Spa Thermal Resort** (*see p156*), where this can happily be done, cold drink in hand.

The sun sets on another day at **El Establo**. *See p148.*

Resources

Bank

Banco Nacional *next to Pensión Santa Elena* *(2212 2000)*.

Hospital

Red Cross *just north of Santa Helena* *(2645 6128)*. Offers good first aid and can help with most problems.

Police

In the Santa Elena central 'Triangle' (2645 5127).

Getting there

By bus

From San José buses leave at 6.30am and 2.30pm daily from Calle 14, between Avenidas 11 and 9, and arrive 4 hrs later in Santa Elena before heading down to Monteverde. From Puntarenas buses leave at 1pm (via Las Juntas) and 2pm (direct) from outside the Banco Nacional. It takes around 3 hrs.
Private shuttle **Interbus** (2645 7007, www.interbus online.com) can be taken from your hotel in San José for US$35, or from other locations in Costa Rica.

By road

The roads up to Monteverde and Santa Elena are bad and only the sturdiest four-wheel drive will do. From the Interamericana the best way is to turn off by the Río Lagarto crossing. For Arenal take the jeep-boat-jeep – a bumpy drive down the mountain to Lago Arenal, a 30min boat ride over, then a jeep-ride the other side to your hotel (www.arenal.net, US$25).

Arenal & La Fortuna

For a country the size of a smallish US state, Costa Rica offers an overwhelmingly impressive wealth of sights and activities. A packed two-week holiday merely scratches the mountainous, fruit-sprouting, lava-spewing surface. So if time is short, and you need a multi-faceted destination offering minimal travel and maximum experiences, Arenal should definitely make the shortlist. Those gagging for an activity-fest have windsurfing, fishing, kayaking, volcano and rainforest hikes, canopy tours, horseriding, quad biking and bungee jumping to work their way through, all in the immediate area. For the more relaxed tropical chill-out, try an indulgent hot spring resort and head to the **Arenal Observatory Lodge** (*see p155*) for an evening drink, and hopefully get a glimpse of Volcán Arenal's nightly show.

The area's main urban centre is the busy tourist focused town of La Fortuna. Considering the scores of tour operators prowling the streets, La Fortuna is surprisingly pleasant and, of course, the surroundings include a looming volcano. Scattered around the Parque Central are several nice bars and eateries, and the park itself has an attractive seating area.

For a spot of relic browsing head 900 metres west of the park to **Museo y Antigüedades Los Abuelos Antique** (2479 7306, www. museolosabuelos.com, US$8), which displays

Toad safety

That a species could become extinct beneath Monteverde's copious canopies is difficult to imagine. The fresh mountain breezes, deep tangled jungle and moisture-rich air seem the perfect recipe for life. Yet a once common resident of the high-altitude cloud forest has made a worryingly rapid departure. The golden toad was discovered in 1966 and, though no more than four centimetres in size, the gleaming orange of the male made it something of a local celebrity.

However, in the 1980s glimpses of the tiny and distinctive amphibian diminished significantly, and the last sighting was in 1989. After much hoping, searching and waiting, it was officially registered as extinct in 2004. The case of the Monteverde golden toad is part of a global plummet in amphibian numbers that has greatly alarmed scientists across the world; more than 150 species are thought to have become extinct since the 1980s and many more are in decline.

The major worldwide factor of destruction of habitat cannot be applied to Monteverde, where every inch of flora is lovingly preserved. The main theory here centres on the super permeability of amphibious skin being acutely sensitive to increasing toxins in the atmosphere, minute climate changes and any increase in UV rays.

Thus, while the cause of the brightly skinned amphibian's demise remains unproven, its sudden absence from Monteverde's misty cloud forest is viewed by many as a chilling indication that global warming is starting to have its long-predicted poisonous effect.

---

a collection of international coins, bank notes and tools from down the ages.

It's a different vibe entirely five blocks east of the park at **Arenal Bungee** (2479 7440, www.arenalbungee.com, US$39). There are a selection of other activities to be sampled too including the 'Rocket Launcher' and the 'Big Swing'. It's open from 9.30am to 9.30pm. About 30 kilometres (19 miles) north-west of La Fortuna is the small lakeside town of Nuevo Arenal. The original Arenal was sacrificed with the expansion of the lake and a new town built at a higher altitude. While Nuevo Arenal is not as bustling as La Fortuna, it is a very picturesque spot with a couple of great restaurants with views. Swing by **Tom's Pan German Bakery** (2694 4547) for delicious cakes, cheeses and sausages. *Photo p158*.

Like a master of ceremonies overlooking proceedings, the conical figure of **Volcán Arenal** is never far away. As well as its defined shape, Arenal's continual splutterings put it up there with the world's top ten most active volcanoes. The peak is often shrouded in cloud, which can be frustrating for eager firework spotters, but if you are fortunate enough to get clear skies, Arenal is very impressive indeed. Just remember to appreciate it from a safe distance (*see p150* **Where there's smoke**…). The volcano is the centre piece of **PN Volcán Arenal** (ranger station 2461 8499) and the surrounding parkland offers the intrepid trekker great trails through the young forests that emerge in a lava-strewn landscape. The entrance is 14 kilometres (nine miles) from La Fortuna and a taxi costs US$20 each way. Taking a tour usually offers the best value. Many operators incorporate a volcano hike with a visit to the hot springs at **Tabacon Grand Spa Themal Resort** (*see p156*).

The glittering 33-kilometre long (20-mile) Lago Arenal completes the stunning scenery and is an attraction in itself. The original lake was enlarged in 1979 for the construction of a dam as part of a hydroelectric project, and today it is a popular spot for catching rainbow bass among many other river fish (*see pp68-70*). It is also considered one of the top windsurfing spots on the globe. **Tico Wind** (2695 5387, www.ticowind.com) offers individual lessons starting at US$50 and also has boards and sails that can be rented.

EXCURSIONS

A popular hike is to **Cataratas de La Fortuna** (US$8), five kilometres (three miles) out of the town they are named after. It is quite a steep walk but the resulting waterfalls are worth the effort. *Photo p154.* To see the area on horseback try **Rancho Arenal Paraíso** (2460 5333, www.arenalparaiso.com) or for petrol heads there's **Off Road Arenal** (2479 9769, www.offroadarenal.com), which runs quad bike tours. Looking for something with even more oomph? See the rainforest from great heights with **Sky Trek** tours (2479 9944, www. arenalreserve.com) at the private **Arenal Rainforest Reserve**, or try a spot of canyoning with **Pure Trek Costa Rica** (2479 1313, www.puretrekcostarica.com, US$90). A further 30 kilometres (19 miles) north-west of La Fortuna are the ancient Venado Caves, with their stalactites, stalagmites and corals. **Bobo Adventures** runs an informative tour (2479 9058, www.geocities.com/boboadventures).

Many use La Fortuna as a base from which to visit the wet and wonderful **Caño Negro** (*see p157*). To appreciate these wetlands a boat trip is necessary. The zone is home to an impressive range of wildlife including jaguars, tapirs, ocelots and several species of monkey, and is considered one of the best places to see birds in the country. This is a beautiful trip and good tour operators include **Canoa Aventura's Real Caño Negro Tour** (2479 8200, www.canoa-aventura.com, US$40-50) and **Mapache Tours** (2479 8333, www.mapache tours.com, US$50). The trips take all day and food is included.

Around two kilometres (1.25 miles) south of La Fortuna town is the ecological centre of **Ecocentro Danaus** (2479 7019, www.eco centrodanaus.com). Stroll through pretty forests and gardens and see many species of butterflyas well as Sloths and caimans. The exhibition of medicinal plants is fascinating. There's also an art gallery and a café.

Overshadowed by Volcán Arenal is the church of **La Fortuna**.

Cataratas de La Fortuna. *See p153.*

Where to eat & drink

Las Brasitas

Parque Central (2479 9819/www.lasbrasitas.com).
Open 11am-10pm Mon-Thur; 6am-11pm Fri-Sun.
Main courses US$15. **Credit** AmEx, DC, MC, V.
Fill up with a fistful of tasty Mexican food at this cheerful restaurant. This top spot for families is clean and friendly. Yes, they may serve a burrito with french fries, but it's a darn good burrito.

La Choza de Laurel

400m east of Catholic Temple (2479 7069/www.lachozadelaurel.com). **Open** 6.30am-10pm daily.
Main courses US$15. **Credit** AmEx, MC, V.
Part of a chain of popular restaurants serving Costa Rican fare and some of the most interesting dishes from neighbouring countries. It has an extensive menu and there will be something cheap and good for most palates. It is also a fantastic place for breakfast with a bewildering selection of *gallos pintos*. There are also branches in Liberia and Guanacaste.

Don Rufino

Opposite petrol station in La Fortuna (2479 9997/www.donrufino.com). **Open** 11am-10.30pm daily. **Main courses** US$16. **Credit** AmEx, DC, MC, V.
This lively international eaterie found in the heart of La Fortuna is run by a family team. The friendly relaxed restaurant is a good bet for a reasonable feed. Customers can either sit in the restaurant section or up at the sweeping cocktail bar while watching staff whip up a fine selection of cocktails. Portions here are typically generous and the avocado-topped ceviche is an ideal starter for two. Complement your meal from the extensive wine list.

Gingerbread

1km east of Gimnasio, Nuevo Arenal (2694 0039).
Open 5pm-9pm Tue-Sat. **Main courses** US$15.
No credit cards.
A perfect spot for innovative cuisine, situated on the edge of Lago Arenal. Freshness here is the key and the ever changing menu has been known to include fresh tuna, mahi-mahi, red snapper, sea bass and jumbo prawns. Everything here is cooked freshly, including the deliciously indulgent home-made desserts. Enjoy the food in private booths or in the open air patio seating. It is also a nice place to stop for a drink. Lunch can be arranged for parties of four or more by reservation. The management has also opened up a small three-room hotel on the premises, each room decorated by a local artist.

Rainforest Coffee House

On the road running left at the bottom of the Parque Central (2479 7239). **Open** 7am-8pm daily. **No credit cards.**
Sugar addicts will adore the selection of milk and ice-cream shakes in this pleasant modern café. It also serves up some small snacks and good pastries, alongside fine coffee, of course.

Soda La Parada

Left of the Parque Central (2479 9547).
Main courses US$3. **Credit** MC, V.
For that spontaneous snack, this place serves the best *casados* in La Fortuna, 24 hours a day. Simple and tasty combinations of beans and rice.

Where to stay

Arenal Country Inn

12mins from La Fortuna on San Ramón road (2479 9669/www.arenalcountryinn.com). **Rates** US$70-$100 double. **Rooms** 20. **Credit** AmEx, DC, MC, V.
The large garden of this peaceful complex has green space aplenty for strolling, sunbathing or gazing at Volcán Arenal. The on-site café is open for food until 10.30pm, and breakfast, included in the room rates, is taken in a separate shaded section near the pool and games area. The resort's air-conditioned rooms are set out as bungalows, each with two double beds, orthopaedic mattresses, private bathroom, safe box and minibar.
Pool (outdoor). Restaurant. TV (cable).

Arenal Observatory Lodge

Lago Arenal, 9km from National Park turn off (2692 2070/www.arenalobservatorylodge.com).
Rates US$70-$140 double. **Rooms** 43. **Credit** AmEx, MC, V.
Without doubt this establishment offers the area's most magnificent volcano views. The grounds of the Arenal Observatory Lodge are situated within PN Volcán Arenal, less than 3km from the mountain. There is a large wooden decking area from which to observe the volcano, and which offers views over Lago Arenal. You can also lava-gaze from the on-site restaurant; however, the food here, considering the quality of the hotel and grounds, should be better. The service is reasonable.
Bar. Disabled-adapted rooms. Pool (outdoor). Restaurant.

Arenal Volcano Inn

6.5km north of La Fortuna church (2461 2021/www.arenalvolcanoinn.com). **Rates** US$95 double. **Rooms** 15. **Credit** AmEx MC V.
This friendly, well-kept resort is a complex of neat bungalows complete with minibars and queen-sized beds. The Garden Spa is on hand for an array of massages and treatments. The on-site restaurant, Que Rica Aquí en Arenal, serves fun, colourful dishes and cocktails. The only small downside to this establishment is that its close proximity to a main road detracts from a feeling of total remoteness, but the views are wonderful and the staff attentive, welcoming and professional.
Bar. Internet (high-speed, wireless). Pool (outdoor). Restaurant. Spa. TV.

Hotel Dorothy

200m south of the church (2479 8068/ www.hoteldorothy.com). **Rates** US$10 per person. **Rooms** 19. **No credit cards.**

The quest for the quetzal

The resplendent quetzal is considered to be the most beautiful bird in the Americas. And it is this beauty that has impacted on society and culture in Central America for centuries and that may have been the inspiration for the legendary phoenix. The Maya of southern Mexico and northern Central America revered the bird as sacred, collecting the male's tail feathers for use in headdresses. Killing the bird, however, was a grave offence. In Guatemala, the significance of the resplendent quetzal extends to the present day. In addition to being the national bird, the quetzal also lends its name to Guatemala's currency.

The biggest impact of the quetzal on Costa Rica, however, has been to stimulate tourism. Researchers' documentation of the sizable quetzal populations around the Monteverde area in the late 1970s and early 1980s triggered the birth of eco-tourism there, and the effect spread throughout the country. And today, the moment when a visitor sees the quetzal 'swimming' through the air will be remembered long after the sunsets fade in the memory.

The male measures 30 centimetres (18 inches) in length but has a 75-centimetre (30-inch) double tail covered with iridescent plumage that sparkles emerald green and turquoise blue. The rest of the bird is equally impressive – the male quetzal sports a greenish-gold Beckham-style mohawk and a brilliant crimson breast. Males, and their attractive, but less stunning female counterparts, swoop through the cloud forest in search of the wild avocado (*aguacatillo*) fruits that serve as their principal food. They nest from March to June in holes in dead trees, taking turns to care for the eggs and later the hatched chicks.

This is a real budget spot south of town. The staff can be quite pushy when selling the tours but at the same time do offer them at good prices.
Internet (shared terminal), Parking. Restaurant

La Mansion Inn

45-min drive west from La Fortuna towards Nuevo Arenal, (2692 8018/www.lamansionarenal. com). **Rates** US$225-$275 double; US$550-$1,750 cottage. **Rooms** 17. **Credit** AmEx, DC, MC, V.
Lake views and lovely private cottages make this small resort a perfect spot for ultimate relaxation. The on-site gourmet restaurant is highly recommendable, serving up a good range of regional and European dishes.
Pools (2, outdoor). Restaurant.

Tabacon Grand Spa Thermal Resort

100m from the Tabacón hot springs (2519 1999/www.tabacon.com). **Rates** US$230-$415. **Rooms** 114. **Credit** AmEx, MC, V.

There can be few experiences evoking a greater sense of indulgent escapism than lying back in naturally heated water and watching rising steam melt slowly into the sunset. Add to that scores of tropical plantlife, garden-fresh cuisine, a superb restaurant and views of a looming lava-spewing volcano, and you'll have some clue as to the appeal of Arenal's five-star hotspot.

Guests staying at the Tabacón Hotel get free reign of the hot springs, otherwise a pass costing US$60 gives a day's unlimited use. The price is also US$60 for an evening soak and impressive buffet at the Ave del Paraíso Restaurant, or simply go all out with an all-day pass including lunch and dinner, priced at US$80. The on-site Grand Spa offers an array of ritzy treatments including volcanic stone massage, mud body wraps and hydrotherapy.
Bar. Disabled-adapted rooms. Internet (US$5 per hr/US$10 per day). Pool (outdoor). Restaurant. Room Service. Spa. TV (cable).

Resources

Bank
Banco de Costa Rica *opposite the church to the left (2284 6600).*

Internet
End of the strip lining the park. 12 flat-screen computers costing US$1 for an hour. Headsets for Skype calls and printing facilities available. **Open** 9am-9pm Mon-Sat.

Getting there

By air
Both **Nature Air** (www.natureair.com) and **Sansa** (www.flysansa.com) have one flight a day in and out of San José.

By bus
The bus to La Fortuna from San José takes around 4 hrs leaving from Calle 12 between Avenidas 7 and 9 , 6.15am, 8.30am, 11.30am.

By road
There are several routes to Arenal, but the easiest is to head west on Highway 1 out of San José and then follow signs to Grecia. From Grecia head through Sarchi, Naranjo, Zarcero and to Cuidad Quesada (San Carlos). From here there are signs.

Los Chiles

Boats, birds and border crossings are why travellers find themselves nearly 200 kilometres (124 miles) north of the capital in the quiet agricultural town of Los Chiles. Situated less than four kilometres from Nicaragua, Los Chiles is an increasingly popular spot for crossing over to Costa Rica's northern neighbour. Although there is a road, it is not for tourist use, and the crossing here is made by a boat trip of one to two hours, with three ferries a day travelling along the San Juan river to San Carlos (Immigration, 2471 1233, 8am-4pm, US$7). *See p313* **Nicaragua**.

While the surrounding area is typically luscious, for those intending to remain within Costa Rican perimeters this small town has little to mark it down as a must-see destination and its best lodging is out of town.

Lying west of the town, the Rio Frio provides the watery route to the area's main attraction, the lush **Caño Negro Refugio Nacional de Vida Silvestre Fauna**. Many people travel to the wetlands as a day trip from La Fortuna (*see p151*), but those staying just 26 kilometres (16 miles) away from the park, in Los Chiles, benefit from an extra couple of hours seeing the wildlife emerge at the crack of dawn. The area's clouds of avian life are famed among bird-watchers and many hotels offer tours.

Los Chiles sits by the **San Juan La Selva Biological Corridor**, which was set up in 2002 between Costa Rica's most northern forest and **Indio-Maíz Biological Reserve** in Nicaragua as part of efforts to conserve the declining Great Green Macaw and the almendro tree. See www.lapaverde.or.cr.

While a seemingly sleepy and calm area, the short distance between this fisherman-founded

Arenal Observatory Lodge – if you think it looks good now, wait until night-time. *See p155.*

agricultural town and abutting Nicaragua has provided Los Chiles with a far more enlivened recent history than its humble environs may suggest. In the early 1980s, it served as a base and supply route for the US-backed Contras (counter-revolutionaries) in their insurgence against the leftist Frente Sandinista de Liberación Nacional (Sandinista National Liberation Front). The Sandinistas, who took their name from Nicaraguan anti-imperialist Augusto César Sandino, ended the 43-year reign of the Somoza dynasty in 1979. In the climate of the Cold War the US was unhappy with the left-wing government and the Sandinistas' open identification with the Cuban Revolution. On taking office in 1981, President Ronald Reagan set about funding the anti-Sandinista Contras with bases in Honduras, El Salvador and Los Chiles, Costa Rica.

Where to stay

Hotel de Campo Caño Negro
Caño Negro, 25km (16 miles) south of Los Chiles (2471 1012/www.hoteldecampo.com). **Rates** US$85 double. **Rooms** 14. **Credit** AmEx, MC, V.
Find activities galore at Hotel de Campo Caño Negro, part of a new outdoors centre for the area. The 14 rooms are set out in seven bungalows with wood finishings and either a king-sized or two double beds. One of its specialities is photography safaris.
Bar. Parking. Pool (outdoor). Restaurant.

Caño Negro Lodge
8km south of Los Chiles (2471 1000/www. canonegrolodge.com). **Rates** US$95 double. **Rooms** 22. **Credit** AmEx, MC, V.
Nestled in the verdant north of the country, Caño Negro Lodge is a nature-lover's dream. This peaceful haven is in a prime location for getting the most from the famed wetlands. The rooms are pleasantly decorated and there is a good restaurant.
Bars (2). Pool (outdoor). Restaurant. Room service. TV.

Resources

Bank
Banco Nacional *north of the football pitch (2212 2000).*

Getting there

By air
There is a landing strip for chartered flights. **Nature Air** (www.natureair.com) runs them from San José.

By bus
Buses leave San José twice a day from Calle 12, between Avenidas 7 and 9. For times call 2460 5032. The bus timetable leaving Los Chiles is anything but formalised, but all buses leave from opposite the park on the main street.

By road
When driving take Highway 35 from Muelle for 90km (56 miles).

It can take hours to choose from the pastries at **Tom's Pan Germany Baker**. *See p152.*

Pacific North

Pacific North

PACIFIC OCEAN

Lago de Nicaragua

Peñas Blancas

La Cruz

R B Isla Bolaños
Playa Jobo
Puerto Soley
Soley
Isla Despensa
R V S Bahía Junquillal
Santa Rita
Playa Cuajiniquil
Isla Los Cabros
Playa Blanca
Península de Santa Elena
Parque Nacional Santa Rosa *See p170*
Isla Pelada
Islas Murciélago
Isla Colorada

Santa Cecilia
Hacienda Inocentes
Brasilia
Birmania
Volcán Orosí
Río Niño
Parque Nacional Guanacaste
San Jos
Santa Clara

El Socorro
Lilas
Parque Nacional Rincón de la Vieja *See p169*
San Isidro
Pueblo Nuevo
Zona Protectora Volcán Miravalles
Potrerillos
Río Ahogados
Volcán Rincón de la Vieja
Hacienda Los Ahogados
Ingaray
Estación Horizontes
Cerro Carbonal
Río Colorado
Pueblo Nuevo
Guayabo
Volcán Miravalles
Bijagu
Fortuna
Río Liberia

Playa Nancite
Playa Naranjo
Playa Cabuyal
Papagayo *See p174*
Islas Palmitas
R V S Iguanita
Morada
LIBERIA *See p163*
Torno
Río Salto
Salto
Río Potrero
Río Piedras
Río Corobía
6

Playa Hermosa
Panamá
Playa Ocotal *See p174*
El Coco
Guardia
Hacienda El Real
Laguna El Palenque
Pijije
Río Blanco
BAGACES
1
Sandill.
Zapotal
Sardinal
Palmira
Río Sardinal
Potrero
Islas Santa Catalina
Isla Plata
Playa Flamingo *See p178*
Brasilito *See p179*
Tempate
FILADELFIA
Belén
Río Tempisque
Hacienda Tamarindo
CAÑAS
Puerto Viejo
Huacas
Porte Golpe
21
Puerto Ballena
Ortega
Bebedero
San Miguel
Cabo Velas
R V S Tamarindo
Playa Tamarindo
Punta Langosta
PNM Las Baulas *See p190*
TAMARINDO *See p186*
Hatillo
Río Cañas
Parque Nacional Palo Verde *See p184*
Monte Potrero
Playa Avellana *See p192*
San José Pinilla
Santa Bárbara
Puerto Humo
Río Lajas
Pargos
Río Seco
SANTA CRUZ *See p183*
San Lázaro
Caballito
Colorado
Paraíso
Diriá
San Vicente
Puerto Moreno
Playa Junquillal
Retallano
Nambi
San Antonio
Parque Nacional Barra Honda
Puerto Jesús
Lagarto
Parque Nacional Diriá
NICOYA *See p181*
Mansión
Isla Chira
Marbella
Río Rosario
Quirimán
Puerto Thiel
Playa San Juanillo
San Juanillo
Río Nosara
Caimital
HOJANCHA
San Pablo Viejo
Isla Berrugate
Playa Ostional
OSTIONAL
Belén
Pilangosta
Zapatal
CARMONA
Playa Nosara
Nosara *See p193*
R V S Ostional
Lajas
Maravilla
Río Ora
Río Dra
Garza
Santa María
Cangrejal
Bellavista
Jicaral
Barco Quebrado
San Martín
Los Angeles
Playa Barco Quebrado
Playa Sámara *See p199*
Estrada
Punta Islita
Bejuco
Jabillo
Isla Chora
Playa Carrillo *See p199*
Pueblo Nuevo
Jabilla
Playa Bejuco
Playa San Miguel
Río Bongo
Río Jabillo
Playa Coyote

0   5   10 miles
0   5   10 km

© Copyright Time Out Group 2008

Getting Started

Costa Rica's most tourist-friendly region still holds a few surprises.

Playa Carrilo. *See p199.*

Thanks to its consistent sunshine, dry heat, plentiful white sand and thrilling water sports, Costa Rica's northern Pacific coast is one of the country's most touristy regions. Liberia's **Aeropuerto Internacional Daniel Oduber Quirós** (*see p167*), opened in 1993, has allowed direct flights from the US to land in the very centre of Guanacaste province, transforming the region from a sparsely populated backwater to the most accessible and well-developed area for tourists – all in little over a decade.

Whether you're a pensioner or a surfer – or perhaps both – the north and south Guanacaste coast has something to offer you. The principal attractions in this area include hiking in several of the country's most interesting national parks, surfing a variety of breaks, scuba diving, sailing, and simplest of all, sun worshipping on tropical beaches. The landscape is fertile and complex, ranging from beach to mountainous cloud forests to tidal mangrove swamps. Volcanoes, waterfalls and hot springs can be visited, and make for good day trips.

There are lots of excursions available into the many wildlife reserves such as at **Isla de Pájaros** (*see p184*), a healthy habitat for numerous birds. **PN Ostional** (*see p193*) is known worldwide for its turtle nesting sites, while off the beach and into the blue sea, the coral reefs around **Playa Sámara** (*see p196*) are a highlight. You can even spend a couple of

nights in the company of monkeys, bats and rangers at the national parks including **PN Rincón de la Vieja** (*see p169*), **PN Santa Rosa** (*see p170*) and **PN Barra Honda** (*see p181*).

Some say this area, with its many grand resorts, finger-snapping service and expensive lots for sale, attracts the more demanding type of tourist. But that's not to say the north Pacific is solely geared towards the idle; there are also plenty of places with a good nightlife. You'll find a fun and sociable crowd as at the capital Liberia, and coastal towns such as **Playa Tamarindo** (*see p186*) or **Playa Flamingo** (*see p178*) are great places for dancing salsa and merengue or meeting like-minded party-goers. Tourists of all types are generously welcomed by local residents and beach towns still retain a friendly unrushed atmosphere.

Further south, the beaches of **Playa Panamá** (*see p174*) and **Playa Carrillo** (*see p199*) are excellent for parasailing, sport fishing or boating. Also at your service are reputable restaurants and bars, most making good use of the ocean's bounty or the vast array of fruit from the forests.

It all sounds like one happy paradise but there has been fierce criticism from environmentalists about what they see as the area's overdevelopment. At the centre of the controversy is the Papagayo Project. In the

The best Pacific North

Things to do

Bury those city-boy blues and take part in a cowboy spectacle of rodeos, horsemanship and folk dancing at a *fiesta cívica* in **Liberia** (*see right*), **Santa Cruz** (*see p183*) or **Nicoya** (*see p181*). Visit one of the country's least frequented parks, **Rincón de la Vieja** (*see p169*), and get close to volcanic activity. Or walk through the country's largest and last remaining dry tropical forest in **PN Santa Rosa** (*see p170*), also the site of William Walker's last stand (*see p168* **Making of a hero**). To get away from the typical beach holiday, make an excursion to **Guaitil** (*see p184*). You can witness the ancient pottery-making techniques of the pre-Columbian-style Chorotega pots. For those looking for a different adventure, explore **PN Barra Honda's** (*see p181*) underground network of limestone eroded caves full of weird mineral formations.

Places to stay

The Península de Papagayo is in general pricey, but you can enjoy luxury accommodation at **El Ocotal Resort** (*see p177*). Those travelling with a group or with a young family should head to quieter Playa Carrillo where **Cabinas El Colibri** (*see p200*) has mini-apartments plus lots of water sports to keep everyone busy. If you're looking for an off-water option, make a reservation at **Hacienda Guachipelin** (*see p170*), a working ranch just five minutes from **PN Rincón de la Vieja**. Treat yourself to the best of holistic therapy at the **Harmony Hotel** (*see p196*) in Playa Guiones near Nosara and come out feeling soft, smooth and relaxed.

Places to eat

The North Pacific is the best area to try typical Costa Rican cuisine. Try any soda along Highway 21 to sample these delicacies. Santa Cruz's **La Fabrica de Tortillas** (*see p186*) makes home-made Guanacastan dishes, specialising in cornflour recipes. For a fish dinner try **Papagayo Pura Vida** (*see p176*) in Playas del Coco. For a good Argentinian-style barbecue head to **Restaurante El Colibri** (*see p200*) in Playa Carrillo. After an action packed day of surfing, regenerate with a smoothie at Shake Joe's (*see p196*).

1970s, the Costa Rican government's tourist board, the Instituto Costarricense de Turismo, set aside a huge swathe of beachfront land in the Golfo de Papagayo and earmarked it as the largest tourist development in Central America. A total of 14,000 hotel rooms were to be built. (There are currently around 13,000 rooms in Costa Rica). Buying land in this area is free from many regulations as long as the development will be beneficial to the tourism industry. Little happened until 1997, when work on the **Four Seasons Resort** (*see p177*) began. The original plan failed to incorporate an environmental impact study, though this has now been rectified. Less than 30 per cent of the dry forest originally slated for destruction will be razed, the number of hotel rooms has been halved and the planned golf courses are to be moved to former cattle pastures. Despite these concessions, the building of luxury resorts and private villas in this area is likely to increase at a much quicker pace than ever before, much to the chagrin of environmentalists.

North Guanacaste is far from a paved and sanitised 'tourist mecca'. The region's heritage lives on in the forms of folk music and dance (*see p171* **A folk tale**) and its working cowboy culture (*see p172* **Costa cowboys**). In the cities of **Santa Cruz** (*see p183*) and **Nicoya** (*see p181*), annual festivals demonstrate the Costa Rican identity, often absent from the pristine Costa Rica many tourists are used to. This is cattle country, and cowboy hats, boots and dusty bottoms are as common as the bikinis and flipflops seen on the beaches.

If you happen to visit this province in the last week in February, you can take part in such cultural celebrations during the week of *fiestas cívicas* (civic parties), a celebration involving local music, parades, a bullring and happy drunken residents decked out in cowboy gear.

A similar ritual is repeated at the end of July, when locals celebrate the anniversary of Guanacaste's independence from Nicaragua in 1824. Both are entertaining examples of Guanacaste pride that is separate and unique from the cultural heritage of the rest of Costa Rica. This strong spirit is embodied in Costa Rica's colourful national dance, the *Punto Guanacasteco*, which orginated from these parts. If you visit such festivals you will no doubt peer over a crowd to see a lot of stomping, skirt twirling and, special to the *Punto Guanacasteco* dance, pauses throughout where rhyming verses are shouted aloud. It is also a time when traditional instruments such as the *chirimia* (like an oboe) and the *quijongo* (a one-stringed bow and gourd) are played. Folk music and dance festivals are often holiday highlights for visitors.

North Guanacaste

Colonial tradition remains alive along the Costa Rican Gold Coast.

The 'White City' of **Liberia** is still a colonial cowboy town.

Liberia City

The capital of Guanacaste province is Liberia, known historically as the 'White City' for the old colonial buildings in its downtown area made from dazzling ignimbrite stone.

Today Liberia might just as well be called Boomtown, Costa Rica. It is the governmental, business and transportation hub for the region and is drawing a huge share of the nation's overall tourism revenue as well as foreign investment in light industry.

Liberia was (and still is) a cowboy town in the heart of Costa Rican ranch country. But the city of almost 44,000 residents also sits astride the Interamericana Highway, which runs south into the Península de Nicoya and provides access, via secondary roads, to some of the most beautiful beaches in the nation. Its location at a key crossroads also makes Liberia a base for one- or two-day trips to nearby sights such as national parks, waterfalls and zip-line tours, as well as for excursions further afield into Nicaragua (*see p309*).

Even more importantly for the development of the city and surrounding province, Liberia is home to a burgeoning international airport that has brought millions of sun-worshipping tourists directly to Guanacaste since it opened in 1993. As a result, Liberia is a city balanced between historic tradition and modernity.

A walk around the city centre exposes visitors to 160-year-old buildings that still serve as private homes, small hotels, restaurants and bars and other businesses. An army fort, built well before Costa Rica abolished its military in 1949, dominates one corner of the Parque Central and still serves as the *Comandancia* or main police station downtown.

A Guanacaste flag still flaps alongside the Costa Rican national flag on the fort, a juxtaposition repeated on other governmental buildings such as the city hall across the street. Guanacaste is the only province with its own flag. The emblem dates back to 25 July 1812, when the province broke away from Nicaragua and was briefly independent before voting to become part of Costa Rica. Some sentiments of

Out of Africa

Living side by side on the baked Costa Rican savannah, giraffes and zebras peacefully chomp at the grass tufts at their feet. Now, before readers in possession of even the most rudimentary zoological or geographical knowledge either guffaw at this ineptitude or explode at the thought that they've planned a much-needed holiday on the advice of those who place zebra on the Central American isthmus, please forget secondary school geography, and believe. In the Guanacastan town of El Salto, just a few kilometres from Liberia, exists an expanse of African-esque savannah on which roam the aforementioned animals, alongside warthogs, zebras, antelopes and gemsbok.

Africa Mia (2666 1111, www.africamia.net) is the realised dream of a Costa Rican family who set about creating a tranquil slice of Africa on the flat Guanacastan plains. In 2007 Africa Mia won the Tourism Enterprise Award from the Costa Rica Chamber of Commerce. But while the sun-soaked stretches and bowing giraffes resemble a scene from the *Lion King*, there is no little Simba. The essence of the project has always been cage-less freedom: so to avoid a carnivorous blood bath (and running out of livestock), the reserve is predator free. While the park's theme and main attractions are

imported from Africa, the draw of native wildlife hasn't been overlooked, and an assortment of monkeys can be found playing alongside wild rabbits and many species of Costa Rica's bird population.

Experiencing this Afro-Costa 'animalgamation' costs US$65 for a wildlife tour or US$15 (children US$10) for basic entry. Visitors can not only watch as the park's eclectic mix of inhabitants roam free, but groups are taken right up to creatures and are allowed to feed the more placid giraffes and deer by hand. As well as the 'savannah', Africa Mia includes rich primary forest, Río La Carana, the six-metre-high (20-foot) El Salto waterfall that crashes into a lagoon, and Lago Victoria, which creates an attractive habitat for migratory birds.

While the park is all about discovering nature, the main building offers the creature comforts necessary for human herds, including bathrooms, a visitor centre and a souvenir shop. Hungry wildlife spotters have a couple of options; La Columnata Restaurant serves international and typical Costa Rican food, and the café has a selection of light snacks. It is located off the Interamericana Highway 12 kilometres (7.5 miles) south-east of Liberia. (Open 8am-6pm daily; last public entry 5pm).

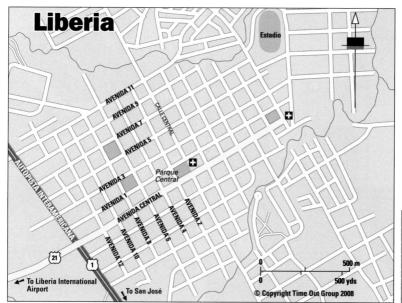

independence still carry on to this day, with some residents claiming that they are Guanacastan not Costa Rican.

Another interesting sight downtown is the **Iglesia de la Agonía** which lies at the end of Avenida Central. The church's location dates from 1769 when town residents built a wooden structure in which their local priest could conduct services. The present building was constructed between 1854 and 1865. Although masses are no longer celebrated there, locals gather at 2.30pm daily to say the rosary. The current location for Roman Catholic services, the **Iglesia de la Inmaculada Concepción**, was built in the mid 20th century and its brilliant white façade and steeple topped with a steel cross dominate one entire side of the central park.

Yet just a few kilometres from all this heritage is the international airport. The development around it is stunning in its scale, the rapidity of its growth and the diversity of the businesses it involves. Across the highway from the airport, several new shopping malls have been built along with a large Hilton Garden Inn that will open to travellers after its scheduled completion in late 2008. Large condominium and housing developments are also planned across Highway 21 in front of the airport. But possibly the most meaningful development is the least visible. Just north of

the airport and down a tree-lined road off Highway 21 is the Ad Astra Rocket Company, a laboratory opened two years ago to develop the plasma rocket fuel that NASA scientists hope will power the first manned flight to Mars. (The company's founder is Costa Rican scientist and former NASA astronaut Dr Franklin Chang Diaz who undertook the business when NASA privatised several of its research and development projects several years ago.) Ad Astra Rocket Company (not open to the public) is arguably one of the most cutting-edge technological initiatives under way in all of Central America. And it's happening in a cowboy town.

EXCURSIONS

There are numerous places to visit on one-day excursions from Liberia. Three national parks – **PN Rincón de la Vieja** (*see p169*), **PN Santa Rosa** (*see p170*) and **PN Palo Verde** (*see p184*) – are close by and can be reached by small tourism vans from various hotels in town.

Africa Mia (2666 1111, www.africamia.net; *see left*) is a private nature reserve offering half-day or full-day tours through an environment similar to an African savannah.

Llanos de Cortez Waterfall makes a decent one-day excursion within an easy drive or bus ride from Liberia to the town of Cortez. Turn right off the Interamericana in Cortez and then turn right a second time. If travelling by

Rustic relaxation at the **Hotel Casa Real**.

bus, the waterfall is about a 15-minute walk from the Interamericana. The 14-metre (40 feet) wide waterfall drops nine metres (30 feet) into a sandy pond surrounded by forest.

Where to eat & drink

Hotel El Bramadero

Corner of Interamericana Highway & Highway 21 (2666 0371/www.hotelelbramadero.com). **Open** 6am-10pm daily. **Main courses** US$10. **Credit** AmEx, DC, MC, V.

This was a restaurant 50 years ago before it tacked on a hotel, and it is still a better place in which to eat than to stay. Well known for its steaks, it also does a brisk breakfast business because of its key location at a main crossroads. It is the Liberia pick-up point for Tica Bus service along the Interamericana for destinations throughout Central America.

Paso Real

Avenida Central, entre Calles Central y 2 (2666 3455). **Open** 11am-10pm daily. **Main courses** US$15. **Credit** AmEx, DC, MC, V.

This second-floor restaurant with balcony seating overlooking the central park is generally considered one of the best places in Liberia to try seafood.

Las Tinajas

Calle 2, entre Avenidas Central y 1 (2666 7569). **Open** 10am-10pm daily. **Main courses** US$8. **Credit** AmEx, DC, MC, V.

This veranda restaurant is popular with locals as a place to enjoy drinks and food while viewing the activity in and around the park, which often includes strolling musicians. Its steak and chicken kebabs are the best dishes on offer here.

Where to stay

Liberia is full of cheap places to stay, many of which are more like backpacker hostels than real hotels. Most are near the central park but the nicest hotels are two Best Westerns outside the downtown area. The more expensive hotels can also help with transfers to the nearby national parks.

Best Western Hotel El Sitio

Highway 21, 200m south-east of Interamericana Highway (2666 1211/www.bestwestern.com). **Rates** US$87 double. **Rooms** 52. **Credit** AmEx, DC, MC, V.

El Sitio has 52 clean, well-equipped rooms, as you would expect from this cookie cutter chain. It has a restaurant, and a small casino should you want to bet away what you saved on the room. Three nightclubs are also close by. Along with the other Best Western facility in town – Hotel Las Espuelas (*see right*) – it represents the high end of accommodation in Liberia.

Bars (2). Gym. Internet (wireless, free). Parking (free). Pool (outdoor). Restaurants (2). Room service. TV (cable).

Best Western Hotel Las Espuelas Hotel & Casino

2km south on Interamericana (2653 0114/ www.bestwestern.com). **Rates** US$87 double. **Rooms** 44. **Credit** AmEx, DC, MC, V.

The Hotel Las Espuelas is surprisingly charming for a chain hotel. This is typified by a 19th-century Costa Rican carriage sitting under the canopied entrance. Inside, the 44 rooms are divided among seven wings separated by open courtyards. The bar is in a large veranda alongside a garden courtyard. The rooms are plain but big with comfortable beds and air-conditioning.

Bar. Business centre. Disabled-adapted rooms. Internet (wireless, free). Parking (free). Pool (outdoor). No-smoking rooms. Restaurant. TV (cable).

Hotel Primavera

Avenida Central, entre Calles Central y 2 (2666 0464). **Rates** US$52-$59 double. **Rooms** 30. **Credit** AmEx, DC, MC, V.

This two-storey, 30-room hotel facing the central park has TV, private baths and air-conditioning in some rooms for a few dollars more per night. It is a basic affair, but recommendable.

Parking (free). TV.

La Posada del Tope and Hotel Casa Real

Calle Central, entre Avenidas Central y 2 (2666 3876). **Rates** US$16-$22 double. **Rooms** 22. **Credit** AmEx, MC, V.

La Posada is a 19th-century house converted into an eight-room hotel with shared bathrooms and fans. Across the street is its sister **Hotel Casa Real** (2606 3876), which has 11 rooms with private baths and TV. Casa Real's rooms are decorated with old furniture and historical photos on the walls. Antique tools such as coffee grinders are mounted on tables in the communal seating area in the courtyard.

Internet (shared terminal, free). Parking (free). Restaurant. TV.

Resources

Medical Services

Hospital Dr Enrique Baltodano *Avenida 1, near stadium on north-east edge of city (2666 0011).*

Internet

Planet Internet *Calle Central, entre Avenidas Central y 2.*

Getting there

By air

Aeropuerto Internacional Daniel Oduber Quirós (12km/7.5 miles south-west of Liberia on Highway 21, 2668 1010) has played a key role in the development of Liberia and Guanacaste Province. All international flights are via the United States with Delta, Continental or American Airlines (*see p314*)

Pacific North

Making of a hero

To many Central Americans, William Walker is history's poster child for US interference and domination in the region. The US-born imperialist and soldier of fortune had unsuccessfully invaded Mexico before turning his attention further south to Central America. His ambition was as much pecuniary as political – to capitalise on a slave-trading centre he intended to set up. And it was a campaign thwarted by the Costa Ricans and, in particular, a drummer boy called Juan Santamaría: the nation's unlikely hero.

On 4 May 1855, Walker, accompanied by about 60 mercenaries, landed by steamship in Nicaragua in the midst of a civil war between the conservative government and liberal insurrectionists. Ironically, the rebels, who had no idea he would seek to become their dictator, invited Walker into the fray.

Walker's force, augmented by the rebel army and new recruits from the United States, turned the tide against the government and captured the Nicaraguan city of Granada, the conservative power base. The government surrendered, and the United States quickly recognised a new puppet government led by liberal president Patricio Rivas. But it was Walker who wielded most of the power by brokering a deal in which he gained command of the Nicaraguan army.

Concerned by Walker's ambitions, the conservative governments of the other four Central American nations agreed to send troops into Nicaragua. Costa Rica went so far as to declare war on Walker in March 1856, but cholera decimated its army, and it withdrew. Encouraged by this, Walker staged a rigged election and installed himself as president of Nicaragua. He decreed English the official language, legalised slavery and called on the United States to annex Nicaragua as a state – drawing support from pro-slavery forces in the United States.

The forces opposing Walker – assisted and armed by Britain because of its desire to blunt US influence in the region – started to gain the upper hand. Walker retreated from his base in Granada, leaving most of the historic colonial city a smoking ruin. At a large ranch in what is now the **PN Santa Rosa** (*see p170*) on the Pacific coast, he and his followers drove south across the border into Costa Rica. Here they were repulsed by a combined force of Costa Ricans, Guatemalans, Hondurans and Salvadorans – united now behind Costa Rican president Juan Rafael Mora. The reconstructed ranch house in the park is a memorial to the victory.

At this house the final battle against Walker took place in April 1857, in the town of Rivas, just north of the Costa Rican border. From their stronghold, Walker's men beat back wave upon wave of attacks by the Central Americans. Then a Costa Rican drummer boy named Juan Santamaría sacrificed his life in a fusillade of gunfire while running across open ground to ignite the building's roof with a torch. He is honoured as a hero in Costa Rica, with the Aeropuerto Internacional Juan Santamaría in San José named after him and a famous statue of him in Alajuela (*pictured*).

Walker was allowed to leave Rivas on 1 May 1857 and return to the United States under escort by the US Navy, which had sent ships to Nicaragua's Pacific coast to protect economic interests. Incredibly, Walker didn't abandon his dreams of an empire. He returned to Central America under various schemes in 1858, 1859 and 1860, when he was finally captured by a British warship as he tried to enter Honduras illegally. The British turned Walker over to Honduran authorities, who executed him.

Arriving & leaving), with daily connections in Atlanta, Houston and Miami. There are also several flights daily to and from San José with Costa Rican carriers **NatureAir** (www.natureair.com) and **Sansa** (www.flysansa.com).

By bus

Liberia has 2 major bus stations that are near each other for easy transfers among the various carriers. **Terminal Liberia** (Avenida 7, entre Calles 12 y 14) handles much of the traffic to and from towns to the south such as Filadelfia, Santa Cruz and Nicoya as well as popular beach communities like Tamarindo, Playa Hermosa and Playa Panama. **Terminal Pullmitan** (Avenida 5, entre Calles 10 y 12) handles much of the traffic north towards Nicaragua and south-east to San José. Schedules frequently change and are seldom available in print. Rely on the schedule listed on the billboard of each terminal's ticket office for the latest accurate times. A ticket from Liberia to San José costs around US$5.

By road

Liberia is 234km (145 miles) north-west of San José on the Interamericana Highway. It is 77km (48 miles) south of the Nicaraguan border via the same highway. Running south-west from Liberia into the Peninsula de Nicoya is Highway 21 (past the airport).

PN Rincón de la Vieja

This park was established in 1973 to help protect the geothermal properties from its two volcanoes, the largest in the Cordillera de Guanacaste. The park is teeming with wildlife and its waterways feed about 30 rivers and streams flowing down into the region. The mildly active volcano from which the park takes its name is 1,895 metres (6,217 feet) tall and has nine eruption points. The nearby **Volcán Santa María** (located within the same park) is dormant and has an elevation of 1,916 metres (6,286 feet).

The park's position means that two ecosystems, the dry Pacific side and the humid Caribbean side, are starkly apparent. Rincón de la Vieja is among Costa Rica's least visited volcanic parks, which makes it that much more appealing for tourist-averse hikers who wish to explore stunning landscape and view abundant wildlife. The park's 141 square kilometres (54 square miles) are home to hot water and volcanic mud springs, as well as waterfalls and archaeological sites containing petroglyphs carved by the early inhabitants of the region.

About 300 bird species live here: toucans, parrots, hummingbirds, quetzals, eagles, owls, woodpeckers – the list goes on and on. Mammals include three species of monkey, armadillos, coatis, tapirs, skunks, deer, squirrels and several wild cat species, although sightings of jaguars and pumas are infrequent.

Hiking trails through the park are well marked and range from easy to strenuous as they lead visitors to their choice of sights. The easiest route is an eight-kilometre (five-mile) circular trail beginning at the park's western entrance into **Las Pailas** (the hot pools sector). The trail takes two to three hours and leads past mud baths, sulphur-belching fumaroles, hot water springs, a waterfall and a *volcancito* (little volcano).

Two other hiking trails start from the same park entrance but each lead to a large waterfall. **La Cangreja** waterfall drops from a cliff into a deep-blue pool (the water contains high concentrations of dissolved copper salts). La Cangreja is a five-kilometre (three-mile) hike each way. **La Escondidas** waterfall is smaller and closer – about four kilometres (2.5 miles) each way – a swim at the end makes it worth it.

For the more physically fit, there is an eight-kilometre (five mile) trail (each way) that leads to the crater of Rincón, past a high-elevation, blue-green lake called Von Seebach. Weather permitting, hikers on this trail can see the Peninsula de Nicoya to the south and as far as Lago Nicaragua to the north. Hikers here are advised to take a light jacket as the temperature drops considerably at higher altitude. Throughout the park, visitors should wear good walking shoes and carry drinking water. Insect repellent may also be needed, and hikers should be wary of snakes. There are plenty around, more so at the lower elevations (the park's minimum is about 600 metres). Towards the eastern side of the park is the Santa Maria entrance. There is a three-kilometre trail through heavy forest, leading past a waterfall and on to sulphurous hot springs. Some visitors dip in the springs, then go for a swim in nearby cold water springs. Also located here is **Casona Santa María**, a late 1800s ranch house that is now the ranger station for this section of the park. PN Rincón de la Vieja is a natural treasure of international significance, and visitors to the Guanacaste area of Costa Rica should not miss the opportunity to see it. A two-day visit with an overnight stay is desirable, but a single-day visit is easy and cheap because of its proximity to Liberia. Admission to the park is US$10. Visitors entering through the **Las Pailas** gate (park rangers 2661 8139) also must pay a US$2 per person toll because the access road crosses private property. The park is open from 7am to 4pm every day except Mondays.

Where to eat & drink

There's no restaurant inside the park, so bring a cooler of food and drinks if driving there or riding with a tour group. Carry drinks and

Parque Nacional Rincón de la Vieja

Volcán ▲
Rincón de
la Vieja

Parque Nacional
Rincón de la Vieja

Río Colorado
Río Liberia
Río Salto

Pueblo Nuevo ○

0   1.5   3 miles
0   1.5   3 km
© Copyright Time Out Group 2008

snacks if you walk into the park from some of the area's lodgings with the intention of hiking a trail or two. There is a small store outside the **Las Pailas** entrance to the park that sells basic supplies. The other option is to eat at one of the hotel restaurants outside the park.

Where to stay

Visitors can camp in the park for US$2 per person per night. Campgrounds at the ranger stations at each park entrance have water, showers, toilets, tables and grills but visitors must bring their own charcoal or wood for cooking. Outside the Las Pailas entrance there are several hotel options. **Hacienda Guachipelin** (2666 8075, www.guachipelin. com, US$133-$143 double) is located about five minutes' walk from the park entrance. It has 52 rooms with hot water and private bathrooms on the site of a large 19th-century ranch that still herds cattle. The hotel has a swimming pool and offers variously priced activity packages including canopy tours, horseriding and river tubing on the ranch's grounds.

El Sol Verde Lodge & Campground (2665 5357, www.elsolverde.com, US$40 double room, US$10 campsite) is a modest but charming establishment in Curubandé. It is eight kilometres (five miles) from the park

entrance, and has three rooms and several concrete base tent sites. The campsite rate includes a tent if needed. Three kilometres (two miles) outside the Santa María entrance of the park, the **Rinconcito Lodge** (2666 2764, www.rinconcitolodge.com, double US$35) has 11 comfortable rooms with private baths and hot water. It is a pleasant hotel and allows guests to get close to the region's natural wonders. It can organise horseriding trips.

Getting there

By road

To get to the park's Las Pailas sector, drive north from Liberia on the Interamericana Highway for 5km (3 miles) and then turn right at the sign indicating the park and the town of Curubandé. Drive 20km (12 miles) on this gravel road to the park entrance. To reach the Santa María entrance to the park, drive along the gravel road from the Barrio La Victoria neighbourhood of Liberia.

Group transportation to and from the park can also be arranged through various hotels in Liberia for about US$15 per person. Try the **Hotel Liberia** (2666 0161) near the city's park.

PN Santa Rosa & around

This park, along the northern Pacific coast of Costa Rica near the Nicaraguan border, was created in 1971 – but more for historic than ecological reasons. It takes its name from **Hacienda Santa Rosa**, a large ranch where, in 1856, a Costa Rican army, augmented by other Central American fighters, defeated a band of mercenary adventurers led by William Walker of the United States (*see p168* **Making of a hero**). The two-storey ranch house that was the centre of the battle remains a focal point of the park's attractions.

The park's 38 square kilometres (15 square miles) also make it one of the largest protected areas in Costa Rica; it contains natural elements that are extremely important for the preservation of the area. Within the confines of PN Santa Rosa is also the largest expanse of dry tropical forest left in all of Central America, and nesting areas for several varieties of sea turtle. It's home to 115 species of mammal, 100 species of amphibian and reptile, 253 species of bird and more than 10,000 species of insect, including 3,140 species of butterfly and moth.

The park stretches from the coast about 20 kilometres (12 miles) inland to the Interamericana Highway, where the main entrance is located (2666 5051). Admission costs US$10, and the park is open from 8am to 4pm daily except Mondays. For more information log onto www.sinaccr.net (in Spanish only).

A folk tale

It's a relatively small place, Costa Rica, but there is a wealth of good music – fed by the varied cultural influences that have melded through the history of the country. The main signposts at the crossroads of Costa Rica's musical world point to the Península de Nicoya to the north-east and the Caribbean coast to the west with its heavy Afro-Caribbean influences and the beat-heavy rhythm known as *sinkit*.

One of the oldest styles in Costa Rican folk music, that invented by the Chorotega indigenous tribe, native to Nicaragua, Honduras and Costa Rica, continues to influence contemporary sounds and dances. Pre-Columbian routines such as the *Danza del Sol* and the *Danza de la Luna* are still performed at *fiestas*.

Many of the instruments used in the folk music of the country reflect the diversity and richness of the area. You might see an oval-shaped, flute-like wind instrument called the *ocarina*; the single-string bow and gourd resonator that is the *quijongo*; a native oboe called the *chirimia*; the xylophone-esque marimba; and the maracas, seed- or bean-filled dried calabash or gourd shells all taking up the rhythm of *coplas*, *cantantas*, *retahilas* and *bombas*.

Several bands have taken the traditional folk music of Costa Rica, mixed it up and played it to a new audience, both nationally and on the international stage.

For 14 years Editus has been tinkling away, mixing styles as diverse as modern jazz, 'new age', classical and authentic traditional Costa Rican sounds, with an academic outlook that has seen them travel the globe plucking and preaching wherever they go. They're the only Tico band to grab a Grammy and in 2003 they won Best World Music Album and Best Tropical Contemporary Album for their wonderful *Mundo* album.

Malpaís (*pictured*), named after a remote town on the Península de Nicoya, mix traditional rhythms and contemporary beats to create a unique sound. Similarly testing the boundaries between genres are Cantares. They take their music to the people and source new sounds and rhythms from the less well-known central region of the country.

While Costa Rican music has yet to make a big impact on the global music scene, the quality is there and, as Jaime Gamboa, lead bassist and backup vocals for Malpaís, says, 'Currently, Costa Rican music is in very good shape. There are many groups from very diverse genres, creating high quality music.'

For CD ideas, *see p328* **Music**. For more about the Papaya music label, instrumental in the resurgence of Costa Rican folk music, *see p42* **Musical differences**.

Pacific North

Costa cowboys

An ox cart driver with a mobile phone pressed to his ear, car traffic yielding to a herd of cows crossing the road, men of all ages sporting ornate belt buckles and a bewildering variety of brimmed leather hats... Guanacaste is cowboy country – 21st century style.

Here the nation's cowboy tradition is not just a celebration of the past but is an active force in daily life. Although there are major rodeos and large horse parades in the Central Valley and elsewhere in the country at various times of the year, present-day Guanacaste remains the heart of cattle and horse ranching. And that means that *sabaneros* (cowboys) are a common sight on the region's roads and expansive pastures.

In the middle of Liberia's main boulevard you'll find a large bronze statue of a *sabanero* on a bucking bronco, and similar statues honouring the cowboy lifestyle can be found in smaller cities in the area such as Santa Cruz. Saddle shops, feed stores and animal vets can be readily found – whether by a tourist shopping for finely crafted leather stirrups or a rancher seeking aid for a sickly calf.

There are numerous civic *fiestas* celebrating the cowboy culture throughout the year in Guanacaste, but the rodeo season from December to April is when it all peaks. Each city and town hosts its own rodeo on a rotating schedule, meaning that visitors can attend a rodeo almost every weekend if they want to. And many people with a penchant for the organised chaos of a Guanacaste rodeo *do* attend week after week.

Experienced cowboys ride horses and bulls for competition, but participation is not limited to real *sabaneros*. Each night during a rodeo – some of them last four or five days – scores of men and an occasional woman enter the hand-built wooden arenas to taunt a bull that is released into the pen. The resulting carnage, while infrequent, is not for the faint-hearted spectator or an animal rights activist.

Scores of people are injured each year, with occasional deaths by goring or trampling. People try to pull the bull's tail or escape his charges at the last second by clambering over the arena fence. Ambulances stand by for the injured, and medical professionals decry the risk to life and limb. But tradition trumps, and one of the best crowd pullers is a bull that has already killed two men.

From the park entrance on the highway, there is a seven-kilometre (4.5 mile) road leading west to the park headquarters where there is an information centre, a small museum, a campground, a one-kilometre (half-mile) circular nature trail and the historic battlefield.

The main building of Hacienda Santa Rosa is **La Casona**, and it was around this structure that much of the fighting occurred. The original building was burned down by arsonists in 2001 but was rebuilt a year later with local timber. The builders used old photographs of La Casona to ensure an accurate reconstruction.

(The arsonists were a local father and son who had been banned from the park for poaching game. They received long prison sentences for destroying a national heritage site.)

A short trail leads from La Casona to the battlefield monument and a nearby viewing platform that provides a panoramic vista of much of the park. Heading west from the park's headquarters towards the coast is a 13-kilometre (eight mile) rough road passable only by four-wheel-drive vehicles or on foot. During the rainy season from May to November, the road is closed to all vehicles. But the hike is well worth the effort, not only for the sights along the way but also because at the end of the road is **Playa Naranjo**, which some people regard as one of the most pristine and beautiful beaches in Costa Rica. At the four kilometre (2.5 mile) point on this road is a scenic viewpoint known as **Mirador Valle Naranjo**, from where the beach can be seen in all of its splendour. There are also short hiking trails leading off the main road to waterfalls. About three kilometres after the mirador, the road branches in two. The right branch takes travellers to a campground at the north end of Playa Naranjo; the left branch leads to a campground on the south end of the beach.

Playa Naranjo is on a bay that is internationally acclaimed for two surfing locations. One is an island jutting out of the bay known as Witch's Rock, while the other is Ollie's Point along the shoreline. Witch's Rock can only be reached by boat from some of the beachfront towns further south along the coast such as **Playas del Coco** (*see p174*). But ardent surfers pay hefty sums for single-day boat trips to Witch's Rock because of its consistent three-metre-high (ten foot) waves.

Ollie's Point can be used by park visitors who are willing to carry in their surfboards. It also provides an interesting reference point about the region's recent history. The point takes its name from Oliver North, the US Marine Corps officer who was involved in supplying arms and other equipment to the Nicaraguan Contras during their 1980s civil war against the Sandinista communist government that had taken control of Nicaragua. A secret airstrip near Ollie's Point was one of several areas in Central America used by US operatives to supply the Contras.

EXCURSIONS
Directly opposite from PN Santa Rosa, on the Interamericana Highway, is **PN Guanacaste**. This 34-square-kilometre (13-square-mile) park was established in 1989 and has two volcanoes, **Orosí** and **Cacao**, within its boundaries. There are rough trails to the summits of both volcanoes, as well as hundreds of pre-Columbian indigenous petroglyphs carved in the rocks.

The park has three biology stations housing scientists and students, but offers little in the way of lodging for visitors. Camping (no facilities) is allowed near the ranger stations for US$2 per person per night.

There are three entrances to PN Guanacaste. One is on Highway 4 about three kilometres (two miles) south of La Cruz after turning east off the Interamericana Highway. A second is east of the Interamericana just south of Santa Rita, in the opposite direction to the road to Cuajiniquil into the north sector of PN Santa

Rosa. The third entrance is nine kilometres (5.5 miles) south of the main Santa Rosa entrance. Turn east from the Interamericana at the town of Potrerillos. Admission to the park is US$10. The park is closed on Mondays.

If you want more time on dry land – or, more commonly, a soggy trail – visit **Refugio de Vida Silvestre Bahía Junquillal**, a wildlife refuge protecting coastal mangroves and tropical dry forest. Overlooking a tiny bay, this small park offers good snorkelling and marine birdwatching. The refuge and the national park offer joint admission for US$10. The wildlife refuge is reached by the same road through Cuajiniquil that takes visitors into the northern section of PN Santa Rosa. But instead of staying on the road west, turn right two kilometres (1.25 miles) past Cuajiniquil on to a dirt road and then go four kilometres (2.5 miles) north into the refuge. Camping costs US$2 per person. There are no toilets and water consumption is seasonally restricted.

Where to eat & drink

Most visitors to PN Santa Rosa – and certainly all who camp – take their own food and beverages. But meals are available in the hotels listed below. There is no store inside the park.

Where to stay

The campground near the park headquarters has potable water, toilets, cold showers, picnic benches and cooking grills. The campgrounds at Playa Naranjo are more rustic – pit latrines, brackish water for showers, no drinking water. Camping costs US$2 per person per night, with a two-night maximum stay at Playa Naranjo.

Visitors with their own transport may wish to stay at one of the hotels outside the park. Most are around the town of **La Cruz**, about 24 kilometres (15 miles) north of the park's main entrance on the Interamericana Highway.

Amalia's Inn (on central park of La Cruz off Interamericana Highway, 2679 9618, US$35 double) is the nicest hotel in town, with seven large rooms, private bathrooms and a pool.

For those willing to drive a bit further and spend a lot more, a dirt road leads south-west from La Cruz about 16 kilometres (ten miles) to Salinas Bay on the coast north of PN Santa Rosa. **Ecoplaya Beach Resort** (2676 1010, www.ecoplaya.com, US$98-$114 double) has amenities, including a huge swimming pool with two jacuzzis and a wet bar. The complex is separated into 16 comfortable villas, ideal for families. There is also a good restaurant. It also offers many activities, and kayaks, mountain bikes and snorkelling equipment can be hired.

Pacific North

Getting there

By road

The main entrance to PN Santa Rosa is 35km (22 miles) north of Liberia on the Interamericana Highway. Visitors usually arrive by private car, small tour vans (US$20 per person round trip from Hotel Liberia) and public buses from Liberia. There is a second entrance to the park about 16 km (10 miles) further north on the Interamericana Highway and just south of the town of Santa Rita. The turn-off road near Santa Rita goes eight km (5 miles) west through the town of Cuajiniquil and then into the northern section of Santa Rosa known as the Sector Murcielago (Bat sector). The last part of the road into the northern park sector is bad. During rainy season it requires a four-wheel-drive vehicle or may be impassable after very heavy rains.

Playa Panama to Playa Ocotal

This is the heart of Costa Rica's so-called 'Gold Coast'. It attracts a large share of the nation's tourism – an estimated 20 per cent or more – as well as a big slice of the country's total foreign investment.

From the southern boundary of the **PN Santa Rosa** (*see p170*) near the Nicaraguan border southwards to Playa Conchal, there are at least 13 named beaches and many more *playas* that are not formally identified or bear only local nicknames.

Thousands of people from the United States, Canada, Europe and South America have moved to the area in the last two decades, and many other foreigners and well-to-do Costa Ricans have built holiday homes in the beachfront communities strung along this stretch of lovely coastline. In total, about 40 per cent of all new construction for the tourism industry in Costa Rica is taking place in Guanacaste and along the central Pacific coast to the south towards Puntarenas province.

The Golfo de Papagayo is at the northern end of this beach zone, with the Península de Papagayo jutting into the gulf. Two of Costa Rica's premier resorts are located here: the **Four Seasons Resort** (*see p177*) and the **Occidental Allegro Papagayo** (*see p177*). When the government and resort corporations launched an iniative, known as the Papagayo Project, to begin developing the peninsula two decades ago, some predicted it would become an international tourist magnet similar to Cancún, Mexico. Instead, the Península de Papagayo has become more like the exclusive resort areas of Hawaii, both in terms of amenities and rates. The all-inclusive resorts of the Papagayo are unmistakably geared towards the well-heeled

visitor, but just south of the peninsula are beach communities attracting travellers on all budgets. From north to south, the first cluster of towns includes **Playa Panama**, **Playa Hermosa**, **Playas del Coco** and **Playa Ocotal**.

Playas del Coco is one of the most popular beach destinations on the Guanacaste Gold Coast. Only 35 kilometres (22 miles) south-west of Liberia and reachable by good road all the way from San José, Coco has become the central hub for the other three beach communities covered in this section.

Coco once was a simple fishing village and its commercial fishing boats still provide fresh seafood for the tables of restaurants and homes throughout the area. But it has also become a focal point for sport fishing, sailing and scuba diving, as well as the primary launching point for boats shuttling surfers further north along the coast to **Witch's Rock** and **Ollie's Point** – two internationally known surf spots in PN Santa Rosa.

The main beach at Coco is not particularly scenic – a long stretch of brown sand between rocky outcrops to the north and south. Nearby, however, and within easy walking distance, is a beautiful small beach that is left off most maps: **Playa Penca**.

The town is also a popular nightlife destination, much like Tamarindo, about 30 kilometres (19 miles) south along the coast, and Jacó on the Central Pacific coast. Playas del Coco's reputation as a party town has attracted some problems: prostitution, drugs and petty theft are all part of the scene. Coco has a wide assortment of hotels (about 20 including B&Bs), restaurants and bars.

Six kilometres from the centre of Playas del Coco, on the main road coming into town, is the turn-off for **Playa Hermosa** and **Playa Panama**, which lie seven and nine kilometres (4.5 and 5.5 miles) north of Coco respectively.

Hermosa is far more laid-back than Coco. There are fewer hotels and restaurants, and much less nightlife. Consequently, it is popular with many foreign retirees and second-home owners. The beach is one of about three dozen around the country that have been honoured by the government with the coveted Blue Flag environmental award for cleanliness (water quality and shoreline attributes). Contrast this with Playa Tamarindo further south along the coast, which lost its Blue Flag status last year.

Just north of Playa Hermosa is **Playa Panama**, a wide black sand beach on a lagoon ringed by hillsides dotted with homes. The beach and lagoon face **Bahía Culebra** and across it the Península de Papagayo with its classy resorts. Playa Panama is an activities beach popular with both locals and tourists for

The living is easy on **Playa Hermosa**.

its shallow calm waters. Swimming, snorkelling, boating, waterskiing, parasailing and kayaking can all be enjoyed, but it is definitely not a surfing beach.

For diving and snorkelling the most recommended outfitter is **Bill Beard's Costa Rica** (www.billbeardcostarica.com), which has been kitting out novices and experienced divers alike since 1974. It specialises in multi-day tours that include accommodation and side trips to national parks and volcanoes, but it also offers individual one-day trips.

Bill can be found in **Villa de Sol** (*see p177*) in Playa Hermosa. Directly in front of the Beach Club is **H2O Water Sports of Costa Rica** (2672 4009), which rents everything from WaveRunner water bikes to Hobie Cats. H2O also books sport fishing charters using local captains and their boats. The company uses top-rate equipment and is very safety conscious. The owner-operators have a lot of experience in water sports businesses in the United States.

Playa Ocotal is a pleasant beach town four kilometres (2.5 miles) south of Coco, known for its sport-fishing outfitters and its views over the Golfo de Papagayo. It can be reached by turning south from the main road into Coco on to a narrow, curving road across from the Coco water utility building. Just follow the road as it meanders south and west into Ocotal, where it ends. This is one of the points along the Guanacaste coastline where the north–south coastal road network is interrupted. To reach beaches south of here, travellers must return to Highway 21, drive south and use other east–west roads to get back to the coast.

Where to eat & drink

Playas del Coco has many restaurants, from sodas to seafood joints; there's also a Mexican eaterie, reflecting the popularity of the cuisine in this area. One of the best restaurants in town is **Sol y Luna** located in the **Hotel La Puerta del Sol** (2670 0195, main courses US$10). It offers simple but well-executed Italian food. The pasta is home-made. There are several restaurants specialising in fish in front of the beach. **Papagayo Pura Vida** (no phone, main courses, US$9) is one of the best, and offers a seafood platter big enough to share.

Playa Hermosa's **Villa del Sueno** (in Villa del Sueno Hotel, 2672 0026, main courses US$13) is an open-air restaurant serving

To infinity and beyond, all from the comfort of a wetbar at the **Four Seasons Resort**.

Mediterranean cuisine. The food is outstanding. During high season the Canadian owners of the hotel and restaurant entertain diners with live music several nights a week. Other hotels are the best bet for food in Playa Hermosa.

The focal point of Playa Panama is the **Beach Club** (2672 1364, main courses US$8). This open-air restaurant and bar serves good food and offers a great view of the lagoon, the larger bay and the peninsula opposite. The other options are, of course, the **Four Seasons Resort** and the **Occidental Allegro Papagayo** (*see below*).

In the tiny town of Playa Ocotal the hotels are undoubtedly the best eating options. Try **El Ocotal Resort** (2670 0321, www.ocotalresort. com, main courses US$9). Its **Roca Bruja** has a stunning view, and the food is well presented and tasty. For a more down-to-earth eaterie try **Father Rooster Bar & Grill** (2670 1246, www.fatherrooster.com, main courses US$6), an old farmhouse that doubles as some of the main social hubs of the town. It is open all day and serves quality *casados* and Mexican-influenced wraps and sandwiches along with barbecued seafood and meats.

Where to stay

On the Peninsula de Papagayo is Costa Rica's most exclusive lodging, the **Four Seasons Resort** (end of the peninsula road, 2696 0000, www.fourseasons.com, US$445-$12,500 double). No, that latter room rate isn't a typo. This all-inclusive resort in a tropical dry forest, set on hillsides with marvellous ocean views, has every amenity – beaches, pools, spas, saunas, bars, restaurants, casinos, tennis courts and a long list of activities ranging from ocean kayaking to cooking classes given by its excellent chefs. There are 145 large rooms and suites designed using indigenous-styled motifs and materials. Some guests never leave the resort grounds (golf carts are used to travel around) during their visit to Costa Rica except for the shuttle bus rides coming in and returning to Liberia's airport.

Occidental Allegro Papagayo (on peninsula road, 2690 9900, www.occidental hotels.com, US$236-$334 double) is another all-inclusive resort. It is pricey, but far less so than the Four Seasons. Occidental has similar amenities, though, including a boat shuttle that transports guests to and from a nearby private beach. The rooms are not as luxurious as those at the Four Seasons, but they are spacious and well-appointed and each has a private patio or a balcony. Every water sport imaginable is offered, including water polo and even water basketball. Scuba diving is also available, with

daily boat trips run to nearby islands, but instruction and equipment rental are additional to room rates.

To reach both resorts head south of Liberia airport on Highway 21, and when you reach a large building supplies centre, turn west and travel for about ten kilometres (six miles).

Near Playas del Coco, **Villa del Sol Bed & Breakfast** (one kilometre north of town plaza, 150 metres from beach, 2670 0085, www.villa delsol.com, US$55-$75 double) is a secluded and well-maintained establishment away from the crowds and noise of the central town nightlife district, yet still within easy walking distance of it, and only a block from the beach. **Hotel La Puerta del Sol** (one block north of the main road into Coco, 2670 0195, www.bbpuertadelsol.com, US$80 double) is a small hotel with a pool and restaurant, **Sol y Luna**, on the premises and eight rooms with air-conditioning.

There aren't many places to stay in Playa Hermosa – most visitors are day-trippers who drive in from nearby Coco – but **Villa del Sueno Hotel** (on southern entrance road into Playa Hermosa, 2672 0026, www.villadelsueno. com, US$75-$140 double) consists of Mediterranean-style buildings set amid lush gardens. It also has a lovely pool area. In addition, there are 14 rental villas across the street grouped around their own pool. Villa del Sueno has a restaurant on site.

Set on the clifftop overlooking Playa Ocotal is **El Ocotal Resort** (2670 0321, www.ocotalresort.com, US$200 double), often referenced as one of the best hotels in the country, especially in this price bracket. Its location provides spectacular views of the ocean and sunsets, from both the rooms and its decked outdoor dining area. El Ocotal has all the usual amenities of a top-flight resort, as well as a scuba diving centre and a sport fishing charter service on the premises. Its breakfasts are a particular treat. **Hotel Villa Blanca** (2670 0448, www.hotelvillacasa blanca.com, US$100-$125 double) is a good, well-priced option in Playa Ocotal. It offers golfing and diving packages with basic but homely Spanish-styled villas, set in beautiful gardens with iguanas and monkeys.

Resources

Bank

Banco Nacional *4 blocks before beach on main road in Playas del Coco (2670 0801).*

Hospital

There is one health clinic on the main road in Playas del Coco (2670 0987).

Playas del Coco – at rush hour. *See p174*.

Internet
Internet Jugo Bar *on main road near beach.*
Open 8am-9pm daily.

Police
Call 2670 0258 for Playas del Coco police, or 911.

Getting there

By bus
A **Pulmitan** (2256 9552) bus leaves from San José, (Calle 24, entre Avenidas 5 y 7), for Playas del Coco 3 times a day: 8am, 2pm and 4pm. The trip takes about 6hrs and costs around US$5. There are also many buses daily from Liberia, only an hour away. Most leave from **Terminal Liberia** (Avenida 7, entre Calles 12 y 14). The tourist bus **Grayline** (2220 2126, www.graylinecostarica.com) leaves San José for all the resorts on the Golfo de Papagayo at 8am daily and costs US$45. Interbus leaves San José at 7.45am and 2.30pm daily and costs US$35.

By road
From San José it's best to head to Liberia (*see p163*) first. Then go west to Santa Cruz along Highway 21

until just after the village of Comunidad. The road splits after 10km (6 miles); continue north to Playa Hermosa or continue west to Playas del Coco. It is all paved. The nearest airport is in Liberia.

Playa Flamingo to Playa Potrero

Playa Flamingo and the three beach communities nearby are a major draw along the Gold Coast. Flamingo was once known as Playa Blanca thanks to its sparkling white sand beach. Many North American retirees and part-time residents have built homes here, including, at one time, Elizabeth Taylor. Now Flamingo has the dubious distinction of being referred to by many locals (both foreign relocators and Ticos) as 'gringo beach'.

The rapid development in Flamingo and some other Pacific coast towns like Tamarindo to the south has spurred the Costa Rican government into passing legislation to greatly restrict building along the entire coastline of

Guanacaste province. In April 2008, at the time of writing, Costa Rica President Óscar Arias approved a law limiting height and density in the construction of all new developments in the area from the coastline to four kilometres (2.5 miles) inland. This is to prevent the Guanacaste coast from becoming what many people say sections of it already resemble – the Florida coastline of the United States, with its walls of high-rise condominiums and hotels. It is a slow movement away from the original plan of vast swathes of resorts covering the entire area that was approved in the 1970s.

Despite the excessive development, Playa Flamingo remains a popular destination. It is not a surfing beach, but is a good swimming location. It is also a premier sport fishing destination, with billfish most abundant in June and July. A new marina has been in the planning stages for a couple of years. Boat charters for snorkelling, and scuba diving

at the nearby Catalina Islands are other popular excursions for visitors.

Playa Brasilito is a small fishing village that has retained its charm despite the heavy development of Flamingo just to the north. Brasilito is a very popular beach among locals and can get quite busy at weekends. There is limited accommodation but it is probably the best value on offer throughout this stretch of beaches and the little towns.

Playa Conchal, immediately south of Playa Brasilito, is considered by some to be one of the most beautiful beaches in Costa Rica. It is set in a cove and is covered with seashells. It is also home to all-inclusive resorts such as Meliá's **Paradisus Playa Conchal** (*see p180*). This complex occupies much of the beach, which is unfortunate (unless you are staying there, of course). **Playa Potrero** is actually a string of three smaller beaches, Prieta, Penca and Potrero, located on a bay seven kilometres

Wet, but not so wild, at the relaxing **Flamingo Beach Resort**. *See p180*.

(4.5 miles) north of Flamingo, and quieter than surrounding areas. The beaches are on a protected bay popular with yacht owners. The town of Potrero is at the beaches' north end.

Where to stay

The **Flamingo Beach Resort** (2654 4444, www.resortflamingobeach.com, US$140-$263 double) is, as the name implies, directly on the beach of Playa Flamingo. The rooms are air-conditioned and have cable television. The pool is large and equipped with a wet bar. The hotel has two bars, a restaurant and a casino. **The Mariner Inn** (2654 4024, marinerinn@ racsa.co.cr, US$40-$70 double) has 12 plain rooms and is the best bargain in Flamingo. Rooms have air-conditioning, cable TV and double beds. As the name suggests, it's popular with the sport fishing crowd. It has a pool and is home to the lively Spreader Bar, a popular local hangout.

In Playa Basilito, **Hotel Brasilito** (2654 4247, www.brasilito.com, US$30-$50 double) offers rooms at bargain prices and is located directly on a small, tranquil beach. This little, two-storey hotel is German-owned and very well kept. **Apartotel Nany** (2654 4320, www.apartotelnany.com, US$65-$110 double) has 12 rooms and apartments with air-conditioning and cable TV. There is a small pool, a restaurant and an internet café on the premises. The hotel is located near the south end of Playa Brasilito.

Paradisus Playa Conchal (2654 4123, www.solmelia.com, US$428-$1,800 double) is part of the giant Spanish hotel and resort company Sol Meliá, which operates 350 facilities in 30 countries. The Paradisus resort has 328 rooms, five restaurants, several bars, a casino, a small shopping mall and a golf course. Guests travel around the resort's ten square kilometres (3.9 miles) on trams.

Close to Playa Potrero, **Cabinas Cristina** (2654 4006, www.cabinascristina.com, US$50-$60 double) is near the north end of the beach. It has a pool, and some rooms have kitchenettes and air-conditioning. The hotel will arrange all manner of activities and tours for its guests. **Bahía Esmeralda** (2654 4480, www.hotel bahiaesmeralda.com, US$55-$93 double) is near the centre of the town of Potrero. It has a pool and a restaurant. There are 20 rental units, each with air-conditioning.

Where to eat

There aren't too many eating options apart from the restaurants of the main hotels. Right on the main beach of Playa Brasilito, **Happy**

Snapper Restaurant (2654 4413, main courses US$9) serves very good seafood and steaks, occasionally to the sound of live music. **Restaurante y Bar Camarón Dorado** (2654 4028) is a highly recommendable restaurant. From the open-air dining room you can watch the waves crash. The service isn't the best, but the seafood is.

In Playa Flamingo, **Mar y Sol** (2654 4151, main courses US$22) is probably the best restaurant in the area. Catalan chef Alain Taulere cooks up exquisite – and pricey – food in the open-air restaurant. Dishes include lobster bisque, and jumbo prawns with steaks. **Marie's** (2654 4136, main courses US$12) offers more down-to-earth, but no less tasty, dishes. Seafood is, of course, the staple, but its meat and chicken dishes are also well prepared.

Getting there

By air

The nearest airport is Tamarindo (*see p186*), a 30min taxi ride away. The international airport in Liberia (*see p163*) is also an option being just a 40 min drive away, albeit along poor, but paved, roads.

By bus

Tralapa (2221 7201) buses pass all these beaches on the twice daily service leaving San José (Calle 20, entre Avenidas 3 y 5) at 8am and 10.30am. It is a 6hr journey. The tourist bus **Grayline** (2220 2126, www.graylinecostarica.com) leaves San José's hotels for Playa Conchal and Flamingo at 8am daily and costs US$35. **Interbus** leaves San José at 7.45am and 2.30pm daily and costs US$29.

By road

Travelling south from Liberia on Highway 21, turn west at the town of Belen on to a paved road and drive 25km (16 miles) to the town of Huacas. (It's worth noting that Huacas is the location of the only petrol station in the area, so if you're driving, fill up here.) From Huacas, a smaller paved road leads for a few more kilometres to Flamingo and the beach towns south of it, Playa Brasilito and Playa Conchal. Playa Potrero is just north of Flamingo on the same smaller paved road.

Resources

Bank

Banco de Costa Rica *in Playa Flamingo (2284 6600).*

Hospital

Santa Fe Medical Centre *in Playa Flamingo (2654 9000).*

Internet

Apartotel Nany *south end of Playa Brasilito (2654 4320/www.apartotelnany.com).* **Open** 9am-10pm daily.

South Guanacaste

Ritzy resorts, world class surf breaks and Costa Rica's folk music capital.

Nicoya

The town of Nicoya has charm and historic interest and makes for an enjoyable day trip. It is also a good base from which to explore the surrounding area. Its main attraction is its 500-year-old landmark, the **Iglesia de San Blas**. Declared a national heritage monument in 1995, this colonial structure is, incredibly, still standing after surviving an earthquake and severe damage from damp rot. It is the town's pride and joy, and has recently undergone the first instalment of a US$300,000 restoration project, funded by the private sector. Venturing inside you will find a little museum housing colonial relics such as a baptismal font dating from 1644, and bronze bells from 1768.

Nicoya is the central service point for neighbouring villages and has banks, grocery stores, a few shops and a hospital. All necessities can be found here, as well as some decent accommodation. There is a pleasant **Parque Central** that serves as the town's meeting point for chess-playing old men, canoodling couples and the odd stray dog. Nicoya is often cited as

the country's only city with both colonial and pre-Columbian heritage. The word 'Nicoya' is the name of a chief of the Chorotega indigenous group who originally inhabited the area when the first Conquistadores arrived. Their legacy can also be seen in the pottery Nicoya is known for. Most of the stores and stalls that line the town's two main streets sell handcrafted Chorotega-style vases and pots.

EXCURSIONS

While most national parks showcase life above the earth's surface, **PN Barra Honda** offers a more underground experience. The park is located 22 kilometres (13 miles) north-east of Nicoya and protects a subterranean network of 42 limestone caves that constitute the largest of such geological formations found in Costa Rica. Only about 50 per cent of the caves have been fully surveyed and you can strap on some climbing gear and descend into their eerie depths (accompanied by a guide). The deepest is Santa Ana, which drops 240 metres (787 feet). La Trampa (the Trap) is a steep 52-metre (170-foot) descent into Hades' Quarters, a more spacious cave with a startling white calcite chamber.

Pacific North

The dazzling beauty of the Península de Nicoya.

Green gold

Costa Rica has long stumped archaeologists on two accounts. First, there are those stone spheres (*see p260* **Circling the square**), and second, there is the presence of a skilled and intricate craftsmanship in the form of jade lapidaries. A whole slew of polished jade objects have been unearthed in Costa Rica, including pendants, blades, jewellery, beads, tubes and miniature vessels; the latter are thought to have been used to hold narcotics during rituals. Jade was revered for its colour, texture and supposed healing qualities by Mesoamerican peoples (the indigenous tribes of what is now Mexico, Honduras and Nicaragua who inhabited these regions from around 1000 BC until the Spanish invasion). Jade was by far the most valuable commodity for the indigenous population. When Hernán Cortés de Monroy Pizarro and his men first encountered the Aztecs in Mexico, they were given, among other gifts, jade objects as welcome presents. The *Conquistadores*, not particularly sensitive to jade's value, were insulted not to be offered gold. But for the Aztecs and other Central American groups, jade was their gold.

It is assumed that jade was held in the same high esteem in pre-Columbian Costa Rica since jade objects excavated there appear to have been buried alongside important tribal members. The earliest example discovered to date is a celt (axe-shaped) pendant found on the Península de Nicoya at a burial site. The top is shaped into the head and torso of a bird, and a small hole at the neck indicates it was meant to be worn on a string. Historians have dated the piece to the mid first millennium BC. Other carved ornaments depict a bird that is thought to be a sacred animal, perhaps one that links the present and the afterworld. Just how such ornaments were carved still induces much stroking of beards. Jade is a hard rock and is extremely difficult to cut, chip or work with in such fine detail. Excavated objects, however, are stunning in design and colour, ranging from white to many shades of green, but examples have been found in light yellow, lavender (very rare), mottled white, pink and black. In Costa Rica the most highly prized objects tended to be in those darker shades and bluish greens; in contrast to Asian societies where light green, almost milky-coloured pieces were favoured.

But the mysteries do not stop here. While small jade pebbles have been found in local riverbeds, the origin of the majority of worked pieces is likely to be the Motagua Valley in Guatemala, thus indicating these ancient peoples practised travel, transport and trade. Another strange fact is that the production of jade items seemed to virtually stop overnight. It is as if carving tools were purposely laid down. It seems gold became the new trend and many historians attribute this to the arrival and influence of the Spanish in the early 16th century.

An incredible amount of this lost art and uncovered objects have been excavated in the northern Pacific offering a glimpse into the lives of the people who once lived on these lands. To see how skilfully crafted Costa Rican jade lapidaries are, visit the **Museo de Jade** (*see p86*) or the **Museo de Oro Precolombino y Numismática** (*see p86*), both in San José.

The Pozo Hediondo (Stinkpot Hole) makes for amusing dinner table conversation – its name comes from the stench of dung deposited by the thousands of bats that nest here.

One cave, named 'the Nicoya Cave', is particularly interesting for history buffs; pre-Columbian human remains and indigenous objects were discovered in five of its chambers. There are various theories as to how they got there, but many assume the bodies were thrown into the cave, since the evidence garnered from the skulls suggests they date from different times. The most explored cave is Terciopelo, 63 metres (206 feet) deep and named after the deadly terciopelo snake (fer-de-lance) found dead at the bottom during the first exploration.

For those who are claustrophobic or for kids under 12, La Cuevita (Little Cave) is a good introduction as it is a smaller cave with an easy descent and has one room with good examples of stalagmite and stalactite formations.

Above ground is the **Cerro Barra Honda**, a limestone hill that rises 450 metres (1,470 feet). There is a trail that continues from the main entrance road of the park. At the top, hikers are treated to a terrific view of the Gulfo de Nicoya and Rio Tempisque. Other trails lead around the caves and through rare tropical lowland dry forest. The park entry fee is US$7, with tours offered for US$40 for up to four people. The gates are open from 8am to 4pm. Camping is allowed and drinking water is available. For a better night's sleep opt for a bed in one of the four cabins a little way up from the main ranger station. Cabins can sleep up to six people and are a handy option for those who want an early start to catch sight of the morning wildlife. To reserve your place, call the ranger station at 2659 1551 or the MINAE office in either Nicoya (2686 6760) or Liberia (2666 0630). If bat noises and salamanders give you the creeps, Nicoya is the nearest town for a less rustic stay. For information on how to get to the park see **Getting there** below.

Half an hour from Nicoya on the way to Puente de la Amistad is **Canopy Tempisque Eco Adventures** (2687 1212/1110), which offers five cables for zip-lining with lunch included for US$35. Sailing along the Rio Tempisque is another activity it offers for US$50 for two hours; the rate includes lunch and a bilingual guide.

Where to eat

Nicoya is a place to stock up on supplies rather than to find gastronomical delights. There are, however, several typical sodas where the best thing to order is a good *casado*. The restaurant of **Hotel Mundi Plaza** (north side of Tribunales de Justicia, 2685 3535, main courses US$4) serves up basic Italian pizza, pastas and lasagne. Nonna back in Italy might be turning in her grave, but it is decent enough quality nevertheless. There are several Chinese restaurants but **Restaurant El Teyet** (Calle 1, entre Avenidas 2 y 4, 2686 6654, main courses US$4) is the best – but don't expect anything really fabulous except for a dollop of chop suey. **Café Daniela** (Calle 3, entre Avenidas Central y 2, 2686 6148, main courses US$4) is a reliable choice for both breakfasts and plates of *casado*.

Where to stay

Cabina Ríos Tempisque (1km north of the crossroads towards Nicoya, 2686 6650, www.hotelriotempisque.com, US$50 double) is a nice place close to PN Barra Honda, with a good sized pool and shady gardens. Rooms are basic but clean and pleasant and equipped with a microwave and minibar. Another bonus is that the restaurant makes some tasty *casados*.

In Nicoya centre, **Hotel Jenny** (100m south of the park, 2685 5050, US$50 double) is clean… and that's about it. The staff won't greet you with a wide smile and a cocktail but the hotel is opposite the town's internet cafés and the rooms have air-conditioning units (which sometimes work). **Hotel Las Tinajas** (100m from Banco Nacional, 2685 5081, US$20 per person) is located in front of the bus stop. It offers

comfortable rooms with hot water and private bathrooms but is a bit dreary. **Hotel Mundi Plaza** (north side of Tribunales de Justicia, 2685 3535, US$40 double) is the best equipped hotel in Nicoya. It comprises three units, with shops and a restaurant. Rooms are air-conditioned, well equipped and reasonable value. It also has an outdoor pool, free internet and room service.

Resources

Bank
Banco de Costa Rica *West side of Parque Central (2284 6600).*
Banco Popular *Calle 3, entre Avenidas Central y 1 (2686 6484).*

Hospitals
Clínica Médica Nicoyana *Calle 3, entre Avenidas Central y 2 (2685 5138).*
Hospital La Anexión *600m north of Parque Central on Calle 3 (2685 5066).*

Internet
Internet el Parque *North side of Parque Central (2642 0169).* **Open** 9am-6pm Mon-Sat.

Police
Nicoya Police (2685 5328).

Getting there

By bus
It is about a 5-6hr ride from San José to Nicoya. The bus leaves you at the entrance of Nacaome village (10km from the park). You will need to take a private taxi to the park entrance. **Transportes Alfaro** (Terminal Alfaro, entre Calle 14 y Avenida 5, 2222 2666) departs from San José at 6.30am, 8am, 10am, 1.30pm, 2pm, 3pm and 5pm. **Tralapa** also leaves hourly from San José (Terminal Tralapa, 400m north of Hospital Nacional de Niños, 2221 7202). There is a daily public bus from Nicoya to Nacoame at 12.30pm.

By car
From San José, take the Interamericana Highway north. Turn left on to Highway 18 towards San Joaquin and past Pueblo Nuevo. Cross the Amistad Tempisque bridge and follow the signs to Nicoya. There are also signposts to Barra Honda, also known as Nacaome. The park has gates and is up a gravel road. If you are coming from Liberia, take Highway 21 south past Santa Cruz down to Nicoya and from there turn off towards Nacaome.

Santa Cruz

Santa Cruz may sit around 30 kilometres (18 miles) from the region's most popular beaches, but a blend of folklore and lasting traditions gives the unassuming town a flash more colour and character than the average beach resort.

Pacific North

In fact, folklore here is so deeply embedded in the ways of the town that the Central American institute of tourism has dubbed it the National Folklore City of Costa Rica. And Santa Cruz continues to live up to this honour with a fitting amount of live music, rodeos, festivals and dances all year round. Two parties to watch out for are the week-long January festival for Santo Cristo de Esquipulas, the patron saint of Santa Cruz, and the popular fiesta of the Dia de Guanacaste on 25 July, commemorating the day the province switched from Nicaraguan to Costa Rican rule in 1825. The town has all amenities required for a convenient restocking on the way to the coast and it is just 30 minutes by car to Aeropuerto Internacional Daniel Oduber Quirós (*see p167*).

EXCURSIONS

PN Palo Verde consists of marshes, mangrove swamps and lagoons near the mouth of the Río Tempisque where it flows into the north end of the Golfo de Nicoya. It is a 200-square-kilometre (77-square-mile) national park, uniquely made up of seasonal wetlands as well as tropical dry forest. About 300 bird species have been reported in the park, including 60 species of wading and aquatic bird. It is considered to be one of the most important marshes in Central America and is a sanctuary for many species of resident and migrant waterfowl as well as for forest birds. Palo Verde is at its best from September to March, when masses of migrant birds arrive to rest and feed. The largest populations include an estimated 25,000 black-bellied whistling ducks, 15,000 migrant blue-winged teals,and 4000 wood storks. The park is a 28-kilometre (17-mile) excursion from the Interamericana Highway and there are no buses to the park entrance, so a hire car or an organised tour are virtually the only ways to get there. A more interesting way into the park is by boat via the crocodile-filled Río Tempisque from Puerto Humo. It is also a great way to get to the Isla de Pajaros. Ask around the dock in Puerto Humo for a ride.

The **Hacienda Palo Verde research station**, eight kilometres (five miles) from the park entrance and run by the Organisation for Tropical Studies (www.ots.ac.cr), has lodging in dorms and a few private rooms (US$55 double), but book ahead as they are often filled with research students. The station also offers meals. The Palo Verde ranger station (2200 0125) has six rooms with several beds in each. Again it is best to book ahead, but it also allows camping (US$7 per person) outside, with easy access to showers and hot water.

Isla de Pajaros, on the Río Tempisque, is an important nesting site for 13 species of water

bird including black-crowned night-herons, jabiru storks, roseate spoonbills, cattle egrets, snowy egrets, white ibis, glossy ibis and muscovy ducks. Apart from the waterfowl, forest birds such as scarlet macaws, crested caracaras, black-headed trogons and thicket tinamous may also be encountered. The endemic mangrove hummingbird may also be found in the mangrove forests of Palo Verde and other mangrove swamps throughout the Pacific coast. To get to the island take Highway 21 from Liberia 35 kilometres (22 miles) south-east to the town of Bagaces, then turn right on to a signed road and drive 28 kilometres (17 miles) to the park entrance (2200 0125, closed Mondays, admission US$15).

Bosque Nacional Diriá is nine kilometres (5.5 miles) south of Santa Cruz. Opened in 2004, this is a relatively new wildlife refuge consisting of virgin dry forest and tropical cloud forest and the three river basins of Río Diriá, Río Enmedio and Rio Tigre. The refuge's value lies in the fact that it is a tract of land that protects natural underground water networks, though of course its beauty is appreciated above ground. Two trails, El Venado and El Escabel, give hikers a chance to pass through thick vegetation leading to the Brasil waterfall. Along the way hikers are likely to spot deer, howler monkeys and some of the 134 species of bird living within these forests. A bunkhouse on site offers sleeping capacity for 25 people. Drinking water and electricity are available, but it is recommended you take a small gas stove and camping food for dinner. There is also a campsite with showers and drinking water. The ranger station is open daily from 8am to 4pm and the entry fee is US$6. For more information, see SINAC's website www.sinaccr.net. An English version of the website is promised soon.

Sightseeing

Santa Cruz is a 12-kilometre (7.5 miles) trot from one of the country's most important craft centres. **Guaitil** is home to 40 families of artisans who are especially renowned for their work in ceramics. Their pieces are produced according to the traditional techniques of the pre-Columbian Chorotegas indigenous group, and are usually adorned with mythical motifs and symbols similar to those used by the Maya. These works were originally used as domestic utensils but are now collectable souvenirs. Although you can buy ceramics throughout the region, it is cheaper to buy them directly from the makers in Guaitil . A taxi from Santa Cruz to Guaitil costs US$6.

Hold that lot

Hear the rumbling of heavy lorries? The creak of a crane? The buzz of a saw? That is the sound of paradise in the making. Since the 1970s, Costa Rica has become a hugely popular location for owners-holiday homes. Aside from the 'oh-my-god-that's-the-nicest-beach-I've-ever-seen-let's-live-here' factor, the presence of a stable government, a reasonable cost of living, high quality public services and minimal red tape have made Costa Rica a very attractive option for the well-heeled. Conveniently for investors, the constitution and laws of Costa Rica also protect private ownership of land and property, which means that foreigners enjoy the same rights as Costa Rican citizens. Unsurprisingly, given its beaches, the most popular region for second homes is the province of Guanacaste.

The boom sector is currently in housing complexes, usually large beachside constructions with golf courses, swimming pools and restaurants. These offer varying financing and ownership options somewhere between outright ownership, timeshares and condominiums.

Cabo Caletas (www.cabocaletas.com)

A two-square-kilometre oceanfront complex located in Esterillos. Plans include 1,000 metres of coastline, an 18-hole golf course, a Bali-themed members only club, private

security, hotel, spa and a commercial centre with restaurants, shops and boutiques.

Los Sueños Resort & Marina (www.lossuenosresort.com)

Los Sueños has 200 moorings, a private beach, a design centre and an 18-hole golf course, Within its grounds, a forest reserve of two square kilometres has been spared from the bulldozer.

Ocotalito Resort & Spa (www.ocotalito.com)

Located in Playa Ocotal, this resort sits on a hillside and is 25 minutes from Liberia's international airport. By 2009, 50 new villas are to be built.

Tamarindo Heights (www.tamarindolifestyle.com)

A private gated community of half a square kilometre featuring 168 residential lots. Amenities will include a supermarket, pharmacy, bank, restaurants, boutiques, spa and resort.

Hacienda Pinilla (www.haciendapinilla.com)

Located near Tamarindo, Hacienda Pinilla is a condo complex of 18 square kilometres. The surrounding scenery incorporates beaches and rainforest. The complex is family oriented, has private security and water sports and includes an exclusive golf course.

Pacific North

Where to stay

The relatively new **Hotel La Estancia** (2680 0476, US$30 double) is a comfortable and affordable option. The hotel is located close to the central Plaza de Los Mangos and its rooms are all air-conditioned. They also have cable TV and private bathrooms. Found in Santa Cruz centre, diagonally opposite the south-west corner of Plaza de Los Mangos, is the simple yet colourful **Hotel La Pampa** (2680 0586, US$40 double). It offers friendly service, private bathrooms, cable TV and air-conditioning. **Hotel Diria** (2680 0080, hoteldiria@ hotmail.com, US$45 double) sits adjacent to Banco Nacional. This hotel is a little out of the centre but has 50 air-conditioned rooms, beautiful surroundings and a swimming pool. Another place built for relaxing is **Hotel La Calle de Alcala** (2680 0000, US$45 double, www.hotellacalledealcala.com). It has air-conditioned rooms with room service, bar and restaurant areas, a pool and secure parking.

Where to eat

Santa Cruz's restaurant scene is oddly abundant in Chinese cuisine. If a brief hiatus from rice and beans with, erm, beans and rice is in order, then try **El Milenio** (100m west of Parque Central, 2680 0586, main courses US$5), whose generous portions of tasty stir-fries and chow meins are extremely popular. For a bit of character and some very tasty *casados,* try **La Fabrica de Tortillas** (200m south of Banco Popular, no phone, main courses US$4). This restaurant, also referred to as Coope-Tortillas, serves great value and authentic Guanacaste food and its busy kitchen is in full view.

Resources

Hospital

Hospital La Anexión *Nicoya, 600m north of Parque Central on Calle 3 (2685 5066).*

Bank

Banco Nacional *3 blocks north of Plaza de los Mangos (2680 0544).*

Internet

Ciberm@nia *100m north of Parque Ramos (2666 7240).* **Open** 8am-7pm Mon-Sat.

Getting there

By bus

A **Tralapa** (2680 0392) bus from San José to Santa Cruz leaves the capital from the Coca-Cola terminal (Avenida 1, entre Calles 16 y 18) every 1-2 hrs from 7am to 6pm. Buses heading to Liberia, Nicoya and San José leave from the terminal on the north side of La Plaza de los Mangos. Buses heading to the region's beaches including Playas Tamarindo, Flamingo and Brasilito leave from the terminal 400m east of La Plaza de los Mangos.

By road

Santa Cruz lies on Highway 21. It can be reached by turning on to Highway 21 from the Interamericana Highway in Liberia, or off the Interamericana on to Highway 18 towards Puente de la Amistad.

Playa Tamarindo

The 'holiday capital of the Gold Coast', Playa Tamarindo attracts surfers, backpackers, honeymooners and hoteliers like ants to a picnic. Easy to reach, with dry heat, sunshine and ideal waves, it is usually one of the first beach towns to be hyped by travel agents and returning holidaymakers. During peak season the town more than doubles in population, which gives an indication of its decidedly not 'Costa Rica's best kept secret' status. While Tamarindo has retained its beach town vibe, it has established amenities, a large community of expats, a decent selection of restaurants, and comfortable hotels.

Tamarindo is also known for its party atmosphere: the town has the best bars in Guanacaste. There is a substantial crowd of backpackers and twentysomethings who frequent the bars that line the main strip. Reggae, local jazz and merengue keep the fun-loving spirit going, with each bar throwing a themed *fiesta* on a designated night of the week.

Tamarindo is also a playground for sport enthusiasts, and is excellent for outdoor pursuits. Often called the 'Hawaii of South America', this region attracts competent professional surfers who carve up the huge waves. Close to the town centre, breaks at the rivermouth such as **Langosta** and **Pico Pequeño** are prime surfing points, and a short drive away lie **Playas Grande** (*see p190*), **Avellanas** (*see p192*) and **Negra** (*see p192*). Experienced surfers will want to try **Witch's Rock** and **Ollie's Point** (*see p173*), both only accessible by boat. These are tempting reef breaks that are internationally acclaimed for their long lefts, rights and hollow waves. If you have never attempted the sport, beginner lessons are available at a number of surf shops. Try **Banana Surf Club** (2653 1270, www.bananasurfclub.com), **Matos Surf Shop** (2653 0845, www.matosfilms.com) or **Blue Trailz Surf Camp** (2653 0221, www.bluetrailz.com).

Sport fishing comes in a close second when it comes to water-based activities. Offshore and around Tamarindo you can go after marlin, sailfish, roosterfish, yellow-fin tuna, wahoo and mahi-mahi (the latter being most tasty on the barbecue). The months from December to February attract marlin chasers and May to November are the better months for sailfish, dorado and tuna. Contact **Vic Tours Flamingo Sport Fishing** (2654 5573, www.vic-tourscr.com) for full- or half-day trips. Its boats are equipped with all the latest in fish finding technology.

Costa Rica Gamefish Sportfishing (2371 4418, www.crgamefish.com) is another outfit that offers trips out on its boat, the Ocean Master, with an experienced captain and crew. A reliable option for snorkelling and scuba diving tours is **Agua Rica Diving Center** (2653 2032). Snorkelling tours cost between US$50 and US$90, and scuba diving from US$125 and US$370. The centre organises clients into small groups of no more than six people, with all equipment provided, as well as boat transfers, guides, drinks and snacks. It also offers certified courses.

Skim the waves on a catamaran with **Marlin del Rey Sailing Tours** (2536 3241) and you might see dolphins, flying fish or even a breaching whale. For anyone who fancies a bit more turf than surf, there are two golf courses: **Hacienda Pinilla** (2680 7000,

www.haciendapinilla.com), an ocean-facing course designed by American architect Mike Young; and **Garra de Leon** at Paradisus Playa Conchal (2654 4123, www.paradisus playaconchal.com), a tropical space by the beach designed by another well-known architect, Robert Trent Jones Jr. Both are 18-hole courses and have well-tended greens.

Not recommended for those with French-tipped manicures, **Off Road Costa Rica** (2653 1969, www.offroadcostarica.com) has a fleet of jeeps that take you into the jungle, affording an opportunity to see otherwise uncharted territory. You can choose from three-hour, five-hour or full-day trips accompanied by knowledgeable staff and ride through the bumpy terrain of the Guanacaste back country, shifting gears through river crossings and quagmires.

EXCURSIONS

Tamarindo is also a superb location for nature exploration, being close to **PN Marino las Baulas** (*see p190*). You can tour the **Estero Tamarindo**, a five-square-kilometre (1.9-square-mile) estuary where saltwater and freshwater mix to create a ecosystem home to dozens of birds and other wildlife, including saltwater crocodiles. Birdwatching and flat boat tours can be arranged, for the early

Watching the sunset, beer in hand, is a pastime on **Playa Tamarindo**.

Pacific North

Surf and song in **Playa Tamarindo**.

morning too. Bring binoculars in the hope of spotting tiger-heron, black-headed trojans or ospreys. Kayak rentals are also readily available. The 'jungle boat safari' at **Tamarindo Bay Tours** (across from Plaza Conchal Shopping Mall, 8821 9987) is a great trip.

Where to eat & drink

Cala Moresca Restaurant
Far west end of Tamarindo (2653 0214/ www.calaluna.com). **Open** 8am-10pm daily. **Main courses** US$50-$90. **Credit** AmEx, MC, V.
Situated next to the pool at the Cala Luna hotel, this top end restaurant specialises in delicious Italian and other Mediterranean dishes. The service is excellent, and the food carefully cooked and well presented. Chose from an extensive wine list and enjoy a romantic candlelit meal. There is also a sushi bar.

Lola's
On Tamarindo beach (2652 9097). **Open** 8am-6pm daily. **Main courses** US$15. **No credit cards**.
Lola's is a chic minimalist restaurant. The menu alters throughout the day, with *batidos* (smoothies) and *queques* (banana bread) from 8am to 10am; a full menu of fish, salads, pizzas and vegetarian hamburgers from 10am to 1pm; and *bocas* (small tapas) from 3pm to 5pm. Lola's is in the same building as the **Avellana Surf School** (www.avellanasurf school.com), which operates from 7am to 6.30pm.

Nogui's Sunset Café
On Tamarindo loop by bus station (2653 0029). **Open** noon-10pm daily. **Main courses** US$9. **No credit cards**.
The ideal place for a sunset dinner. This eaterie is popular with locals – always a good sign. Its menu of salads, hamburgers, fish fillets and huge breakfasts changes all the time.

Tabú
70m north of Hotel Barceló (2653 1422). **Open** 5-10.30pm. **Main courses** US$12. **No credit cards**.
Relaxed Tico-run restaurant serving up some high quality dishes including starters of lobster bisque or tuna wrapped in chard. Complement your meal from the extensive wine and drinks menu.

Tango Grill
Opposite bar Voodoo (2653 0189). **Open** 6-10.30pm. **Main courses** US$9. **Credit** AmEx, MC, V.
Experience some live tango dancing and enjoy a slab of meat and a slosh of Argentinian wine at this typical joint straight from the River Plate. Wenceslao, also the owner of La Botella de Leche (*see right*), cooks the meat and offal to perfection.

El Voodoo
Tamarindo (2653 0100/www.elvoodoo.com). **Open** 5pm-2.30am days. **Main courses** US$17. **Credit** MC, V.

El Voodoo is the coming together of fine dining, live music and DJs. The menu, created by Spanish chef Pablo Pose Buongiorno, mixes delicately flavoured seafood dishes such as mahi-mahi fillets on garlic calamari with meat dishes like wasabi-crusted rack of lamb. The desserts are equally adventurous – pumpkin carpaccio with coconut ice-cream or pineapple pastry with lychee ice-cream. Once the kitchen has closed, the decks are loaded and the music is turned up with live DJs from Thursday to Saturday nights.

Where to stay

Los Altos de Eros
Tamarindo (8850 4222/www.losaltosdeeros.com). **Rates** US$395-$595 double. **Rooms** 5. **Credit** AmEx, MC, V.
Located on top of a hill 20 minutes out of Tamarindo, Los Altos has peace and quiet guaranteed. It also has gorgeous rooms, an infinity pool, tropical jungle, massages with complimentary champagne and dried fruits, yoga and valley views. There is a spa too, with incredible views towards the sea and all manner of treatments. The rate includes breakfast, lunch, dinner from Tuesday to Sunday, and unlimited wine and beer. Transfers to the beach and to Tamarindo are also included.
Bar. Gym. Internet (wireless, shared terminal, free). Parking. Pool (outdoor). Restaurant. Room service. Spa. TV.

La Botella de Leche
Tamarindo (2653 0189/www.labotelladeleche.com). **Rates** US$24 double. **Rooms** 8 cabins. **Credit** AmEx, DC, MC, V.
A relaxed hostel with private and shared air-conditioned cabins. A communal kitchen, open patio and pool surrounded by hammocks are great spots to meet fellow travellers. The young Argentinian owners Marina and Wenceslao can also organise tours and surf classes – at US$20 per hour.
Internet (wireless, shared terminal, free). Pool (outdoor). TV.

Cala Luna Boutique Hotel & Villas
Far west end of Tamarindo (2653 0214/ www.calaluna.com). **Rooms** 20 (plus 22 villas each with 2 or 3 rooms). **Rates** US$185 double. **Credit** AmEx, DC, MC, V.
Character oozes from this stylish hotel located just a few metres from Playa Langosta. The colourful interior and tropical wood furnishings are complemented by the bright and welcoming service, plus one of the best restaurants in the area, the Cala Moresca (*see left*). The 21 villas offer privacy and can comfortably accommodate four people. Each has a private swimming pool and small park area, and there are three larger villas for six guests. The hotel can arrange plenty of activities including surfing, fishing, boating, golf and nature tours.
Bar. Internet (shared terminal, free). Parking. Pool (outdoor). Restaurants (2). Room service. TV.

Hotel Capitán Suizo

Tamarindo (2653 0075/www.hotelcapitansuizo.com).
Rates US$190-$210 double. **Rooms** 22; 8
bungalows. **Credit** AmEx, DC, MC, V.
A charming hotel that is part of the Small Distinctive
Hotels group. The grounds are a haven of greenery
set against the blue of the nearby ocean, and the
hotel's restaurant has an understandably good
reputation. There are 22 spacious and tastefully
decorated rooms and eight bungalows set back in
the jungle. All this is topped off with almost
flawless service. The hotel also almost exclusively
hires Costa Ricans to ensure it benefits the local community. The restaurant uses only organic ingredients where possible and serves up some interesting
dishes such as cucumber gazpacho with natural
yoghurt and prawns as well as some other good
seafood plates.
Bar. Business centre. Disabled-adapted rooms.
Internet (shared terminal, free). Parking. Pool
(outdoor). Restaurant. Room service. Spa. TV.

Sueño del Mar Bed & Breakfast

Playa Langosta (2653 0284/www.sueno-del-
mar.com). **Rates** US$195-$250 double. **Rooms** 6.
Credit AmEx, DC, MC, V.
This is an intimate hotel, with an abundance of candles. The swimming pool area is a lovely place to
take Sueño del Mar's breakfasts. A seating area with
hammocks has excellent views of the sea. An extra
plus is the special dinner nights. A highly recommended hotel for a relaxing few days.
Internet (shared terminal, free). Pool (outdoor).
Room service.

Villa Deveena

Villa Deveena, on the north side of Alan's surfboard
repair workshop, Los Pargos. **Rates** US$85 double.
Rooms 9. **Credit** AmEx, MC, V.
A stylish new addition to the Tamarindo hospitality
scene is Villa Deveena, run by a couple who spent
30 years running a private club in California. The
delicately decorated rooms have king-sized beds,
open-air showers and bathrooms. All rooms overlook the saltwater swimming pool, and at the end of
the large central patio there is a specially designed
deck for massage and reiki sessions.
Bar. Gym. Internet (wireless, free). Pool (outdoor).
Restaurants. Room service. TV.

Witch's Rock

Tamarindo (2653 1262/www.witchsrocksurfcamp.
com). **Rates** US$70-$160 double. **Rooms** 10. **Credit**
AmEx, MC, V.
Named after the famous Tamarindo break, Witch's
Rock is surf-oriented accommodation at its best.
While the rooms here are all comfortable, the
emphasis is on surfing – so don't expect to find a TV
anywhere. The meeting spot is typically the central
patio restaurant Eat@Joes, which serves up some
great fast food from sushi to hamburgers. This surf
camp is popular for week-long packages.
Bar. Internet (wireless). Pool (outdoor). Restaurant.
Room service.

Resources

Bank

Banco Nacional *(2653 0366).* Can change dollars.

Internet

Next to Banco Nacional. **Open** 9am-9pm daily.

Police

Call 2653 0283 or 911 for emergencies.

Getting there

By air

There are up to 8 flights a day from San José with
both **Sansa** (www.flysansa.com) and **Nature Air**
(www.natureair.com). Prices are around US$89 for
a single, US$178 for a return.

By bus

Buses from the Empresas Alfaro office at the
Coca-Cola bus station (Avenida 1, y Calle 16) in San
José leave for Tamarindo sporadically throughout
the day. **Fantasy Tours/Gray Line**
(www.fantasy.co.cr) has a daily bus to Tamarindo,
which departs from several San José hotel locations
every morning.

By road

From San José the best route is via Belén, off the
Interamericana at Liberia. From Huacas it is a poor
but paved road. The whole journey takes 4-5hrs.

PN Marino las Baulas & Playa Grande

A 30-minute drive north of Tamarindo will lead
you to **Playa Grande**, a key turtle nesting site
within **PN Marino las Baulas**. Playa Grande
has less of a party atmosphere and a more
remote feel than Tamarindo. There are a few
shops and a couple of pizzerias, but it's the
glorious oceanfront that is the attraction here.
Because the town is within the park's protected
range, development is closely regulated, with
few hotels allowed along the shoreline.

Unless you are a surfer, the real reason for
coming here is PN Marino las Baulas, named
after the endangered leatherback turtles
(*baulas*) that nest here (*see p194* **Turtle
power**). Officially declared a park in 1990, five
kilometres (three miles) of coastline and 220
square kilometres (85 square miles) of ocean
make up this protected turtle nursery. From
October to February female turtles haul
themselves out of the ocean to lay their fragile
eggs – still an attraction for poachers – on one
of the three nesting beaches in the park, Playas
Langosta, Grande and Ventanas. There are no
marked trails in the park grounds and camping
is strictly forbidden. To witness the

leatherbacks laying eggs, you can either make reservations through your hotel, which will arrange the transport and entry fee, or register at the park entrance at 9.30am (take your passport) and return at night (around 10pm) to see the turtles in action. The park has a small museum with a thorough compilation of interesting turtle facts including an informative video. Audio tours are available in English. On the night tour wear dark clothes, whisper, and remember that the use of flashlights is prohibited so as not to disturb the creation of more than 100 (per mother) endangered baby turtles. The entry fee is US$7 plus another US$7 for the night tour.

Where to eat & stay

Playa Grande is a great place for smaller, family-run hotels, the kind of places where you genuinely feel welcome. One prominent hotel on the beach is **Hotel Las Tortugas** (2653 0423, www.lastortugashotel.com, US$105 double), which was erected before park status was conferred on the area and whose owner, Louis Wilson, was one of the key figures in fighting for the protection of the region's turtle nesting sites. It is an 11-room building right in front of the best surf break. There is a pool and a palm-roof respite ranch, which was set up to allow guests to take in the tropical air and listen to the waves. The hotel supports and practises sustainable tourism and funds community projects, but its focus has always been on wildlife; this was the first enterprise in town to voice concern over turtle welfare. It also has a good, cheerful restaurant.

Just south of Hotel Las Tortugas is **Rip Jack Inn** (2653 0480, www.ripjackinn.com, US$93 double), a secluded but more basic option with eight decent sized rooms tucked away in its gardens. Onsite activities include yoga. The hotel's second-floor open-air bar and restaurant is usually filled with guests and non-guests sampling its top-notch cooking. **Hotel Bula Bula** (2653 0975, US$140 double) is a favourite for couples thanks to its quirky layout, brightly decorated rooms and excellent restaurant, the **Great Waltini's**.

Resources

Most of the resources are in Playa Tamarindo (*see p186*).

Internet

Matos Films This surf shop is also the only internet café in Playa Grande. **Open** 9am-7pm daily.

Getting there

By boat

Many people visit the turtle beaches and Playa Grande from Tamarindo. The quickest way to get there is by boat across the estuary. There are always

The swinging scene of **Playa Avellana**.

boats waiting. They charge around US$1.50 a head, sometimes less if the boat is full.

By road
From San José the best route is via Belén, off the Interamericana Highway at Liberia. From Huacas it is a poor but paved road to Playa Tamarindo. From there it is a 30min drive north to Playa Grande.

Playa Avellana to Playa Azul

The legendary status of the beaches of **Playa Avellana**, **Playa Azul**, **Playa Negra** and **Playa Junquillal** was cemented in 1994 with the release of the surfing film *Endless Summer 2*. The film opened with the boarder Robert August – and star of the first *Endless Summer* – taking the two protagonists to these beaches and showing them the perfect swells (*see p72* **Making waves**), hollow curls and Hawaiian-style breaks (some even call the area Little Hawaii). Non-surfers will enjoy the long, relatively empty, beaches and the forest scenery a few hundred yards inland. The night scene tends to centre on surf shacks and sodas serving cold beers, where surfers chat away about the day's waves.

There are some good basic places to stay. The best options for eating are also in the hotels along the coast.

Where to eat & drink
If you want to eat well, reserve a table at one of the hotel's reastaurants; eateries along the beach only offer basic fast food. Recommendable among the latter is **Lola's on the Beach** (Playa Avellana, 2658 8097, main courses US$11), which serves large portions and sandwiches, its tuna sandwich is a particular highlight. You can get good fish at **Café Playa Negra** (in Playa Negra, 2658 8034, main courses US$8); it specialises in Peruvian food and sushi and is open from 7am to 9pm daily. For pizza try **La Vida Buena Pizzeria** (Playa Negra, 2658 8082, main courses US$4). It's open from 4pm Monday to Thursday, and from 11am on Saturdays.

Where to stay
A good choice for nature lovers is **Cabinas las Olas** (2652 9315, www.cabinaslasolas.co.cr, US$80 double). Its nature trails allow guests to spend some time among jungle wildlife while Playa Avellana beckons sun worshippers out front. Its ten airy rooms have comfy beds, lots of light and free wireless access. A little way down the bumpy road from Playa Avellana to Playa Negra is **Café Playa Negra B&B**

Surfers sizing up the swells from the beach at **Hotel Playa Negra**.

(2652 9351, www.playanegracafe.com, US$58 double). Run by a friendly Peruvian family, it offers six rooms decorated with artwork and colourful fabrics. A large shared patio lets you relax and socialise. **Hotelito Si Si Si** (Playa Junquillal, 2658 9021, www.hotelitosisisi.com, US$103 double) offers three rooms and one cottage. It is a private and tidy place with lots of appeal. There is a stylishly designed pool, a small gym and a tennis court.

Hotel Playa Negra (2652 9134, www.playanegra.com, US$80 double) is probably the finest resort in this area. Its ten brightly coloured round cabins are set in a green garden close to the beachfront. Each has a queen-size bed and two singles. It is popular among surfers for its proximity to some excellent waves.

Resources

Internet
Café Internet *in Playa Negra across from La Vida Buena Pizzeria.* **Open** 9am-7pm daily.

Getting there

By road
There are no buses to Playa Avellana or Playa Negra, but these beaches are accessible by a bumpy road south from Tamarindo. This road continues south to Playa Junquillal. If coming from inland, you need to go to Santa Cruz (*see p183*) either for buses or to take the road. Half of the route is paved and the rest is accessible by four-wheel drive only. In the height of the rainy season it is often impassable.

Nosara

Beautiful beaches, lush forests and some rather confusing roads make up the Nosara area, one of Guanacaste's most alluring destinations. Each of the four local beaches, **Playa Nosara**, **Playa Pelada**, **Playa Guiones** and **Playa Ostional**, offers something different, from snorkelling to swimming to turtle watching to plain lazing. The area was the victim of major deforestation, with forests cleared for cattle raising, but these days the emphasis is on reforesting the land and preserving what is left of the zone's flora. A large amount of the land is protected by restrictions on urban development, championed by residents not wanting this area to succumb to the built-up resort-look adopted by several of the country's other famed coastal spots. Nosara is a collection of basic amenities and a soccer field found six kilometres (3.5 miles) from the water, and is a convenient point to replenish stocks if travelling through. There is, however, plenty of decent lodging in the area for those who need it.

The surfing spot of the area is Playa Guiones, which stretches between Punta Pelada and Punta Guiones. The waves crash hard, and beginners need to be wary of strong currents. Sitting behind this seven kilometres (4.5 miles) of beach are restaurants, bars and hotels. North of Guiones are the white sands and palm trees of Playa Pelada. Dolphins also swim close to this small piece of curving coastline and local fishermen sometimes take parties out.

EXCURSIONS
Those wishing to venture into the surrounding greenery should try **Reserva Biológica Nosara** (US$6 for entry and guided tour) next to Rio Nosara. Look out for 200 species of bird and monkeys in the foliage and canopies, and some crocodiles lurking in the nearby waters and mangrove swamps. The major Olive Ridley sea turtle nesting site, **Refugio Nacional de Fauna Silvestre Ostional**, is eight kilometres (five miles) north-west of Nosara. If you are lucky enough to catch an *arribada* (arrival), you'll see droves coming ashore (*see p194* **Turtle power**).

Those more interested in wave-riding should try **Safari Surf School** (2682 0573, www.safarisurfschool.com). This company is the area's top spot for everything surf-related. A post-surf massage can also be provided. If meditation is more your style, call in on the **Nosara Institute** (2682 0071, www.nosara yoga.com), which holds internationally recognised yoga classes for those of all levels.

Where to eat

Café de París
Main road on way into Nosara (2682 0087/ www.cafedeparis.net). **Open** 7am-7pm daily. **Main courses** US$9. **Credit** AmEx, MC, V.
A tasty European bakery where you can pick up some French bread or croissants on the way to the beach and some quality vegetarian or traditional food on the way home.

La Luna Bar & Grill
Playa Pelada, 200m north of Olga's (2682 0122). **Open** 11am-11pm daily. **Main courses** US$10. **No credit cards.**
This is the right place for those looking for a varied menu with lots of international influences. Head here for a lively atmosphere and great cocktails.

Marlin Bill's
Playa Nosara (2682 0458). **Open** 11am-2.30pm, 6-11pm Mon-Sat. **Main courses** US$10. **Credit** MC, V.
Come equipped with a large appetite as the portions here are made to fill. The menu offers a good selection of meat and fish dishes, and the service is friendly and welcoming.

Turtle power

As the sun rises over the Península de Nicoya, hundreds of hands scrabble the sand searching for pockets of newly laid turtle eggs, thrusting the glistening balls into bags. These eagerly gathered treasures are dispatched to restaurants and bars across Costa Rica. The eggs are regarded not only as delicious – they are also said to be a potent aphrodisiac.

This periodic mass egg hunt on the Pacific beach of Ostional is not, however, a mass act of illegal poaching but is the only time and place anywhere in the world where the ban on collecting sea turtle eggs is temporarily lifted.

Created in 1982, the Ostional Wildlife Refuge protects a key nesting spot for the Olive Ridley sea turtle. During the prime nesting season from August to December, mass *arribadas* (arrivals) occur for up to seven days at a time. As nearly all eggs laid during the first couple of days are destined to be scrambled by the ensuing droves of nesting turtles, the local community is permitted to harvest the initial batches laid during the first 36 hours, a mere one per cent of the eggs from each *arribada*. In exchange the community plays an active part in the protection of Ostional, keeping the beach clear and patrolling for poachers.

During peak season, *arribadas* can occur up to twice a month, with each female depositing around 100 eggs. Once hatched (after around 50 days) the fledgling turtles must make the treacherous journey to the waterline, running the gauntlet of vultures and other predators. In an attempt to keep Ostional's scuttling infants safe from harm, they are accompanied to the water's edge by local schoolchildren. The few turtles that make it to adulthood will return to their birthplace in 10-15 years to lay eggs of their own.

The main threats to turtles, and the main reasons why only a tiny percentage of the hatchlings reach maturity, are predictably man-made. Egg poaching, the hunting of turtles for the meat and shell, unethical fishing practices and the destruction of nesting grounds through beach development, continue to bore into the world's turtle population. The largest of all turtles, the mighty leatherback, shared the planet with the dinosaurs. Yet since the 1980s the number of nesting females is thought to have dropped from 115,000 to less than 26,000.

In the Pacific, once a prolific spot for the leatherback, the population is estimated at less than 3,000. Reserves and organisations protecting these animals are vital in order to ensure their future.

The reserve at Ostional is one of the world's most important nesting sites for the olive ridley, the smallest of the sea turtles. The rainy season sees around 200,000 creatures haul their egg-laden bodies on to the shore. The 15-kilometre (9.5 mile) beach strip is also visited in lesser numbers by the critically endangered green turtle. Another principal nesting ground for the distinctive leatherback is Tamarindo's Playa Grande, part of **Parque Marino las Baulas** (*see p190*). The turtles nest there from November to February.

The defining feature of this marine giant is its thick leathery shell, which is unlike the hard shell generally associated with turtle species. This design innovation allows the leatherback to withstand much colder temperatures than its cousins. But despite their solid form and seeming durability, they are one of the most endangered animals on earth. While leatherbacks are rarely killed for food, they frequently mistake plastic bags floating in the water for their dietary favourite, jellyfish, and choke. It is the green turtle that has the unlucky honour of being the most delicious – it is the main ingredient in most turtle soup recipes. The Caribbean haven of **PN Tortuguero** (*see p279*) is a sanctuary for the green turtle, which nests there from June to September.

Five species of marine turtle frequent Costa Rican shores. Both coasts are home to green, hawksbill and leatherback turtles. The olive ridley is found on the Pacific coast, and the loggerhead on the Caribbean coast. Visitors to the country can have a hands-on experience of turtle conservation projects through the many volunteer programs set up.

The environmental organisation Earthwatch (www.earthwatch.org) runs an active and acclaimed leatherback monitoring programme in the Guanacaste region. The beautiful **Pacuare Nature Reserve** (2224 8568, www.turtleprotection.org) is another haven for the endangered leatherback.

Asociación WIDECAST runs several programmes throughout Costa Rica including the Ostional sea turtle project (2224 3570, www.latinamericanseaturtles.org).

Olga's

On Playa Pelada (no phone). **Open** 8am-7pm daily. **Main courses** US$4. **No credit cards**.
Try huge *casados* and other typical food in this restaurant overlooking the sea. The *sopa pescado* (fish soup) is highly recommended and is made with locally caught fish. Olga's is a local institution.

Restaurant del Harmony Hotel

Playa Guiones (2682 4114/www.harmonynosara. com). **Open** 7am-10.30am, noon-3.30pm, 6-9pm daily. **Main courses** US$15. **Credit** AmEx, MC, V.
Lovely open-air restaurant serving up to 40 guests. Produce used here is, where possible, organic and local, and the menu incorporates fresh seafood and fruits and vegetables, with exotic flavours such as wild ginger and coconut.

Where to stay

Giardino Tropicale

Playa Guiones (2682 4000/www.giardino tropicale.com). **Rates** US$70-$90 double. **Rooms** 10. **Credit** MC, V.
The driving principle behind this charming hotel is green holidaying. Measures such as solar-powered water heaters and grey water waste systems keep the establishment's environmental impact down to a minimum. The restaurant has excellent pizzas cooked in a wood-fired oven as well as an extensive international menu. Owners Myriam and Marcel, who live on the premises (and have lived in the area for years) will be able to advise you on the best tours.

The deluxe rooms have a private balcony and there is one apartment with a fully equipped kitchen. *Bar. Business centre. Internet (wireless, free). Gym. Pool. Restaurant.*

Gilded Iguana

Playa Guiones (2682 0259/www.gildediguana.com). **Rates** US$75-$115 double. **Rooms** 6. **Credit** AmEx, MC, V.
Just 30m from Playa Guiones, this friendly hotel is a popular choice for visitors to Nosara thanks to its large rooms that are ideal for families and surfing groups. Relax in the swimming pool area, which has its own 'waterfall' and wet bar. Surf lessons, Spanish classes, live music, kayak tours and fishing charters are available.
Bar. Parking. Restaurant.

Harmony Hotel

Playa Guiones (2682 4114/www.harmony nosara.com). **Rates** US$320 double. **Rooms** 24. **Credit** AmEx, MC, V.
The name suggests what visitors should expect from the Harmony Hotel, and, thanks to the efforts of the owners, those expectations are largely met. Prospective guests can choose from the Coco Rooms, opening out on to a private patio with heated shower and seating area; open layout bungalows complete with rocking chairs and hammocks; and the Harmony House, with infinity pool, king-sized beds and lovely views. The open-air restaurant serves dishes of organic seafood, fruits and vegetables. It has an interesting art collection.
Internet (wireless). Pool. Restaurant. Spa.

The balance between art and design is captured in **Harmony Hotel**.

L'Aqua Viva Resort & Spa

Playa Guiones (2682 1084/www.lacquaviva.com).
Rates US$185-$375 double. **Rooms** 36. **Credit**
AmEx, DC, MC, V.

This resort is situated in the tropical forest of the
Nosara Civic Association, just a 1km walk from the
white sand beach. The main buildings play with
open spaces and have various levels, all topped with
a thatched roof that would not look out of place in
Bali. There is an exotic garden to wander through,
and a private collection of artwork including the
sculpture *Sophia* made by the master Jorge Jiménez
Deredia. There are ten suites, six master suites and
two ample villas.

*Bar. Gym. Internet (wireless, shared terminal, free).
Parking. Pool (outdoor). Restaurant. Room service.
Spa. TV.*

Villa Tortuga

*Playa Guiones (2682 4039/www.villatortuga
nosara.com).* **Rates** US$120-$205 double. **Rooms** 7.
Credit AmEx, MC, V.

The main house of this villa is split into
two units and four suites with a varying number of
rooms in each. The units, Casa Tortuga and Casa
Pelicano, are spacious, have living and dining
rooms, full kitchens, two master bedrooms and
one bedroom with two single beds. The four suites
– Del Sol, Del Mar, Del Mono, De La Luna –
each have one bedroom along with living and
dining areas that mimic those of the units. Staff
can also organise surf lessons, canopy tours
and fishing trips.

Internet. Pool (outdoor). TV/DVD player.

Resources

Bank

Banco Popular *in the shopping centre near Playa
Guiones.* In Nosara village, travellers' cheques can be
changed at Super Nosara, at the south-west corner of
the football pitch .

Hospital

Red Cross provides emergency treatment.

Internet

Frog Pad Nosara *Villa Tortuga (2682 4039/
www.thefrogpad.com).* Has several internet stations,
surf board and bicycle rental, surfing classes, fishing
charters and canopy tours. **Open** 9am-9pm daily.

Police

*South-east corner of Nosara football field.
(2682 0317).*

Getting there

By air

Sansa (www.flysansa.com) flies from San José to
Nosara for around US$90 one-way. **Nature Air**
(www.natureair.com) flies from San José 3 times a
day, and from Liberia to Nosara twice a day.

By bus

A 6hr ride with **Alfaro Bus** from San José that
departs daily at 5.30am from the Coca-Cola terminal
(Avenida 1, y Calle 16) in the centre of the city.
US$10. **Interbus** (www.interbusonline.com) also has
private shuttles from San José direct to Nosara daily.
Leaving at 8am from San José it provides pick-ups at
designated hotels and lodges in the area for US$45.
Additional fees for extra luggage and surfboards.

Playa Sámara

Playa Sámara has long been a draw for sun
worshippers with its seven-kilometre (4.5 mile)
band of white sand beach. It is also an excellent
swimming beach as the shore stays calm
thanks to a protective reef further out. There
are plenty of activities to partake in if you get
bored of the beach. **Sámara Adventures**
(2656 1054, www.samarabeach.com/
samaraadventures), specialises in tailor-made
trips and arranges for transport to and from the
airport as well as offering a whole host of tours.
Tio Tigre Tours (2656 0098, tiotigre@
samarabeach.com) located 100 metres north of
the post office, offers numerous sea creature-
loving tours. Trips include dolphin and whale
tours and turtle nesting observation.

As the swell on this part of the coast is tame,
it makes a good spot for beginner surfers.
Jesse's Sámara Beach Surf School (2656
0055, US$40 per person) gives professional
instruction aimed at beginners. It is one
kilometre down the beach from central Sámara
near Hostel Fénix. **C&C Surf School** (2656
0628, www.ticoadventurelodge.com, US$40 per
person) also offers encouraging instruction. It is
located 200 metres east of the police station.

Where to eat

Coco's (on the main street, 2656 0922,
main courses US$25) has a varied menu but
specialises in whatever has been hauled out of
the sea that day. It is open daily from noon until
sunset. Located directly on the beach is **El
Lagarto Bar & Restaurant** (2656 0750, main
courses US$25), which runs a sociable beach
barbecue from 5pm to 11pm and sizzles up
steaks and grilled fish. Live music is often
featured. During the day it is an excellent place
to sip a fruit daiquiri while gazing out on to the
ocean. **El Ancla** (2656 0254, main courses
US$8) is another beachfront restaurant that
grills fresh fish.

For healthy shakes and fresh sandwiches
go to **Shake Joe's** (2656 0252, main courses
US$8). Located 50 metres east of the main
entrance to the beach, this restaurant is on a
mission to be the town's only chill-out lounge,

a place to unwind, hangout and eat in peace. It is open from 11am to 9pm.

If you want something more down-to-earth try **El Samareño Restaurant** (2656 0419, main courses US$25) located close to Licorera Las Olas, on the road to Carrillo. It serves excellent plates of *gallo pinto* and other soda favourites. It is a good place to pad the stomach before a morning surf lesson – it opens at 7am. The tapas at **Las Brasas** (2656 0546, main courses US$13) are well prepared along with other Spanish dishes such as paella.

Where to stay

Entre dos Aguas B&B (300m from main street along the beach, 2656 0998, www. hoteldosaguas.com, US$50-$60 double) has seven spacious rooms set among tropical gardens. There are hammocks around the swimming pool to laze in.

Hotel Giada (2656 0132, www.hotelgiada. net, US$75 double) is a centrally located option with 24 rooms and facilities that include two swimming pools, a restaurant and bar. Rooms are airy and have pretty balconies and cable TV. Outside of town is **Villas Playa Sámara** (2656 0104, www.villasplayasamara.com,

US$200-$300 double), an upscale resort often used for wedding ceremonies and popular with honeymooners. There are 59 private well-equipped villas facing the ocean.

On the far east side of Playa Sámara is the brightly painted **Cabinas Villa Kunterbunt** (2656 0235, www.cabinas-villa-kunterbunt.com, US$25-$50 double) with its ten simple but colourful rooms, some with shared bathrooms. You'll need to take a cab into town.

The **Flying Crocodile** (near Playa Buenavista, 2656 8048, www.flying-crocodile. com, US$80) is six kilometres (3.5 miles) from the town centre, and has four Gaudi-inspired cabins with quality beds. The landscaping and interior design of the hotel is beautiful, featuring a nice pool, a bar and a restaurant, with friendy and attentive staff. It's great for anyone looking for a tropical bolthole that isn't on the beach, and it can also arrange ultralight flying tours.

Resources

Banks

Banco Nacional *50m west of the Catholic church downtown (2656 0089)*. ATM machine and money transfers.

Reflect on the beauty of **Playa Sámara**.

CABINAS "El Colibri"

Carrilla beach is a bay of your dreams where white sands are surrounded by beautiful palm trees. Relax and enjoy incredible sunsets in th paradise.

Located just 200 metres from the sea, El Colibri has big and comfortable rooms and min appartments. All of the rooms are surrounded thick vegetation and have fantastic tropical view

Rooms can sleep from 1 to 4 people with doubles and single beds. Private bathrooms, hot showers, fans and air-conditioning.

All the bedrooms and mini-appartments are fully-equipped and are kept extremely clean.

Breakfast, lunch and dinner available in our fancy restaurant where you can enjoy Argentinian steaks and barbecues.

Playa Carrillo * Guanacaste * Costa Rica.
Tel.: (+506) 2656-0656 * colibricarrillo@yahoo.co
www.cabinaselcolibri.com

Playa Carrillo.

Hospitals

Centro Médico Sámara *in the town centre north of the plaza (2656 0123)*. There is also a pharmacy here.

Internet

Se@net Internet Café *next to the football pitch and ReMax Real Estate*. **Open** 9am-9pm daily.
Sámara Travel Center *on the main street next to Coco's*. **Open** 9am-6pm Mon-Sat.

Police

Police station is just off the beach on Main Street. Call 911 for emergencies.

Getting there

By air

Daily flights into Sámara with **Sansa** (www.flysansa.com) and **Nature Air** (www.natureair.com). There is a small air strip in Sámara.

By bus

Alfaro buses (Alfaro bus station, 150m north-west of Coca-Cola Station, 2222 2666, US$8) leave San José daily at 12.30pm, returning at 3.45pm Mon-Sat and 1pm Sun. From Nicoya there are daily buses that leave from three blocks east of Nicoya Park at 8am, 3pm and 4pm and return at 5.30am, 6.30am, 7.30am, 1.30pm and 4.30pm. Private tourist buses can also be hired for a more comfortable journey. **Interbus** (2283 5573, www.interbusonline.com, US$35) and **Gray Line** (2220 2126, www.graylinecostarica.com, US$35) both have shuttle buses and convenient schedules.

By road

From San José take the Interamericana Highway to the Tempisque Bridge 'Puente de la Amistad' turn-off. Keep driving to Nicoya and from there head south to Sámara. The trip will take around 5hrs.

Playa Carrillo

Only three kilometres (two miles) from Playa Sámara is the little beach town of Playa Carrillo. Just as beautiful as Sámara but less populated, Carrillo is a secluded destination for those who don't want any hassles: just the beach, a stiff cocktail and no irritations. Retirees and couples make up most of the tourists here but there are still enough activities to keep you occupied for a day or two.

There are reputable tour companies in Carrillo that can hook you up with just about anything from zip-lining to real estate viewing. **Carrillo Tours** (2656 0543, www.carrillotours.com) offers a wide selection of activities. We recommend its horseriding trip (US$35 per person), which makes the most of this area's scenic landscape. Its four-hour kayak tours along the Río Ora are also good fun, and good for birdwatching. **Popo's Tours** (2656 0086, www.camaronal-cr.com/popos) offers surfing, turtle watching, kayaking and more.

EXCURSIONS

Tension is an unheard-of concept in Carrillo except when it comes to fishing lines. Sport fishing is a popular activity off this beach and there are several professional outfitters able to take you out on to the ocean, where you can wrestle it out eye to eye with marlin. **Captain Rob Gordon** (2656 0170, www.sportfishcarrillo.com) will take you out on the *Kitty Kat* for either half-day or full-day fishing trips. The going rate is about US$650 for half a day and US$900 for a full day.

Where to eat

There are more restaurants in Playa Sámara, than in Playa Carrillo. The best tend to be in hotels (you don't have to be a guest to eat in them). **Hotel El Sueño Tropical** (2656 2150, main courses US$15) has a good restaurant with a menu featuring sushi, gourmet pizzas, grilled lobster and excellent tuna steaks. It also has a thorough wine list. **Restaurante El Colibri** (2656 0656, main courses US$9) at Cabinas El Colibri specialises in Argentinian barbecue, including *chimichurri* (spicy sauce) and chorizos. With its friendly service, excellent meat and attractive wine list, the restaurant could easily be mistaken for a Buenos Aires *parrilla* (steakhouse) – except, of course, that it's situated in front of a beautiful beach. At **Carrillo Club Hotel** (2656 0316, main courses US$10) you will get top service and one of the best views in town. It is a good choice for a romantic lunch.

Where to stay

Cabinas El Colibri (2656 0656, www.cabinaselcolibri.com, US$80 double) has six tidy rooms and mini-apartments conveniently located 200 metres from the beach. There is nothing too fancy here, but it's excellent value, safe, quiet and clean. The hotel has a friendly atmosphere and is good for friends travelling together or for small families. If you are looking for a larger hotel try **Hotel Carrillo Club** (2656 0316, www.carrillo club.com, US$85 double), located on the top of the highest hill in the area and thus offering terrific views across the bay. It has 19 spacious rooms and nine apartments with quality beds and private patios. Some rooms come with their own kitchenettes and all look out on to the ocean below. There is a pool and a gym, and the hotel organises outdoor activities such as fresh air aerobics and surfing.

Recently renovated, **Hotel Esperanza** (2656 0564, www.hotelesperanza.com, US$120 double) has seven airy rooms, a brand new pool, a courtyard and, that rarity of rarities in Costa Rica, disabled access. Columned hallways and landscaped grounds add an elegant feel to a small hotel. It is a handy base camp being so close to both the beach and the town's amenities. **El Sueño Tropical** (2656 0151, www.elsuenotropical.com, US$107 double) has 12 rooms and four apartments in uncluttered and peaceful surroundings. The hotel features two swimming pools and three acres of tropical garden. There is also a good restaurant serving international dishes including hamburgers, pizzas and pastas and sushi.

Hand of God! at the Argentinian **El Colibri**.

Central Pacific

Getting Started

Deserted islands or nightclubs? Surfing swells or fine dining? You decide.

Sunset over **Playa Santa Teresa**. See p210.

The sunny Central Pacific coast region is a popular destination for both tourists and Ticos for two main reasons. Firstly, it has beaches – lots of beaches. Secondly, it is easy to get to, only a two-hour drive from San José. It is a well-developed area, and while mass-tourism facilities and retirement condominium constructions are saturating the coastline, the interior continues to be off the package holiday trail and can still deliver seclusion and escape.

This coast includes a thumb-like chunk of land called the **Península de Nicoya** (*see p204*). It is a region enjoyed by sunbathers, birdwatchers and sporty types. It's also territory for those into sport fishing, surfing or sailing; a number of hotels and (usually excellent) outfitters cater for clients addicted

to those pursuits. In the section devoted to Península de Nicoya we cover the area from **Islita** in the province of Guanacaste, around the Golfo de Nicoya, to **Puntarenas** (*see p220*) on the mainland. Puntarenas south to **Quepos** (*see p230*) and **PN Manuel Antonio** (*see p233*) is covered in Central Pacific Mainland.

Alongside the natural beauty is a certain amount of unnatural ugliness in the shape of boilerplate tourism infrastructure. The region seems to have transformed itself from remote paradise to tourist centre, and locals and even expats worry that the process of land clearance and hotel construction is going too fast. The region is no longer Costa Rica's best kept secret, and many believe the influx of foreigners has still not peaked. That said, there are many areas that are yet to be troubled by the bulldozer and the buzz-saw. Zones such as **Reserva Natural Absoluta Cabo Blanco** (*see p211*) and **Refugio Nacional de Vida Silvestre Curú** (*see p218*) are protected to ensure that indigenous endangered species are studied and, if possible, preserved.

If you have bee-lined to this zone and have nothing in mind but beach bumming, you've come to the right place – choosing a beach around the Península de Nicoya on which to lap up some sun is as easy as finding a restaurant that serves rice and beans. On the west side, **Islita** (*see p204*), **Playa Coyote** (*see p204*) and **Playa Caletas** (*see p204*) have good surf and a sense of isolation (with basic amenities), while eastern beaches such as **Playa Cabuya** (*see p215*) and **Playa Tambor** (*see p217*) appeal to families and couples due to the number of water-based activities like kayaking and snorkelling that are on offer.

Across the Golfo de Nicoya the vibe is very different. On the Central Pacific mainland lies a ribbon of party towns where flocks of sun-seekers descend for steamy weekends of sun, sex and surf. **Puntarenas, Jacó** (*see p223*) and **Quepos** are prime targets for mojito-guzzling hedonists; at these resorts lounging around the beachfront until sunset and dancing like a maniac at one of the clubs until dawn is virtually compulsory. A particularly festive event is the *Día de la Virgen del Mar* (Day of the Virgin of the Sea) on 19 June when decorated fishing boats cruise along the coast of Puntarenas paying homage to the patron saint

Central Pacific

of the city, the Virgen de Monte Carmelo. Fireworks and debauchery are guaranteed.

The gay scene along the Central Pacific coast is the best developed in Costa Rica, especially in the town of Manuel Antonio (*see p234* **Chasing rainbows**) where locals are welcoming the constant influx of 'pink' dollars. Otherwise, for the most part this area, with its clubs, wet T-shirt contests and beach cafés, attracts young monosyllabic types who roar and squeal a lot; but if you venture away from the urban centres there are enough wholesome leisure activities to keep families and honeymooners happy. **PN Carara** (*see p222*) and **PN Manuel Antonio** (*see p233*) are two worthwhile nature-based excursions where sightings of Three-toed sloths, White-faced Monkeys and binocular-worthy birds are common. Both these parks, as well as several private reserves, have trails for hiking – a perfect cure for a weekend of bingeing or a good way of keeping that outdoorsy tag-along friend occupied. Lodges and high-end hotels, usually situated amid outstanding scenery, are often easy to come by and offer restful stays. These types of hotels have extras such as trained chefs and private exercise classes, and many offer spas, beauty treatments and all kinds of massage in house.

The shores of the Central Pacific are frequented not only by those who love to party but by foodies as well. This coast guarantees some deliciously messy seafood to get your fingers sticky with. Many restaurants specialise in freshly caught fish that is so tasty all that needs to be done is to scrape off the scales and spark up a barbecue. Point your nose in the air in **Jacó** or **Manuel Antonio** and follow the smoky zephyrs produced by grilled meat, fish and jumbo garlic prawns.

Finally, it probably goes without saying that with all the easy access to shoreline, water sports are hugely popular. Sea-kayaking, sailing and surfing are available in every town and on every roadside, but for quality instruction and equipment it is always best to book with a reputable hotel or use our listed services. In general, beginner surf lessons are given privately or in small groups of two to three people and last from one to two hours (the going rate is around US$30 per hour).

Jacó (*see p223*) is generally considered Costa Rica's surf central, with the world-famous Crazy Rock and Playa Hermosa attracting advanced surfers and professionals. Playa Jacó has good learning waves. Downtown Jacó itself can get a little seedy at night but is, nonetheless, a great base for surfers wanting to explore some of the lesser known beaches, or for beginners wanting to find patient teachers and gentle swells.

The best Central Pacific

Things to do

Settle into the Costa Rican pace of life on the Península de Nicoya with a long beach stroll and a hammock nap. Explore by kayak or boat the deserted (and, according to some, haunted) islands off the Gulfo de Nicoya (*see p218*). Find your forgotten or current youth by taking off your shoes and taking on some booze in the popular party town of **Jacó** (*see p223*). Put on some hiking boots and explore **PN Manuel Antonio** (*see p233*) where you can go sloth spotting or sunbathing.

Places to stay

Let **Hotel Punta Islita** (*see p209*) take the weight off your shoulders with impeccable service and luxury spa treatments. During a morning yoga class at **Ylang Ylang Lodge** (*see p212*) in Manzanillo, you can breathe in the scent of the bloom – also known as the Chanel No.5 flower – from which the hotel takes its name. Soak in a jacuzzi bubblebath or sip a refreshing cocktail under a star-spangled night in Jacó's **Hotel Villa Caletas** (*see p229*), in an idyllic setting and art deco vibe that will make for a carefree stay. For a great night's sleep and tip-top service, look no further than **Gaia Hotel & Reserve** (*see p237*), a luxury hotel within its own nature reserve by PN Manuel Antonio.

Places to eat

Used as a film set for its regal decor, **1492** (*see p206*) in Hotel Punta Islita serves up organic traditional dishes fused with international staples. For a strictly fish-laden menu try **Tanga's** (*see p207*) on Playa Coyote, rumoured to have some of the best fish dishes in all of Costa Rica. Couples and healthy eaters can't skip Montezuma's **Playa de los Artistas'** (*see p215*) for a romantic setting and organic specialities. Spicy food-lovers must try **Jacó Taco** (*see p227*) for the most authentic Mexican food in the area, including *real* tortilla chips. For a substantial steak, make your way to **La Yunta Steakhouse** (*see p223*), a safe bet away from surf shack specials in Puntarenas. But for a non-pretentious vibe with fresh Tico food, go to the lovable **Soda Sánchez** (*see p231*) in Quepos.

Península de Nicoya

The crowd is in, the surf is up – and the secret is definitely out.

Central Pacific

Islita to Playa Caletas

Not long ago the coastline from Islita to the beaches of Coyote and Caletas was well off the tourist trail. In fact, it was the most isolated and pristine part of the Península de Nicoya, and was virtually inaccessible until 1994.

Islita, once a sleepy off-the-map inland town, was introduced to the modern world when the Punta Islita Resort set up camp. Domestic flights were introduced; publicity about the region's beauty spread fast; and hotel developers began pouring concrete into the least spoilt parts to meet the tourism demand. Vitalised by this new service industry – which was generally welcomed by locals – the Caletas area flourished into a myriad small communities. Today, although well known, it still retains some of its isolation – or, to put it another way, has positioned itself in the market for those looking for tranquillity rather than an action-packed holiday. It's a fine spot for relaxation and meditation.

Officially, Islita lies on the border of the province of Guanacaste and belongs to the *cantón* of Nandayure, but it has much more in common with its southern counterparts than with the touristy, highly developed Guanacaste beaches to the north. The panorama is made up of winding rugged roads, squiggly rivers and secluded beaches. Activities include kayaking among the mangrove swamps in the estuary, walking through teak plantations, exploring farms by horseback, and occasionally sighting olive ridley sea turtles nesting on the shore. From **Playa Camaronal**, north of Islita, to **Playa Corozalito** and **Bejuco** and further south to **Playa San Miguel**, **Playa Coyote** and **Playa Caletas**, the scenery is unforgettable. These last two beaches have white sand and are separated by the mouth of the Río Jabillo. There are no nearby coastal villages – the nearest town with facilities (a *pulpería*, petrol station and internet) is in San Francisco de Coyote, five kilometres (three miles) inland.

SIGHTSEEING

Beaches, beaches and more beaches is the name of the game here, and there is little else. The coast from Islita to Caletas is the kingdom of doing sweet nothing, so get out the sunblock, throw down your towel and hit the sand.

Exploring *playas* (at low tide they can become 200 metres wide) by foot or by renting a quad bike makes for an enjoyable day out. Take your time on the waterways by kayaking on the Río Ora at Playa Camaronal or on the Río Jabillo at Playa Coyote. Surfing in the breaks off San Miguel and Punta Coyote is an irresistible pull for many but it's also pretty quiet and a good place to practise. Animal-lovers should check out Playa Caletas, a nesting site for olive ridley sea turtles (*see p194* **Turtle power**) – the months from September to December are peak nesting season. Anyone who prefers their sand in neatly arranged bunkers can head over to **Hotel Punta Isilita** (*see p209*), which has a nine-hole golf course in its expansive grounds that is open to non-guests.

EXCURSIONS

Tumbleweed may appear prone to roll through Islita but it deserves a visit if only for its highly colourful **Museo de Arte Contemporáneo al Aire Libre** (*see p206* **Frescoes al fresco**). It is funded by the **Hotel Punta Islita**.

Horseriding is another popular activity and can be arranged through any local hotel. (We recommend you check how healthy the horses are in advance. If they are skinny and tired you can decline and look elsewhere.) **Casa Caletas** (*see p207*) organises pleasant day rides within its farm and teak plantation. Jet skiing and canopy zip-lining are also offered by numerous hotels. Lastly, there is always surfing. If you're a beginner, ask your hotel for lessons. Experienced surfers should head down the road to Playa Coyote where there is a challenging, consistent and crowd-free break.

Up from Playa San Miguel, in the tiny community of Pueblo Nuevo, is the **Jungle Butterfly Farm** (www.junglebutterfly.com, entrance US$10). This large outdoor butterfly sanctuary is dedicated to rearing and releasing butterflies native to Costa Rica. Managed by Michael Malliet, a former Air Force entomologist in the US military, this project will give you a real taste of Costa Rican flora and fauna. There is a self-guided tour through the land, which is frequented by Howler Monkeys, agoutis and iguanas. It is open from 9am to 4pm daily and costs US$10 for adults and US$6 for children under 12. There is a snack bar and a gift shop.

Frescoes al fresco

It's hard to believe but 20 years ago Islita was a dusty, almost abandoned little town with no electricity or water. Income was low, and hardly anyone completed secondary education. Since 1994, however, standards of living have risen sharply, in large part thanks to the farsighted management of the Hotel Punta Islita where more than 150 locals work. The hotel has harnessed the latent energies of the community through various sustainability programmes, none more visible than an inspirational art project that involves every aspect of village life. From trees to house façades, this economically depressed village has been transformed into a colourful and self-sufficient community.

The project began with a simple mission: to gather local artworks and sell them to tourists. But instead of aggressively hawking the items, the point was to educate the visitor by introducing them to the artists and showing them the natural materials used to make the pieces. The idea took off and today this village is proud to hold the **Museo de Arte**

Where to eat & drink

There are fewer eating options around Islita than in other parts of the peninsula and it is usually best to go to a small hotel and ask for the fish of the day or a reliable *casado*. Listed below are some alternatives to soda staples.

1492

Hotel Punta Islita (2661 3324). **Open** 7am-9.30pm daily. **Main courses** US$25. **Credit** AmEx, MC, V.

With a magnificent 15-high (50ft-)high thatched palm roof and an open layout that leads to an infinity pool and the bay below, this structure is impressive. Its colonial-style decor was used as a set for *1492*, a film about Christopher Columbus that was partly shot in Punta Islita. The restaurant delivers Costa Rican fine dining: Tico fusion cuisine using fresh locally caught seafood, superb drinks (two bars) and a decent wine list.

Bar Co Nico

On the turn-off from San Francisco de Coyote to northern Playa Costa de Oro (2655 1205/www.barco-nico.com). **Open** 10am-10pm Wed-Mon. **Main courses** US$6. **No credit cards**.

With a downstairs bar serving cocktails and cold beers and an upstairs terrace facing the beach, this bar has a lovely setting and an extensive menu of appetisers, fresh seafood, meat and pizzas. The cocktail list is quite short, but the drinks are well mixed. Those not wishing to escape entirely can take advantage of the high-speed internet and a large screen TV.

Contemporáneo al Aire Libre, the first open-air contemporary art museum in Central America. The museum is a powerhouse of creativity and currently runs a programme that pairs prominent Costa Rican artists, such as Florencia Urbina, Loida Pretiz and Zulay Soto, with local artists to produce unique murals, paintings, textiles and ornaments. The result has turned the entire village into a living art project; streets, houses and even trees are adorned with art.

A positive side effect has been the growth and active participation of local art groups. Bosquemar, for example, comprises a group of artists who use driftwood to make sculptures, lamps and ornaments. Las Papaturras consists of women who regularly meet under a *papaturro* tree to create intricate collages out of materials such as seeds, shells and stones. Las Papaturras' group leader Doña Cecilia sums it up: 'Besides complementing the family income, my involvement in Las Papaturras has instilled a sense of pride in my community.' The co-operative theme has also prompted residents in the community to participate by learning English or getting involved with computer and art classes. The programme has also funded a library, university scholarships, environmental education programmes and a recycling centre.

You can view the work at Casa Museo in the village and in the Hotel Punta Islita gift shop. Hotel Punta Islita's involvement has won it the Investor in People category of the World Travel and Tourism Council's Tourism for Tomorrow Awards.

Caletas Bar & Restaurant

Casa Caletas Hotel, Playa Caletas (2655 1271/ www.casacaletas.com). **Open** 7.30-10.30am, noon-3pm, 7-9pm daily. **Main courses** US$15. **Credit** AmEx, MC, V.
Caletas is a well-stocked bar and restaurant that serves up good quality and well-presented Tico food. It is worth a visit, especially for a romantic meal, as the restaurant is next to the hotel pool with views of the estuary that flows into the ocean.

Mirador Barranquilla

2km south of Hotel Punta Islita (no phone). **Open** 10am-10pm Wed-Mon. **Main courses** US$6. **No credit cards**.
Set on a tropical hilltop, this restaurant has some of the best views of the bay and is a great spot to grab a light dinner, enjoy a beer and watch the sunset.

Tanga's

On the beach at Playa Coyote (2655 1107). **Open** 7am-7pm daily. **Main courses** U$S6. **No credit cards**.
Owners Mayela and Carlos first set foot on this Pacific shore more than 20 years ago, and, lured by the good fishing, they never left. This simple soda uses fresh produce that Carlos (aka Tanga) catches at sunrise. The seafood soups, snapper fillet, octopus and stews are widely praised.

Where to stay

Casa Caletas

Punta Coyote (2655 1271/www.casacaletas.com). **Rates** US$192-$698 double. **Rooms** 9. **Credit** V.

High on a hilltop, next to the mouth of the Río Jabillo, lies this exquisite boutique hotel with an excellent restaurant. Each room has its own terrace with a view over the estuary or the ocean. Behind, there is an expansive area to be explored by foot or on horseback. This is a private and romantic setting, perfect for honeymooners.
Bar. Restaurant. Pool (outdoor). TV.

Casitas Azul Plata

Pilas de Bejuco at Playa San Miguel (2655 8209/ www.casitasazulplata.com). **Rates** US$70-$90 double. **Rooms** 2 apartments. **No credit cards.**
This secluded getaway is a good choice for families, especially ones with small children. Casitas offers fully equipped apartments sleeping up to four people, each with terrace, plunge pool and ocean views. It's a fairly basic operation but a clean and comfortable choice.
Pool (outdoor). TV.

Eco Hotel Arca de Noé

1km north from Playa San Miguel (2655 8065/www. hotelarcadenoe.com). **Rooms** 15. **Credit** AmEx, MC, V.
This clean mid-range Noah's Ark-styled hotel is a great find. It has simple, quiet rooms at very good rates and is set in beautiful surrounds. A colonial-style restaurant and inviting pool add touches of glamour to a wholesome vibe. Spa treatments are available in the 'centre of well-being'.
Bar. Pool (outdoor). Restaurant. Spa. TV.

Hotel Punta Islita

On the hillside in Islita (2231 6122/www.hotelpunta islita.com). **Rates** US$280-$727 double. **Rooms** 47. **Credit** AmEx, MC, V.
This is the most luxurious hotel on the peninsula. It was designed by internationally renowned Ronald Zürcher (creator of the first Four Seasons in Costa Rica). It is the oldest hotel in the area and has fully equipped suites, villas and rental houses spread along the hill above Playa Islita. The top-of-the-range service and surroundings are hard to beat.
Bar. Gym. Internet (shared terminal, wireless, free). Pools (2, Outdoor). Restaurants (2). Spa. TV.

Resources

Internet

Centro de Internet Comunitario *Islita.* **Open** 9am-7pm daily.
Soda Familiar *in San Francisco de Coyote village has wireless access.* **Open** 7.30am-6pm daily.

Post office

At Eco Hotel Arca de Noé, Playa San Miguel.

Getting there

By air

The most convenient option is to take a domestic flight with **Nature Air** (www.natureair.com) or **Sansa** (www.flysansa.com). Both fly once daily from several destinations to a small airstrip in Punta Islita for around US$50-$90.

By bus

Empresa Arsa (Terminal del Atlántico Norte, Calle 12, entre Avenida 7 y 9, 2650 0179) runs buses that depart at 6am and 3.30pm daily from San José for San Miguel, San Francisco de Coyote and Bejuco.

By road

After crossing the Golfo de Nicoya from Puntarenas, continue through Jicaral to San Francisco de Coyote. Continue along to San Miguel and Bejuco and from

Central Pacific

Hotel Punta Islita is hidden among the tropical dry forest of Guanacaste.

Drinking, dancing and defintely no dust at the **La Lora Amarilla** in Santa Teresa. *See p212.*

Bejuco to Islita. In normal conditions it can take up to 6hrs from San José. Cars, even four-wheel drives, can struggle at certain points on the road and at certain times of the year: the Río Ora can only be crossed in dry weather and at low tide. In the rainy season the Río Jabillo sometimes floods the road and turns it into a quagmire that can be impassable for weeks.

Mal País, Manzanillo & Santa Teresa

It is a 20-kilometre (12-mile) drive along a winding stretch of road from the border of the **Reserva Natural Absoluta Cabo Blanco** (*see right*), the southernmost point of the peninsula, to the quiet fishing bay of **Playa Manzanillo**. Running alongside this solitary route, through Mal País and Santa Teresa, are the picturesque shores of white sand beaches.

From **Cóbano** on Highway 160, the road continues to **Playa Carmen**, also known as 'El Cruce' (the crossroad). To the south lies Mal País, to the north Santa Teresa; and though the whole area is one long coastal town, it is commonly referred to as Mal País.

Just 20 years ago Santa Teresa and Mal País were isolated villages almost impossible to reach (this is just one of many theories why such a scenic place is named Mal País – 'badland'). But with consistent waves, an increasing amount of upscale accommodation

and a multicultural atmosphere, both the towns of Mal País and Santa Teresa attract more and more visitors every year; surfers, yoga enthusiasts, nature-lovers, honeymooners, real estate barons and celebrities travelling incognito comprise the bulk.

Mal País centre is a residential area where private holiday houses, boutique hotels and several restaurants dot the roadside. The end of the line is at the fishermen's port where you can buy fresh *pargo* (red snapper) or *atún* (yellowfin tuna) to barbecue later for lunch. Fishing trips around **Isla Cabo Blanco** are popular excursions and you can often catch glimpses of manta rays, dolphins and whales while out boating. For the water weary, **Canopy del Pacífico**, a few metres before the reserve's entrance (2640 0360, www.costarica-beachrentals.com), organises zip-lining adventures between trees by the ocean.

Santa Teresa is the hip counterpoint to the serenity of Mal País. There is a wide range of lodging here from top resorts to camping, and handy shops, supermarkets, bars and tour agencies populate the main road. Beginner surfers should head to **Playa Carmen** with entrances to the beach at **Bar La Lora Amarilla** and at **Suck Rock** (also the entrance for camping at Rocamar).

For some seclusion make your way to the last beach, **Playa Hermosa** (if you're lucky –

or not, depending on your point of view – you may come across a supermodel practising her boardwalking here). Kiteboarding is another popular activity in this area and is good fun to watch. For instruction call **Pachamama Mal País** (2640 0195, www.pacha-malpais.com). It costs US$50 per hour or US$380 for three days of instruction with International Kiteboarding Organisation certification. On Saturday afternoons the **Heart & Honey's Organic Market** at **Playa Carmen** is a fun meeting point and is frequented by both locals and tourists. The scene consists of an amusing mix of people, goods, clothes made by local designers and dogs sniffing for scraps.

The last beach town on this sandy strip is **Manzanillo**. Although it has a large expat community, it still maintains a quaint village mood. With a broad bay and calm waters it proudly hosts an annual sandcastle competition in March or April. Manzanillo is also a popular place with nature-lovers. White-faced capuchin and howler monkeys, iguanas, raccoons, hummingbirds and deer are commonly spotted, and some people rate the fauna here above that of the **Reserva Natural Absoluta Cabo Blanco** (*see below*).

SIGHTSEEING

Mal País and Santa Teresa are as laid-back as they come. Sightseeing by quad bike, bicycle or foot, or beachcombing at low tide (when up to 200 metres – 328 feet – of beach is revealed) can really get you into the *pura vida* swing of things. There are natural pools for snorkelling, such as at **Playa de los Suecos** (beyond the fishing port at the end of the road in Mal País) or at **Poza del Cambute** (in front of El Rey Patricio Hotel in Playa Hermosa). And when rock pools lose their novelty, have a surf lesson at one of the many surf camps or take a yoga class at an ocean-front dojo.

The towns fill up with visitors mainly in the dry season, from November to April. And although there is a good social atmosphere, it is probably not the best time to visit the surrounding forests as the traffic from the main road kicks up a lot of dust and makes visibility poor. On the other hand, come the rainy season, the dirt roads turn to mud traps making four-wheel-drive vehicles essential, not that outdoor enthusiasts are perturbed; the wet season is the ideal time to traverse the area's many nature trails in its lush forests.

EXCURSIONS

At the end of the main road at the Mal País border lies **Reserva Natural Absoluta Cabo Blanco**, a nature reserve made up of 12 square kilometres (4.6 square miles) of forest and more

Star gazing

In the beginning it was Flea. Yep, the bassist from the Red Hot Chili Peppers was one of the first to come to Santa Teresa to ride the waves more than ten years ago. Back then, no one but hardcore (or West Coast neo-funk) surfers could point to this beach on a map, and you could count the number of passable hotels and eateries on the strings on a guitar. Nowadays this area has been graced with the presence of more than 100 celebrities – and counting.

Word of this secret paradise has quickly spread in Tinseltown, with *Forbes Magazine* recently declaring Mal País as one of the 'ten most beautiful beaches in the world'. Other publications such as *Vogue* and *Condé Nast* praise its luxury hotels, and now Hollywood stars aplenty are looking to this tiny tip of the southern Península de Nicoya when in need of a tropical getaway.

Don't be surprised if your sunbathing is disturbed by an invasion of paparazzi or if you bump into Leonardo DiCaprio at the local *pulpería,* or see Gwyneth Paltrow whizz past on a canopy tour. UK enfant terrible Kate Moss has been known to rock up for a discreet fix of – horror of horrors – karaoke, while Brazilian supermodel Gisele Bündchen surfs at her summer house in Playa Hermosa. American football players the Olsen twins are also keen, as are Matthew McConaughey and Mel Gibson (who recently brought Britney Spears here). The list of celebrities is a long one.

than 15 square kilometres 5.8 square miles) of protected ocean. It covers the entire southern tip of the Peninsula de Nicoya. The reserve is the oldest in the country, founded in 1963 thanks to the effort of Danish-Swedish couple Karen Morgensen and Olof Wessberg, both of whom were among the first conservationists in Costa Rica. The park first opened for visitors in 1980. The reserve has two hiking trails (maps and guides are available at the entrance). One makes a loop inside the park and takes about an hour. The more challenging trail is five kilometres (three miles) long, a two-hour trek, through forest that will leave you on the pristine shores off Isla del Cabo Blanco. Monkeys, squirrels, sloths and iguanas, and occasionally armadillo, deer and peccaries can all be spotted here. Make sure to bring your own food and plenty of water as they are not available in the park. Camping is not permitted. Contact the ranger station (2642 0093, cablanco@ns.minae.go.cr) for specific queries and for official maps. The entrance fee is US$6 and the park is open Wednesday to Sunday from 8am to 4pm.

Where to eat & drink

The numbers of new restaurants and sodas swell in high season between Manzanillo and Mal País. While most don't last more than a summer, the places listed here are still going strong. For superb seafood, try **Langosta Paraíso** (8353 5120, main courses US$8), located 600 metres east of Playa Manzanillo and open from 10am to 10pm Monday to Wednesday. Meaning 'lobster paradise', this little restaurant is tucked away in Bello Horizonte, a tiny village up from Playa Manzanillo, and does some of the best seafood and, of course, lobster in the area. Dishes are also reasonably priced. **Al Chile Viola** (2640 0248, www.elreypatricio.com, main courses US$10) is a new local favourite that serves up Mediterranean fusion dishes. Its popularity forced it to relocate to the El Rey Patricio Hotel and it now serves food from an impressive 12-metre-high (39-foot) open-air restaurant that looks out on to the beach's natural tide pools.

For even more upscale dining, head four kilometres (2.5 miles) north of El Cruce where you will find the elegant **Néctar** (2640 0032, main courses US$20) at the Flor Blanca Hotel (*see right*). It specialises in delicious (if small) assortments of sushi and Asian-fusion dishes as well as grilled New York steaks and celestial desserts. The setting is fancy but relaxed. Another 400 metres north of the Santa Teresa school is **Venga Restaurant Supernatural** (2640 0701, main courses US$10), a good vegetarian option with a Middle Eastern approach. Think houmous wraps and falafels.

Cheaper downtown options are typically pizza joints such as **Tomato** (2640 0200) and **El Pulpo** (2640 0685). If your taste buds are crying out for meat, try Argentinian-styled barbecued chicken and beef at **Las Piedras** at Playa Carmen (2640 0453, main courses US$8). **Ritmo Tropical** (2640 0174, main courses US$10) is another good option in Playa Carmen with an extensive menu specialising in Italian dishes.

Just three kilometres (two miles) south of Playa Carmen is **Soda Piedramar** (2640 0069), a Mal País classic lunch stop. It's a simple, fisherman's eaterie with excellent food in an impressive setting perched next to crashing waves. For partying, try **D&N Beach Bar**

(2640 0353), 100 metres north of Playa Carmen, and open from sunset to 2am. Friday night at **Mar Azul** restaurant (2640 0075), located three kilometres south of Playa Carmen, is another nightlife hot spot. But for authentic Tico fun **La Lora Amarilla** (2640 0132), three kilometres (two miles) north of Playa Carmen, is a cool bar right in the heart of Santa Teresa that plays excellent local music. Grab a beer in one hand and a salsa partner in the other and you'll fit right in.

Where to stay

From hidden away boutique hotels to insanely expensive celebrity playgrounds to no-frills hostels, this part of the Península de Nicoya has a pad for everyone. For longer stays, holiday rental companies have a plethora of week- and month-long rental accommodation. Go to **www.costaricabeachrentals.com**, **www.playacarmen.net** or **www.malpais-beach-rentals.com**. For secluded locations, try rentals in Manzanillo, north Santa Teresa or Playa Hermosa.

One example of hidden hillside bliss is **Ylang Ylang Lodge** (8359 2616, www.lodgeylang ylang.com, US$170 double). Discreetly set up in Manzanillo one kilometre (half a mile) north of the Bello Horizonte soccer pitch, this lodge has five teak bungalows with full amenities including kitchenettes and DVD players. Tack on great views, a swimming pool next to the private restaurant and a yoga platform suspended from a tree and the wow factor is pretty high. In north Santa Teresa, seven kilometres (4.5 miles) north of Playa Carmen on Playa Hermosa, is **Villas Hermosas** (2640 0360, www.villashermosas.com, US$200-$250 double), a selection of luxury beachfront cabins and a very private option. Other luxury options include the exclusive **Flor Blanca Hotel** (4640 0232, www.florblanca.com, US$675-$950 double), which was the first high-end boutique hotel in the area, and **Milarepa** (2640 0023, www.milarepahotel.com, US$198-$233 double), a Zen-like nest of four bungalows popular with the model set. For groundlings, a more affordable option but with all amenities is **Esencia Hotel & Villas** (2640 0420, www.esenciahotel.com, US$105 double) in Santa Teresa in front of La Lora Amarilla Bar.

Blue Surf Sanctuary (2640 1001, www. bluesurfsanctuary.com, US$125 double) next to Rocamar camping is a new hotel and surf school located in front of one of the best surf points in Santa Teresa. Beach bums may prefer to lounge in Playa Carmen at the striking blue **Casa Azul** (2640 0379, www.hotelcasaazul.com, US$75-$125 double) with its beachfront swimming pool.

Sand, surf and organic spuds in chilled-out **Santa Teresa**.

Nature's alarm call: a Howler Monkey in **Reserva Natural Absoluta Cabo Blanco**.

In Mal País the three best options are: **The Place** (2640 0001, www.theplacemalpais.com, US$78-$290 double), located 500 metres south of Playa Carmen; **La Hacienda B&B** (2640 0103, www.lahaciendademalpais.com, US$150 double) three kilometres (two miles) south of Playa Carmen; and **Moana Lodge** (2640 0230, www.moanalodge.com, US$135 double), two kilometres south of Playa Carmen. All are within walking distance of the Mal País beach.

For budget travellers and backpackers, Santa Teresa offers countless sociable options. Among them is **Casa Zen** (2640 0523, www.zencostarica.com, US$12 dorm, U$24 double), which has shared and private rooms plus a cosy restaurant and bar.

Cuesta Arriba (2640 0607, www.cuesta arribahostel.com, US$12 per person), 150 metres north of La Lora Amarilla Bar, is a good choice

for the surf mad. North of the Santa Teresa football pitch is **Brunellas** (2640 0321, US$10 per person), which fits the bill for anyone in, or yearning for, their twenties – be prepared for boozy nights.

Resources

Bank
Banco Nacional de Costa Rica *At the Centro Comercial Playa Carmen (2212 2000).*

Hospital
Emergencias 2000 *Cóbano (2642 0208).* For emergencies call 2642 0950.

Police
Cóbano, beside the post office (2642 0770). The OIJ also has an office in Cóbano *(2642 0480).*

Montezuma & Cabuya

Around 30 years ago, bohemians and artists, disenchanted with San José life, crossed the Golfo de Nicoya and discovered a little bay where they decided to set up camp and live the hippie life. It was the standard utopian dream of a peaceful community living off fresh fruit, communing with nature and smoking lots of pot. At least that was the idea until the rainy season came and, like, bummed everyone out. The hippies subsequently opted to use the area more as an occasional retreat than a permanent commune.

Montezuma grew from a picturesque village situated around a pretty bay to *the* party town of the southern peninsula. It's still, however, a favourite destination for creative thinkers, with a lively arts scene and enough funky cafés and bars to keep the children of the aforementioned hippies happy. The artistic flair of the town is demonstrated every afternoon along the side of the road where artisans display their work, half hoping to sell a piece, half hoping not to have to part with one. A downside of Montezuma's healthy tourist trade is that it has placed strain on the city's street planning, and pollution along the beaches and waters is a constant worry.

This bayside town is not just about hippies and high fives – Montezuma is a worthwhile two-day retreat due to its main attraction, three waterfalls over the Montezuma river, just a five-minute walk from town. It's a fun excursion, especially because the main waterfall has a naturally deep swimming hole.

For a monkey's-eye view of the Montezuma river, book a place on the enjoyable **Waterfall Canopy Tour** (2642 0808, www.montezuma traveladventures.com, US$35).

Another waterfall worth a visit is **El Chorro**, which flows straight into the ocean. By foot it is an hour-and-a-half north and is located on the beach between Montezuma and Tambor. Many local tour agencies such as **Aventuras en Montezuma** (2642 0050, www.zumatours.com) and **Cocozuma Traveller** (2642 0911, www.cocozuma.com) offer horseriding through private reserves to get to El Chorro.

Other activities such as fishing excursions, kayaking and quad bike rental can easily be arranged. For underwater exploration, a thrilling day trip is the full-day snorkelling excursion to **Isla Tortuga** (*see right*) and to the **Reserva Natural Absoluta Cabo Blanco** (*see p211*) just ten kilometres (six miles) south of Montezuma.

Continue south and you will come to the village of **Cabuya**, which sits flush on the border of the Reserva Natural Absoluta Cabo Blanco and is renowned for its impressive, lush scenery. Although there are rumours of multi-chain hotels and marinas eager to move in, daily village life remains relaxed, and the only thing that ruffles feathers is a gust of ocean breeze. Trekking and wildlife watching within the reserve are the main activities on offer here. Walkers can stroll up the Río Lajas, see the waterfalls or pay a visit to Isla Cabuya, a tiny island accessible only at low tide that houses the local cemetery. The beaches surrounding Cabuya – Los Cedros and Los Almendros – are secluded surfing spots, but rocky. Ultimately, if it is privacy you're looking for, then there is nothing better than taking it easy on the peninsula tip.

EXCURSIONS

Isla Tortuga is not an island teeming with turtles. The name comes from the fact that the land mass resembles a gigantic turtle – if you see it from the air and squint a little. Isla Tortuga, located in front of Punta Curú, half an hour by boat from Montezuma, is actually made up of two islands, Alcatraz and Tortuga. The main island, Tortuga, is a favourite day excursion for visitors due to its coral reefs and picture perfect beaches. Since 1974, it has been managed by the Cubero Fernández family and every day dozens of boats deposit tourists on its idyllic grounds. Overnight stays are not allowed and there are no restaurants or facilities. There may not be any island bistros, but somehow souvenir shops, beach chairs and kayak rentals have crept in. Tour operators along the peninsula offer half-day snorkelling trips to Tortuga with a barbecue lunch including drinks for about US$45 per person. Try **Chico's Tour** (2642 0673), a reliable outfitter located in the centre of Montezuma. Opt for a weekday; on the weekends the island becomes overrun with tourists, boats and the odd group of misguided kids desperately looking for turtles.

Where to eat & drink

Playa de los Artistas (2642 0920, main courses US$15) is regarded as one of Montezuma's, and indeed the peninsula's, best restaurants. The tables are made from wood collected from the beach, and lighting comes from coconut lamps and candles. The seasonal menu changes each day. Vegetarians looking for decent cooking should head downtown, where across the street from the church is **Orgánico** (8359 4197, main courses US$7). Here you'll find salads and *batidos* (smoothies) made with home-made sugar and milk-free ice-cream.

Central Pacific

Lounge lizards should head straight for **Montezuma**.

Cocolores (2642 0348, main courses US$14) is another classic beachside restaurant. It offers good Italian and Mexican dishes, and occasionally hosts live music. **Restaurant Moctezuma**, on the main beach (2642 0657, main courses US$10), is one of the oldest establishments in town and serves excellent paella and *ceviche* (raw seafood marinated in lime juice). It is also a popular bar. For the freshest of seafood try **Lucy's Restaurant** (2642 0956, main courses US$9) on your way back from the waterfall, and enjoy a simple but hearty meal with a fantastic view.

At night in the heart of Montezuma, **Chico's Bar** always serves cold beers, plays good tunes and has pool tables. **Hotel Luz de Mono** hosts regular reggae and electronic music nights at its bar.

In Cabuya, less than a kilometre from the reserve, is **El Rancho** (2642 0226, main courses US$5), a typical eaterie where you can regain your strength after visiting the reserve.

Where to stay

Montezuma has options for every budget, mostly located around the town centre. **Hotel El Jardín** (2642 0548, www.hoteleljardin.com, US$95 double) is built on a hillside and has 15 rooms and villas with ocean views. **Hotel Los Mangos** (2642 0384, www.hotellosmangos.com, US$35-$75 double) appeals to groups as it offers both shared rooms and private bungalows. Yoga classes take place in the peaceful setting, and there is a big pool. Close to the entrance of the waterfall is **Amor de Mar** (2642 0262, www.amordemar.com, US$70 double), which offers dark caoba wood rooms and a manicured garden that leads to a big tide pool next to the Rio Montezuma.

Just outside of town is **Horizontes de Montezuma** (2642 0534, www.horizontes-montezuma.com, US$64 double) with its seven bright and comfortable rooms. It is also a centre for professionally taught Spanish courses. **Nature Lodge Finca Los Caballos** (2642 0124, www.naturelodge.net, US$90 double), further along the road to Cóbano, has the most private setting with rooms looking out on to the expansive ranch, and, that local rarity, sturdy, well-fed horses for riding.

In Cabuya, **Hotel Celaje** (2642 0374, www.celaje.com, US$82 double) is an upscale option with airy bungalows spaced around a swimming pool; it prides itself on its superb Belgian cuisine. The hotel closest to the nature reserve is **El Ancla de Oro** (2642 0369, www.caboblancopark.com/ancla, US$40-$60 double), a Dutch-owned 'jungalow' hotel with tree-house-like rustic thatched bungalows on stilts. Its proximity to the Reserva Natural Absoluta Cabo Blanco is its major plus point, but it also has kayaks and snorkelling equipment for rental. The newest addition is the **Howler Monkey Hotel** (2642 0303, www.caboblancopark.com/howler, US$60 double), situated next door to the reserve. It features very basic bungalows with kitchenettes for limited self-catering.

Resources

Bank
Banco Nacional de Costa Rica *in Cóbano (2212 2000).*

Hospital
Emergencias 2000 *Cóbano (2642 0208).* For emergencies call 2642 0950. It has first aid and ambulance services.

Internet
Pizza Net *Montezuma (2642 0096).* Open 9am-9pm daily.

Police
On the road to the waterfall.

Post office
Cóbano, on the road to Paquera (2642 0047). Open 8am-4pm Mon-Sat.

Getting there

By air
Both **Nature Air** (www.natureair.com) and **Sansa** (www.flysansa.com) have daily flights from several destinations to Tambor airport for around US$70.

By bus
From the Coca-Cola Terminal in San José (Calle 16, y Avenida 1), the **Hermanos Rodríguez** bus service departs daily at 7.30am, 11am and 3.30pm (2642 0740) for Montezuma and Mal País and Santa Teresa, making stops in Paquera and Tambor. It costs US$10 per person. Ferry tickets are not included. Alternatively, there are private door-to-door shuttles that run once a day from San José to the area, for example **Montezuma Expeditions** (2440 8078, www.montezumaexpeditions.com, US$40 per person one way, ferry tickets included).

By road
From San José, take the Interamericana Highway to Puntarenas. From Puntarenas port catch the ferry to Paquera (2hrs). There are 8 daily crossings that leave every 2hrs starting at 4.30am and the trip takes about 1hr 30mins. **Ferry Naviera Tambor** (2661 2084) and **Ferry Peninsular** (2641 0515) take passengers for US$1.50 per person and US$20. From Paquera take the road to Tambor, and once there follow the road to Montezuma.

Bahía Ballena

Bahía Ballena, one of the largest bays in Costa Rica, includes two small popular beach communities: **Pochote**, and **Playa Tambor** on the Golfo de Nicoya. The bay itself is known for its calm waters and silver sands, ideal for kayaking and swimming. This scenic waterfront has attracted several condominium projects to the surrounding hills and there is talk of building a large marina.

Accommodation is aimed at the retired and moneyed, and includes the Spanish hotel group Barceló, which has two extensive, all-inclusive resorts (Hotel Barceló Tambor and Los Delfines Golf & Country Club), not wildly popular with conservationists. Tambor is also home to an airport that serves the whole peninsula. This area specialises in resort hotels, where people sport clean, white tennis shoes rather than battered flipflops. If you are not planning on practising your backhand or mooring daddy's yacht, a day's visit is enough time to take in the sights.

Where to sleep & eat
Barceló Playa Tambor (2683 0303, www.barcelo.com, US$160 double) is an all-inclusive option preferred by Ticos and families on holiday. **Tango Mar Beach & Golf Resort** (2683 0001, www.tangomar.com, US$268 double) is a more upscale resort with a golf course, spa and a swanky restaurant. It was once used as the location for the reality show *Temptation Island.* Most of its suites open out on to the beach while its more basic rooms have an ocean view and a small balcony. It is a popular choice for honeymooners.

A more affordable option is the **Hotel Costa Coral** (2683 0105, www.hotelcostacoral.com, US$105 double). Located at the entrance to Tambor, 200 metres from the beach, it is a colonial-style ten-room hotel with terrace, pool and small restaurant. **Cabinas Tambor Beach** (2683 0057, US$30 double) is a basic budget hotel with private rooms and inexpensive meals.

Head south of Tambor to where the Rio Pochote empties into the bay and you'll find **Bahía Ballena Yacht Club** (2683 0213, main courses US$15). Relaxing place to chat and sip drinks with locals. Its restaurant specialises in simple fresh food such as fish and roast chicken and the club includes a bar, pool tables and satellite TV. If you are looking for a dance club – Tico style – then head to **KHU** disco at **Los Delfines Country Club** (2683 0304). It is only open at the weekends.

Isle of fright

On arrival it looks like an attractive, if deserted, tropical island. But the story behind **Refugio de Vida Silvestre Isla San Lucas** just off the south-eastern tip of the peninsula is far from pretty.

After the arrival of the Conquistadors, the sound of birds and lapping waves here became interspersed with the clinking of shackles and the screams of desperate men. For centuries, like a Costa Rican Alcatraz, this island once housed a jail. The Spanish invaders were the first to bang people up here: San Lucas was originally a detention centre for indigenous Costa Ricans. Its use as a penitentiary continued under Costa Rican dictator Tomás Guardia Gutiérrez in the late 1800s, and from then on the infamous reputation of San Lucas only grew. It would eventually come to be known as the 'Island of Unspeakable Horrors' and was regarded as one of the cruelest prisons in Latin America – and that's saying something. San Lucas remained open as a functioning prison until 1992.

Its history is well known among Costa Ricans, thanks mainly to the novel *La Isla de Los Hombres Solos* (The Island of Lonely Men), an internationally acclaimed memoir by Costa Rican writer and former inmate José León Sánchez, published in 1984. Born in 1930, at the age of 19 León Sánchez was sentenced to 30 years in prison after being convicted of stealing La Negrita (the Virgin of Los Ángeles, located in the Basílica in Cartago; *see p134* **Myths and miracles**) and killing a guard; he has always pleaded his innocence.

León Sánchez recounted how he began writing the book: 'Prisoners were not allowed to send more than single sided letters, and we were not permitted to express feelings of sadness or discomfort to the outside world. And if you did, you were charged five cents per sheet which was expensive and discouraging. Then one day a new prisoner was brought in. He was already a very old man by the name of Juan Valderrama. He handed me cement bags to write on, a large pencil and said "Fool, you write our story and I'll pay you good money".

'With this encouragement I started writing, and at night over oil lanterns and dice games I'd read chapters to my fellow prisoners. They were all enthusiastic about it and we would discuss what I'd written. It was really the first Costa Rican novel of oral tradition and this is the way it all happened.'

In this furtive, ad hoc manner, *Isla de Los Hombres Solos* was created. The book was published while Sánchez was still incarcerated even won him literary contests. In 1980 he was released, but continued to write. He went on to win the Premio Nacional de Literatura five times and has written more than 20 novels. It was not until 1998, 48 years after being sentenced, that León Sánchez was officially recognised as innocent, by the Supreme Court, of the Basílica crime. *La Isla de Los Hombres Solos* has been reprinted more than a hundred times and a (dreadful) Mexican film, based on the book, was made in 1974. The novel is considered one of the best in the Costa Rican canon, is a school curriculum classic that has sold more than two million copies.

Today the prison walls are crumbling ruins taken over by birds and lizards. The tourist board is considering making the jail a tourist attraction with guided walks, shuttle boats and even a restaurant. It is proposed that US$3 million will be spent to restore the prison cells and main building. Until these plans come into play, however, casual tours are available if you ask around; if not, ask the island's caretaker and he might let you look around and give you a few bits of information on its bleak past.

Paquera & Golfo de Nicoya

Paquera is a small beachless town, four kilometres (2.5 miles) from the ferry terminal. It is no more than a pit stop where you can refill your petrol tank and take out some cash. If you want to tour the islands off the gulf it is best to head to Tambor or Montezuma. Paquera is, however, the closest town to the **Refugio Nacional de Vida Silvestre Curú** and is as an eye-opener into a typical Costa Rican town.

The Golfo de Nicoya contains around 15 mostly uninhabited islands that are best explored by sea kayak or by boat. Boat tours depart from Puntarenas; for example, **San Lucas Transportes Marítimos** (2661 1069, www.coonatramar.com). Anyone with an interest in birds or ghost stories should plan a day trip out to these islands; they have little human history but contain some spooky ancient and recent burial grounds. The most accessible islands are around **Bahía Gigante**, south of

Playa Naranjo. **Isla San Lucas** is the largest and most infamous. Its six square kilometres (two square miles) once housed a tropical version of Alcatraz; a prison that was open from 1873 to 1992, it inspired *La Isla de los Hombres Solos* (The Island of Lonely Men) by Costa Rican author and former prisoner José León Sánchez (*see left* **Isle of fright**). **Isla Gitana**, aka **Isla Muertos**, is an abandoned Indian burial site (now Christianised with crosses) that is – surprise, surprise – said to be haunted. **Isla Jesusita** is the island closest to the Paquera ferry landing and an old graveyard can be seen peeking out from behind sandy beaches. Locals only stopped burying their dead here recently. Unless you're really into cemeteries, the most attractive of these islands are the ones grouped in the biological corridor, such as **Isla Guayabo**, **Isla Negritos** and **Isla Los Pájaros**. The latter is home to the largest colony of Brown Pelicans in Costa Rica and is a nesting area for many other seabirds. By far the most popular island in the area is **Isla Tortuga**, a white sand, palm lined oasis; the type of place that adorns office cubicle screen savers. In reality it's even prettier.

EXCURSIONS

Located seven kilometres (4.5 miles) south of Paquera on the main road is the **Refugio Nacional de Vida Silvestre Curú** (2641 0004, www.curuwildliferefuge.com). Declared a wildlife refuge in 1983, it is a small sectioned piece of protected jungle. It conserves and regenerates dwindling habitats of beaches, coral reefs, deciduous and semi-deciduous forests and mangroves in which live white-faced capuchin monkeys, scarlet macaws, white-tailed deer and collared peccaries. Attractions include a 200-metre-wide (650-foot) beachfront, mangrove estuaries and clean rivers.

The rest of the reserve consists of protected forest (75 per cent) and low-impact agriculture (20 per cent). Since 1933, the refuge has been managed by a Tico family, the Schutts, whoencourage tourists to visit the grounds and hike along the 17 different nature trails. Deer, monkeys, ocelots and anteaters live in the forests, and some 232 species of bird have been recorded. The Schutts are involved in environmental projects, from reintroducing monkeys and macaws to creating an artificial reef and maintaining low-impact tourist development.

Tours by horse or kayak, together with boat trips to Isla Tortuga and Playa Quesera, are available. You can stay the night at the reserve in one of the rustic cabins for US$30 per person, meals included (arrange in advance). Volunteers and researchers are also welcome. It is open daily from 7am to 3pm and entry is US$8.

Where to stay & eat

Downtown Paquera has a number of budget *cabinas* (cabins). They are usually great value, but make sure you have a nose around first. The best option, however, is **Cabinas & Restaurante Ginana** (2641 0119, US$20 double) with 30 simple and clean rooms, some with private bathrooms and air-conditioning. Its restaurant has huge *casados* and other typical dishes for around US$5 per main course.

Outside Paquera, nine kilometres (5.5 miles) on the road to Playa Naranjo, is **Hotel Bahía Luminosa Resort** (2641 0386, www.bahia luminosa.com, US$57 double). It has 15 rooms set on the hills overlooking the bay, complete with a pool. To get your fill of fresh fish, **Mariscos Macho** (2641 0262, main courses US$5) is excellent. It's in front of the school house.

Resources

Bank
Banco Popular *50m east from the Clinic (2641 0075).*

Hospital
Clínica de Paquera *(2641 0107).*

Police
In front of Hotel Ginana in Paquera town centre.

Getting there

By air
Both **Nature Air** (www.natureair.com) and **Sansa** (www.flysansa.com) have daily flights from several destinations to Tambor airport, the nearest to this area, for around US$70.

By bus
From the Coca Cola Market in San José, the **Hermanos Rodríguez** bus service departs daily at 7.30am, 11am and 3.30pm (2642 0740) for Montezuma and Mal Pais and Santa Teresa, making stops in Paquera. It costs US$10 per person. Ferry tickets are not included. Private shuttles run once a day from San José to the area, for example **Montezuma Expeditions** (2440 8078, www.montezuma expeditions.com, US$40 per person one way, ferry tickets included).

By road
From San José, take the Interamericana Highway to Puntarenas. From Puntarenas port catch the ferry to Paquera port. There are 8 daily crossings every 2 hours starting 4.30am, and the trip lasts about 1.5hrs. **Ferry Naviera Tambor** (2661 2084) and **Ferry Peninsular** (2641 0515) take passengers for US$1.50 per person and cars for US$20. The road from Paquera heads to Tambor and then on to Montezuma.

Central Pacific

Central Pacific Mainland

Party, surf, party and surf some more.

Puntarenas

The city of Puntarenas (meaning 'sand point') is a 16-kilometre (ten-mile) peninsula jutting out into the Golfo de Nicoya. It is also the capital of the province of the same name that extends along the Pacific coast from the Golfo de Nicoya all the way to the border with Panama. Puntarenas was previously Costa Rica's main port. However, as shipping routes develop along the Caribbean coast, it is no longer as busy as it once was.

The town is generally used by visitors as a base from which to explore the surrounding area. Historically, there have been problems with pollution, both in the streets and on the beach. The provincial government, however, has made an effort to clean up the city, and the water is now safe for swimming. Though Puntarenas can still be a nasty place to be on rubbish pick-up day, it is improving.

The city's tourist heart runs along the oceanfront on the well-policed **Paseo de los Turistas**. Puntarenas is now an important port for cruise ships, which seems to be the most popular mode of arrival for foreign tourists. The business district is three blocks inland on Avenida Central, a wide stretch occupied by shopping malls, government agencies and restaurants and, at night, home to Costa Rica's ubiquitous prostitutes and drug hustlers. Considering its size, Puntarenas is a relatively safe city, but it's probably safer to travel in pairs outside the Paseo de los Turistas.

Most of what the city has to offer can be seen in an afternoon. Start with a walk along the Paseo and visit the stalls selling jewellery and souvenirs, then stop off for a snack or ice-cream at one of the many kiosks by the long cruiser wharf. Another option is the **Parque Marino del Pacífico** (500m east of the wharf, 2661 5272, www.parquemarino.org, US$8), a

Coming soon to a restaurant near you: **Puntarenas**' catch of the day.

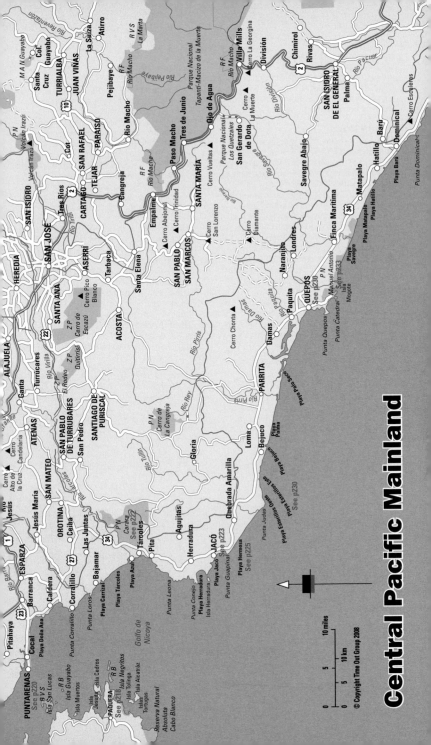

Central Pacific Mainland

small aquarium with marine life native to the Central Pacific. Or if you're looking for some art, take a trip to the town's cultural centre, **La Casa de Cultura** (2661 1394), which puts on plays and musical events, and has a small museum devoted to the area and its inhabitants.

EXCURSIONS
Many future plans are on the drawing board for Puntarenas, such as a US$10 million expansion to the aquarium and a new tourist pier on the Paseo. However, right now, if you're looking for something other than urban sprawl and (admittedly incredible) seafood, it would be wise to journey out of the city and into the forest. **Travel Agency Alova** (75m north of the hospital, 8335 4040/8308 1360) offers many great tours to **PN Volcán Poás** (*see p118*), **Sarchi** (*see p123*) and around – canopy tours, horseriding, rafting, rental minibuses, and so on – and it generally has a rep on the pavement outside Restaurante Imperial. Just south of Puntarenas is **Playa Doña Ana**, a small beach area with a resort set up by the Costa Rican national tourism institute. Showers and parking are open to the public, and it's also home to the second longest surf break in the country, after **Pavones** (*see p272*).

Along the road from Puntarenas to Jacó you'll pass **PN Carara** (2383 9953), important because it links the dry northern Pacific lowlands to the wet southern Pacific lowlands, making the park a kind of halfway house for dry forest and rainforest species. The 52-square-kilometre (20-square-mile) is home to white-throated magpie Jays reach their southern limit; they can happily raid nests of birds such as shining honeycreepers and white-shouldered tanagers who reach their northern limit here. Scarlet macaws can also be spotted, along with roseate spoonbills, anhingas and northern Jacanas.

Named after the indigenous word for crocodile, the park also protects monkeys, armadillos, peccaries, opossums, sloths, boas, jaguars, white-tail deer and and ocelots. It has two main hiking trails, and you can park a kilometre south of the bridge at Río Grande de Tárcoles by the ranger station. The five-kilometre (three mile) Araceas Nature Trail that begins here runs parallel to the Río Grande de Tárcoles and has short branches to the Laguna Meandrica and marshes.

Rain Forest Aerial Tram (2257 5961, www.rfat.com) has gondola rides over where the tropical dry forest meets the tropical rainforest.

The **Golfo de Nicoya** contains around 15 islands that are best explored by boat.

Where to eat & drink

Bar Restaurante Chirripó
In bus terminal (2661 2397). **Open** 6am-9pm daily.
Main courses US$4. **No credit cards.**
A great place for a snack before your bus leaves,
serving delicious *naturales* (freshly squeezed juices).

Bar Restaurante Mar Abierto
*Next to the ferry terminal, Barrio El Carmen (2661
6196).* **Open** 7am-8pm daily. **Main courses** US$5.
No credit cards.
One of Puntarenas's many seafood specialists. It's
standard Costa Rican fare, but with the freshest fish.

Restaurante Imperial
*Paseo de los Turistas, 100m west of bus station
(2661 0955).* **Open** 7am-10pm daily. **Main courses**
US$8. **Credit** AmEx, DC, MC, V.
A popular eaterie among locals, Imperial has a broad
choice of dishes including some gigantic prawns. It's
a typical Costa Rican set-up with the bar as the
centrepiece and stool seating around.

La Yunta Steakhouse
Paseo de los Turistas, y Calle 21 (2661 3216).
Open 10am-6am daily. **Main courses** US$12.
Credit AmEx, MC, V.
La Yunta offers upscale atmosphere and a great
selection of steaks and seafood in large portions.
Reservations recommended on weekends.

Where to stay

Alamar Hotel
*Paseo de los Turistas, 300m before the point (2661
4343/www.alamarcr.com).* **Rates** US$94 double.
Rooms 34. **Credit** AmEx, MC, V.
The Alamar comprises handsomely laid-out villas
and standard rooms overlooking a central pool and
jacuzzi. Most have ocean views, with a clean and
smart design.
*Bar. Internet (shared terminal, free). Parking (free).
Pool (outdoor). Restaurant. Room service. TV.*

Hotel Las Brisas
*Paseo de los Turistas, 200m before the
point (2661 4040/www.lasbrisashotelcr.com).*
Rates US$120-$160 double. **Rooms** 36.
Credit AmEx, DC, MC, V.
Just acing it over the Alamar, this is the nicest hotel
in Puntarenas. The upstairs rooms have wonderful
sunset views of the gulf. Facilities include a great
central pool with fountains, and one of the better
restaurants in town. Renovations were under way
at the time of writing, with plans to add new rooms,
jacuzzis and a small gym.
*Bar. Gym. Internet (wireless, free). Parking (free).
Pool (outdoor). Restaurant. Room service. TV.*

Hotel Familiar Macarena
*Avenida Central, 100m west from Motel Alajuela
(2661 6161).* **Rates** US$30 double. **Rooms** 10.
Credit MC, V.

Owned by the same family as Soda Macarena, this
place is certainly no palace. It is somewhere to stay
mainly for sleep and security rather than comfort.
Rooms have air-conditioning and feel very safe and
secure due to the complete absence of windows.

Resources

Bank
Banco Nacional *Avenida 3, y Calle 1
(2661 9200).*

Hospital
Hospital Monseñor Sanabria *8km east of town
(2663 0033).*

Internet
Soda Macarena *50m west of bus station (2661
1415).* **Open** 7am-6pm daily.

Police
Behind Banco de Costa Rica (2661 0640).

Post office
Avenida 3, y Calle 1 (2661 2156).

Tourist information
*Paseo León Cortés, y Calle Central in the former ICE
building by the beach (2661 6408).* Office hours are
utterly random.

Getting there

By boat
There are passenger and drive-on ferries to Paquera
and various points on the Peninsula de Nicoya from
the tiny 'fishing village' 200m from the point on the
north side of the Puntarenas peninsula (**Ferry
Coonatramar**, 2661 1069, www.coonatramar.com).

By bus
From San José, Calle 16, between Avenidas 10 and
12, Barrio Los Ángeles. Buses leave every hour from
6am to 7pm, take about 3hrs and cost US$6 (2222
0064 in San José, 2661 2158 in Puntarenas). Buses to
the southern zone leave from across the street from
the Puntarenas covered bus station.

By road
Go west out of San José on the Interamericana
Highway, past the airport and Alajuela, and follow
signs to Puntarenas. The drive takes about 2hrs
along good roads.

Jacó & Around

Jacó Beach, 117 kilometres (73 miles) west
of San José, is one of Costa Rica's more
bacchanalian destinations. With its 24-hour
discos, strip clubs, drug pushers and
prostitutes, it is much like a year-round US
spring break. The clientele is, therefore, much
as you'd expect – boozing North Americans
and partying surfers.

Be sure to drop in on the spectacular **PN Manuel Antonio**. *See p233.*

That said, the near five kilometres (three miles) of beach, nestled between two steep, rocky points, is very pretty. Jacó offers some of the best surf on the Pacific coastline, and if you're interested in learning to ride the waves or just improving your skills, stop by **WOW Surf** (Jacó Centro across from Economy Car Rental, 2643 3844, www.wowsurf.net) for one of its specialised, three-part lessons (US$65 per person for three hours). Even if you're a strong swimmer, be careful of the riptides out there. The area is also a sport fishing mecca. Contact **Hooked On Costa Rica**'s Captain Josh Foster (8372 2627, www.hookedoncosta rica.com) for fishing trips close to Jacó's shores or out of nearby Los Sueños marina.

Almost everything in Jacó is within walking distance along the main street, Avenida Pastor Diaz (also known as Calle Principal). Shops and bars seem to proliferate by the minute. Despite what is frequently written about the town, Jacó is relatively safe, and if you're out in the daytime you shouldn't have any problems. At night it is a different story, however, and your ears will quickly ring from the shouts of drug dealers whose sales pitch – 'Weed, coke! Weed, coke!' – is tried on every passing tourist.

The world's oldest profession is going strong here too, due to the large numbers of middle-aged foreign 'fishermen' who 'holiday' here. The divide between rich and poor is stark in Jacó, and it can occasionally be a little saddening. If you feel the need, you can escape into one of the many elegant hotels and restaurants. The drinks are expensive, but many restaurants allow patrons to take their own alcohol. Like anywhere, you can always spend a little more to elevate yourself away from the shadier side.

EXCURSIONS

Jacó has a high concentration of expats (mainly North American and European), many of whom have interesting travel experiences to share. The streets are lined with tour booths. **Green Tours** (2643 1984, ecishing_greentour @costarricense.co.cr) offers boat tours on its 'fiesta party' boat to nearby Isla Tortuga, where staff lay on kayak and snorkelling expeditions. The trips include lunch and transport and cost US$79 per person. **Ricaventura** (25m east of Subway, 2643 3395, www.ricaventura.com) has quad-bike tours and motorcycle rental.

Alternatively, be your own tour guide by renting a bicycle or taking the bus south to nearby **Playa Hermosa**, about five kilometres Three miles) away. Sea turtles lay their eggs here from July to December (*see p194* **Turtle power**). If you're a surfer, take your

The best Surf breaks

Only two hours away from San José by car, the best time for these beaches is during the rainy season months of April to November when the south swells pump up the waves. However, these waves are known to go off high all year round.

Boca Barranca The dark water is only rainwater runoff, and that's great because this rivermouth break is a very long left and is ranked favourably in Costa Rica. Just south of Puntarenas.

Playa Tivives and Valor This area provides a variety of waves including Tivives' beach breaks to the rocky point of Valor, with good quality rights and lefts. To get to Valor you will need to paddle across the river then walk along the trails.

Playa Escondida Accessible only by boat from Playa Herradura, but with a good swell, this excellent point break peaks up forming a very good left and a nice right.

Playa Jacó An excellent learners spot. A beach break when the surf is small.

Crazy Rock A kilometre south of Jacó. To get to this rocky point you will need to climb down a steep cliff and paddle out across a rocky strait. Be careful: the wave breaks right over submerged, shallow rocks. Definitely needs swell.

Playa Hermosa The crown jewel of the area. One of the most consistent beach breaks on the Pacific coast.

board – the beach is known for its great break that is often better than Jacó's. Playa Hermosa is also a great spot for birdwatching; it is home to the Snowy Egret and five species of heron.

Another option is the town of **Parrita**, about 40 kilometres (25 miles) away on the coastal highway. There's not a great deal to see, but from there you can head east seven kilometres (4.5 miles) to the small town of Pocares. From Pocares you'll see signs to **Rainmaker Conservation Project** (2777 3565, www.rainmakercostarica.org, US$70 per person), a collection of boardwalks and elevated observation platforms that give bird's-eye views of waterfalls and rich rainforest vegetation. There are six sections of suspension bridge, with a total walking distance of 250 metres (820 feet). The project attempts to have as little impact as possible on the natural habitats below. Take swimming togs for a quick dip in the waterfall.

Central Pacific

Endless summer of love

It should have been the usual story. Boy meets girl. Boy falls in love with girl. Boy and girl get married. Except for a couple of remarkable facts: the boy is Costa Rica's male surf champion. And the girl? Costa Rica's female surf champion. It was a relationship that blossomed on the perfect beaches splashed by the perfect swells of the Pacific Ocean.

Central Pacific

When Lisbeth Vindas was a 13-year-old hanging out with a bunch of kids in her hometown of Jacó Beach, she asked 14-year-old Diego Naranjo to give her a surf lesson. She fell in love with surfing and, after years of surfing together, she fell in love with Naranjo too. On 23 June 2007, they married at the Parroquia de Jacó church in front of their family and pretty much the entire Latino surf community, including Magnum Martínez from Venezuela, Otto Flores from Puerto Rico, Kalle Carranza from Mexico and Gary Saavedra from Panama, all of whom made the journey to join the Costa Rican surf fraternity in celebrating this love born on the waves.

After an almighty reception in the Hotel Los Sueños Marriott in Playa Herradura, newlyweds Diego and Betty (as Lisbeth is known to her friends) and the wedding party headed to Nicaragua (an up-and-coming surf spot) for a holiday riding the waves. However, it wasn't just a honeymoon. Naranjo, who has been instrumental in Costa Rica's development of its competitive surf circuit, took the opportunity while in Nicaragua along with his wife and friends Martínez, Flores, Carranza and Saavedra to participate in organised surf clinics for the local surfers.

The goal was to help them deal with different aspects of competitive surfing, an important task given that Nicaraguan surfers also form part of the Central American Surfing Federation along with Costa Rica and Panama.

Their real honeymoon (snowboarding in Bariloche, Argentina), however, has been postponed due to their hectic competitive surfing schedules. Betty has to retain her five national women's championships and two Central American female championships, and Naranjo his national surfing trophy. And, together, they must surf in the Costa Rican national team, which is currently ranked eighth in the world.

'Well, now we have to surf more than ever to pay the bills,' Betty laughs. 'Everything has been great: We moved into our house, we're really doing a lot of things and it's really fun. Hopefully, it will stay that way.'

'I'm very happy with this new stage of my life, and I'm really grateful for being able to enjoy it with my friends,' Naranjo adds before heading back down to the beach and out on to the waves.

Where to eat & drink

Café Del Mar

Avenida Pastor Díaz, y Calle Bribrí (2653 1250).
Open 7am-midnight daily. **Credit** AmEx,
DC, MC, V.
Delicious hot and cold espresso drinks and pastries.
The porch area is right on the main walkway and
makes a good spot for morning people-watching.
The café has free Wi-Fi.

El Hicaco Restaurant

*Calle Hicaco, y Avenida Pastor Díaz (2643 4104/
elhicaco@racsa.co.cr).* **Open** 11am-11pm daily.
Main courses US$14. **Credit** AmEx, DC, MC, V.
Probably the most upscale restaurant in Jacó, El
Hicaco can be a little pricey but it makes for a fun
evening. It's a huge place, seating 200, with tables
just above the beach. If you're there on a Wednesday,
go for the 'all you can eat lobster feast' (US$60, from
6pm) including mahi-mahi, a salad bar, sushi and
alcoholic drinks (beer, wine and margaritas).

Jacó Taco

*Avenida Pastor Díaz, at northern entrance to town
(2643 1313/www.jacotaco.com).* **Open** 24hrs daily.
Main courses US$9. **Credit** MC, V.
The Mexican food here is great, and authentic – 80%
of it is imported directly from Mexico. There's live
music Thursday to Sunday. The upstairs bar (pool
tables, foosball) opens late in the day and has a nice
view of the ocean. Staff offer a free golf cart shuttle
to the restaurant from the sea and give a free margarita upon arrival.

Soda Jacó Rústico

Just before El Hicaco Restaurant (2643 2117).
Open 7am-7pm daily. **Main courses** US$4.
No credit cards.
Highly recommended by locals, Soda Jacó Rústico
serves up great *casados*. Not much of a menu but a
sure-fire bet for good, cheap food.

Sunrise Restaurant

Jacó Centro in front of Monkey Bar (2643 3361).
Open 6.30am-12.30pm daily. **Main courses** US$7.
No credit cards.
The best breakfast in town, featuring a variety of
North American and international wake-up dishes.
It also serves and delivers pizza in the evenings
(6pm-3am, closed Tue).

El Tabacón

*Jacó Centro in front of Restaurante Colonial (2643
3097).* **Open** 4pm-1am Mon-Thur; 11am-1am Fri-
Sun. **Main courses** US$12. **Credit** MC, V.
The food here is expensive for what you get but is
still pretty good. It's more popular as a drinking
establishment among both locals and tourists, with
two pool tables alongside the bar. Unlike at some
other venues in town, you won't be approached by
prostitutes. There is live music in the evenings from
Thursday to Sunday.

Escape the party scene in Jacó at the nearby retreat of **Ama Tierra**. *See p229.*

Central Pacific

Jaco Beach, Costa Rica
(over one million years in the making.)

WYNDHAM
JACO BEACH
RESORT & CONDOMINIUMS

Introducing "Guilt-free Ownership" in our five-star luxury resort.
Jaco Beach, Costa Rica has long been a paradise for those who love high-end sport fishing and for passionate surfers. Amidst abundantly green mountains, exotic animals, flowers and of course, world-class beaches with turquoise waves, the idea of building a luxury resort was irresistible.

Now with **pre-approved financing through HSBC Bank***, the freedom to come and go as you like and the opportunity to rent your resort residence in one of the largest reservations systems in the world, we think you can enjoy ownership in a new way. So stop waiting and discover life at Wyndham Jaco Beach. **You can't afford not to.**

Pre-Construction Prices from the $300k's
Costa Rica 506 2289 9419 • U.S. Toll Free 1 888 CRWYNDHAM
Info@WyndhamJacoBeach.com • www.WyndhamJacoBeach.com

Where to stay

Ama Tierra

2km before San Pablo de Turrubares, 20km from Puriscal (2419 0110/www.amatierra.com). **Rates** US$189 double. **Rooms** 10 cabins. **Credit** MC,V.
This nature retreat offers visitors ten nicely decorated private cabins. With yoga classes, delicious organic meals and a holistic approach to healthy holidaying, Ama Tierra is an ideal choice for those seeking well-being and outdoor exploration. It is also a good way of getting some distance between yourself and the party nuts in Jacó. Day trip hiking includes trails to hot springs and freshwater streams. *Photo p227.*
Internet (wireless, free). Pool (outdoor). TV.

Las Camas Hostel

Jacó opposite Kentucky Fried Chicken (2643 1607). **Rates** US$14 for dorm bed, US$30 for private double. **Rooms** 6. **Credit** MC, V.
What? A hostel with air-conditioning? Yes, it has it in every room. It also has a cool rooftop hang-out area with barbecue. There is free internet and wireless, hot water and shared cable TV, bathrooms and kitchen. The owners are Edit and Csaba from Hungary – they are very sweet and can help you set up tours and find your way around.
Bar. Internet (wireless, free). Parking (free).

Hotel Canciones del Mar

Calle Bribri on the beach (2643 3273/www.canciones delmar.com). **Rates** US$95-$120 double. **Rooms** 11. **Credit** AmEx, DC, MC, V.
The best value hotel in Jacó, 'Sea Shanties' offers ocean- or pool-view suites with all amenities. It is a well-maintained property right on the beach with extremely helpful staff. The new Saca Gomas rooftop bar has wonderful sunset vistas and a jacuzzi. The jungle grounds also attract a fair amount of birds and wildlife.
Pool (outdoor). TV.

Hotel Poseidón

30m towards ocean on Calle Bohio (2643 1642/ www.hotel-poseidon.com). **Rates** US$75-$120 double. **Rooms** 14. **Credit** AmEx, DC, MC, V.
The rooms are pleasant and well appointed, but quite small for the price. Each has air-conditioning, two double beds with an extra bed available on request, and a fridge. There is a swimming pool in the centre of the complex (with wet bar) and a lovely North African-style bar and restaurant. Free wireless internet and continental breakfast are included. The US owners Chrissy and Tim also offer three- and six-day packages that include canopy tours and a trip to PN Manuel Antonio.
Bars (3). Disabled-adapted rooms. Concierge. Internet (shared terminal, wireless, free). Restaurant. TV.

Villa Caletas

8km from Playa Jacó & 4km from Playa Herradura (2637 0505/www.hotelvillacaletas.com). **Rates** US$193-$495. **Rooms** 52. **Credit** AmEx, DC, MC,V.
This luxury hotel offers first-rate services and surroundings. Rooms and suites are dotted around a mountain top and look out over flowering orchids and the ocean. Oversized bath towels, fresh fruit breakfasts and impressive design accents enhance the experience.
Bars (2). Gym. Pool. Restaurants (2). Spa. TV.

Villas Estrellamar

Avenida Pastor Díaz after Payless Car Rental (2643 3102/www.estrellamar.com). **Rates** US$80-$129 double. **Rooms** 24. **Credit** AmEx, DC, MC, V.
Pleasant and comfortable villas complete with kitchenettes, set in a large property. There is a nice pool, and breakfast is included.
Bar. Pool (outdoor). Restaurant. TV.

Vista Pacifico

Lomas de Jacó (2643 3261/www.vistapacifico. com). **Rates** US$64-$163 double. **Rooms** 9. **Credit** DC, MC,V.
Pacifico, owned by two happy-go-lucky Canadians, offers clean, family-friendly apart-hotels complete with kitchens. Ocean views and pool-side barbecue nights add to the easgoing atmosphere. Pets are welcome but ask first before booking. There is also an ample book and game lending library.
Disabled-adapted rooms. Parking (free). Pool (outdoor). TV.

Resources

Bank

Banco Nacional *100m south of Mas-X-Menos supermarket (2643 1123).*

Hospital

Red Cross *Avenida Pastor Díaz 15m north Importadora Monge (2643 3090).*

Internet

Mexican Joe's *Avenida Pastor Díaz, across from Bar La Bruja (2643 2141).* **Open** 8am-10pm daily.

Police station

Calle Bohio (2643 3011).

Tourist information

No public office but countless tour agency offices on Avenida Pastor Díaz. A good resource is www.hookedoncostarica.com.

Getting there

By bus

From San José, buses leave the Coca-Cola terminal (Calle 16, entre Avenidas 1 y 3). They leave 8 times a day, cost US$3 and take about 3hrs with **Transportes Jacó** (2223 1109 in San José and 2643 3135 in Jacó). From Puntarenas station on the beach, buses take about 3 hrs, cost US$2.50 and leave 6

Central Pacific

It's not all birdwatching and surfing. Party time at **Arco Iris** in Quepos.

times daily – **Transportes Quepos
Puntarenas** (2661 1345).

By road

From San José take the highway to Escazú and Santa
Ana and pass through Puriscal and Orotina where
you'll see signs for Jacó. From Puntarenas go south
on the Costanera (Coastal Highway).

Esterillos to Quepos

South-east of Jacó along the coastal Costanera
Highway are the three small villages of
Esterillos (West, Central and East) that begin
about 22 kilometres (14 miles) from Jacó and sit
right on the beach or only slightly inland. There
are good surf breaks along here and the buses
will stop if you know where you want to get off.
It's a beautiful drive, dipping in and out of the
coast, and there are more than a few hotels and
restaurants worth checking out along the way.
La Dolce Vita (Esterillos Oeste Beach, 50m
from the bus stop, 2778 7015, www.resortla
dolcevita.com, US$72 double) features seven
apartments and a decent bar and restaurant
just a short walk from the beach.

For most tourists, **Quepos** is little more
than a gateway into the national park and area
around Manuel Antonio. But it's also one of the
region's top party towns, and the residents are
the first to get up and dance at almost any time
of the day. After the demise of the banana trade

in the 1970s, Quepos underwent a serious
decline, rescued partly by palm oil plantations,
but mainly by tourism.

The oceanfront facing Quepos, comprising a
gravel road just above a boulder embankment
with a sand spit for a view, is poor compared
with the beaches around the town; but if the
moon is big, the reflection on the tiny lapping
waves is certainly worth checking out.

The town itself is not quite as manic as Jacó,
so you won't be hassled as much. But you should
still take care of your belongings – there are
occasionally problems with theft. The town is
packed full of bars and restaurants, most of them
good. It's often reported that this area of the
country has different prices for gringos and
Ticos, so make sure you are not paying more
than the listed cost. Nearly everyone who works
in tourism around here speaks English, so even
if you speak little or no Spanish, you should be
able to get by fairly easily.

Where to eat & drink

A popular bar, restaurant and general hangout
for local expats and holidaying fishermen,
El Gran Escape (2777 0395, www.elgran
escape.net, main courses US$12) is just below
sea level opposite the oceanfront entrance into
Quepos Centre and specialises in seafood and
Mexican dishes. Even better is local favourite

Soda Sánchez (next to Red Cross, 2777 2635, main courses US$7). Soda Sánchez's owner, Don Sánchez, is always delighted to chat; both he and his establishment are Quepos legends. Another popular place with the locals is **Restaurante El Jardín del Mar** (diagonally opposite the Banco Nacional, 2777 0104, main courses US$6). El Jardín dares to go beyond the soda standard *comida típica* with dishes such as chicken stroganoff. The location right in the middle of town offers some good people-watching opportunities.

As for the nightlife, there are a surprising number of options in a town that is essentially six square blocks. If you're any kind of party animal, hit the **Arco Iris** disco (500m north of Quepos Centre along the waterfront, US$6). The place isn't not overly keen on big groups of foreign tourists but it's a fun evening regardless, and if nothing else a bit of an adventure. **Republik Lounge** (50m west of Banco Nacional) is another hotspot. The drinks are expensive, and it's obviously built for the tourist dollar (it looks like a teenager's idea of a ritzy New York hair salon), but you'll have fun. Mingle with tourists and Manuel Antonio tour guides before you all head over to Arco Iris at closing time. Or have a go at **WackyWanda's** (Quepos Centre, 2777 2245), which is deceptively straight. The air-conditioning is kept on high, so it's a good place to relax.

Where to stay

At the entrance into Quepos, facing the water, sits the **Best Western Hotel & Casino Kamuk** (2777 0811, www.kamuk.co.cr, US$90-$125 double). It's one of the most reliable hotels in Quepos. It may not look much from the outside, but air-conditioning, cable TV, Wi-Fi, hot water and breakfast are all included. There's a nice central pool and an open-air bar and restaurant overlooking the waterfront.

On the next block you'll find **Hotel El Pueblo** (Quepos Centre after El Gallo Más Gallo, 2777 1003, US$35 double), a simple place with air-conditioned rooms and a good restaurant. The management at **Hotel La Sirena** (50m west of Banco Nacional, 2777 0572, www.la sirenahotel.com, US$65 double) is under the impression that its establishment has been voted 'best budget hotel in Quepos', but no one is quite sure why. It's comfortable enough but nothing out of the ordinary. If you're travelling on a tight budget, **Widemouth Frog** backpacker hostel is a good choice (one block east of bus station facing the school, 2777 2798, www.widemouthfrog.org, US$9 dorm, US$24 double). It is way above par by Costa Rican standards with complimentary breakfast, free internet, a swimming pool, shared kitchen, plenty of board games, and lockers.

Beans, rice and good chat at the legendary **Soda Sánchez**.

Resources

Bank
Banco Nacional *opposite fire station (2777 1157).*
Coopealianza *next to the Red Cross (2777 0400).*
More reliable for ATM withdrawals.

Hospital
4km south-west on the road to Dominical (2777 0922, for emergencies 911).

Internet
Compunet *from the main ocean entrance by Hotel Kamuk, go east, take first left, 20m on left (2777 4698).* **Open** *9am-10pm Mon-Sat.*

Police station
100m south of Quepos public park (2777 0196).

Post office
In front of Rancho Grande (2777 1471).

Tourist information
No public office. **Iguana Tours** (2777 2052, www.iguanatours.com) comes highly recommended and is willing to answer general questions. On the road to Manuel Antonio in front of Quepos soccer field. **Open** 7am-9pm daily.

Getting there

By air
Sansa (2290 4100, www.flysansa.com) has 5 daily flights to Quepos for US$72 per person from Juan Santamaria International Airport. **Nature Air** (2521 5226, www.natureair.com) has 2 to 3 flights daily, leaving from the Aeropuerto Tobias Bolaños in Pavas Airport in the city of San José. Flights cost around US$60 one way.

By bus
From the San José Coca-Cola terminal (Calle 16, entre Avenidas 1 y 3), buses take about 3 hrs, cost US$5.50 and leave 6 times daily to Quepos's main downtown station. **Transporte Morales** (2223 5567 in San José, 2777 0263 in Quepos). From Puntarenas station on the beach, buses take about 3 hrs, cost US$3 and leave 6 times daily (via Jacó) to the Quepos main station. **Transportes Quepos Puntarenas** (2661 1345).

By road
From San José it's about a 3 hr drive: take the road out of San José to Alajuela then follow it through La Garita, Atenas, Orotina, Jacó, Parrita and Quepos.

Parque Nacional Manuel Antonio

The seven-kilometre (4.5-mile) road from Quepos to Parque Nacional Manuel Antonio rolls through lush jungle foliage, down hills and up valleys, along what is one of the most popular tourist routes in the country. Since the 1980s, international investors and hoteliers have scrambled to purchase what little land is left in an area with unbelievable ocean views. Fortunately, the region is vast and it hardly seems populated until you arrive at the main beach and village just before the national park. Accommodation and eating options are decidedly more upscale than the rest of the country, but there are prices to suit most budgets.

The main attraction in Manuel Antonio is the many beautiful beaches, the best among them

Central Pacific

The view from the Mirador trail of **PN Manuel Antonio** is worth battling the bugs for.

Chasing rainbows

Though Costa Ricans are, in general, more liberal-minded than many of their Central American neighbours, certain parts of the country are still fairly backward when it comes to sexual preferences. Fortunately, this is not the case in Manuel Antonio. In the past decade or so, Manuel Antonio and the surrounding area have become bastions of gay tourism in the country, and indeed in Central America as a whole. The scene initially seems to have been formed around 'Playitas', a section of beachfront within the national park that, until recently, was popular spot for chaps, particular gay ones, to go and partake in a little nude sunbathing. Being only accessible for brief periods at low tide, it became popular for its remoteness.

It's worth noting that nude bathing has always been illegal in Costa Rica, but it's only been in the past couple of years that anyone seemed to be concerned with this particular point. So why ruin the fun? Many think that change of heart could be down to a new, family-oriented hotel built with a direct view of Playitas. Now there is more chance of being fined or arrested for skinny dipping here, and the gay community isn't happy about it. Yet the naked bathing still continues, as does Manuel Antonio's expanding gay-friendly community.

Erwin Pérez, the Manuel Antonio-born general manager of the very successful gay-owned **Hotel Villa Roca** (2777 1349, www.villaroca.com, US$95-$190 double), explains how he first became aware of the area's gay scene as a teenager in the late 1980s – by going to the **Arco Iris** (see p231) disco in Quepos. He had in the past always heard of the nude beach, and at the disco he met employees of the first gay-owned hotel in Manuel Antonio, La Mariposa (still there but no longer specifically gay). Discoing homophobes initially fought with Mariposa's gay staff, pejoratively dubbing them *playitos*, but as time went on, tolerance grew. 'Year by year, the people of Manuel Antonio got used to gay people,' Pérez explains, 'and now homophobia is no longer a problem.'

Olga Sánchez, manager of **Hotel Casa Blanca** (2777 0253, www.hotel-casa blanca.com, US$90-$130 double), which caters to gay and lesbian tourists, moved to Manuel Antonio 14 years ago. 'Manuel Antonio is a very open area,' she explains.

'When I moved here even San José wasn't as open.' José Chávez, a partner in both **Gay Tours** (2294 0606, www.gaytourscr.com) and *Circuito Playita*, a free, bi-monthly bulletin on gay life in Costa Rica, seems to agree with Olga Sánchez. 'Even 25 years ago there was gay development in Manuel Antonio,' he says. 'Gay tourism grew stronger and respect grew in Tico culture because Costa Ricans are very tolerant of foreign cultures. In Manuel Antonio today you don't feel any homophobia.'

Some of the more popular nightlife spots among gay locals and tourists include **Bar Tutu** (2777 5040) inside Hotel Eclipse and **Cantina Salsipuedes** (2777 5019), described by its owners as 'a gay-friendly tapas place with an incredible ocean view and Latin music' (which pretty much covers all bases). Like most 'gay destinations' in Latin America, gay men are far more visible than lesbians, although there are signs that the girls are starting to move in on the act. The prevailing opinion in Manuel Antonio is that the town is less a specifically 'gay' destination, and more a haven for people who don't care who does what with whom.

Other nearly exclusively gay/lesbian and gay-friendly hotels:

Hotel del Mar

Manuel Antonio (2777 0543/www.gohotel delmar.com). **Rates** US$70 double. **Rooms** 12. **Credit** AmEx, DC, MC, V.
Just 200m from Manuel Antonio's famous beach, Hotel del Mar's location is its highlight. The rooms are basic but comfortable and spacious. Choose the one with a private balcony for an opportunity to see the abundant wildlife that makes its home in the gardens.

La Plantación

Manuel Antonio (2777 1332/www.bigrubys. com). **Rates** US$150-$180 double. **Rooms** 23. **Credit** MC, V.
The Plantation is an excellent value hotel with tasteful and well-appointed rooms, several of which have their own balcony. High on the hillside overlooking a protected cove moments away from PN Manuel Antonio, there can be few more beautiful spots in the area.
Bar. Internet (wireless, free). Pool (outdoor). TV.

Surf's up in the pristine waters of **PN Manuel Antonio**.

being **Playa Espadilla Norte**, just north of the national park. It is rather crowded, and those in search of a more secluded beachfront may have better luck at one of the beaches inside the park itself, although they too can be busy in high season. Some of the beachfront restaurants at Northern Espadilla offer chairs and umbrellas for rent – arrive early for the prime real estate.

The village surrounding Playa Espadilla Norte offers many restaurants, drinking establishments and a few hotels. Although the local authority makes an effort to keep the place clean, the streets and beach are sadly often littered with rubbish. The pavements are lined with vendors hawking hand made jewellery, T-shirts and other goods designed to separate tourists from their coinage. People are generally friendly but this isn't a crime-free utopia, so hang on to your wallet.

From the village it is a short five-minute walk to the park entrance. On the way you will pass the **Asoguinama** (Asociación de Guías Naturalistas del Parque Nacional Manuel Antonio) tour guide office on the left side (2777 5194, asoguinama@hotmail.com, tours US$20 per person). The office also sells more detailed maps (US$3) than those available at the park entrance, and though there are a plethora of other companies and private guides, it is a safe bet. From here, walk on to the beach and through the shallow stream, over a short hill to the park. The entrance fee is US$10, and it is open from 7am to 4pm Tuesday to Sunday.

PN Manuel Antonio was founded in 1972 and currently has approximately 18 square kilometres (6.9 square miles) of land within its borders. Although tourists are generally drawn by the park's incredible beaches, there is

Towering trees reach high into the canopy of **PN Manuel Antonio**.

also a wide range of wildlife to be seen. It is recommended you arrive early to see the mammals and birds, among them the white-nosed coati, mantled howler monkey, white-faced capuchin monkey, toucans, guacos and fishing sparrow hawks. The park also provides a home for the endangered titi monkey, a subspecies endemic to Costa Rica with very little natural habitat remaining.

The park has showers, toilets, picnic tables and phones. The trails go from flat and sandy to steep concrete steps, a few of which are pretty difficult even for people in reasonable shape.

The recommended sights include **Playa Puerto Escondido** and blowhole, the **Mirador Trail** (with a greats views from the park's highest point over the ocean) and **Cathedral Point** (just beyond the entrance). There are also streams and lagoons throughout and more difficult unmarked trails for the experienced trekker. Most of the park can be seen in around four hours. Be aware of rising tides that can leave you stranded – a poor way to end your day trip.

EXCURSIONS

For a bit more adventure, the highly recommended rafting and kayaking outfitters **Amigos del Rio** (2777 0082, www.amigos delrio.net) offer all manner of soaking action on the Class III Rio Savegre and Class III/IV rides down the Rio Naranjo through an overgrown canyon. Its kayaking trips skirt the PN Manuel Antonio and offer a tranquil way to see wildlife from a different angle. To get wetter try waterfall rappelling with **Xtreme Tours** (2777 4926, extremetours@latinmail.com).

Sunset Sails (2777 1304, www.sunsetsails tours.com) cruising tours take you along the coast of the park with the chance to see whales, giant sea turtles and dolphins. All tours include an on-board meal, cold beers and a cocktail or two. Snorkelling gear is provided.

Where to stay & eat

As you follow the road from Quepos into Manuel Antonio, one of the first eateries you'll pass on the left will be **Bambu Jam** (2777 3369, www.bambujam.com, main courses US$10). Probably the most popular spot for nightlife, Bambu Jam offers live music on Tuesdays and Fridays and gets crowded with tourists and locals.

Next, about one kilometre in, you'll come to **Mono Azul Hotel & Restaurant** (2777 2572, www.hotelmonoazul.com, US$35-$105 double); the reasonably sized rooms include cable TV and hot water, and most have balconies. There are also three swimming pools on site. The

place could do with a revamp, but for the price it probably can't be beaten. It's a good restaurant stop, especially for vegetarians.

Restaurante Kapi Kapi (2777 5049, kapikapi@racsa.co.cr, main courses US$10), 100 metres before Tulemar on the road from Quepos, has a romantic feel and serves delicious international dishes with on-the-ball service.

The sparkling new **Arenas del Mar** (2777 2777, www.arenasdelmar.com, US$256-$675 double) is two kilometres (1.25 miles) from the port of Quepos in Manuel Antonio. It has 38 rooms, smiling staff and lovely views over the national park. Each room and suite has a flatscreen TV, air-conditioning and wireless internet access. The hotel is situated on a cliff and has access to two secluded white sand beaches. Its upscale restaurant, El Mirador, is known for seasonal ingredients and freshly caught fish. It also holds a certificate for sustainable tourism and warms the water with solar energy and reuses grey water for irrigation.

Continue through the hills (three kilometres from Quepos) and you'll come to **Gaia Hotel & Reserve** (2777 2239, www.gaiahr.com, US$350-$850 double), Manuel Antonio's only five-star resort. The complex offers guests complimentary tours through its private reserve and includes everything you'd expect from a top-dollar establishment. The staff are eager to aid in your every whim (within reason) as you relax by the three-tiered waterfall pool on a near-cliff overlooking the Pacific. The spa is world class, the wine list extensive, and the delicious tapas and ceviche (available from 3 to 6pm) are downright cheap. The sleek, open-air dining room is open to the public 24 hours a day, provides probably the best panorama of the beach and features a surprisingly economical menu (main courses US$20). The highlights include local jumbo prawns with polenta and a tasty mango-pineapple chutney all mopped up with some home-made bread. It is a good choice for honeymooners and couples in need of some extended silence – youngsters under 16 are not permitted. There's also a business centre.

Just a couple of hundred metres down the road from Gaia, and about a five-minute drive west on a narrow gravel road, is **Ronny's Place** (2777 5120, www.ronnysplace.com, main courses US$13), one of the best restaurants in the area. The food is good (sandwiches, meats, seafood and pasta), although not quite as cheap as the locals would have you believe, but the place's real charm is its jocular staff – the owner himself often pops in to chat and joke with the customers. The red snapper and Mahi-mahi are recommended.

Playa Manuel Antonio. *p233.*

For restaurant views, we'd suggest **Barba Roja** (2777 0331, www.barbaroja.co.cr, main courses US$16) and its 'global fusion' menu. This comfortable, relaxed and gay-friendly place claims to have the 'best sunset view in town', and there are few more appealing ways to watch the sun go down than with a cocktail on Barba Roja's wooden deck bar.

Just beyond Barba Roja, also on the right, you'll find the road to **La Mansion Inn** (2777 3489, www.lamansioninn.com, US$250-$300 double), a strange and delightful maze of walkways, rooms and restaurants (one for each meal). The view of the beaches looking south from the pool bar and the rooms' balconies are, of course, stunning. La Mansion is a bit more laid-back than Gaia but doesn't quite provide the service you'd expect for the price. There are amusing perks, though, like the hotel's bat cave, a tiny medieval-style bar built into the exposed rock (open to the public 6pm to midnight). From here, continuing down the side road there are more fine hotels, and it's a short but rigorous ten-minute walk to the less crowded Vizan Beach.

Back down the main road is **Hotel Karahe** (2777 0170, www.karahe.com, US$116-$150 double), which has satisfactory rooms with air-conditioning, comfortable beds and balconies (on the ocean side) overlooking the nicely maintained, expansive property and pool. This is a good choice for families, who will appreciate the spacious villas. The hotel's most impressive feature is its proximity to the national park, a 15-minute walk along the beach.

Down the hill from Karahe begins Manuel Antonio village and the entrance to **Cabinas Hermanos Ramírez** (2777 5044, US$12 hostel beds, US$30-$60 double), one of the country's best budget hotels with an incredible location. The current owner's father opened it back in 1961 and at the time it was the second business in Manuel Antonio. The rooms all have porches and a padlock to secure the welded rebar gates. All things considered, the rooms are a bargain and equivalent to many 'high-class' hotels in less-visited areas of the country. There's a pathway directly to Playa Espadilla Norte, and **Restaurante Balu** (2777 0339, main courses US$10) is a good budget beachfront restaurant that serves great pizzas.

Resources

Internet

Espadilla Tours *next to liquor store in front of Playa Espadilla Norte (www.espadillatours.com).* **Open** 8am-8pm daily.

Tourist information

No public office. **Iguana Tours** (2777 2052, www.iguanatours.com) is recommended and is willing to answer general questions. On the road to Manuel Antonio in front of Quepos soccer field. **Open** 7am-9pm daily. For park information call 2777 5185. The ranger station can provide maps and guides.

Getting there

By bus

From the Quepos bus station there are buses every 30mins to Manuel Antonio (US$0.25 one-way).

By road

From Quepos go east through town, turn right on the road to Manuel Antonio. It is only 7km (4.5 miles long), but winds along quite a dangerous road.

Southern
Pacific

Southern Pacific

Cerro Bobocara ▲
Reserva Biológica
Hitoy Cerere

Puerto V

Bribrí

R F
Río Macho

Río Telre

Suretka

BRATSI

Río Sik

Cerro La Georgina ▲

Río Chirripó

Río Coen

Amubri

Katsi

Cerro
La Muerte ▲

Río Lari

San Gerardo de Rivas
See p245

Cerro
Chirripó ▲

Parque Nacional Internacional
La Amistad
(Sitio Patrimonio Mundial)
See p267

Río Uren

Rivas

Parque Nacional
Chirripó

SAN ISIDRO
DE EL GENERAL
See p242

Cerro Etna ▲

Cerro Durika ▲

Río Celto

PANAM

Palma

Río Convento

Reservas
Indígenas
Ujarrás

Cerro Dika ▲

Cerro Kamuk ▲

Platanillo

Río General

Hacienda Barú

Río Volcán

Volcán

Dominical
See p247

China Kicha

BUENOS AIRES

Hacienda Bahía

Río Pejibaye

Río General

2

Río Cabaga

Punta Uvita
P N
Marino Ballena
Isla Ballena

Brujo

Ojochal
See p249

Térraba

Playa Tortuga

Coronado

Boruca

Paso Real

Río Singri

Zona Protectora
Las Tablas

34

Palmar Norte

Isla Bocabrava

Palmar Sur
See p252

Río Colón

Jabillo

Río La Palma

Palmira

PUERTO
CORTÉS

Isla Bocachica

Parque Esferas
Precolombinas

Col. Gutiérrez Braun

Río Negro

Mellizas

Isla Zacate

H N
Térraba-Sierpe

Sierpe
See p254

Venecia

Río Sierpe

Chacarita

Unión

Río Jaba

SAN VITO

Unión

Sabalito

Isla Violín

Sábalo

Humedal Nacional
Térraba-Sierpe

Río Limón

Punta Sierpe

Río Chocuaco

Mogos

Riyito

Agua Buena

Cañas Gordas

Punta Ganadito
Bahía Drake

Chocuaco ▲

Bahía Drake
See p255

Punta
Islotes

Parque Nacional
Piedras Blancas

Villa Briceño

Río Claro

Punta Aguijitas

Rincón

Punta Esquinas

Río Claro

CIUDAD NEILY

Punta
San José

Puerto Escondido

Punta Adela

R V S Golfito

Corredor

Los Planes

Palma

Punta
Gallardo

GOLFITO
See p264

San Pedrillo

Río Corcovado

Parque Nacional
Corcovado
See p258

Agujas

Punta Agujas

Parruja

Río Colorado

Punta
Llorona

Laguna de
Corcovado

Puerto Jiménez
See p260

Punta Voladera
Puntarenitas

Trenzas

Zancudo
See p270

Pueblo Nuevo

Playa Corcovado

Dos Brazos
de Río Tigre

Río Nuevo

Punta
Zancudo

Pavones
See p272

La Cuesta

Playa Sirena

Sirena

Madrigal

Río Platanares

Golfo Dulce

Laurel

Punta Salsipuedes

Carate
See p263

Agua
Buena

Punta Tigre

Bahía
Pavón

Puerto Pilón

Punta
La Cancha

Playa Carate

Punta Sombrero

El Higo

Río La Vaca

Playa Matapalo

Punta Matapalito
Cabo Matapalo
See p261

Punta
Banco

PACIFIC OCEAN

Clarita

0   5   10 miles
0   5   10 km

Punta Gorda

© Copyright Time Out Group 2008

Getting Started

Costa Rica's highest peak, its best beaches and its most diverse national park.

The Southern Pacific region gives travellers who prefer to avoid crowds and tourist traps a chance to witness the natural and unspoiled hinterlands of Costa Rica. And with three major national parks already in this area (**Parque Nacional Chirripó**, **Parque Nacional Marino Ballena**, **Parque Nacional Corcovado**) and several more reserves secured in the south, it looks like the government is keen to keep it that way. Small-scale hotels too have realised that by promoting green accommodation they can bolster interest in their businesses. Bear in mind that, this being the least developed part of the country, some destinations do require disc jolting journeys on rocky roads, and woozy boat rides; but once you get there the stunning views will immediately quell any motion sickness.

The scenery of the south is diverse, ranging from cloud rainforests to tropical jungles to paradisiacal beaches. Outdoor types can hike up Costa Rica's highest peak, **Mount Chirripó** (*see p243* **High climbers**), which rises to 3,819 metres (12,532 feet) in the protected rainforest of PN Chirripó.

This unique neotropical ecosystem is found within the Talamanca range, for example along the **Cerro de la Muerte**, the highest point on the Interamericana highway and home to the country's most famous bird, the resplendent quetzal. If virgin rainforest rich with life is not your thing, then head to the beaches of **Dominical** (*see p247*) and **Pavones** (*see p272*) and refresh your spirit in the ocean spray. Surfing, snorkelling or simply snoozing on the beach are the order of the day. Local fauna consists of sarong-clad expats who have swapped being chairman of the board for being shaman on a surfboard. Furrowed brows defurrow, slicked-back hair turns blonde and socks become long-forgotten objects of a long-forgotten wardrobe.

From **Playa Tortuga** (*see p251*) down to **Bahía Drake** (*see p254*) the ocean views are mesmerising. The Pacific coast is a sapphire dream with picturesque lagoons ideal for swimming and long stretches of sand where couples walk hand-in-hand as if auditioning for a perfume advertisement.

Isla del Caño (*see p59* **Treasure Island**) off the mainland in the biological reserve is an underwater wonderland for scuba divers and snorkellers. Head on to **Cabo Matapalo** (*see p261*) and **Carate** (*see p263*) for some serious surf swells and into the pristine waters of **Golfo Dulce** (*see p264*) for world-class sport fishing.

When you've had your fill of salt, be that from too much surf or too many margaritas, head inland into the jungle. Virtually every hotel, B&B or hostel offers tours into Costa Rica's primal depths. Thanks to the conservation drive, species such as the white-faced capuchin monkey, scarlet macaw and white-nosed coati are now commonly spotted.

The remote **PN Corcovado** (*see p258*) has lush trails to explore, giving you a chance to release your inner Indiana Jones. The jungles are exotic, busy with leafcutter ants, decorated with orchids and filled with soundtracks composed by monkeys and birds. And after exercising your brain by researching the flora and fauna, you can kick back in the spa of a luxury hotel.

The best Southern

Things to do

Explore one of Costa Rica's greatest natural treasures, the magnificent **PN Corcovado** (*see p258*). Some of the Pacific's best swells hit the shores of the southern zone around **Dominical** (*see p247*) and **Pavones** (*see p272*). And there are some huge billfish to catch around **Puerto Jiménez** (*see p260*).

Places to eat

For a good whack of entertainment along with some top-quality Italian cuisine, the talented blues-playing chef at **La Puerta Negra** (*see p270*) in Pavones will quite happily sing a few songs to accompany your post-meal grappa.

Places to stay

Many of the lodges in this area are stunning. **La Paloma** (*see p257*) in Bahía Drake is a luxury option. For those who want to get closer to nature, the conservation-conscious **Hacienda Barú** (*see p247*) is a must.

Southern Pacific

San Isidro & Around

Climb Costa Rica's highest mountain and gasp at the elusive quetzal.

A white-knuckle ride south on the Interamericana will take you along one of the highest routes through the Talamanca mountain range and into the cloud forests of southern Costa Rica. The drive is a bit hairy but passengers will be treated to beautiful views and scenes of lush greenery. Protected masses of primary forest such as the **PN Chirripó** (*see p245*) make this area a hiker's haven. The climate is a refreshing change for those returning from the beach, or for gung-ho trekkers who intend to traverse the parks' many trails. It's a good idea to pack a few woollies since at night the temperature drops dramatically. Nature-lovers, in particular birdwatchers, make their way here to enjoy the range of wildlife and to tick it off their must-see lists. The freshwater rivers are also ideal for fly fishing – or simply gathering your thoughts and taking deep gulps of pure air.

The foreboding name Cerro de la Muerte (Death Peak) does not originate from the rollercoaster road and the kamikaze drivers who use it but from the cold climate that townspeople would face when they crossed over on foot or horseback. (When the sun sets, the temperature can dip below zero.) The mountain is shrouded in mist and is a protected habitat for many rare species of bird, the quetzal being its most famous resident. Many visitors drive through this area without taking advantage of the several convenient cabins and hostels en route. Those who do are practically guaranteed a sighting of this beautiful and mythical bird, respected for its inability to live in captivity. Along the Interamericana, **Albergue de Montaña Tapantí** (turn off near marker km62, 2290 7641) and **Mirador de Quetzales** (turn off near marker km70, 2381 8456) both offer homey cabins as well as guided tours for around US$45 per person per night.

San Isidro de El General

If you've just made the drive from San José along the Cerro de la Muerte this is the town where you'll open your eyes, unclench your fists, swiftly cross yourself and knock back a cold one. Serving the nearby towns, San Isidro (known to locals as Pérez Zeledón) is the region's largest city, with a population of 50,000. Here, hotel owners stock up on supplies,

teenagers attend school and locals get their errands done. Tourists, on the other hand, tend to hang around for one night only (if that), using the city as a recoup stop en route to Dominical (*see p247*) or as a launching point for PN Chirripó. It's not the prettiest of towns but has all the essentials (banks, bus station, medical service, and so on) along with a rather oddly designed cathedral, which looks something like a Duplo Lego piece plonked in the main square.

Where to eat & drink

There are no street signs to guide you, but the following restaurants are located on the west side of the cathedral, facing the main square. Most restaurants in town serve regional food that is light on beef and heavy on rice and beans. **Soda Chirripó** (Calle 1, y Avenida 2, main courses US$4) is the 'heart of San Isidro' – or at least so it states on its menus – and serves big steaming mugs of the liquid ambrosia that is Costa Rican coffee and plates brimming with the Tico breakfast staple *gallo pinto* (rice mixed with beans). **Restaurant Chirripó** (next to Soda Chirripó, main courses US$4) is not as quaint or as culturally enlightening as its neighbour but dishes out the basic favourites and makes some refreshing *batidos* (smoothies) – try the pineapple one. If you're looking for something other than *gallo pinto,* try **México Lindo** (Centro Comercial Pedro Pérez, 2771 8222, closed Sun, main courses US$8), a more upscale (the menus aren't laminated) Mexican option. For those who savour the authentic, there is also a **Mercado Central** on Avenue 4 and Central, which has tasty local soups.

San Isidro is not the sort of town where you are going to find the perfect martini. Cold Imperial, it does have. We recommend sticking to restaurants and ordering a drink along with your meal rather than making for a random bar.

Where to stay

Overall, accommodation in San Isidro is basic but clean and aimed at in-transit clientele. **Hotel Chirripó** (diagonally opposite to the cathedral on the west side, 2771 0529, hotelchirripo@ice.co.cr, US$15-$25 double) with 40 rooms is a bit like your old university

High climbers

Parque Nacional Chirripó is located in the Talamanca mountain range and climbing Mount Chirripó is a great way to experience the surrounding environment. With a little bit (OK, a lot) of sweat you will be in the thick of one of the world's rarest ecosystems. The hike takes you through low-lying swampy lands, cloud forest and into sub-alpine *páramo* (moorland). The mountain has three peaks, the highest reaching over 3,820 metres (12,532 feet), making it Costa Rica's highest point. The difference in altitude has created numerous habitats, resulting in a plethora of wildlife; monkeys, peccaries, tapirs, 263 species of amphibian and reptile, and around 400 bird species have been recorded here. Although no professional hiking gear is required, doing the full circuit is a demanding excursion – but the scenery is unlike anywhere else in Costa Rica.

The best time to attempt the trek is between December and April, the dry season. At any other time the route will be a slippery uphill battle of mud, torrential rain and more mud. The park is shut during May. Don't forget that you are in a cloud forest and it is a damp and cold journey no matter what time of year. The full route takes two or three days, depending on your fitness.

A few words of warning. Firstly, you must reserve your entry through the San Isidro park service office (see p245) as much as one month in advance. On the day before your hike you must confirm your reservation at the Chirripó ranger station. Please note that if you have not made a reservation there is little staff can do; the ranger station in this situation is merely the middleman. After a big ol' dinner and a good night's sleep, attack the mountain early because the main gate only stays open between 4am and 10am. Lastly, note that it gets cold. Wear layers and take a warm hat. If you're the type of person who feels the cold, pack long-johns. Don't forget to take plenty of water and to pack lightweight snacks – it's a good 16 kilometres (ten miles) uphill to the hostel. The midway rest point known as Llano Bonito is the next place to take on water and offers some shelter if the weather is dire.

The hostel, rustic at best, sleeps 60 in dorm rooms and has extra blankets for rent. There is a communal kitchen but nothing other than crisps and soda is available, so be thankful for that trail mix in your pack. From the hostel, the summit is another four kilometres (2.5 miles) and on flatter terrain. Most hikers leave their packs at the hostel for this final stretch. When you eventually reach the summit you will be standing on Costa Rica's highest peak and will be rewarded with stellar views. All that sweat and swearing will have been worth it. If the weather is clear you can see both the Pacific Ocean and the Caribbean Sea.

After taking in the landscape, inhaling the fresh air and patting your mate on the back for not having had a cardiac arrest, you'll need to squeeze out just a little more energy from somewhere because going down is just as tough as climbing up. Godspeed.

Southern Pacific

It is a long drive up to **San Gerado de Rivas**, but the flora makes it worthwhile.

residence, but if you ask for a room overlooking the plaza, you'll get a bearable night's sleep. For something more roomy and private, try **Hotel Los Crestones** (south-west side of the municipal stadium, 2770 1200, www.hotel loscrestones.com, US$57 double), a motel-hotel with 20 decent rooms, a pool and restaurant.

Resources

Banks
Banco Nacional *on the east side of the square* (2212 2000). ATM and changes travellers' cheques. **Banco de Costa Rica** *on Avenue 4, y Central* (2284 6600).

Hospital
100m north of the Municipal Stadium (2771 7115).

Internet
On the west side of the cathedral in the Centro Comercial Pedro Pérez. **Open** 8am-9pm Mon-Fri; 8.30am-8pm Sat; 10am-4pm Sun.

Police Station
100m north of the Municipal Stadium.

Post Office
Calle 1, entre Avenidas 6 y 8.

Tourist information
Calle 2, entre Avenidas 4 y 6 (2771 3155). **Open** 8am-noon, 1-4pm Mon-Fri.
There is no tourist information point in the city, but the regional park service office can give you information on parks.

Getting there

By bus
Buses from San José leave every hour on the half hour from 5.30am to 6.30pm every day. The bus company is called **Musoc** (2222 2422) and the terminal is in the south of the city at Central Avenue and 22, across the street from the Hospital de las Mujeres. A taxi fare from downtown San José to the Musoc terminal should cost no more than US$2. A one-way trip to San Isidro de El General (Pérez Zeledón) costs CRC1,845, approximately US$3.75. The trip takes three hrs with a pit stop at the half-way point where you can pick up some fresh fruit and nuts. Buses from San Isidro to San José leave from 5.30am to 4.30pm every hour on the half hour. The Musoc terminal in San Isidro is just west of the Interamericana highway, about 200m north of the cathedral plaza.

By car
If you are coming from San José by car, take the Interamericana (Highway 2), passing through the Cerro de la Muerte. It is a two-to-three-hour drive of 136km (85 miles). Along the way there are a few viewpoints and large restaurants to stop at. Not recommended at night.

San Gerardo de Rivas

High up in the mountains, San Gerardo is a scenic little village where hikers and birdwatchers set up camp for their treks into Chirripó. There are lots of lovely small hotels and B&Bs, most of which are careful about their environmental impact. Typically, visitors only stay for a few nights as it is the park that draws tourists, but if it's a nature-lover's trip you're after, there are plenty of trails, tours and good outdoor fun to keep you busy, especially if you want a break from the heat.

Volunteers interested in forest preservation, reforestation and habitat research are welcome to visit the **Cloudbridge Project**. Contact the organisation in advance for applications by visiting its website at www.cloudbridge.org.

Where to eat & drink
Thankfully, after a long day's hike you'll find several small restaurants to refuel at. Take note that, being a mountain *pueblito* (village), once the sun sets owners shut shop for the night around 8pm. One of the best restaurants in the area is **Pelícano Albergue de Montaña Restaurant** (main courses US$6), which has particularly scrummy fajitas and friendly servers. **Talamanca Hotel** restaurant (main courses US$6) is new and bright with a good stash of wine and substantial meals. The smell of stone-baked pizzas made with home-made dough and fresh toppings will draw you in to **Robino's Pizza** (main courses US$7). The restaurant is upbeat, friendly and has a gorgeous view of the river below. Pastas, healthy dips and smoothies are also available.

Where to stay
The following lodgings are listed in sequential order according to where they lie on the main road. The last is closest to the park entrance.

Down the main road past Canaán you'll find **Talari Mountain Lodge** (2770 0341, www.talari.co.cr, US$59-$79 double), a property made up of 11 cabins neatly arranged among fruit trees and next to a bubbling river. Fresh pesticide-free bananas are brought to your door, which can be consumed or used to attract birds. The restaurant is open for dinner from 6pm to 8pm (lunch is on request only) and serves healthy organic dishes (main courses US$14).

Across the road is **La Botija** (2770 2147, www.ranchobotija.com, US$66 double), a family-oriented holiday spot with large rooms, a small outside pool and plenty for the kids to do. (It's closed between 24 December and 1 January.) It has a well-regarded restaurant

Southern Pacific

serving Tico staples that is open from 9am to 5pm, Tuesday to Sunday.

Coming into San Gerardo itself, on the left is **Pelícano Albergue de Montaña** (2742 5126, www.hotelpelicano.net, US$17 per person, US$50-$75 cabin), a family owned and operated property that originally started out as a gallery for dad's curious wooden sculptures. Today there is a large chalet-style building, five cabins and a birder's windowed restaurant. The rooms are frill free but high and dry with tree-house-like appeal. Further on, across from the football pitch is **Robino's apartments** (2742 5205, donrobino@hotmail.com, US$25-$50 cabin). Curly topped Robino has built two fully equipped (including washing machines) apartments overlooking the ravine. They are new and funky, decked out with stone floors, carved furniture and comfortable rooms; an excellent find if they are not booked up. For those who prefer a more pampered approach to the rainforest, there is **Talamanca Reserve Hotel** (2742 5080, www.talamancareserve.com, US$69-$79 cabin) set on 1.6 square kilometres (0.6 square miles) of private land. If you don't think you can hack Mount Chirripó this is a good alternative to explore the surroundings. Its ten squeaky clean cabins facilitate a very comfortable stay.

The last place to stay before the gateway to Mount Chirripó is **Hotel Casa Mariposa** (2742 5037, www.hotelcasamariposa.net, US$25 double), a lovely little hostel with a warm and friendly atmosphere. It was constructed from an old Tico house – originally built into the stone – and has cosy rooms, and thick blankets for the cold nights. It has two kilometres (1.25 miles) of scenic trails and caves to explore. Home-made granola bars and 'I climbed Mount Chirripó' T-shirts are also sold here.

Resources

Tourist information

First house in main village.
Not strictly a tourist information office but it has a wealth of knowledge. It also has books in English, *National Geographic* magazines to borrow, and a curiosity corner for kids. This project also serves the local indigenous community, with classes for children in computers and English. Old clothes are gratefully accepted; they go to the local community. **Open** 9am-2pm Wed; 8am-8pm Sat; 8am-4pm Sun.

Getting there

Bus company **Jenifer**, a fleet of old American school buses (now painted blue and white), only leaves San Isidro twice a day, at 5.30am and 2pm, to San Gerardo de Rivas for CRC850 or approximately US$1.70 one way. The bus terminal is located on the same block as the central market and is known as the El Mercado terminal. The guy loitering about with a clipboard and cigarette is who you buy tickets from. Just ask for San Gerardo de Rivas.

Take in a hearty breakfast at **Pelícano Albergue de Montaña** before climbing Chirripó.

Southern Pacific

Dominical & Around

Catch a wave, spot a whale or just unwind on a deserted beach.

For visitors who have come to Costa Rica to escape the colder climates of their native countries, this area is the postcard-perfect antithesis of snow, sleet and seasonal affective disorder. This coast has the type of beaches where you sip piña coladas and watch the sun slowly dunk itself into the Pacific; deadlines, rush hour and drizzle could not be further away. For surfers of all levels, the waves off **Dominical** await your board; for less active sun worshippers, the beaches along **Playa Tortuga** will be your throne. **Parque Nacional Marino Ballena** has stunning people-free beaches as well as outdoor pursuits like whale watching. Alternatively, fascinating excursions into the rainforest are fun days out where you can't help but appreciate the complexity and natural beauty of jungle life.

peccaries. Arriving in southern Costa Rica at the beginning of the 1970s, Jack's initial plan was to make a living as a cattle rancher, but before long the rainforest became his passion, and he decided to return the land around Hacienda Barú to nature.

Almost 40 years later Hacienda Barú has become a model for sustainable eco-tourism around the world. The refuge is a popular destination for its tours with local guides, which include trips to birdwatching platforms, night excursions and a particularly vertiginous but insightful tree climbing tour. Zip-lines, canopy tours, a butterfly house and typical Tico restaurant all add up to a great day out. It is a good, light-hearted destination for those who like a bit of fun with their nature. The refuge is three kilometres (two miles) from Dominical, on the road towards Quepos.

Dominical

Surfers long ago commandeered this one-road beach town and it is now the social centre for bronzed young things. Walking around, you're as likely to hear 'dude' as 'amigo'. Plenty of surf schools, bars and burger joints line the well-trodden road leading to the beach, along with useful amenities such as a chemist, mini-market and post office.

The most recommended place to get surf lessons is **Costa Rica Dive & Surf** (2319 5392, www.costaricadiveandsurf.com). These chilled-out operators charge US$40 per person for two hours. Another well-established outfit is **Green Iguana Surf Camp** (2787 0157, www.greeniguanasurfcamp.com), also charging US$40 per person for two hours.

If you are so attracted to Dominical you want to stay longer, there are Spanish lessons at **Adventure Education Centre** (2787 0023, www.adventurespanishschool.com). It charges US$20 per hour or US$315 per week. There are also branches in the tourist centres of Turrialba and Arenal.

EXCURSIONS
Owner Jack Ewing can remember when all that was around **Hacienda Barú National Wildlife Refuge** (2787 0003, www.haciendabaru.com) was fields. Today the reserve comprises of 3.3 square kilometres (1.3 square miles) of thriving secondary forest, buzzing with monkeys, sloths, toucans, anteaters and, proudly, the recently returned

Rooftop iguanas in **Hacienda Barú**.

Southern Pacific

Humans and wildlife hang out in harmony at **Hacienda Barú**.

Where to eat & drink

You won't have any problems finding decent grub in Dominical, which has a good selection of beach resto-bars that dish up 'I'm on holiday' favourites. For some Tex-Mex and Corona beer head to **San Clemente Bar & Grill** (main courses US$8). Vegetarians should hit **Maracatú** (main courses US$6), which serves big soya burgers, wraps and fresh juices. Jam night on Tuesdays, Ladies Night on Wednesdays and reggae on Thursdays keep this bar busy, but it has been known to get a bit rough at night. **Tortilla Flats** (2787 0147, www.tortillaflatsdominical.com, main courses US$5) is a popular, tried and tested surfer hangout that mixes killer margaritas and serves ridiculously huge portions of nachos topped with everything. With its cool and savvy bartenders, laid-back atmosphere and good food, this place is the definitive beachside bar. Locals and tourists have unofficially chosen it as the gathering point to watch the sunset as the surfers catch their last waves of the day.

Where to stay

Apart from swanky resort **Villas Río Mar** (on the first small road on the right as you enter town, 2787 0052, www.villasriomar.com, US$88-$110 double), which has all creature comforts laid out including a pool, restaurant and spa, most of the nicer (and bass-beat free) hotels are a ten-minute drive from Dominical. The furthest along the road, **Albergue Alma de Hatillo** (6km/3.5 miles north of Dominical, 8850 9034, www.cabinasalma.com, US$70 double) is one of these. Here, friendly owner Sabina, has three charming cabins and eight rooms surrounded by untouched forest. It's a verdant place where guests can enjoy home-made chocolate and jams for breakfast. Take a dip in the chlorine-free pool and breathe in the fresh ylang-ylang scented air. The view of the ocean is captivating and there is a large screened cabin ideally suited for yoga and the latest vipassana meditation retreats.

Three kilometres back towards Dominical is **Hacienda Barú** (2787 0003, www.hacienda

baru.com, US$70 cabin) the first eco-lodge in the area. Set among its impressive reserve are six large cabins – with more being built at the time of writing – each of which is modern and comfortable, with private showers and kitchens. With its open-air restaurant and easy access to the gorgeous coastline, and boasting some of the best tours in the area, Hacienda Barú delivers a memorable and educational stay. For those wanting a basic room to stash their towels and surfboard, Dominical has plenty of hang-ten establishments such as **Tortilla Flats Rooms** (2787 0147, www.tortillaflats dominical.com, US$30 double), which is probably the best budget option. There is a series of cabins behind the main restaurant and bar that offer basic but clean accommodation.

Resources

Bank
Banco de Costa Rica *Centro Comercial Plaza Pacifica (2787 0381).* **Open** 8am-4pm Mon-Fri. ATM machine. Money can be changed here.

Internet
Internet Emmanuel & The Back Porch Café *Centro Comercial (2787 4022).* **Open** 7am-8pm daily. It has dvds and a computer repair service, plus a small café out back.

Police
2787 0011.

Post office
Located at San Clemente Bar & Grill.

Tourist information
There is no official tourist information centre but one of the many tour agents will help.

Getting there

By bus
Transport Blanco bus company (2771 2550) from San Isidro leaves for Dominical at 5.30am, 9am, 11.30am and 3.30pm daily, returning from Dominical at 6.45am and 2.45pm. The bus stop is at the turn-off into Dominical town on the Costanera Sur. Transfer to another bus company in San Isidro to continue on to San José. For a more comfortable journey at US$30 one way, you can book a shuttle bus with **Easyride** (2524 0889/8812 4012, www.easyridecr.com), which leaves from San José to Dominical at 7am and 4pm. It returns from Dominical at 6.30am and 3pm.

By car
From San Isidro de El General head west on to the Costanera Sur highway. Cross over the concrete Rio Barú bridge and into Dominical town. Head south-east along the Costanera Sur to get to Uvita, Parque Marino Ballena and Palmar Norte.

Southern Pacific

The whole town converges to watch the sunset over the Pacific from **Dominical**'s beach.

Costa Ballena

Just 15 minutes down the Costanera Sur you will reach the hamlet of **Bahía Uvita** (also called Punta Uvita), which is dotted with tour companies specialising in whale watching, a few scruffy bars and some naff souvenir stalls. Bahía Uvita doesn't have an 'in scene' like the one in Dominical, but thanks to the tourist traffic, Uvita proper is turning into something of a boom town, with new restaurants, hairdressers and shops popping up faster than you can say 'buildquickwhilethegoingisgood'. The beaches in the area are perfect for swimming: long and shallow with less undercurrent than those in Dominical.

EXCURSIONS

Famous for the humpback whales that migrate here to rear their young in the warmer waters, the **PN Marino Ballena** has beautiful stretches of shoreline for walking, swimming and, of course, whale watching (the season is from February to April). Long sandy beaches, rock pools and mangrove swamps make up its 110 hectares (270 acres), which lie between **Playa Hermosa** and **Playa Piñuela**. Fragile rock and coral reefs create special habitats for marine life and with a reputable tour company you can explore these waters. The shoreline also has a diverse cast of characters such as green marine iguanas, ibises, frigate birds and, between May and November, olive ridley and hawksbill turtles, who lay their eggs there.

For a scenic escape, at low tide you can walk around the peninsula (conveniently enough for the local tourist board, shaped like a whale's fluke) and to an island that is only accessible when the sand bar is exposed – beachcombing heaven. Entry into the park costs US$6. The ranger station is at the end of the dirt road in Punta Uvita. To get out on to the water, **Dolphin Tours** (2743 8013, www.dolphintourcostarica.com, US$65-$95 per person) has a range of tours to choose from or you can ask the park guard, who runs a four-hour boat tour leaving at 7.30am every day (US$65 per person).

Where to eat & drink

Getting to restaurants requires a car, as they are spread out along the Costanera Sur. **Kem Vari Soda**, about a kilometre south of Puente de Uvita (Uvita Bridge), is a great little soda bar with typical dishes such as *casados* and freshly grilled fish. Main courses from US$6. **La Parcela** (Sunset Point off the Costanera Sur, 2787 0016, www.laparcela.net, main courses US$15) is perched on a cliff above the Costa Ballena and combines lovely views with some of the best food you will find in the south (rumour has it even Mel Gibson was impressed). High-end hotels and resorts have excellent restaurants open to the public. **Cuna del Angel** (main courses US$5-$12) and **Cristal Ballena** (main courses US$8-$15) are both first-rate eateries and widely recognised in the area for their innovative fusion cuisine.

Where to stay

Bahía Uvita caters to a backpacking crowd. **Steve's Hotel Toucan** (100 metres east of the Banco de Costa Rica intersection, 2743 8140, www.tucanhotel.com, US$27-$33 double) has a sociable, youthful vibe. Further south along the highway, often down long rocky roads, are the posher places. **Cuna del Angel** (2787 8012, www.cunadelangel.com, US$188-$230 double) has 16 grand and ornately decorated rooms with plush beds, all mod cons and extra thick walls for a quiet stay – nothing is amiss. Polished halls are dimly lit to continue the peaceful ambience, which also plays into the no children rule. A relaxing stay is key and there is a fully equipped spa with professionals ready to administer a large selection of treatments, facials and massages.

Equally indulging is **Cristal Ballena Hotel Resort** (2786 5354, www.cristal-ballena.com, US$73-$204 double), a high-end hotel that offers guests 23 large rooms set among manicured surroundings. Beauty spa, large pool and gourmet restaurant complete this option. **Finca Bavaria** (8355 4465, www.finca-bavaria.de, US$59-$69 double) wows guests with its outstanding ocean view. Comfortable bungalows, pool and charming surroundings make this an ideal place to enjoy the Costa Ballena. **La Cusinga Eco Lodge** (2770 2549, www.lacusingalodge.com, US$135 double) has lovely airy rooms decorated with smooth wood furniture made by local craftsmen, and river-stone floors. The property gets the green stamp of approval by its use of hydroelectricity, solar panels and planned low impact construction. The atmosphere is natural and unspoilt; sit back and enjoy the enchanting reserve or spend days wandering through the trails and spotting the wildlife at close quarters.

At marker km170 on the Costanera Sur is **Mar y Selva** (2786 5670, www.mary selva.com, US$112-$122 double), which has ten new eco-friendly cabins high up in the jungle with a breathtaking view of the ocean below. A good-sized pool, wholesome food and massage treatment make this a great spot for the health-conscious tourist. Cabins are fully equipped, spotless and have new beds and

Beers, burritos and very strong margaritas at **Tortilla Flats**. *See p248.*

mattresses – perfect for flopping down on after a day of jungle walks and beach fun. A final feature is the long balcony in the main building from which to watch the sunset, or spy on the whales, or other wildlife, with the telescope.

Resources

Bank
There are three banks in Uvita, all of which have reliable ATMs. **Banco Nacional de Costa Rica** is across the street from Don Israel Supermarket, **Banco de Costa Rica** is next to La Corona Supermarket and **CoopeAlianza** is 100m west of **Banco de Costa Rica.**

Getting there

By road
Uvita is a short drive from Dominical. Head south along the Costanera Sur. Taxis can do the trip for around US$10 one way. There is a shuttle service with **Shuttle Osa** (8825 6788, www.shuttleosa.com, US$30), which is another option to and from San José.

Ojochal

Blink-and-you-miss-it Ojochal is 30 minutes south of Dominical and 30 minutes north of Palmar Norte. It's a pretty mountain village with enough necessities such as internet cafés, restaurants, a petrol station, medical care and a grocery store that you don't feel cut off from the rest of the world. The area is popular with foreigners, and many, particularly French-Canadians, have bought property here. There are a surprising number of cabins for rent considering the town's size. New and central **Filibustero** (100 metres after the bridge, 2786 5118, arokea@hotmail.com, US$49 cabin) is a good rest stop with pretty wood cabins complete with bathrooms, kitchenettes and screened windows. Tours can be booked for both the nearby rainforest and beach, such as scenic horse riding with **Don Lulo's** (2787 8013, www.cataratasnauyaca.com) and snorkelling with the **Mystic Dive Center** (2786 5217, www.mysticdivecenter.com).

EXCURSIONS
Hidden between Playa Dominical and Palmar Sur, **Playa Tortuga** is usually deserted, making it a wonderful destination for those wishing to get away from it all. Its long beaches and shallow waters shout out for beachcombers and sunbathers. For adrenaline junkies, numerous scuba diving and sport fishing tours can be booked. Access is limited to car or taxi but the area is well worth a visit.

Facing the past

The Boruca (also known as Brunka) indigenous community, from the villages of Rey Curré and Boruca along the Térraba river, is made up of 2,000 people whose traditional craft of mask making has become a leading form of Costa Rican art. Masks are intricately carved from cedar or balsam and either left bare, tinted in natural earth tones, or, for modern tastes, brightly accentuated with paints. The origin of this style is hazy, but within the past decade the craft has been reintroduced and taught to young Boruca by local craftsmen whose designs typically portray teeth-baring, quite fearsome visages (somewhat similar to the Maori masks of New Zealand). Masks depicting nature scenes such as vibrant jaguars and macaws are a new take and are popular with hotels as decorative objects. The resurgence of this traditional craft is an important tool in keeping Boruca culture alive, as well as a means of providing extra income to reservations where jobs are sparse.

During the annual **Festival Danza de los Diablitos** (Festival Dance of the Little Devils) Boruca masks are on display as revellers re-enact the Spanish conquest. Masked dancers portray their ancestors (called 'little devils' by the invading Spanish) and fight off the *Conquistadores*, who are

represented by a costumed bull. Throughout the festivities *chicha*, a fermented corn moonshine, and *cacique*, a sugarcane, based drink, are consumed. (The masks are said to endow their wearers with magical powers, which may simply be a testament to the strength of the cacique.) The festival takes place between 30 December and 2 January. Though culturally intriguing, it

A day trip to **Nauyaca Waterfalls** can be both exhilarating and tranquil. At eight metres (26 feet) wide and 40 metres (131 feet) high, the falls, with their clear, cascading water, are a magical sight. Swimmers are permitted to splash about in the deep base pool after an enjoyable six-kilometre (3.5 mile) hike. It is also a great environment for birdwatching. Tour companies in Ojochal and Uvita can arrange a guided trek with food included.

Palmar Norte & Sur

At the crossroads where the Costanera Sur (Highway 34) joins the Interamericana, this cluster of buildings is an important transport hub. It sits between the Panama border and the Costa Ballena. Palmar Norte tend to be thought of as nothing more than a pit stop and is more populated with drivers taking a break than

with gringos seeing the sights. However, if you have a long drive ahead of you – for instance, if you are going on to PN Corcovado – it is a suitable place to rest.

Across the Térraba river is Palmar Norte's homely sister, Palmar Sur. (You will pass through here if you are driving to Sierpe.) The majority of its residents work and live on the nearby banana and palm oil plantations, their houses faded two-storey wooden buildings originally constructed by the United Fruit Company (*see p16* **Bitter fruit**) for its labourers. Apart from the plantations and empty football pitches, there is not much to see, yet Palmar Sur has a tourist attraction that will only take a minute of your time. The central park has an example of a stone sphere where you can get out and take a few snaps. Similar spheres can be seen in front of civic buildings across the area. *See p260* **Circling the square**.

Southern Pacific

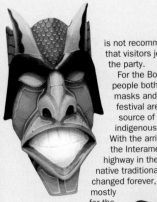

is not recommended that visitors join the party.

For the Boruca people both the masks and the festival are a source of indigenous pride. With the arrival of the Interamericano highway in the 1940s native traditional life changed forever, mostly for the worse. The Boruca language is virtually extinct as there are no elders alive who speak it as a mother tongue. It is taught to local schoolchildren in the same way English kids learn French, but from modern assimilation, Spanish is now their first language. Deforestation and pollution are other factors that have had a negative impact on Boruca culture. As vegetation and animals disappear so does traditional daily life. Hunting, culinary dishes (river fish are inedible due to high toxicity levels), bonding activities and ritual celebrations can no longer be practised. As time goes by more and more villagers go in search of prosperity in urban centres leaving many homes in the community abandoned. The natural landscape has changed too, and as it is turned into farmland more species are lost, and the Boruca names forgotten. Myths and creation stories, common to many native tribes across Central America, are sadly non-existent. Visiting Rey Curré and Boruca as a tourist destination is not encouraged, as tourism only eats away at the already fragile culture. However, there are 'working holiday' projects carefully managed by various grassroots organisations. We advise that you check that the organisation is legitimate. The best way to help the reservation is to buy Boruca-made masks available at most fine craft stores, or often sold at artisan fairs.

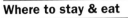

Where to stay & eat

Typical Tico sodas and other fast food places line the streets. **Soda Diquis** (main courses US$4) across from the Banco Nacional is the most popular, with grilled chicken dishes and have-some-more *gallo pinto*. Chinese food is available at **Wah Lok** (main courses US$6) across from the petrol station. There are several mid-range hotels in town. **Brunka Lodge** (2786 7489, www.brunkalodge.com, US$45-$60 double), located off the Interamericana coming into town, is a crowd-pleaser with nicely decorated rooms and a lovely pool.

Resources

Bank
Banco Nacional de Costa Rica
next to the petrol station (2212 2000).

Getting there

By air
Across the Térraba river is Palmar Sur where the airport is located. There are daily flights to and from San José with **Nature Air** (www.natureair.com) and **Sansa** (www.flysansa.com).

By bus
Buses leave San José and San Isidro for Palmar Norte 7 times a day with **Tracopa** bus company (7221 4214). Returning from Palmar Norte, buses leave from the bus stop on the east side of the Interamericana. One bus goes to Dominical at 8am. Buses depart from Supermercado Térraba five times a day for Sierpe, the earliest at 7am. Buses to Puerto Jiménez depart in front of the Banco Nacional.

By car
From Dominical continue south-east past Uvita on the Costanera Sur road until reaching a T-junction which is right in the middle of Palmar Norte.

Bahía Drake

Accessible by boat only, this hidden peninsula is a pristine paradise.

Thanks to its remote location, **Bahía Drake** (Drake Bay) is not overrun by big hotels and monstrous rental SUVs. Its natural beauty is truly remarkable. Perfect beaches look out on to deep-blue waters, with **Isla del Caño** enticing you in the distance. You can picture Francis Drake aboard the *Golden Hind*, pockets filled with loot, checking his compass and throwing the anchor overboard for a few days' rest, as he reputedly did in 1579. And what a place to rest. Disturbance is minimal – the closest you will hear to a disruptive ringtone are the squawks from the scarlet macaws flying overhead. Hotel lodges use the impeccable environment to their advantage, tucking eco-cabins into uncontrived rainforest landscapes or simply setting up large tents on the beach as accommodation. The amount of wildlife that thrives here is the core element of the area, attracting tourists for rainforest walks, scuba diving, snorkelling and dolphin and whale watching – even tours involving some pretty hefty insects (*see p256* **A bug's life**). The unique **Parque Nacional Corcovado** (*see p258*) can also be reached from Bahía Drake.

Sierpe

This unassuming *pueblito*, 15 kilometres (nine miles) south of **Palmar Sur** (*see p251*), is the exit point for the Sierpe River, which flows out to Bahía Drake. There are several hotels and restaurants but the majority of hustle and bustle happens on the dock where a number of tour companies and hotel shuttles ferry tourists to and from their coastal destinations. It is the best place to head in order to reach the bay. There is a road to Bahía Drake but it is terrible, and besides, the boat journey is a highlight.

Where to eat & drink

Across the road from the town park there are a couple of basic sodas and a mini-market, **Pulpería Fenix**, but the most action is at **Las Vegas Restaurant & Bar** (2788 1082, main courses US$8), a large building sitting in front of the dock that also roofs the internet café and souvenir shop. It has plenty of cold beer and specialises in fish dishes.

The view from **Drake Bay Wilderness Resort**. No wonder Francis Drake took a break here.

Where to stay

Hotel Oleaje Sereno (2788 1082, www.lasvegassierpe.com, US$25 double) attached to Las Vegas Restaurant has ten rooms in need of a revamp, but it's convenient, clean and cheap. For something more upmarket try **Veragua River House** (2788 1460, notelveragua@rasca.co.cr, US$50 double).

Resources

Car park
To travel to Bahía Drake you must leave your car in Sierpe. Leaving your car keys behind the desk at the Las Vegas Bar with a man you've never met before might seem foolhardy, but rest assured that for US$6 a day your vehicle is in safe hands. Those paranoid about encountering a Ferris Bueller situation upon returning to collect their vehicle might do well to note the mileage before they leave.

Internet
Las Vegas Restaurant & Bar has three fast computers. **Open** 9am-10pm daily.

Getting there & away

By air
From the Palmar Sur airstrip a taxi can take you to Sierpe. **Nature Air** (www.natureair.com) and **Sansa** (www.flysansa.com) fly to Palmar Sur. These companies also connect to San José and other towns.

By bus
Tracopa buses go to Palmar Norte. From Palmar Norte (see p251), a local bus departs for Sierpe from outside **Supermercado Térraba** 5 times a day, the earliest at 9am. A US$15 taxi ride will get you from Palmar Norte to Sierpe. Leaving Sierpe you can catch the bus from Pulperia Fenix that leaves at 5.30am, 10.30am, 1.20pm, 3.30pm and 6pm.

By road
From Palmar Norte cross the bridge into Palmar Sur and turn right off the Interamericana just before the mechanic's garage on your right and continue through the palm oil plantations. You will pass 2 very narrow bridges leading directly into Sierpe.

Bahía Drake & around

Bahía Drake is no more than a small inlet with a few T-shirt stalls, a general store and a public phone. There are actually two towns on the lip of the bay: Drake and Agujitas. It is a good base for tours but the accommodation in town, although clean and satisfactory, is aimed at budget travellers. Most of the more expensive lodges are found on the outskirts of town and have access to prettier beaches. They are also well hidden within the rainforest.

EXCURSIONS
The diminutive **Isla del Caño** is easily visible from Bahía Drake. A dedicated biological reserve, excursions to this island (the peak of an underwater mountain) can be arranged by all the lodges in Bahía Drake. Even if you are not staying at any of them, the lodges below can organise tours. Popular activities on the island include excellent snorkelling and scuba diving, activities largely impossible in the rough shores around the bay. The island is also of crucial importance to archaeologists studying the Diquís indigenous group, who buried some of their dead here, and the lithic spheres are entrancing. See p260 **Circling the square**.

Where to eat

As all food and supplies are brought in by boat, it has not been in Drake's economic interest to turn this town into a culinary nexus. The hotels will provide you with three, usually excellent, meals a day, but if you are experiencing some cabin fever most hotel restaurants are open to anybody on request and it is a fun way to check out the competition. **Aguila de Osa Inn** (2296 2190, www.aguiladeosa.com, main courses US$12) has an inviting open air restaurant with gourmet chefs who are trained for tourist taste buds, but if you prefer more traditional nosh head to restaurant **Amapola** (main courses US$8), which is over the football field.

Where to stay

Luxury accommodation seems to be Bahía Drake's speciality, so be prepared to experience paradise in style. If your wallet is feeling a tad thin there are plenty of budget options in town, such as the spotless and bright cabins at **Manolo's** (400 metres from the beach in Agujitas, 8885 9114, www.cabinasmanolo.com, US$30 double). At the opposite end of the financial spectrum is **Aguila de Osa Inn** (2296 2190, www.aguiladeosa.com, US$180 double), a rather grand establishment with luminous rooms, polished wood floors and quality service.

Continuing along the path and across a very wobbly suspension footbridge is **Drake Bay Wilderness Resort** (8384 4107, www.drake bay.com, US$65-$130 double), which sits on the peninsula with an amazing 180-degree view of the ocean. Charming rooms face the water and have private bathrooms and balconies. There is free rental of kayaks – useful for getting up close to the crocodiles in the river. Its gorgeous surroundings and owner Marleny's very moreish chocolate chip cookies have kept this hotel a favourite with returning guests.

Southern Pacific

A bug's life

Did you know the Chinese gave Queen Victoria a dress made entirely out of spider silk? Or that the US government enlisted cockroaches in the Vietnam War? And did you know that some male insects sing with their, erm, insecthood? Welcome to the fascinating world of arachnids and amphibians, snakes and skunks. And if you are in Costa Rica reading this, chances are you are currently surrounded by more bugs than you could ever imagine.

Enlightening, amusing and mildly terrifying curious visitors to Bahía Drake for 12 years, Tracie Stice, known simply as 'the Bug Lady' (the cockroach is predictably called Roachy), offers one of the best night wildlife tours in the country.

Every evening Tracie and her eagle-eyed husband Gianfranco Gomez arm themselves with head torches and cameras to scour the rainforest around the lodges of Bahía Drake for all manner of creepy crawlies. Each find inspires Tracie to regale gripping stories, sometimes funny (spiders on LSD), occasionally gross (without spoiling it, NEVER EVER swat a moth on the back of your neck) and always beguiling. Not that the tour is without its cuteness, as anyone who has ever seen a sleeping hummingbird will testify.

Tracie, a biologist, first arrived in Bahía Drake 14 years ago. For someone who'd specialised in entomology (the study of insects), Bahía turned out to be bug heaven and Tracie never went home. She met naturalist and nature photographer Gianfranco and married him in 2005. They now regularly find new species and spend their days documenting the phenomenal array of life.

But by night, the pair point out bugs that defy description, stunningly colourful and other-worldly. (In fact, it is estimated that the 38,000 identified species of spider in Costa Rica are a mere 25 per cent of all those thought to exist.) Scorpions that glow in the dark, trap-door spiders, possums, red-eyed tree frogs and snakes are all regular sightings, with some lucky folk witness to ocelots, armadillos and, on one occasion, a puma.

Their insatiable enthusiasm comes across on every tour and they are easily as thrilled as you by everything that moves in this unique area. And don't forget to ask for the story about the goat, the spider and the US army.

● Tours with Tracie 'the Bug Lady' Stice can be booked for US$35 through any lodge in Bahía Drake or on www.thenighttour.com.

Stunning sunsets and thrilling hiking at **Bahía Drake**.

One beach over, at Playa San Josecito, is **Corcovado Adventure's Tent Camp** (8384 1679, www.corcovado.com, US$65 tent) where 24 large tarpaulin-covered tents (proper beds inside) are arranged along the beach for an unpretentious and enjoyable stay.

Further along the coast, about two beaches down, is **Poor Man's Paradise** (2788 1442, www.poormansparadiseresort.com, US$60 cabin, US$45 tent) whose slice of heaven beachfront is best enjoyed with a boogie board. It has a sociable atmosphere, a small bar and helpful staff. They can arrange tours into PN Corcovado and to Isla del Caño. Introductory sport fishing tours here are cheaper than most other places.

The most luxurious accommodation in the bay is **La Paloma Lodge** (2293 7502, www.lapalomalodge.com, US$1,100-$1,400 per person three-night package). It is the acme of a luxury eco-lodge with 11 beautifully designed rooms and seven *ranchos* (bungalows) surrounded by nature. Large open windows, private balconies complete with hammocks, and floors made from teak, almond and purple heart wood create a natural look, harmonious with the rainforest outside. The restaurant and reception area are housed in an impressive colonial-style lodge, tastefully furnished and topped off with a magnificent ocean view. Stone paths weave throughout the grounds highlighting tropical flowers and enormous palms harbouring an array of wildlife.

Getting there

By air
It is possible to take a small plane in and out of Bahía Drake with **Nature Air** (www.natureair.com) and **Sansa** (www.flysansa.com) airlines.

By boat
From Sierpe you have to get a boat to take you to your hotel. All the hotels provide this shuttle service but if you have not made prior arrangements ask around **Las Vegas Restaurant** (*see p254*) for a boatman. The going rate is US$20 per person one way. It's best to leave no later than 4pm. The boat journey is a scenic two-hour trip through the mangroves.

By road
Bahia Drake can be reached by road, but only in a quality high-clearance four-wheel-drive vehicle and then only during the dry season, because there are several river crossings. To get there head south on the Interamericana to Chacarita. Turn left at the junction signposted to Puerto Jiménez and go to Rincón where the road splits to Bahía Drake, via Rancho Quemado.

Península de Osa

Visit what is thought to be the most biologically diverse place on the planet.

Parque Nacional Corcovado

Bahía Drake

Puerto Escondido

San Pedrillo

Río Bruto

Parque Nacional Corcovado

Río Corcovado

Río Rincón

Playa Llorona

Río Sirena

Los Patos

Laguna de Corcovado

Río Claro

Dos Brazos de Río Tigre

Playa Corcovado

Río Tigre

Playa Sirena ○ Sirena

La Leona

Punta Salsipuedes

Playa Madrigal

○ Carate

Punta La Cancha

PACIFIC OCEAN

If you make your way to the Península de Osa make sure your camera batteries are juiced up because the scenery on this land mass is simply faultless. Rainforests buzz with life – rare butterflies, birds and mammals roam the bush – while offshore the waters teem with fish and endangered marine species and whales.

Parque Nacional Corcovado

Encompassing 425 square kilometres (164 square miles) of rainforest, PN Corcovado is often regarded as Costa Rica's most diverse and exciting national park. It is one of the last remaining reserves of lowland tropical rainforest in the world as well as the largest chunk of primary forest in Central America. As you have probably read, *National Geographic* has dubbed it the 'most biologically intense place on the planet'.

Here primeval forests sprawl on to pristine beaches giving it the feel of a land forgotten by time. As well as the nearly 400 species of bird recorded here, it is the best place in the country to see critically endangered mammal species such as baird's tapirs, squirrel monkeys and

white-lipped peccaries. A well-marked trail system takes visitors through old growth; secondary forest as well as primary forest. Endangered harpy eagles, ornate hawk- eagles, black-and-white hawk eagles and other large raptors make their home in the park.

Other species include: white-throated shrike-tanagers, little tinamous, bare-throated tiger-herons, great curassows, crested guans, white hawks, double-toothed kites, marbled wood-quails, scarlet macaws, mealy parrots, baird's trogons, chestnut-mandibled toucans, fiery-billed aracaris, white-necked puffbirds, rufous-tailed jacamars, red-capped manakins and all three species of honeycreeper. This is also a good place to see the indigenous clack-cheeked ant-tanager, which lives only in the Península de Osa area.

You can immerse yourself in this world by taking a trek on one of the park's three major routes via the central **Sirena ranger station**. These trails can be walked with or without a guide but be forewarned: a lot of it is hot and sticky hiking with difficult terrain, and people can – and have – got hopelessly lost in the jungle. We do not recommend hiking alone and it is always safest to go in a three-person party.

Apart from **La Leona Lodge** and **Corcovado Tent Camp**, which have cushy beachfront lodgings, you'll be roughing it in the mosquito-ridden, ant-covered bush at night. It is possible to do day visits to the fringes of the park from all the lodges listed in Carate (*see p263*), Bahia Drake (*see p254*) and Puerto Jiménez (*see p260*), but most people opt for the two- to three-day 'become one with nature' experience, hiking from one ranger station to another. The park has six ranger stations, five of which have camping areas, bunkhouses, drinking water and can occasionally provide hot food on request.

Dry season is from January to April, and although it is also open from May to December, rainfall can close off some trails. Obviously, it is best to check in advance which trails are accessible before you go. The park entry fee is US$8 plus US$5 extra per night for camping.

You must book your reservation well in advance, usually six weeks ahead at either the Puerto Jiménez offic,e the **Oficina de Área de Conservación Osa** (opposite the airfield, 2735 5036, corcovado@minae.go.cr), or via the

Fundación de Parques Nacionales in San José (2257 2239, fpn_cr@racsa.co.cr). In order to ensure your needs will be met, it is a good idea to get advice first at the Puerto Jiménez office with regards to which trails are best suited for you, whether to take your own food, whether to go with a tour group, and so on. It is worth noting that freak accidents very rarely occur, but visitors still have to be careful of basking crocodiles being aggressive on the trails or the odd shark in the waters; however, your greatest danger is dehydration so make sure you take sufficient quantities of water.

Osa Aventura (www.osaaventura.com) and **Costa Rica Expeditions** (www.costarica expeditions.com) both offer guided treks and tours into NP Corcovado. They can also arrange accommodation and food.

Where to eat & drink

There are two options when it comes to camp cuisine. One is to take your own food and remember to string it up – there are a lot of hungry animals out there. The other is to prearrange to eat with the rangers, who, for around US$6-$12 per meal, cook basic but filling hot lunches and suppers.

Where to stay

La Leona Eco-Lodge (2735 5705, www. laleonaecolodge.com, US$25-$55 double) and **Corcovado Tent Camp** (2257 0766, www. costaricaexpeditions.com, US$43-$60 double)

are alternatives for those who like a bit of space between their body and the jungle undergrowth. The **Sirena Biological Station**, which must be booked through the park's Puerto Jiménez office (*see right*), is another padded option. Otherwise, it's a night under the stars, or a rustic night's sleep at one of the ranger station bunkhouses.

Getting there

By air
Planes fly from Puerto Jiménez into Carate (*see p263*). The airstrip is a 3km- (2-mile) walk from the La Leona ranger station.

By boat
You can take a boat from Bahia Drake to **San Pedrillo ranger station** or Playa Llorona for around US$20 per person. All lodges in Bahia Drake (*see p254*) should be able to arrange this.

By foot
It is a tough, but easy to follow, 18km (11-mile) walk along the coastline to the **San Pedrillo ranger station**.

By road
There are 3 ways to get into PN Corcovado from a road. The closest access point to San José is via La Palma on the Rincón to Puerto Jiménez road, off the Interamericana. But it is a 14km (8-mile) hike to the **Los Patos ranger station**. Four-wheel-drive vehicles may be able to go further down the road. The most common entrance is from Carate (*see p263*), via a terrible road from Puerto Jiménez (*see p260*). From here it's a 3km-hike to **La Leona ranger station**.

Southern Pacific

A ring-tailed coati clinging on in **PN Corcovado**.

Circling the square

Those perfectly round stones you may have spotted on mansion lawns or outside government buildings are not chichi garden features. They are mysterious artefacts left behind by the little understood Díquis civilisation and are believed to date back to between 200 BC and AD 1500. Known as the 'Díquis spheres', they were discovered in the 1930s when the United Fruit Company started to clear the jungle for plantations. Unfortunately, during plantation clearance virtually all of these stone balls were removed from their original locations or destroyed, making it a nightmare for archaeologists to study their purpose. There are only six standing in their original locations, yet several questions have floated the idea that they were originally placed in a specific alignment for either ceremonial purposes or perhaps to be used as an astrological calendar. Several strange factors will forever remain unanswered such as: Who made them, and why? How did they carve such perfect spheres out of a type of granite not found in the area? Another unusual feature is that the balls are all expertly polished, an advanced technique the makers must have acquired. (The Incas never learned how to polish their balls.) The Spanish made no reference to these spheres; nor is there evidence as to their use in the rituals of any existing tribes today. Get Mulder and Scully on the case.

Puerto Jiménez

On the dusty high street of this small town are stalls selling flip-flops, a few bars with even fewer barflys and one large supermarket. For most people it is either a stock-up town before heading into the incredible PN Corcovado or out on to the Golfo Dulce. It no longer retains its frontier town attitude, but is beginning to welcome wealthy tourists for its sport fishing. The Corcovado national park office here is the headquarters where you can get information on the park's trails, weather conditions, maps, hiking advice and book your entrance (2735 5063, corcovado@minae.go.cr). It is open from 8am to 4pm daily and is across from the airstrip on the west side.

Where to eat & drink

Carolina's (main courses US$4) on the main drag rustles up *gallo pinto* and other basic staples. There are two public telephones outside. A livelier recommendation is **Juanita's Mexican Bar & Grill** (main courses US$6), which has happy hour from 4pm to 6pm with beers for US$1.20. It is found at the first intersection past the football field as you come into town, and serves surprisingly good burritos and home-made tortilla chips. It gets a bit rowdy in the evening but is fun. **Café La Onda** (main courses US$4) is a healthy option specialising in smoothies and granola bars. It is opposite **BM Corcovado supermarket** at the far end of the airstrip.

Where to stay

Along the beachfront are a slew of basic budget hotels. It is on the outskirts of the town centre where you will find the higher end accommodation. **Iguana Lodge** (8829 5865, www.iguanalodge.com, US$180 double) has stylish bright rooms and cabins perfect for those who enjoy the finer things in life.

Crocodile Bay Resort (2733 1115, www.crocodilebay.com, US$200 double) is an established favourite among celebs (David Hasselhoff and NFL players) where sport fishing is the priority. It has a fleet of boats ready to serve the most enthusiastic of fishermen, and at the end of a day wrestling marlin, there is an excellent restaurant (all meals are included) and pool, complete with bar and waterfall, to unwind in. Staff are exceptionally friendly (all speak English), making this luxury resort a popular choice for families and first-time travellers. They can also organise any tour you can think of.

However, if fishing is not your thing, one of the highlights of this place is its award-winning spa, open to non-residents. The masseurs are extremely professional and exceptional at their job. Even if you are not staying here stop for a massage. Choose a treatment from the menu and lie back.

Resources

Bank
Banco Nacional *opposite the Santo Domingo de Guzman church (2735 5020).* Has an ATM machine. **Open** 8.30am-3.45pm Mon-Fri.

Internet
In the Surfdog Tours building. **Open** 8am-8pm Mon-Fri; 8am-6pm Sat; 8am-4pm Sun.

Getting there

By air
Daily flights from San José to Puerto Jiménez with **Nature Air** (www.natureair.com) or **Sansa** (www.flysansa.com).

By boat
A ferry departs Golfito to Puerto Jiménez from the municipal dock (*muelle*) 6 times a day from 5am to 5pm and costs either US$2 or US$4 depending on the boat you get. The first return from Puerto Jiménez is at 5.45am, the last at 4pm. It is a 90-min crossing.

By bus
Tracopa buses (2222 2666) depart daily from San Isidro de El General to Puerto Jiménez at 6.30am and return at 1pm. It is a 5-hr journey. Tracopa leaves Puerto Jiménez for San José at 5am and 11am from the bus station west of the football pitch.

By road
From San Isidro de El General continue south on the Interamericana highway past Palmar Norte to just beyond Chacarita where you turn west on Highway 245 for Puerto Jiménez. It is a slow and rocky ride for most of the journey.

Cabo Matapalo

At the southern nose of the Península de Osa is one of the most beautiful collections of isolated beaches famed for excellent surfing – strictly well-heeled experts – and turquoise lagoons popular for those fed up with manufactured packages. There are no real amenities, but hotels can provide food.

The quay to great sport fishing? Walk the plank from **Crocodile Bay Resort**.

Southern Pacific

Lie in the lap of luxury at **Lapa Rios**, set high above the Pacific.

Where to eat & drink

There aren't many restaurants to choose from along this route, but all the lodges mentioned below turn out decent gourmet cooking. For something different try **Buena Esperanza Bar Restaurant** (on the main road just before Cabo Matapalo, main courses US$10). Open from 9am, this funky restaurant bakes fresh bread for hearty sandwiches and also makes great Tico dishes. It is also the town's only nightspot of note and gets busy in the evenings. Note that it closes during the wet season from September to November.

Where to stay

There are a number of houses for rent along the main road, a good idea if you are travelling with a group of friends and plan to stay for a week. **Kapu Rancho Almendros** (johnhannegan@hotmail.com, US$90-$125 per person) has two colourful bohemian houses for rent and two rustic *ranchitos* (open cabins) with individual rooms: a lovely option for those who appreciate smaller 'grassroots' enterprises. **Encanta La Vida Rainforest Lodge** (2735 5678, www.encantalavida.com, US$87-$120 per person) has seven pretty cabins designed for a mellow atmosphere. There is a small pool and restaurant set among the jungle flora. It's a coconut's throw from the beach.

Cranking it up a luxurious notch or two is **Lapa Rios** (2735 5130, www.laparios.com, US$325 double), which has 16 thatched bungalows sitting atop a mountain. For easy wildlife spotting, the reception-cum-restaurant lodge has a winding staircase that takes you up to a majestic viewing tower. Impeccable service is at the snap of your fingers, delivering everything from fruit juices to personal yoga instruction. Book ahead, though – this place is always filled solid.

Bosque Del Cabo (2735 5206, www.bosque delcabo.com, US$175-$225 cabin, US$350-$450 house) is another divine property with tidy lawns, cabins overlooking the ocean below and, best of all, fun outdoor – but completely private – showers.

For those with a heightened environmental consciousness, **El Remanso Rainforest & Wildlife Lodge** (2735 5569, www.elremanso. com, US$140-$165 per person) has probably the best green CV in the area. Not only does the owning family include a former captain of Greenpeace's *Rainbow Warrior*, but also the entire hotel runs on less energy than an average US household and is set among uncut rainforest and sublime coastline. It has a romantic vibe and is a popular pick for honeymooners.

Getting there

By bus

There is a public bus – a big 4x4 truck with wooden benches – that trundles along the main road, from Puerto Jiménez to Cabo Matapalo. It leaves the Puerto Jiménez bus station at 6am and 1.30pm (US$7).

By car

From Puerto Jiménez take the main road which follows the coast to Cabo Matapalo. This road is extremely tough going and the journey takes 1-2 hrs each way, depending on the shape your car is in. Four-wheel-drive taxis are available for US$50.

Carate

Carate is a remote village near the **La Leona ranger station** in the **PN Corcovado**. Its isolated location attracts a few tourists, most of whom are there for its proximity to Corcovado. Several secluded hotels are tucked away in the surrounding primary rainforest and on the superb coastline, which has some of the most extraordinary beaches in the country. The local *pulpería* has simple snacks and meals, but other than this cornerstone of culinary excitement, hotel restaurants are the sole option.

Where to sleep

Luna Lodge (8380 5036, www.lunalodge.com, US$135-$175 per person) has seven luxury cabins positioned on the hillside, each with a viewing platform. This hotel specialises in yoga retreats and inside-out well-being. Organic meals, a massage cabin and meditation clinics encourage healthy minds in a healthy outdoor setting. The **Lookout Inn** (2644 5967, www.lookout-inn.com, US$115-$175 per person) is another luxurious choice with scenic views. There are nearby waterfalls and a 'Stairway to Heaven' track up to a trail high on a ridge.

Getting there and away

By air

Locally owned **Alfa Romeo Air Charters** (2735 5178, www.alfaromeoair.com, US$175) can take up to 4 people directly from Puerto Jiménez to Carate.

By bus

There is a public bus that leaves the Puerto Jiménez bus station at 6am and 1.30pm (US$9).

By car

The main coastal road from Puerto Jiménez leads to Carate. It is a long and very bumpy 4-hr drive. A private taxi can also make this same trip for US$70 per car one way.

Golfo Dulce & Around

Shhhhhhh! This area has some of the best surfing in Costa Rica.

Southern Pacific

This tropical gulf possesses perhaps the most visually stimulating jungles, arguably the best sport fishing and certainly the longest, most consistent left-hand break in Costa Rica. The land is so fertile that the United Fruit Company (*see p16* **Bitter fruit**) extended its monopoly of the banana plantations here from the Caribbean coast to the Zona Sur, constructing its headquarters in Golfito. Birdwatching, guided walks and zip-lining are all popular activities within the numerous national parks and reserves found in the area, including: **PN Piedras Blancas** (*see right*), **PN La Amistad** (*see p267*) and **Refugio Nacional de Fauna Silvestre Golfito** (*see right*).

Fishermen fly here to take on the marine beasts, appreciating the lack of crowds – in fact, virtually the bulk of Golfito's (the largest town) tourist infrastructure is dedicated to this sport. Past **Golfito** towards **Pavones**, verdant hills turn to dark sandy beaches where surfers flock to its ideal swells and where well-travelled holidaymakers traverse bumpy roads in search of sun drenched *playas* (beaches) removed from the norm. It's an adventurous and exciting area.

Golfito

From 1938 to 1985, Golfito was in the hands of the United Fruit Company (UFC), an almighty US banana empire. Situated in the natural harbour of Golfo Dulce, Golfito became the headquarters of the UFC. Its location was a convenient point for the company to unload its banana trains from around the southern Pacific area and ship them around the world. The UFC constructed the town and governed its every aspect. Streets and houses were built and maintained, running water and electricity installed, a city hospital was erected, even the football league was funded – all by the UFC.

On the surface it was a prosperous and happy community. However, the city was divided into three neighbourhoods: banana workers in one section, foremen in another, and the *zona americana*, named after the North American bosses who lived there and whose white mansions still stand. Every *centavo* earned depended on the UFC; likewise every *centavo* spent went straight into its pockets (citizens could only spend their wages in UFC

A rickety river crossing on the way to **Pavones**. See p272.

owned stores). By the late 1970s banana production had decreased and was slowly being replaced with palm oil plantations, a crop that does not need nearly as much manpower as the fruit. By 1984, the UFC had abandoned the area, cutting off all train services, refusing to cover infrastructural costs and had sold off its land and assets. In a flash, Golfito's bustling banana business became defunct.

Today Golfito is a skeleton of its former glory. Its dozy streets are shouldered with washed-out turquoise houses and dingy bars. To boost the economy, the government promotes it as a duty-free zone, which attracts shoppers, mostly during the holidays. The town stands still, hoping for better days to come – or at least for more of the sport fishing fraternity who flock to the gulf. Its clear waters are irresistible and all the hotels cater for the influx of fishing tourism; even if the sportspeople don't stay, they are at least passing through before hopping on a boat bound for Puerto Jiménez. **Sportfishing Golfito** (364 4499, www.sportfishinggolfito.com, US$1,100 full day) is a good bet for marlin-hunters.

EXCURSIONS

Protecting the last of the lowland rainforest near Golfito, the **Refugio Nacional de Fauna Silvestre Golfito**'s ample biodiversity is particularly exciting for botanists, where examples of an endemic species in the genus *Caryodaphnopsis* (part of the Lauraceae or laurel family and related to the avocado) grow. Over 400 different varieties of tree, including cristobal and purple heart, attract all sorts of animals, such as raccoons, coatis, collared peccaries, pacas and four types of monkey.

There is excellent birdwatching and opportunities to view rare species such as the black-cheeked ant-tanager and golden-naped woodpecker living in these forests. Although there are no public facilities, camping is allowed and can be arranged through the Rio Claro office (2789 9092).

Trails for hiking are accessible from Golfito, one starting at Tower Road near the cemetery or behind Banco Nacional; a second at the north end of the town, off the road towards La Gamba. The landscape is rugged and mountainous (which is why it was spared from the banana plantations) but thick and alive with nature's sounds. At the top, 520 metres (1,640 feet) above sea level, the views are fantastic and look out on to the Golfo Dulce.

Casa de Orquídeas is located at San Josecito beach, and only accessible by boat. Ron MacAllister, his wife Trudy and their daughter Melanie offer visitors an unusual and enjoyable three-hour tour of their carefully tended botanical garden. Self-taught botanists, for more than 30 years they have planted, grown and cared for unique plant and tree species on their 28-hectare (70-acre) farm, free from modern annoyances. The tour begins at 8am and along the route you will come across a bemusing array of exotic plant life: rare orchids, the 'Chanel No.5' flower (a ylang-ylang), palms and numerous fruit trees.

You are encouraged to use your senses by tasting the fruit (who knew cashew fruit was so dry and bitter?) and opening your nostrils (the scrumptious scent of vanilla). This living salad of flora also attracts many birds, especially hummingbirds, as well as other wildlife. Private guided tours cost US$20 or, if there is a group of four or more, US$5 per person (Saturday to Thursday). Any hotel or lodge in the area can arrange for your visit via radio communication (there is no phone or website).

Seven kilometres (4.5 miles) outside of Golfito towards La Gamba is the delightful **Esquinas Rainforest Lodge** (2741 8001, www.esquinas lodge.com, US$105 per person), an eco-lodge partly owned by the University of Vienna (and therefore popular with visiting Austrians) and hidden within the **PN Piedras Blancas**. Close your eyes, imagine a rainforest, and this is it. It is an ideal retreat for nature-lovers with numerous rainforest trails and guided tours. There is a spring-fed pool and a (separate) pond that is home to two caimans, Lorenzo and Chicitita (who get shockingly close). Cosy cottages with board games and hand-woven blankets make for enjoyable respite during the heavy rain showers. The food is particularly delicious – healthy, great tummy fillers for a day's adventure of wildlife watching. The knowledgeable guides can point out all the usual suspects, especially on their night tours. Open for day visits too.

Where to eat & drink

For local surf and turf, walk along Golfito's five-kilometre (three-mile) strip which has fast food huts and greasy cafés where waitresses are ready to serve up monstrous portions of *gallo pinto* and *casado*. Don't flash your money about though, this area is near the red light district (highlighted on the city sponsored map with a cartoon drawing of a hooker, no less). If you want to upgrade try **Las Gaviotas Hotel** (2775 0062, main courses US$10-$20) which has a pleasant restaurant that looks out on to the bay; or stock up at the supermarket Mega Super, a little way past Banco Nacional.

Golfito seems to be a general watering hole for the down and out. We recommend beers at your hotel bar at night.

The beauty and the beast around the **Esquinas Rainforest Lodge**. *See p265.*

Where to stay

Just outside Golfito is the hamlet of La Purruja where **La Purruja Lodge** (2775 5054, www.purruja.com, US$40 double) provides five sweet cabins spaced out along a cropped lawn. It is excellent value for this charming accommodation, including fresh breakfasts, a peaceful landscape and birding territory.

In Golfito itself, **Las Gaviotas** (2775 0062, lasgaviotas@hotmail.com, US$50 double) is your best bet for clean sheets and a good night's sleep. It has a direct view of the once busy harbour, a large tiled pool and satisfactory service. Although in need of a lick of paint, this is a reliable hotel and a hangout for sport fishermen. **Samoa del Sur** (2775 0264, www.samoadelsur.com, US$93 double) has 14 tired looking but roomy cabins just off the public pier. Cable TV, a pool, bar and restaurant make this another fisherman's favourite – tattoos and tall tales are rife here.

If you are not spending the night in Golfito, there are idyllic beachside and rainforest lodges around Playa San Josecito. **Golfo Dulce Lodge** (8821 5398, www.golfodulcelodge.com, US$95-$115 per person) and **Playa Nicuesa Rainforest Lodge** (2258 8250, www.playa nicuesa.com, US$170-$190 per person) are good options in the area.

Resources

Banks

Banco Coopealianza *across from Hospital de Golfito (2473 3020)*. ATM and Western Union. **Banco Nacional** *big white building on the main road heading south from the hospital (2212 2000)*. Has an ATM.

Hospital

On the main road south of the airport.

Internet

At Golfito Hotel (2775 0192) next to the public pier. **Open** 9am-10pm daily.

Tourist information

Cámara Ecotourism de Golfito (2775 1820), on the main road before Las Gaviotas. **Open** 10am-6pm Mon-Sat.

Getting there

By bus

Tracopa bus company (2222 2666) leaves San José at 7am and 3pm (US$4 one way). It is an 8-hr journey. Buses to San José depart from the bus station at the Ecotourism Centre at 10am and 3pm. Buses depart from Golfito's municipal dock for Zancudo and Pavones at 10am and 3pm and return at 5am and 12.30pm (US$2 one way).

By car

From Palmar Norte continue on the Interamericana (Highway 2) to Rio Claro and take Highway 14 south to Golfito.

By boat

A passenger ferry runs daily between Puerto Jiménez and Golfito. It departs from Puerto Jiménez at 5.45am, 6am, 6.10am, noon, 3pm and 4pm. From Golfito: 5am, 9.30am, 11.30am, 3.30pm, 4pm and 5pm. It costs either US$2 or US$4 depending on which boat turns up. Private water taxis are also available to and from Golfito.

Parque Nacional La Amistad

This very remote national park, named 'the Friendship', is Costa Rica's largest, with more than 200,000 hectares (494,000 acres) of land that links into the Talamancan mountain range encompassing tropical lowland rainforest, cloud forest and *páramo* (moorland). Its untouched forests extend into Panama and it has been estimated that about two-thirds of the total species found in Costa Rica live here. A large population of baird's tapirs, all six species of neotropical cats – jaguar, puma, ocelot, margay, oncilla and jaguarundi – as well as monkeys, coatis, more than 600 bird species, 115 species of fish and almost 300 reptile and amphibian species inhabit this unique environment. The protected area also includes reserves for the Bribri and Cabecar indigenous tribes. Being the biggest forest reserve in Central America also makes it one of the least explored. New species of both flora and fauna are recorded yearly (three new species of salamander were recently discovered in the park).

The park has been declared a UNESCO Biosphere Reserve and is also included on the World Heritage Site list. Exploring this park is for hardcore hikers only – the terrain is pretty rugged. Trails are not clearly marked and sheltered lodgings are few and far between. However, if you are determined, step one is to contact one of the local park offices either in San Vito (2773 4090) or San Isidro de El General (2771 3155). You can also try the **Fundación de Parques Nacionales** office in San José (2257 2239). These offices will reserve your entry, give you advice about weather and trail conditions and can book a guide. Entry is US$6 plus US$3 for camping. The best time for hiking is from January to April and it is recommended to take your own gas stove, tent and warm sleeping bag.

The park headquarters (2200 5355) is found in the village of **Altamira** (20 kilometres – 12 miles – north of Guácimo). There is a ranger

Southern Pacific

Those Italian food blues at **La Puerta Negra** Italian restaurant. *See p270*.

there who can point you in the right direction and give you last-minute trail tips. Getting to Altamira in itself is an adventure, as the roads are barely drivable, even with a big four-wheel drive. But if you make it, there are trails that lead to Valle del Silencio, Gigantes del Bosque, Canasta and Sabanas Esperanza, all of which have good camping sites. In Valle del Silencio there are very rustic cabins that include shower facilities, tables and drinking water.

Other entrances are from **Sector Tres Colinas** (2730 0846) two hours south of Buenos Aires on the San Vito road, via Potrero Grande; **Sector Santa María de Pittier** (2773 3955) at 45 kilometres (28 miles) from the Paso Real turn-off on the Interamericana. **Sector Biolley** (2742 8090) is another 20 kilometres (12 miles) past Potrero Grande and **Sector Santa María** is by its namesake village south of Santa Marta de Brunka. Each has a park office open from 7am to 4pm and rangers who can advise on trekking conditions. For more information (in Spanish for now, but an English translation is promised) visit www.sinaccr.net.

EXCURSIONS

Not far from San Vito is the **Wilson Botanical Garden** (www.ots.ac.cr, US$10), a beautifully groomed botanical garden bordered by primary forest that shelters more than 1,000 genera in 212 plant families. Originally started by an American couple in 1963 and now run by the Organisation for Tropical Studies, these gardens serve as an important biological station and educational grounds. On site there is accommodation for both researchers and visitors (US$82 double), a lab, experimental sites for studies in biology and ecology as well as guided trails. Those who choose to stay overnight are treated to unique educational walks, such as the 'early bird tour' where species such as the Scarlet-thighed Dacnis, Silver-throated Tanager, Blue-headed Parrot and Violaceous Trogon can be sighted. A memorable stop on any itinerary.

Where to eat

Bring your own camp food if you are not staying in a lodge (*see below*) or at the Wilson Botanical Garden.

Where to stay

The great outdoors is your bed for the night unless you stay at **La Amistad Lodge** (2228 8671, www.laamistad.com, US$85 per person), an eco-lodge and organic coffee farm that practises sustainable development. Its rates include three daily meals, access to its private reserve plus a local guide. It has have ten comfortable double rooms with private bathrooms and electricity. The lodge is located just outside Las Mellizas. If you reserve ahead, staff will arrange for your transport.

A new fragrance by Costa Rica

When asked what she wore to bed, Marilyn Monroe reportedly replied: 'Why, two drops of Chanel No.5 of course.' Chanel's legendary perfume has continued to be the world's most recognisable fragrance since its creation in 1921 by Ernest Beux. Coco Chanel asked Beux to create 'the ideal smell for a woman'. She immediately chose number five out of a choice of six samples. And what is this alluring aroma's secret ingredient? Its top notes include the ylang-ylang flower, a historically bewitching blossom that grows in tropical climates – and which can be found almost all over Costa Rica.

The gorgeous scent of Chanel No.5 is instantly recognisable as you pass a ylang-ylang tree with its drooping branches and long sherbet-yellow petals that hang like ladies' kidskin gloves. Ylang-ylang flowers are used in the production of perfume, fragrant soap, candles or, best of all, simply placed in a bowl as a natural air freshener. For perfume, the flowers are picked at night when their aroma is at its strongest and turned into essential oil through a two-part distillation process. Other perfumes that use the ylang-ylang are Aqua de Gio by Giorgio Armani, Diorissimo by Christian Dior and Carolina Herrera by Carolina Herrera. **Wilson Botanical Gardens** (*see p268*) and **Casa de Orquídeas** (*see p265*) both have examples of the Ylang-ylang tree whose creamy flowers blossom all year round.

Another intoxicating flower found in Costa Rica and used in perfumes is the passiflora, or passion flower. First recorded by 17th-century Spanish missionaries in South America and named for the Passion of Christ, this exotic looking five-petal blossom has a captivating aroma. Herbalists often prescribe the passion flower as a mild sedative to people suffering from insomnia or anxiety. (It's also worth noting that because of this flower's exquisite anatomy it has been adopted in Japanese culture as a symbol of homosexuality. Take another look at its bold organs and you'll understand why.) The passion flower aroma is found in many perfumes such as In Love Again by Yves Saint Laurent, Fleur de la Passion by Calvin Klein and Dazzling Silver by Estée Lauder. This purple flower thrives in Costa Rica and is commonly sighted along the side of roads, in gardens and up trellises.

If you happen to enjoy midnight strolls, you will probably encounter a wiff of Reina de la noche (Queen of the night) aka Angel's Trumpet. This example of Brugmansia is an endemic species in Costa Rica and is recognisable by its white fairytale flowers that hang from large shrubs. These trumpet shaped flowers have evolved to open only during the night, taking advantage of nocturnal bats that spread their pollen.

Brugmansia are toxic and have been used for recreational experimentation and in indigenous religious ceremonies. The high, however, has been known to be unpredictable, usually resulting in a bad trip and in some cases has been fatal. Inhaling its fragrance, however, is a pure pleasure and perfectly harmless. Ineke Rühland's perfume Evening Edged in Gold uses this flower in its top notes. It was selected as the perfume's base because 'it has a wonderful, rich scent that wafts on the evening breeze'.

Costa Rica is a perfumer's Garden of Eden with vast jungles home to numerous flowering flora. The sweet smells in the air are part of the experience and it's comforting to know you can take a piece of Eden away with you, as you pass through duty free. But be careful in the forests apart from some poisonous plants there are also some not-so-nice smelling species, such as the Dracontium flower, a remarkably fragrant blossom that mimicks the odour of faeces to attract flies for pollination.

Southern Pacific

Getting there

Transportation to park entry points is poor. There are no buses into the park, so most visitors choose to hire four-wheel-drive taxis from San Vito to as far as the vehicle will go and then walk into the park. Bus company **Alfaro** (2222 2666) departs from San José to San Vito daily at 5.45am, 8.15am, 11.30am and 2.45pm, and returns at 4.30am, 7.30am, 8.30am, 10am and 3pm. The trip takes 8hrs.

Playa Zancudo

A subdued beachside town, Playa Zancudo is home to a number of expats who hail from colder climates, as well as Ticos on holiday. The waves, although not as great as at Pavones, are a draw for surfers and perhaps even better suited to beginners and swimmers, the tide not being excessively strong. The vibe is one of a stress-free small town where the biggest excitement usually arises from visiting divorcees who've had one cocktail too many. Sport fishing, surfing and other water sports keep tourists busy during the day, while at night quaint bars fill up with the sunburned and shrivelled where tales of 'the one that got away' (fish or betrothed) filter through the air. It is a perfect place for long beach walks and evenings spent reclining with a cocktail.

For surf lessons, **Surfer Mike** (2776 0217, US$20) offers excellent one-on-one instruction where beginners are given Mike's tentative promise that they will stand up by the end of the hour. (His wife also makes excellent barbecued chicken to take away at the church at the north end of town past the police station and football pitch). Experienced masseuse Kate is more than happy to help de-knot those surf-sore muscles (2776 0191, US$30).

Where to eat & drink

The restaurants in this tropical twilight zone are surprisingly good. For some strange reason there is a rather high percentage of Italians who have left their European kitchens to become pizza and pasta chefs here, and they are very good at it. Other expat-run places offer mostly good food, and always in a lovely environment. They are listed according to where they lie along the road towards the peninsula.

Bar Coquito

(No phone). **Open** varies. **No credit cards**.
As close to a club as Zancudo can get, this open-sided *rancho* pumps out cumbia and reggaeton for a Tico crowd, but Anglo-Saxon hips are more than welcome to come and attempt to gyrate.

Bar Sussy

No phone. **Open** varies. **No credit cards**.
This bar seems to be a favourite of locals and long-term expats. Some real characters keep the bar stools warm here talking about ex-wives and ex-lives. Amusing drunken anecdotes flow as fast as the rum and cokes.

Coloso Del Mar

2776 0050. **Open** 7am-9pm daily. **Main courses** US$5. **Credit** MC, V.
A screened roadside café with friendly service and popular surf snacks like cheese quesadillas, fishcakes and beer with lime in the top.

Iguana Verde

2776 0921. **Open** 8am-8pm daily. **Main courses** US$8. **No credit cards**.
This feelgood bar and restaurant is famous for its grilled cheese sandwiches. DJ Andy spins a mean mix of indie and soul and, as the sun sets, might invite you to join him for a shot of some lethal rum.

Oceano Cabinas Bar & Restaurant

2776 0921. **Open** 11am-9pm daily. **Main courses** US$8. **Credit** MC,V.
Filled daily with both tourists and locals this restaurant serves fresh and healthy meals with excellent service. It is proud to make the best burgers in town, and the Sunday brunch, with bloody marys and eggs benedict, is a secret treat.

La Puerta Negra

2776 0181. **Open** 6-10pm daily. **Main courses** US$10. **No credit cards**.
Italian owner and chef Alberto will greet you with his catchphrase, 'Viva la pizza!' This is possibly the best Italian food in Costa Rica and is a real highlight in Zancudo. After the meal and a few shots of Limoncello, Alberto often shows off his guitar skills on his Dobro guitar, belting out not Italian folk but deep south blues, with his dog, Can-Can, snoozing at his feet. There is also one small *cabina* for rent, although so close to the restaurant it's not for those on Weight Watchers or who turn in really early.

Sol y Mar

2776 0014. **Open** 7am-9pm daily. **Main courses** US$9. **No credit cards**.
An open air beach hut featuring a centre bar that gets busy during the evening. Fairy lights and Wi-Fi lure in the homesick and chat addicted. On occasion they have barbecue nights. A good space for larger groups or families.

Where to stay

Along Playa Zancudo's main road, choices for accommodation are easy. Most deliver your beachside fantasy of palm-leaf huts and ocean views with friendly laid-back owners. The following are listed according to where they lie along the road towards the peninsula.

Rural real estate going cheap in **Pavones**. *See p272.*

Cabinas los Cocos

2776 0012/www.loscocos.com. **Rates** US$70 cabin.
No credit cards.
Four charming cabins, each with their own kitchen
and bathroom, have been lovingly decorated. Two
are restored banana workers' houses transported
from Golfito. Beautiful hardwood floors, hammocks
and colourful deckchairs create a relaxing ambience
where you can lounge and enjoy the beachfront
location, which is probably the nicest in town. Artist
owners Susan and Andrew also have five three-bedroom houses for rent, between US$700 and $1,500
per week. Boat tours (US$45) and boat taxis to and
from Golfito or Puerto Jiménez (US$15) are other
services provided. In addition, Susan founded a
charity that funds secondary education for local
children in the community. Any donations are
greatly appreciated.

Cabinas Sol y Mar

2776 0014/www.zancudo.com. **Rates** US$25-$50
cabin. **No credit cards**.
Comfortable screened cabins with long balconies,
great for sun-seekers and social holidaymakers. This
is a hotspot at night thanks to its inviting bar and
restaurant, which also has a stash of board games
and a good book exchange.
Bar. Restaurant.

Coloso Del Mar

(2776 0050/www.coloso-del-mar.com). **Rates** US$40-
$45 cabin. **Credit** MC, V.
A sunny plot of land that features four cheerful
wooden cabins each with private bathroom and
screened windows. There is also a raised gazebo,
perfect for taking in the sunset or to get away from
the noon heat. Good rates and lovely lodging equal
a slice of *pura vida*.
Restaurant.

Iguana Verde

2776 0902/www.iguanaverde.net. Closed Oct.
Rates US$60 cabin. **No credit cards**.
With a welcoming atmosphere and three spotless
cabins situated just off the beach, this is a good find.
All cabins have air-conditioning and private bathrooms with hot water. Knowledgeable and helpful
staff are more than happy to offer advice on local
tours, surfing, and other activities. An excellent bar
makes this place a lot of fun.
Bar. Restaurant.

Oceano Cabinas Bar & Restaurant

2776 0921/www.bestcostaricavacations.com. Closed
15 Sept-1 Nov. **Rates** US$69 double. **Credit** MC, V.
Above the successful restaurant are two rooms
furnished with comfy beds, pretty mosquito nets

Southern Pacific

and soft pillows. Both have modern bathrooms. Super friendly Torontonians Mark and Stephanie work hard to keep guests happy. They check daily to make sure all is well, lend out their boogie boards and personally cook the meals.
Bar. Restaurant. TV.

Resources

Internet
Oceano Cabinas Bar & Restaurant has a computer with internet access. **Cabinas Sol y Mar** has Wi-Fi.

Police
On the north side of Zancudo village, past Soda Katherine (2776 0166).

Getting there

By boat
Ronny's Golfito boat to Zancudo departs from the municipal dock at noon from Monday to Saturday (US$5). It leaves Zancudo at 7am from Palmera de Oro. Private water taxis are a more convenient and flexible means of getting there: Cabinas los Cocos (2776 0012) charges US$15 per person to and from Zancudo.

By bus
Buses from Golfito to Zancudo depart daily from the municipal dock at 10am and 3pm (US$2 one way).

By car
From Golfito take the road out of town towards Rio Claro. About 13km (8 miles) out of Golfito at Bar Rodeo the road forks; head south-east. After 20km (12 miles) you reach the most exciting part of the journey – the river crossing. The charge is CRC800 per car (US$1.60). A rusty cable barge, powered by a boat motor, crosses the murky river with 3 cars per load. It's a 5-min ride so queues rarely form. Continue south down the road (mind the potholes), which becomes a dirt track. Keep turning right at the intersections and into Playa Zancudo.

Playa Pavones

A magnet for surfers, this rocky 1.6-kilometre (one-mile) beach boasts one of the longest left-hand breaks in the world. It's a long barreling wave that, on a good day, can offer rides of up to three minutes. During the rainy season (April to October) waves are at their biggest and surfing machismo heats up. Pavones is part of the National Surf Circuit and in February attracts some big names to its annual contest. For non-surfing people and partners out there, there are pretty rock pools to explore, or turn away from the ocean and the rainforest stares back at you. It's a difficult place to reach but many swear it is one of Costa Rica's best kept secrets. Activities such as horseriding and hiking provide active alternatives, but Pavones is and will always be centred around surfing. If you feel like you're missing out, professional surfer Laura gives two-hour lessons for US$50 per person. Ask anyone in town for 'pro surfer Laura'; there is no phone or website.

Where to eat & drink

Other than a couple of sodas and a supermarket, there are not too many food options to choose from. Hotels provide decent meals and local sodas usually feature typical surfer grub like nachos and burgers.

Where to stay

Attracting the young and sporty, most hotels are of the cheap and cheerful type, but for a touch of luxury try **Casa Siempre Domingo** (8820 4709, www.casa-domingo.com, US$80 double) whose modern rooms have big beds and classic ocean views. The hotel is built high up on a private ridge where the fresh air and excellent service will take any load off your shoulders.

Cabinas Mira Olas (8393 7742, www.miraolas.com, US$30-$45 double) has four cabins set in a tropical garden. Butterflies and birds flutter about the fruit trees on this five-hectare (12.5-acre) farm. The Rio Claro trickles through the property, with river pools perfect for taking a dip in. Hikes and horse rides through the back hills of the Guaymi Indian reservation can be arranged.

For top-of-the-range comfort, head to **Tiskita Jungle Lodge** (2296 8125, www.tiskita-lodge.co.cr, US$130 double). It's an impressive eco-lodge, whose owner, a conservationist, has planted over 125 species of fruit tree and now works to reforest nearby cleared land. The rich jungle surrounds wood cabins built from fallen mahogany, purple heart and rosewood trees. Screened windows, porches with hammocks and stunning views keep guests in a bubble of happiness and relaxation.

Getting there

By bus
Buses depart Golfito's municipal dock for Pavones at 10am and 3pm and return at 5am and 12.30pm (US$2 one way).

By car
From Golfito head over the ferry crossing. You will then head through the small town of Conte. About 1km after that, the road forks. Turn left at the fork. Follow this road for 18km (11 miles) and it will lead you straight into Pavones. As are almost all in this area, it is a very bad road and a four-wheel drive vehicle is essential.

Caribbean

Getting Started

The little-visited Caribbean coast is 200 kilometres of paradise.

Costa Rica's Caribbean coast is the backbone of the vast and sparsely populated province of Limón, which stretches over some 200 kilometres (125 miles) of mostly untamed land south from Nicaragua and down to the Panamanian border. The region has a zesty, multicultural flavour that is worlds apart from the Spanish-derived lifestyle of the rest of the country. It is a culturally diverse zone, the result of generations of cohabitation between Jamaican and Carib immigrant workers, and the area's indigenous tribes.

These days dreadlocked Rastafarians live a slow pace of life reminiscent of that of the islands; reggae and calypso pipe from beachfront dwellings, Spanish and English mingle with rhythmic Patois (*see p285* **Patois patter**) and aromas of spicy Creole cooking seep into the streets from tiny family restaurants. The people are friendly and fun-loving and visitors are never treated with contempt. The Caribbean coast receives fewer visitors than the Pacific coast but it is a good destination for eco-tourists.

In 1502, Christopher Columbus became the first known European to land on this coast when he set foot on Isla Uvita, a kilometre off the coast of Puerto Limón. Presumably fantasising about an unlimited wealth of gold to satisfy his Midas complex, he dubbed the land 'Costa Rica' or 'rich coast'. Pirates, rumrunners and gunrunners followed, infiltrating the region until the mid 18th century. Some of this motley crew settled along the coastal lowlands, bringing with them slaves who had their own Caribbean dialects and traditions, which have been passed down to today's culture. (It is said that the local dish *rondón* derives its name from the expression 'whatever the cook can 'run down').

Development was shaped by the construction of the railway, and by the banana trade. In 1871, a railway was constructed that connected San José to the coast via the Cordillera Central in order to export coffee to Europe more efficiently. American Minor Keith (*see p16* **Bitter fruit**) was commissioned to build the 'jungle train', and it was his idea to plant the

Only the splash of waves disturbs the silence and serenity on **Manzanillo**. *See p299.*

Caribbean

Caribbean

Punta Castilla

AGUA

n Juan

Barra del Colorado
See p278

Colorado

La Zapota
de Vida Silvestre
a del Colorado

Zona Protectora
Tortuguero

Río Suerte

Boca del Río Tortuguero
Cerro Tortuguero ▲

Tortuguero
See p281

Río Tortuguero

Parque Nacional
Tortuguero
See p279

CARIBBEAN SEA

La Pavona

Cariari

Pueblo Nuevo

Roxana

PILES

Río Parismina

Laguna Salvadora

Parismina

Caño Blanco

ACIMO

Parismina

Carmen

San Rafael

Tres Millas

Río Pacuare

Boca Río Matina

SIQUIRRES

Río Reventazón

Matina

Estrada

Boca del Pantano

Barbilla

32

Cocal

Punta Piuta

PUERTO LIMÓN
See p284

Isla Uvita

Nacional
rialba
lcán Turrialba

M A N Guayabo

10

Col. Guayabo

P N
Barbilla

Río Pejé

Río Victoria

Westfalia

Bomba

TURRIALBA

Pacuare

Río Zent

Bananito Sur

Playa Vizcaya

AN VIÑAS

La Suiza

Río Banano

San Clemente Nuevo
San Clemente Viejo

Bonifacio

P N Cahuita

Pejibaye

Moravia

Reserva
Indígena
Taini

Río Chirripó

Pandora

Cahuita
See p288

Punta Cahuita
Puerto Vargas

R F

Río Estrella

P N Cahuita

Río Macho

Reserva de
Vida Silvestre
La Marta

Río Pacuare

Cerro Bobocara ▲

Hone Creek

Playa Negra

Punta Uva

Manzanillo
See p299

Reserva Forestal
Río Macho

Reserva Biológica
Hitoy Cerere

Uatsi

Puerto Viejo
See p293

R V S

Parque Nacional
antí-Macizo de la Muerte

Bribri

Sandoca Manzanillo

R F Río Macho

Río Telre

Suretka

BRATSI

Río Sixaola

32

Villa Mills
Cerro La Georgina ▲

Parque Nacional
Chirripó

Amubri

Boca Uren

Río Yorkin

Daytonia

División

▲ Cerro Chirripó

Reserva
Indígena
Talamanca

SIXAOLA
See p308

Rivas

Parque Nacional Internacional
La Amistad
(Sitio Patrimonio Mundial)

Río Coen

SAN ISIDRO DE EL GENERAL

▲ Cerro Etna

▲ Cerro Durika

Río Larí

Palma
namaste

Río General

Río Convento

Río Icílán

▲ Cerro Bika

▲ Cerro Kamuk

Río Uren

PANAMA

Ujarrás

Volcán

0	5	10 miles
0	5	10 km

Things to do

Tourism on the Caribbean coast is defined by either eco-friendly holidays to **PN Tortuguero** (*see p279*), a thriving national park home to a bewildering array of wildlife and, of course, the largest turtle-nesting site in the Western hemisphere, or relaxing in a hammock on a pristine beach, sipping a cocktail out of a coconut shell. **Puerto Viejo** (*see p293*) is the place to head for the typical Caribbean vibe: dreadlocks and Bob Marley dominate the scene. Experienced surfers around the world will have heard of the Hawaiian-style Salsa Brava wave (*see p293*), and anyone who has held a fishing rod more than likely knows about the **Barra del Colorado** (*see p278*) tarpon run.

Places to stay

At the northern end of the coast, in the wilds of PN Tortuguero, the best accommodation is luxury lodges. The most comfortable is **Pachira Lodge** (*see p282*). Five minutes from the national park entrance, this good-value hotel also organises quality tours. Towards the south, the best accommodation is between Puerto Viejo and Manzanillo. The bungalows in **Shawandha** (*see p300*) are basic, but tranquil, comfortable and carefully appointed. The most interesting hotel in the area has to be the **Tree House** (*see p301*). Although not actually built aloft in the canopy, this large house is built from found hardwood and is a masterpiece of environmental architecture that has won awards for sustainability. Equally unusual are the 'tents' at **Almonds and Corals** (*see p301*). Although many may baulk at the idea of hunkering down under canvas, bear in mind that this lodging comes specced with a jacuzzi and a minibar.

Places to eat

Food along the Caribbean is Costa Rica's tastiest. Any run-down shack will serve up good spicy Caribbean food. The favourites, however, are: **Miss Junie's** (*see p281*) in Tortuguero, for authentic dishes and great views; **Miss Edith** in Cahuita (*see p290*), whose coconut infused stews are almost legendary; and **Chile Rojo** (*see p295*) in Puerto Viejo, which has upmarket Caribbean food.

banana crop throughout the lowlands, bringing in flocks of immigrant labourers both to work the crops and lay the tracks. A deadly bout of yellow fever wiped out many of the workers, so thousands of African labourers from Jamaica and the Caribbean islands – thought to be immune to the fever – were contracted to finish the railway line. Most stayed to work on the banana plantations during the banana boom, and over time it was they who established the first villages along the coast, setting the scene for today's Puerto Limón and Puerto Viejo.

The province can be divided into two distinct regions: the North, and the south of Puerto Limón. The North is an area made up of an intricate system of waterways that slice through thick jungle and pour out to a straight strip of coast that continues all the way to Nicaragua. Sloths, monkeys, birds, caimans and a host of other beasts reside in and along the canals and mangrove swamps that reach out to **Refugio Nacional de Fauna Silvestre Barra del Colorado** (*see p278*) and **PN Tortuguero** (*see p279*). The waterways serve as transportation routes and are navigated by motorised canoes and water taxis. They also make for good day trips as you can rent a canoe and paddle about in search of wildlife.

To the far south, lush jungle meets turquoise waters on expanses of sparsely settled beach. Stretches of coast are cut by headlands and the sea shelters vast coral reefs. If you want that 'Caribbean feel', head to Cahuita and to Manzanillo. This is where you'll find those beaches, the relaxed Rasta vibe, welcoming cafés and the ability to wile away hours without doing very much at all.

You have two options to choose from if you do visit the Caribbean. Either take part in one of the numerous outdoor activities or succumb to the slow pace and planless afternoons in beach towns like Cahuita or Puerto Viejo. These delightful hamlets, and the many stretches of sand that lie to the south, are havens for surfers in search of gnarly waves, backpackers looking for a party and Rastas seeking Jah. Other visitors come to the Caribbean to see monkeys, snorkel the reefs of **PN Cahuita** (*see p288*), visit the **Refugio Nacional de Vida Silvestre Gandoca-Manzanillo** (*see p300*) or to explore the swampy waterways and spot turtle hatchlings in **Tortuguero** (*see p279*). A serious sport fisher will want to head north to **Barra del Colorado** (*see p278*) where the tarpon fishing is world renowned. Inland, and often overlooked, is some of the best whitewater rafting in the Americas on Limón's numerous river rapids. **Reserva Punta Mona** (*see p300*), off the coast, makes a good alternative to happy hour and salsa lessons.

Caribbean North

Home to the world's largest turtle nesting site and top-quality sport fishing.

Guápiles

Heading east from San José, the Guápiles Highway (Highway 32) climbs out of the highlands and then runs north-east, winding its way 104 kilometres (64 miles) to Puerto Limón and down the Caribbean coast. Rugged landscape changes to jungly lowland as you traverse the Cordillera Central and head towards the sea. About 62 kilometres (38 miles) north-east of San José, and just off the highway, is the industrial town of Guápiles, a transport hub for the Río Frío banana plantations and the first real town you hit en route to Puerto Limón. This dusty town is no cultural or geographical highlight but is a satisfactory base from which to visit the area's main attraction, the **Rainforest Aerial Tram** (*see p222*), 20 kilometres (12 miles) away.

Just north of Guápiles is the tiny banana town of **Cariari**, the gateway to the water routes to Tortuguero. There's no reason to stay here, and you probably won't be in town for more than a couple of hours while waiting for a boat, but there are a few bakeries and *sodas* scattered around the bus terminal. There are also some very basic cabins if you get stuck here overnight.

Heading towards Puerto Limón along the banana highway lies another blink-and-you'll-miss-it town. Located about 12 kilometres (seven miles) east of Guápiles, **Guácimo** has little to offer the typical tourist but is home to one of the best private universities in Latin America for studies in agricultural sciences and natural resources, the **Escuela de Agricultura de la Región Tropical Húmeda** (2713 0000, www.earth.ac.cr/turismoeducacional@earth.ac.cr). Students come here from all over the world to study the tropics close-up. You can tour the campus and its jungle and stay the night (US$60 double).

EXCURSIONS

If you're in a rental car, turn off Highway 32 at the Servicentro Santa Clara where you'll see the **Las Cusingas Botanical Garden** (2710 0114, admission US$5), a private plot of land featuring more than 80 species of medicinal plant, 80 species of orchid, various bromeliads and over 100 documented species of bird. A two-hour tour will educate you on local culture and conservation in addition to providing botanical information. Gentle walking trails lead around the premises and there is also a small cabin in which you can arrange to stay with advance booking. Just north of Guácimo is **Costa Flores** (3.5km north of Guácimo en route to Río Jiménez, 2716 6457, costaflor@sol.racsa.co.cr, admission US$19), another botanical adventure open from 6am to 4pm daily with tours available with advance booking. It is a popular day trip for masses of cruise ship holidaymakers and can get busy, but it is a large place featuring more than 500 varieties of flower.

Where to stay & eat

Most people simply pass through these towns, and the few hotels in the area really only cater to temporary workers (hint: they have thin walls and charge by the hour). There are a few notable exceptions should you get stuck here or want to break up your trip. At **Casa Río Blanco Ecolodge** (1.5km south of turn-off west of the Rio Blanco Bridge, 5km west of Guápiles, 8382 0957, www.casarioblanco.com, US$65 double), four pretty cabins sit on the edge of a cliff 20 metres (66 feet) above the Río Blanco in the canopy. The owners offer guided hikes on private trails through primary forest that lead past waterfalls and a bat cave. You can also swim and tube in the river below.

Just outside Guápiles, the **Hotel & Country Club Suerre** (150m from town centre past the *lavandería*, 2710 7551,www.suerre.com, US$65-$155 double) caters to executives, country clubbers and package tourists. Rooms have air-conditioning, phones and cable TV. There is an Olympic-sized swimming pool, spa, tennis courts and a decent open-air restaurant (main courses US$9). The more modest **Cabinas Quinta** (past turn-off to Cariari leaving town, 2710 7016, US$32-$45 double) has surprisingly clean and comfortable cabins on a large property with private trails to explore.

Sodas and pizzerias come and go in these towns, but there's always some form of decent eaterie. About half a kilometre east of the university, **Hotel & Restaurant Las Palmas** (2760 0330, www.hotelriopalmas.com, main courses US$10) has the best restaurant in the area and the hotel provides comfortable tiled-roof cabins for very decent rates.

Sit back and enjoy the sunset on the slow boat to the Caribbean.

Resources

Hospital
Clínica del Caribe *Guápiles (2710 1445).*

Getting there

By bus
Buses going from San José to the coast, and vice versa, pass through Guápiles regularly. All intercity buses arrive and depart from the **Guapileños Bus Station** in the southern part of town, while local buses leave for nearby towns from various points. Buses for Guácimo leave regularly from the Terminal Caribe in San José almost every hour from 6am to 6.30pm and from Limón every 30mins from 6am to 7.30pm. To get to the university, take a **Siquirres** or **Pocora** bus and ask to get off at the university.

By car
From San José take Highway 32 to Guápiles.

Barra del Colorado

Sprawled in a swampy maze of waterways and dense rainforest running all the way up to the Río San Juan that marks the border with Nicaragua, **Refugio Nacional de Fauna Silvestre Barra del Colorado** is Tortuguero National Park's remote northern twin. Named for its location at the gaping mouth of the Río Colorado, this 912 square-kilometre (352 square-mile) reserve largely comprises the Río San Juan delta from which the Río Colorado flows, and it is

ecologically similar to its Tortuguero counterpart 35 kilometres (22 miles) to the south. The region shares a similar climate, vegetation and fauna. Sloths, monkeys, crocodiles and birds populate the canals. Notable populations of hawksbill, leatherback and green sea turtles also nest on Barra's beach from July to September. But the reserve's real claim to fame is phenomenal 'tarpon-guaranteed' sport fishing. Dozens of tributaries create a network of waterways, making the area accessible only by air or boat.

The village itself is a ramshackle scattering of littered dirt pathways and raised-stilt houses, split into slivers of land on the north and south banks of the river. Fishing lodges, minimal amenities and an airstrip make up Barra del Sur, while Barra del Norte is primarily residential, inhabited by Ticos from diverse ethnic backgrounds as well as fishing expats and Nicaraguan immigrants, many of whom fled across the border during their nation's violent civil war. Locals rely on the fishing industry, either through fishing or fishing-related tourism. It is also no secret that a fair amount of drug trafficking takes place.

Most visitors make the effort to come here for the world-famous sport fishing in the reserve's tarpon, snook and gar filled waters. All the area's lodges cater to sport fishermen, mostly operating through prearranged multi-day packages that include meals, transportation and guided tours. The best time

or tarpon fishing is from February to May,
while snook fill the waters in September and
October; but the waters are so full of life all
year round that you're sure to catch something
no matter when you come. Lodges can also
arrange wildlife tours with expert guides.

Packages can be arranged in San José or
online and generally consist of three to five
nights of accommodation, meals, equipment
and boat trips. A handful of upscale fishing
lodges line the river; the following are the most
recommendable. The **Río Colorado Lodge**
(Barra del Sur, 2232 8610, www.riocolorado
lodge.com, US$450 per person, US$120 for
non-fishing guests) has air-conditioned rooms
linked by covered walkways. It offers a
number of diversions for landlubbing guests
and their children, including a television and
games room, a hot tub, a mini zoo and a
riverfront restaurant.

Some 300 metres up the river, the more
modest **Silver King Lodge** (300m upriver
from Rio Colorado Lodge, 2381 1403, www.
silverkinglodge.net, US$130 per person) has
very comfortable rooms in duplexes scattered
along a maze of walkways that lead to a small
swimming pool and lounge area. The only
place that comes close to catering for travellers
on a budget who still fancy a bit of fishing is
Tarponland (30m from dock by the airstrip,
2710 2141, US$20 per person). Most people
around the village, however, will know
it as 'Memo's'.

Getting there

By air

Most travellers come on packages with lodges
that often operate charter flights or will organise
air transport for you. **Sansa** (www.flysansa.com)
makes the 30min flight from San José's Juan
Santamaria International Airport daily. **Nature Air**
(www.natureair.com) flies from the Tobias Bolaños
International Airport in Pavas, sometimes stopping
first in Tortuguero.

By boat

After taking the bus to Cariari, connect to Barra
via the bus to Pavona that departs at 6am, noon
and 3pm, then catch the boat from Pavona to Barra.
Leaving from Tortuguero, you can take a 1hr boat
to Pavona, which departs at 6am, but you will then
have to wait for the 2pm boat to Barra. Private boats
from Tortuguero can also be hired at negotiated (but
generally high) prices. A less common option, and a
rather expensive one, is to travel to Barra by boat
from Puerto Viejo de Sarapiquí. Several of the lodges
operate private shuttles between Puerto Viejo de
Sarapiquí, Limón and Barra. Contact the Rio
Colorado Lodge (*see above*) for more information
(you don't need to be a guest).

Parque Nacional Tortuguero

Parque Nacional Tortuguero is a unique
waterworld of canals, coastal mangrove
swamps and lagoons surrounded by rainforest,
and almost all of it is accessible only by boat
or plane. The 266 square kilometres (102 square
miles) of coastal terrain and 456 square
kilometres (176 square miles) of marine area
comprise one of the most varied parks in the
Costa Rican system. Here you are likely to see
howler monkeys, toucans, caimans, anteaters,
kinkajous, tapirs and a host of other creatures
(many endangered or close to extinction) in the
park's grounds.

Spotting such wildlife is always a heart-
racing delight but Tortuguero's true majesty is
that it protects the largest marine turtle nesting
site in the Western hemisphere. Of the eight
species of marine turtle that exist on the planet,
six can be found in Costa Rica, and four of
those come to 'desove' (lay their eggs) in
Tortuguero. No one is entirely sure what lures
them specifically to Tortuguero's beaches;
some locals will tell you it's the warmth of the
black sands, while scientists believe the sand
has particular qualities that make an imprint

on the turtles, causing them to return year after year. *See p194* **Turtle power**.

The **Caribbean Conservation Corp** (CCC) (1km north of docks, 2709 8091, www.cccturtle.org, admission US$1 donation), open from 10am to noon and from 2pm to 5.30pm from Monday to Saturday, and from 2pm to 5.30pm on Sunday, was the first organisation to bring international attention to the nesting turtles and to the threats to their survival in the 1950s. The campaign eventually led to the founding of the national park in the 1970s. The CCC continues to monitor turtle populations today. You can visit the centre at the northern end of the village, where a small history museum has lots of information in English and Spanish. It also offers an 'adopt-a-turtle' programme in which you can sponsor your own tagged turtle and chart her journeys. The CCC can also arrange participation programmes allowing volunteers to be involved in the tagging process, though these must be organised in advance though its Florida office (see website). March to October is turtle season and the peak nesting months are July and August; needless to say, with the turtles comes the high tourist season.

The park's headquarters and main entrance are at its northern tip, at the southern end of Tortuguero village. Follow the main path through the village and over a tiny footbridge and you'll come to the **Cuatro Esquinas Ranger Station** (2709 8086, admission US$10). The park's hours are 5.30am to 6pm daily with last entry at 4.30pm. The less frequented **Jalova Ranger Station** sits on the canal at the southern end of the park.

There's a good one-hour walk along the **Sendero El Gavilán**, a muddy two-kilometre (1.25 mile) loop that winds from the Cuatro Esquinas ranger station, through the forest and out to the beach. You can attempt to explore several other trails on your own, but they're a bit confusing so it's best to get a map and ask for guidance from the rangers before setting out. **Bony Scott** (50m south of docks, 2709 8193, bonietravels2004@yahoo.com) is a friendly local bilingual guide who will take you into the park, on the canals, up the *cerro* (peak) or out to sea for sport fishing. He can also provide transport information and organise transfers. Similarly, **Ernesto Tours** (25m south of Bony Scott Tours, 2709 8070) is good for organising transport and also rents canoes at US$20 per hour. While most guides are respectful of the wildlife, it is inevitable that some are in the business for the money and couldn't care less about their boat wakes and noise. Most abide by set rules to limit wildlife disturbance, but if yours doesn't, pipe up and tell him or her to slow down.

If you've come to Tortuguero, you've probably come to turtle watch. Thousands of visitors arrive every season to walk along the beach in search of mother turtles looking for a good nesting spot. You must be accompanied by a guide to visit the beach at night during nesting times; turtle tours leave at 8pm and 10pm nightly during the season (US$10 per person). Any of the tour companies mentioned can hook you up with a tour, or you can just show up at the ranger station a few minutes before the tour begins and tag on to a group. Wear dark clothing and note that no torches or cameras are allowed as they can distract and confuse the turtles and lure predators.

Meet the arboreal mangrove tree crab.

Tortuguero

The colourful houses and fuchsia borders of Tortuguero Village sit to the north of the park. It is connected by gravel pedestrian paths and wooden plank walkways, with one main 'avenue' running the length from the Caribbean Conservation Corp at the northern tip, all the way down to the park entrance at the Cuatro Esquinas ranger station. For its tiny size and remote location, there are a surprising number of restaurants, lodgings, and tourist services on offer, yet it manages to maintain a local charm, despite the overwhelming number of visitors. The western side of the park has a different ambience since it is continually threatened by logging, hunting and commercial interests; the community battles proposals for roads; and pollution is a problem.

The helpful **Tortuguero Info Center** (100m south of northern docks, 2709 8015, tortuguero_info@racsa.co.cr) next to the yellow Casa Marbella is manned by local guide and information guru Victor Barrantes, who also runs **Cabinas Tortuguero** (*see p282*). Victor is the go-to guy for flights and transport details: stop in for free information and to set up tours and activities. The centre is open from 8am to 6pm daily. In the same building Canadian biologist and guide Daryl Loth, the owner of the lovely **Casa Marbella**, also offers tours and is extremely knowledgeable about the area and its wildlife. If all the peace and quiet has you craving an adrenaline rush, the ICT approved **Tortuguero Canopy** (at Evergreen Lodge, 2709 8215, US$35), part of the Pachira enterprise, is a safe and fun choice for zip-lining. Wind down with a massage or chocolate body treatment at the **Tortuguero Jungle Spa** (at Anhinga Lodge, 2709 8187) or try **Natural Beauty Massage** (next to park entrance, 2872 5375).

EXCURSIONS

Cerro Tortuguero hill is about six kilometres (3.5 miles) from the village and is good hiking territory. The main route is an easy 119-metre (390-foot) climb to the highest point, great for panoramic views. You'll need a guide to reach the hill by boat.

This area is also renowned for impressive fishing hauls, and sport fishermen often return with snapper, tarpon, snook, rainbow bass, grunt and other big swimmers. Several operators in town offer fishing trips. **Caribbean Fishing** (Pachira Lodge, 2709 8215) runs trips to Barra del Colorado, Barra del Parismina and Barra del Tortuguero, where fresh and salty waters merge. **Caribeño Fishing Tour** (50m south of Miss Junie's, 2709 8026) offers similar trips and nightly turtle tours. **Tortuguero Sports Fishing** (2709 8072, http://tortuguerosportfish.tripod.com) charges US$200 for up to three people for a full-day tour but will also take you out on shorter expeditions for US$65 per hour.

Most travellers cruise past the tiny fishing hamlet of **Parismina**, wedged between the Río Parismina and the Caribbean Sea, 50 kilometres (31 miles) south of Tortuguero. Fishing opportunities in quiet waters and prime turtle watching on less touristy beaches make this little village worthy of note. The waters and an offshore reef teem with life, great for both anglers and snorkellers. From the dock a dirt path leads to the village. Very basic services, a church and soccer field comprise the town centre. Lodging is backpacker friendly and makes a change from the usual all-inclusive fishing lodges.

Like its counterparts to the north, Parismina is only accessible by boat. Public boats meet buses from Siquirres (4am and noon Monday to Friday; 6am and 2pm Saturday and Sunday) at Caño Blanco. After a two-hour bus trip it's a 15-minute boat ride. You can also hire a boat from Caño Blanco or jump on a boat heading to Tortuguero and ask to be let off at Parismina.

Where to eat & drink

For a town that can only be reached by boat via a messy network of canals or by plane, Tortuguero has a good number of decent restaurants, though prices are generally higher than in the rest of the country due to the logistical challenges of bringing supplies to the area. If you stay at any of the outlying lodges, (very good) meals will probably be included, although it's worth skipping a buffet or two to explore the Caribbean offerings in the village. Probably the most famous eaterie in town is **Miss Junie's** (100m north of Paraiso Tropical dock, 2709 8102, main courses US$10), a tropical dining room that has evolved from the canteen started by Junie's mother, Miss Sibella, in the 1940s. Miss Junie Martinez herself can be found in the kitchen at all hours of the day, simmering down coconut milk for dishes like coconut curried mackerel and jerk chicken.

Miss Miriam II (100m south of football pitch, 15m in from beach, 2709 8107, main courses US$7) is a decent restaurant with cabins, although it is often closed during the low season. Just up from Miss Miriam's on the north-west corner of the football field, **La Casona** (2709 8092, main courses US$6) is a great place to meet fellow travellers and grab a relatively cheap hearty meal in an outdoor dining room lit with paper lanterns. For a

Caribbean

complete change of scene, **Budda Café** (next to police station, 2709 8084, main courses US$7) is a relaxed bohemian pad overlooking the river that feels more like a lounge spot you'd find in the East Village or Brick Lane. Ignore the trendiness for a bit and enjoy tasty pastas, crêpes, salads and fancy cocktails, amid the aroma of *nag champa* incense. Heading past the police station and towards the Paraíso Tropical dock, **Dorling's Bakery & Coffee Shop** (100m south of Muelle Paraíso Tropical, 2709 8132, main courses US$5) serves up fancy coffee drinks to wash down the best baked goods in town. Try the guava pie, or sit down for a simple meal in the tiny dining area.

Where to stay

There are basically two types of lodging in Tortuguero: package resorts and surfer crash pads. The more expensive hotels – catering to organised tour packages – are across the canal and are accessible only by boat. The budget options and a few B&Bs that cater to the independent traveller are generally more basic, but make convenient bases for both the park and beach. Camping is possible near the Cuatro Esquinas ranger station, but be prepared to rough it at the marshy site.

Among the nicest lodges are those belonging to the well-run Pachira group. **Pachira Lodge** (Tortuguero Lagoon, 2256 7080, www.pachiralodge.com, US$188-$445 per person) is a complex of 88 large and breezy rooms in wooden cabins, all with two double beds (the six honeymoon suites have kings) and simple, locally inspired bamboo furnishings. An extension of the Pachira complex offers similar rooms at **Anhinga Lodge**, which has identical facilities plus the **Jungle Spa** (2709 8187) for appointments by guests and non-guests alike. Also part of the Pachira family, the **Evergreen Lodge** (on the canal, 2256 7080/2257 2242, www.pachiralodge.com, US$55 per person basic package), situated across the canal, offers less of a resort experience with its quiet network of 36 bungalows in the jungle.

The combination of classy lodge and village can be found at only one place in Tortuguero, **Mawamba** (1km north of Tortuguero village, 2293 8181, www.grupomawamba.com, US$198-$263 per person). Perfectly pruned gardens sit on a sand bar between the Tortuguero lagoon and Caribbean Sea, within walking distance of the village and park.

Princesa Cabinas & Restaurant (100m north of football field on the beach side, 2709 8131, US$15-$25 per person) is what used to be Cabinas Sabina and is now owned by Miss Miriam's kids, who run all the 'Miriams' and

'Princesas' in town. Princesa has a strip of decent double rooms near the restaurant of the same name and a newer complex next door dubbed Princesa Resort with spacious and mercifully air-conditioned rooms.

The cheapest of the Princesa offerings is at **Cabinas Princesa Río**, south of the public dock, which has nine quiet rooms hanging over the river – a bargain at US$10 per person considering the location. For a few bucks more staff will make you breakfast.

Also a decent budget spot, **La Casona** (north-west of football pitch, 2709 8092, lacasonatortuguero@yahoo.com, US$20 double) has nine basic doubles with fans and a good restaurant. Located closer to the park, **Cabinas Tortuguero** (150m north of the park entrance, 2709 8114, www.cabinastortuguero.com, US$25 double) is a well-kept place with 11 clean doubles plus hot water, fans and hammocks.

Resources

Hospital
EBAIS Health Clinic & Emergency Care
across from Super Las Tortugas (8841 8404).

Internet
Café Internet *50m south of school (2709 8058).* **Open** 9am-9pm daily.

Police station
The blue police station 75m north of public dock (2709 8199).

Getting there

By air
Sansa (www.flysansa.com) and **Nature Air** (www.natureair.com) have flights from San José.

By boat
The most popular way to get to Tortuguero is to take a boat from Moín. Package tours often depart from here, as do the 3pm boats run by **Ruben Viajes Bananero S.A.** (Tortuguero information centre, 100m north-east of park entrance, 8382 6941, www. viajestortuguerocostarica.com). More expensive private boats depart throughout the day. For Barra, you can take a boat from Tortuguero to Pavona at 6am then wait for the 2pm boat to Barra. Another option is to travel to Barra by boat from Puerto Viejo de Sarapiquí. Several lodges operate private *lanchas* (launches) between Puerto Viejo de Sarapiquí, Limón and Barra. Contact the Río Colorado Lodge (*see p279*) for more information.

By bus
The cheapest route is via bus to Cariari, then on to Pavona. Take the local bus from Pavona to Tortuguero with **Viajes Clic Clic** (8844 0463/2709 8155); boats to Tortuguero at 8.30am, 1pm and 4pm.

Caribbean South

Afro-Caribbean sounds and smells infuse this gorgeous corner of Costa Rica.

Balmy, palmy **Puerto Limón**.

The city of Puerto Limón and the southern Caribbean coast is where the true soul of Costa Rica's Afro-Caribbean culture resides. Spirit and colour really come alive here. Until relatively recently this region was cut off from the rest of the country. It was not until 1987, when the Guápiles Highway was completed, that it could be easily accessed from other provinces. The remote location and strong Afro-Caribbean heritage nourished a distinctive culture. The food is spicier here, infused with coconut and curry. Stilt houses are brightly painted, and reggae and calypso drift in and out of windows. Lazy surf hamlets fed with ocean breezes are hard to leave, and the unscarred landscape attracts outdoor enthusiasts, nature aficionados and those curious to see a different wildlife.

While Puerto Limón itself is run-down and of little interest to most tourists, it serves as the gateway to a host of enchanting beach spots and impressive national parks. The popular **PN Cahuita** (*see p288*) was founded to preserve 20 square kilometres (7.7 square miles) of coral reef and coast, and is excellent for snorkelling. You can hike along a wide trail that divides the beach from the jungle and continues all the way out to **Punta Vargas** (*see p288*). Further south, **Puerto Viejo** (*see p293*) is a lively beach town where you can surf waves or gyrate your hips on reggae nights. People love to dance here and after a cocktail or two, you'll find it's hard to resist. The town's cosmopolitan vibe can make for a fun few days. Further down the coast, **Refugio Nacional de Vida Silvestre Gandoca-Manzanillo** (*see p300*) is a section of protected land and sea. And the 12-kilometre (7.5 mile) stretch between Puerto Viejo and **Manzanillo** (*see p299*) has some of the coast's prettiest beaches.

A tropical climate with average annual temperatures of 26°C (79°F) means this region is always warm, but it is also rainy. A colossal 2,997mm to 5,080mm (118 to 200 inches) is the average annual rainfall and generally there is no guaranteed best time to visit, although from August to November it tends to stay a little drier (but bring your rain jacket).

Puerto Limón

A lively tropical port city with a dodgy reputation, Puerto Limón – or simply Limón as it is more commonly called – has little to offer the typical tourist. It is often either passed through or used as a jumping-off point for more attractive destinations such as Tortuguero to the north, or the beaches to the south. Cruise ships dock here regularly – but it is a disappointment for passengers, who come off the boat looking for another Caribbean paradise only to find a gritty industrial port.

Josefinos (San José residents) badmouth Limón as being dirty and unsafe, but the residents of Limón are proud of their heritage and, like most provincials everywhere, couldn't give a fig about what the capital-dwellers think. This is especially evident during **Día de la Raza** (Heritage Day, also known as Columbus Day) on 12 October, when thousands of Ticos flock to the centre during five days of Carnival festivities (*see p286* **Life's rich carnival**) that involve street parades, drinking, dancing and plenty of hooting and hollering chaos. Hotels are booked well in advance, although options further down the coast may still have availability.

Sadly, the Costa Rican government has generally neglected the region. An earthquake in 1991 didn't help matters, demolishing an already poorly maintained infrastructure. Among the casualties was the famous jungle train that once linked Limón to San José. While roads and bridges have since been rebuilt, this region is still the poorest in the country, and political and cultural tensions between Limón and the capital are constant. There is talk of regeneration and some major investment in the area, but no one is holding their breath.

While Limón doesn't live up to its hyped reputation as a haven for criminals, muggings, thefts and some impressively creative con-artist scams do happen. Don't flaunt valuables or hang out in the park or on the streets after dark, and be sure to lock up your belongings and your room. Take the usual precautions and you should have nothing to worry about. *Avenidas* (avenues) run east to west in sequential order, parallel to the railway tracks that run to the port. *Calles* (streets) intersect the avenues and run from north to south perpendicular to the waterfront.

Sightseeing

Take a wander for a few blocks and you'll see some interesting architecture, and the people-watching is good too. The main drag is Avenida 2, more often referred to as **Market Street** since this is where vendors hawk everything from clothing to electronics to pirated CDs. The pedestrian mall continues into the **Mercado Central** (Avenida 2, entre Calles 2 y 3), an entertaining and bustling local market that is great for grabbing a bite to eat and watching typical Tico life.

Down by the water, **Parque Vargas** (entre Avenidas 1 y 2) is the city's main attraction, though it's really nothing to brag about. It's an eerie plaza with towering royal palms and a scattering of benches surrounding a small, crumbling bandstand. Still, it's a pleasant escape from the city and you may even spot tropical birds or sloths hanging out in the trees overhead. Facing the sea, at the easternmost end of the park, a mural depicts the region's tumultuous history since the pre-Columbian era. Waves crash on the long stone *malecón* (sea wall) that winds its way north of the park. Following the wall makes for a pleasant stroll with views of the headland, though you should steer clear of this area at night, as it's a popular mugger hangout.

On the north side of Parque Vargas is the **Municipalidad** (Town Hall), a pale and peeling old building. A few blocks away, the **Black Star Line Hall** (Avenida 5, y Calle 6) was built as a steamship company office in 1922 and is the oldest building in town. Today it serves as a restaurant with authentic Caribbean dishes (*p45* **Spice up your rice**).

EXCURSIONS

There are no nice beaches in town and the puny spots of sand that lie across from the Hotel Continental and the Park Hotel are littered with rubbish; the water is also highly polluted. **Portete** and **Playa Bonita** four kilometres (2.5 miles) north of town are significantly cleaner and people often swim here, but beware of the dangerous riptides. While it doesn't begin to compare to the beaches further south around Puerto Viejo, Bonita sometimes has decent waves, and it has a picnic area and several bars and restaurants that spill out on to the beach. Be very careful if walking on the stretch of road between Limón and Playa Bonita, as drivers carelessly tear down the windy road.

Serious surfers or those just looking for a little offshore adventure will want to visit the undeveloped craggy coast of **Isla Uvita** a kilometre offshore, the site of Christopher Columbus's first landing. Private boats can be hired from the port to make the 20-minute trip. If you haven't yet experienced one of the quintessential Costa Rican canopy tours, book a trip with the pioneer of the pack, **Original Canopy Tour Limón** (Liverpool, 2291 4465, www.canopytour.com), whis has set up zip-lines 45 minutes outside of Limón.

Where to eat & drink

A variety of *sodas* in town and a few nicer places generally serve a mix of local and international food, often throwing in a few random Chinese dishes for good measure. Cheap eats can be found in the Mercado Central, or head up the coast toward Playa Bonita for a nicer meal by the sea in one of the hotels along the way. A few forgettable bars in town provide seedy evening entertainment – you're better off having a drink in a restaurant.

Bar y Restaurant Washington

Avenida 2, y Calle 2 (2758 0509). **Open** 10am-midnight daily. **Main courses** US$8. **No credit cards.**
A sailors' haunt that attracts a mixed crowd and the occasional tourist. It's better for a caipirinha than a *asado*, but the menu offers OK local food and a scattering of Chinese dishes. Karaoke from 7pm to midnight is an experience.

Bio Natura Soda & Café

Calle 6, entre Avenidas 3 y 4 (2798 2020). **Open** 8am-5.45pm Mon-Sat. **Main courses** US$5. **No credit cards.**
A vegetarian haven of crunchy macrobiotic meals, offering tofu, sandwiches and a juice bar. This place doesn't seem to fit in with local offerings but no one's complaining – it's good. The menu doesn't reflect all the day's options so ask what's available.

Black Star Line

Avenida 5, y Calle 5 (2798 1948). **Open** 7.30am-10pm Mon-Sat; 11am-5pm Sun. **Main courses** US$5. **No credit cards.**
Taxi drivers will tell you about this one, a local haunt housed in an old turquoise steamship company building. There are no printed menus but you can point to simple Caribbean classics like rice and beans and boiled plantains from a buffet-style serving bar. And there is always the ol' Tico faithful, *sopa de mondongo* (tripe soup). Don't shy away from the spicy pickled vegetables on every table.

Brisas del Caribe

Avenida 2, north side of Parque Vargas (2758 0138). **Open** 10am-9pm daily. **Main courses** US$6. **Credit** AmEx, DC, MC, V.
Located in the park, this bar-restaurant resembles a cross between a school cafeteria and a local Chinese joint, but serves better food than either. The set buffet with its extensive variety is a good way to sample various local plates. The sprawling tables – and there are lots of them – are good for large groups (though be ready to get attention from the bored riff-raff hanging out on the benches).

El Cevichito

Avenida 2, entre Calles 2 y 3 (8375 2826). **Open** noon-3am daily. **No credit cards.**

Patois patter

Like most elements of culture on the Caribbean coast, the language here is a hybrid of influences. A mix of Spanish, English and English-based patois forms what linguists have dubbed Limón Coastal Creole, also called Mekatelyu (a transliteration of 'make I tell you,' or 'let me tell you' in English) or Limón English.

The unique influence of patois was brought by Jamaican migrant workers and is similar to Jamaican Creole, borrowing many words from English. Though most Caribbean residents speak the nation's official language of Spanish, English infused with Coastal Creole is just as common, if not more so, and often you get a strange mix of the three. Common English words tend to take on new meanings, such as 'alright' normally used for 'hello', and 'okay', which in Limón is often substituted for 'goodbye'. Even some Spanish words get warped in meaning; it comes as a surprise to tourists when they are greeted with a confusing 'adios!' Don't fret about linguistics, though; it is safe to say that since many locals are involved in tourism, most understand and use English as commonly as Spanish.

This is a popular dive that attracts all sorts of people; it has a lively Caribbean feel and friendly bar staff. Loud 1980s elevator music during the day clashes with the Bob Marley posters, but it's a good spot to grab an afternoon cold one and watch passers-by. Nights, with their unbalanced guy to girl ratio, can get predictably rowdy.

Quimbamba Bar & Restaurant

Playa Bonita (2795 4805). **Open** 10am-11pm Mon-Sat; 10am-9pm Sun. **No credit cards.**
An open-air deck on the beach next to Reina's, this bar attracts more Ticos than its posher neighbour and serves regional delights such as fried fruit bread with beans.

Reina's Restaurant

Playa Bonita (2795 0879). **Open** 8am-midnight Mon-Fri; 8am-6am Sat; 8am-8pm Sun. **Main courses** US$13. **No credit cards.**
Located right on Playa Bonita and hands down the swankiest place around, Reina's is a big open-air bar and restaurant serving pricey prawn cocktails, ceviche, seafood and international dishes, all to the sound of waves and the omnipresent reggaeton. Saturday night beach parties go on until dawn with DJs and dancing. It also rents scooters, jet skis,

Caribbean

Life's rich carnival

Take the Mardi Gras party spirit, add a touch of the circus, a splash of history and swarms of parading sequin-clad dancers and you get one of the most culturally exciting events in Costa Rica. Welcome to Puerto Limón's Carnival. This unique celebration draws tens of thousands of Ticos and tourists to this otherwise unassuming port city each October. But the Limón Carnival differs from many other Catholic-derived events.

Historically, the event commemorated Chrisopher Columbus's arrival in the New World on 12 October, but sentiments throughout the Americas have shifted focus and now it is known as Día de la Raza (Day of the Races) – or its more politically correct title Día de las Culturas (Day of the Cultures). It is a celebration of all the races, cultures and peoples that make up Costa Rica and a salute to what it is to be Costa Rican. It is a time to mingle with fellow compatriots, have fun and celebrate. Something that, even up until the 1940s, was forbidden, as Costa Rica's ruling elite prohibited blacks from entering the Central Valley and highlands. Today such thinking is forgotten and Limón's carnival is an event that signifies friendship and tolerance.

The dancing, food, drink and drums pay tribute to indigenous, Afro-Caribbean, European, Asian and other customs and traditions, all of which shaped the identity and culture of the nation. It is also a great excuse for one epic party. The festivities were initiated by a Limónese man named Arthur King who, inspired by Panama's Columbus Day celebrations, wanted to create something similar at home in Limón.

Over time the party lengthened and it now lasts for a staggering four to five intense days that are filled with dancing in the streets, elaborate costumes, decked-out floats, parades, water fights, boozing and fireworks. Food vendors line the streets, dishing out

everything from sizzling Chinese specialities to Tico *mondongo* (tripe soup) and Afro-Caribbean *rondón* (a spicy coconut stew). Balconies shake beyond capacity as party-goers dance to the sounds of calypso, reggaeton, folk music and rap. The celebratory mood is infectious and people take to the streets and shake it until late into the night. While most of the town boozes from dawn until dusk, there is a designated alcohol-free zone on 'Cultural Street', which runs from the Black Star Line down through town and has carnival games and substance-free fun for kids and their parents.

The centrepiece, however, is the *Gran Desfile* (main parade), usually held on the Saturday preceding 12 October. Seemingly endless streams of bangled, feathered and sequinned dancers take over the streets in a colourful exhibition of booty shaking, drumming and singing. At the end of the day the show winds down with a spectacular fireworks display over the port.

boats, mopeds, motorbikes and just about any other land or water toy you can think of.

Soda Meli

Avenida 3, entre Calles 3 y 4 (2758 1149). **Open** 10am-10pm Mon-Sat; 10am-8pm Sun. **Main courses** US$5. **No credit cards**.
Here you'll find Chinese dishes, seafood platters and the usual *soda* fare featuring rice with anything and everything. The place would have a family feel if it

weren't for the beer-girl and Ferrari posters straigh out of the 1980s peeling off the wall. Smalle portions are available and you can get a good frui smoothie for US$1.50.

Where to stay

There's plenty of budget accommodation in town, though most places tend to be cheap – as in horrible – rather than cheap as in good value.

If you're planning to spend any amount of time here, it may be worth splurging on a beachside hotel up the road towards **Playa Bonita**, or at least paying a little extra for a room that's a bit more comfortable.

Hotel prices increase as much as 50 per cent during Carnival week – around 12 October – and rooms book up fast. You shouldn't have much trouble finding somewhere even at the last minute. Several places close down during the rainy season, but the ones we have listed here remain open. We've listed secure and clean options; if bottom-of-the-barrel cheap is what you're after, you'll find it with ease.

Cocorí Hotel Bar & Restaurant

500m south of Playa Bonita (2795 1670). **Rates** US$40 double. **Rooms** 26. **Credit** AmEx, DC, MC, V.
A two-storey lime green building with clean and simple rooms. Rates include breakfast, and rooms numbered 23 to 26 share a balcony that looks over the sea. The open-air terrace restaurant looks across to Playa Bonita and is not too bad, with reasonable prices and a happy hour (6.30am-10.30pm Mon-Sat; closes earlier Sun; main courses US$6). The place fills up with Tico weekenders on Fridays and Saturdays when the restaurant doubles as a disco, so book ahead and bring earplugs.
Bar. Parking (free). Restaurant.

Hotel Continental

Avenida 5, entre Calles 2 y 3 (2798 0532). **Rates** US$12-$15 double. **Rooms** 12. **No credit cards**.
A Limón budget staple that probably hasn't changed or been renovated since it opened, although its quiet location off the main drag near the water gives it some credibility. Dorms with four beds and two double rooms don't have hot water or aircondi-tioning; only one spacious room has airconditioning. An airy hallway gives the place an institutional feel but lets in much needed light. The owners offer similar rooms at Nuevo Hotel Inter-nacional (2758 0434, US$12 double) across the street.
Parking (free).

Hotel Maribú Caribe

3km north-west of Limón en route to Moín (2795 2543/maribucaribe@hotmail.com). **Rates** US$78 double. **Rooms** 56. **Credit** AmEx, DC, MC, V.
A cluster of comfortable bungalows perched on a hilltop overlooking the ocean a few kilometres north-west of Limón is one of the nicer options in the area, popular with business travellers, families and package tourists. Rooms of varying quality have airconditioning, TV and huge showers with steam-ing hot water, almost making up for the shamelessly tacky 1960s decor. There is no beach access, but the location is very pretty and you can hear the waves lapping the shore while you're eating in the restaurant (open 6.30am-10pm Mon-Sun; main courses US$7).
Bar. Business centre. Parking. Pool (outdoor). Restaurants (2). TV.

Hotel Miami

Avenida 2, entre Calles 4 y 5 (2758 0490/ hmiamiLimón@yahoo.com). **Rates** US$27 double. **Rooms** 35. **No credit cards**.
This freshly painted green building is the best mid-range option around, with clean and light rooms, all with private baths, fan, TV and phones, and some with air-conditioning.
Internet (wireless, free). TV.

Hotel Palace

Calle 2, entre Avenidas 3 y 4 (2758 1068). **Rates** US$20 double. **Rooms** 3. **No credit cards**.
There are three simple doubles at the Palace, each with a private bathroom. A shared balcony on the second floor of this crumbling, but architecturally lovely, building faces the street. Sweet and helpful owner Lilian lives at the back of the hotel with her family and could be anyone's granny (although it could be argued that she went a little overboard with the crucifix scheme in the common area). Still, it feels safe and this is one of the best budget options in town if you overlook the shortcomings.

Park Hotel

Avenida 3, entre Calles 1 y 2 (2798 0555/parkhotel Limón@ice.co.cr). **Rates** US$54-$57 double. **Rooms** 32. **Credit** AmEx, MC, V.
This is the fanciest place in town but is still rather basic. The building is flamingo pink and features 32 nondescript rooms with private bathrooms. A few dollars extra buys more space with a sea view and a balcony. The rooms don't make up for the charm the desk staff lack, though they are cleaner and bet-ter equipped than any other hotel in the centre.
Bar. Gym. Internet (shared terminal, free). Parking (free). Restaurant. TV.

Resources

Hospital

Hospital Facio *Avenida 6 at the Malecón (2758 2222/ 0580 emergencies).*

Internet

Internet Pascal *north of park on Avenida 2 with second location west of Mercado Central in centre (2758 8079).* **Open** 8am-11pm Mon-Sat; 9am-11pm Sun.

Police station

Avenida 3, y Calle 8 (2799 1437).

Post office

Avenida 2, y Calle 4. **Open** 7.30am-5pm Mon-Fri; 8am-noon Sat.

Getting there

By air

Sansa (www.flysansa.com) and **Nature Air** (www.natureair.com) offer regular daily flights from around the country to a small airstrip 4km south of town, from where you can take a taxi into town.

Caribbean

By road

Daily buses leave San José from the **Gran Terminal del Caribe** (Avenida Central, entre Calles 15 y 17) every half hour from 5am to 7pm and arrive at **Terminal Caribeño** (Avenida 2, entre Calles 7 y 8) 3hrs later. Local buses depart from Sixaola in the south, passing through Puerto Viejo (2hrs) and Cahuita (1.5hrs) every hour from 5am to 6pm. There are also 5 daily buses from Manzanillo (2.5hrs). They pass through Puerto Viejo and Cahuita before arriving at **Autotransports Mepe** (Avenida 4, y Calle 2) in Limón.

Cahuita

Once a sleepy Rastafied beach village, Cahuita is now slowly waking up. New restaurants and nicer accommodation options have gradually turned the town into a decent tourist stop-over. Its location also helps since it's the first place you hit heading down the coast from Limón. The 'town' is really just two potholed gravel roads running parallel to the coast, with a few restaurants and hostel-dotted streets. From here south it's full-on island holiday mode. That's not to say that there isn't plenty to keep you active. The big draw is **PN Cahuita** (*see right*), one of the coast's best national parks and home to one of the few remaining healthy coral reefs; there's great snorkelling here from March to June and from September to November. Off **Playa Vargas** marine life includes tropical fish, coral, crustaceans, shellfish, lobsters and larger mammals. Landlubbers can hike or bike and watch for howler monkeys, white-faced capuchins, sloths, iguanas, birds and snakes along park trails that lead through thick jungle to sandy beaches with calm waters ideal for swimming.

Just up the coast, the mysterious dark sand of **Playa Negra** is another place to get wet and catch some waves. Surfboards and kayaks can be rented (US$10 for two hours) across from the Reggae Bar. A trail through the jungle behind Playa Negra leads to **Long Beach**, a more secluded nook further up the coast past the headland, which has people-free snorkelling. A number of places around town offer similar day trips, including glass-bottomed boat rides and snorkelling in the park; tours to indigenous reserves and chocolate factories; deep-sea fishing adventures; guided hikes; and toucan and turtle tours. Shop around for the best prices. **Mister Big J's** (2755 0353) next to Cabinas Palmer in the middle of town is a trusted name for local expeditions. 'Big J' (the very friendly Mr Joseph Spencer) has been taking visitors on every kind of trip imaginable for years; 'One stop info? I'm the man!' exclaims the yellow sign at his shop. **Tourística Cahuita** (2755 0071, dltacb@racsa.co.cr)

opposite the supermarket on the main strip is run by Thomas and Tommy Thompson, a father-son duo from California who offer similar tours at competitive prices. Across the way, Willie at **Willie's Tours** (8843 4700, www.willies-costarica-tours.com) speaks German, English and Spanish with a bit of a grunt, but is especially knowledgeable about local indigenous villages and will take you there for US$35. He also gives free internet use with any tour. Serious sport fishers and those looking to get out on deep water will want to hunt down Roberto, one of the top fishing guides in the area, at **Roberto's Tours** (75m south of the park centre, 2755 0117). Roberto offers a variety of shore-based and deep-sea excursions along with a host of other local trips for the non-fisherman, and he'll even bring back your snapper and cook it up in his restaurant next to the agency.

Cahuita Tours (50m south of police station, 2755 0000/ 0232), located towards the end of the strip as you head to Playa Negra, is one of the oldest outfitters in town, and offers the usual array of excursions. Finally, if you're looking to customise your own adventure or simply want the excuse to talk to one of the most interesting and knowledgeable people in the area, local taxi driver, guide, character and jack-of-all-trades **Pino** (8351 7927) will pick you up and take you wherever you want to go while telling you about it in four languages (Italian, German, English and Spanish).

In town, 25 metres from the Supermarket Safari is **Kid's Corner** (2755 0372, 3-10pm daily, admission by donation), a tiny volunteer-run community centre with table football, domino and backgammon tables, board games and other non-electronic sources of entertainment. It's designed to be a safe – no alcohol or smoking allowed here – alternative to brain cell-burning arcade games.

EXCURSIONS

Most people come to this area to visit **PN Cahuita**, ten square kilometres (3.9 square miles) of protected ocean and land that make up one of the country's smallest but most frequented national parks. Fourteen kilometres (nine miles) of beach divide mangrove swamps and a towering canopy on one side from one of Costa Rica's few living coral reefs, about 500 metres offshore. A footbridge leads into the park at the southern end of Cahuita village, passing through the **Kelly Creek Ranger Station** (2755 0461, admission by donation). It's open from 6am to 5pm daily. From here you can access the beach, or walk along seven kilometres (4.5 miles) of nature trails where you're likely to spot a variety of jungle wildlife.

o chance of missing the tree-dwelling yellow eyelash viper.

he main park entrance at **Puerto Vargas anger Station** (2755 0302, admission US$6) about three kilometres south of Cahuita off ighway 36 and is open from 7am to 4pm uesday to Sunday. You can walk from one end : the park to the other, but be careful with coming tides that can catch visitors off guard. he living coral reef between **Punta Cahuita** d **Puerto Vargas** draws the most attention d makes for some stunning underwater xploration. Snorkellers can swim out through e calm waters from Puerto Vargas, or hire a uide to go out further by boat, to explore this rea of protected marine life, home to some 500 pecies of warm-water fish, dazzling corals, rustaceans and two interesting shipwrecks. Be ure to ask rangers where to go – or take a local uide – as tides can be dangerous. Remember ot to touch the reef or its inhabitants, both of which are fragile and increasingly protected by w. Other nearby wilderness dangers include e white-faced capuchin monkeys on Playa argas, who sometimes form gangs and ggressively search for snacks. Too much ttention from tourists has turned the biting uggers into a real problem – food isn't good or their health or manners. Camping is no nger permitted.

A good stop on the way to or from Limón, or y arranged tour from Cahuita, is **Aviarios el Caribe** (2750 0775, www.ogphoto.com/ aviarios, admission US$30) 31 kilometres (19 miles) south of Limón on Highway 32 and open daily from 6am to late afternoon. It is a small, privately owned wildlife sanctuary and sloth refuge on an island in the Río Estrella delta. The centre features a unique sloth research centre, rescued sloths, canoe tours through the delta and a comfortable B&B should you want to make more than a day out of it. You are guaranteed to spot creatures here, including any number of the over 320 species of bird (and counting) that have been recorded. Regrettably, over recent years this refuge has begun to cater to big tourist groups, but it is still worth at least half a day's visit.

Another worthy destination for the nature enthusiast is the **Reserva Biológica Hitoy Cerere** (2758 5855, admission US$6) 15 kilometres (nine miles) west from the end of the Valle de la Estrella bus line and 60 kilometres (37 miles) south of Limón. Opening hours are from 8am to 4pm daily. Located in the Río Estrella valley, it is one of the wettest and least visited parks in the country. It is, nonetheless, a wonderland of drooping mosses, waterfalls, streams and steep trails. Camping is permitted, though there are no facilities. There is a sign at the turn-off from the road to Valle de la Estrella and from there it is another 15 kilometres (nine miles) to the reserve. Transport and tours can also be arranged from Cahuita.

Show a clean pair of wheels at **PN Cahuita**.

Where to eat & drink

A surprising variety of fresh local food and international offerings can be found at the open-air restaurants scattered around the village along the way to Playa Negra. Start your day at **Café del Parquecito** (behind the central square, 2755 0279, main courses US$6) where a 6am opening and lightning quick service mean you don't have to skip breakfast to make that early morning snorkel tour. Delicious crêpes are overstuffed with fresh fruit, and it also serves lunch and hosts festive Caribbean barbecue dinner parties. Next door, the Italian-inspired **Cocorico Cafeteria** (8997 5459/8313 7502, main courses US$4) is a newcomer on the block, a mother-and-daughter owned establishment serving cappuccinos, home-made pastries, pizzas and ice-creams. Movies or music play in the background and there are books and games for when it rains. The most famous place in town is **Miss Edith's** (50m north of the police station, 2755 0248, main courses US$14), a guidebook favourite that locals rave about too. The restaurant overlooks the ocean and the food is divine, especially the stews. Miss Edith swears the secret is in letting the coconut milk simmer, and judging by how long it takes to get your food, she must be doing a good job.

It's also worth noting that Miss Edith now offers cooking classes, and that the restaurant doesn't serve alcohol.

Restaurant La Fe (next to the central square, 2755 0078, main courses US$10) is just as good for Afro-Caribbean specialities, though it's a bit pricey. Ask Walter for the premier Plato Bumbata, a mixed seafood dish steeped in special sauce. Also on the expensive side, but serving tasty food, is **Coral Reef Restaurant** (next to Cocos, 2755 0133, main courses US$10) which serves big portions of seafood such as red snapper in coconut sauce. It has an airy outdoor dining room upstairs. For good local eats on the cheap, head around the corner on the main perpendicular side street, where **Restaurante Tranquilo** (8887 1325, main courses US$5) serves fresh *casados* and hearty meals on a mariner-themed porch.

When Caribbean fare starts feeling heavy, the Colombian and vegetarian **restaurant Natural Ingrid** (across from Supermarket Safari, 2755 0409, www.cahuita.biz, main courses US$6) makes 'everything with love'. Making 'pizza not war' is the task up the road at **Pizza 'n' Love** (150m from the park entrance towards town, 2755 0317, main courses US$6-$12), and they do it well with stupidly named but intelligently made pies like 'Revolution' nd 'LSD' (with prawn, mushrooms and sweet peppers). Reggae rules here and a big screen shows soccer games and music videos. The fusion food at **Cha Cha Cha** (north end of village centre, 2394 4153, main courses US$8) is a delightful escape from typical cuisine, where glowing lanterns hang over intimate outdoor tables, making this place the most romantic dining experience in the area. International dishes from antipasto to TexMex to Jamaican jerk chicken take you around the globe and, if in doubt, there's always tofu.

For more fusion food with an Asian-African focus, try the new **Sambal Restaurant** across from the Salón Comunal in the centre, 833 8553, main courses US$10). Two-for-one cocktails are served alongside spring rolls and curries from 5pm to 7pm in a classy lounge area decorated with African motifs. Up at the end of Playa Negra, chunky and fresh home-made meals are served alongside a tranquil porch backed by rainforest at **Bananas** (2km north of Cahuita village at Cabinas Algebra, 2755 0057, main courses US$6).

If you're looking to party, head to nearby **Puerto Viejo de Talamanca**, as Cahuita has only a few good spots to grab a beer and listen to (often live) music. **Coco's** (town centre, 2755 0437) is undeniably the main bar and party place. Live music on Mondays, Fridays and some Saturdays brings in a big crowd and you'll want to get your groove on, or at least grab one of the tables outside and watch. Music varies but includes plenty of reggae, and there's karaoke on Sunday. Although women may get lots of attention from locals on the prowl, the threshold from annoying to threatening is rarely crossed. **Ricky's Bar** (2755 0228) next door doesn't get quite as wild but brings in live bands and has a well-used and abused dancefloor. Up the beach, **Chao's Paradise** (next to Cabinas Reggae at Playa Negra, 8828 6814, main courses US$11) is another Jah-loving haven and sometimes has live calypso. It also serves fresh food featuring the day's catch. Next door, the crew at **Reggae Restaurant & Bar** (main courses US$7) are fun to chat to over a drink, but ordering food takes time.

Where to stay

These days there are a number of places to stay in town, most of which are dotted along the route north-west to Playa Negra. The cheapest places are in the town centre, while pricier hotels, bungalows and a few more modest cabins are a kilometre or two from the village.

In the centre of town, **Cabinas Palmer** (50m east of the central square, 2755 0435,

cabinaspalmer@gmail.com, US$20 double) is a quality backpacker hangout with 16 rooms that have fans, private bathrooms and added touches like soaps and fancily folded towels. Rooms have their own hammocks and surround a courtyard. Down on the shore, **Spencer Seaside Lodging** (on the water at the end of the street from the central square, 2755 0219, hernanspencer@hotmail.com, US$16-$20 double) is a two-storey block of concrete cookie-cutter rooms, but bathrooms have piping hot water and the place couldn't be much closer to the lapping waves. Shell out the extra four dollars for a nicer double room upstairs. The **Hotel Belle Fleur** (50m from the park entrance next to Super Vaz, 2755 0283, hotelbellefleur@hotmail.com, US$20-$50 double, dorms US$8 per person) has almost as much character as its lively manager Mustafa, who can hook you up with tours and recommend the best places in town. There are ten rooms, all of which are cheap, clean and hideously decorated. (Local artist Franciso Ureña's fascinating murals depicting local indigenous culture on the building's exterior make up for it, though.) Hot water showers are big enough to party in, and several smarter suites in separate buildings have kitchens, air-conditioning and TV. Across the road, **NP Cahuita Hotel & Restaurant** (at the park entrance, 2755 0244, www.cahuitanational parkhotel.com, US$45 double) is rather nondescript, but you could skip rocks across the waters of the park from the balcony (don't). Rooms are well kept and are equipped with safes, air-conditioning, mini-fridges and – on the way at the time of writing – TVs. There's a tour agency on site – **Caribe Tropical** (2755 0065), which offers all the usual excursions – and a good open-air restaurant downstairs with reasonable prices, given its touristy location.

Across the road, to the right as you face the park entrance, sits a cluster of fine hostels and bungalows at varying prices. The nicest is **Alby Lodge** (150m around the corner from the park entrance, 2755 0031, www.albylodge.com, US$40-$50 double), a jungle arrangement of four bungalows with peaceful seating areas in immaculately kept grounds. Cabins have a private feel with overhanging palms and flower hedges and are spaciously situated around a meditation pond. The feel is easygoing with a communal gazebo kitchen and dining area. About 50 metres down the same side road, **Villa Delmar** (100m west of the park entrance, 2755 0392, www.villadelmarcr.com, US$18-$25 double) houses an eclectic array of wildly varying rooms. From private bungalows with TVs and mini-fridges – a snip at US$18 – to rooms in a house of four, the choice is yours.

(Sadly, you have less control over the decor, which is uniformly underwhelming.) Next door, a hibiscus-covered archway leads to **Cabinas Linda's Secret Garden** (150m west of the park entrance, 2755 0327, US$17-$20 double), one of the strangest places in town (and certainly the only one that sounds like it was named after a pulp erotic novel), with plenty of character and plenty of characters. Its five slightly musty double rooms and a dorm for four have private bathrooms and feature creative artwork. This place is quirky to say the least, but is a clean and secure budget option.

If dirt cheap is your priority you'll find a row of choices just past the old bus stop towards the ocean. **Cabinas Smith** (50m from the old bus stop, 2755 0068, US$12-$16 double) is unquestionably the best bet out of the three options here. Lovely owner Joyce keeps five clean rooms with newly remodelled bathrooms and a shared kitchen in good nick. A row of four double rooms at **Cabinas Bobo Shanti** (50m from the old bus stop, 2755 0198, US$8 per person) are decorated with Jamaican flag colours and they face the rooms at Cabinas Smith as if in a stand-off (Cabinas Smith wins). The dark rooms at **Cuartos Jabirus** (no phone, US$7 per person) are the cheapest in town, which is probably all we need to say.

Heading up the beach toward Playa Negra the options are better, though the trade-off is you'll have to make the hike (or bike) into town. It's still an easy walk from the French-Canadian owned **El Encanto B&B** (300m from the fork to Playa Negra, 2755 0113, www.elencanto bedandbreakfast.com, US$75 double), which has three nicely decorated rooms in a modern bungalow, three additional rooms in a house with a shared kitchen, and one apartment that sleeps four, centred around a pretty pool. Buddha statues are placed around tropical gardens and several clusters of caged parakeets hang shrine-like in the centre of the grounds. Staff speak French, English and Spanish.

Further along as you approach Playa Negra are four colourful bungalows at **Centro Turístico Brigitte** (50m from Playa Negra, 2755 0053, www.brigittecahuita.com, US$25-$65 double). The bungalows are simple but well cared for and are painted with cheerful murals. One larger house has a kitchen and sleeps up to six. Swiss native Brigitte also keeps horses on the premises and gives tours along the beach to a waterfall, the moonlight tour being a special highlight. Around the corner on the same road, **Coral Hill Bungalows** (200m from Playa Negra, 2755 0479, www.coralhillbungalows.com, US$105-$116 bungalows) provides some of the most pleasant – if not the nicest – accommodation in the area. American-Swiss couple Joe and Chris Cannon have extensive experience working on luxury yachts and have made it their mission to pay meticulous attention to personalised service and detail – and they don't miss a step. Three boutique bungalows are designed to make guests feel like they're in their own mini-jungle oasis, with quality mattresses, tiled walk-in showers, home-made soaps and hand-painted sinks. A delicious breakfast featuring local breads and tropical fruits is served outdoors among aromatic blossoms. Also fabulous at the upscale end is **Hotel La Diosa** (1.5km north of Cahuita past the end of Playa Negra, 2755 0055, www.hotel ladiosa.net, US$64-$110 double and bungalow). Scattered across tidy grounds and tended gardens are bright bungalows of various sizes and several elegant double rooms – one with a jacuzzi. A path through flowering trees leads to a few park benches overlooking a small private patch of coast. The owners have also just opened a yoga and meditation centre deeper in the jungle (www.thegoddessgarden.com).

Just before La Diosa, **Chalet & Cabinas Hibiscus** (100m north of Playa Negra, 2755 0021, www.hotels.co.cr/hibiscus.html, US$50-$60 bungalows) sits on the water overlooking a pretty stretch of dark coral. Several simple wood and stone bungalows are adequate for the price, but the two chalet-style houses sleeping up to ten are great value for families or groups on extended stays. Families on a budget will also like the German-owned **Cabinas Algebra** (1.5km from Cahuita and 100m north of Playa Negra, 2755 0057, www.cabinasalgebra.com, US$18-$33 cabin). The rustic cabins are built on old farmland and feel far from civilisation. The owners serve wholesome food at a small porch restaurant, **Bananas**, which is also a good place to sit and read (there's a lending library with English and German books).

Resources

Hospital
Clinica Hone Creek *5km north of Puerto Viejo at El Cruce (2750 0220).*

Internet
Spencer Seaside Lodging *on the water at end of street from central square (2755 0027/0210).* **Open** 9am-9pm daily.
Centro Turístico Brigitte *50m from Playa Negra (2755 0053).* **Open** 9am-6pm Mon-Sat.

Police station
Guardia Rural *150m north of village centre (2755 0217).* Call 911 for emergencies.

Post office
150m north of village centre next to police station (2755 0096).

Watching the fishing boats come in around **Puerto Viejo**.

Getting there

Buses from San José pass Limón before continuing on down the coast to Cahuita and on to Sixaola. Local buses depart from Limón every hour from 5am to 6pm. Petrol can be hard to come by in the south, so be sure to fill up when you have the chance.

Puerto Viejo

Call it brilliance in science, a blessing from the powers that be, or pure geographical luck; this is one of those paradisiacal spots that has you squinting your eyes tight every once in a while, only to reopen them to make sure you're really there. Wedged between tourmaline-green waters and the dense jungle-covered hills of Baja Talamanca, Puerto Viejo is a funky surfer town 18 kilometres (11 miles) south-east of Cahuita that sees plenty of tourists but has somehow managed to hang on to its spirit – a seductive mix of tranquillity and vivacity. The scenery is straight out of a Club Med brochure – blue ocean meets palm-lined sandy beaches – but this is offset by a cooler vibe. Puerto Viejo has a colourful culture and a unique rhythm influenced by the turtle fishermen who founded the town, the Afro-Caribbean traditions of the Antillean people who came to work on Limón's railway and a scattering of nearby indigenous communities. Then there is a good handful of eccentric expats who probably couldn't make it anywhere else in the world (or wouldn't want to), a constant convoy of backpackers and surfers and a palpable general sentiment that life is good. Bright hand-painted signs point to restaurants and cabins down gravel roads, local kids bask in tidal pools while their parents bring in the day's catch, and the streets are lined with small markets where vendors sell local handicrafts made of shells and seeds. Get wild in town on reggae night or relax on a quiet beach and watch the sunset behind your bungalow.

Surfing is one of the biggest draws here – the famous **Salsa Brava** wave booms from December to March and again in June and July, and there are gentler waves to play on a little further south. There's plenty for non-surfers to do too: good swimming at Playa Negra, in the protected natural pools in front of Stanford's restaurant and along the string of beaches to the south; kilometres of nature trails behind the beach that lead to others in the **Refugio Nacional de Fauna Silvestre Gandoca-Manzanillo**; indigenous reserves, botanical gardens, butterfly farms and waterfalls to explore; gorgeous strips of secluded sand to nap on; and tours that will take you snorkelling, diving, kayaking, dolphin watching, zip-lining, canyoning, rafting, four-wheel driving and fishing. Notable restaurants fill the village

Caribbean

Gracias a Jamaica!

The vibe of the Caribbean coast just wouldn't be the same if it weren't for the chilled-out sounds of Bob Marley playing in every other bar and the rhythmic reggaeton shrills pumping from passing cars. You can feel the deep roots of Jamaica and the islands in the music played in towns like Limón and Puerto Viejo. Reggae has had a strong influence on these towns and it further distinguishes this region from the rest of the country. Bars and restaurants are hung with images of Bob Marley, and tributes to Jah (Rastafarian for God) are ever present. The colours of the Jamaican flag, red, yellow and green, are seen everywhere from windows to table tops.

Reggae became popular in Jamaica during the 1950s and 1960s, when crowds would gather in the streets and dance to the sounds of experimental DJ backbeats. The poetic lyrics served as the voice and vision for the oppressed, bringing political views and issues to the masses. Back then reggae drew on the Bible and in a sense offered spiritual guidance by praising Jah and the powers of ganja (marijuana). Reggae gained international attention and world following in the 1970s through the legendary Bob Marley and the Wailers, who are still worshipped today as some of the most iconic musical figures of the century.

The 1980s saw the faster reggae-inspired rhythms of dancehall, which combined rap influences with more abrasive beats and lyrics. Then came the digital era, when ragga,

or raggamuffin, a sub-genre of dancehall, used electronic samplings and instrumentation – laying the roots for the more recent explosion of reggaeton, a new generation of blended reggae and dancehall with Latin American styles such as bomba, plena, bachata, salsa and merengue. Though its exact origins are a subject of debate, reggaeton was the Latin American response to North American hip hop, first taking off in rough Puerto Rican neighbourhoods and Panama before skyrocketing throughout Latin America. Highly versatile beats are marked by an interplay of a steady kick drum and syncopated snare, a track derived from the Dem Bow beat produced during the rise of the underground genre in Puerto Rico. The first productions by icons like Daddy Yankee and Master Joe featured a Spanish rapper accompanied by electronicised reggae beats, performed in the famous Playero 37 and Noise clubs. Reggaeton's distinctive rhythms represent a hybrid of many different musical influences and have become wildly popular in Costa Rica and around the globe. These days the most popular tracks are played on loop everywhere on the Costa Rican coast, with songs about everything from streetlife to love, gangs and dancing. It's the top musical choice in dance clubs and parties, where groups (usually of women) face each other and put their back into it, and couples get down and grind, though the versatile beats mean you can dance about any way you want.

---

and line the route heading south to Manzanillo, and the town is also home to the hottest nightlife on the coast.

This region has a reputation for drugs, and not totally without reason. While the weed is cheap and may be tempting to some, it is illegal. Undercover policemen have been prowling around town looking to bust tourists over the past few years and they haven't been afraid to make arrests. It's safe to say that the average Costa Rican jail is the antithesis of the average Costa Rican beach.

EXCURSIONS

A bicycle is the best way to see the area. There is much to explore within 12 kilometres (seven miles) or so in either direction from town and two-wheelers are convenient, fun and cost only US$4 per day. **Playa Cocles** (2km east of town) is home to 'Beach Break' and some

gentler waves for surfers not out to brave Salsa Brava. The surf shop at **Totem Hotel** (Playa Cocles, 2750 0758, www.totemsite.com) rents quality boards and has a surf school, though there are several other spots along the coast that offer the same. When the surf's not good, the snorkelling and diving usually is. Don't miss the spectacular underwater reef world off Manzanillo and to the north near Cahuita. **Reef Runner Divers** (100m east of bus stop, 2750 0480, www.reefrunner divers.com) offers a number of dives and certification courses and is a reputable outfit, as is **Aquamor** (*see p300*), whose shop is down in Manzanillo. Swimmers will want to check out **Punta Uva** and the beach there, one of Costa Rica's most stunning strips of coast, some seven kilometres south of Puerto Viejo. It's possible to walk all the 13 kilometres (eight miles) from Puerto Viejo to Manzanillo if ou're willing to rough it around rocky points nd through a few detours.

This is also a good jumping-off point for afting trips on the Rio Pacuare. **Exploradores Outdoors** (2222 6262, www.exploradores utdoors.com) runs good trips and will pick you up and drop you off at your Puerto Viejo hotel.

You can make your own chocolate the raditional way and learn about the bean and its use at **Cacao Trails** (2756 8186, www.cacaotrails.com, admission US$20) just off the main highway at Hone Creek. There are botanical gardens, a cacao farm, a Caribbean culture museum, a nature trail and canoe tours US$47) through the canals of Cahuita. A four-hour tour includes transport. Learn about exotic fruits and plants at **Finca de la Isla Botanical Garden** (1km west of Puerto Viejo and 200m west of El Pizote Lodge, 2750 0046, ardbot@racsa.co.cr, admission US$5-$10). Open from 10am to 4pm Monday to Friday, the finca cultivates and collects native and imported varieties, and will invite you to sample whatever's ripe.

The **Kekoldi indigenous reserve** is home o some 200 Cabécar and Bribri people, and has opened its community to visitors. The **Asociacíon Talamanca de Ecoturismo y Conservación** (ATEC) (25m west of Café Viejo, 2750 0191, www.ateccr.org) is a grassroots organisation that trains locals as guides for cultural and nature tours of their native Talamanca region, in an effort to promote culturally sound tourism and small ocally owned businesses. Among its highly recommended tours are trips to the reserve, which can include visits to an iguana farm, a community chocolate making project and a waterfall. ATEC's office in Puerto Viejo is open from 8am to 9pm Monday to Saturday and from 10am to 6pm on Sundays. It also has regional and travel information, internet and phone, as well as a small library and gift shop.

If you haven't yet zip-lined through the rainforest canopy by the time you get to Puerto Viejo, the professional (and insured) **Terraventuras** (100m south-west of bus stop, 2750 0750, www.terraventuras.com) will take you to its cabled rainforest oasis. It also offers canyoning into a waterfall in primary forest and other adventures. For water expeditions head 100 metres east of the bus station where you'll find **Juppy & Tino Adventures** (2750 0761/ 0621, closed Sunday), which takes groups out in kayaks on the Sixaola and Estero Negro rivers, out to the Gandoca Lagoon, and around Punta Uva. You can also rent a boat and head out on your own. These and a number of other operators in town offer scores of other tours, from snorkelling and dolphin spotting tours

in Manzanillo to tarpon fishing and four-wheel driving expeditions. Shop around for tours or try **Tropical Tales** (2750 2069, www.tropical tales.co.cr) opposite from the bus stop. Open from 8am to 8pm daily, it is a sort of 'information consolidator' that can give you the latest scoop on all tours, lodging, transport and answer any other questions you have about the area. It also publishes the quirky *Tropical Tales*, a free mini English paper that is worth looking out for.

Where to eat & drink

You can taste the multiculturalism of this region in some of the best cuisine on the coast. Lots of earthy expats and travellers have kept up demand for organic food and healthy eats; Italians brought in fresh pasta; the Afro-Caribbean influence means everything is coconut infused and spicy, and there are even a couple of sushi spots in town. For local delights like *rondón* (a sweet and starchy seafood stew) and *budin* (a moist fruitcake) ask around for the best in town – Miss Lidia dishes out big plates of sizzling Caribbean coconut concoctions at decent prices at **Soda Lidia's Place** (200m south of police station, 2750 0598, closed May, main courses US$5). Next door, **Miss Sam's** (190m south of police station, 2750 0108, main courses US$6) is a travellers' favourite and used to be the best soda in town, though lately it seems to be slacking. A livelier bet is **Soda Tamara** (50m east of Café Viejo, 2750 0148, main courses US$6) where local hero Edwin Patterson started a tiny soda back in the day and saw it evolve into this spot with wholesome home cooking that locals still come for.

You'll be hard pressed to find a Bob Marley-free bar, and the face and music of this reggae hero everywhere. This is most evident at **Jammin'** (100m east of bus station, 2750 3083, main courses US$5), a 'juice and jerk joint' whose menu includes jerk chicken and reads 'Jah bless your path!' It also has surprisingly good breakfast specials. **Chile Rojo** (100m west of Salsa Brava, 2750 0025, main courses US$8) has somehow managed to compile all the global favourites you miss on to a one-page menu, then douse them with a touch of local flavour, with dishes like pad thai with Caribbean lobster, spicy chicken coconut curry, calamari with tahini sauce, and falafel pitta plate. It has recently moved round the corner next to the artisan markets before Salsa Brava, but has plans to move back down the road. Natural foods and local ingredients are almost an obsession at the highly recommended **Bread & Chocolate** (200m south of El Chino, 2750 0723, main courses US$5), where delicious

Caribbean

Life's just swell along **Playa Cocles**. *See p294.*

cinnamon oatmeal pancakes, home-made peanut butter and jam and freshly squeezed lemonade with ginger are served on an open patio. The only place that might give Bread & Chocolate a run for its money on the breakfast front is **Café Rico** (250m south of police station, no phone, main courses US$5), a mellow coffee house (with excellent Costa Rican coffee) serving granola fruit bowls and sandwiches from dawn until 1pm, followed by tea in the afternoon. It also has a few cabins for rent and an eco-friendly laundry service. For bakery goods on the go or an afternoon snack, **Pan Pay** (next to Johnny's Place, 2750 0081, main courses US$3) bakes up croissants and snacks for a song, though options are a bit limited later in the day. **Café Red Stripe** (next to the bus stop, no phone, main courses US$5) has recently reopened with a simple menu featuring smoothies, breakfasts, burritos, and vegetarian snacks that make excellent grab-and-go snacks. (Take note that marijuana ice-cream is no longer served.)

Also cooking vegetarian, vegan and raw macrobiotic dishes with a Caribbean touch is **Veronica's Place** (150m south of Stanford's, 2750 0132, main courses US$5). It also has a closet-sized health food store selling granola goodies and vitamins. **El Loco Natural** (200m south-east of Stanford's on the route to Manzanillo, 2750 0530, main courses US$9),

delivers one of the best overall dining experiences on the coast, and perhaps in the country. Spectacular tropical infusion meals with exotic garnishes are served on a romantically lit veranda with live music on Thursdays and Sundays. The cooks aren't afraid to spice things up if you ask for it *picante*, so you can put the Tabasco back in your bag. Back towards town, **El Parquecito** (a landmark itself on the main strip, 2750 0748, main courses US$12) also has live music on most nights and is a popular spot to kick off the night, though the atmosphere is better than the pricey and so-so food. Down the block, the Italian **Café Viejo** (another landmark at the other end of the block from El Parquecito, 2750 0817, mains US$16) is the classiest spot in the town centre, where mostly gringos and city weekenders go to sip cocktails and eat gourmet pizzas and home-made pastas with fresh mozzarella. But if you're willing to spend that kind of money, better Italian food can be had at the enchanting **Lucia's Restaurant of Amimodo** (200m from Stanford's on the point at Salsa Brava, 2750 0257, main courses US$15), where candlelit tables spill out into sprawling outdoor gardens. **Beto's Pizza & Bar** (same listings as above) in front of the complex is run by Lucia's daughter Michela and her husband and is lower key. Keeping it European is the new **Le Bistrot du Port** (next to markets on main strip, 2750 2079, main courses US$10), which serves French cuisine and offers a set menu including an appetiser, main and dessert for US$10.

Many restaurants double as drinking holes at night, and several feature live music. The Old Bamboo has closed down but **Baga Yaba** (150m south of police station, 8388 4359) has taken over the famous Sunday reggae night, and **Johnny's Place** (25m east of police station, 2750 0445) is still a local staple, though it's a bit run-down. **Salsa Brava** (just off the wave of the same name, 2750 0241/ 0382, main courses US$12) has a fantastic location for a sunset happy hour (deals daily from 5pm to 7pm), but these days it is a better place for a drink than for food.

Though Stanford's has been around for ever, the town's hottest (and only) discotheque has undergone a major makeover and is a bit nicer now. At the end of any Saturday night it still has the best dance party in town and goes on until the small hours when tipsy travellers spill out on to the sand. A bit quieter, **Maritza Bar** (across from the park near bus stop, 2750 0184) has a Wednesday night open jam, salsa on Saturday and live calypso on Sunday. It is also a hotel with decent doubles for US$50, should the night get away from you. A skip away, and churning out live calypso on Thursdays, the **Sunset Bar** (next to the bus stop on the beach, 8311 5610) is a self-proclaimed 'sunny place for shady people' but really attracts all types. Table football and a pool table turn the lower level into a sports bar, while upstairs serves simple, fast(ish) food.

Where to stay

The town centre is full of rooms and cabins, mostly in the middle price range with a handful of more modest options. All sorts of accommodation – including the luxurious – speckle the coast all the way down to **Manzanillo** (*see p299*). With so many options in the area, even the most basic cabins step it up a notch, and **Cabinas Jacaranda** (150m inland of Café Viejo, 2750 0069, www. cabinasjacaranda.net, US$35-$45 double) goes a bit further. There's something calming about the place. Warm colours glow through the Japanese lanterns and mosaic tiling leads you through the gardens. Murals wind around the walls of rooms and mosquito nets take on a more decorative purpose to give what could have been just another hostel an enchanting feel and consequently make it a popular choice.

Just as charming and right around the corner, **Cabinas Guarana** (75m south, 25m west of Café Viejo, 2750 0244, www.hotelguarana.com, US$38 double) is run by a lovely Italian couple who live on the premises and treat the place as an ongoing art project. Adorable cabins with hammock-strung porches and arty touches look over pretty gardens. Friendly staff, free coming and going of guests to the kitchen and friendly attention from Samba, the resident cat, make this place feel like a second home.

Cabinas Tropical (200m south, 25m east of Stanford's, 2750 0283, www.cabinastropical. com, US$40 double) has ten clean and simple rooms on immaculately kept grounds. German owner Rolf is a biologist and can take visitors birdwatching or on wildlife tours. He also runs **Bushmaster Expeditions** (2750 0645/8841 0298) out of the hotel.

Towards the town centre, the tranquil **Casa Verde Lodge** (200m south, 50m east of police station, 2750 0015, www.casaverdelodge. com, US$62-$70 double) is a top pick in its range. Although centrally located it feels far away from it all. Large, breezy bungalow rooms have been made nicer in recent years as is reflected in the higher rates, but you really get what you pay for. Colourful tiled walkways cut through spacious grounds, leading to a landscaped pool area surrounded by bromeliads, orchids and heliconia flowers. There are safes and secure parking, and the Swiss-Costa Rican management speaks English, German and Spanish.

High on a hill behind town and set in the rainforest, **Cashew Hill Jungle Lodge** (100m south-east of football pitch, 2750 0001, www. cashewhilllodge.co.cr, US$75-$125 bungalows) has seven spectacular, individually designed, one- to three-bedroom cottages set in the lodge's wild surroundings without sacrificing the comforts. It's great for couples, families and for long stays. Each bungalow has a fully equipped kitchen, large tiled walk-in showers, custom-made furniture and bohemian decor. All look out into the jungle and several, including the Salsa Brava Cottage, have views of the sea. There is even wireless internet by the dipping pool.

The long-running backpacker favourite is down the beach at **Rocking J's** (600m south of bus station, 2750 0665/0657, www.rockingjs.com, US$4 camping; US$20 cabins), an eccentric mix of quarters in a tree house, budget dorm rooms, and private digs of wildly varying shape and decor (including at least one with a mirrored ceiling). It is also known for its famous 'hammock hotel' where you can rock and snooze to the ocean breezes. Perks include a free taxi service from the bus stop, lots of common areas and a sociable kitchen. Although the place may not be quite as rockin' as it once was, it's still a strong contender among budget options in the area.

Chocolate and bananas are the main crops in the **Reserva Indigena KéköLdi**. *See p295*.

Less remarkable but right in the centre of town, **Cabinas Grant** (100m south of bus stop, 2750 0292, cabinasgrant@costarricense.cr, US$20 double) has basic rooms that sleep from two to six that draw in the skint backpacker crowd. It's worth noting that some of the once highly recommended hostels in town are now the cheapest of the cheap and have crumbled into near coke dens, so be sure to check your choice out in advance to know what you're getting into (we haven't listed any of them here). You shouldn't have a problem finding a place, but reserve during surf season.

Resources

Hospital
Clínica Sunimedica *next to BCR bank in the town centre (2750 0079).*

Internet
Jungle Internet Café *50m south of Café Parquecito (2371 3196/www.junglec.com);* high-speed internet with skype and cameras, international calls and wireless (at cost). **Open** 9am-7pm daily.
ATEC *25m west of Café Viejo (2750 0191/ www.ateccr.org).* **Open** 8am-9pm Mon-Sat; 10am-6pm Sun.

Police station
Guardia Rural *next to Johnny's Place (2750 0230).*

Post Office
Next to BCR bank in the town centre (2750 0404).

Getting there

By bus
Buses from San José to Limón continue on down the coast, stopping at Puerto Viejo. Local buses from Limón depart for the south hourly from 5am to 6pm. **Interbus** (2283 5573, www.interbusonline.com) operates a private fleet of minibuses from San José for US$35 one way.

By car
Drive 13km (8 miles) south from Cahuita until you reach an obvious fork: right heads to Bribri and Sixaola, left takes you another 5km (3 miles) into Puerto Viejo, passing Playa Negra 100m before the village.

Puerto Viejo to Manzanillo

To the east of Puerto Viejo are some 12 kilometres (seven miles) of the prettiest beaches and peaceful hamlets on the coast. A paved but potholed road winds along the coast, skirting the outer edges of the **Reserva Indígena KéköLdi** *(see p295)* and ending at the **Refugio Nacional de Vida Silvestre Gandoca-Manzanillo**, just past the tiny fishing village of **Manzanillo**. On the way,

narrow paths off the route give way to vast expanses of beaches protected by rocky headlands and tiny nooks where towering palms and jungle vines drape over caramel-coloured sands. The public bus only passes every few hours, and though cars do traverse the route, bikes are the far more common means of local and tourist transport and make for a great hop-on, hop-off means of exploring.

Just south of Puerto Viejo, **Playa Cocles** is a long stretch of sand popular with surfers and day-trippers. There are lifeguards. **Playa Chiquita** picks up some four kilometres east, blending with Cocles somewhere along the way but becoming more secluded as you head south, where the jungle starts spilling out to the sea, creating lovely private coves. About eight kilometres east of Puerto Viejo lies **Punta Uva**, easily the prettiest beach on the coast and excellent for swimming. Caimans sometimes hang out in a swampy estuary behind the beach where a river meets the sea. From here it's another five kilometres or so of darker sands to **Manzanillo**, a tiny fishing village and gateway to the spectacular Gandoca-Manzanillo Wildlife Refuge.

The refuge – which stretches from Manzanillo south-east to the Panamanian border and out to sea – is one of the area's top attractions and is well worth a day's exploring. Bike to it, hike through it, boat or snorkel back along the reef, or take a horseriding tour that dips through the refuge's forests and heads out along the beach. **Seahorse Stables** (Punta Cocles, 2750 0468, www.horseback ridingincostarica.com) offers such excursions, along with multi-day trips to Gandoca and other non-horse activities.

Also worth a visit if for nothing else but the scenic location and pleasant hosts is the **Mariposaria** (Punta Uva, 2750 0086, admission US$6) butterfly farm, open from 8am to 4pm. The place is not very commercially oriented but welcomes visitors to explore a screened-in wonderland of Morphos and more than 20 other fluttering species, depending on the time of year. Butterflies are just one excuse to spend time on the property as toucans, sloths, birds and monkeys also dwell here. Nearby is the **Reserva La Ceiba** (off Punta Uva, 2750 0278/8854 2602, www.rpceiba.com, admission with tour US$35). It offers guided trips into the interior of the rainforest on a private reserve. There are also three houses that can be taken over by couples or groups up to six.

EXCURSIONS
Hopping from beach to beach and exploring the sunny nooks and wandering jungle paths

on bike or by foot are the highlights here. Tours in this area are generally the same ones as those offered in **Puerto Viejo** (*see p293*), but it can be cheaper to book water and Manzanillo-Gandoca Refuge excursions directly from Manzanillo. Often they use the same local guides so go directly to boat pilots hanging around Maxi's and on the beach in Manzanillo. Or try **Aquamor** (Manzanillo centre, 2759 9012, aquamor1@racsa.co.cr), which offers diving trips and courses but also organises local guides for other water and land adventures, or Clint at **Pangea** (100m south of Aquamor, 2759 9204, www.megatarponheaven.com).

The pristine nature of this region is largely attributed to the **Refugio Nacional de Vida Silvestre Gandoca-Manzanillo**, 501 square kilometres (193 square miles) of land and 443 square kilometres (171 square miles) of sea, which also include Manzanillo beach and village. The refuge was created in 1985 and covers a variety of habitats, 65 per cent of which is tropical forest and home to a diverse range of species. The park includes one of Costa Rica's two living coral reefs (the other is Cahuita), which extends out five kilometres (three miles) offshore to a barrier reef, where over 400 species of fish, crustaceans, numerous larger marine mammals and five kinds of coral can be seen. Leatherbacks and other endangered marine turtles nest on the beaches between Punta Mona and Sixaola from March to July. You'll also find the nation's only red mangrove swamp and two jolillo palm swamps in the refuge.

A shady trail weaves along the coast in and out of the forest from Manzanillo to Punta Mona and you can stop off and swim along the way. The trail is backed by 40 square kilometres (15 square miles) of life-filled swampland at its south end. At Punta Mona it's worth visiting the **Punta Mona Center for Sustainable Living and Education** (8391 2116, www.puntamona.org), an organic farm and educational centre teaching sustainable farming techniques, where over 200 edible plants are grown. The complex accepts volunteers and is open for day visits and tours on Tuesdays, Thursdays and Saturdays by advance arrangement only.

Where to stay & eat

Tasty eats and the area's nicest lodgings can be found along the route to Manzanillo, with numerous places lining the first part of the way from Puerto Viejo down to Playa Chiquita. Of the more interesting, **La Costa de Papito** (Playa Cocles, 2750 0080, www.lacosta depapito.com, US$69 double) comprises 13 bungalows scattered around a Polynesian themed complex that resembles a summer camp for big kids. You won't be roughing it on bunks here, however; spacious wood-finished rooms with two to five comfy beds have huge tiled baths and private porches. The complex is linked by colourful mosaic tiled paths that lead to the restaurant **Que Rico Papito** (serving breakfast and dinner), a good place to grab a bite to eat and catch some live music (sporadic nights) whether you're staying here or not. Boogie boards can be hired for the day. At the hotel's **Pure Jungle Spa** (at La Costa de Papito, 2750 0536) local cocoa and other natural ingredients are used for luxurious body treatments, massages and facials all in a tranquil thatched bungalow in the middle of the forest.

Somewhere along the way Playa Cocles officially ends and Playa Chiquita begins, stretching east for the next three kilometres (two miles). Near here, the charming **Aguas Claras** (Playa Chiquita, 2750 0131, www.aguasclaras-cr.com, US$70 bungalows) has five pastel-coloured gazebo-style bungalows housing from two to eight, all with full kitchens and set apart on private lots across spacious grounds. **Miss Holly's Deli & Café** (2750 0131, snacks and light meals US$5) on the premises bakes scrumptious goodies and lunches from 8am to 3pm, and has Wi-Fi.

Located on the road to Playa Chiquita, the **Miraflores Lodge** (4km south of Puerto Viejo, 2750 0038, www.mirafloreslodge.com, US$30-$50 double) has rustic rooms in houses on an old cocoa plantation and was one of the first ecological and sustainable tourism lodges in the area, originally built in 1988 with money the owner Pamela made selling exotic plants. Get her to tell you about the heliconia gardens of medicinal plants and the small labyrinth on the grounds, or ask her to set up a trip to a sweat lodge ceremony on the Bribri reserve, with which she is connected. Directly across the street, **Shawandha** (Playa Chiquita, 2750 0018, www.shawandhalodge.com, US$90-$110 bungalow) has some of the nicest digs in the area, with 13 bungalows with luxury touches connected by a maze of wooden walkways, each secluded in its own little pocket of forest. Huge tiled bathrooms have walk-in showers and the room's high ceilings maximise space and keep them cool. An excellent upscale tropical fusion restaurant of the same name is set romantically under a thatched palm roof with low lighting. Try the tropical sea bass, bursting with an inexplicable combination of local flavours.

Beyond Playa Chiquita, some seven kilometres east of Puerto Viejo, Punta Uva begins. It is the most beautiful of Caribbean beaches, with calm waters in a protected cove

Volunteer to help at the **Punta Mona Center for Sustainable Living and Education.**

fantastic for swimming. With its own stretch of sand, the **Tree House** (Punta Uva, 2750 0706, www.costaricatreehouse.com, US$200-$350 double) is one of the most interesting accommodation options in the area, featuring a multi-dimensional house constructed around a massive live sangrio tree. The luxurious cabin sleeps six, and several other options sleep groups of up to that number. It's a pricey but unique lodging experience if you have the cash, though some of the staff aren't as cheery as the surroundings. Cheaper digs and decent eats are available at **Selvin's** (Punta Uva, 2750 0664, US$20-$30 double), where 12 run-down cabins with private bathrooms are located right by the beach. The restaurant has the usual fare and is open at weekends during low season.

If you are staying more than a few days and are looking for an instant home away from home, the highly recommended **Casa Viva** (Punta Uva, 2750 0089, www.puntauva.net, US$50-$130 houses) has three two-bedroom handcrafted homes. Each has a wrap-around porch and hammocks overlooking the beach.

Further down the beach is the very smart camping affair **Almonds and Corals** (2km before Manzanillo, 2759 9032, www.almonds andcorals.com, tent suites US$200-$350 including meals) where screened 'tents'

on stilted platforms have jacuzzis and minibars. An extensive wooden maze of torch-lit walkways connects the jungle suites to a restaurant, spa and the resort's private forest.

At the end of the line in Manzanillo, **Maxi's** (Manzanillo centre, 2759 9061, main courses US$9) has long served as the village's social centre. Locals hang out and play cards downstairs while tourists wander in and out, grabbing a drink at the bar or a bite upstairs.

Several basic cabins are available, though these days there are better sleeping options around the village. Of the best is **Cabinas Faya Lobi** (200m inland of beach, 2759 9167, www.cabinasfayalobi.com, US$25-$30 double) a cheerful two-storey yellow affair with five tidy and quiet rooms surrounding a spick and span open-air kitchen. Stop by the bamboo house next door for moist banana cake (only 75 cents). **Cabinas Bucus** (100m down 1st street on right as you enter village, 2579 9143, meltema1981@yahoo.de, US$25 double), has several lovely simple wood-finished rooms, stone-walled bathrooms and cosy touches. Down the road on the right, **Soda El Rinconcito** (no phone, main courses US$3) gives Maxi's some competition with fajitas, burgers and breakfasts.

Jackass bitters and other cures

The indigenous and other rural peoples of Costa Rica have long relied on plants of the rainforest to cure everything from headaches and parasites, to diabetes and cancer. There are an estimated 265,000 species of flowering plant on the planet and only 0.5 per cent of them have been studied exhaustively by the modern world for their medicinal value. While Western botanists have much to research, indigenous peoples have always lived in harmony with their forests and can describe specific medical uses for as many as 49 to 82 per cent of the plant species in their environments.

Empirically obtained knowledge of native plants and their medicinal uses has evolved through centuries of use by indigenous groups. There is much to learn from their knowledge of medically useful or even life-saving native plants. Many of our common pharmaceuticals are derived from tropical plants, and there are likely to be numerous undiscovered medicines still lurking among the myriad plant species in the world's rainforests. Unfortunately, this invaluable resource is in danger of being lost forever as forests are bulldozed and burned, leaving indigenous groups facing a losing battle to preserve their traditional knowledge and culture. It is already a sad reality that there remain but a few elderly community leaders who retain such knowledge about the identification, collection processes, preparation and medicinal use of plants found in Costa Rican soil.

Some local medicinal plants you may see on your visit are:

Guarumo (*trumpet tree*) A narrow tree with greyish bark, lobed leaves and clusters of pinkish-white spikes. Used as a decongestant and to calm symptoms of asthma.

Chillis (Panama chilli) A hot chilli pepper used as a stimulant.

Gavilana (*jackass bitters*) A scraggly shrub with numerous branches, narrow three-pointed leaves and tiny yellow flowers. Used to combat parasites and fungi; as a douche or bath to fight vaginitis and other infections. And when it is made into a tea, it is thought to cleanse the blood.

Madera negro (*black wood tree*) A thick tree with waxy leaves, purplish flowers and tiny fruits. Leaves are mashed and applied to ulcers, wounds and nappy rash.

Banano (*banana*) The easily digestible fruit we all know is helpful for soothing uneasy stomachs, diarrhoea and ulcers.

Anisillo (*cow foot*) A tall tree with soft leaves and tiny flowers. Leaves are steeped into a calming tea; also used as toilet paper.

Jengibre (*ginger*) Fleshy tuber with pale yellow flowers. The raw root can be chewed or made into tea for relieving digestive problems, vomiting and gas. It can also be applied topically to alleviate muscle pains and stomach cramps.

Bamboo Tall stocks are thought to transform negative energy.

Culantro (*cilantro or coriander*) Herb with bright green serrated leaves, often used as a condiment. Said to combat gas, indigestion, upset nerves and diarrhoea.

Golondrina weed Made into a tea to cure headaches, fevers, colds, flu, urinary tract infections and fatigue.

Curcuma (*turmeric*) Herb applied topically to treat bruises and wounds, and taken internally like an antibiotic to inhibit the growth of bacteria.

Just south of Aquamor dive shop, **Pangea** (100m south of Aquamor, 2759 9204, www.megatarponheaven.com, US$40 double) is the place to stay if you're looking to get out on big waves and do some fishing.

Resources

Hospital
Clinica Sunimedica *next to BCR (2750 0079).*

Internet
Café Rio Negro *before 2nd bridge heading east in Playa Cocles (2750 0801).* **Open** 10am-8pm Mon-Sat.

Police station
Guardia Rural *next to Johnny's Place (2750 0230).*

Post office
In Puerto Viejo next to BCR bank (2750 0404).

Getting there

By bus
Buses from Cahuita pass through Puerto Viejo, then continue on to Manzanillo 3 times daily, and you can get off at any point along the way. Bikes are the most common means of transport and can be rented at a number of shops along the route; look for signs.

By road
Highway 36 continues to the border at Sixaola from Puerto Limón. About 7km after the village of Cahuita the road forks. For Punta Uva and Gandoca-Manzanillo take the left (east) fork onto a rough road that ends at Punta Mona.

Further Afield

Panama

The stunning archipelago of Bocas del Toro is worth the trip over the border.

Less developed and sometimes referred to as the 'Poor Man's Costa Rica', Panama surprises apprehensive visitors with its beauty and what it has to offer. The tourist draw is similar to Costa Rica's, with activities such as canopy tours, jungle and mountain trekking, birding and water sports. Beach vacations and luxury lodges are its strong suit, but for many, Panama's appeal is its relatively untraversed status – it's a Central American secret. The most common destination from Costa Rica is the archipelago of **Bocas del Toro** on the Caribbean side. On the Pacific side, visitors travelling by road must pass through the unlovely David (*see p307*). This guide also includes details about **Panama City** (*see p307*).

Bocas del Toro

Bocas del Toro is the name given to the north-western province of Panama and the sprinkling of islands that lie a few kilometres off its coast. While the Caribbean and Pacific coasts of Costa Rica feel over developed, this mini-paradise of turquoise waters and thriving wildlife offers scenery fit for a James Bond movie (it was recently used as the backdrop for the TV series *Survivor*). For years it remained a treasured secret, the sort of place that visitors would only tell their dearest friends about, in fear of provoking an onslaught of tourism. But in recent years the effects of globalisation and, more directly, the increase in chartered flights from San José and Panama City have placed Bocas firmly at the forefront of many a glossy travel brochure.

How times have changed. When Christopher Columbus first nosed his way through the archipelago, the islands were inhabited by native indigenous groups. Devoid of gold, the region held little interest for the Spaniards and was quickly taken over by the English and immigrating Jamaicans. By the turn of the 19th century, mass plantations of bananas, sugar cane and coconut trees gave the region strategic importance – at its economic zenith, the area boasted consulates from all over the world and three local newspapers. But in the late 1930s, a rare and incurable pest ravaged the plantations and the region slipped into economic decline. Then a series of fires, storms and, in 1991, an earthquake wreaked havoc on many of the main towns and their historical Caribbean buildings. It was time to look beyond the plantations and blue horizons for a more secure source of income: the tourism industry was born.

In the summer months, from November to April, beds are mainly occupied by American and Canadian tourists seeking respite from their harsh winters. Others, tired of the soaring costs of real estate, have sold up at home and bought their own property here. For many, the appeal of Bocas del Toro is similar to that of Key West 20 years ago – and without the Atlantic cruisers or partying students.

Isla Colón is the centre of the archipelago and the most populated island. The American dollar is still king here and you can enjoy a hearty breakfast with maple syrup and hash browns for next to nothing. Happy hour is another budgetary perk, offered at plenty of hotel bars where bottled beer and rum and cokes cost less than a dollar.

From Isla Colón, small boats zip in and out, ferrying visitors to the surrounding islands, many of which are uninhabited. On these islands, you'll find a huge variety of flora and fauna. On Isla Bastimentos, the national park provides sanctuary to white-faced capuchin monkeys, sloths, poisonous frogs, caimans and giant sea turtles. For US$100, a day's guided tour will lead you to their habitats.

Terrific spots for snorkelling, diving and swimming are to be found off Hospital Point, Coral Key and Dark Wood Reef, while surfers can get their kicks from the large and consistent waves breaking over the coral reef at Silverbacks. The more sedentary can kayak around mangrove-covered islands or take a walk along one of the many hidden beaches where your footprints are likely to be the first to mark the sand. Waters teem with over 200 species of fish making fishing another popular sport, though most of the bigger catch, big-eye tuna, yellow-tail snappers and the delicious wahoo, can only be caught in the deeper waters between April and June.

Where to stay

Around Isla Colón accomodation includes everything from lively youth hostels to luxurious waterfront hotels built on stilts.

Local residents row gently around Bastimentos in **Bocas del Toro**.

At **Cocomo-on-the-Sea** (Avenida Norte y Calle 6A 507 757 9259, www.panamainfo@ yahoo.com, US$60-$75 double) you'll find four clean and comfortable rooms and a sea-facing wooden deck where breakfast is served. It's as relaxing and informal as you can get; even the owner naps in the afternoon while guests enjoy the views from hammocks, iced rums in hand. (Booking ahead is crucial.)

The island's best hotel is probably the architecturally Caribbean-inspired **Tropical Suites** (Calle Primera, 507 757 9081/9880, www.tropical-suites.com, US$175-$225 double). Sitting in the heart of the main waterfront, 16 self-contained condominiums offer peerless views and all mod cons.

On a cheaper scale, the popular **Mondo Taitu Hostel & Bar** (Avenida G, 507 757 9425, beds from US$7) has standard shared rooms and a rocking bar that regularly gets packed to the rafters. But the real draw for the backpacking fraternity lies five minutes from the main island on the tip of Isla Bastimentos.

Aqua Bar and Lounge Hostel (Isla Bastimento, no phone, US$20 per person) is an impressive complex that includes shared accommodation, a sunken swimming pool, an open-air bar and wooden decks that border the sea.

For some peace and quiet hop on to a Jampan boat (507 757 9619, www.jampanresort.com, transport from 6am to 11pm) and take the 30-minute ride (US$10) to the **Garden of Eden Resort** (Private Island, Bocas del Toro, 507 700 0352, www.gardenofedenbocaspanama.com, US$140-$160 double), a hotel built on a private island. The story is as good as the venue. American owners Bob and Helena uprooted and, with supplies and help provided by the locals, built this amazing hotel in the space of six months. As well as a private beach, the rates include free kayaks, snorkelling and some amazing views across the bay. Jump off any one of the piers into waters that hum with tropical fish before returning to the pool for a well deserved cocktail. Recommended.

Reasons to love **Bocas del Toro**.

Where to eat & drink

There are plenty of seafront restaurants and bars on Isla Colón, but for perfectly cooked fish and a fruity cocktail it's hard to beat the **Lemon Grass Bar & Restaurant** (Calle Principal, main courses US$12), an Asian inspired restaurant and a top spot on a moonlit night. The pick of the menu is the red tuna steak cooked in wasabi and soy sauce, or the lobster is also excellent, cooked in green curry sauce. Close to the main plaza, on the main street, you'll find the romantic and unpretentious **El Pecado de Sabor** (Calle 3, above the Mangrove Roots shop, 6597 0296, set menus US$17-$20). The chef dabbles in an eclectic mix of cuisines (Thai, Lebanese, Mexican), but he is at his strongest when putting together seafood-based dishes such as prawns in a caramel and ginger sauce. For those wanting to push the boat out, again, the lobster here is particularly good.

On the other side of the headland (a 15-minute walk from the centre) is the equally popular **El Ultimo Refugio** (100m past the Ferry Dock, 6726 9851, www.ultimorefugio.com, main courses US$14), a small wooden restaurant that serves up well-executed, inspired dishes such as sesame seared tuna steaks, Asian prawns, and salmon in a creamy mint sauce. It is open from 6pm from Tuesday to Saturday. For nightlife, on Isla Colón's main sea-facing strip, you'll find plenty of bars like the **Pirate Bar**, which serves beers and cocktails at university bar prices, and as such gets pretty lively. After happy hour, punters often teeter on to the ferries and head over to **Aqua Bar & Lounge Hostel** (*see p305*) to continue the revelry in the stunning setting.

Getting there

By air

Nature Air (506 2299 6000, www.natureair.com) has 4 flights a week to and from San José to Bocas Del Toro in low season (21 Apr to 30 Nov) and daily flights in high season. A return ticket costs around US$140. Make sure you book in advance.

By road and sea

From the border, you can take either a 35km (22-mile) taxi ride to Almirante (US$40) or, the shorter and better option, to Changuinola (US$20). Leaving the small pier at Changuinola (US$6), the spectacular 1hr boat trip leads you through thick mangroves and jungle, across the river and out into the open sea. If you are going to miss the last boat (5pm), then travel further south to Almirante (US$4) where boats leave every hour, arriving at Isla Colón in 25mins.

A little over an hour across the border, **David** is a small city renowned for its frontier feel. It is the centre of cattle farming countryside and convenient place to break your journey.

Where to stay & eat

There are plenty of small eateries in David; **Bocas Caribbean Restaurant** (Avenida 2 Este, entre Calle Central y Calle A Norte, main courses US$6) makes good seafood dishes. **Churrasco's Place** (Avenida 2 Este, entre Calle Central y Calle A Norte, main courses US$7) is an open-air barbecued meat affair. For families the pick of the lodging in David is **Gran Hotel Nacional** (Calle Central, entre Calle A Sur y Avenida 8 de Enero, 507 775 2221, www.hotelnacionalpanama.com, US$78) located in the business area.

Panama City

The capital of the Republic of Panama is a busy modern metropolis. Founded as an important trade route stopover (it was the first European settlement on the Pacific coast) for the Conquistadores and more recently known for its shady money laundering past, it is an intriguing city. Luxury hotels, a thriving arts scene and, of course, the Panama Canal attract tourists from all corners of the world.

Where to stay & eat

For local fare try **El Trapiche** (Avenida 2a B Norte, y Vía Argentina, El Cangrejo, 507 269 4353, main courses US$10). For healthy and fresh food try **Greenhouse** (Calle Uruguay, entre Calle 47 y Bella Vista, 507 264 6846, main courses US$12).

There are plenty of sleeping options. If you want sleek, go to the 20-storey **Panama Marriott Hotel** (Calle 52, y Ricardo Arias, Area Bancaria, 507 210 9100, www.marriott. com, US$291 double). The rooms are large and well appointed and there is a business centre and casino. **Hotel deVille** (Calle 50, y Beatriz M de Cabal, www.devillehotel.com, 573 636 5231, US$225 double) is a converted mansion in a great location. It offers comfort and style with attentive staff, classy rooms and a minimalist-styled restaurant, Ten Bistro. A concierge, internet and free parking make for a well-equipped stay. Around the corner from trendy Vía Argentina is **Hotel Milan** (31 Calle Eusebio A Morales, 507 263 6130, US$35 double), a cheaper option that has clean quiet rooms and satisfactory amenities.

Panama's borderlands share Costa Rica's incredible wildlife.

Getting there

Panamanian law requires travellers either to purchase a tourist card from the airline serving Panama or to get a visa from a Panamanian Embassy or consulate before travelling to the country. Most people buy the tourist card (US$5) at border control, though this may soon not be an option. Contact the Panamanian embassy in San José before you go (Calle 38, entre Avenidas 7 y 9, 2441 1000). To get a tourist card or visa show a departure date such as on a return ticket originating from Panama. This is not always checked, but if you are questioned, buy a cheap return ticket from one of the bus companies. The process of entering Panama can take a frustrating few hours as it usually involves lengthy queues, closed desks and general disarray.

By air

International flights fly into Panama City's **Aeropuerto Internacional de Tocumen** (www.tocumenpanama.aero).

By bus

There are 3 official border crossings into Panama. **Paso Canoas** is the busiest border point and accessible by direct bus from San José. The professional **Tica Bus** (2223 8680, www.ticabus.com, US$37) departs daily at 12pm and arrives in Panama City at approximately 3pm the following day. **Tracopa** (2222 2666, US$30) bus company

leaves from its main terminal at 7.30am daily for the city of David. **Panaline** (2256 8721, www.pana linecr.com, US$35) departs daily at 1pm from its terminal in San José, 250m north of the San Juan de Dios Hospital and arrives in Panama at 5am the following day.

Sixaola is on the Caribbean coast and is slightly less hectic than Paso Canoas. Tourists visiting **Bocas del Toro** use this entry point. Border guards on both the Costa Rican and Panamanian side are notorious for their lengthy lunch breaks, so arrive early in the morning. The border is open from 7am to 5pm. Buses depart at 6am, 10am, 12pm, 2pm and 4pm from the Terminal Caribeños in San José (Calle Central, y Avenida 13) with **Transportes Mepe** and stop in Puerto Viejo. From Puerto Viejo a bus leaves at 1.30pm for Sixaola. If the buses are full in San José, take a different bus to Puerto Limón and walk 5 blocks across town to catch the bus that heads down to the border. In Sixaola there are basic hotels lining the streets and a handful of sodas.

San Vito is a small village in the Talamanca Mountains popular with hikers trekking into PN la Amistad (*see p267*). It is very remote, there are no regular public buses and very little accommodation or amenities. This is a hassle-free crossing as the border officials are usually over the moon to have something to do. The border control is 5km (3 miles) past San Vito and chances are you'll have to hitch there. It is open from 8am to 6pm and once across and into Río Sereno there are buses to Concepción and David (*see p307*).

Nicaragua

North of the border are more great beaches and the unique Isla Ometepe.

The largest country in Central America is beginning to shine: after decades of dictatorships, civil war and natural catastrophes, it is experiencing rapid development. Tourism – and in particular ecotourism – is finally taking off with many eager to explore this 'land of lakes and volcanoes'.

The country's proximity to the popular Guanacaste province in Costa Rica makes Nicaragua a perfect side-trip for a couple of days. It is also very popular with travellers wanting to renew their Costa Rican visa by staying 72 hours outside the country (*see p326* **Visas & immigration**).

San Juan del Sur

Twenty kilometres (12 miles) from the frontier with Costa Rica, San Juan del Sur used to be a tiny fishing village with dozens of deserted beaches to satisfy every surfer dream. Today, upscale hotels and condominiums are sprouting up in the hills surrounding the bay.

International cruises arrive in San Juan, and it is becoming the hottest beach destination in Nicaragua, while also maintaining its fishing town vibe. Head to Bahía Majagual by taxi boat (from outside Bar y Restaurant Buen Gusto) to lie on a deserted beach with cold beers or surf the breaks at Popoyo, Maderas or Ocotal. Fishing tours are also popular. Any agency in town can arrange a night tour to the nearby **Refugio de Vida Silvestre La Flor** (at El Ostional, 18 kilometres – 11 miles – south of San Juan del Sur, 505 563 4264). Entry to the refuge costs US$15 and the place is particularly popular when the paslama turtles are nesting.

Where to stay & eat

For a luxurious stay, **Morgan's Rock Hacienda & Ecolodge** (Costa Rica office 506 2232 6449, www.morgansrock.com, US$219 per person) is one of the premier all-inclusive resorts in the country and is a good example of sustainability. **Piedras y Olas** resort is located on a hill near the town and has great views, classy food and all the neccessary amenities (505 568 2110, www.piedrasyolas. com, US$225-$280 double). If you're on a budget, try **Casa Oro** hostel. It has a relaxed

atmosphere and the best deals for tours around San Juan (505 458 2415, www.casaeloro.com, US$8 dorm). The small restaurants and bars along the beach boulevard all serve fresh seafood; **Josseline** restaurant (505 568 2151, main courses US$6), in particular, stands out.

Granada

Known as the Great Sultaness, this colonial city 90 kilometres (56 miles) north of the border is one of the oldest in Central America, founded in 1524. Baroque churches, old colonial houses turned into chic boutique hotels, year-round art and culture festivals and the ocean-like **Lago Cocibolca**, tight on the doorstep, make this a lovely destination. On Lago Cocibolca are the Isletas, more than 300 tiny islands. Go to the **Reserva Natural Volcán Mombacho** for a zip-line adventure or trek (505 552 5858, www.mombacho.org, entry US$10). Another popular trip is to Laguna de Apoyo, at the km37 marker on the road to Masaya. This crater-formed lagoon has crystal-clear waters, the dockside restaurant of **Norome Resort & Villas** (505 270 7154, www.noromevillas. com, US$72-$127 double) and the **Crater's Edge** hostel (505 895 3202, www.craters-edge.com, US$22-$44 double). **Hotel Darío**, named in homage to Rubén Darío, the poet and national hero, is the finest converted colonial mansion in town (505 552 3400, www.hotel dario.com, US$100 double). **El Patio del Malinche** (505 552 2235, www.patiodel malinche.com, US$76 double) is a beautiful and well-equipped house.

To try *guapote*, a fish local to Lake Cocibolca, head to **Las Colinas Sur** (505 552 3492, main courses US$8) for classic Nicaraguan fare. Once night falls, **El Tercer Ojo** (505 552 6451) and **El Club** (505 552 4245, www.elclubnicaragua. com) see a lot of drinking, dancing and flirting.

Granada has become a centre for social projects and houses a growing number of volunteers from all over the world. One such scheme is the the **Building New Hope** project that runs **Café Chavalos** (505 852 0210, www.buildingnewhope.org), a school-cum-restaurant where former street kids learn about business while serving up decent dishes from US$14.

Further Afield

Isla Ometepe

This magnificent land mass on Lake Cocibolca, apparently loved by Mark Twain, is the world's largest island within a freshwater lake. It has a curious figure of eight shape and two giant volcanoes, Concepción and Maderas, at either end. Ometepe is starting to cater to tourists but it still feels like a remote paradise, with lush greenery and natural freshwater pools such as Ojo de Agua and Charco Verde. There are also mysterious petroglyphs, or stone etchings, scattered over the island, rivers to spend hours birdwatching by, and deserted beaches such as **Santo Domingo**. The main attraction is climbing the volcanoes, the easiest of which is Maderas, covered by thick forest. It can take up to four hours to reach the magnificent emerald lagoon at the top. Most hotels in the area can arrange a full-day guide with lunch for less than US$25.

At Santo Domingo beach, **Hotel Villa Paraíso** (505 563 4675, www.villaparaiso.com.ni, US$46-$63 per person) is the most organised lodging option, with basic amenities and a decent – if slightly expensive – restaurant. For a truly Nicaraguan experience of co-operatives, farming practices and rural tourism, go to the impressive 100-year-old **Finca Magdalena** in Balgüe (505 880 2041, www.fincamagdalena.com, US$6 dorm). It is a backpacker favourite, with great views of the lake and the Concepción volcano. There are petroglyphs around the area.

Managua

An earthquake in 1972 destroyed 90 per cent of Nicaragua's capital, but several important buildings surround the Plaza de la Revolución. These include the **Palacio Nacional de Cultura** and the **Teatro Nacional Rubén Darío**. Except for international fights, a stop isn't required in Managua to travel to Nicaragua's more interesting destinations, but there are several good hotels. **Casa Real** (505 278 3838, www.hcasareal.com, US$75 double) and **Villa Americana** (505 267 5005, www.hvillamericana.com, US$58 double) are the best options, and staff can arrange tours of the city.

For some Nicaraguan dishes try **La Cocina de Doña Haydée** (road to Masaya km4, 505 270 6100, www.lacocina.com.ni, main courses US$9). Another traditional but classy restaurant is **Intermezzo del Bosque** (5km south of Colegio Centroamérica, 505 883 0071, www.intermezzodelbosque.com, main courses $16), located on a hill just outside downtown Managua with the city lights shining below.

Getting there

There are two border crossing to Nicaragua: **Peñas Blancas** and **Los Chiles**. By far the most common is Peñas Blancas. All international buses go through this point and all cars must go this way. Crossing the border by foot or by bus is a simple process. The stamping takes less than an hour if you go by international transport. A US$7-$9 entrance tax must be paid on the Nicaraguan side.

The Los Chiles crossing (Immigration 2471 1233; *see p157*) is open from 8am to 4pm. It is pedestrian only, and the crossing must be made by boat along the San Juan river (US$7 one way, 3 ferries daily) to San Carlos port in Nicaragua. It is a hassle, but an adventure in itself.

By air

From San José international flights to Aeropuerto Internacional de Managua are run by **TACA** (www.taca.com; *see p314*).

By bus

Peñas Blancas (Immigration 2677 0064) is the principal border post to cross into the Pacific half of Nicaragua. Both sides are open daily from 6am to 7pm. Buses depart from San José to La Cruz and Peñas Blancas daily from 5am and the journey takes about 5hrs. Try **Transporte Deldú** (Calle 16, entre Avenidas 3 y 5, 2256 9072, ticket US$5).

Long distance international bus services that run between San José and Managua are more comfortable than buses that just travel over the border. They depart daily from San José, make several stops en route and take about 9hrs.

A return ticket costs US$25 and the most reliable companies are **Tica Bus** (2221 3318, www.ticabus.com), **Transnica** (2223 4242, www.transnica.com) and **King's Quality** (2221 3318). All these buses stop at Granada on the way. The bus company will take care of organising passport stamps and crossing procedures.

For **San Juan del Sur** get any bus at Rivas, about 10km from the border, and take a local bus to the destination. For **Isla Ometepe**, get off at Rivas and take a taxi or local bus to the nearby port of San Jorge (5 km/3 miles) and then take one of the 10 daily ferries. It is about a 1hr trip to Mogoyalpa port in Ometepe and costs US$2.

By car

Peñas Blancas is the only border crossing that allows vehicles into Nicaragua. Be warned: make sure that you have all vehicle documentation; immigration is very strict and it can sometimes take gruelling hours under the hot Nicaraguan sun, only to end in refusal to cross without reasonable explanation.

By foot

If walking, cross the border and take one of the taxis waiting on the other side. Make sure you agree the price before getting in. A 1.5hr hour taxi ride to **Granada** should cost around US$20, while a 30min trip to **Rivas** or **San Juan del Sur** (*see p309*) should be around US$10.

Directory

Features

Directory

Planning Your Trip

Getting started

The first decision to take when planning a trip to Costa Rica is whether to go independently or with a tour operator.

Organised packages are time efficient, as transfers, entrance to attractions and guided tours are pre-planned. Getting around may also be smoother as independent travel can be tricky due to the state of the roads.

Volunteer programmes are also becoming a popular way to get involved on a deeper level with the country. The best ones are listed below; for programmes with turtles *see p194* **Turtle power**.

Tour operators

High on adventure and relatively easy on the bank account, Costa Rica is today one of the world's hot travel destinations. As a result of the country's tourism boom, there are many general and specialist travel agencies operating in the area.

Photography safaris, sport fishing packages, surf schools, conservation volunteer programmes, family resort deals, or simple luxury getaways for honeymooners or couples are all readily available. It's just a matter of finding the right one.

We list below a selection of companies that offer holidays to Costa Rica. Each has a different focus, or offers travel to a different area. Apply the usual checks and criteria in selecting a holiday company. Specialist adventure outfitters can be found in the **Outdoor Pursuits** chapter; *see pp51-78*.

In the UK

Audley Travel *01993 838638/ www.audleytravel.com.*
Established small group tour operator offers a 15-day 'Colours of Costa Rica' journey, either in the north-west of the country or the Caribbean coast.
Cox & Kings *020 7873 5000/ www.coxandkings.co.uk.*
High-end luxury tours for private travellers in small groups.
Journey Latin America *020 8747 8315/ www.journeylatinamerica.co.uk.*
Tailor-made holidays, Spanish courses, family trips and wildlife-focused tours all available. Reputable and very well established.
LATA *020 8715 2913/www.lata.org.*
The Latin American Travel Association online; a worthwhile first point of call for information on travel to the region. Includes several links.
Foto Verde Travel *2253 1161/www.fotoverdetours.com.*
Highly recommended photography tours around Costa Rica focusing on wildlife and landscapes.

In the US

Ecoventures Nature Tours & Travel *1-800 743 8352/ www.ecoventurestravel.com.*
Eco-friendly tours from birdwatching to photography safaris. Family learning adventures also available.
Latin American Escapes *1-800 510 5999/www.latinamerican escapes.com.*
Customised itineraries, featuring good value natural history trips.
SATA USA *www.sata-usa.com.*
The South and Central American Travel Assocation's website. Not as many members as LATA, but has a useful online facility for sending questions about travel in the region to participating members.

Volunteer trips

Globe Aware *1-877 588 4562 (from US)/www.globeaware.org.*
The company offers participants the chance to experience village life in the rainforest and help communities establish sustainable living away from the tourist spots.

Global Volunteers *1 800 487 1074 (from US)/www.global volunteers.org.*
Hands-on work within the Santa Elena community involving anything from renovating public spaces to sprucing up classrooms.
Monteverde Institute *2645 5053/www.mvinstitute.org.*
Conservation and community based programmes around the Monteverde cloud forest.
United Planet *1-800 292 2316 (from US)/www.unitedplanet.org.*
Runs environmental and social projects in Costa Rica such as working in national parks, homeless children centres and hospitals.
uVolunteer *2447 6856/ www.uvolunteer.org.*
Costa Rican programmes include teaching English, sports coaching, turtle conservation, working in orphanages and an ecological farm.
Volunteers for Peace *1-802 259 2759 (from US)/www.vfp.org.*
Community art projects and helping in national parks.
World Teach *1-800 483 2240 (from US)/www.worldteach.org.*
Year-long post-grad volunteer programme teaching English at small public primary schools.

Accommodation

The phenomenal growth in tourism to Costa Rica has inevitably led to a marked increase in accommodation options for visitors. They vary from all-inclusive luxury lodges, popular in out-of-the-way places, to cheap cabins, often added on to a bar. Large corporate hotels dominate the San José scene. Be careful, particularly in the capital, as several of the cheaper options, not recommended in this guide, also double up as brothels but it will be immediately apparent when looking around. Bungalows and cabins are also commonplace, particularly ones that can be rented by four or more people.

It is best to book ahead if travelling during peak periods,

.ch as between December
.d April, long weekends
e p326 **Public holidays**)
.d especially Easter week
emana Santa). Some lodgings
ose for a month or two,
.ually in September or
.ctober when flooding is
.ely. Periods of the year
hen establishments we
.ature are closed are
.entioned in the guide.

ricing

.here is a huge variance in
.ices in Costa Rica. Beach
.bins and the type that most
.urs or restaurants offer can be
.nted for as little as US$10 a
.ght. Hostels will also charge
.similar price for a bed in a
.rm room. Nicer cabins cost
.round US$40-$100 a night,
.nd usually are well equipped
.ith kitchens and televisions.
.any of these provide great
.alue, especially if self-
.atering or with families.

Probably the most popular
.pe of accommodation is the
.l-inclusive lodge. One price
.ill buy a cabin or room, all
.inners, drinks and usually
.couple of tours to nearby
.ational parks. These places
.ften charge per person per
.ight. Those travelling alone
.ill usually pay a single rate.
.any larger bungalows and
.abins will have prices for
.ultiple occupancy.

Prices do drop during the
.hort low season, but there
.re not usually considerable
.avings to be had.

All hotels and lodges will
.harge in US dollars, although
.he equivalent in colones is
.kely to be accepted. Even
.asic hotels are likely to accept
.redit cards.

Sales tax (Impuesto al Valor
.IVI) is 13.39 per cent and
.sually is not included in
.rices. Hotels sometimes
.dd a three per cent tourist
.urcharge to the sales tax. The
.rices in our **Where to stay**
.ections include IVI.

Apart hotels

In Costa Rica Apart Hotels
have standard hotel features,
but larger rooms with
kitchenette and small living
and eating area.

B&Bs

Bed and breakfasts are
becoming hugely popular in a
country still catching up with
the tourist influx. They are
particularly prevalent in urban
areas such as Heredia, Alajuela
and the outskirts of San José –
useful before leaving the
country from the San José
airport. They are rooms in
a family home.

Cabins

Cabin complexes are extremely
common all across Costa Rica
and often provide good value
and are very well appointed.
Some are laid out like a motel,
with several cabins under one
roof, while others have
individual cabins hidden
among the jungle. Cabins
generally have a master
bedroom, living room,
sometimes a small kitchen.
Some cabins have secondary
bedrooms to sleep children or
more people. The complexes
often include a restaurant
and swimming pool and
can arrange tours.

Camping

There are few camping options
in Costa Rica, but many towns
have some sort of municipal
camp ground, but don't expect
excellent facilities. Most
national parks have campsites
but usually offer little in the
way of facilities, except for
drinking water. They usually
charge around US$2 per pitch.
Camping is also usually
allowed around the ranger
stations; some even have basic
beds and indoor facilities that
can be used. The law also

allows free camping anywhere
within five metres of the sea.
However, in practice this may
not always be allowed,
especially among the resorts
of Guanacaste. Ask first.

Hostels

There are hostels in most
towns and Costa Rica is
generally a backpacker-
friendly country. Most hostels
are well looked after and
equipped with all modern
facilities. Many can be booked
with www.hostelworld.com.

Hotels

Hotels are the same here as
anywhere else in the world,
and you should take the same
precautions when choosing
where to stay. Always see the
room, particularly in San José
and along the Caribbean coast.
There are many good cheap
hotels but some are real
horrors once you get inside.
The star rating system is not
the best guide to quality.

Resorts

Resorts make up a large
section of Costa Rica's lodging
options. Mostly they offer
packages, which can include
a plane transfer from San José.
All meals will be included and
there are usually a couple of
tours thrown in. Bear in mind
that meal times are fixed and
tours will be with other guests.

Information

Under each destination in
this guide we have provided
the details of the local tourist
office and, in relevant sections,
the national parks offices.
The state-run Instituto
Costarricense de Turismo
can be found at www.visit
costarica.com. *See p325*
Tourist information
and *p329* **Websites** for
useful contacts.

Directory

Getting Around

Arriving & leaving

By air

Costa Rica is served by two international airports. The most important is the **Aeropuerto Internacional Juan Santamaría** (2443 0840, 2437 2626, www.alterra.co.cr), located in Alajuela, 17 kilometres (ten miles) north-west of San José. Most of the principal international airlines arrive here. The Alajuela-San José bus passes frequently in front of the airport but the cab company located at the only arrival gate, **Taxi Aeropuerto** (2221 6865, www.taxiaeropuerto.com), is the best and safest choice to travel into San José. A regular trip into downtown costs around US$20 and is pre-paid in the airport office.

Major hotels usually offer free shuttles from/to the airport as do companies that provide direct shuttles to other parts of the country, such as **Interbus** (2283 5573, www.interbusonline.com), although they are often considerably more expensive.

Just beside the airport is the terminal of **Sansa**, the major domestic airline company (2290 4100, www.flysansa.com). Sansa charters fly to 17 destinations (around the country and also locations in Panama and Nicaragua), most of them several times a day. Flight time is usually less than an hour. The other domestic charter company, with similar destinations, frequency and rates is **Nature Air** (2299 6000, www.natureair.com). Nature Air flights depart from **Aeropuerto Tobias Bolaños** (2232 2810), located in the suburb of Pavas, eight kilometres west of downtown San José.

The other main international airport is **Aeropuerto Internacional Daniel Oduber** (2668 1010), located 13 kilometres (eight miles) west of the city of Liberia, province of Guanacaste, in the north-west of Costa Rica.

A departure tax is charged on international departures, currently US$26 and paid before you check in.

The following airlines fly into Costa Rica.

American Airlines *2257 1266/ www.aa.com*
Air Canada *www.aircanada.ca* No office in Costa Rica.
Air France *2280 0069/ www.airfrance.com*
Alitalia *2293 6820/ www.alitalia.com*
British Airways *2256 6509/ www.britishairways.com*
Continental Airlines *2296 4911/www.continental.com*
Copa Airlines *2223 2672/ www.copaair.com*
Delta Airlines *2256 7909/ www.delta.com*
First Choice Airlines *2667 0922/www.firstchoice.co.uk* Flies into Aeropuerto Internacional Daniel Oduber.
Iberia *2257 8266/ www.iberia.com*
KLM *2240 4111/www.klm.com*
Lufthansa *2256 6161/ www.lufthansa.com*
Martinair *2232 3246/ www.martinair.com*
TACA *2223 4314/www.taca.com*

By rail

Costa Rica has no national rail network but some commuter train lines do exist within San José and there is a tourist train from the capital to Puntarenas (*see p220*).

By road

The Interamericana Highway 1 is the gateway to San José and the main road towards most destinations around the country. Tourists arriving by car must pay a road tax, insurance stamp, and obtain car entry permit. Drivers can use a licence issued by their home country if the visa has not expired. Four-wheel-drive vehicles are recommended, especially outside San José and during the rainy season.

By sea

Costa Rica is a stopover point for many international cruises at the ports in Puntarenas, Caldera and Limón. There are also many private marinas along the Pacific coast where it is possible to arrive by private yacht or boat.

Public transport

Costa Rica has an extensive public bus system. It is a popular and inexpensive way of getting around, if rather slow. Distant beaches and the borders with Nicaragua and Panama can all be reached with a little time. More remote roads are often in terrible condition, therefore schedules cannot be relied on 100 per cent. Patience and double-checking departure times are essential.

Competing with them are numerous private shuttles and van transfers to travel outside San José. Although more expensive, these are comfortable, fast and safe and particularly popular if you're heading to the Arenal area.

Buses

To travel within the city, San José has several bus routes, usually identified with the name of the route (for example San José to Zapote, Sabana to Cementerio) on the front of the bus, which stops every two to three blocks. Tickets usually cost around US$0.50, or round US$1 to go to the nearby cities of Alajuela or Heredia. Express services to those towns can be identified by a *directo* sign visible in the front window.

Local buses operate in most urban locations including Puntarenas, San Isidro, Golfito, Puerto Limón, Liberia and Península de Nicoya. Buses need to be waved down by passengers and any local should be able to advise about times. The tickets are usually around US$1-$5.

To travel from San José to other destinations, there is no central terminal: each company has a specific departure point and these are located around the city. However, there are three major long distance bus stations in San José where most of these companies are located: the popular **Terminal de la Coca Cola** (Calle 16, entre Avenidas 1 y 3) and the **Terminal de Puntarenas** (Avenida 12, y Calle 16) with departures to the Pacific coast; and the **Terminal del Caribe** (Avenida 13, y Calle Central), with departures to the Caribbean coast. Under the getting there section of each destination is information as to which terminal the buses depart from. Most of the tickets are bought in kiosks or at desks in the terminals. Each will have a list of the destinations that it serves.

Take care of belongings in terminals. It is preferable to carry luggage on board, although this is not always possible. Tickets for long journeys are around US$10 to 15. With some exceptions, you ought to be prepared to travel without air-conditioning or bathrooms on board, though usually drivers make one or two pit stops on long journeys where food and bathrooms are available.

Long distance buses to Nicaragua (*see p309*) and Panama (*see p304*) cross the border at Peñas Blancas (to Nicaragua) and Paso Canoas (to Panama) on a daily basis for around US$15 for a one way ticket. **Ticabus** (2221 8954, www.ticabus.com) and **Transnica** (2223 4242, www.transnica.com) are the most popular companies.

The **Instituto Costarricense de Turismo (ICT)** has an updated master bus schedule with contact information at **www.visit costarica.com**, or check out **www.costaricabybus.com**. Buses usually depart early if they are full. To be safe, arrive at least half an hour before departure time.

Water transport

Ferries connect the Central Pacific coast with the southern tip of Península de Nicoya. There are two routes: Puntarenas to Playa Naranjo with **Coonatramar**, which has five car ferry departures a day (2661 1069, www.coona tramar.com). **Naviera Tambor** (2661 2084) and **Ferry Península** (2641 0515) sail from Puntarenas to Paquera eight to ten times daily. The timetable often changes, especially during holidays, so it is advisable to call ahead. The journey is about one-and-a-half hours long. Tickets cost US$2 per person, and around US$20 per car including driver. **Lancha Don Bernardino**, a passenger ferry, crosses from the Mercado de Puntarenas to Paquera twice a day (2641 0515) at unreliable hours.

In the Southern Pacific area, two passenger ferries run daily (*see p267*) between Golfito and Puerto Jiménez across the Golfo Dulce, and **Asociación de Boteros** water taxis travel to Zancudo and Playa Cacao (2775 0357). Tickets are US$3.

There are also many private boat charters, particularly between Jacó and Montezuma,

linking the Central Pacific area and the Península de Nicoya (*see p204*), and bus-and-boat services such as between Cariari and Tortuguero on the Caribbean coast (*see p279*).

Taxis

Licensed taxis in Costa Rica are red with a yellow triangle on the door and licensed plates. If in San José or around, try to avoid the early morning and late afternoon when traffic jams are the rule and cab journeys are not only endless but expensive too.

Be aware that taxi drivers should use the meter (*maría*), and if they don't, ask them. During the night, some drivers can try to charge outrageous rates and generally speaking do not use the meter. Prices can be arranged before getting in. Safest, however, is to call a radio taxi. In San José and around, good options are **Coopetico** (2224 7979) or **Alfaro** (2221 8466).

Outside the city or for long journeys, taxis do not have meters and usually have a set rate – although this may change with the number of passengers. The conditions of the cars vary and many locals use their own car as a taxi service in remote areas.

Cars and drivers can be hired for the day for about the same rate or less than a rental car service, and due to the bad condition on most roads, especially in remote places, it is a good alternative. Hotels can often recommend reliable drivers with cars for you. Or, alternatively, enquire at a taxi office.

Driving

Driving in Costa Rica can be a tricky experience, yet the advantage of seeing scenery and reaching destinations impossible to get to by bus makes it worthwhile. A valid driver's licence from abroad is accepted in Costa Rica for 90 days. After that it is necessary to get a Costa Rican driver licence, a one day errand that requires the home licence and some other papers. To bring a car into the country, a long and expensive 'vehicle nationalisation' procedure is required after the initial six-month permit has expired.

Driving in Costa Rica is on the right hand side. On all primary roads the speed limit is 100km/h (62 mph) and 60km/h (37 mph) or less on other roads. Front seatbelts are compulsory. Minimum driving age is 18.

Traffic police control is common on main roads. They usually ask for your licence, along with a valid passport and visa if the migration and traffic police are making a joint operation. Fines can be paid at any national bank. By law, police are not allowed to ask for bribes – but it's not unheard of.

A vast majority of roads, especially out of San José, are unpaved or very pot-holed. Expect to come across herds of cattle, cyclists and many trucks and traffic jams. Roads are often unmarked or have inaccurate signs. Always ask about road conditions: many require crossing rivers, easy in the dry season but impassable during the rainy season. Driving in the dark can also be dangerous for these reasons. For maps, go to the **Instituto Costarricense de Turismo** (*see p326* **Tourist information**) or to the **Instituto Geográfico Nacional** (located inside the Ministerio de Transporte, MOPT, 2523 2619/2257 7798).

Car hire

Minimum age to rent a car is 21, and requires a valid driver's licence, passport and credit card. International and local rental agencies are located in San José and all major tourist destinations, and cars can be dropped off or picked up at the airport. Prices start at around US$400 per week including unlimited mileage and basic insurance. Most rental vehicles are manual shift.

It is recommended to always rent a four-wheel-drive vehicle if leaving San José: ordinary cars are useless in most destinations around the country, and especially during rainy season.

Adobe *2259 4242/ www.adobecar.com*
Budget *2223 3284/ www.budget.co.cr*
Dollar *2443 2950/ www.dollarcostarica.com*
Economy *2299 2000/ www.economyrentacar.com*
Hertz *2221 1818/ www.costaricarentacar.com*
Toyota *2258 5797/ www.toyotarent.com*

Fuel stations

They are commonly named *bombas* and are usually found on main roads, but are hard to find in remote areas or small towns where petrol and diesel are usually sold from a drum or small grocery shops known as *pulperías*. Regular petrol is often soiled, so use super instead. Check the distance to the next station when you fill up. The cost of petrol in early 2008 was around US$1 per litre but the price usually goes up or down several times a year.

Parking

Parking in San José during the day is only allowed in a few streets. Car parks are called *parqueos* and cost around US$2-$3 an hour. In the street, you may be approached, especially during the night, by an unofficial *guachimán*, someone offering to look after your car in exchange for a few coins. If you're not happpy

about this arrangement it's best just to find somewhere else to park.

It goes without saying that you should never leave any belongings inside the car.

Cycling

Professional cyclists are commonly seen pedalling the roads in almost any town. Lago Arenal (*see p152*), Turrialba (*see p139*) and Península de Nicoya (*see p205*) are popular destinations. The scenery makes cycling a great way to travel around, although the roads and weather conditions can be difficult. Mountain bikes are widely available for rent, with prices starting at around US$10 a day. The coast-to-coast Ruta de los Conquistadores race (www.adventurerace.com), held every November, is the main cycling event.

Walking

Costa Rica is a small but hilly country (*see pp54-59* **National Parks & Trekking**). For local maps, the tourist board, **ICT** (*see p326*), is the best choice. Commonly, each park has a free simple map for trekkers and the main routes are well signposted. Robberies have been reported in some parks and every year walkers without a guide get lost – therefore it is best to go in a group or with a guide.

Hitch-hiking

Take the same care in Costa Rica as you would anywhere else, especially if you're travelling alone or on main roads, and especially at night. You can get a lift almost anywhere by sticking a thumb up. Offering to pay is the courtesy rule, but the offer will be waved aside most of the time.

Resources A-Z

Addresses

Costa Rica is a country where addresses are not usually known by numbers or names, instead they rely on landmark directions, for example, '100 metres north of the football pitch'. For postal services most residents have a numbered post office box.

In San José, *calles* (streets) are numbered with odd numbers moving west from the Calle Central (sometimes known as Calle 0) with even numbers to the east. *Avenidas* (avenues) have odd numbers north of the Avenida Central and even numbers south. House numbers are rare. Along roads, addresses are given as kilometre road markers, or with rivers as the landmark.

Age restrictions

Legally, Costa Ricans become adults at 18 years old and this is also the legal age for smoking, drinking and having sex, although these laws are rarely adhered to.

Attitude & etiquette

Costa Ricans are sociable, friendly and often interested in meeting foreigners. There are also more foreigners in Costa Rica than in any other country in Central America and they are part of everyday life. In a population of around four million people, almost one million are foreigners. Ticos make friends easily with foreigners. But there are occasional misgivings about the rate of development and the fact that locals are often priced out of the housing market. Ticos place great value on friendship and personal contacts, and don't generally like to argue; indeed, many will shut down if anger or aggression is expressed. They also tend to avoid conflict, saying 'yes' even if they mean 'no', just to leave a good impression.

Ticos are formal: when meeting somebody they will shake hands and use the traditional *usted* form rather than the *vos* (informal). *See pp326-327* **Language & Vocabulary**. Kisses and hugs are reserved for family and close friends.

Any attempt to speak Spanish and to show an interest in local culture will always be appreciated in any situation. 'Con mucho gusto' is a polite often-used expression meaning 'You are very welcome'. 'Pura Vida!' (pure living) is also a very common and well-appreciated way of saying thank you, or finishing off a conversation. 'Don' and 'Doña' titles are used with first names and show respect and familiarity at once.

Costa Ricans are casual dressers, usually jeans and a nice shirt will be fine in tourist venues. When travelling or going to the beach, women should avoid wearing short skirts or just a swimsuit – local men are not afraid to stare, and comments to women in the street such as 'mi reina' (my queen) or 'corazón' (sweetheart) are common. Usually, Ticos are tolerant of foreigners; topless bathing is not common but is permitted in some secluded beaches. However, Ticos will become noticeably cool with visitors who break social norms such as taking drugs, or drinking heavily.

'Tico time' refers to Costa Ricans' lack of punctuality: more often than not everything will start at least 15 minutes late, usually much later. 'Ahorita' (right now) is a popular expression that can mean in a minute or…who knows when.

Business

Most business meetings take place in San José and around, though there are convention centres in most upscale hotels around the country, especially in the North Pacific. Business attire is often smart-casual due to the heat (shirt and trousers)

Travel advice

For up-to-date information on travel to a specific country – including the latest news on safety and security, health issues, local laws and customs – contact your home government's department of foreign affairs. Most of them have websites packed with useful advice for would-be travellers.

Australia
www.smartraveller.gov.au

New Zealand
www.safetravel.govt.nz

UK
www.fco.gov.uk/travel

Canada
www.voyage.gc.ca

Republic of Ireland
http://foreignaffairs.gov.ie

USA
http://travel.state.gov

Directory

most of the time. Do not expect to solve a business deal in one meeting: the proverbial Costa Rican easy attitude and bureaucratic steps tend to delay proceedings, but patience goes a long way in Costa Rican commerce. Many business professionals speak English well and are happy to conduct business in English. *See pp327-328* **Language & vocabulary** for the basics. For more information about business in the country see **www.bizcostarica.com**.

Conventions & conferences

Conventions are commonly held in upscale hotels that can provide suitable rooms, internet access and catering. Here are a few of the best:
Ramada Plaza Herradura Hotel & Convention Center San José (*2209 9800/www.ramada herradura.com*).
Barceló San José Palacio San José (*2220 3034/www.barcelo sanjosepalacio.com*). *See p105.*
Hotel Camino Real Intercontinental Escazú, San José (*2208 2100/www.inter continental.com*). *See p111.*
Four Seasons Resort Costa Rica Península de Papagayo, North Pacific (*2696 0000/www.four seasons.com*). *See p177.*

Couriers & shippers

Also *see p323* **Postal services**.

DHL
Edificio Meridiano, 1st floor, Escazú, San José (2208 7000). **Open** 7.30am-7.30pm Mon-Fri; 8am-1pm Sat. **Credit** AmEx, DC, MC, V.
The San José branch of 3 DHL drop-off points in Costa Rica. The others are at José Santamaria International Airport in Alajuela (open 8am-3.30pm Mon-Fri) and in Jacó, in front of the Hotel Tangerie (open 8am-5.45pm Mon-Fri; 9am-noon Sat).

FedEx
Zona Franca Metropolitana, Local 1B, Heredia (800 463 3339). **Open** 8.30am-5pm Mon-Fri. **Credit** AmEx, DC, MC, V.
International door-to-door express delivery. Up to 68kg.

Office services

If you need to use a telephone, fax or internet, it is best to go to one of the *locutorios* (call centres) throughout Costa Rica. They are handy and inexpensive. In more remote areas, hotels and large resorts are the best bets and generally allow non-residents to use their services. To rent office space **www.vacationcity.com** (2290 0798) can arrange premises in San José, Heredia and other selected towns around the country.

The English-language newspaper the **Tico Times** (www.ticotimes.net) has a comprehensive classified section including commercial properties for rent. For translation services contact your embassy, or one of the following are recommended: **Idioma International** (2290 1229, www.idiomacr.com) based in Uruca, San José. **Language Solutions** (2232 9710, www.soluciones idiomaticas.com) and **Official Translation Services** (2241 6758, traduccionescr @gmail.com) are also based in the capital.

Useful organisations

Costa Rican American Chamber of Commerce (AMCHAM) *Sabana Norte (2220 2200/ www.amcham.co.cr).*
Bolsa Nacional de Valores (Costa Rica National Stock Market) *Parque Empresarial Forum, Autopista Próspero Fernández, Santa Ana (2204 4848/www.bnv.co.cr).*
CADEXO (Costa Rica Exports Chamber) *100m south, 150m west from Veinsa (Mitsubishi), Curridabat, San José (2280 8033/www.icoexonline.org).*
CINDE (Costa Rican Investment Promotion Agency) *Plaza Robles, Edificio Los Balcones, 4th floor, Guachipelín, Escazú (2201 2800/www.cinde.org).*
PROCOMER (Foreign Trade Promotion Institute) *Edificio Centro de Comercio, Paseo Colón, San José (2299 4700/ www.procomer.com).*

Consumer

Consumers in Costa Rica are protected by the Ley 7472 de Promoción de la Competencia y Defensa Efectiva del Consumidor, a law introduced in 1995. In the event of a problem, the following organisations should be able to provide help and give advice:

Comisión Nacional del Consumidor
Avenida 3, entre Calles 30 y 32 (800 266 7866 freephone/ www.consumo.go.cr).
A state-run organisation that depends on the Economy Ministry and helps consumers make complaints and provides a special phone number for advice.

Consumidores de Costa Rica (CONCORDI)
Avenida 3, entre Calles 1 y 3, Edificio Cristal, office 9 (www.consumidores decostarica.org).
A non-profit organisation that integrates and promotes fair relationships between the state, commerce and citizens. A phone line for consumers is in the works.

Defensoría de los Habitantes
Avenida 7, y Calle 22, Barrio México (800 258 7474 freephone/2258 8585/www.dhr.go.cr).
Created by law in 1992, this is a state-run organisation whose goal is to promote citizen's rights in the presence of public institutions.

Customs

Entering Costa Rica you can bring in the following without paying import duties: 200 cigarettes or 500g of tobacco, five litres of alcohol and up to six rolls of film. Cameras and sporting equipment are readily allowed into the country. No customs duties are charged on personal luggage. Costa Rica law requires checked-in luggage to be screened and travellers to fill out customs declarations stating the value of any item in their possessions, including fruits, vegetables, biological products such as vaccinations.

Directory

UK Customs and Excise allows each person 200 cigarettes, 60cc of perfume, two litres of table wine, one litre of spirits and £145 worth of all other goods and souvenirs. US Customs and Border Protection allows one litre of any alcohol duty free.

Disabled

Travel to Costa Rica implies a physically involved holiday. The most difficult part is getting around. Access can be tricky throughout the country and even in San José problems should be expected, but the situation is improving. Although there is a law that enforces equality for disabled people, buses and other transport are often not prepared for people with disabilities, and just a few hotels have the minimum requirements for wheelchair users. Special phones for hearing impaired people or signs in Braille are practically non-existent.

Unpaved roads and unmarked pot-holed streets make it difficult to get around in a wheelchair. Private transfers such as minibuses and domestic flights are the best option to travel.

The **Association of Costa Rican Special Taxis** (2296 5443) offers cars equipped for wheelchair travellers. **Grayline Tours** also has disabled equipped bus tours available (2220 2126, www.graylinecostarica.com).

Organisations offering special trips and information for disabled travellers to Costa Rica include **Vaya Con Silla de Ruedas** (2454 2810, www.gowithwheelchairs.com), **International Institute of Creative Development** (2771 7482, www.empowermentaccess.com), **Kosta Rhoda** and **Accessible Journeys** (in USA, www.disabilitytravel.com).

Drugs

All drugs are illegal in Costa Rica, whether large amounts or for personal consumption. Although police often turn a blind eye to soft drug use among tourists, they carry out operations in bars and beaches by night and will make arrests. If you are carrying an amount considered more than for personal use, penalties are severe (three to 25 years).

Electricity

Electricity in Costa Rica is 110 volts. Most sockets take only flat pins. Europeans need to bring travel adaptors.

Embassies & consulates

Australian Embassy
The Canadian diplomatic mission gives consular assistance to Australian citizens.

British Embassy
Edificio Centro Colón, 11th Floor, Avenida Central, entre Calles 38 y 40 (2258 2025/www.britishembassy. gov.uk). **Open** 8am-4pm Mon-Thur; 8am-1pm Fri.

Canadian Embassy
Apartado 351-1007, Centro Colón 3rd Floor, Avenida Central, entre Calles 38 y 40 (2242 4400/ www.dfait-maeci.gc.ca/sanjose). **Open** 7.30am-4pm Mon-Thur; 7.30am-1pm Fri.

United States Embassy
Avenida Central, y Calle 120, Pavas (2519 2000/www.usembassy.or.cr). **Open** 8am-4.30pm Mon-Fri.

Emergencies

For every emergency, call 911, available nationwide. Here are some other useful numbers.

Ambulance
128

Burns unit (Unidad de Quemados)
2257 0180

Fire
911 or 118

National Insurance Institute (Instituto Nacional de Seguros)
800 800 8000
For reporting car accidents if the vehicle is insured.

Intoxication Centre
2223 1028

Police
911 or the OIJ, Judicial Investigative Police on 2295 3463. See p323 **Police**.

Traffic Police
800 872 6748/2222 9330

Gay & lesbian

In general terms, Ticos are more open to gay visitors than other Central American countries. Some beaches, such as Manuel Antonio in the Central Pacific, reflect a curious mix of conservatism and openness: for several years it has been a favourite destination for straight families as well as for gay couples. Public displays of affection are often frowned upon but trouble is unlikely. On the web, **www.gaycosta rica.com** has links to gay-friendly lodging, and links to dozens of sites with gay tourist information, including the useful **www.orgullogay cr.com** and **www.dons costarica.com**.

GLBT counselling organisations include **UNO@DIEZ** (2258 4561, www.1en10.com) and **CIPAC-DH** (2280 7821, www.cipacdh. org), the main gay activist organisation. **Gaytours Costa Rica** (2777 1910, www.gaytourscr.com) and **Tiquicia Travel** (256 6429) organise excursions into San José gay nightlife as well as around the country. Gay magazines such as **Gente 10** (www.gente10.com) can be picked up for free in gay bars in San José.

Directory

Health

Healthcare standards in Costa Rica are generally higher than in other Central American countries but travel insurance is highly recommended. Tap water is drinkable almost everywhere, but bottled water will always be safer.

The US government recommends vaccinations against hepatitis and typhoid, although these diseases are as rare in Costa Rica as in any developed country. As well as recommending these vaccinations, the only two diseases the UK Foreign & Commonwealth Office (FCO) warns visitors about are Dengue fever and malaria.

Malaria isn't common but a handful of tourists are affected every year. Visitors to the Caribbean coast are most susceptible and many doctors will recommend prophylactics (usually chloroquine – marketed in Costa Rica as Arelen) to be taken two weeks before you arrive. Most visitors, however, do not take malaria tablets.

Dengue fever, also transmitted by mosquitoes, is an increasing problem, with San José and the Central Valley the most affected areas according to the FCO. There is no vaccination or immunisation against Dengue fever, but precautions such as using repellent containing DEET, sleeping under mosquito nets and avoiding stagnant water can be taken. The risk of being infected is higher during the rainy season (May to November). The fever is characterised by flu-like symptoms and severe body pain for more than two weeks.

If you are on medication of any kind, bring a supply to last the trip. Standard pharmaceuticals are widely available, but often under different names. Sunburn is the most common problem.

Accident & emergency

See under **Resources** in each section for local hospitals but small towns will have a centre of primary attention, called **EBAIS**, which are usually well stocked. For a basic emergency consultation, expect to pay around US$35.

CIMA-Centro Internacional de Medicina *Autopista Próspero Fernández, in front of Plaza Tskazú, on the road to Santa Ana (2208 1144/www.hospital sanjose.net).*

Hospital Clínica Bíblica *Calle Central, entre Avenidas 14 y 16, San José (2258 7184/ www.clinicabiblica.com).*

Hospital San Juan de Dios *Calle 14, y Avenida Central, San José (2257 6282).*

Hospital de Niños (Children's hospital) *Calle 14, y Avenida Central, San José (2222 0122/www.hnn.sa.cr).* Only for children 12 and under.

Complementary medicine

Alternative and holistic healthcare is popular all over the country. Holistic centres, reiki and homeopathic practices are all growing (*see below*), and yoga is also popular. Alternative and organic supplies are also commonplace; the most popular is the **BioLand** (www.bioland.org) line of toiletries and food, sold at many supermarkets.

Centro Médico Victoria *200m north of Muñoz y Nanne, San Pedro, San José (2224 0654/www.clinica victoria.com).*

Hotel los Mangos *Montezuma, Península de Nicoya (8811 7582www.montezumayoga.com).*

Hacienda del Sol *San Juanillo, Road to Nosara (8828 4080/www.sunvacation.org).*

KASASANA *200m north of the Centro Cultural Norteamericano, Barrio Escalante, San José (2253 8322/www.kasasana.com).*

Nosara Yoga Institute *Playa Guiones, road to Nicoya (2682 0071/ www.nosarayoga.org).*

Pia Plant *Playa Santa Teresa, Península de Nicoya (2640 0307).*

Contraception & abortion

Abortion in Costa Rica is illegal. Contraceptives like the pill and condoms are offered free of charge in most public hospitals and EBAIS (*see left*). You can also get all types of contraceptives from pharmacies (*see below*).

Dentists

Even small towns will have at least three or four dentist clinics to choose from. In San José, many dentists cater to foreigners as they offer high quality procedures at lower costs than in the UK or US. The **Colegio de Cirujanos Dentistas de Costa Rica** (www.colegiodentistas.org, 2256 3100) offers an up-to-date list of registered dentists in Costa Rica.

Hospitals

The main hospitals are listed left and under Resources in the relevant section. Check with medical insurers for other doctors and hospitals.

Opticians

Opticians are found in every town of any size and will be able to fulfil most prescriptions.

Pharmacies

Pharmacies can be found in all towns, although the brand names are likely to differ. Most major supermarkets also have pharmaceutical sections or an on-site chemist.

STDs, HIV & AIDS

It is estimated that 8,000 people in Costa Rica live with HIV/AIDS. Hospitals are the best choice for starting treatment. **Clínica Bíblica** (*see above*) has free HIV/AIDS

Directory

tests. Other institutions offer access to medication and group therapy support:
Agua Buena Human Rights Association *2234 2411/www.aguabuena.org*
UNAIDS *2220 1100 ext. 1703/maria.tallarico@undp.org*
REDES – HIV *2280 7821/cipacdh@racsa.co.cr*

Helplines

The following helplines are for English speakers, or should have someone on duty to support English speakers:
Alcoholics Anonymous *2220 4076*
Association of Foreigner Residents *2233 8068*
Narotics Anonymous *2256 8140*
Asociación de Mujeres Costarricenses (Women's helpline) *2233 5769*

ID

Identification must be carried at all times, but this may be a photocopy of the photo page of a valid passport and the visa page. Police (Fuerza Pública) are tolerant with visitors but Migration Police are likely to ask for ID on long distance buses, especially during high season and near the country's borders.

Insurance

All visitors to Costa Rica are strongly advised to take out comprehensive travel insurance before travelling, including medical insurance. A high-risk policy is needed if doing dangerous sports.

Internet

In the past five years, internet access has spread across the country and internet cafés (*cybercafés* or just *ciber*) can be found even in the smallest of towns. It usually costs around US$1 per hour but tends to be more in remote areas. Wi-Fi access is common in San José, in main cities and

in large hotels, but expect it to be rather slow.

Language

Most people involved with tourism speak excellent English, but outside this industry a little Spanish can go a long way. (*See p323* **Study** and *pp327-328* **Language & Vocabulary**).

Left luggage

It is best to travel light in Costa Rica. There is no left luggage storage at the airport and the ones at bus stations are, at best, unreliable. Most hotels and hostels will store items for you for a small fee, if you are going on a short trip. *See right* **Lost property**.

Legal help

Although there are plenty of solicitors in Costa Rica with experience of dealing with foreigners, their area of expertise is usually business and real estate, so it is still best to contact your consulate or embassy for any legal help (*see p319* **Embassies & consulates**).

Libraries

The largest libraries in Costa Rica are the **Biblioteca Nacional** and the **Archivo Nacional** (National Library and National Archive, *see below*). Most of its archive is in Spanish but it does have some material in English. Other libraries with English material are listed below:
Biblioteca Nacional Miguel Obregón Lizano *Avenida 3, entre Calles 15 y 17, San José (2221 2436). Open 8am-4.30pm Mon-Fri.*
Archivo Nacional de Costa Rica *Avenida Central, 9 blocks east of Plaza del Sol, Curridabat, San José (2234 7223). Open 8am-3pm Mon-Fri.*
Mark Twain Library at the Centro Cultural Norteamericano *Calle 37, 200m*

north of the petrol station, Barrio Dent, San José (2207 7575). **Open** *8am-8pm Mon-Fri; 8am-5pm Sat.*
Biblioteca David Kitson *Behind the EBAIS, Nosara (2682 0211).*

Lost property

In general, if you have lost it, forget it. Recovering stolen or lost property depends on the good nature of the person who finds your belongings. In small towns, you may be able to ask locals to tell you where thieves discard what they don't want. Bear in mind too that just because something isn't worth pinching in London, that the same applies in Costa Rica.

Always carry copies of your passport and airline tickets, along with any traveller's cheques you might have, and report losses to local police as soon as possible for insurance claims if nothing else.

If you have lost something on public transport, the operator should, in principle, hold on to it. Radio taxis are more reliable as they have driver identity regulations, so take note of the cab number just in case. There is a Lost Property counter at the airport.

Media

Magazines and newspapers are sold on the streets and in grocery stores (*pulperías*). There are only a few magazine shops in San José and the main airport sells international publications: try **Papyrus** (at the Mas x Menos supermarket in La Sabana, 2221 4664, and at Mall Internacional in Alajuela, 2442 7770) and also **Casa de la Revista** (at Plaza del Sol Mall, Curridabat, 2283 0822).

La Prensa Libre, the most important Nicaraguan tabloid, is also sold on the streets. In tourist destinations such as Tamarindo, Quepos or Mal País regional bilingual or English publications can be found usually for free.

Directory

Magazines

Rumbo
A weekly news magazine with cultural articles as well as a synopsis of the main news stories of the week.

SoHo
A leading monthly magazine, aimed at men, that focuses on interviews, chronicles and humour.

Newspapers

La Nación
Founded in 1946 and part of Grupo Nación, La Nación is the most important media corporation in Costa Rica. It's the staple read for most middle-class Ticos and has an extensive classified listing and two glossy magazines on Sunday.

Extra
A bestselling tabloid, with sensational crime stories and gruesome accidents.

Tico Times
The leading English language newspaper founded in 1956. It is current, concise and useful.

Radio
There are more than 100 radio stations, but few in English. The leading English language station is **Real Rock Radio** 107.9 FM.

Television
Cable companies (AMNET, CableTica and DIRECT TV) have a wide variety of international programmes and are beamed into most hotels. The most important Costa Rican local TV channels are listed below:

TELETICA 7
Found on channel 7, TELETICA is probably the most widely viewed TV channel. Primarily a news channel, it also shows quality programmes from around the region as well as broadcasting US sport.

REPRETEL
On channels 4, 6 and 11, this is a private news channel.

Channel 13
Costa Rica's state-owned channel.

Money

The Costa Rican currency is the colón (CRC) – in plural, colones – named after Christopher Columbus. It hovers around CRC500 to one US dollar, and CRC975 to one British pound. Denominations of bank notes are 1,000 (red), 2,000 (light green), 5,000 (green) and 10,000 (blue). There are coin denominations of 500, 100, 50, 25, 20, 10 and 5 colones. There are two types of coin for 25, 10 and 5 denominations, some large and heavy, others light, silver in colour. A one colón coin also exists but is rarely used.

Credit cards are widely accepted in supermarkets, car rentals, restaurants and tourist shops, but not in small towns.

Banks & ATMs

There are several local and international banks in San José. The principal state-owned banks are Banco Nacional and Banco de Costa Rica. Foreigners are allowed to open a bank account but it is getting increasingly difficult to do so without a residency. The main requirements are an ID, a utility bill, purpose of the stay, an initial deposit as well as professional letters of reference.

There are ATMs around the country, but it is recommended you take cash out when you find one that works. Most accept foreign cards, especially the international banks such as HSBC and Scotiabank.

Western Union is a common option for receiving money, with almost 100 offices around the country.

Bureaux de change

Travellers' cheques are occasionally accepted at places that otherwise only accept cash, but are increasingly uncommon. You can change

them in banks and bureaux de change (practically nonexistent outside San José, though many small businesses do change money) but the rates are worse than for cash. American Express cheques are the easiest to change. The dollar is almost as widely accepted as colones. If you ask first, you can often pay in dollars almost anywhere from restaurants to tours to hotels.

Credit cards

Most tourist haunts, especially top-end hotels and quality restaurants, accept credit cards, but check in advance and make sure their machine is working. The most accepted cards are VISA (V) and MasterCard (MC); American Express (AmEx) and Diners Club (DC) are less common.

Lost/stolen credit cards

VISA *800 011 0030*
MasterCard *800 011 0184*
American Express *800 012 3211*
Diners Club *2295 9393*

Tax

Sales tax (Impuesto al Valor) is 13.39 per cent and usually not included in prices. When it is included, the price is marked 'IVI'. Occasionally, restaurants, shops and hotels charge it illegally, so always ask for a receipt. Service charge is ten per cent and is usually on the final bill. Hotels sometimes add a three per cent tourist surcharge to the sales tax. The prices in our **Where to Stay** sections include IVI.

Natural hazards

Costa Rica is located in the so-called 'Cinturón de Fuego del Pacífico', a seismic area that runs through all the countries on the Pacific coastline, and lies on the edge of active tectonic plates, meaning occasional earthquakes and minor earth tremors. Active volcanoes such as the Arenal have erupted in the past but are safe as long as you follow instructions on hotel and park trails. Hurricanes and prolonged rains are common on the Caribbean coast, and may lead to floods. Flooding in other parts of the country is also increasing due to deforestation. Always follow local instructions on Costa Rican waters, whether rivers (which can flow stronger than you think, and can contain crocodiles) or the ocean, where dangerous riptides are common and can be fatal.

If you are hiking, always do so in a group, be sure to stay on the marked trails, bring water and use sturdy boots to minimise the risk of being bitten by snakes or scorpions.

Opening hours

Shops usually open from Monday to Saturday from 8 or 9am until 6 or 7pm. Shopping malls open around 10am, closing at 10pm. Lunch hours can vary but are typically between 1pm and 3pm. Government offices should be open Monday to Friday from 8am to 4pm. Banks are open on weekdays from 8.30am to 3.45pm and on Saturday until 1pm. This can vary in coastal towns where banks are often open until later. Restaurants normally close the kitchen between 9 and 10pm. Most bars and clubs stay open until 2am, later in some coastal towns. However, overall Costa Ricans tend to turn in early.

Police

There are two different types of police in Costa Rica. The OIJ is the investigative branch, and the Fuerza Pública is the preventive branch who patrol the streets. Call 911 for

emergencies. See useful contacts for both below. *See p319* **Emergencies** for more information.
Oficina de Investigación Judicial (OIJ – Judicial Investigative Police) *2295 3463.*
Ministerio de Seguridad Pública - Fuerza Pública *2586 4000*
Tourist Police *2286 1473*
Fuerza Pública Puntarenas *2663 3791.*
Fuerza Pública Limón *2758 0365.*

Postal services

Correos de Costa Rica is the state-owned postal company and handles most mail in Costa Rica. It has an office in almost every town. They are open normal office hours on weekdays and most of them are open until noon on Saturday. Mail prices within Costa Rica start at about US$0.25 for the first 2g, and US$0.35 for international delivery. It takes about three days to a week for a letter to be delivered inside Costa Rica and ten to 15 days to arrive abroad. Correos de Costa Rica also has national and international courier services, starting at US$15 for international delivery. For a full list of branches log on to: www.correos.go.cr.

Other courier companies such as FedEx and DHL can be found in San José. *See p318* **Couriers & shippers**.
Correo Central *Calle 2, entre Avenidas 1 y 3 (2223 7436).*
Escazú *100m north of the Municipality (2289 9564).*
Puntarenas *In front of Banco de Costa Rica, Puntarenas Centre (2661 0440).*
Puerto Viejo *Beside Licorera Mane (2750 0444).*
Quepos *North corner of Plaza Rancho Grande (2777 1471).*
Puerto Jiménez *Beside the GAR (2735 5045).*

Religion

Catholicism is the official and largest religion of the country, and the Virgin Mary remains

greatly revered, especially among older people. Evangelical Christians are the second largest denomination. On the Caribbean coast, there are a minority of Protestants and also some Jewish residents, mainly in San José. The constitution deems that everyone can practise any religion peacefully.

Safety & security

Thousands of tourists arrive in Costa Rica every year and most never encounter any problems. Crime is, however, rising as tourism grows. According to the FCO the most common crime is pickpocketing and theft of valuables and passports. This is closely followed by breaking into cars and hotel rooms. Never leave anything in a car and always use the safe in a hotel room.

It is rare to be a victim of violent mugging, especially outside San José. If you are in San José do not flaunt valuable accessories such as jewellery or purses and closely watch your cameras and luggage.

Smoking

Costa Rica does not yet have the stringent anti-smoking laws that are in place across much of Europe and the US and smoking is only banned on public transport. That said, many restaurants have non-smoking sections, and a few are totally non-smoking.

Study

Hundreds of students from all around the world come to study in Costa Rica, spending anything from a few months to a year, while many Costa Ricans study abroad, mainly in the US and Europe.

Exchanges can be organised through academic institutions in your home country and

Directory

many organisations have links with local universities. The largest universities in Costa Rica are public and are the most likely to receive foreign students. Public universities and several private institutions with exchange programmes are listed here.

Universidad de Costa Rica (UCR) *San Pedro Campus, San José (2207 5634/www.ucr.ac.cr).* Also university centres in Puntarenas, Limón, San Ramón and Turrialba.
Universidad Nacional (UNA) *Calle 1, y Avenida Central, Heredia. (2277 3199/www.una.ac.cr).* Campuses also in Pérez Zeledón (San Isidro de El General) and Guanacaste.
Instituto Tecnológico de Costa Rica (ITCR) *1km south of the Basílica de Nuestra Señora de Los Ángeles, Cartago (2550 2218/ www.itcr.ac.cr).* Centres in San Carlos and San José.
Escuela de Agricultura de la Región Tropical Húmeda (Earth School) *Guácimo, Limón (2713 0000/www.earth.ac.cr).*
Business Administration Institute (INCAE) *La Garita, Alajuela (2437 2305/www.incae.edu).*
Universidad Creativa *Sabanilla, San José (2283 6880/www.ucreativa.com).*
Universidad Veritas *Zapote, San José (2283 4747/www.uveritas.ac.cr).*

Language classes

Costa Rica is an excellent country in which to learn Spanish, with dozens of language schools around the country. Individual and intensive classes can be found as well as special programmes that include learning a sport, visiting different tourist destinations or home stays with local families. Some of the most recognised institutions are listed below.

Academia Latinoamericana de Español *Avenida 8, entre Calles 31 y 33, Los Yoses, San José (2224 9917/www.alespanish.com).*
ILISA Language Institute *400m south and 125m east from Banco Nacional, San Pedro, San José (2280 0700/www.ilisa.com).*
Institute for Central American Development Studies (ICADS) *Colegio de Arquitectos, Curridabat (2234 1381/www.icads.org).*
Montaña Linda Language School & Hostel *Valle de Orosí*

(2533 3640/www. mountanalinda.com).
Spanish Language & Environmental Protection Centre (SEPA) *San Isidro de El General (2770 1457).*
Centro Panamericano de Idiomas (CPI) *Playa Flamingo, North Guanacaste (2654 5001).*
Escuela de Idiomas D'Amore *Manuel Antonio (2777 1143/ www.escueladamore.com).*
Horizontes de Montezuma *Montezuma (2642 0534/ www.horizontes-montezuma.com).*

Telephones

All communications in Costa Rica are regulated by a state-monopoly institution, the Instituto Costarricense de Electricidad (ICE), but the newly approved Tratado de Libre Comercio (TLC) with the US has a strong emphasis on opening the communications industry to private investors.

Dialling & codes

From April 2008, all telephone numbers in Costa Rica have eight digits. All phones except mobile phones start with a 2 (for example, 2642 0137). Mobile numbers begin with an 8 followed with a 3 or another 8 (for example, 8345 5678). There are no area codes; the country code is 506.

Mobile phones

There are two systems in use in Costa Rica; TDMA and the European GSM type, which work on the 1800mHz frequency. Most phones from the UK will work with global roaming, although the price of using it can be high. However, the GSM system can be slow and unreliable in Costa Rica, although coverage is said to be around 80 per cent.

Mobile (cellular) phones are only sold to residents by authorised ICE dealers; often a resident will buy a phone and then sell it on.

Many hotels rent mobile phones, as do car rental

companies. Also try **Cellular Costa Rica** (www.cell phonescr.com), which can deliver phones to the airports in Alajuela and Liberia, and **Cellular Telephone Rentals** (2290 7534, www. cellulartelephonerentals.com) rents out phones in most major tourist destinations.

Operator services

Dial 116 for international operator and collect calls. To make international calls, dial 00 and then the country code. To call Costa Rica from abroad, dial 00 and then the country code (506). The directory enquiries number is 113. For international information dial 124.

Public phones

Every rural one-street town has at least one public phone, and they are numerous in San José and other major towns. Some accept coins, or a magnetic card, or a chip card only. The easiest way to use them is to buy a 'Colibrí 197 card' (priced from CRC500) for local calls or a 'Colibrí 199 card' (from CRC3,000) for international and mobile phone calls. They are sold in supermarkets, grocery shops and community shops. Dial 197/199 and then the long number on the card. Instructions are in Spanish or English. The cards can be used at any phone.

Time

Costa Rica time is six hours behind GMT. There is no daylight savings and sunset is around 6pm all year long.

Tipping

Costa Ricans are not big tippers. Restaurants and bars with table service will add a ten per cent service charge to

Climate chart

Average daily temperatures		San José	Península de Nicoya	Península de Osa	Puerto Limón
Jan	max	24°C/75°F	32°C/90°F	33°C/91°F	28°C/82°F
	min	14°C/58°F	27°C/80°F	22°C/72°F	22°C/73°F
Feb	max	24°C/75°F	33°C/91°F	34°C/93°F	28°C/82°F
	min	14°C/58°F	26°C/79°F	21°C/70°F	22°C/73°F
Mar	max	25°C/77°F	35°C/95°F	34°C/93°F	29°C/84°F
	min	14°C/58°F	26°C/79°F	21°C/70°F	23°C/75°F
Apr	max	26°C/79°F	35°C/95°F	33°C/91°F	29°C/84°F
	min	16°C/61°F	27°C/80°F	21°C/70°F	24°C/75°F
May	max	26°C/79°F	32°C/90°F	31°C/88°F	29°C/84°F
	min	17°C/62°F	27°C/80°F	21°C/70°F	25°C/77°F
June	max	27°C/80°F	31°C/88°F	31°C/88°F	29°C/84°F
	min	17°C/62°F	26°C/79°F	21°C/70°F	23°C/75°F
July	max	26°C/79°F	31°C/88°F	31°C/88°F	28°C/82°F
	min	17°C/62°F	25°C/77°F	21°C/70°F	25°C/77°F
Aug	max	25°C/77°F	31°C/88°F	32°C/90°F	28°C/82°F
	min	16°C/61°F	23°C/73°F	20°C/68°F	24°C/75°F
Sept	max	26°C/79°F	31°C/88°F	32°C/90°F	30°C/86°F
	min	21°C/61°F	23°C/79°F	21°C/70°F	24°C/75°F
Oct	max	26°C/79°F	28°C/82°F	31°C/88°F	29°C/84°F
	min	16°C/60°F	25°C/79°F	21°C/70°F	24°C/75°F
Nov	max	25°C/77°F	28°C/82°F	31°C/88°F	28°C/82°F
	min	16°C/60°F	25°C/77°F	21°C/70°F	24°C/75°F
Dec	max	24°C/75°F	31°C/88°F	33°C/91°F	27°C/80°F
	min	14°C/58°F	26°C/79°F	21°C/70°F	22°C/71°F

Average monthly rainfall	San José	Península de Nicoya	Península de Osa	Puerto Limón
Jan	25mm	10mm	6mm	13mm
Feb	10mm	8mm	5mm	9mm
Mar	38mm	9mm	8mm	8mm
Apr	50mm	35mm	11mm	10mm
May	220mm	200mm	19mm	11mm
June	240mm	240mm	17mm	11mm
July	200mm	180mm	19mm	17mm
Aug	240mm	235mm	22mm	12mm
Sept	300mm	305mm	22mm	6mm
Oct	300mm	250mm	28mm	7mm
Nov	127mm	110mm	23mm	14mm
Dec	50mm	30mm	12mm	16mm

the bill automatically. Usually, Ticos don't leave any additional tip, but it is appreciated and it is becoming expected for visitors to do so. It is not customary to tip taxi drivers but it is welcome especially if you hire a driver for the day.

Toilets

Public toilets are practically non-existent. Even in bus stations, a small amount will always be charged, usually a CRC50 or CRC100 coin but it could be up to CRC500, and is usually in exchange for paper.

Tourist information

The main source of tourist information is the Instituto Costarricense de Turismo (ICT), a government-run tourist board with two offices in San José. It has no regional offices except on the borders with Nicaragua and Panama. There are also up to 60 tourist chambers and associations (see **www.visitcostarica.com** for detailed information) that can give some insight into the areas but, more often than not, little else.

Instituto Costarricense de Turismo (ICT) *Correo Central office, Calle 2, entre Avenidas 1 y 3 (2258 8762/www.visitcostarica.com).* **Open** 8am-4pm Mon-Fri.
Plaza de la Cultura office *Calle 5, entre Avenidas Central y 2 (2222 1090).* **Open** 9am-5pm Mon-Fri.
Cámara Nacional de Turismo (CANATUR) *Office at the Aeropuerto Juan Santamaría (2234 6222/www.canatur.org).* **Open** 8am-10pm Mon-Sun.

Visas & immigration

Visitors from the United Kingdom, Canada, New Zealand, Ireland and USA don't need a visa to enter Costa Rica. They can stay with a passport for up to 90 days, along with subjects of most European countries. Australian and New Zealand citizens can stay up to 30 days without a visa. Other nationalities may require a visa from a Costa Rican embassy or consulate before arriving. Visit **www. migracion.go.cr** for full details. Every visitor needs a passport valid at least six months prior to arrival.

If you over-stay, you may be fined when you leave Costa Rica and possibly banned from re-entering for a certain amount of time. Migration police may also deport those who overstay their visa. The easiest way to extend your stay is to leave the country for 72 hours and your visa will be automatically extended when you re-enter Costa Rica. Requirements vary depending on the officers you come across, so it is wise to carry an outbound ticket from Costa Rica (usually a US$20 bus

ticket to Nicaragua or Panama City) to show in case they ask how you will be leaving the country. Although officially required, it isn't always enforced. *See p309* **Nicaragua** and *p304* **Panama**.

Weights & measures

Costa Rica has a surprisingly open approach to measurement: inches, centimetres and feet, gallons and litres, pounds and kilograms are used indiscriminately by locals, but the metric system is the standard for weight, distances and measures. Petrol is measured in litres, temperature is given in celsius and *gallo pinto* is dished out in mounds.

When to go

Climate

Climate in Costa Rica varies greatly for such a small country. When the Caribbean lowlands are flooding, Guanacaste can be bone dry. Sudden and heavy rains often make roads muddy and inaccessible (sometimes due to mudslides) as is most common along the remote Península de Osa. Along the coast in peak season, temperatures soar into the 30s, while in the mountains the air tends to be cool.

In general terms, there are two different seasons: a dry season (summer) from December to April, and a rainy season (winter or 'green season') from May to November, when the rain begins to fall at night, and increases as the season goes on, especially in the Southern Pacific region. Most of the rain falls during September and October, making the transitional months of August and November fresh and lush, and a beautiful time to visit.

Public holidays

Catholic holidays are the most widely celebrated, often taken seriously by the devout and used as an excuse to party by the non-devout. Semana Santa (Easter week) is the most revered holiday (both religiously and beach party-wise). Also *see pp48-50* **Festivals & Events**.
1 Jan New Year's Day.
11 April Juan Santamaría Day.
March/April Semana Santa (Easter week).
1 May Labour Day.
29 May Corpus Christi Day.
25 July Annexation of Guanacaste.
2 Aug Virgin of los Angeles.
15 Aug Mother's Day.
15 Sept Independence Day.
12 Oct Cultures' Day and Limón Carnival.
8 Dec Inmaculate Conception.
25 Dec Christmas Day.

Women

Although the Latin American macho male mentality exists in Costa Rica, it is less intense than in other Central American countries. Women can put an end to any insistent Tico male whistling by simply ignoring them, and although staring at foreign women is common (and occasional hissing), it isn't usually intimidating. Women travelling alone must follow all the normal precautions as in any other part of the world. Beware of travelling alone at night and avoid hitchhiking.
Hospital de la Mujer *Calle Central y Avenida 22, San José (2257 9111).*

Working in Costa Rica

To work in Costa Rica you must cut through a thick bureaucratic web to get a temporary work permit. It is difficult to do this without a lawyer and takes time and money. Tourism related businesses, English teaching, media and arts are the main employment opportunities in the country.

Language & Vocabulary

Ticos living and working in tourist areas usually speak some English and generally welcome the opportunity to practise with foreigners. That said, most tourist destinations were rural towns until a few years ago and some people working now in tourism don't speak English. So a bit of Spanish goes a long way, and making the effort to use even a few phrases will be greatly appreciated and respected.

As in other Latin languages, there is more than one form of the second person (you) to be used. In Costa Rica the polite form *usted* is used more commonly than in many other Latin countries. It is even used between people very familiar with each other and is not necessarily a form of politeness or an indication of the formality of the situation. You may even hear small children talking to each other using *usted*. The local variant of the informal, the *voseo*, differs from the *tú* that you may know from European Spanish. Both forms are given here, *usted* first, then *vos*. *Tú* is used and understood, but isn't as common.

Pronunciation

Spanish is easier than some languages to get a basic grasp of, as pronunciation is largely phonetic. Look at the word and pronounce every letter, and the chances are you will be understood. As a rule, stress in a word falls on the penultimate syllable, otherwise an accent indicates where the stress lies. Accents are omitted on capital letters, though still pronounced.

The key to learning Costa Rican Spanish is to master the correct pronunciation of a few main letters and all of the vowels.

Vowels

Each vowel is pronounced separately and consistently, except in certain vowel combinations known as diphthongs, where they combine as a single syllable. There are strong vowels: a, e and o, and weak vowels: i and u. Two weak vowels, as in *ruido* (noise), or one strong and one weak, as in *piel* (skin), form a diphthong. Two strong vowels next to each other are pronounced as separate syllables, as in *poeta*, poet.

a is pronounced like the **a** in apple.
e is pronounced like the **a** in say.
i is pronounced like the **ee** in beet.
o is pronounced like the **o** in top.
u is pronounced like the **oo** in mood.
y is usually a consonant, except when it is alone or at the end of the word, in which case it is pronounced like the Spanish **i**.

Consonants

Pronunciation of the letters f, k, l, n, p, q, s and t is similar to English. y and ll are generally pronounced like the **y** in English, just like the European Spanish pronunciation. ch and ll have separate dictionary entries. ch is pronounced as in the English chair.
b is pronounced like its English equivalent, and is not distinguishable from the letter v. Both are referred to as be as in English bet. b is **long b** (called *b larga* in Spanish), v is known as **short b** (*b corta*).
c is pronounced like the s in sea when before **e** or **i** and like the English **k** before all other vowels.
g is pronounced like a guttural English **h** like the **ch** in loch when before **e** and **i** and as a hard g like **g** in goat otherwise.
h at the beginning of a word is silent.
j is also pronounced like a guttural English **h** and the letter is referred to as jota as in English hotter.
ñ is the letter **n** with a tilde and is pronounced like ni in English onion.
r is pronounced like the English **r** but is rolled at the beginning of a word, and rr is pronounced like the English **r** but is strongly rolled.
x is pronounced like the **x** in taxi in most cases, although in some it sounds like the Spanish **j**, for instance in Xavier.

hello *hola*
good morning *buenos días*
good afternoon *buenas tardes*
good evening/night *buenas noches*
OK *está bien*
yes *sí*
no *no*
maybe *tal vez/quizá(s)*
how are you? *¿cómo le va?* or *¿cómo te va?*
how's it going? *¿cómo anda?* or *¿cómo andás?*
Sir/Mr *Señor*
Madam/Mrs *Señora*
please *por favor*
thanks *gracias*
thank you very much *muchas gracias*
you're welcome *de nada*
sorry *perdón*
excuse me *permiso*
do you speak English? *¿habla inglés?* or *¿hablás inglés?*
I don't speak Spanish *no hablo castellano*
I don't understand *no entiendo*
speak more slowly, please *hable más despacio, por favor* or *habla más despacio, por favor*
leave me alone (quite forceful) *¡déjeme!* or *¡déjame!*
have you got change? *¿tiene cambio?* or *¿tenés cambio?*
there is/there are *hay/no hay*
good/well *bien*
bad/badly *mal*
small *pequeño/chico*
big *grande*
beautiful *hermoso/lindo*
a bit *un poco*; a lot/very *mucho*
with *con*
without *sin*
also *también*
this *este*; that *ese*
and *y*; or *o*
because *porque*; if *si*
what? *¿qué?*; who? *¿quién?*; when? *¿cuándo?*; which? *¿cuál?*; why? *¿por qué?*; how? *¿cómo?*; where? *¿dónde?*; where to? *¿hacia dónde?*
where from? *¿de dónde?*
where are you from? *¿de dónde es?* or *¿de dónde sos?*
I am English *soy inglés* (man) or *inglesa* (woman); Irish *irlandés*; American *americano/ norteamericano/estadounidense*; Canadian *canadiense*; Australian *australiano*; a New Zealander *neocelandés*
at what time/when? *¿a qué hora?/¿cuándo?*
forbidden *prohibido*
out of order *no funciona*
bank *banco*
post office *correo*
stamp *estampilla*

Emergencies

Help! ¡auxilio! ¡ayuda!
I'm sick estoy enfermo
I need a doctor/policeman/
hospital necesito un médico/un
policía/un hospital
there's a fire! ¡hay un incendio!

On the phone

hello hola
who's calling? ¿quién habla?
hold the line espere en línea

Getting around

airport aeropuerto
station estación
train tren
ticket boleto
single ida
return ida y vuelta
platform plataforma/andén
bus/coach station terminal
de colectivos/omnibús/micros
entrance entrada
exit salida
left izquierda
right derecha
straight on derecho
street calle; avenue avenida;
motorway autopista
street map mapa callejero;
road map mapa carretero
no parking prohibido estacionar
toll peaje
speed limit límite de velocidad
petrol gasolina; unleaded sin plomo

Sightseeing

museum museo
church iglesia
exhibition exhibición
ticket boleto
open abierto
closed cerrado
free gratis
reduced rebajado/con descuento
except Sunday excepto
los domingos

Accommodation

hotel hotel; bed & breakfast
pensión con desayuno
do you have a room (for this
evening/for two people)? ¿tiene
una habitación (para esta noche/para
dos personas)?
no vacancy completo/no hay
habitación libre; vacancy
desocupado/vacante
room habitación
bed cama; double bed
cama matrimonial
a room with twin beds
una habitación con dos camas
a room with a bathroom/shower
una habitación con baño/ducha

breakfast desayuno;
included incluido
lift ascensor
air-conditioned
con aire acondicionado

Shopping

I would like... me gustaría...
Is there a/are there any?
¿hay/habrá?
how much? ¿cuánto?
how many? ¿cuántos?
expensive caro
cheap barato
with VAT con IVI (13.39 per cent
valued added tax)
without VAT sin IVI
what size? ¿qué talle?
can I try it on?
¿me lo puedo probar?

Numbers

0 cero
1 uno
2 dos
3 tres
4 cuatro
5 cinco
6 seis
7 siete
8 ocho
9 nueve
10 diez
11 once; 12 doce; 13 trece;
14 catorce; 15 quince; 16 dieciséis;
17 diecisiete; 18 dieciocho;
19 diecinueve;
20 veinte; 21 veintiuno; 22 veintidós
30 treinta
40 cuarenta
50 cincuenta
60 sesenta
70 setenta
80 ochenta
90 noventa
100 cien
1,000 mil
1,000,000 un millón

Days, months & seasons

morning la mañana
noon mediodía; afternoon/evening
la tarde
night la noche
Monday lunes
Tuesday martes
Wednesday miércoles
Thursday jueves
Friday viernes
Saturday sábado
Sunday domingo
January enero; February
febrero; March marzo; April
abril; May mayo; June junio;
July julio; August agosto;
September septiembre;
October octubre; November

noviembre; December
diciembre
spring primavera
summer verano
autumn/fall otoño
winter invierno

Others

Costa Rica is Spanish-speaking. But as anyone arriving from Spain or Mexico can attest, the local slang and speed of speaking can, at times, make communicating a somewhat tricky experience, especially in areas that still don't receive very many foreign visitors.

Talking among friends, Ticos will start every few sentences with 'mae' ('hey, you' or 'mate') in the monotonous way Southern California skateboarders say 'dude'. You will hear 'mae' almost every two or three phrases. But don' confuse it with 'maje'; if you do they are unlikely to be your mate for much longer.

Ticos have lots of slang words, some of them originating from Mexico, and others as a result of corruption of English words or phrases. Queque (cake), guachimán (watchmen), and tuanis (too nice), a common way to greet among young people, fall into this category.

A few choice words or expressions you might hear only in Costa Rica include: suave (mellow, commonly used 'suave, mae' as in 'take it easy, man'), harina (money), chante (home), jama (food), Chepe (San José), yodo (coffee), chema (shirt), cara e'picha (a very serious insult, like 'son of a bitch'. Picha means balls), birra (beer), agüevado (to be in a bad mood, or a sad mood), hablar paja (to speak bullshit), qué es la vara (what's up).

And then there is, of course, pura vida (pure living) and con mucho gusto, meaning 'you're welcome', which is said after saying thank you. Polite bunch, the Costa Ricans.

Further Reference

Books

Non-fiction

Oscar Arias and Mark Wainwright *The Mammals of Costa Rica: A Natural History and Field Guide* In depth illustrations and detailed information on Costa Rica's mammal population.

Priscilla Barrett, David Beadle and Les D Beletsky *Costa Rica, Travellers' Wildlife Guides* Pin-pointing the country's most commonly sighted amphibians, reptiles, mammals and birds plus information on species conservation.

Dr Robert Dressler *Fieldguide to the Orchids of Costa Rica and Panama* Solid introduction to the national flower of Costa Rica.

Jack Ewing *Monkeys are Made of Chocolate; Exotic and Unseen Costa Rica* Ewing's fascinating Costa Rican experiences from over 30 years.

Michael Fogden and Patricia Fogden *Hummingbirds of Costa Rica* All-inclusive guide to the country's beautiful avian inhabitant.

Michael Fogden, Patricia Fogden and Jay M Savage *The Amphibians and Reptiles of Costa Rica: A Herpetofauna Between Two Continents, Between Two Seas* In-depth studies of amphibian and reptile life from Savage's work spanning more than four decades.

Richard Garrigues *Birds of Costa Rica* Step by step companion for even the most inexperienced spotter.

James Kavanagh and Raymond Leung *Costa Rica Butterflies & Moths: An Introduction to Familiar Species* Pocket sized guide to the fragile and fluttering.

Ivan Molina and Steven Palmer *The Costa Rica Reader: History, Culture, Politics* A diverse collection of over 50 texts predominantly from Costa Rican voices.

Simona Stoppa *Costa Rica: The Land Between Two Oceans* Stunning pictorial journey through the multifarious landscape.

Paul Theroux *The Old Patagonian Express* His late 1970s railroad trip from Boston to Patagonia remains a travel writing paragon.

Mark Wainwright *Birds of the Cloud Forest and Highlands* Field guide with illustrations of over 100 birds sighted from higher grounds.

Willow Zuchowski *Tropical Plants of Costa Rica: A Guide to Native and Exotic Flora* The Monteverde botanist's authoritative introduction to the country's impressive array of flora.

Fiction

Miguel Benavides and Joan Henry *The Children of Mariplata* A collection of short tales depicting little fragments of Costa Rican life.

John Howard Davies *Costa Rica Capers: A Romp Across the Pan-American Isthmus* Gripping, witty novel, drawing on experiences of a pre-tourist boom Costa Rica.

Carlos Luis Fallas *Mamita Yunai: el infierno de las bananeras* Colourful portrayal of gruelling life on Limón's banana plantations.

Enrique Jaramillo Levi *When New Flowers Bloomed: Short Stories by Women Writers from Costa Rica and Panama* Showcasing some of the country's most acclaimed female literary voices including Carmen Naranjo and Yolanda Oreamuno.

Tatiana Lobo *Assault on Paradise* An historical novel on the devastating effect of Spanish colonists on indigenous life.

Barbara Ras *Costa Rica: A Traveller's Literary Companion* Charming anthology of 26 stories by Costa Rican writers.

Yasmin Ross *La Flota Negra* Hailing from Mexico, Ross moved to Costa Rica, and this nautical tale has become a popular piece of fiction in her adopted homeland.

Film

1492: Conquest of Paradise (Ridley Scott) Released to commemorate the 500th anniversary of the discovery of the Americas, this Scott blockbuster shows the struggle between European and indigenous peoples…epic-style.

Carnival in Costa Rica (Gregory Ratoff) Innocent musical following the capers of four young lovers.

Endless Summer Two (Bruce Brown) Surfs up yet again in the *Endless Summer* sequel. Surfing, windsurfing and body boarding from the world's best surf spots, including the Costa Rican coast.

Paso a paso: a sentimental journey (Julio Molina and Daniel Ross) A glimpse into the country's afrocaribbean community.

The Chosen One (George Sluizer) Lighthearted comedy starring Rob Schneider about a dissatisfied car salesman given meaning to his life by a shaman and an indian. Though the Indians are said to be from Colombia, filming took place in Costa Rica for safety precautions.

Tropix (Percy Angress and Liva Linden) Tense action thriller.

Music

December's Cold Winter *Decaying Recollections* Debt album from melodic metallers.

Editus *Decada Uno* Debut release from jazz classcal and folk trio.

Evolución *Mundo de Fantasia* The top selling album which brought the San José band to the fore.

Gandhi *Ciclos* Latest album from the latin infused rockers.

Insano *Drain* Current album and third thrashing release from the popular metalcore group.

José Capmany *Volando Alto/La Historia Salvaje* Double disc of hits from before the singer's untimely death in 2001. Plus unreleased songs.

Malpaís *En Vivo* Lilting live tracks from the Costa Rica favourites.

Manuel Obregon *Simbiosis* Ambient piano music interfused with wondrous sounds from Monteverde.

Ray Tico *Solo para Recordar* Songs from the bolero guitar legend.

Various *Costa Rican Rock and Pop* Journey through 20 years of Costa Rican rock and pop.

Various *Guanacaste al Atardecer* Lounging rhythms for the perfect sunset soundtrack.

Walter Ferguson *Dr Bombodee* Lilting sounds hailing from the carribean coastal town of Cahuita.

Websites

www.arenal.net Swat up on Volcan Arenal, and the action packed surrounds.

www.costarica.com A plethora of info on travelling, business and living in Costa Rica.

www.costarica-online.com/costarica-board/ Active message forum.

www.infocostarica.com Over 150 articles plus live forum.

www.monteverdeinfo.com Facts and figures on the misty Reserva Biologica Bosque Nuboso de Monteverde and the picturesque Reserva Santa Elena.

www.puravida.com Everything from animal conservation to typical recipes.

www.therealcostarica.com Costa Rican life through the eyes of a gringo whose been living in the country for several years.

www.visitcostarica.com Official and comprehensive tourist board website in Spanish, English, German and French.

www.tourism.co.cr Facts and articles a plenty to satisfy the impending visitor.

Directory

Index

Note: Page numbers in **bold** indicate section(s) giving key information on topic; *italics* indicate photos.

Accommodation

Caribbean
Cocori Hotel Bar & Restaurant 287
Hotel Continental 287
Hotel Maribú Caribe 287
Hotel Miami 287
Hotel Palace 287
Park Hotel 287

Central Pacific
Alamar Hotel 223
Ama Tierra *227*, 229
Camas Hostel, Las 229
Casa Caletas 207
Casitas Azul Plata 209
Eco Hotel Arca de Noé 209
Hotel Canciones del Mar 229
Hotel del Mar 234
Hotel Familiar Macarena 223
Hotel Las Brisas 223
Hotel Poseidón 229
Hotel Punta Islita 209, *209*
Plantación, La 234
Villa Caletas 229
Villas Estrellamar 229
Vista Pacifico 229

Central Valley
Arenal Country Inn 155
Arenal Observatory Lodge 155, *157*
Arenal Volcano Inn 155
Caño Negro Lodge 158
Hotel de Campo Caño Negro 158
Hotel Dorothy 155
Hotel Mi Tierra 121
Jardin Tropical 121
La Paz Waterfall Gardens 121
Mansion Inn, La 156
Pura Vida 121
Tabacon Grand Spa
  Thermal Resort 156
Vida Tropical 121
Xandari Resort 121

Pacific North
Altos de Eros, Los 189
Aqua Viva Resort & Spa, L' 196
Best Western Hotel Las Espuelas
  Hotel & Casino 167

Botella de Leche, La 189
Cala Luna Boutique Hotel & Villas
  189
Giardino Tropicale 195
Gilded Iguana 195
Harmony Hotel 195, *195*
Hotel Capitán Sulzo 190
Hotel Casa Real *166*, 167
Hotel Primavera 167
Posada del Tope, La 167
Sueño del Mar Bed & Breakfast 190
Villa Deveena 190
Villa Tortuga 196
WItch's Rock 190

San José
Aurola Holiday Inn 93
Canal Grande Hotel 109
Casa Cambranes 99
Casa Roland 103
Clarion Amón Plaza 93
Colours Oasis Resort 105
Crowne Plaza Hotel Corobici 105
De Luxe Backpackers 93
Gran Hotel Costa Rica 93
Hostel Bekuo 99
Hotel 1492 99
Hotel Alta 109, *111*
Hotel Balmoral 93
Hotel Barcelo Palma Real 105
Hotel Boutique Jade 100
Hotel Britannia 93
Hotel Don Fadrique 100
Hotel Dunn Inn 93
Hotel Grano de Oro 93
Hotel Las Orquideas 100
Hotel Le Bergerac 100
Hotel Milvia 100
Hotel Parque del Lago 93
Hotel Quality 111
Hotel Rincon de San José 94
Isla Verde 105
Marriott Courtyard 111
Mi Casa Hostel 105
Pangea 94
Paseo del Rosa, La 94
Real Intercontinental 111
Tennis Club 105
Villa Escazú B&B 11

Southern Pacific
Cabinas los Cocos 271
Cabinas Sol y Mar 271
Coloso Del Mar 271
Iguana Verde 271
Oceano Cabinas Bar & Restaurant
  271

Eating & Drinking

Caribbean
Bar y Restaurant Washington 285
Bio Natura Soda & Café 285
Black Star Line 285
Brisas del Caribe 285
Cevichito, El 285
Quimbamba Bar & Restaurant 285
Reina's Restaurant 285
Soda Meli 286

Advertisers' Index

Please refer to the relevant sections for contact details.